Research Methods in the Social Sciences

SECOND EDITION

Research Methods in the Social Sciences

SECOND EDITION

DAVID NACHMIAS

CHAVA NACHMIAS

St. Martin's Press
New York

Library of Congress Catalog Card Number: 80–52386
Copyright © 1981 by St. Martin's Press, Inc.
All Rights Reserved.
Manufactured in the United States of America.
54321
fedcba
For information, write St. Martin's Press, Inc.,
175 Fifth Avenue, New York, N.Y.   10010

cover design: James M. Wall
typography: RFS Graphic Design, Inc.

ISBN: 0–312–67621–2

To our daughter, Anat

Contents
in Brief

Contents
in Detail

Preface

When the First Edition of *Research Methods in the Social Sciences* appeared in 1976, we stated that it was our goal to offer a comprehensive treatment of the scientific approach to the social sciences. Our goal in the Second Edition has not changed; we continue to emphasize the relationship between theory, research, and practice, and to integrate the various research activities in a systematic framework. We have, however, made very substantial additions to the text. A variety of new concerns and developments have come to the fore in the five years since the appearance of the First Edition, and we have had the benefit of suggestions for improved coverage from a considerable number of instructors in research methods courses across the country, including both users and nonusers of our First Edition. As a result, *Research Methods in Social Sciences* has been expanded from its original thirteen chapters to eighteen. We should add that an Instructor's Manual and an optional Study Guide for the student are now available to accompany the text.

Social science research is, in our view, a cyclical, self-correcting process consisting of seven interrelated stages: the research problem, the hypothesis, the research design, measurement, data collection, data analysis, and generalization. The text leads the reader through each stage of this process.

Chapter 1 examines the foundations of knowledge, the aims of scientific research, and the assumptions of the scientific approach. Chapters 2 and 3 discuss the basic issues of empirical research and the relationship between theory and research. Included are such topics as concept formation, functions and types of theories, models, variables, and the various sources for research problems and hypotheses.

Chapters 4 and 5 present the research design stage. A research design is a strategy that guides researchers throughout their investigations; it is a logical model for inferring causal relations. Experimental designs are discussed and illustrated in Chapter 4 and pre- and quasi-experimental designs are examined in Chapter 5. Chapter 6 is concerned with measurement and quantification. The issues of validity and reliability, which are inseparable from measurement theory, are also discussed in this chapter.

Chapters 7 through 10 are devoted to the various methods of data collection available to social scientists. Controlled and noncontrolled observational methods are the subjects of chapter 7, and survey research in general and the mail questionnaire, the personal interview, and the telephone interview in particular are examined in Chapter 8. Chapter 9, which explains how to construct a questionnaire, focuses on such topics as the content of questions, types of questions, and question format and sequence. Chapter 10 is devoted to the various forms, uses, and limitations of unobtrusive measures.

The next five chapters are concerned with data processing and analysis. In Chapter 11 we present methods for constructing coding schemes and for preparing data for computer processing. Chapter 12 introduces the univariate distribution, measures of central tendency and dispersion, and the various types of frequency distributions. Chapter 13 examines the concept of relationship and measures of nominal, ordinal, and interval relations. The major topics of multivariate analysis, statistical techniques of control, and interpetation and methods of causal inferences are the subjects of Chapter 14. Chapter 15 explores the techniques used in constructing indexes and scales that are used to measure complex phenomena.

Chapters 16 and 17 examine methods of statistical inference. In Chapter 16 we present the principles of sampling theory and the most commonly used sample designs. Chapter 17 is devoted to a discussion of the strategy of hypothesis testing and the frequently used parametric and nonparametric tests. The significance-test controversy, also discussed in this chapter, serves as a vivid illustration of the evolving nature of social science methodology.

As the scope of the social sciences has expanded, and as our models of research and analysis have become more sophisticated, concerns have arisen about the ethics of social science research. Chapter 18 examines these ethical considerations and suggests ways to ensure the rights and the welfare of those who participate in research experiments.

Our literary debts are testified to in the bibliography. Many students, instructors, reviewers and colleagues offered useful ideas and comments. We are particularly grateful to Michael Baer, Sandra Baxter, Bruce S. Bowen, Jeffrey Brudney, Scott Greer, Glenn A. Harper, Ronald Hedlund, Norman R. Kurtz, D. E. Pilant, Lawrence Rosen, Mack C. Shelley, and George Zito. We are also grateful to the Literary Executor of the late Sir

Ronald A. Fisher, F. R. S., to Dr. Frank Yates, F. R. S., and to Longman Group Ltd., London, for permission to reprint appendixes from their book *Statistical Tables for Biological, Agricultural and Medical Research* (6th edition, 1974).

Finally, we wish to thank Bertrand W. Lummus, Senior Editor at St. Martin's Press, for his conscientious work on behalf of this edition, and Richard Steins, Project Editor, for his fine editorial guidance.

PART 1
Foundations of Empirical Research

CHAPTER PREVIEW

CHAPTER 1
The Scientific Approach

INTRODUCTION

What does the scientific approach have to offer to those who take an interest in the problems of society? How can we acquire reliable knowledge about those aspects of the human experience that are considered "social," "political," "economic," and "psychological"? More specifically, how can the scientific approach be of value in understanding phenomena such as inflation, unemployment, democratic governance, bureaucracy, deviance, or self-actualization?

One way to answer these questions is first to define *science* and then to take a close look at the scientific approach, its assumptions, goals, and attributes and compare these with other approaches to knowledge. In this chapter we first define science and then compare the scientific approach with three other approaches to knowledge. We discuss the assumptions of science, its aims, and the role of methodology in the scientific approach. We then present the ideas of scientific revolutions, discoveries, and scientific progress. The last section presents a model of the research process, the stages of which are discussed throughout this book.

WHAT IS SCIENCE?

Unfortunately, *science* cannot be easily defined. Laypersons, journalists, policymakers, scholars, and scientists themselves define the term *science* in different ways and employ it in different contexts. To some, science connotes a prestigious undertaking; to others, science denotes a body of true knowledge; to still others, it means an objective investigation of empirical phenomena.

3

The difficulty encountered in attempting to define *science* arises from the tendency to confuse the content of science with its methodology. Although science has no special subject matter of its own, we do not view every study of phenomena as science. For example, astrology studies the positions of the stars and various events in human life and tries to establish relations between them and to predict future phenomena. These goals and activities do not qualify astrology for admission into the family of the various sciences. Even if a prestigious university would decide to establish a Department of Astrology, recruit faculty, develop a curriculum, and offer a Master of Science degree, astrology would not qualify as a scientific discipline. The reason that we reject astrology as a science is not because of its subject matter, but rather because the methodology used by astrologists is considered to be unscientific. Whenever a branch of supposed factual knowledge is rejected by science, it is always on the basis of its methodology. Furthermore, much of the content of science is constantly changing; knowledge regarded as scientific at present may become unscientific in the future. Science is not any general or particular body of knowledge; science is united not by its subject matter, but by its methodology. For these reasons we shall use the term science throughout this book to mean all knowledge collected by the means of the scientific methodology.

APPROACHES TO KNOWLEDGE

The word *science* is derived from the Latin word *scientia*, itself from Latin *sciens*, the present participle of *scire*, "to know." Throughout history, knowledge has been acquired by various modes. The scientific approach is by no means the only mode by which people have attempted to understand their environment and themselves. There are three other general modes that have served the purpose of acquiring knowledge: the authoritarian mode, the mystical mode, and the rationalistic mode. A major distinction among these modes is the manner in which each vests confidence in the producer of knowledge (that is, *Who* says so?); the *procedure* by which knowledge is produced (that is, *How* do you know?), and in the *effect* of the knowledge produced (that is, *What* difference does it make?)[1] A brief description of these modes provides a comparative perspective for the evaluation of the scientific approach.

Authoritarian mode. In the authoritarian mode, knowledge is looked for by referring to those who are socially or politically defined

---

1. Walter L. Wallace, *The Logic of Science in Sociology* (Chicago: Aldine-Atherton, 1971), p. 11. See also, Morris R. Cohen and Ernest Nagel, *An Introduction to Logic and Scientific Method* (New York: Harcourt, Brace, 1934), pp. 193–195.

as qualified producers of knowledge. These may be oracles in tribal societies, archbishops in theocratic societies, kings in monarchical societies, and individuals occupying scientific roles in technocratic societies. Within any society, different authorities may be sought to produce knowledge for different phenomena. For devout Catholics, the pope possesses undisputed authority on matters viewed as religious. Undisputed authority is also possessed by the Soviet Academy of Sciences, which in 1950 decreed that statistical theories based on probability are nonscientific; this decision was an abortive attempt to resolve the contradiction between the determinism of dialectical materialism and theory of probability. In the authoritarian mode, the knowledge-seeker attributes the ability to produce knowledge to the social or political authority of the knowledge-producer. The procedure whereby the seeker solicits this authority affects the nature of the authority's response, but not the seekers's confidence in the response. Furthermore, although the effects of an item of knowledge obtained by this mode can lead to the eventual replacement of authority, a large number of refutations is required before this happens.

Mystical mode. In the mystical mode, knowledge is solicited from prophets, divines, gods, mediums, and other supernaturally knowledgeable authorities. In this sense, the mystical mode is similar to the authoritarian mode. However, it differs from the latter in its dependence on manifestations of supernatural signs and on the psychophysical state of the knowledge-consumer. For example, the rites surrounding the process of astrological prophecy are aimed at persuading the consumer of the astrologer's supernatural powers. The mystical mode depends, to a large extent, on applying ritualistic and ceremonial procedures to the consumer. Moreover, under conditions of depression, helplessness, and intoxication, the knowledge-consumer is most willing to accept items of knowledge produced by the mystical mode. The confidence in the knowledge produced in this manner decreases as the number of disconfirmations increases or as the educational level of a society advances.

Rationalistic mode. Rationalism is a school in philosophy that holds that the totality of knowledge can be acquired by strict adherence to the forms and the rules of logic. The underlying assumptions of rationalism are that (1) the human mind can apprehend the world independently of observable phenomena and (2) that forms of knowledge exist that are prior to our experiences. In other words, the concern of the rationalistic mode is with what *must be true in principle*, and what is logically possible and permissible.

To the rationalist, abstract logic is a normative master science, which makes it possible to separate scientific propositions from unsound thinking. According to classical rationalists, Aristotle had explored once and for all the entire subject matter of logic and thus the structure of knowledge and truth. The German philosopher Immanuel Kant (1724–1804) declared of logic:

> Since Aristotle it has not had to retrace a single step, unless we choose to consider as improvements the removal of some unnecessary subtleties, or the clearer definition of its matter, both of which refer to the elegance rather than to the solidity of the science. It is remarkable also, that to the present day, it has not been able to make one step in advance, so that, to all appearances, it may be considered as completed and perfect.[2]

Kant elaborated the theory that our minds impress a certain pattern on the observational world. This pattern is in terms of space and time and certain "categories," a term whose meaning we need not consider now. What is of interest to us is that the statements of logic and mathematics tell us, according to Kant, something about our experiences. Such statements of knowledge are produced by pure reason, for it is the mind that stamps them upon reality.

The notion that a priori knowledge exists and that it is independent of the human experience did not end with classical rationalism. The supreme embodiment of rationalism in contemporary social sciences is abstract, pure mathematics. Pure mathematics consists of statements that are universally valid, certain and independent of the empirical world. For example, the statements of pure geometry are considered to be absolute and true by definition. Pure geometry says nothing about reality; its propositions are tautological, that is, true by virtue of their logical forms alone. Contemporary rationalists are more concerned with pure mathematics than with empirical content. Although pure mathematics and formal logic are important instruments to the scientific approach, their value for the social sciences "exists only in so far as they serve as means to fruitful progress in the subject-matter, and they should be applied, as complex tools always should, only when and where they can help and do not hinder progress."[3]

THE ASSUMPTIONS OF SCIENCE

The scientific approach is grounded on a set of fundamental assumptions that are unproved and unprovable. They are necessary prerequisites for the conduct of scientific discourse and represent those issues in the area of the philosophy of science that is termed *epistemology*—the study of the foundations of knowledge. By examining these assumptions, we can

2. Immanuel Kant, *Critique of Pure Reason*, trans. by Max Muller (London: Macmillan, 1881), p. 688.

3. Kurt Lewin, *Field Theory in Social Science* (New York: Harper, 1951), p. 12.

better understand the scientific approach and its claim for superiority over other approaches to knowledge.

Nature is orderly and regular. The basic assumption of the scientific approach is that there exists a definite regularity and order in the natural world; events do not occur haphazardly. Even within a rapidly changing environment, it is assumed that there is a degree of order and regularity and that change itself displays patterns that can be understood.

The concept of nature does not refer to omnipotent or supernatural forces. In science, nature denotes all those empirically observable objects, conditions, and phenomena that exist independently of human intervention but include the human being as a biological system. The laws of nature do not prescribe, but rather describe, what actually is happening. Furthermore, order and regularity in nature are not necessarily inherent in the phenomena. For example, there is no logically compelling reason why spring should follow winter, winter follow autumn, autumn follow summer, and summer follow spring. But they do, and regularly so, and this regularity underlies observable conditions and phenomena, such as growing seasons.

We can know nature. The assumption that we can know nature is no more provable than is the assumption that nature is orderly and that there are laws of nature. It expresses a basic conviction that human beings are just as much part of nature as other natural objects, conditions, and phenomena and that, although we possess unique and distinctive characteristics, we can nevertheless be understood and explained by the same methods by which we study nature. Individuals and societal phenomena exhibit sufficient recurrent, orderly, and empirically demonstrable patterns to be amenable to scientific investigation. The human mind is not only capable of knowing nature, but also of knowing itself and the minds of others.

Knowledge is superior to ignorance. Closely related to the assumption that we can know nature and ourselves is the idea that knowledge should be pursued both for its own sake and for perfecting human conditions. The contention that knowledge is superior to ignorance does not mean that everything in nature can or will be known. Rather, it is assumed that scientific knowledge is tentative and changing. Things that we did not know in the past we know at present, and current knowledge might be modified in the future. Truth in science is relative to the evidence, the methods, and the theories employed.

The contention that relative knowledge is superior to ignorance is diametrically opposed to ideologies based on absolute truth. As Gideon Sjoberg and Roger Nett put it, "Certainly the ideal that human dignity is enhanced when man is restless, inquiring, and 'soul searching' conflicts with a variety of belief systems that would strive toward a closed system, one based on absolute truth. The history of modern science and its clash with absolute systems bears testimony to this proposition."[4] True believers already "know" all that there is to know. Scientific knowledge threatens the old ways of doing things; it is detrimental to tranquillity, stability, and the status quo. And, in exchange, the scientific approach can offer only tentative truth that is relative to the existing state of knowledge. These are both the strength and weakness of the scientific approach:

> It is a strength in the sense that rational man will in the long run act to correct his own errors. It is a weakness in that scientists, not being so confident of the validity of their own assertions as is the general public, may, in those frequent periods when social crises threaten public security, be overturned by absolutists. Science is often temporarily helpless when its bastions are stormed by overzealous proponents of absolute systems of belief.[5]

All natural phenomena have natural causes. The assumption that all natural phenomena have natural causes epitomizes the scientific revolution. It has placed the scientific approach in opposition to fundamentalist religion, on the other hand, and spiritualism and magic on the other. The assumption implies that natural events have natural causes or antecedents. It rejects the counterassumption that forces other than those found in nature operate to cause the occurrence of natural events. Moreover, until scientists can account for the occurrence of phenomena in natural terms, they reject the argument that some other supernatural explanation is necessary. The main function of this assumption is to direct scientific research away from omnipotent supernatural forces and toward the regularities and order that underlie natural phenomena. Once delineated, such regularities can serve as evidence for cause-and-effect relationships.

Nothing is self-evident. Scientific knowledge is not self-evident; claims for truth must be demonstrated objectively. Tradition, subjective beliefs, and common sense could not be exclusively relied upon in the verification of scientific knowledge. Possibilities for error are always present, and even the simplest notions call for objective verification. It is not incidental, therefore, that scientific thinking is skeptical and critical.

Knowledge is derived from the acquisition of experience. If science is to tell us anything about the real world it must be *empirical*; that is, it must rely on perceptions, experience, and observations. Perception is a fundamental tenet of the scientific approach, and it is achieved

4. Gideon Sjoberg and Roger Nett, *A Methodology for Social Research* (New York: Harper & Row, 1968), p. 25.

5. Ibid., p. 26.

through our senses: "Science assumes that a communication tie between man and the external universe is maintained through his own sense impressions. Knowledge is held to be a product of one's experiences, as facets of the physical, biological, and social world play upon the senses."[6]

This assumption should not be interpreted in the narrow definition of the five senses—touch, smell, taste, hearing, and seeing. Many phenomena cannot be directly experienced or observed. Observation is not "immediately given" or entirely detached from scientific terms, concepts, and theories. As the British philosopher of science Sir Karl Popper wrote:

> The naïve empiricist . . . thinks that we begin by collecting and arranging our experiences, and so ascend the ladder of science . . . But if I am ordered: "Record what you are experiencing" I shall hardly know how to obey this ambiguous order. Am I to report that I am writing; that I hear a bell ringing; a newsboy shouting; a loudspeaker droning; or am I to report, perhaps, that these noises irritate me? . . . A science needs points of view, and theoretical problems.[7]

Still, from a historical perspective, the assumption that scientific knowledge should be based upon empirical observations was a reaction against the belief that knowledge is innate in human beings or that "pure reason" alone is sufficient to produce verifiable knowledge.

AIMS OF SOCIAL SCIENCES

Having explicated the assumptions of science, we are now in a position to address the question raised earlier: What does science have to offer to those who take an interest in societal problems? The ultimate goal of the social sciences is to produce an accumulating body of reliable knowledge. Such knowledge would enable us to _explain, predict,_ and _understand_ empirical phenomena that interest us. Furthermore, a reliable body of knowledge could be put to use to ameliorate the human condition. But what are scientific explanations? When can we make predictions? When are we justified in claiming that we understand empirical phenomena?

Scientific Explanation

Why are per capita government expenditures higher in Sweden than in the United States? Because, some persons might respond, "Swedes want

6. Ibid.

7. Karl R. Popper, _The Logic of Scientific Discovery_ (New York: Science Editions, 1961), p. 106.

their government to spend more." Whereas such an explanation might satisfy the layperson, it would not satisfy social scientists unless they could employ the same reasoning to explain per capita government expenditures in other political systems. In fact, per capita government expenditures in Britain have decreased since the Conservative party won the national elections, although most Britons are reported to want their government to spend more.

The social sciences aim to provide general explanations to "Why?" questions. When social scientists ask for an explanation of why a given phenomenon has taken place, they ask for a systematic and an empirical analysis of those antecedent factors in the given situation that are responsible for the occurrence of the phenomenon.

Ever since David Hume, such an application of the term *explanation* has been considered to be a matter of relating the phenomenon to be explained with other phenomena by means of *general laws*. General laws set the framework from which a particular explanation can be derived. In the words of Richard Braithwaite:

> The function of science . . . is to establish general laws covering the behavior of empirical events or objects with which the science in question is concerned, and thereby to enable us to connect together our knowledge of the separately known events, and to make reliable predictions of events as yet unknown . . . If science is in a highly developed state . . . the laws which have been established will form a hierarchy in which special laws appear as logical consequences of a small number of highly general laws . . . if the science is in an early stage of development . . . the laws may be merely the generalizations involved in classifying things into various classes.[8]

As scientific disciplines make progress, their forms of explanation change. Carl Hempel made an important distinction between two basic types of explanations: *deductive* and *probabilistic*. The classification is based upon the kinds of generalizations that the explanation employs.[9]

Deductive explanations. A deductive explanation calls for a universal generalization, a statement of the conditions under which the generalization holds true, an event to be explained, and the rules of formal logic. In a deductive explanation, a phenomenon is explained by demonstrating that it can be deduced from an established universal law. For example, a physicist's explanation for the return to earth of an object thrown into the air would be based on the law of gravitation. He or she will point out that if *all* objects exercise a mutual attraction on one an-

8. Richard B. Braithwaite, *Scientific Explanation* (New York: Harper, 1960), p. 1.

9. Carl G. Hempel, *Philosophy of Natural Science* (Englewood Cliffs, N.J.: Prentice-Hall, 1966), chapter 5.

other, then any given object is expected to behave in the same way with reference to earth. The essential feature of a universal law is that it purports to encompass all cases that fall within the class to which it applies— present, past, and future.

Probabilistic explanations. Not all scientific explanations are based on laws of universal form. Thus, a particular increase in government expenditures in the United States might be explained by suggesting that it happened in response to adverse economic conditions and that in the past increased expenditures followed severe economic conditions. This explanation links the phenomenon to be explained to an earlier occurrence—the country's economic conditions. The latter is suggested to provide an explanation because there is a connection between economic conditions and government expenditures. That connection, however, cannot be expressed by a law of universal form because not every case of adverse economic conditions brings an increase in government expenditures. What can be suggested is only that there is a high probability that severe economic conditions will bring increases in government expenditures or that in a high percent of all cases that were investigated, severe economic conditions led to increases in government expenditures. General explanations of this type are referred to as *probabilistic* or *inductive* explanations, and they derive from probabilistic generalizations. In other words, a probabilistic explanation makes use of generalizations that express an arithmetical ratio between phenomena or generalizations that express tendencies. For example, a probabilistic generalization can take the form "n percent of X is Y," or "X tends to be Y."

The chief limitation of probabilistic generalizations, in comparison to universal laws, is that certain conclusions cannot be drawn about a particular unit (for example, an individual, a group, a society, a government, an event) of a set from properties of the whole set. If, for instance, one has the information that 70 percent of the members of an ethnic group voted for the Democratic party for the past twenty years, one still cannot conclude with certainty that the probability that a particular member of the group voted Democratic is 7/10. Other factors, besides membership in the given group of which the generalization is true, may influence the behavior in question. The particular person may also be a member of a social group with a long tradition of Republican political leaning, and this, in turn, may outweigh the influence of his or her ethnic identification.

Prediction

Deductive and probabilistic explanations constitute one important component of scientific knowledge. Prediction constitutes the other. In fact, the ability to make correct predictions can be viewed as the first quality for identifying what science is: "If one knows something to be true, he is in a position to predict; where prediction is impossible, there is no knowledge."[10] For example, if one knows that two times six is twelve, one can predict the outcome of a count of two combined groups of six objects. If one knows that the freezing point of water is 32°F or 0°C, one can predict what will happen to his or her car if an antifreeze treatment is not applied to the water in the radiator during the freezing season. If one knows that governments increase their spending in economic recessions, one can predict that the 1980–1981 recession (and future recessions) would bring increases in government spending. If one knows that manpower programs solve unemployment problems, one can predict that current rates of unemployment are temporary and unemployment is bound to disappear.

The expectation that scientific knowledge should lead to accurate predictions is based upon the argument that *if* it is known that X causes Y, and that X is present, *then* the prediction that Y will occur can be made. Underlying this argument is the assumption that if a universal law or a probabilistic generalization is *both* known and true—that the antecedent conditions are sufficient for predicting the outcome—then the only reasons for failure in prediction can be (1) the law or the generalization is not true or (2) the antecedent conditions are incorrectly perceived. Thus, if, say, the problem of unemployment remains unsolved, it is either because the generalization that manpower programs solve unemployment problems is not true or because the activities aimed at solving unemployment are erroneously perceived as manpower programs.

Recalling the deductive mode of explanations, we can see that the process of prediction is, logically speaking, the *reverse* of the process of explanation. The antecedent observations are merely recording the fact that the initial conditions are present. Universal laws or probabilistic generalizations are used to justify the prediction that if the initial conditions are present, then the consequent must follow.[11]

The logical structure of scientific explanations and predictions can now be explicated. This structure consists of the following parts:

1. A statement E describing the specific phenomena or event to be explained.
2. A set of statements A_1 to A_n describing specific relevant conditions that are antecedent to, or causally related with, the phenomenon to be described by E.

10. Adrian D. De Groot, *Methodology: Foundations of Inference and Research in the Behavioral Sciences* (The Hague, Netherlands: Mouton, 1968), p. 20.

11. George J. Graham, *Methodological Foundations for Political Analysis* (Waltham, Mass.: Xerox College Publishing, 1971), pp. 226–228.

3. A set of universal laws or probabilistic generalizations L_1 to L_n that state: "Whenever events of the kind described by A_1 to A_n take place, then an event of the kind described by E occurs."

In order for these three parts to constitute an explanation of the event or the phenomenon, they must fulfill at least two conditions:

1. The E statement must be deducible from the A and L statements together, but not from either set of statements alone, and
2. The A and L statements must be true.

A symbolic presentation of the logical structure of scientific explanations and predictions looks like the following:

$$L_1........,L_n$$
$$\underline{A_1........,A_n}$$
Therefore E

The logical structure of explanation and prediction is identical. The only difference between them is the temporal vantage of the scientist. In the case of explanation, the E is a past event relative to the scientist's present temporal vantage point, and he or she seeks the appropriate L's and A's under which to deduce it; in the case of prediction, the scientist already has the L's and A's, and he or she seeks for an event that the former imply.[12]

Sense of Understanding

The third component of social scientific knowledge is a sense of understanding. The meaning of the term *understanding* is not agreed upon, and it is being used in two radically different senses—*Verstehen* (or empathic understanding) and predictive understanding. These different usages evolved from the fact that the social sciences are both humanistic and scientific and that social scientists are observers as well as participants in the subject matter of their disciplines. In the words of Hans Zetterberg:

> Symbols are the stuff out of which cultures and societies are made . . . For example, a sequence of conception, birth, nursing and weaning represents the *biological* reality of parenthood. But in analyzing human parenthood we find, in addition to the biological reality, a complex of symbols dealing with the license to have children, responsibilities for their care and schooling, rights to make some decisions on their behalf, obligations to launch them by certain social rituals . . . Our language thus contains codifications of what parents

12. Richard S. Rudner, *Philosophy of Social Science* (Englewood Cliffs, N.J.: Prentice-Hall, 1966), p. 60.

are and what they shall do and what shall be done to them, and all these sentences in our language represent the *social* reality of parenthood. Social reality, in this as in other cases, consists of symbols.[13]

But are symbols and, by implication, human behavior amenable to investigation by the same scientific methodology that is used in the natural sciences? Is the subject matter of the social sciences so complex and distinct that a unique scientific methodology ought to be developed? Do social scientists, unlike natural scientists, have to "get inside" their subject matter in order to understand it?

The Verstehen tradition. According to the *Verstehen* (the German term for empathy) tradition, the natural and social sciences are distinctive bodies of knowledge because of the divergence in the nature of their subject matter. From this assumption the argument was developed that natural scientists and social scientists must employ different methods of research. For example, the social scientist must take cognizance of both the historical dimension of human behavior and the subjective aspects of human experience. The German sociologist Max Weber (1864–1930) argued that if social scientists are to understand the behavior of individuals and groups, they must learn to "put themselves into the place of the subject of inquiry." They must gain an understanding of the other's view of reality: his or her symbols, values and attitudes.[14]

More recently, the *symbolic interactionist* approach emerged as an offspring of the *Verstehen* tradition. Herbert Blumer, a proponent of the approach, espouses the view that the subject matter and thus the structure of the scientific method in the natural and the social sciences are radically different. Blumer emphasizes not only the subjective component of human behavior but also the evolutionary creativeness of the "social act." For him, individuals are continually remaking their social environment; the social order is constantly in the state of becoming. Consequently, scientists cannot impose fixed, rigid explanations or prediction upon an ever-changing social world.[15]

Predictive Understanding

In contrast to the *Verstehen* tradition, *logical empiricists* take the position that social scientists can attain objective knowledge in the study of the natural as well as the social world. The social and the natural

13. Hans L. Zetterberg, *On Theory and Verification in Sociology*, 3rd enlarged ed. (Totowa, N.J.: Bedminster Press, 1965), pp. 1–2.

14. Max Weber, *The Theory of Social and Economic Organization*, trans. by A. M. Henderson and Talcott Parsons (New York: Free Press, 1964).

15. Herbert Blumer, "What is Wrong with Social Theory?" *American Sociological Review*, 19 (February 1954): 3–10.

sciences are amenable to investigation by the same scientific methodology. Furthermore, logical empiricists do not take issue with the argument that empathic understanding may be a helpful way for discovery. But discoveries must be verified if they are to be integrated into the scientific body of knowledge. (The idea of discovery *versus* verification is discussed in greater detail later in this chapter.)

THE ROLE OF METHODOLOGY

Science is not united by its subject matter but rather by its methodology. What sets the scientific approach apart from other modes of acquiring knowledge are the assumptions upon which it is based and its methodology.

The scientific methodology is a system of explicit rules and procedures upon which research is based and against which claims for knowledge are evaluated. This system is neither closed nor infallible. Rather, the rules and procedures are constantly improved; scientists look for new methods and techniques of observation, inference, generalization, and analysis. As these are developed and found to be congruent with the underlying assumptions of the scientific approach, they are incorporated into the system of rules that make the scientific methodology. The scientific methodology is first and foremost self-correcting:

> Science does not desire to obtain conviction for its propositions in *any* price. Proposition must be supported by logically acceptable evidence, which must be weighed carefully and tested by the well-known canons of necessary and probable inference. It follows that the *method* of science is more stable, and more important to men of science, than any particular result achieved by its means. In virtue of its method, the scientific enterprise is a self-corrective process. It appeals to no special revelation or authority whose deliverances are indubitable and final. It claims no infallibility, but relies upon the methods of developing and testing hypotheses for assured conclusions. The canons of inquiry are themselves discovered in the process of reflection, and may themselves become modified in the course of study. The method makes possible the noting and correction of errors by continued application of itself.[16]

The methodology of the social sciences has evolved in a slow process of growth. In this process criticism has always performed an important function. Through the continuous interchange of ideas and information it became possible to formulate commonly accepted rules and procedures and to develop corresponding methods and techniques. This system of rules and procedures is the *normative* component of the scientific

16. Cohen and Nagel, *An Introduction to Logic and Scientific Method*, pp. 395–396.

methodology. It defines the "rules of the game"; and these, in turn, enable communication, constructive criticism, and scientific progress.

Methodology as Rules for Communication

Anatol Rapoport illustrated the general problem of communication between two people who have not shared a common experience with the following anecdote:

> A blind man asked someone to explain the meaning of "white."
> "White is a color," he was told, "as, for example, white snow."
> "I understand," said the blind man. "It is a cold and damp color."
> "No, it doesn't have to be cold and damp. Forget about snow. Paper, for instance, is white."
> "So it rustles?" asked the blind man.
> "No indeed, it need not rustle. It is like the fur of an albino rabbit."
> "A soft, fluffy color?" the blind man wanted to know.
> "It need not be soft either. Porcelain is white, too."
> "Perhaps it is a brittle color, then." said the blind man.[17]

A major function of methodology is to facilitate communication between scientists who either shared or want to share a common experience. Furthermore, by making the rules of methodology explicit, public, and accessible, the framework for replication and constructive criticism is set forth. Replication, that is, the repetition of the same investigation in exactly the same way either by the same scientist or other scientists, is a safeguard against unintentional error or deception. Constructive criticism implies that as soon as one makes claims for knowledge, we can ask questions, such as the following: "Does the explanation (prediction) follow logically from the assumptions?" "Are the observations correct?" "What were the methods of observation?" "Was the testing valid?" "Weren't other factors interfering in drawing conclusions?" "Shouldn't the findings be taken as evidence that another explanation is correct?" and so forth. We shall see throughout this book that such queries form the criteria for evaluating claims for scientific knowledge.

Methodology as Rules for Reasoning

Though empirical observations are fundamental to the scientific approach, they must be related and assembled into systematic logical structures. Empirical observations or facts don't "speak for themselves." The scientific methodology explicates the logical foundations of reasoned knowledge. The most essential tool of the scientific approach, along with factual observations, is logic—the system of valid reasoning about factual

---

17. Anatol Rapoport, *Operational Philosophy* (New York: Wiley, 1967), p. 12.

observations that permits reliable inferences to be drawn from them. Logic, as the study of the foundations and principles of reasoning, is so crucial to the scientific approach that the science of many subject matters is called the logic of them—for example, bio*logy*, anthropo*logy*, soci-*ology*, crimino*logy*, geo*logy*, and so on.

The scientific methodology demands competence in logical reasoning and analysis. Rules for classification and definition, forms of deductive and probabilistic (inductive) inferences, theories of probability, sampling procedures, systems of calculi, and rules of measurement are the methodological tool kit of the social scientist. Furthermore, through the use of logic science progresses systematically rather than haphazardly, and the scientific body of knowledge is itself systematic. The logical procedures inherent in the scientific methodology take the form of closely interwoven series of procedures that support each other or, at least, do not contradict each other. In this way, the scientific methodology enhances the internal consistency of claims for empirical knowledge.

Methodology as Rules for Intersubjectivity

Logic is concerned with valid reasoning, not with empirical truth or verified facts. A fact is either certainly or probably true when objective evidence exists to support it. On the other hand, a claim for knowledge is valid when the conclusion necessarily follows from the assumptions made originally. Thus, scientists can make an erroneous inference from verified facts (truth statements) if they reason incorrectly. But they can just as easily make an erroneous inference by reasoning correctly (logically valid reasoning) if they do not employ verified facts: "The truth of an assertion is related to experience; the validity of an assertion is related to its inner consistency or its consistency with other assertions."[18]

Recall the forms of deductive and probabilistic explanations (predictions) discussed in the last section. It should now be obvious that they relate only to logically valid reasoning. The validity of their conclusions followed strictly from their antecedent assumptions. Their truth cannot be established or verified solely on logical grounds. Truth has to be verified with objective evidence. As the following syllogism demonstrates, strict adherence to logical reasoning without studying the objective facts can lead to absurdities:

All human beings are power-motivated organisms,
All power-motivated organisms are destructive.
Therefore: all human beings are destructive.

The scientific methodology explicates the *accepted criteria* for empirical objectivity (truth) and the methods and techniques for verifica-

18. Ibid., p. 18.

tion. These two are highly dependent: empirical objectivity depends on verification so much so that the scientist cannot make claims for objectivity until verification has been carried out.

Given that the criteria for empirical objectivity and the methods for verification are products of the human mind (in contrast to the belief that truth is an absolute given), the term *intersubjectivity* is more appropriate than *objectivity*. To be intersubjective, knowledge in general and the scientific methodology in particular have to be transmissible: "A type of knowledge that can be transmitted from any person who has such knowledge to any other person who does not have it but who can grasp the meaning of the symbols (words, signs) used in communication and perform the operations, if any, described in these communications."[19] Thus, if one scientist conducts an investigation, another scientist can replicate it and compare the two sets of findings. If the methodology is correct and (we assume) the conditions have not changed, we would expect the findings to be similar. Indeed, conditions might change and new factors emerge. But the significance of intersubjectivity is that one scientist can understand and evaluate the methods of others and perform similar observations so as to verify empirical facts. The methodological requirement for intersubjectivity is the evidence that empirical observations are uncontaminated by any factors save those common to all observers: "The methodological question is always limited to whether what is reported as an observation can be used in subsequent inquiry even if the particular observer is no longer a part of the context."[20]

SCIENTIFIC REVOLUTION

Scientific knowledge is knowledge provable by *both* reason and the evidence of the senses (experience). The importance of the scientific methodology is primarily to be found in institutionalizing a language for communication, rules for reasoning, and procedures and methods for observation and verification. In this sense, methodology demands conformity: claims for knowledge are rejected if they do not conform to the rules and procedures explicated by the methodology. But does not methodological conformity hinder new discoveries and, by implication, scientific progress? Furthermore, scientists are members of scientific communities governed by conventions, norms, rituals, and power relations that may be incompatible with the objective pursuit of knowledge. Do scientific communities hinder scientific progress?

19. Arnold Brecht, *Political Theory* (Princeton, N.J.: Princeton University Press, 1959), p. 114.

20. Abraham Kaplan, *The Conduct of Inquiry* (San Francisco: Chandler, 1964), p. 128.

Philosophers of science and social theorists have long been concerned with the dangers of dogma in science. As Scott Greer put it, "If we are lucky and our scientific knowledge accumulates, it may spiral upward; it may also revolve at the same level, a merry-go-round of fashion; or it may spiral downward, from theory to doctrine to dogma."[21] Among the various attempts to describe scientific revolutions from a sociological-political perspective, Thomas Kuhn's thesis is provocative and worth outlining in some detail.

Normal Versus Revolutionary Science

Basic to Kuhn's image of the scientific enterprise is the distinction between *normal science* and *revolutionary science*. Normal science is viewed as the routine verification of the dominant theory in any historical period. Verification and testing become part of a puzzle-solving activity. In Kuhn's words:

> "Normal science" means research firmly based upon one or more past scientific achievements, achievements that some particular scientific community acknowledges for a time as supplying the foundation of its practice. Today such achievements are recounted, though seldom in their original form, by science textbooks, elementary and advanced. These textbooks expound the body of accepted theory, illustrate many or all of its successful applications, and compare these applications with exemplary observations and experiments.[22]

Such works socialize students and practitioners into the scientific community. They define the kinds of research problems to be investigated, the kinds of assumptions and concepts to be employed, and the kinds of research methods to be used. Historically such works ". . . were able to do so because they shared two essential characteristics. Their achievement was sufficiently unprecedented to attract an enduring group of adherents away from competing modes of scientific activity. Simultaneously, it was sufficiently open-ended to leave all sorts of problems for the redefined group of practitioners to resolve."[23] Kuhn terms achievements that share these two attributes *paradigms* and suggests that they are closely related to the idea of normal science:

> By choosing it [the term *paradigm*], I mean to suggest that some accepted examples of actual scientific practice—examples which

21. Scott Greer, *The Logic of Social Inquiry* (Chicago: Aldine, 1969), pp. 3–4.

22. Thomas S. Kuhn, *The Structure of Scientific Revolutions*, 2nd ed. (University of Chicago Press, 1970), p. 10.

23. Ibid., p. 10.

include law, theory, application, and instrumentation together—provide models from which spring particular coherent traditions of scientific research . . . The study of paradigm . . . is what mainly pre-
pares the student for membership in the particular scientific
community with which he will later practice.[24]

Furthermore, because the scientist joins a scientific community
whose mentors learned the same conceptual and methodological foundations of their discipline from the same sources, his or her subsequent
research will rarely evoke disagreement or criticism over fundamentals.
Scientists whose research is grounded on a shared paradigm are psychologically committed to the same rules, norms, and standards for scientific practice: "That commitment and the apparent consensus it produces are prerequisites for normal science, i.e., for the genesis and
continuation of a particular research tradition."[25]

Instead of unbiased scientists, normal science potrays scientific communities as groups of partisans advocating and defending the established
order or the paradigm. Yet, adherence to a paradigm should not necessarily imply hindrance to scientific progress. Paradigms are necessary;
without them scientific research could not take place as a collective enterprise, for science needs an organizing principle: "Acquisition of a
paradigm and of the more esoteric type of research it permits is a sign
of maturity in the development of any given scientific field."[26]

Revolutionary Science

In contrast to normal science, Kuhn views revolutionary science as the
abrupt development of a *rival paradigm* that can be accepted only gradually by a scientific community. Paradigm transformation is what is revolutionary in science. For example, the paradigm that human intelligence is a product of both the sociocultural environment and genetic
processes transformed the paradigm that advanced the view that intelligence is entirely determined by genetic mechanisms. This, in turn,
revolutionized the study of personality and human behavior and has
been the cornerstone for many social, educational, and economic public
policies.

The process of rejecting a dominant paradigm begins, according to
Kuhn, as the paradigm is verified; for as scientists empirically test the
various dimensions and implications of a dominant paradigm, its compliance with research findings becomes tenuous. Kuhn terms such in-

24. Ibid.

25. Ibid., pp. 10–11.

26. Ibid., p. 11.

congruences *anomalies* and proposes that anomalies become more recognizable as the process of verification or problem-solving activities continues. At some point a rival candidate for a paradigm is constructed. Conflict ensues between the supporters of the old and the new paradigm, culminating finally in the acceptance of the new paradigm and reestablishment of the normal science. The period of transition from old to new paradigms produces uncertainty and splits in the scientific community. The transition period is characterized by random research, aimless verification, and accidental discoveries.

Scientific revolutions are infrequent. Most of the time devoted to the pursuit of science is devoted to normal science. A scientific revolution is a long time a-building and occurs only rarely because most scientists are *not* trying to refute dominant paradigms; they do not perceive anomalies right away. Perceptions are easily slipped into mental categories established prior to experience of verification. Scientists see what they come to see; long after a dominant paradigm fails to be congruent with empirical findings, it remains the accepted paradigm.

Is There a Logic of Discovery?

In Kuhn's view there can be no logic of discovery, but only sociopsychology of discovery: anomalies and inconsistencies always abound in science, but a dominant paradigm secures puzzle-solving activities until it is overthrown by a crisis. But is there a rational cause for the appearance of crisis? Why do scientists suddenly see a crisis? How is a rival paradigm constructed? Kuhn's thesis does not address these questions: There is no logic of discovery but rather group struggle within scientific communities.

In sharp contrast to Kuhn's descriptive view of science is Karl Popper's normative position. Popper maintains that the scientific community ought to be, and to a considerable degree actually is, an open society in which no dominant paradigm is ever sacred. Science ought to be a revolution in permanence; and criticism, the heart of the scientific enterprise. Refutations of claims for knowledge constitute revolutions:

> In my view the "normal" scientist, as Kuhn describes him, is a person one ought to be sorry for . . . The "normal" scientist . . . has been badly taught. He has been taught in a dogmatic spirit: he is a victim of indoctrination. He has learned a technique which can be applied without asking for the reason why. . . .[27]

Popper admits that at any moment scientists are "prisoners" caught

---

27. Karl R. Popper, "Normal Science and Its Dangers," in *Criticism and the Growth of Knowledge*, ed. by Irme Lakatos and Alan Musgrave (New York: Cambridge University Press, 1970), p. 53.

in their paradigms, expectations, past experiences, and language. But "we are prisoners in a Pickwickian sense: if we try, we can break out of our framework at any time. Admittedly, we shall find ourselves again in a framework, but it will be a better and roomier one; and we can at any moment break out of it again."[28]

It is helpful at this point to distinguish two contexts of scientific activities—discovery and justification.[29] The *context of justification* refers to the activities of scientists as they attempt logically and empirically to verify claims for knowledge. The scientific methodology establishes the logic of justification. Methodology is indifferent to how scientists arrive at their insights, but asks only whether they are justified in reaching claims for knowledge. The activities of the scientist within the *context of discovery*, however, are not limited by methodology. The scientific methodology may facilitate activities that lead toward discovery, but for the present no formalized rules or logic for discovery can be explicated. Creativity, insight, imagination, and inspiration are of enormous importance in science. Although these can be cultivated, they cannot be reduced to rules: "There is no science which will enable man to bethink himself of that which will suit his purpose."[30]

THE RESEARCH PROCESS

Scientific knowledge is knowledge provable by both reason and experience (observation). Logical validity and empirical verification are the criteria employed by scientists to evaluate claims for knowledge. These two criteria are translated into the research activities of scientists through the *research process*. The research process can be viewed as the overall scheme of scientific activities in which scientists engage in order to produce knowledge; it is the paradigm of scientific inquiry.

As illustrated in Figure 1.1, the research process consists of seven principal stages: *problem, hypothesis, research design, measurement, data collection, data analysis,* and *generalization*. Each of these stages is interrelated with *theory* in the sense that it is affected by it as well as affects it. Throughout this book we will discuss extensively each stage and the transitions from one stage to the next. For the moment, we will limit ourselves to a general overview of the research process.

The most characteristic feature of the research process is its *cyclic nature*. It usually starts with a problem and ends in a tentative empirical

28. Ibid., p. 56.

29. See Hans Reichenbach, *The Rise of Scientific Philosophy* (Berkeley: University of California Press, 1959), pp. 230–231, and Kaplan, *The Conduct of Inquiry*, pp. 12–18.

30. John Stuart Mill (quoted in Kaplan, *The Conduct of Inquiry*, p. 16).

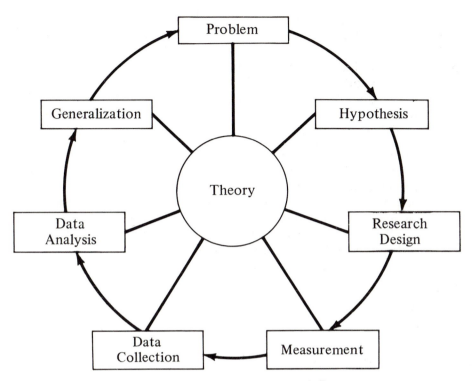

FIGURE 1.1.   The Principal Stages of the Research Process

generalization. The generalization ending one cycle is the begining of the next cycle. This cyclic process continues indefinitely, reflecting the progress of a scientific discipline.

The research process is also *self-correcting*. Tentative generalizations to research problems are tested logically and empirically. If these generalizations are rejected, new ones are formulated and tested. In the process of reformulation all the research operations are reevaluated because the rejection of a tentative generalization might be due not to its being invalid, but to deficiencies in performing the research operations. For example, a generalization that economic crises lead to increased government spending will be rejected if it cannot be logically validated and empirically verified. But the generalization might also be rejected, *even if it's true*, if procedures for validation and verification (for example, research design, measurement, data analysis) are deficient. To minimize the risk of rejecting true generalizations, one reexamines each of the stages in the research process prior to the formulation of new generalizations.

Finally, the reader should be aware of the fact that the research process, as presented here, is somewhat idealized; that is, it is a rational reconstruction of scientific practice: "The reconstruction idealizes the logic of science only in showing us what it *would* be if it were extracted and refined to utmost purity . . . [But] . . . not even the greatest of scientists has a cognitive style which is wholly and perfectly logical, and the most brilliant piece of research still betrays its all-too-human divagations."[31]

In practice, the research process occurs

(1) sometimes quickly, sometimes slowly; (2) sometimes with a very high degree of formalization and vigor, sometimes quite informally, unself-consciously, and intuitively; (3) sometimes through the interaction of several scientists in distinct roles (of, say, "theorist," "research director," "interviewer," "methodologist," "sampling expert," "statistician," etc.), sometimes through the efforts of a single scientist; and (4) sometimes only in the scientist's imagination, sometimes in actual fact.[32]

Thus, our logical reconstruction of the research process is not intended to be inflexible, but rather to convey the underlying themes of social science research.

THE PLAN OF THIS BOOK

This book is organized along the major stages of the research process. Chapters 2 and 3 cover the conceptual foundations of empirical research and the relationships between theory and research. They focus on the ideas of concepts, definitions, the functions and structures of theories, models, relations, variables, and the construction of research hypotheses.

In Chapters 4 and 5 we discuss the research design stage. A research design is the strategy that guides the investigator throughout the process of research. It is a logical model of proof that allows the drawing of inferences concerning the causal relations among the phenomena under investigation. As you will see, there are various types of research designs, each of which explicates the conditions for accepting or rejecting causal inferences.

Chapter 6 is concerned with the measurement stage. Measurement is the procedure of systematically assigning symbols (in particular, numbers) to empirical observations. These symbols are, in turn, amenable to logical, mathematical, and statistical manipulations that reveal information and relations that otherwise could not have been revealed. Numbers can be added, subtracted, percentaged, correlated, and used as *means* for describing and analyzing phenomena and for generalizing.

31. Kaplan, *The Conduct of Inquiry*, pp. 10–11.

32. Wallace, *The Logic of Science in Sociology*, p. 19.

Chapters 7, 8, 9, and 10 cover the data collection stage. In this stage empirical observations are being made and recorded. Data (observations) can be collected by different methods, including structured observation, nonstructured observation, personal interviewing, impersonal surveys, public records, or private records. There is neither one foolproof data collection method nor one method that will suit all research problems. Different problems call for the employment of different methods, and each method displays certain advantages but also certain inherent limitations.

Chapter 11 discusses major topics of data processing, the latter being the link between data collection and data analysis. Data processing involves the transformation of observations gathered in the data-collection stage into a system of conceptual categories and the translation of these categories into coding schemes that are amenable to quantitative analysis. These codes can then be recorded and processed through the computer. The central issues involved in coding and automatic data processing are also covered in this chapter.

In the next stage of the research process, the concern is with quantitative, statistical analyses. We view statistics as numbers that can be used to summarize, evaluate, or analyze a body of information. It is useful to distinguish two categories of statistics with different functions: *descriptive statistics* and *inferential statistics*. Descriptive statistics are procedures used to organize, describe, and summarize data. Chapter 12 covers descriptive univariate distributions; Chapter 13 focuses on bivariate distributions; and in Chapter 14 multivariate data analysis techniques are presented. In Chapter 15 we present methods of index construction and scaling. Inferential or inductive statistics make possible generalizations beyond the data in hand, the evaluations of differences among groups, and the estimation of unknown values. Chapter 16 covers major topics of sampling and sample designs, and in Chapter 17 we discuss hypothesis-testing and statistical inferences.

The concern of the last chapter is with ethical and moral dilemmas involved in the conduct of social science research. Questions such as "Is it unethical not to acquire participants' informed consent for all research?" "What are the limits of an investigator's responsibility for participants?" "Should promises of confidentiality always be kept?" and "Should research data have legal protection?" have become increasingly salient and are discussed in this chapter.

SUMMARY

Science is united by its methodology, not by its subject matter. What sets the scientific approach apart from other modes of acquiring knowledge are the assumptions upon which it is grounded and its methodology.

The assumptions of the scientific approach are these: Nature is orderly; we can know nature; knowledge is tentative but superior to ignorance; natural phenomena have natural causes; nothing is self-evident; knowledge is derived from the acquisition of experience.

The methodology of the scientific approach serves three major purposes: rules for communication; rules for logical and valid reasoning; rules for intersubjectivity. These three systems of rules allow us to understand, explain, and predict our environments and ourselves in a manner that other systems for generating knowledge (that is, the authoritarian, the mystical, and the rationalistic) cannot allow us to do.

Scientific knowledge is knowledge provable by *both* reason and the evidence of the senses. The scientific methodology requires strict adherence to the rules of logic and observation. Such adherence should not be seen as encouraging conformity and dogma. The research process is cyclistic and self-correcting. Rational criticism should be the heart of the scientific enterprise, and science ought to be a revolution in permanence. Obviously, scientific communities, like other social communities, are involved in power struggles that are not always conducive to the progress of science. Perhaps such power struggles are inevitable. But claims for knowledge are accepted only in so far as they are congruent with the assumptions of science and its methodology.

KEY TERMS FOR REVIEW

Science
Rationalism
Epistemology
Assumptions of
  science
Empirical
Explanation
Deductive
  explanations

Probabilistic
  explanations
Prediction
Verstehen
Logical empiricists
Methodology
Replication
Intersubjectivity
Normal science

Paradigm
Revolutionary
  science
Context of
  justification
Research process

ADDITIONAL READINGS

Brown, Robert. *Explanation in Social Science.* Chicago: Aldine, 1963.

Kemeny, John G. *A Philosopher Looks at Science.* Princeton, N.J.: D. Van Nostrand, 1959.

Madge, John. *The Origins of Scientific Sociology.* New York: Free Press, 1962.

McLain, Carvin, and Erwin M. Segal. *The Game of Science.* Belmont, Calif.: Brooks Cole, 1969.

Meehan, Eugene. *The Theory and Method of Political Analysis.* Homewood, Ill.: Dorsey, 1965.

Polanyi, Michael. *Personal Knowledge: Towards a Post-Critical Philosophy.* New York: Harper Torchbooks, 1964.

Popper, Karl R. *Conjectures and Refutations: The Growth of Scientific Knowledge.* New York: Harper & Row, 1963.

Scheffler, Israel. *Science and Subjectivity.* New York: Bobbs-Merrill, 1976.

Winch, Peter. *The Idea of a Social Science.* New York: Humanities Press, 1967.

CHAPTER PREVIEW

CHAPTER 2
Conceptual Foundations of Research

INTRODUCTION

Scientific knowledge is knowledge provable by both reason and experience. This implies that social scientists operate at two distinct but interrelated levels—conceptual-theoretical and observational-empirical. Social science research is the outcome of the interaction between these two levels. This chapter covers the basics of the conceptual-theoretical level and the relations between theory, models, and empirical research.

CONCEPTS

Thinking involves the use of language, which is a system of communication composed of symbols and a set of rules permitting various combinations of these symbols. One of the most significant symbols in language, especially as it relates to research, is the *concept*. Science begins by forming concepts to describe the empirical world. A concept is an abstraction representing an object, a property of an object, or a certain phenomenon. For example, "social status," "role," "power," "bureaucracy," and "relative deprivation" are common concepts in political science and sociology. Concepts such as "intelligence," "perception," and "learning" are common among psychologists. Every scientific discipline develops its unique set of concepts; to scientists, this constitutes a language; outsiders call it a "jargon."

Functions of Concepts

Concepts serve a number of important functions in social science research. First and foremost, they are the foundation of communication and thought. Without a set of agreed-upon concepts, intersubjective communication is impossible. Concepts are abstracted from sense impressions or percepts and are used to convey and transmit perceptions and information. It should be stressed that concepts do not actually exist as empirical phenomena; a concept is not the phenomenon itself, but rather a *symbol* of the phenomenon. Treating concepts as though they are the phenomena themselves leads to the *fallacy of reification*—to the error of regarding abstractions as actual phenomena. For example, it is erroneous to regard a concept such as "power" as having drives, needs, or instincts.

Second, concepts introduce a point of view—a way of looking at empirical phenomena: "Through scientific conceptualization the perceptual world is given an order and coherence that could not be perceived before conceptualization."[1] The concept enables scientists to relate to some aspect of reality and give it a common quality:

> It permits the scientist, in a community of other scientists, to lift his own idiosyncratic experiences to the level of consensual meaning. It also enables him to carry on an interaction with his environment; he indicates to himself what a concept means and acts toward the designation of that meaning. The concept thus acts as a sensitizer of experience and perception, opening new realms of observation, closing others.[2]

Third, concepts are means for classification and generalization. Scientists categorize, structure, order, and generalize their experiences and observations in terms of concepts. As John McKinney puts it,

> All phenomena are unique in their concrete occurrence; therefore no phenomena actually recur in their concrete wholeness. The meaning of identity is always "identical for the purpose in hand." To introduce *order* with its various scientific implications, including prediction, the scientist necessarily ignores the unique, the extraneous, and nonrecurring, and thereby departs from perceptual experience. This departure is the necessary price he must pay for the achievement of abstract generality. To conceptualize means to generalize to some degree. To generalize means to reduce the number of objects by conceiving of some of them as being identical.[3]

For example, we can ignore the ways in which pine, oak, spruce, fir, palm, and apple differ from each other and grasp their generic resem-

1. Norman K. Denzin, *The Research Act* (Chicago: Aldine, 1970), p. 36.

2. Ibid.

3. John C. McKinney, *Constructive Typology and Social Theory* (New York: Appleton-Century-Crofts, 1966), p. 9.

blance via the concept "tree." Tree is the general concept by means of which we grasp a multiplicity of unique aspects and comprehend them within an order. Tree is also an abstract concept in the sense that the specific differences between pine, oak, spruce, fir, palm, and apple are lost in the conceptualization process. This process of abstraction and generalization enables scientists to delineate the essential attributes of empirical phenomena. At the same time, once the concept is formed, it cannot be a perfect symbol of that which it stands for because its content is inevitably reduced to those attributes that the scientist considers to be essential.

The fourth function of concepts is to serve as the building blocks of theories and thus of explanations and predictions. Concepts are the most critical elements in any theory because they define the shape and content of theories. For example, the concepts "power" and "legitimacy" define the shape and content of theories of governance. The concepts "individualism" and "Protestantism" defined and shaped Durkheim's suicide theory. The theory predicts conditions under which suicide rates would be high and low by specifying the relationships between individualism and religion. The concept "relative deprivation" is central in theories of violence, and "supply" and "demand" are pillar concepts in economic theory. Such concepts when linked in a systematic way lead to theories; concept formation and theory formation are closely related.

DEFINITIONS

If concepts are to serve the functions of communication, sensitization of experience, generalization, and theory construction, they have to be clear, precise, and agreed-upon. Indeed, the problem with everyday language is that although it is not totally arbitrary, it is vague, ambiguous, and imprecise. Concepts such as "power," "bureaucracy," or "satisfaction" mean different things to different people and are used in different contexts to designate various things. Usually, this does not create major problems in everyday communication. But neither scientific communication nor the other three functions of concepts can be served with ambiguous and imprecise language.

Any scientific discipline is necessarily concerned with its vocabulary. The social sciences have sought to distinguish a clear and precise body of concepts (abstractions) to characterize their subject matter. In the process, thousands of concepts were invented, refined, used, and discarded. Upon an examination of this volume of concepts one is likely to find a great deal of ambiguity and inconsistency in the meaning of many of these concepts. This should not be too surprising. Social scientists are faced with the problem of distinguishing their concepts from those popularly and indiscriminately used by the publics they want to study. But as the social sciences progress, so will their vocabulary. As Carl Hempel wrote,

> In the initial stages of scientific inquiry, description as well as generalization is stated in the vocabulary of everyday language. The growth of a scientific discipline, however, always brings with it the development of a system of specialized, more or less abstract, concepts and of a corresponding technical terminology.[4]

Clarity and precision in the usage of concepts are achieved by definitions. Two types of definitions are important in social science research—*conceptual* and *operational*.

Conceptual Definitions

Definitions that describe concepts using other concepts are conceptual definitions. For example, "power" has been conceptually defined as the ability of an actor (for example, individual, group, state) to get another actor to do something that the latter would not otherwise do. The concept "relative deprivation" is defined as actors' perception of discrepancy between their "value expectations" and their "value capabilities." "Value expectations," in turn, are defined as the goods and conditions of life to which people believe they are rightfully entitled, and "value capabilities" are defined as the goods and conditions people think they are capable of getting and keeping.[5]

In these examples a number of concepts were used to define other concepts. But the process of definition might not stop here. In the case of "relative deprivation," a person unfamiliar with the theory is likely to ask, "What are 'capabilities,' 'expectations,' and 'perceptions'?" These concepts call for further clarification. "Expectations," for instance, can be defined as a manifestation of the prevailing norms set by the immediate economic, social, cultural, and political environment. But what is meant by "norms," "immediate," "social," "cultural," "economic," and "political"? These concepts can be defined by still other concepts, and so on. At a certain point in this process one will encounter concepts that cannot be defined by other concepts. These are called *primitive terms*. For example, colors, sounds, smells, and tastes are primitive terms. Primitive terms are those on which there is shared agreement as to their meaning. Usually, their meaning is conveyed by indicating examples. Such demonstrative definitions are called *ostensive definitions*.

---

4. Carl G. Hempel, *Fundamentals of Concept Formation in Empirical Science* (Chicago: University of Chicago Press, 1952), p. 1.

5. Ted R. Gurr, *Why Men Rebel* (Princeton, N.J.: Princeton University Press, 1970), p. 24.

They must be used in order to develop basic language terms. An ostensive definition can be visualized by an attempt to teach a child the meaning of, say, "red." We point to "red" objects until the child realizes that only the quality of "redness" is shared by all of the objects.

Conceptual definitions consist of primitive and *derived terms*. Derived terms are those that can be defined by the use of primitive terms. Thus, if there is an agreement on the primitive terms "individual," "interact," "two or more," and "regularly," we can define "group" (derived term) as two or more individuals that interact regularly. The main advantage of derived terms is that their use is more efficient; they require less effort than the set of the primitive terms that compose the definition of the derived term.[6]

Conceptual definitions are neither true nor false. As pointed out earlier, concepts are symbols permitting communication. Conceptual definitions are either useful for communication, or they are not. Indeed, one may criticize the intelligibility of a definition or question whether it is being used consistently. But there is no point in criticizing a conceptual definition for not being true; the definition is what the definer says it is. Conceptual definitions that enhance communication share the following essential attributes:

☐ A definition must denote the distinctive characteristics or qualities of that which is defined. It must be inclusive of all things covered by it. At the same time, it should be exclusive of all things *not* being denoted by it.

☐ A definition should not be circular; that is, it must not contain itself any part of the thing being defined. Defining "female" as a person having feminine qualities or "power" as a quality shared by powerful people does not enhance communication.

☐ A definition should be stated positively whenever possible. Defining "intelligence" as a property that lacks color, weight, and character obviously does not contribute to communication because there are many other things that lack color, weight, and character.

☐ A definition should be stated in clear, unequivocal terms. A term such as "conservative" means different things to different people, and unless there is an agreement on its meaning, it should not be used in a definition.

Operational Definitions

It is often the case that the empirical properties or events that are represented by concepts cannot be directly observed. For example, the con-

---

6. Paul D. Reynolds, *A Primer in Theory Construction* (New York: Bobbs-Merrill, 1971), pp. 45–48.

cepts "power," "relative deprivation," "intelligence," and "satisfaction" and, in general, nonbehavioral properties (for example, perceptions, values, attitudes) cannot be directly observed. In such cases, the empirical existence of a concept has to be inferred. Inferences of this kind are made with operational definitions. Through operational definitions concepts are given empirical referents.

An operational definition is a set of procedures that describe the activities one should perform in order to establish empirically the existence or degree of existence of a concept. Through such definitions the meanings of concepts are specified; operational definitions explicate the testing procedures that provide criteria for the empirical application of concepts. Thus, operational definitions bridge the conceptual-theoretical level with the empirical-observational level. They tell *what to do* and *what to observe* in order to bring the phenomenon defined within the range of the researcher's experience: "The thing or quality defined is not assumed to exist a priori. Rather its existence or reality follows from the operations performed and resides in the invariants observed."[7]

The idea of operational definitions was developed by the operationist school of thought as exemplified in the works of the physicist P. W. Bridgman. His central idea was that the *meaning* of *every* scientific concept must be specifiable by indicating a definite testing operation that provides a certain criterion for its application. The meaning of a concept is fully and exclusively determined by its operational definition. In Bridgman's words,

> The concept of length is therefore fixed when the operations by which length is measured are fixed: that is, the concept of length involves as much as and nothing more than the set of operations by which length is determined. In general, we mean by any concept nothing more than a set of operations; *the concept is synonymous with the corresponding set of operations.*[8]

Thus, an operational definition of "length" would specify a procedure involving the use of a ruler for determining the length of the distance between two points. An operational definition of "weight" would specify *how* weight is determined by means of an appropriate instrument, for instance, a scale. Similarly, the term "harder than" as applied, say, to minerals, might be operationally defined as follows: "To determine whether mineral m_1 is harder than mineral m_2, draw a sharp point of a piece of m_1 under pressure across the surface of a piece m_2 (test

7. Anatol Rapoport, *Operational Philosophy* (New York: Wiley, 1967), p. 29.

8. Percy W. Bridgman, *The Logic of Modern Physics* (New York: Macmillan, 1961), p. 5 (Bridgman's italics).

operation); m_1 will be said to be harder than m_2 just in case a scratch is produced (specific test result)."[9] An operational definition of "intelligence" could consist of a test to be administered according to specifications; the test results are the responses of the individuals tested or a quantitative summary of the responses.

The structure of operational definitions is straightforward. If a given stimulus (S) is applied to an object, consistently producing a certain reaction (R), the object has the property (P), this being an operational definition. In the last example, an intelligence test (stimulus) is applied to respondents producing test scores (R); intelligence (P) is inferred from, or defined by, the test scores.

Many concepts used by social scientists are operationally defined solely on the strength of reactions to specific stimuli, conditions, or situations because the physical manipulation of individuals or events is either impossible or unethical. Even if we could manipulate individuals through certain operations—say, induce fear in a laboratory situation— it would involve a number of critical ethical dilemmas, including the rights of scientists to do so and the personal rights of the researched individuals. (The ethical dilemmas involved in social science research are discussed in Chapter 18.) In such cases, concepts are operationally defined by reactions to stimuli such as tests, questionnaires, or aggregate indicators that will be discussed in later chapters.

Example: The Definitions of Alienation

Let's see how the very abstract and complex concept "alienation" has been empirically researched. In a pioneering work, Melvin Seeman argued that alienation was conceptualized in the literature as "a sense of the splitting asunder of what was once held together, the breaking of the seamless mold in which values, behavior, and expectations were once cast into interlocking forms."[10] This conceptualization, he suggested, attributes five meanings to alienation, and thus five conceptual definitions are called forth:

1. Powerless—the expectancy by individuals that their behavior cannot determine the occurrence of the outcomes or reinforcements they seek.
2. Meaninglessness—perception by individuals that their minimal standards for clarity in decision making are not met.

9. Carl G. Hempel, *Philosophy of Natural Science* (Englewood Cliffs, N.J.: Prentice-Hall, 1966), p. 89.

10. Melvin Seeman, "On the Meaning of Alienation," in *Continuities in the Language of Social Research*, ed. by Paul Lazarsfeld, Ann Pasanella, and Morris Rosenberg (New York: Free Press, 1972), pp. 25–34.

3. Normlessness—high expectancy that socially unapproved behaviors are required to achieve certain goals.
4. Isolation—assignment of low reward value to goals and beliefs that are typically highly valued in society.
5. Self-estrangement—the degree of dependence of the given behavior upon anticipated future rewards that lie outside the activity itself.

In later research these five concepts, or dimensions of alienation, were operationally defined by constructing questionnaire items for each dimension; the responses of individuals to the entire questionnaire defined the empirical existence of each of the five dimensions. As a means of operationalizing "powerlessness," the following question was used: "Suppose your town was considering a regulation that you believed to be very unjust or harmful. What do you think you could do?" Individuals who responded that they could do nothing were defined as powerless. Other questions used to define powerlessness operationally are these: (1) If you made an effort to change this regulation, how likely is it that you would succeed? (2) If such a case arose, how likely is it that you would actually do something about it? (3) Would you ever try to influence a local decision? (4) Suppose Congress were considering a law that you believed to be very unjust or harmful. What do you think you could do? (5) Would you ever try to influence an act of Congress?[11]

Figure 2.1 illustrates the process of transformation from the conceptual to the observational level, using the example of alienation. The concept "alienation" cannot be directly observed; its empirical existence can, however, be inferred. In order to establish its empirical existence, we first delineate its conceptual components or dimensions. There are five distinct dimensions of alienation, each of which is conceptually defined; the conceptual definitions are indicative of the fact that the dimensions refer to different empirical aspects. Next, operational definitions are constructed; in this example they are questionnaire items. The questionnaire items serve the purpose of transforming the conceptual definitions into the observational level. Finally, the questionnaire items (operational definitions) are administered; from the responses to the questionnaire we infer the extent to which the five dimensions of alienation exist on the empirical level.

The Congruence Problem

Two important issues arise with the transition from the conceptual level to the empirical-observational level. The first is connected with the degree of congruence between conceptual definitions and operational def-

11. David Nachmias, "Modes and Types of Political Alienation," *The British Journal of Sociology*, 24 (December 1976): 478–493.

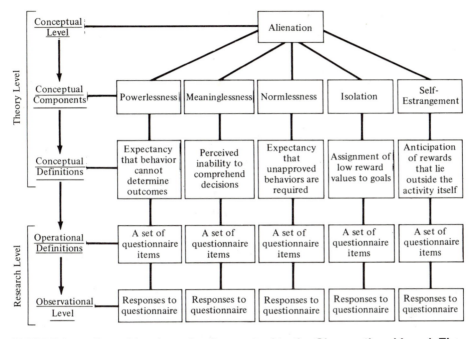

FIGURE 2.1.   Transition from the Conceptual to the Observational Level: The Case of Alienation

initions. If "intelligence" is defined conceptually as "the ability to think abstractly" and operationally by an intelligence test, what is the degree of congruence between the two definitions? Does the score achieved by a certain individual in an intelligence test represent everything that the conceptual definition of "intelligence" conveys. The degree of congruence between a conceptual definition and an operational definition can be evaluated with the aid of validity tests discussed in Chapter 6. At this stage, it should be pointed out that there is no absolute criterion for checking congruence, and there can indeed be situations in which an operational definition does not exhaust all the ramifications contained in a conceptual definition. Improving operational definitions and extending the degree of congruence between them and conceptual definitions constitute important challenges to social scientists.

Theoretical Import

The second issue involved in the transformation from the conceptual to the observation level arises when concepts cannot be operationally defined; that is, they cannot be either directly or indirectly observed. For example, "ego," "Oedipus complex," "dialectical materialism," "subconscious," "marginal utility," "public interest" are concepts for which no satisfactory operational definitions have yet been constructed.

According to the orthodox operational approach, a concept that cannot be operationally defined (at least, in principle) should not be used in scientific research because it is not amenable to intersubjective verification; such a concept necessarily leads to meaningless research; the scientific meaning of a concept can be established only by constructing a set of operations (instruments of observation); to know these operations is to understand a concept and to be able to investigate empirically the phenomenon that it represents. Historically this approach fulfilled the important function of stressing the empirical concern of science—of demarcating the physical from the metaphysical. But when carried to its extreme, the orthodox operational approach becomes problematic.

Scientific concepts should not be evaluated only in terms of their observability but also in terms of their theoretical import; that is, some concepts gain meaning only in the context of the theory in which they are introduced. For example, the concept "anomie" becomes meaningful in the context of Durkheim's suicide theory; the concept "ego" gains meaning within the context of psychoanalytic theory, and "public interest" cannot be viewed independently from a theory of democracy. Carl Hempel's idea of "systematic import" has influenced current practice:

> Scientific systematization requires the establishment of diverse connections, by law or theoretical principles, between different aspects of the empirical world, which are characterized by scientific concepts. Thus, the concepts of science are the knots in a network of systematic interrelationships in which laws and theoretical principles form the threads . . . The more threads converge upon, or issue from, a conceptual knot, the stronger will be its systematizing role, or its systematic import.[12]

Scientific concepts are to be evaluated not only with reference to their observability, but their theoretical import needs also to be considered:

> Empirical import as reflected in clear criteria of application, on which operationalism rightly puts much emphasis, is not the only desideratum for scientific concepts: systematic import is another indispensable requirement—so much so that the empirical interpretation of theoretical concepts may be changed in the interest of enhancing the systematic power of the theoretical network. In scientific inquiry, concept formation and theory formation must go hand in hand.[13]

12. Hempel, *Philosophy of Natural Science*, p. 94.

13. Ibid., pp. 96–97.

In other words, concepts gain empirical meaning from operational definitions and gain theoretical meaning within the context of the theory within which they are employed. Theory, as indicated in Figure 1.1, plays a vital and central role in the research process. It is not only an important source for the generation of problems and hypotheses, as discussed in Chapter 3, but the meaning and significance of some concepts are interpreted in the context of a theory.

THEORY: FUNCTIONS AND TYPES

Having discussed concepts, conceptual and operational definitions, and the idea of theoretical import, we now turn to the place of theory in empirical research. Although social scientists are in agreement that one of the most important functions of empirical research is to contribute to the development and refinement of theory and that theory enhances the goals of science, there is little agreement on what theory is. George Homans made the following observation on the state of theory in sociology: "Contemporary sociologists have been preoccupied with 'theory,' yet have seldom tried to make clear what theory *is* . . . We sociologists show our confusion about the nature of theory both by what we say about theory in general and by what kinds of theories we actually produce."[14] Similar statements have been made by social scientists in other disciplines.

Theory means different things to different people. Some social scientists would identify theory with any kind of conceptualization. Such concepts as "power," "social status," "democracy," "bureaucracy," or "relative deprivation," when defined and used in interpretations of empirical phenomena, are equated with theory. In this sense, any conceptualization as opposed to observation is theory. Other social scientists equate theory with the "history of ideas." Still others view theory in a narrow sense: a *logical-deductive* system consisting of a set of interrelated concepts from which testable propositions can be deductively derived. Before we discuss what theory is and what types of theory are prevalent in the social sciences, it is useful to point out three common misconceptions of theory.

What Theory Is Not

The layperson usually contrasts "theory" and "practice." The adage "all right in theory but it won't work in practice" conveys the idea that theory is unrealistic. As Arnold Brecht put it, "The relation between practice and theory is well indicated in the popular saying that we learn best through 'trial and error.' Trial is practice; error refers to theory. When

14. George C. Homans, "Contemporary Theory in Sociology," in *Handbook of Modern Sociology*, ed. by R. E. L. Faris (Chicago: Rand McNally, 1964), pp. 951–977.

theory miscarries in practical trials it needs correction . . ."[15] But theory is *of* practice, and in this sense it will be accepted or rejected by scientists with its practicality provided only that the method and contexts of its application (practice) are logically and explicitly pointed out. In principle, there is no contrast between theory and practice. A sound theory is the conceptual foundation for reliable knowledge; theories help us to explain and predict phenomena of interest to us and, therefore, to make well-founded, practical decisions.

Another misconception of theory results from the substitution of "theory" for "philosophy." Thus, the writings of classical scholars such as Plato, Aristotle, Locke, Marx, and Pareto are identified as "theory." In fact, prior to World War II, theory in the social sciences almost exclusively implied philosophy in its various forms, with particular emphasis on moral philosophy; that is, how things *ought* to be. Plato's presentation of the ideal, just state in which absolute knowledge of the philosopher-king is prescribed as the standard for political and social behavior is perhaps the most familiar example.

Moral philosophies state value judgments. They are neither true nor false because they cannot be empirically verified. If one strongly believes that capitalism is the best economic system, no amount of empirical evidence can prove or disprove one's belief. Unlike philosophical works, scientific theories are abstractions representing certain aspects of the empirical world; they are concerned with the *how* and *why* of empirical phenomena.

Types of Theory

There is no one simple definition of theory that would be agreed upon by all social scientists. This is so because there are many different kinds of theories serving different purposes. David Easton, for example, suggested that theories can be classified according to their *scope*—whether they are macro- or micro-theories; according to their *function*—whether they seek to deal with statics or dynamics, with structure or process; according to their *structure*—whether they are postulational systems of thought with closely knit, logical interrelations or whether they constitute a more loosely defined set of propositions; or according to their *level*—"by the relationship of the behavioral systems to which they refer as ranked on some hierarchical scale."[16] Our classification is based on the Parsons and Shils distinction among four *levels* of theory: ad hoc

15. Arnold Brecht, *Political Theory* (Princeton, N.J.: Princeton University Press, 1959), p. 19.

16. David Easton, "Alternative Strategies in Theoretical Research," in *Varieties of Political Theory*, ed. by David Easton (Englewood Cliffs, N.J.: Prentice-Hall, 1966), pp. 1–13.

classificatory systems, taxonomies, conceptual frameworks, and theoretical systems.[17] (A fifth level, empirical-theoretical systems, is somewhat arbitrarily distinguished from theoretical systems by having a precise empirical base.)

Ad Hoc Classificatory Systems

An ad hoc classificatory system consists of arbitrary categories constructed in order to organize and summarize empirical observations. For example, the classification of individuals' responses to the questionnaire item "All groups can live in harmony in this country without changing the system in any way" into four categories "Strongly Agree," "Agree," "Disagree," "Strongly Disagree" constitutes an ad hoc classificatory system.

Taxonomies

The second level of theory is the *categorical system,* or taxonomy. It consists of a system of categories constructed to fit the empirical observations so that relationships among categories can be described. Often there is an interdependence between categories so that classification into one category calls for conceptual treatment in another. A taxonomy bears a close relationship to the empirical world, and in this sense the categories mirror the reality described. Parsons' analysis of social action exemplifies this level of theory. He suggested that behavior has four attributes: It is goal-oriented, occurs in situations, is normatively regulated, and involves an expenditure of energy. When behavior is so organized, it is said to constitute a social system. Furthermore, social systems take three forms: personality systems, cultural systems, and social systems.[18] Parsons carefully defined these seven categories and then explicated their logical interrelations. Eventually, empirical observations have been fitted to the categories.

Taxonomies perform two important functions in social science research. By careful definitions they specify the unit of empirical reality to be analyzed and indicate how the unit may be described (in Parsons' taxonomy, social systems). The goal of a taxonomy

> is an orderly schema for classification and description . . . When faced with any subject of research, [one] can immediately identify its crucial aspects or variables by using his taxonomy as a kind of a "shopping list." To "test" his taxonomy, he takes a fresh look at

17. Talcott Parsons and Edward A. Shils, *Toward a General Theory of Action* (New York: Harper & Row, 1962), pp. 50–51.

18. Ibid., pp. 247–275.

subject X and shows that the general terms defining his dimensions have identifiable counterparts in X.[19]

The second function of the taxonomy is to "summarize and inspire descriptive studies,"[20] such as those concerned with the empirical distributions of one or more categories of the taxonomy. Taxonomies, however, do not offer explanations; they only describe empirical phenomena by fitting them into a set of categories. To know the concepts that represent phenomena (for example, "government spending") and their distributions (for example, how much is being spent on various items) is not to explain or predict phenomena (for example, why our government spends more on defense and less on education).

Conceptual Frameworks

The third level of theory is conceptual frameworks. Here descriptive categories are systematically placed within a broad structure of explicit as well as assumed propositions. Communication theory serves as an example of conceptual frameworks. Concepts such as "signal transmission," "destination," "communication net," and "channel noise" are used to analyze and explain empirical observations, and a systematic image of the world is assumed. The framework is yet too imprecise to permit the systematic derivation of propositions, but deductions are possible. Although the empirical verifications in the conceptual framework are of varying quality, there is continuous interaction between the framework and empirical observations.

One version of communication theory—cybernetics—is illustrated in Figure 2.2.[21] In this framework the central concepts are "information source," "transmitter," "channel noise," "receiver," and "destination." These are suggested to be sequentially related with feedback performing the function of continuity. A number of different propositions are offered to explain how messages are transferred, how efficiency is enhanced, and why communication systems adjust themselves upon receiving feedback.

This conceptual framework stands above taxonomy because its propositions summarize and provide explanations and predictions for vast amounts of empirical observations. Much of what is considered theory in the social sciences consists of conceptual frameworks that direct sys-

---

19. Hans L. Zetterberg, *On Theory and Verification in Sociology*, 3rd enlarged ed. (Totowa, N.J.: Bedminster Press, 1965), p. 26.

20. Ibid., p. 26.

21. Based on Warren Weaver, "The Mathematics of Communication," in *Communication and Culture*, ed. by A. G. Smith (New York: Macmillan, 1966), p. 17.

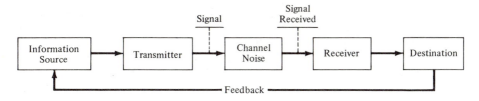

FIGURE 2.2. A Conceptual Framework for Communication

tematic empirical research. However, the propositions derived from conceptual frameworks are not rigorously and deductively arrived at. Consequently, their explanatory and predictive powers are limited, and their usefulness for future research is impaired. For instance, issues such as the communication of intentions and the perceptions and interpretations of the messages by the receivers cannot be effectively explained with the conceptual framework presented in Figure 2.2.

Theoretical Systems

Theoretical systems represent combinations of taxonomies and conceptual frameworks, but now descriptions, explanations, and predictions are combined in a systematic manner. At this level theory meets its narrow classical definition: a system of propositions that are interrelated in a way that permits some to be derived from others. When such a theoretical system exists, social scientists can claim to have explained and predicted the phenomena at hand.

A theoretical system is one that provides a structure for a complete explanation of empirical phenomena; its scope is not limited to a particular aspect. It consists of a set of concepts, some of which are *descriptive*, showing what the theory is about (for example, "relative deprivation," "suicide," "political participation"), and others that are *operative* or empirical properties (for example, "the *extent* of relative deprivation," "suicide *rate*," "*incidence* of political participation"). These empirical properties are termed *variables*. (A detailed discussion of variables and their types is found in Chapter 3.) A theoretical system also consists of a set of *propositions*, that is, statements of relationships between two or more empirical properties that can be verified or refuted: such a set of propositions forms a *deductive system*. In other words, the set of propositions forms a *calculus*, and, according to the rules for the manipulation of the calculus, some propositions are deduced from others. When propositions are so deduced, they are said to be explained as well as to provide predictions. Finally, some of the propositions of a theoretical system must be *contingent* in the sense that "experience is relevant to their truth or falsity or to that of propositions derived from them."[22] Indeed, acceptance or rejection of theoretical systems depends on whether their propositions are empirically true or false.

Durkheim's theory of suicide, as presented by George Homans, provides a classic example of a theoretical system:[23]

1. In any social grouping, the suicide rate varies directly with the degree of individualism (egoism).
2. The degree of individualism varies with the incidence of Protestantism.
3. Therefore, the suicide rate varies with the incidence of Protestantism.
4. The incidence of Protestantism in Spain is low.
5. Therefore, the suicide rate in Spain is low.

In this example, proposition 3 is deduced from propositions 1 and 2, and proposition 5 is deduced from 3 and 4. Furthermore, if, for example, one did not know what the suicide rate in Holland was, but did know that the incidence of Protestantism was low, this observation, together with proposition 3, would allow him or her to predict that the suicide rate was also low. Thus, the theoretical system provides both an explanation and a prediction of suicide rates.

Axiomatic Theory

One form of theoretical systems that deserves special mention is the *formal* or *axiomatic* theory. An axiomatic theory contains the following:

1. A set of concepts and definitions—conceptual and operational.
2. A set of existence statements that describes the situations in which the theory can be applied.
3. A set of relational statements, divided into
   a. Axioms—untestable statements or assumptions assumed to be true. For example, the axioms in geometry need not apply to the empirical world.
   b. Theorems—propositions *deduced* from the axioms and amenable to empirical verification.
4. A logical system that is used to
   a. Relate *all* concepts with statements.
   b. Deduce theorems from axioms, combinations of axioms, and theorems.

Hans Zetterberg's reformulation of Durkheim's theory is an early and often referred to example of axiomatic theory. Zetterberg explicated

---

22. Homans, "Contemporary Theory in Sociology," p. 959.

23. Ibid.

the following ten propositions:

1. The greater the division of labor, the greater the consensu
2. The greater the solidarity, the greater the number of asso< member.
3. The greater the number of associates per member, the greater the consensus.
4. The greater the consensus, the smaller the number of rejections of deviants.
5. The greater the division of labor, the smaller the number of rejections of deviants.
6. The greater the number of associates per member, the smaller the number of rejections of deviants.
7. The greater the division of labor, the greater the solidarity.
8. The greater the solidarity, the greater the consensus.
9. The greater the number of associates per member, the greater the division of labor.
10. The greater the solidarity, the smaller the number of rejection of deviants.[24]

He then selected the last four propositions as axioms and argued that the remainder can be deduced from this combination of axioms: 7 and 8 generate theorem or proposition 1; 7 and 9 render 2; 8 and 2 render 3; 8 and 10 lead to 4; 7 and 10 generate 5; and 9 and 5 render 6. Thus, with the four axioms, all the theorems were deduced.

The most critical problem in axiomatic theory involves the selection of axioms. What criteria should be used to choose certain propositions and treat them as axioms? Why did Zetterberg choose the last four propositions and not others to constitute his set of axioms? One criterion of selection is *consistency*: No two axioms, or any combination of axioms, should generate conflicting theorems. Another criterion is to select the smallest set of axioms from which *all* other theorems can be deduced. This criterion reflects a preference for *parsimony* or simplicity when constructing substantive theories. The third criterion for the selection of axioms—and the one that makes the construction of axiomatic theory in the social sciences most difficult—is to choose as axioms only those propositions that have achieved the status of laws. However, propositions that become laws must have considerable empirical support *before* they are considered laws. At present very few propositions in the social sciences have achieved such status. This, in turn, is a serious obstacle to the construction of substantive axiomatic theories.

In recent research the practice is to select as axioms that set of in-

24. Zetterberg, *On Theory and Verification in Sociology*, pp. 159–160.

dependent propositions that makes the substantive theory explicit and easiest to understand, no matter how large. This is achieved when those propositions that describe a *direct causal* relationship between two concepts are employed as axioms. As Hubert Blalock put it, "An axiom might be stated somewhat as follows: An increase in X will produce (cause) an almost immediate increase in Y; this increase in Y will, in turn, result in further increase in X, but with a delayed reaction."[25] Using the rule of direct causal relationships, Blalock restated Zetterberg's four axioms in the following way:[26]

1. An increase in the number of associates per member will produce an increase in the division of labor.
2. An increase in the division of labor will produce an increase in solidarity.
3. An increase in solidarity will produce an increase in consensus.
4. An increase in solidarity will produce a decrease in the number of rejections of deviants.

These causal axioms, in turn, lead to the generation of empirically testable theorems or propositions.

Advantages of Axiomatic Theory

Given that only very few propositions in the social sciences have achieved the status of laws, why construct axiomatic theories?

There are several advantages to axiomatic theory. First, it calls for a careful description of substantive theory, for the explication of the central concepts and assumptions used in a theory. Second, each concept has to be clearly defined, using both primitive and derived terms and operational definitions. Third, axiomatic theory can provide a parsimonious summary of actual and anticipated research. It is a way of economizing; instead of having a large number of independent propositions, an axiomatic theory presents only the essential ones. Fourth, an axiomatic theory can be used "to coordinate research so that many separate findings support each other giving the highest plausibility to the theory per finding."[27] Because the theory consists of a set of interrelated propositions, empirical support for any one proposition tends to provide support for the entire theory. Fifth, the axiomatic form allows the researcher to examine *all* the consequences of his or her axioms; this, in turn, helps in determining what parts of the theory are verified and what parts call

25. Hubert M. Blalock, Jr., *Theory Construction* (Englewood Cliffs, N.J.: Prentice-Hall, 1969), p. 18.

26. Ibid., p. 19.

27. Zetterberg, *On Theory and Verification in Sociology*, p. 163.

for further research. This is particularly useful when we want to locate research topics that will contribute most to theory. Finally, the axiomatic form is compatible with causal analysis, described in Chapter 14.

MODELS

Closely related to the idea of theory as a systematic conceptual organization is the notion of models. Often conceptual organization is attempted by models. A model can be viewed as a likeness of something. For example, an engineer might have a model of a machine such as an aircraft. The aircraft model is a miniature reproduction of the real aircraft, including scale representation of some of the real airplane's features—its structure—but omitting other aspects, such as its control instruments. The model aircraft serves to represent physically and visibly the structure and the features of the aircraft. The model can be used in place of the real machine for experimentation and testing. For example, the engineer might subject the model to the effects of a wind tunnel (itself a model) to determine the aircraft's performance.

In the social sciences, models usually consist of symbols rather than of physical matter; that is, the characteristics of some empirical phenomenon, including its components and the relationships between the components, are represented in logical arrangements among concepts. Thus, we can more formally define a model as an imitation or an abstraction from reality that serves the purpose of ordering and simplifying our view of the reality while still representing its essential characteristics:

> A characteristic feature in the construction of a model is abstraction; certain elements of the situation may be deliberately omitted because they are judged irrelevant, and the resulting simplification in the description of the situation may be helpful in analyzing and understanding it. In addition to abstraction, model-building sometimes involves a conceptual transference. Instead of discussing the situation directly, it may be the case that each element of the real situation is simulated by a mathematical or physical object, and its relevant properties and relations to other elements are mirrored by corresponding simulative properties and relations . . .; a city's traffic system may be simulated by setting up a miniature model of its road net, traffic signals, and vehicles.[28]

A model, then, is a representation of reality; it delineates certain aspects of the real world as being relevant to the problem under investigation; it makes explicit the significant relationships among the aspects, and it enables the formulation of empirically testable propositions re-

28. Olaf Helmer, *Social Technology* (New York: Basic Books, 1966), pp. 127–128.

garding the nature of these relationships. After testing, a better understanding of some part of the real world can be attained. Models are also used to gain insight into phenomena that cannot be directly observed. In policy analysis, for example, models pertaining to the structures and processes of decision making are constructed and propositions relating to the behavior of the decision makers are generated. These propositions are then evaluated with empirical data. Also in policy analysis, models are used to estimate the value of various alternative courses of action on which a decision maker might take action. The models provide a more explicit basis for choice than subjective judgment.

Example: A Model of Policy Implementation

Thomas Smith's model of the policy implementation process provides an interesting example of modeling complex and directly nonobservable aspects of the real world.[29] Many laypersons believe that once a public policy has been made (for example, the passage of a bill by Congress), implementation will follow orderly and even automatically to achieve the goals desired by the policy makers. This does not always happen. Problems of implementation are widespread, and in many cases policies are not implemented in the manner intended by decision makers. Public bureaucrats, interest groups, and affected individuals and organizations often attempt to force changes in policy during the implementation process.

The model developed by Smith abstracts certain aspects of the implementation process and focuses on four components:

1. The idealized policy, that is, the idealized patterns of interaction that those who have defined the policy are attempting to induce.
2. The target group, defined as those who are required to adopt new patterns of interaction by the policy. They are the individuals most directly affected by the policy and who must change to meet its demands.
3. The implementing organization, usually a government agency, responsible for the implementation of the policy.
4. The environmental factors, those elements in the environment that are influenced by the policy implementation. The general public and various special interest groups are included here.

These four components and their postulated relations are diagrammed in Figure 2.3. The policy-making process produces public policies; these serve as a tension-generating force in society: while policies are imple-

---

29. Thomas B. Smith, "The Policy Implementation Process," *Policy Sciences*, 4 (June 1973): 197–209.

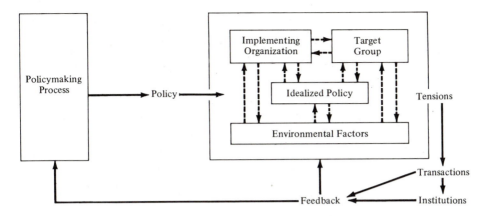

FIGURE 2.3.   A Model of the Policy Implementation Process

mented, tensions, strains, and conflicts are experienced by those who are implementing the policy and by those affected by it. Tensions lead to transactions, Smith's concept for the responses to tensions and conflicts within and between the components of the policy implementation context. The feedback generated by transactions and institutions is suggested to influence future policy making as well as the four components of the implementation process.

THEORY, MODELS, AND EMPIRICAL RESEARCH

The social sciences as scientific disciplines rest on two major components—theory and empirical research. Social scientists qua scientists operate in two "worlds"—the world of observation and experience and the world of ideas, or theories and models. Establishing a systematic connection between these two worlds enhances the goals of the social sciences. But how should this connection be established? Should we first construct our theories and models and then move to the world of empirical research? Or alternatively, should theory follow research?

Theory-then-Research

According to one school of thought, theory should come first, to be followed by research; this is often referred to as the Theory-then-Research strategy. Karl Popper has developed most systematically this strategy. Popper argues that scientific knowledge would advance most rapidly through the development of ideas (conjectures) and attempts to refute them through empirical research (refutations).[30] Popper denies the sys-

30. Karl R. Popper, *Conjectures and Refutations* (New York: Harper & Row, 1963).

tematic bearing of empirical research on theorizing; research cannot generate new ideas nor serve as a logical method for theory construction. Theories ". . . can only be reached by intuition, based upon something like an intellectual love of the objects of experience."[31] A similar position was taken by Watson:

> At first we operate only with thought abstractions, mindful of our task only to construct inner representation-pictures. Proceeding in this way, we do not as yet take possible experiential facts into consideration, but merely make the effort to develop our thought-pictures with as much clarity as possible and to draw from them all possible consequences. Only subsequently, after the entire exposition of the picture has been completed, do we check its agreement with experiential facts.[32]

Although somewhat simplified, the Theory-then-Research strategy involves the following five stages:

1. Construction of an explicit theory or model.
2. Selection of a proposition generated by the theory or model for empirical investigation.
3. Designing a research project to test the proposition.
4. If the proposition derived from the theory is rejected by the empirical data, changes in the theory or the research project (for example, research design, measurement; see Figure 1.1) are to be made. The scientist returns to stage 2.
5. If the proposition is not rejected, one selects other propositions for testing or attempts to improve the theory.

Research-then-Theory

In sharp contrast to the Theory-then-Research strategy, Robert Merton, a proponent of the Research-then-Theory strategy argued as follows:

> It is my central thesis that empirical research goes far beyond the passive role of verifying and testing theory; it does more than confirm or refute hypotheses. Research plays an active role: it performs at least four major functions which help shape the development of theory. It initiates, it reformulates, it deflects, and it clarifies theory.[33]

31. Karl R. Popper, *The Logic of Scientific Discovery* (New York: Science Editions, 1961), p. 32.

32. W. H. Watson, "On Methods of Representation," in *Philosophy of Science*, ed. by Arthur Danto and Sidney Morgenbesser (Cleveland: World Publishing Co., 1960), pp. 226–244.

33. Robert K. Merton, *Social Theory and Social Structure*, rev. and enlarged ed. (Glencoe, Ill.: The Free Press, 1957), p. 103.

Empirical research suggests new problems for theory, calls for new theoretical formulations, leads to the refinement of existing theories, and serves the function of verification. The Research-then-Theory strategy consists of the following:

1. Investigation of a phenomenon and delineating its attributes.
2. Measurement of the attributes in a variety of situations. (Measurement and measuring procedures are discussed in Chapter 6.)
3. Analysis of the resulting data to determine if there are systematic patterns of variation.
4. Once systematic patterns are discovered, a theory is constructed. The theory may be of any of the types discussed earlier, although a theoretical system is preferred.

Clearly, these two strategies aim at theory and regard it as a manifestation of scientific progress. The dilemma is over the place of theory in the research process. It is our contention that a firm commitment to either of the two strategies is not essential in the conduct of research. The social sciences have progressed in spite of this controversy, and scientific undertakings are being pursued under both strategies. In fact, theory and research are constantly interacting, as suggested in Chapter 1 in Figure 1.1. Furthermore, as Ernest Nagel maintains, the contrast between the two strategies is more apparent than real:

> Distinguished scientists have repeatedly claimed that theories are "free creations of the mind." Such claims obviously do not mean that theories may not be *suggested* by observational materials or that theories do not require support from observational evidence. What such claims do rightly assert is that the basic terms of a theory need not possess meanings which are fixed by definite experimental procedures, and that a theory may be adequate and fruitful despite the fact that the evidence for it is necessarily indirect.[34]

SUMMARY

One of the most significant symbols in science is the concept. Science begins by forming concepts to describe the empirical world and advances by relating these concepts into theoretical systems. Concepts enable effective communication, they introduce a point of view, they are means for classification and generalization, and they serve as the building blocks of propositions, theories, and hypotheses, which will be discussed in the following chapter.

To serve their functions, concepts have to be clear, precise, and agreed-upon. This is achieved by conceptual and operational definitions.

34. Ernest Nagel, *The Structure of Science* (New York: Harcourt, Brace, and World, 1961), p. 86.

A conceptual definition describes concepts using primitive and derived terms. Operational definitions explicate the set of procedures and activities that one should perform in order to observe empirically the phenomena represented by concepts. Operational definitions connect the conceptual-theoretical level with the empirical-observational.

Although social scientists are in agreement that theory is the ultimate achievement of scientific undertakings, there are divergent views concerning the meaning and structure of theory. At present four levels of theory can be distinguished: ad hoc classificatory systems, taxonomies, conceptual frameworks, and theoretical systems. One form of theoretical system is the axiomatic theory. It contains a set of concepts and definitions, a set of existence statements, a set of relational statements divided into axioms and theorems, and a logical system used to relate concepts with statements and to deduce theorems from axioms.

Models are often used by social scientists to represent systematically certain aspects of the real world. Models are abstractions from reality that serve the purpose of ordering and simplifying our view of the reality while still representing its essential attributes. Models are also used to gain insight of phenomena that cannot be directly observed, such as the United States economic system.

The establishment of systematic connections between the empirical and the conceptual worlds has been achieved with the aid of two general strategies: Theory-then-Research and Research-then-Theory. Although there is a lively controversy as to which strategy most rapidly enhances scientific progress, our position is that theory and research should be constantly interacting and that the contrast between the two strategies is more apparent than real.

KEY TERMS FOR REVIEW

Concept
Fallacy of
   reification
Conceptual
   definition
Primitive term
Ostensive
   definition
Operational
   definition

Theoretical import
Ad hoc
   classificatory
   system
Taxonomy
Conceptual
   framework
Theoretical system
Axiomatic theory
Model

Theory-then-
   research
Research-then-
   theory

ADDITIONAL READINGS

Abell, Peter. *Model Building in Sociology*. London: Weidenfeld & Nicholson, 1971.

Braithwaite, R. B. "Models in the Empirical Science." In *Readings in the Philosophy of Science*, ed. by Baruch A. Brody. Englewood Cliffs, N.J.: Prentice-Hall, 1970. Pp. 268–293.

Dubin, Robert. *Theory Building*. New York: Free Press, 1969.

Hage, Jerald. *Techniques and Problems of Theory Construction in Sociology*. New York: Wiley, 1972.

Isaak, Alan C. *Scope and Methods of Political Science*. Homewood, Ill.: Dorsey, 1969. Chapters 5 and 8.

Stinchcombe, Arthur L. *Constructing Social Theories*. New York: Harcourt, Brace, and World, 1968.

Tullock, Gordon. *Toward a Mathematics of Politics*. Ann Arbor: University of Michigan Press, 1967.

CHAPTER PREVIEW

CHAPTER 3
Basic Elements of Research

INTRODUCTION

Whether carried out under the Theory-then-Research or the Research-then-Theory strategy, the terms *research problem, variable, relation,* and *hypothesis* are perhaps the most used words in social science research. They are the basic elements of research; they help transform an idea into concrete research operations. In this chapter we define, discuss, and exemplify the use of these basic terms in the context of the research process.

RESEARCH PROBLEMS

In the beginning is the problem: "The scientist is a man with a problem or he is nothing."[1] A problem is an intellectual stimulus calling for an answer in the form of scientific inquiry. For example, "Who rules America?" "What incentives lead to energy conservation?" "How can inflation be contracted?" or "Does social class influence voting behavior?" are all problems amenable to scientific research.

Not all intellectual stimuli can be empirically studied, and not all human behavior is guided by scientific knowledge. In fact, we saw in Chapter 1 that the assumptions of science themselves are empirically nonresearchable; they are neither proved nor provable. Similarly, questions such as "Will Western civilization disappear?" "Is blue nicer than green?" or "Is Impressionism the most advanced form of art?" cannot be empirically investigated. In general, problems that cannot be empir-

---

1. Scott Greer, *The Logic of Social Inquiry* (Chicago: Aldine, 1969), p. 4.

ically grounded or that are concerned with subjective preferences, beliefs, values, or tastes are not amenable to empirical research.

The observation that our subjective preferences cannot be studied scientifically should not, of course, imply that social scientists in their roles as concerned citizens, parents, friends, and so on do not have subjective preferences about many things, just as nonscientists do; they justify and advocate such preferences as other people do. However, such preferences are not empirically verifiable, and thus they do not constitute scientific knowledge.

Certain subjective preferences or biases can be approached in exactly the same way as scientists approach empirical phenomena—as factual problems to be investigated by the scientific approach. For example, one could study why some people believe that Western civilization will disappear and why others do not share this view or whether the preference for Impressionism is related to social class.

In addition to being empirically grounded, research problems have to be clearly and specifically articulated. For example, the problem "What incentives lead to energy conservation?" is too general and too ambiguous. It means different things to different people. It does not specify the types of incentives (for example, economic, social, patriotic) or the sources of energy (for example, crude oil, gasoline, natural gas, coal). It also does not distinguish between industrial and residential conservation. The lack of clarity and specificity may lead to ambiguous findings that can be interpreted in different and contradictory ways.

UNITS OF ANALYSIS

In the formulation of a research problem, serious consideration also has to be given to the units of analysis. These are entities to which our concepts pertain and which influence subsequent research design, data collection, and data analysis decisions. Does the research problem call for the study of perceptions, attitudes, or behavior? Should we concentrate on individuals or groups? Institutions or societies? Abraham Kaplan termed the problem of selecting the units of analysis the "locus problem":

> The locus problem may be described as that of selecting the ultimate subject-matter for inquiry in behavioral science, the attribute space for its description, and the conceptual structure within which hypotheses about it are to be formulated. Quite a number of alternatives present themselves, and have been selected in various inquiries: states of conscious acts, actions (segments of meaningful behavior), roles, persons, personalities, interpersonal relations, groups, classes, institutions, social traits or patterns, societies, and cultures. With

respect to each of these, there is the associated problem of unit, *that is, of what constitutes the identity of the element selected. Are legal institutions, for example, quite distinct from the institution of the state or part of it, and if so, in what sense of "part"?*[2]

In principle there are no limitations on the selection of units to be employed in a research project. But once a selection has been made, subsequent research operations, including the level of theorizing, are to be congruent to the units selected. Each unit of analysis has its distinct properties, and it is often problematic to shift from one unit to another. In fact, one of the difficulties in social science research involves the explanation of cross-unit relationships, for example, the relations between individual properties such as perceptions and attitudes and group properties such as power and cohesion. When the unit of analysis is the individual, the research focus might be with individuals in various roles, disregarding the groups to which they belong. One might ask, say, whether urban residents are more likely than suburbanites to vote for Democrats. On the other hand, when the unit of analysis is a group, the individuals who compose it are disregarded. One might ask, for instance, whether groups that are socially cohesive are necessarily also nonhierarchical (cohesion and hierarchy being group properties). Here the purpose of the research would be to describe, compare, and assess relationships among properties of groups.

The Ecological Fallacy

One type of fallacy that results from analyzing groups but making inferences on the behavior or properties of individuals was termed by William Robinson the *ecological fallacy*.[3] Robinson showed that there are great differences between findings obtained with aggregate data (for example, census data) and those obtained using individual data. Group data is inappropriate when the research problem focuses on the individual.

The Individualistic Fallacy

The converse of the ecological fallacy is the atomistic or the *individualistic fallacy*. This might result if inferences about groups, societies, or systems in general are drawn from individuals. For example, to count the percentage of individuals who agree with particular statements on democracy and to take this as an indicator of the degree to which a political system is democratic is to commit the individualistic fallacy. A

2. Abraham Kaplan, *The Conduct of Inquiry* (San Francisco: Chandler, 1964), p. 78.

3. W. S. Robinson, "Ecological Correlations and the Behavior of Individuals," *American Sociological Review*, 15 (June 1950): 351–357.

political system can be authoritarian even if most of its citizens have democratic opinions.

VARIABLES

Research problems are conveyed with a set of concepts. We saw in Chapter 2 that concepts are abstractions representing empirical phenomena. In order to move from the conceptual to the empirical level, concepts are converted into *variables.* It is as variables that our concepts will eventually appear in hypotheses and be tested.

Concepts are converted into variables by *mapping* them into a set of values. For example, assigning numbers (one type of values) to objects is a mapping of a set of objects into a set of numbers. A variable is an empirical property that takes two or more values. If a property can change in value or kind, it can be regarded as a variable. For example, "social class" is a variable because it can be differentiated by at least five distinct values: lower, lower middle, middle, upper middle, and upper. Similarly, "expectations" is a variable because it can be assigned at least two values: "high" and "low." When a variable has only two values, it is termed a *dichotomous variable.* For purposes of research it is important to make an analytic distinction among dependent, independent, and control variables and between continuous and discrete variables.

Dependent and Independent Variables

The variable that the researcher wishes to explain is regarded as the *dependent variable.* The variable expected to explain change in the dependent variable is referred to as the *independent variable.* The independent variable is the explanatory variable; it is the presumed cause of changes in the values of the dependent variable; the dependent variable is the expected outcome of the independent variable. (Dependent variables are also termed *criterion variables*; and independent variables, *predictor variables.*)

In the language of mathematics we mean by a dependent variable whatever variable happens to appear on the left-hand side of an equation. For example, if we write $Y = f(X)$, we are considering Y to be the dependent and X the independent variable. In this case, we say that Y is a *function* of X; that changes in the values of X cause changes in the values of Y, or that X yields Y (via f). For example, a researcher might want to explain why some people participate in politics more than others. Based on the theory of social stratification, the researcher may deduce that the higher an individual's social class, the more likely that person is to participate in politics. In this case, political participation is hypothesized to be the *outcome* of social class; social class is presumed to cause variations in political participation. Accordingly, political participation is the dependent variable, and social class is the independent variable.

It should be stressed that the distinction between dependent and independent variables is analytic and relates only to the research purpose. In the empirical world, variables are neither dependent nor independent; the researcher decides how to view them, and his or her decision is based on the research objective. An independent variable in one investigation may be a dependent variable in another, and the same researcher in different projects may classify the same variables in different ways. If one wants to explain variations in political participation, the latter will be his or her dependent variable. One variable that explains variations in political participation is social class, and this will be regarded as an independent variable. But if one wants to explain variations in social class (for example, why some individuals are in the lower class and others are in the middle), the latter will be now regarded as a dependent variable. One variable that may be hypothesized to explain variations in social class is educational attainment, which will now be regarded as an independent variable.

Most of the phenomena investigated by social scientists call for the assessment of the effects of several independent variables on one or more dependent variables. This happens because one independent variable usually explains only a certain amount of the variation in the dependent variable, and more independent variables have to be introduced in order to explain more variation. For example, when political participation is studied as a dependent variable, social class explains why some people participate in politics more than others. This explanation, however, is incomplete because there are other reasons in addition to social class that explain variations in political participation. Such additional independent variables are age, sex, interest in politics, and political efficacy (that is, the extent to which individuals believe that their participation will affect political outcomes).

Control Variables

The function of control variables in empirical research is to reduce the risk of attributing explanatory power to independent variables that *in fact are not* responsible for the occurrence of variation in the dependent variable. Control variables are used to test the possibility than an empirically observed relation between an independent and a dependent variable is *spurious*. A spurious relation is a relation that can be explained by other variables. In other words, if the effects of all relevant variables are eliminated (or controlled for) and the empirical relation between the independent variable and the dependent variable is maintained, then the relation is nonspurious. It implies that there is an in-

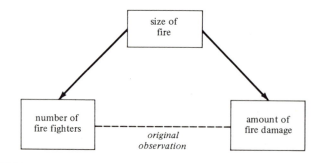

FIGURE 3.1.

herent, causal link between the variables and that the observed relation is not based on an accidental connection with some associated phenomena.

Suppose one observes that the number of fire fighters is related to the amount of fire damage. The more fire fighters at the fire site, the greater the amount of fire damage. Obviously, fire fighters are not the cause of the damage. Accordingly, the amount of fire damage should not be explained by the number of fire fighters at the site, but by another variable, namely, the size of the fire. Large fires call forth more fire fighters and also cause more damage. Thus, the original observed relation between the number of fire fighters at the fire site and the amount of fire damage is spurious because a third factor, the size of the fire, explains it. In this case, the size of the fire is a control variable. Without the influence of the control variable, no relation would have been observed between the number of fire fighters (the independent variable) and the amount of fire damage (the dependent variable). This is illustrated in Figure 3.1.

Another example illustrating the significance of control variables is the empirical relation observed between political participation and government expenditure. Is the amount of government expenditure (dependent variable) caused by the extent of political participation (independent variable)? Seemingly yes. But when Hayward Alker examined economic development as a control variable, he found that the empirical relation between political participation and government expenditure vanished.[4] The level of economic development influences *both* government expenditure and political participation. Without the influence of economic development, no relation would have been observed between political participation and government expenditure. Control variables thus serve the purpose of testing whether the observed relations between independent and dependent variables are nonspurious.

4. Hayward R. Alker, *Mathematics and Politics* (New York: Macmillan, 1965).

Continuous and Discrete Variables

One other important attribute of variables is their being either continuous or discrete. This attribute, as we shall see in later chapters, affects subsequent research operations, particularly measurement procedures, data analysis, and methods of inference and generalization.

A variable is *continuous* if it does not have a minimal size unit. Length is an example of a continuous variable because there is no minimal unit of length. A particular object may be 10 inches long, it may be 10.5 inches long, or it may be 10.5431697 . . . inches long. In principle, we can speak of a tenth of an inch, ten-thousandths of an inch, or ten-trillionths of an inch. Although we cannot measure all possible different length values with absolute accuracy (some values will be too small for any measuring instrument to register), it is possible for objects to exist at an infinite number of different lengths.

Unlike continuous variables, *discrete* variables do have a minimal size unit. The amount of money in your bank at this moment is an example of a discrete variable because currency has a minimal unit. One can have \$101.21 or \$101.22, but not \$101.21843. Different amounts of money cannot differ by less than the minimal size unit. In general, all quantities of a discrete variable are multiples of the minimal unit size. The number of children per family is another example of a discrete variable because the minimal unit is one child. Families may have three or four children, but not 3.5 children. If some quantity of a variable cannot be subdivided, the variable is discrete.

RELATIONS

In earlier chapters we saw that scientific explanations and predictions involve relating the phenomena to be explained (dependent variable) to other explanatory phenomena (independent variables) by means of general laws or theories. But what is a relation?

A *relation* in research always means a relation between two or more variables. When we say that variable X and variable Y are related, we mean that there is something *common* to both variables. For example, if we say that education and income are related, we mean that the two "go together," that they covary. The *covariation* is what education and income have in common: Individuals with higher education have higher incomes. Establishing a relation in empirical research consists of determining which values of one variable covary with values of one or more other variables. The researcher systematically pairs values of one variable with values of other variables. For example, the two sets of observations given in Table 3.1 report the values of education (operationally defined by years of schooling) and income of six individuals. The table

TABLE 3.1   Relation Between Education and Income

Observations	Years of Schooling	Income
Dan	16	$35,000
Ann	15	30,000
Marie	14	27,000
Jacob	13	19,000
Phillip	12	15,000
Suzanne	11	12,000

expresses a relation because the two sets of values have been paired in an orderly way; they covary: higher education is paired with higher income; and lower education, with lower income.

Kinds of Relations

We say that two variables are related when changes in the values of one systematically bring changes in the values of the other. In the last example, changes in years of schooling brought changes in income. Two properties of relations are always of concern in empirical research—direction and magnitude.

Direction

When we speak of *direction* we mean that the relations between variables are either positive or negative. A *positive relation* means that as values of one variable increase, values of the other also increase. For example, the relation between education and income is positive because increases in years of schooling lead to higher income. There is also a positive relation between interest in politics and political participation: As individuals become more interested in politics, they tend to participate more in political activities. A positive relation has also been found between economic development and government expenditures, as pointed out earlier.

A *negative relation* indicates that as values of one variable increase, values of the other decrease. High values for one variable are associated with low values for the other. For instance, the interest rate for a house mortgage is negatively related to the number of new home loans: as the interest rate increases, the number of new home loans decreases. There is also a negative relation between education and racial prejudice: People with higher levels of education tend to be less prejudiced. A negative relation also exists between bureaucratization and political participation:

as the political system becomes more bureaucratized, the level of political participation falls.

The relation between an independent variable and a dependent variable can be illustrated with the aid of orthogonal axes. Following mathematical custom, X, the independent variable, is represented by the horizontal axis, and Y, the dependent variable, by the vertical axis; X values are laid out on the X axis, and Y values on the Y axis. A very common way to observe and interpret a relation is to plot the pairs of XY values, using the X and Y axes as a frame of reference. Let us suppose that in a study of academic achievement we have two sets of measures: X measures the number of hours a student devotes to studying each day, and Y measures the number of excellent grades attained by a student in a given semester. Hypothetical data of nine students on the two measures are presented in Table 3.2, and the measures are plotted in Figure 3.2.

The relation between the number of daily hours of study (independent variable) and the number of excellent grades (dependent variable) can now be made visible: high values on the X axis are related to high values on the Y axis; medium values on the X axis are related to medium values on the Y axis; and low values on the X axis are related to low values on the Y axis. The relation between the independent variable (X) and the dependent variable (Y) is depicted by the joint distribution of values. The straight line passing through the points representing pairs of values indicates the direction of the relation. Furthermore, with the aid of information about the characteristics of the straight line (its slope and intercept), the researcher can predict the values of the dependent variable according to the values of the independent variable. (For methods of calculating the slope and the intercept, see Chapter 13.)

TABLE 3.2. Number of Hours of Study per Day and Number of Excellent Grades (Hypothetical Data)

Number of Hours of Study per Day (X)	Number of Excellent Grades (Y)
8	5
7	5
6	4
5	3
4	2
4	1
3	1
2	0
1	2

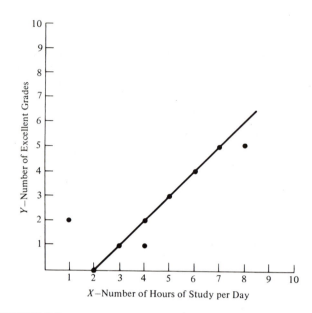

FIGURE 3.2.

Thus, for example, if the slope of the straight line is known, as well as the value of the point at which it intersects the Y axis, it will be possible to predict how many daily hours of study will produce how many excellent grades.

Magnitude

Relations between variables are characterized not only by direction, but also by *magnitude*. The magnitude of a relation is the extent to which variables covary positively or negatively. The highest magnitude of relation is a *perfect relation*, in which knowledge of the value of one or more independent variables determines exactly the value of the dependent variable. Physical laws such as $E = mc^2$ (Einstein's mass-energy law) are examples of perfect relations because there are no exceptions to the rule. The hypothetical example in Table 3.1 displays a perfect relation: there are no exceptions to the rule that increases in years of schooling bring increases in income.

At the other extreme is the lowest magnitude of relation, the *zero relation*. No systematic covariation between the values of an independent variable and a dependent variable can be discerned; that is, the variables are not related; changes in the values of one variable do not affect the values of the other.

The vast majority of relations studied in the social sciences range in magnitude between zero and perfect. The relation between education and income is positive but not perfect: Individuals who have higher education *tend* to have higher income, but there are many exceptions. The relation between education and racial prejudice is negative but not perfect: not all highly educated persons are nonprejudiced, and not all persons with lower education are prejudiced. (Precise measures of magnitude such as coefficients of correlations are presented in Chapters 13 and 14.)

Having discussed variables and relations, we are now in a position to elaborate more fully on the idea and the characteristics of hypotheses.

HYPOTHESES

Hypotheses are tentative answers to research problems. They are expressed in the form of a relation between independent and dependent variables. Hypotheses are tentative conjectures because their veracity can be evaluated only *after* they have been tested empirically. When a researcher suggests a hypothesis, he or she has no assurance that it will be verified. A hypothesis is constructed, and if it is rejected, another one is put forward; if it is accepted, it is incorporated into the scientific body of knowledge.

Hypotheses can be derived deductively from theories, directly from observations, intuitively, or from a combination of these. The sources from which researchers derive their hypotheses are of little significance in comparison with the way in which they reject or fail to reject them. Thus, there are those who believe that it was the apple falling from the tree that brought Newton to suggest the hypothesis about gravitation. However, it was not this episode that induced scientists to accept the hypothesis, but the empirical data.

Research hypotheses share four common characteristics. They are *clear, value-free, specific*, and *amenable to empirical testing* with the available research methods. It is useful to examine these characteristics in greater detail in order to help you construct your own hypotheses and be able to evaluate the hypotheses of others.

Hypotheses must be clear.   Clarity is achieved by means of conceptual and operational definitions as discussed in Chapter 2. In order to test a hypothesis empirically, one has to define operationally all the variables in the hypothesis. The professional literature and experts' opinions can be of great help when one is constructing hypotheses and defining the variables. For example, if the hypothesis is that alienation is negatively related to political participation, then the independent variable is alienation and the dependent variable is political participation. An examination of the professional literature will help one see how other researchers defined the variables. Among these definitions, one is likely to find one suitable to his or her research hypothesis. If the definitions do not satisfy the investigator, he or she can always build on others' experience while defining the variables in a way that expresses one's own understanding. In any case, operational definitions must be specific and precise so that observation and replication are made possible.

Scientific hypotheses are value-free. In principle, the researcher's own values, biases, and subjective preferences have no place within the scientific approach. However, given that research in the social sciences is to a certain extent a social activity whose problems are affected by the milieu in which it takes place, the researcher must be aware of his or her personal biases and make them as explicit as possible. As Myrdal wrote:

> The attempt to eradicate biases trying to keep out the valuations themselves is a hopeless and misdirected venture . . . There is no other device for excluding biases in the social sciences than to face the valuations and to introduce them as explicitly stated, specific, and sufficiently concretized value premises.[5]

Hypotheses are specific. The investigator has to explicate the expected relations among the variables in terms of direction (that is, positive or negative) and the conditions under which these relations will hold. A hypothesis stating that X is related to Y is too general. The relation between X and Y can be positive or negative. Furthermore, relations are not independent of time, space, or the unit of analysis. As we saw earlier, the observed relations between variables may vanish when the unit of analysis changes (for example, the ecological fallacy). Thus, the relations between, say, education and political participation can be studied at the individual or the group level; these different levels of analysis require different conceptualizations and different operational definitions. The hypothesis will express the expected relations between the variables as well as the conditions under which the relations are expected to be manifested. Here theory becomes especially important in generating researchable and fruitful hypotheses.

Hypotheses are testable with available methods. One can arrive at clear, value-free, and specific hypotheses and find that there are no research methods to test them. How, for example, are we to test the hypothesis that object A is longer than object B without a ruler? Or how are we to test the hypothesis that the excretions of microbe C have a positive relation to disease D without an instrument permitting the identification of the microbe? Or how are we to test the relation between education and political participation without having instruments to observe these variables systematically?

5. Gunnar Myrdal, *The American Dilemma* (New York: Harper, 1944), p. 1043.

The simplicity of these examples should stress our claim that the evaluation of hypotheses depends on the existence of methods for testing them. Indeed, progress in science is closely related to the development of new research methods, methods of observation, data collection, data analysis, and generalization.

Some social scientists attach little value to methods for fear of being enslaved by them. It is, of course, possible to become enslaved by some method of research if one employs it blindly, without regard to the research problem at hand, or if the method is regarded as an end unto itself. Even hypotheses that lack methods of testing may have a place in the scientific approach if they are innovative. However, their verification depends on the ability to test them, which, in turn, depends on the availability of methods of research.

EXAMPLES OF PROBLEMS AND HYPOTHESES

Problems are questions about relations among variables, and hypotheses are tentative, concrete, and testable answers. A few examples will further clarify the distinction between problems and hypotheses and illustrate how hypotheses are constructed and expressed.

Problems are general questions about relations among variables. The following are examples of research questions:

- Who rules America?
- What causes inflation?
- Why does bureaucracy threaten democracy?
- Is the 55 m.p.h. speed limit law achieving its objective?
- Does racial school integration enhance educational attainment?
- What factors determine urbanization?
- What causes political violence?

Such general questions are operationalized into a series of hypotheses. For example, the question on political violence has been answered by Ted Gurr with a series of hypotheses, including the following:[6]

- The potential for collective violence increases as the intensity and scope of relative deprivation among members of a collectivity increases.
- The potential for political violence varies strongly with the intensity and scope of normative justifications for political violence among members of a collectivity.

6. Ted R. Gurr, *Why Men Rebel* (Princeton, N.J.: Princeton University Press, 1970), pp. 360–367.

- The potential for political violence varies strongly with the intensity and scope of utilitarian justifications for political violence among members of a collectivity.
- The potential for specifically political violence varies strongly with the potential for collective violence generally.
- The magnitude of political violence varies strongly with the potential for political violence.
- The intensity of relative deprivation varies strongly with the average degree of perceived discrepancy between value expectations and value capabilities.

Another example of hypothesis construction is the Gibbs and Martin study on the causes of urbanization.[7] The authors hypothesized that

- The degree of urbanization in a society varies directly with the dispersion of objects of consumption.
- The degree of urbanization in a society varies directly with the division of labor.
- The division of labor in a society varies directly with the dispersion of objects of consumption.
- The degree of urbanization in a society varies directly with technological development.
- Technological development in a society varies directly with the dispersion of objects of consumption.

SOURCES OF PROBLEMS AND HYPOTHESES

Research problems and hypotheses can be derived from theories, directly from observation, intuitively, or from a combination of these. Probably the greatest source of problems and hypotheses is the professional literature. A critical review of the professional literature would familiarize the researcher with the state of the knowledge; with problems and hypotheses that others studied; with concepts, theories, major variables, conceptual and operational definitions; and with the research methods used. This will also contribute to the cummulative nature of scientific knowledge.

As thousands of articles and books in the social sciences are being published every year, it is best to begin any search with one of the guides to published literature. These guides are increasingly computerized and include bibliographies, indexes, and abstracts.

---

7. jack P. Gibbs and Walter T. Martin, "Urbanization, Technology, and the Division of Labor: International Patterns," in *Urbanism, Urbanization and Change,* ed. by Paul Meadows and Ephraim H. Mizruchi, 2nd ed. (Reading, Mass.: Addison-Wesley, 1976), pp. 132–145.

Bibliographies, Indexes, Abstracts

Useful bibliographies and indexes to published professional literature in the social sciences are the following:

The library card catalogue, subject guide.

National Union Card Catalogue
International Bibliography of the Social Sciences
Social Science Index
Public Affairs Information Service Bulletin

Social Science Citation Index: Subject Index
Biography Index
Book Review Index
Cumulative Book Index
Education Index
Index of Economic Journals

These bibliographies and indexes list the complete citation necessary to find the literature that one is searching for. In addition, there are abstracts that include short summaries of the work cited. Useful abstracts include the following:

Dissertation Abstracts International
International Political Science Abstracts
Historical Abstracts
Sociological Abstracts
Psychological Abstracts
Public Administration Abstracts

Journal of Economic Abstracts
SAGE Urban Studies Abstracts
The Universal Reference System: Political Science Government and Public Policy Series

Professional Journals

There are today so many social science journals that one must use abstracts, indexes, and other guides to locate the literature that interests him or her. For information purposes, however, there follows a list of some of the major journals by discipline:

Political Science
American Political Science Review
American Journal of Political Science
American Politics Quarterly
Comparative Political Studies
European Journal of Political Research
Journal of Politics
Policy Sciences

Policy Studies Journal
Political Science Quarterly
Polity
Public Administration Review
Public Interest
Public Opinion Quarterly
Public Policy
Urban Affairs Quarterly
Western Political Quarterly
World Politics

Sociology

*American Journal of
  Sociology*
*American Sociological
  Review*
Human Relations
*International Journal of
  Comparative Sociology*

*Journal of Mathematical
  Sociology*
Journal of Social Issues
Social Forces
Social Problems
Sociological Quarterly
Sociometry

Psychology

*American Behavioral
  Scientist*
*Journal of Applied
  Behavioral Research*

*Journal of Applied
  Psychology*
*Journal of Applied Social
  Psychology*
Psychological Bulletin

Administration and Management

*Academy of Management
  Journal*
*Administrative Science
  Quarterly*
Administration and Society
*Advanced Management
  Journal*
Decision Sciences
Evaluation

Evaluation Quarterly
Harvard Business Review
Management Science
*Midwest Public
  Administration Review*
Personnel Administration
*Public Administration
  Review*

Economics and Business

American Economic Review
*Bell Journal of Economics
  and Management Science*
Econometrica
Economic Journal
Fortune
*Journal of Political
  Economy*

*Quarterly Journal of
  Economics*
*Review of Economics and
  Statistics*
*Socio-Economic Planning
  Sciences*

Statistical Sourcebooks

Among the most useful statistical sourcebooks are these:

U.S. Bureau of the Census. *Historical Statistics of the United States:
Colonial Times to 1957. A Statistical Abstracts Supplement.* Washington,
D.C.: U.S. Government Printing Office, 1960. Arranged in twenty-six
chapters: population; vital statistics and health and medical care; mi-
gration; labor; prices and price indexes; national income and wealth;

consumer income and expenditures; social statistics; land, water, and climate; agriculture; forestry and fisheries; minerals; construction and housing; manufactures; transportation; communication; power; distribution and services; foreign trade and other international transactions; business enterprise; productivity and technological development; banking and finance; government; colonial statistics. Index of names and subjects.

U.S. Bureau of the Census. *Historical Statistics of the United States: Colonial Times to 1957—Continuation to 1972 and Revisions.* A Statistical Abstract Supplement. Washington, D.C.: U.S. Government Printing Office, 1972. Arranged in two parts: continuation of series in "historical statistics," revisions of series in "historical statistics." Source notes.

U.S. Bureau of the Census. *Statistical Abstract of the United States, 1979.* 100th ed. Washington, D.C.: U.S. Government Printing Office, 1979. Arranged in thirty-three sections: population; vital statistics, health, and nutrition; immigration and naturalization; education; law enforcement, federal courts, and prisons; area, geography, and climate; public lands, parks, recreation, and travel; labor force, employment, and earnings; national defense and veterans affairs; social insurance and welfare services; income expenditures, and wealth; prices; elections; federal government finances and employment; state and local government finances and employment; banking, finance, and insurance; business enterprise; communications; power; science; transportation—land; transportation—air and water; agriculture—farms, land, and finances; agriculture—production, marketing, and trade; forests and forest products; fisheries, mining and mineral products; construction and housing; manufactures; distribution and services; foreign commerce and aid; outlying areas under the jurisdiction of the United States; comparative international statistics. Three appendixes. Index of names and subjects.

United States Census of Population by States. Washington, D.C.: U.S. Government Printing Office, 1973. Contains the following information for most urban places of 2,500 or more: size of population by sex; major occupational groups by sex; color of population by sex; age of population by sex; years of school completed; marital status of males and females, fourteen years and above; country of birth of foreign-born whites (a decennial publication).

World Handbook of Political and Social Indicators by Charles L. Taylor and Michael C. Hudson. Rev. 2nd ed. New Haven: Yale University Press, 1972. An extensive compilation of seventy-five variables for 133 countries and colonies based on indexes covering human resources, government and politics, communication, wealth, health, education, family and social relations, distributions of wealth and income, and religion.

City Directories. Often useful in giving a wide range of information about industries and social organizations of the community. Contain alphabetical lists of persons and typically list occupation and address of each adult.

The County and City Data Book. Washington, D.C.: U.S. Government Printing Office. Lists numerous tables for each county and cities of 25,000 or more. Contains tables on such areas as labor force, income, elections, banking and finance, business enterprises, and education.

The Municipal Year Book. Chicago: International City Managers' Association. (Issued yearly.) Authoritative reference book on municipal governments. Facts available about the role of city governments (including education, housing, welfare, and health) make it possible to compare any city with other cities on hundreds of variables.

Handbooks

There are several excellent handbooks that describe in great detail the sources of problems, hypotheses, and data available to social scientists. These include the following:

Bart, Pauline, and L. Frankel. *The Student Sociologist Handbook.* Cambridge, Mass.: Schenkman, 1975.

Bottomore, T. B. *Sociology: A Guide to Problems and Literature.* 2nd ed. London: Allen & Unwin, 1971.

Holler, Fredrick. *Information Sources of Political Science.* Santa Barbara, Calif.: American Bibliographical Center–Clio Press, 1971.

Hoselitz, Berthol. *A Reader's Guide to the Social Sciences.* New York: Free Press, 1970.

Kalvelagem, Carl; Morley Seagal; and Peter Anderson. *Research Guide for Undergraduates in Political Science.* Morristown, N.J.: General Learning Press, 1972.

Mason, John Brown. *Researcher Sources: Annotated Guide to the Social Sciences.* Vol. 1, 1960; Vol. 2, 1972. Santa Barbara, Calif.: American Bibliographical Center–Clio Press.

Merritt, Richard L., and Gloria J. Pyszka. *The Student Political Scientist's Handbook.* Cambridge, Mass.: Schenkman, 1969.

Miller, Delbert C. *Handbook of Research Design and Social Measurement.* 3rd ed. New York: McKay, 1977.

White, Carl M. *Sources of Information in the Social Sciences.* Chicago: American Library Association, 1973.

SUMMARY

Research problems are intellectual stimuli calling for an answer in the form of a scientific inquiry. Problems amenable to research are empirically grounded, clear, and specific. In the problem formation stage, one should also give serious consideration to the units of analysis. These are the entities to which our concepts pertain and which influence subsequent research operations. Two fallacies, the ecological and the individualistic, are possible when one analyzes certain units but makes inferences to other units.

In order to move from the conceptual to the observational level, concepts are converted into variables by mapping them into a set of values. A variable is an empirical property that takes two or more values. For purposes of research, a distinction is made between independent, dependent, and control variables. An independent variable is the presumed cause of the dependent variable, and a dependent variable is the presumed outcome of the independent variable. Control variables serve the purpose of testing whether the observed relations between independent and dependent variables are spurious. Variables can also be continuous or discrete. A discrete variable has a minimal size unit; a continuous variable does not have a minimal size unit.

A relation in empirical research always means a relation between two or more variables. When we say that two variables are related, we mean that there is something common to them. Establishing a relation consists of determining which values of one variable covary with values of other variables. Two properties of relations should be stressed: direction and magnitude. When we speak of direction, we mean that the relation between the variables is either positive or negative. The magnitude of a relation is the extent to which variables covary positively or negatively.

Hypotheses are tentative answers to research problems. They are expressed in the form of a relation between dependent and independent variables. Research hypotheses are clear, value-free, specific, and amenable to empirical testing with the available research methods.

Research problems and hypotheses can be derived from theories, directly from observation, intuitively, or from a combination of these. But the greatest source for problems and hypotheses is the professional literature. One should be informed of the major guides to published research, including bibliographies, indexes, abstracts, journals, and statistical sourcebooks.

KEY TERMS FOR REVIEW

Research problem
Units of analysis
Ecological fallacy
Dependent variable
Independent
  variable
Control variables
Discrete variables

Continuous
  variables
Relations
Negative relations
Magnitude of a
  relation
Hypothesis

ADDITIONAL READINGS

Abell, Peter. *Model Building in Sociology.* London: Weidenfeld & Nicholson, 1971.

Dubin, Robert. *Theory Building.* New York: Free Press, 1969.

Glazer, Myron. *The Research Adventure.* New York: Random House, 1972.

Graham, George J. *Methodological Foundations for Political Analysis.* Waltham, Mass.: Xerox College Publishing, 1971.

Hannan, Michael T. *Aggregation and Disaggregation in Sociology.* Lexington, Mass.: Lexington Books, 1971.

Merton, Robert K. "Problem-Finding in Sociology." In *Sociology Today,* ed. by Robert K. Merton, Leonard Broom, and Leonard Cottrell. New York: Basic Books, 1959.

Polanyi, Michael. *Personal Knowledge.* New York: Harper & Row, 1962.

Reynolds, Paul D. *A Primer in Theory Construction.* New York: Bobbs-Merrill, 1971.

Smith, Mapheus. "Hypothesis vs. Problem in Scientific Investigation." *Philosophy of Science,* 12 (October 1945): 296–301.

CHAPTER PREVIEW

CHAPTER 4
Research Designs: Experiments

INTRODUCTION

Once the research objectives have been determined, the hypotheses explicated, and the variables defined, the researcher confronts the problem of constructing a research design that will make possible the testing of the hypotheses. A research design is the program that guides the investigator in the process of collecting, analyzing, and interpreting observations. It is a logical model of proof that allows the researcher to draw inferences concerning causal relations among the variables under investigation. The research design also defines the domain of generalizability, that is, whether the obtained interpretations can be generalized to a larger population or to different situations.

In this chapter, we first discuss the research design as a logical model of causal inference and then distinguish among several research designs. In the first section an example of how an experimental research design is implemented is given. In the second section the structure of experimental designs is explicated. The third section deals with the four components of research designs: comparison, manipulation, control, and generalizability. Finally, in the last section, some commonly used experimental designs are presented.

THE RESEARCH DESIGN: AN EXAMPLE

Any researcher who is about to test a hypothesis faces some fundamental problems to which solutions must be provided before the project can be started. These problems are as follows: Whom to study? What to observe? When will observations be made? How will the data be collected? The research design is the "blueprint" of research that enables the investigator to come up with solutions to these problems. It is a logical model of proof that guides the investigator in the various stages of the research.

The purpose of this section is to describe what processes are involved in designing a study and how a decision to adopt a specific research design helped in structuring the collection, analysis, and interpretation of data. We will describe a study based on an experimental design called *Pygmalion in the Classroom.*[1] This study is an attempt to test the effect that others' expectations have on a person's behavior. The central idea of the study has been that one person's expectation for another's behavior may serve as a self-fulfilling prophecy. This is not a new idea, and anecdotes and theories can be found to support it. The most notable example is George Bernard Shaw's play *Pygmalion.* To use Shaw's own words:

> . . . You see, really and truly, apart from the things anyone can pick up (the dressing and the proper way of speaking, and so on, the difference between a lady and a flower girl is not how she behaves, but how she's treated. I shall always be a flower girl to Professor Higgins, because he always treats me as a flower girl, and always will; but I know I can be a lady to you, because you always treat me as a lady, and always will.

Many studies on animal behavior support Shaw's shrewd observations. In these studies, when experimenters were led to believe that their animal subjects were genetically inferior, these animals performed poorly. On the other hand, when the experimenters were led to believe that the animals were genetically superior, the animals excelled in their performance. In reality, there were no genetic differences between the two groups of animals.

Rosenthal and Jacobson, who conducted the *Pygmalion in the Classroom* study, argued that if animal subjects believed to be brighter actually became brighter because of their trainers' expectations, then it might also be true that school children believed by their teachers to be brighter would indeed become brighter because of their teachers' expectations.

To test this hypothesis, the investigators selected one school—Oak School—as a laboratory in which the experiment would be carried out. The school selected was a public elementary school in a lower-class community. On theoretical grounds, the study had to examine the effects of teachers' favorable or unfavorable expectations on their pupils' intellectual competence. However, on ethical grounds, only the hypothesis

---

1. Robert Rosenthal and Lenore Jacobson, *Pygmalion in the Classroom* (New York: Holt, Rinehart & Winston, 1968).

that teachers' favorable expectations will lead to an increase in intellectual competence was tested.

The independent variables of the study were the expectations held by the teachers. The expectations were manipulated by the investigators by using the results of a standard nonverbal test of intelligence. This test was presented to the teachers as one that would predict intellectual "blooming." At the beginning of the school year, following a schoolwide pretesting, the teachers were given the names of about 20 percent of Oak School's children, in their respective classrooms, who in the academic year ahead would supppsedly show a dramatic intellectual growth. These predictions were allegedly made on the basis of these children's scores on the "intellectual blooming" test. However, the names of the potential bloomers were actually chosen randomly. Thus, the difference between the "special" children and the ordinary children was only in the mind of the teacher.

The dependent variable was the intellectual ability of the children. It was measured by using the standard IQ test that allegedly predicted intellectual growth. All the children of Oak School were retested with the same test after a full academic year. (The tests were given after one semester and after two academic years, but we will refer here only to the first retest.) For the "special" children and for all the other children, gains in IQ from the first to the second testing were computed. Advantage resulting from positive teachers' expectations was defined by the degree to which IQ gains by the "special" children exceeded gains by all other children. After the first year of the experiment, a significant gain was observed among the "special" children, especially those in the first and second grades.

In interpreting the results of the experiment, Rosenthal and Jacobson concluded that the favorable expectations held by the teachers of the "special" children account for their significant gain in IQ. In summarizing their results, the investigators attempted to account for this process:

> . . . We may say that by what she said, by how and when she said it, by her facial expression, postures, and perhaps by her touch, the teacher may have communicated to the children of the experimental group that she expected improved intellectual performance. Such communications together with possible changes in teaching techniques may have helped the child learn by changing his self concept, his expectations of his own behavior, and his motivation, as well as his cognitive style and skills.[2]

Let us now introduce some of the terms employed in discussions

2. Ibid., p. 180.

on experimental research designs. In the next section we will look at the Pygmalion experiment as an example of a classic experimental design.

THE CLASSIC EXPERIMENTAL DESIGN

The classic research design consists of two comparable groups: an experimental group and a control group. These two groups are equivalent except that the experimental group is exposed to the independent variable (also termed the treatment) and the control group is not. Assignment of cases to either the experimental or to the control group is based on chance. Cases are randomly assigned to either group. To assess the effect of the independent variable, researchers take measurements on the dependent variable, designated as scores, twice from each group. One measurement, the pretest, is taken prior to the introduction of the independent variable in the experimental group; a second, the posttest, is taken after exposure has taken place. The difference in measurements between the posttest and pretest is compared in each of the two groups. If the difference in the experimental group is significantly larger than in the control group, it is inferred that the independent variable is causally related to the dependent variable.

The classic design is often diagrammed as in Table 4.1, where X designates the independent variable; O_i, the measurements on the dependent variable; R, the random assignment of subjects to the experimental group and the control group; and d_e and d_c, the difference between the posttest and pretest in each group.

Why Study Experiments?

The classic experimental design is usually associated with research in the biological and physical sciences. We are used to associating experiments with the study of chemicals in the laboratory rather than with the study of group behavior or voters' political preferences. Why then do we spend considerable time discussing experiments? The reasons are twofold: First, the classic experimental design helps us understand the logic of all research designs. But the experiment is treated here not only as a model against which we can evaluate other designs. The significance of the experiment is that it allows the investigator to draw causal inferences and observe, with relatively little difficulty, whether or not the independent variable caused the dependent variable. With other research designs, this cannot be easily determined. Thus, when we understand the structure and logic of the classic experimental design, we can also understand the limitations of other designs.

The experiment is used less widely in the social sciences, primarily because its rigid structure cannot often be adjusted to social science

TABLE 4.1. The Classic Experimental Design

		Pretest		*Posttest*	*Difference*
Experimental group	R	O_1	X	O_2	$O_2 - O_1 = d_e$
Control group	R	O_3		O_4	$O_4 - O_3 = d_c$

research. Thus social scientists frequently use designs that are weaker for drawing causal inference, but that are more appropriate to the type of problems they examine. Designs that are identified as quasi experiments (discussed in Chapter 5) are more commonly used.

Yet, as we see from the examples discussed in the previous and following sections, experiments are certainly used in the social science. As a matter of fact, in some social science fields, such as social psychology, experiments are the predominant design. Moreover, over the past few years the use of experiments has become more widespread in policy analysis and evaluation research.

The Structure of the Classic Experimental Design

To illustrate the application of the classic experimental design in a social setting, let us examine again the Rosenthal and Jacobson study on the self-fulfilling prophecy. All the Oak School children participated in the experiment. The children defined by the investigator as "potential bloomers" were in the *experimental group* whereas all the other children were in the *control group*. The decision as to who will be in either group was determined randomly (designated as *R* in Table 4.1). Children were randomly assigned to the experimental group or the control group. Twenty percent of the Oak School children were in the experimental group, and all the rest were in the control group. All the children were pretested (designated as O_1 and O_3) with the standard nonverbal test of intelligence. Following the pretest, each of the participating teachers was given the names of the children "expected" to show intellectual growth. These predictions were allegedly made on the basis of an intellectual blooming test and created the positive expectations of teachers, which was the independent variable of the study (designated as *X* in Table 4.1). All the children in the two groups were retested again (posttest) with the same intelligence test after one year (O_2 and O_4), and gains in intelligence were measured. The gains in intelligence were defined as the dependent variable. A significant difference between the pretest and the posttest was found only among the children of the experimental group. This finding led the investigators to conclude that the positive expectations of teachers accounted for the intellectual growth of the children in the experimental group.

Another interesting policy example, based on an experimental design, is The Manhattan Bail Project initiated by the Vera Institute in New York City.[3] The Vera Institute sought to furnish criminal court judges with evidence that many persons could be safely released prior to trial and without bail provided they had strong links to the community through employment, family, residence, and friends. The population examined included persons accused of felonies as well as misdemeanors; individuals charged with very serious crimes were excluded from the experiment. New York University law students and Vera staff reviewed the defendants' records of employment, families, residences, references, current charges, and previous records to decide whether a pretrial release without bail should be recommended to the court. The total group of recommendees was split randomly into experimental and control groups, and recommendations were made to the judge only for persons in the experimental group. The independent variable was pretrial releases granted, and the dependent variable was the default rate.

The recommendation for pretrail release without bail for the experimental group was accepted by the judges in the majority of the cases. The results of the experiment were clear-cut. Between 1961 and 1964, when the experiment ended, less than 1 percent of the experimental group failed to show up in court for trial—a rate considerably lower than that for similarly charged defendants who had posted bail, suggesting that the relaxation of the bail requirement did not result in unacceptable default rates. Following this experiment, the New York Probation Department extended this program to criminal courts in all five boroughs of the city.

CAUSAL INFERENCES

Both the Pygmalion experiment and the Manhattan Bail project are tests of causal hypotheses. Indeed, at the heart of all scientific explanations is the idea of causality; that is, an independent variable is expected to produce a change in the dependent variable in the direction and of the magnitude specified by the theory. However, an observation that whenever the independent variable varies, the dependent variable varies too does not necessarily mean that a cause-and-effect relationship exists. As Hubert M. Blalock has observed, "If X is a cause of Y, we have in mind that a change in X produces a change in Y and not merely that a change in X is followed by or associated with a change in Y."[4]

3. The following account leans on Bernard Botein, "The Manhattan Bail Project: Its Impact in Criminology and the Criminal Law Process," *Texas Law Review*, 43 (February 1965): 319–331.

4. Hubert M. Blalock, Jr., *Causal Inferences in Nonexperimental Research* (Chapel Hill: University of North Carolina Press, 1964), p. 9.

Consider, for instance, crime-control policies. A major objective of such policies is to deter crime. Deterrence, in turn, is viewed as the prevention of behavior that can be said to have had a realistic potential of actualization. Now, does the observation that a person does not commit a crime imply that he or she has been effectively deterred from doing so by a government policy? Obviously, the answer depends on whether the individual was inclined to engage in criminal behavior. Furthermore, even if the person were inclined to commit a crime, was he or she deterred by the possibility of apprehension and punishment or by other factors such as the lack of opportunity or peer group influence? Accordingly, even if researchers observe that with the enactment of more aggressive crime-control policies the frequency of actually committed crimes declines, they cannot safely conclude that the two are causally related.

In practice, the demonstration of causality involves three distinct operations: (1) demonstrating covariation, (2) eliminating spurious relations, and (3) establishing the time order of the occurrences.[5]

Covariation

Covariation simply means that two or more phenomena vary together. For example, if a change in the level of education is accompanied by a change in the level of income, one can say that education covaries with income, that is, that individuals with high levels of education have higher incomes than do individuals with lower levels of education. On the other hand, if a change in the level of education is not accompanied by a change in the level of income, education does not covary with income. In scientific research, the notion of covariation is expressed through measures of relations commonly referred to as correlations or associations. Thus, a correlation between phenomena is necessary evidence for a causal interpretation. For example, if relative deprivation is not correlated (does not covary) with violence, it cannot be a cause of violence.

Nonspuriousness

The second operation requires the researcher to demonstrate that the observed covariation is *nonspurious*. As defined in the preceding chapter, a nonspurious relation is a relation between two variables that cannot be explained by a third variable. In other words, if the effects of all relevant variables are controlled for and the relation between the original two variables is maintained, then the relation is nonspurious. A nonspurious relation implies that there is an inherent causal link between variables, and that the observed covariation is not based on an accidental

5. Julian Simon, *Basic Research Methods in Social Science*, 2d ed. (New York: Random House, 1978), pp. 341–353.

connection with some associated phenomena. As we saw in Figure 3.1, the observed covariation between the number of fire fighters at a fire and the amount of fire damage is spurious because a third variable—the size of the fire—explains the covariation.

Time Order

The third operation, *time order*, requires the researcher to demonstrate that one phenomenon occurs first or changes prior to another phenomenon. For example, in a number of studies it has been shown that the covariation between urbanization and democratic political development is nonspurious. To establish that urbanization is causally related to democratic development, one must also demonstrate that the former precedes the latter. The implicit assumption here is that phenomena in the future cannot determine phenomena in the present or past. In many cases, there is little difficulty in determining the time order of phenomena. Thus, the status of parents influences the educational expectations of their children, and not vice versa; an interest in politics precedes political participation; and depression precedes suicide. In other cases, the time order is harder to determine. Does urbanization precede political development, or does political development occur prior to urbanization? Does achievement follow motivation, or does a change in the level of motivation follow achievement? In the following section, the methods employed to determine the time order of events will be discussed. At this point, we merely want to stress the significance of the time-order criterion when formulating causal explanations.

THE COMPONENTS OF A RESEARCH DESIGN

The classic research design consists of three components: comparison, manipulation, and control. These components are necessary to establish that the independent and dependent variables are causally related. Comparison allows us to demonstrate covariation, manipulation helps in establishing the time order of events, and control enables us to determine that the observed covariation is nonspurious. In this section we shall discuss each of these components as a distinct research operation.

Comparison

The process of comparison underlies the concept of covariation: an association between two or more variables. A comparison is an operation required to demonstrate that two variables are correlated. (Association and covariation are also termed correlation.) A common example is the correlation between cigarette smoking and lung cancer, which means that the smoking of cigarettes is associated with a greater risk of getting lung cancer. To test this hypothesis, one may compare the frequency of cancer cases among smokers and nonsmokers or, alternatively, compare the number of cancer cases in a population of smokers before and after they started smoking. Or suppose that a relationship exists between a teaching method X and the achievement of students; one would then expect to find a *joint occurrence* of both the teaching method and a certain degree of achievement; that is, students will achieve more after being exposed to the teaching method than before. Similarly, those students who are studying under teaching method X will have higher achievement than those students who are not. Thus, to assess the joint occurrence of the teaching method and achievement, one makes a comparison of a group of students exposed to method X with one that is not, or of the group's achievement before and after the introduction of method X. In other words, to assess covariation, one evaluates the students' scores on the dependent variable before and after the introduction of the independent variable, or one compares a group that is exposed to the independent variable with one that is not. In the former case, a group is compared with itself; in the latter case, an experimental group is compared with a control group.

Manipulation

The notion of causality implies that if Y is caused by X, then an induced change in X will be followed by a change in Y. It is hypothesized that the relations are asymmetrical: that one variable is the determing force, and the other is a determined response. For this to be established, the induced change in X would have to be prior to the change in Y, for what follows cannot be the determining variable. If teaching method X is to influence achievement, then it has to be demonstrated that improvement in achievement takes place only after exposure to the method. This can be accomplished by some form of control over the introduction of the method, so that the investigator can measure achievement before and after the introduction. In experimental settings, especially in laboratory experiments, researchers can introduce the experimental treatment themselves; in natural settings, on the other hand, this is not always possible. In both cases, the major evidence required to determine the time sequence of events, that is, that the independent variable precedes the dependent variable, is that a change occurred only after the activation of the independent variable.

Control: The Internal Validity of Research Designs

The third criterion of causality requires that other factors be ruled out as rival explanations of the observed association between the variables under investigation. Such factors could invalidate the inference that the variables are causally related. Donald Campbell and Julian Stanley have termed this the problem of *internal validity,* which is the sine qua non of research; it refers to the question of whether the independent variable did, in fact, cause the dependent variable.[6]

The factors that may jeopardize internal validity can be classified into those that are extrinsic to the research operation and those that are intrinsic and impinge upon the results during the study period.

Extrinsic factors. Extrinsic factors refer to the possible biases resulting from the differential recruitment of research participants to the experimental and control groups. They are designated as *selection* factors that produce differences between the experimental and control groups *prior* to the research operation. For example, to investigate the changes occurring in the social life of slum families as a result of their rehousing in public housing projects, Chapin compared an experimental group of families who had been rehoused with a control group of families who were still living under slum conditions.[7] The findings showed a marked improvement in the social life of the experimental group, leading to the conclusion that public housing projects change the lifestyle of their inhabitants. However, a rival explanation of the observed change in the rehoused families is that the people in new housing projects were *initially different* from the families serving as a control group. Perhaps the groups differed in type of employment, level of education, size of family, or attitudes. These initial differences could have accounted for the observed differences between the experimental group and the control group.

Selection effects are especially problematic in cases in which the individuals themselves decide whether to participate in an experiment. In such cases, the investigator cannot tell whether the independent variable itself caused the observed differences between the experimental and control groups or whether other factors related to the selection procedures were responsible for the observed effects. In fact, many social programs (for example, Head Start and Medicaid) are available on a self-selection basis to a larger target population. Assessment of the effectiveness of such programs is problematic because, among other things, of the selection effects. Selection factors must be controlled before the investigator can rule them out as rival explanations. Later in this section, we shall discuss methods for controlling selection factors.

Intrinsic factors. Intrinsic factors refer to changes in the individuals or the units studied that occur during the study period, changes in

6. Donald T. Campbell and Julian C. Stanley, *Experimental and Quasi-Experimental Designs for Research* (Chicago: Rand McNally, 1963), p. 3.

7. F. Stuart Chapin, "An Experiment on the Social Effects of Good Housing," *American Sociological Review,* 5 (December 1940): 868–879.

the measuring instrument, or the reactive effect of the observation itself. The following are the major intrinsic factors that might invalidate a causal interpretation given to research findings.[8]

1. *History.* History refers to all events occurring during the time of the study that might affect the individuals studied and provide a rival explanation for the change in the dependent variable. For example, in a study attempting to assess the effect of an election campaign on voting behavior, the hypothesis might be that propaganda to which voters are exposed during the campaign is likely to influence their voting. The voting intentions of individuals are compared before and after exposure to propaganda. Differences in voting intentions of the two groups—one that has been exposed to propaganda and another that has not—could result from differential exposure to the propaganda or, alternatively, from events that occurred during this period, for example, additional taxes levied, governmental conflicts, international crises, or rapid inflation. The longer the time lapse between the pretest and the posttest, the higher the probability that events other than the independent variable will become potential rival hypotheses.

2. *Maturation.* A second group of factors that may become plausible rival explanations is designated as maturation and includes biological and psychological processes that produce changes in the individuals or units studied with the passage of time. These changes could possibly influence the dependent variable and lead to erroneous inferences. Suppose one wants to evaluate the effect of a specific teaching method on student achievement and records the students' achievement before and after the method was introduced. Between the pretest and the posttest, students have gotten older and perhaps wiser; this change, unrelated to the teaching method, could possibly explain the difference between the two tests. Maturation, like history, is a serious threat to the validity of causal inferences.

3. *Experimental mortality.* Experimental mortality refers to dropout problems that prevent the researcher from obtaining complete information on all cases. When individuals drop out selectively from the experimental or control group, the final sample on which complete information is available may be biased. In a study on the effect of the media on prejudice, for instance, if most dropouts were prejudiced individuals, the impression rendered could be that exposure to media reduced prejudice, whereas, in fact, it was the effect of experimental mortality that produced the observed shift in opinion.

4. *Instrumentation.* Instrumentation designates changes in the measuring instruments between the pretest and the posttest. To associate the difference between posttest and pretest scores with the independent

8. Campbell and Stanley, *Experimental and Quasi-Experimental Designs for Research.*

variable, one has to show that repreated measurements with the same measurement instrument under unchanged conditions will yield the same result. If this cannot be shown, observed differences could be attributed to the change in the measurement instrument and not necessarily to the independent variable. The stability of measurement is also referred to as *reliability,* and its absence can be a threat to the validity of experiments. (See Chapter 6.) For example, if a program to improve cognitive skills were evaluated by comparing preprogram and postprogram ratings by psychologists, any changes in the psychologists' standard of judgment that occurred between testing periods would bias the findings.

5. *Testing.* The possible reactivity of measurement is a major problem in social science research. The process of testing may itself change the phenomena being measured. The effect of being pretested might sensitize individuals and improve their scoring on the posttest. A difference between posttest and pretest scores could thus be attributed not necessarily to the independent variable but rather to the experience gained by individuals while taking the pretest. It is known, for example, that individuals may improve their scores on intelligence tests by taking them often. Similarly, through a pretest, individuals may learn the socially accepted responses either through the wording of the questions or through discussing the results with friends. They might then answer in the acceptable direction on the posttest.

6. *Regression artifact.* The regression artifact is a threat that occurs when individuals have been selected to the experimental group on the basis of their extreme scores on the dependent variables. When this happens and measures are unreliable, individuals who scored below average on the pretest will appear to have improved upon retesting. Conversely, individuals who scored above average on the pretest would appear to have done less well upon retesting. The most familiar demonstration of this problem is taken from our own experience in test taking. Most of us have sometimes performed below our expectations on an academic test because of factors beyond our control that had nothing to do with our academic ability. For example, we may have had a sleepless night just before taking the test or were distracted by some serious personal problems. These factors, which do not reflect true ability, are defined as errors. It is very likely that the next time the test would be taken, our performance would improve without any additional studying. Viewed more generally, regression artifact can become a threat to the validity of a study whenever the treatment is expected to produce a change in individuals whose scores on the dependent variable are extreme to begin with. If children were chosen to participate in a compensatory program such as Head Start because their cognitive development was extremely low, it is very likely that they will show improvement in the posttest

even without being affected by the program simply because they cannot get worse. There is a risk, then, that their improvement will be erroneously attributed to the effect of the program.

7. *Interactions with selection.* Many of the intrinsic factors that pose a threat to the internal validity of experiments can interact with *selection* and present added threats to the validity of the study. The factors that are most commonly cited are *selection-history* and *selection-maturation.*

Selection-history results when the experimental group and the control group are selected from different settings so that each might affect their response to the treatment. Suppose, for example, that a study is designed to test the effect of manpower training on the transition of the hard-core unemployed into nonsubsidized jobs. Participants in the program (the experimental group) were inadvertently selected from regions where several industrial plants had closed down just when the training program terminated, making it very difficult for program graduates to obtain employment. Thus it would seem that the program had no effect, whereas it was the interaction of the specific economic condition in the region and the selection of participants from that region that produced these results.

Selection-maturation refers to a situation where the experimental group and the control group mature at a different rate. For example, suppose the cognitive development of males and females is compared at the pretest and posttest. It is possible that the rate of development for females is faster than for males, and this accounts for their better performance at the posttest.

Procedures of Control

Extrinsic and intrinsic factors that threaten the internal validity of causal inferences may be controlled by several procedures. Two methods of control are employed to counteract the effect of extrinsic factors. The first, matching, controls for variables that are known to the investigator prior to the research operation. The second, randomization, helps to offset the effect of unforeseen factors.

Matching. Matching is a way of equating the experimental and control groups on extrinsic variables that are known to be related to the research hypothesis. There are two methods to match the groups: *precision matching* and *frequency distribution.* With the first method (also known as pairwise matching), for each case in the experimental group, another one with identical characteristics is selected for the control group. As a means of controlling the effect of age, for example, for every individual in a specific age category in one group, there should be one in the same category in the second group. Having matched on the extrinsic variables, the investigator can conclude that any difference found between the experimental and control groups cannot be due to the matched variables.

The main drawback in this method is the difficulty in matching a large number of variables. For example, if we wanted to control for age, sex, race, and education, for every black male thirty years old with a college degree in the experimental group, we would have to find an individual with the same combination of characteristics for the control group. Therefore, when there are many relevant characteristics that need to be controlled, it is difficult to find matching pairs. Indeed, precision matching often causes a loss of about 90 percent of the cases for which an appropriate match cannot be found.

An alternative and more efficient method of matching is frequency distribution. With this method, the experimental and control groups are made similar for each of the relevant variables *separately* rather than in combination. Thus, instead of a one-to-one matching, the two groups are matched on central characteristics. For example, when one is matching for age, the average age of one group should be equivalent to that of the other. If sex is controlled, care should be taken that the two groups have the same proportion of males and females. Thus, the two groups are matched separately for each extrinsic factor. Although somewhat less precise, frequency distribution matching is much easier to execute than precision matching and enables the investigator to control for several factors without having to discard a large number of cases.

The most basic problem in using matching as a method of control is that ordinarily the investigator does not know which of *all* the relevant variables are critical in terms of explaining the independent-dependent variable relationship. Furthermore, one is never certain that *all* the relevant variables were considered.

Randomization.   Matching is a method of controlling for a limited number of predefined extrinsic factors. However, even if it were possible to eliminate the effects of all the relevant factors, one can never be sure that all factors that may be associated with the variables under investigation have been identified. There may be other factors the investigator is unaware of that may lead to erroneous causal interpretations. This problem can be avoided by resorting to randomization, a process through which cases are assigned to the experimental and control groups. Randomization can be accomplished either by flipping a coin, by using a table of random digits, or by any other method that assures that any of the cases has an equal probability of being assigned to either the experimental group or the control group.

Suppose a researcher is examining the hypothesis that the participation of workers in the decision-making process of their place of work is conducive to production. Workers are divided into experimental and control groups; the experimental group is allowed to participate in decisions concerning the work schedule and its organization. The production level of both groups is measured at the beginning and at the end of the experiment. The objective is to see whether workers who took part in the decisions are significantly more productive than workers in the control group. However, a difference in the production level can be accounted for by numerous factors other than the independent variable (participation) whose effect is directly examined. Obviously, there are a number of personal factors, such as age, personal fitness, intelligence, and motivation that could account for the difference. (The highly motivated, the more intelligent, the more physically fit, and the younger workers could be more productive.) Without a controlled assignment of the workers to the groups, perhaps the most motivated, intelligent, and fit among the younger participants would volunteer for the experimental group, a fact that might account for the improved production level.

One way to counteract the effect of these variables is by pairwise matching. Another is to randomize the groups by flipping a coin or using a table of random digits to decide which workers are assigned to the experimental group and which to the control group. The latter process assures similar distributions of all prior characteristics of the workers in both groups. It is expected in the long run that motivation, intelligence, physical fitness, and average age will be about the same in the two groups. Consequently, any difference in production between the groups can be interpreted as the effect of the experimental variable. (See Appendix B for a table of random digits.)

The Control Group. Randomization cancels out the effect of any systematic error due to extrinsic variables that may be related to the dependent or independent variables. The advantage of this method is that it controls for numerous factors simultaneously even without the research's awareness of what they are. With randomization, the investigator can equalize the experimental and control groups on *all* initial differences between them. Control of intrinsic factors is facilitated by the employment of a control group from which the experimental stimulus is withheld. Ideally, the control and experimental groups are selected randomly or by matching so that they will have the exact same characteristics and are also under identical conditions during the study except for their differential exposure to the independent variable. Thus, features of the experimental situation or external events that occur during the experiment are likely to influence the two groups equally and will not be confounded with the effect of the independent variable.

We will discuss briefly the way in which each of the intrinsic factors is controlled by the use of a control group. First, history cannot remain a rival hypothesis, for the control and experimental groups are both exposed to the same events occurring during the experiment. Similarly, maturation is neutralized because the two groups undergo the same changes. The inclusion of a control group does not necessarily avoid the mortality problem because the loss of cases might be differential and bias the results. However, the acceptable procedure is to include in the final sample only cases for which complete information is available. The influence of instrument change can be avoided by a control group; if the change between posttest and pretest scores is a result of the instrument's unreliability, this will be reflected in both groups. Yet only when the groups are exposed to identical testing conditions does this method of control provide a solution to the instrumentation problem. Using a control group is also an answer to the matter of testing. The reactive effect of measurement, if present, is reflected in both groups and leaves no grounds for misinterpretation.

The use of a control group will help in counteracting effects of factors that interact with selection (selection-maturation, selection-history, and other interactions) only if it is used in conjunction with methods that control for extrinsic factors, such as matching and randomization. Such methods assure that the group being treated and the control group have the same properties and that they experience identical conditions during the experiment.

Generalizability: External Validity

Internal validity is indeed a crucial aspect of social research. An additional significant question concerns the extent to which the research findings can be generalized to larger populations and applied to different social-political settings. Surely, most research is concerned not only with the effect of one variable upon another under the particular setting studied, but also with its effect in a natural setting and on a larger population. This concern is termed the *external validity* of research designs. Two issues of external validity involve the representativeness of the sample and the reactive arrangements in the research procedure.

Representativeness of the Sample. Randomization contributes to the internal validity of a study. However, it does not necessarily assure representativeness of the population of interest. Results that prove to be internally valid might be specific to the group selected for the particular study. This possibility becomes likely in situations where the recruitment of cases to the study is difficult. Consider an experiment on college students that is carefully planned yet is based on volunteers. This group cannot be assumed to be representative of the student body, let alone the general population. To make possible generalizations beyond the limited scope of the specific study, one should take care to select the sample, using a sampling method that assures representation. Probability methods such as random sampling would make generalizations to larger and clearly defined populations possible, as discussed in Chapter 16. In theory, the experimental and control groups should each constitute a probability sample of the population. In practice, however, drawing a probability sample for an experiment often involves problems such as high cost and high rate of refusal to cooperate.

Reactive arrangements. The results of a study are to be generalized not only to a larger population but also to a real-life setting. This cannot always be accomplished, especially when a study is carried out in a highly artificial and contrived situation such as a laboratory. For example, Muzafer Sherif's famous study on group influences upon the formation of norms was designed to assess the influence of the group on individuals placed in an unstable situation in which all external bases of comparison were absent.[9] Sherif created an unstable situation experimentally by using the autokinetic effect, which can be produced in complete darkness. The autokinetic effect is produced when a single ray of light introduced to the room cannot be localized; it seems to move erratically in all directions and to appear at different places in the room each time. The investigator examined the norms as to the movement of the light that were evolving in this context of uncertainty. However, it can be claimed that an experimental situation in which persons are placed in a dark room and are required to respond to a moving ray of light does not represent ordinary social situations and that the observed results might very well be specific to an artificial situation alone. (See also Chapter 7 on observation methods.)

In addition to the possible artificiality of the experimental setting, various features in the setting might be reactive and affect the external validity of the study. For example, the pretest may influence the responsiveness of individuals to the experimental stimulus; its observed effect would thus be specific to a population that has been pretested.

TYPES OF DESIGNS

Research designs can be classified by the extent to which they meet the criteria discussed thus far. Some designs allow for manipulation but fail to employ methods of control or an adequate sampling plan; others may include control groups but have no control over the manipulation of the independent variable. Accordingly, three major types of designs can be distinguished: *experimental, quasi-experimental,* and *pre-experimental.* In experimental designs, individuals or other units of analysis are randomly assigned to the experimental and control groups and the independent variable is introduced only to the experimental group. Such designs allow for comparison, control, manipulation, and, in most cases,

9. Muzafer Sherif, "An Experimental Approach to the Study of Attitudes," *Sociometry,* 1 (1937): 90–98.

generalizability. Quasi-experimental designs usually include combinations of some of these elements but not all of them. Typically, these designs lack possibilities for manipulation and randomization. Pre-experimental designs include even fewer safeguards than quasi-experimental designs, and in this sense they provide the least credibility as to whether two or more variables are causally related. Some commonly used experimental designs are discussed in the next section; pre-experimental and quasi-experimental designs will be presented in Chapter 5.

Controlled Experimentation

The classic experimental design presented in Table 4.1 is one of the strongest logical models for inferring causal relations. The design allows for pretest, posttest, and control-group-experimental-group comparisons; it permits the manipulation of the independent variable and thus the determination of the time sequence; and, most significantly, by including randomized groups, it controls for most sources of internal validity. However, this classic experimental design is weak on external validity and does not allow for generalizations to be made to nontested populations. There are two variations of this design that are stronger in this respect: the Solomon Four-Group Design and the Posttest-Only Control Group Design.

The Solomon Four-Group Design

The pretest in an experimental setting has advantages as well as disadvantages. Although it provides an assessment of the time sequence as well as a basis of comparison, it can have severe reactive effects. By sensitizing the sampled population, a pretest might in and of itself affect posttest scores. For example, measuring public attitudes toward a government policy *prior* to its implementation may sensitize individuals to respond differently from nonpretested persons. Furthermore, there are circumstances under which a premeasurement period is not practical. In education, for instance, entirely new methods for which pretests are impossible are often experimented with.

The Solomon Four-Group Design, presented in Table 4.2, contains the same features as the classic design plus an additional set of control and experimental groups that are not pretested. Therefore, the reactive effect of testing can be directly measured by comparing the two experimental groups (O_2—O_5) and the two control groups (O_4—O_6). These comparisons will indicate whether X has an independent effect on groups that were not sensitized by a pretest. If it can be shown that the independent variable had an effect even with the absence of the pretest, the results can be generalized to populations that were not measured prior to exposure to X. Moreover, as Campbell and Stanley suggest, "not

TABLE 4.2. The Solomon Four-Group Design

	Pretest		Posttest
R	O_1	X	O_2
R	O_3		O_4
R		X	O_5
R			O_6

only is generalizability increased, but in addition, the effect of X is replicated in four different fashions: $O_2 > O_1$, $O_2 > O_4$, $O_5 > O_6$, and $O_5 > O_3$. The actual instabilities of experimentation are such that if these comparisons are in agreement, the strength of the inference is greatly increased."[10]

"The Selling of the Pentagon"—An Example

An interesting application of the four-group design is a study on the effect of public affairs television in politics.[11] Throughout the early 1960s, most political scientists clung to the theory of minimal consequences, which relegated television and all mass media to a position of relative impotence. This position was beginning to change in the late sixties when, during the war in Vietnam and the student revolution, television journalism became a new focus. This study addresses the issue of public television and politics. It asks several questions: "Does public affairs television affect the national political ethos? Has it fostered cynicism, feelings of inefficacy? Has it influenced a national election?"

The researcher adopted the Solomon-Four Group Design to test the impact of the CBS documentary "The Selling of the Pentagon" upon individual opinions about the military, the national administration, and the media. (Actually, there were two sets of experiments—one set for testing effects of program, the other set for testing effects of commentary presented at the end of the program. We shall discuss only the first set of experiments.)

To test the program effects, the design included two experimental groups and two control groups. A pretest was administered to some, but not all, of the participants. Posttests were administered to the experi-

10. Campbell and Stanley, *Experimental and Quasi-Experimental Designs for Research*, p. 25.

11. Michael J. Robinson, "Public Affairs Television and the Growth of Political Malaise: The Case of 'The Selling of the Pentagon,'" *American Political Science Review*, 70 (1976): 409–432.

mental groups immediately following presentation of "The Selling of the Pentagon." Control groups were tested just prior to exposure. A follow-up test was administered to all groups two months later. The design is presented in Table 4.3. The pretest and posttest were a questionnaire, which tapped opinions about the behavior and credibility of (1) social and political institutions, (2) public officials, (3) private citizens, and (4) new organizations. The follow-up questionnaire tapped similar dimensions but was shorter in length.

The analysis of the results demonstrates some of the practical realities involved in social science research. The Solomon design was originally selected because it provides unusually greater power for controlling virtually all potential factors that may provide alternative explanations for the results. Yet the inclusion of an experimental and a control group that were not pretested raised some serious problems. It turned out that Group B and Group D, which were not pretested, were far less likely to arrive and participate later on than were those who had been questioned earlier. Thus, the dropout rate from these two groups was so serious that the investigator had to rely only on the pretested group for the analysis of the results.

The results confirmed that "The Selling of the Pentagon" changed beliefs about the behavior of the American military, rendering those beliefs less positive. The experimental groups perceived the military as more likely to get involved in politics and more likely to seek special political advantage than these subjects had previously believed. The control group showed no significant change on any of the items. The experimentally induced change is significant because it was in the direction of "disloyalty," that is, change in beliefs about governmental misconduct.

More recently, Robert Lana has demonstrated through a series of experiments that, across a wide variety of attitudes and opinions, either

TABLE 4.3. "The Selling of the Pentagon" Experiment

	Pretest (Nov. 1971)	Mode of Exposure	Posttest (Dec. 1971)	Follow-up (Feb. 1972)
Group A	Yes	Program	Yes	Yes
Group B	No	Program	Yes	Yes
Group C	Yes	Control	Yes	Yes
Group D	No	Control	Yes	Yes

Adapted from Michael J. Robinson, "Public Affairs Television and the Growth of Political Malaise: The Case of "The Selling of the Pentagon." *American Political Science Review,* 70 (1976): 412

TABLE 4.4 The Posttest-Only Control Group Design

		Posttest
R	X	O_1
R		O_2

(1) there was no difference in experimental effects between pretested and posttested-only groups or (2) where differences were found, smaller changes occurred for the pretested than for the posttested-only groups. If anything, pretest measurements tended to result in underestimates rather than in overestimates of effects.[12] These findings lead to the general conclusion that whereas sensitization may logically threaten the internal and external validity of experiments, the actual effects are rather small.[13]

The Posttest-Only Control Group Design

Although the Solomon Four-Group Design is a strong experimental design, it is often impractical to implement or too costly, or the pretests might be reactive. The Posttest-Only Control Group Design is a variation of both the classic design and the Solomon design; it omits the pretested groups altogether. The design is diagrammed in Table 4.4. It is identical to the last two groups of the Solomon Four-Group Design, which are not pretested. Individuals are randomly assigned to either the experimental or the control group and are measured during or after the introduction of the independent variable.

Suppose, for example, that a researcher examining the effects of a racist film on racial prejudice selects a sample of people who are randomly assigned to either of the two groups. One group is shown the film, and later both groups are interviewed and their responses compared. The occurrence of prejudice in the experimental group is compared with its occurrence in the comparison group. A significant difference will indicate that the film had an effect on prejudice. The time order can be inferred from the randomization process used to assign the individuals to the different groups. This procedure removes any initial differences

---

12. Robert E. Lana, "Pretest Sensitization," in *Artifact in Behavioral Research*, ed. by Robert Rosenthal and Ralph L. Rosnow (New York: Academic Press, 1969), pp. 119–141.

13. See Ilene N. Bernstein et al., "External Validity and Evaluation Research," in *Validity Issues in Evaluation Research*, ed. by Ilene M. Bernstein (Beverly Hills, Calif.: Sage, 1976), p. 116.

between the groups, and it can, therefore, be inferred that the observed difference was caused by the film.

The Posttest-Only Control Group Design controls for all intrinsic sources of invalidity. With the omission of the pretest, testing and instrumentation become irrelevant sources of invalidity. It can also be assumed that the remaining intrinsic factors are controlled, for both groups are exposed to the same external events and undergo the same maturational processes. In addition, the extrinsic factor of selection is controlled by the random assignment of individuals, which removed an initial bias in either group.

Experimental Designs to Study Effects Extended in Time

In all the experimental designs described thus far, it was assumed that the effect of the independent variable on the dependent variable can be observed immediately or within a very short period of time. But sometimes we can expect long-range effects that are spread out over time. This is particularly evident in policy studies and in research in which the dependent variable is an attitude. For example, the effect of an educational program upon racial attitudes may be delayed, and thus the observation of changes should be spread out over a long period of time. Another example taken from the field of the sociology of religion deals with the effects that persuasive religious communication in a revival setting has on religious beliefs. The central concern in research on this topic would be to test and specify the conditions under which persons experience change in their religious beliefs. Yet the change cannot be expected to occur immediately, and thus the measurement of religious belief will have to be of a longer duration.

One solution to a delayed effect study would be to introduce additional posttest periods, such as six months and a year later. This is a convenient solution in research taking place in school settings, for example, where posttest measures such as grades would be collected anyway. However, as Campbell and Stanley have indicated, ". . . when the posttest measures are introduced by the investigator the repeated measurements on the same subjects could have the same invalidating effect as the pretest would. Therefore a better solution would be to set up separate experimental and control groups for each time delay for the posttest."[14] An illustration is presented in Table 4.5.

The same duplication of the experimental group can be incorporated in other types of research designs.

14. Campbell and Stanley, *Experimental and Quasi-Experimental Designs for Research*, p. 32.

TABLE 4.5. An Experimental Design for Delayed Effect

	Pretest		Posttest	Posttest
R	O_1	X	O_2	
R	O_3		O_4	
R	O_5	X		O_6
R	O_7			O_8

Factorial Designs

In all the designs discussed until now, there was only one independent variable (the treatment), which was introduced in the experimental group and withheld from the control group. For example, the independent variables have been either a teaching method, a movie, or a social integration program. In either case, only the effect of a single variable was observed systematically. Often, more insight might be gained if the effect of two or more independent variables is studied simultaneously. For example, research on organizations suggests that the size of the organization is related to the members' morale. Larger organizations are more likely to present their members with situations that lead to stress and lowered morale. However, though size is an important determinant of morale, it cannot be considered independently of other organizational variables. The effect of size will be different in different types of organizations. Large organizations vary in structure, and the negative effects of size can be minimized through decentralization.

Examining the effect of more than one independent variable will require a large number of experimental groups. Suppose we use size and decentralization as our independent variables and morale as the dependent variable. If each independent variable had only two possible values (dichotomous variables), four experimental groups are necessary in order to study all combinations of these two variables. We can diagram the combinations as in Table 4.6.

TABLE 4.6. Possible Combinations in a Two Independent-Variable Design

		Size	
		Large	Small
Decentral-ization	High	1	2
	Low	3	4

The four experimental groups have four different "treatments" representing all possible combinations of values of the two variables: (1) large size—high decentralization; (2) small size—high decentralization; (3) large size—low decentralization; (4) small size—low decentralization. Any of the designs discussed previously can be applied to this problem. For example, in Table 4.7 the posttest-only control group design is applied. The four different "treatments" illustrated in Table 4.6 are represented by X_1 to X_4. As usual, the cases have been randomly assigned to the four groups. The different treatments are represented by X_1 to X_4, and O_1 to O_4 are posttest measures on morale.

The External Validity of Factorial Designs

The chief advantage of factorial designs is that they may considerably broaden the range of generalizability. Instead of "controlling for everything," as in single-variable experiments, additional relevant variables are introduced, each at two or more different levels. Consequently, the researcher is not restricted by some constant level of each of these relevant variables when generalizing on the effect of an independent variable. Rather, the investigator is in a position to infer that the effect occurs similarly across several levels of the variables or, alternatively, that the effect is different at different levels of one or another of these variables. Factorial designs, then, increase the external validity of experiments because, as Ronald A. Fisher has suggested:

> Any conclusion . . . has a wider inductive basis when inferred from an experiment in which the quantities of other ingredients have been varied, than it would have from any amount of experimentation, in which these had been kept strictly constant. The exact standardization of experimental conditions, which is often thoughtlessly advocated as a panacea, always carries with it the real disadvantage that a highly standardized experiment supplies direct information only in respect of the narrow range of conditions achieved by standardization. Standardization, therefore, weakens rather than strength-

TABLE 4.7. A Factorial Design to Test the Effects of Size and Decentralization on Morale

		Posttest
R	X_1	O_1
R	X_2	O_2
R	X_3	O_3
R	X_4	O_4

ens our ground for inferring a like result, when, as is invariably the case in practice, these conditions are somewhat varied.[15]

Interaction Effects in Factorial Designs

Another advantage of the factorial design is that it allows us to assess systematically how two (or more) independent variables interact. Interaction is present when the effect of one independent variable upon the dependent variable depends upon the value of the second independent variable.

For example, if large organizational size is associated with low morale of members *only* in organizations that are low on decentralization, it means that "size" and "decentralization" interact. On the other hand, if large size leads to lowered morale whether or not the organization is more or less decentralized, then the effect of size on morale is independent of decentralization, and there is no interaction. The test for interaction makes it possible to expand greatly our understanding of the effect of independent variables upon the dependent variable. It allows us to qualify the conclusion on their effects in an important way because the researcher studies the simultaneous operation of the two independent variables.

SUMMARY

A research design is the program that guides the investigator in the process of collecting, analyzing, and interpreting observations. It allows inferences concerning causal relations and defines the domain of generalizability.

The classic research design consists of four components: comparison, manipulation, control, and generalization. A comparison is an operation required to demonstrate that the independent and dependent variables are related. Manipulation involves some form of control over the introduction of the independent variables, so that the time order between the variables can be determined. Control requires that other factors be ruled out as rival explanations of the observed associations between the independent and dependent variables.

The process of control is related to the internal validity of the research design. Factors that may jeopardize internal validity are intrinsic or extrinsic to the research operation. Extrinsic factors are called selection effects. They are biases resulting from the differential recruitment of respondents to the experimental and control groups. Intrinsic factors are history, maturation, experimental mortality, instrumentation, testing,

15. R. A. Fisher, *The Design of Experiments*, 8th ed. (New York: Hafner, 1971), p. 106.

regression artifact, and factors that interact with differential selection of subjects to the experimental and control group.

Two methods of control are employed to counteract the effect of extrinsic factors. The first, matching, controls for variables that are known to the investigator prior to the research operation. The second, randomization, helps to offset the effect of foreseen as well as unforeseen factors. Control of intrinsic factors is facilitated by employment of a control group.

Generalization addresses the problem of the external validity of research designs. It concerns the extent to which the research findings can be generalized to larger populations and applied to different settings.

Experimental research designs are the strongest model of proof in that they permit the manipulation of the independent variables and provide maximum control of intrinsic and extrinsic factors. In this chapter we have discussed the classic experimental design and two of its variations: the Solomon Four-Group Design and the Posttest-Only Control Group Design. We also examined designs that allow us to study effects extended in time, as well as factorial designs, which allow the researcher to examine the effects of more than one independent variable. The advantage of factorial designs is that they strengthen the external validity of the study and allow the assessment of interaction between the independent variables.

KEY TERMS FOR REVIEW

Research design	Manipulation	Experimental
Experimental	Control	mortality
research design	Internal validity	Instrumentation
Experimental group	Extrinsic factors	Matching
Control group	Intrinsic factors	Randomization
Pretest	History	External validity
Posttest	Maturation	Factorial design
Comparison		

ADDITIONAL READINGS

Anderson, Barry. *The Psychology Experiment.* Monterey, Calif.: Brooks/Cole, 1971.

Aronson, Elliot, and James Carlsmith. "Experimentation in Social Psychology." In *The Handbook of Social Psychology,* ed. by Lindzey Gardner and Elliot Aronson. Reading, Mass.: Addison-Wesley, 1968.

Campbell, Donald T. "Factors Relevant to the Validity of Experiments in Social Settings." *Psychological Bulletin,* 54 (1957): 297–312.

Chapin, Stuart F. *Experimental Design in Sociological Research.* New York: Harper, 1955.

Cochran, William G., and Gertrude M. Cox. *Experimental Designs.* 2nd ed. New York: Wiley, 1957.

Festinger, Leon. "Laboratory Experiments." In *Research Methods in the Behavioral Sciences,* ed. by Leon Festinger and Daniel Katz. New York: Holt, Rinehart and Winston, 1953. Pp. 140–146.

Katz, J.; A. M. Capron; and E. S. Glass. *Experimentation with Human Beings.* New York: Russell Sage Foundation, 1972.

Madron, Thomas William. *Small Group Methods and the Study of Politics.* Evanston, Ill.: Northwestern University Press, 1969.

Riecken, Henry W., and Robert Boruch. *Social Experimentation: A Method for Planning and Evaluating Social Intervention.* New York: Academic Press, 1974.

Verba, Sidney. *Small Groups and Political Behavior.* Princeton, N.J.: Princeton University Press, 1961. Chapters 3 and 4.

Wood, Gordon. *Fundamentals of Psychological Research.* Boston: Little, Brown, 1974.

CHAPTER PREVIEW

CHAPTER 5
Research Designs: Pre-Experiments and Quasi Experiments

INTRODUCTION

The controlled experiment allows the most unequivocal evaluation of causal relations between two or more variables. However, many phenomena that are of interest to social scientists are not amenable to the straightforward application of experimental designs. Furthermore, social, political, and ethical considerations may impede or make impossible the application of controlled experiments. For example, although we can induce fear in laboratory situations and experimentally manipulate other individuals, the question whether we have the right to do so, even for the sake of science, is extremely important. In general, the experimental design cannot be employed if randomization and experimental control cannot be applied.

Taking the experimental design as the strongest model of logical proof, this chapter presents a number of commonly used pre-experimental and quasi-experimental research designs. These are designs in which one or more of the sources of internal and external validity are not controlled for, and, therefore, their causal inferential powers are impaired. Before we discuss pre- and quasi-experimental designs, it is useful to make a distinction between stimulus-response and property-dispositions relations and see how these are related to research designs.

TYPES OF RELATIONS AND DESIGNS

Some years ago Morris Rosenberg made an important distinction between two kinds of relationships.[1] The one is a *stimulus-response* relationship, characterized by an independent variable that is external, specific, and well defined, with a dependent variable being a particular response to it. For example, relationships between reward and satisfaction or between advertisement and consumption patterns are of the stimulus-response type. The second type is between *property* (usually some background characteristic) and *dispositions*, such as attitudes, values, and orientations. Examples are the relations between social class and political tolerance or between race and prejudice.

Whereas stimulus-response relationships are well suited for experimental investigation, property-disposition relationships are not. The reason lies in the inherent differences between them on four issues: time interval, degree of specificity, the nature of comparison groups, and the time sequence of events.

Time interval.   The first difference relates to the time interval between the effect of the independent variable and the response to it. In a stimulus-response relationship, the time interval is relatively short, whereas with the property-disposition type it can extend over a long period. For example, the response to a drug or an advertising campaign can be observed within a short period, but the effects of properties such as age, race, and social class are not of such an immediate nature.

Degree of specificity.   The second difference is the degree of specificity of the independent variable. A stimulus is usually easy to isolate and identify, and its effect can be concretely delineated. However, a property such as social class is more general and incorporates various factors, including prestige, occupation, and education, each exerting its relative influence. Therefore, it is often difficult with this type of variable to define the relevant causes and to manipulate them experimentally.

Nature of comparison groups.   The nature of the comparison groups is the third difference between stimulus-response and property-disposition relationships. In the first, comparisons can be made of two similar groups: one that has been exposed to the stimulus and one that has not; and of a group before and after its exposure to the stimulus. In the second kind of relationship, a before-after comparison is practically impossible, especially with properties that do not change, such as sex and race. Similarly, it is difficult to assume that two groups having different properties are comparable in any other respect. Indeed, a lower-class group and an upper-class group differ in various aspects other than class: value orientations, child-rearing practices, voting behavior, and so on.

1. Morris Rosenberg, *The Logic of Survey Analysis* (New York: Basic Books, 1968), chapter 1.

Time sequence of events. With the stimulus-response kind of relation, the direction of causation is relatively clear, especially when the research design allows for before-after comparisons. But the time sequence is harder to establish with some properties. With fixed properties such as race and sex there are more difficulties because these can only be the determining factors but not the determined effects. However, this is not the case with properties that are acquired, including intelligence, education, and political orientations. These properties can both determine and be determined by other factors. All the same, the time order cannot be easily established.

Owing to these difficulties, the components of research designs—comparison, manipulation, control—cannot be applied to property-disposition relations in the pure experimental sense. Not all the phenomena that are of interest to social scientists can be experimentally manipulated by them. Moreover, units of analysis cannot always be randomly assigned to experimental and control groups; and many social, political, and economic processes can be studied only after a relatively long period of time. Yet social scientists have been trying to approximate the experimental model by employing specialized data-analysis techniques that compensate for the limitations inherent in property-dispositions relations. Let's turn now to the weakest research designs—the pre-experimental.

PRE-EXPERIMENTAL DESIGNS

Pre-experimental designs are the weakest kinds of research designs because most of the sources of internal and external validity are not controlled for. Indeed, the risk of drawing causal inferences from pre-experimental designs is extremely high. The first type of pre-experimental design to be considered is the one-shot case study.

The One-Shot Case Study

The One-Shot Case Study involves an observation of a single group or event at a single point of time, usually subsequent to some phenomena that allegedly produced change. For example, the study might be an observation of a community after an urban renewal program, a political system after general elections, or a school after it has been exposed to an innovative teaching method.

The case of Head Start vividly illustrates the pitfalls of the One-Shot Case Study. In January 1965, President Lyndon B. Johnson informed the public that a preschool program named Head Start would be established as part of the Community Action Program. Initially, $17 million were to be committed for the summer of 1965 to enable 100,000 children to participate.[2] The publicity given Head Start generated a large volume of demands for funds from numerous localities. The Office of Economic Opportunity (OEO) met these demands by committing $103 million to provide places for 560,000 children during the summer of 1965. Later in the year, Head Start was made a permanent part of the antipoverty program. According to President Johnson, Head Start had been "battle-tested" and "proven worthy" and, as a result, was expanded to include a full-year program. In 1968, $330 million were allocated to provide places for 473,000 children in summer programs and another 218,000 in full-year programs, turning Head Start into the largest single component of the Community Action Program.

As late as mid-1967, no reliable evidence existed regarding the effectiveness of the program. Members of Congress, the Bureau of the Budget, and OEO officials were, however, pressing for evidence. Consequently, the evaluation division of the Office of Research, Plans, Programs and Evaluations (RPP&E) proposed a study design for Head Start in which children who had participated in the program and were currently in the first, second, and third grades of school would be observed through a series of cognitive and affective tests. Performance on these tests would serve as evidence of the effectiveness of Head Start. The proposed design can be illustrated in the following way.

$$X \quad O_1$$

where X represents Head Start and O_1 observations that are carried out subsequently.

Head Start officials opposed the proposed study on the grounds that such a design cannot provide solid evidence for inferring causality. There are numerous rival explanations and hypotheses that could explain differential performance in cognitive and affective tests. Observations made only at the testing period would have no meaningful basis of comparison, and comparison is an essential component of making causal inferences. Furthermore, this design fails to provide any evidence of whether the program had *any* impact on the children. For drawing valid causal inferences, it is necessary to have observations made *prior* to the implementation of the program. The design has no control over extrinsic and intrinsic factors. It also does not allow for before-after or control-group–experimental-group comparison. The One-Shot Case Study cannot be used for testing causal relations.

The One-Shot Case Study is useful in exploratory research. It may lead to insights that, in turn, could be studied as research hypotheses.

2. This account draws on Walter Williams and John W. Evans, "The Politics of Evaluation: The Case of Head Start," *Annals of the American Academy of Political and Social Science*, 385 (September 1969): 118–132.

But in the case of Head Start, this weak design was used to test the effectiveness of the program, and when the research findings were made available they were ignored precisely because of "problems in research design."[3]

The Pretest-Posttest Design

The second pre-experimental design is the Pretest-Posttest. This design can be diagrammed as follows:

$$O_1 \quad X \quad O_2$$

The obvious advantage of the Pretest-Posttest design is that a variable is compared with itself: the variable is measured before the occurrence of a phenomenon (O_1); after its occurrence the same variable is measured again (O_2). The difference in scores is examined to assess the causal impact of the phenomenon (X). In the case of Head Start, the children's performance, say, on cognitive tests, could have been measured before their participation in the program and compared with the scores obtained after participation.

The major drawback of the Pretest-Posttest design is that changes might have been produced by other events, not necessarily because of the independent variable. The longer the time lapse between the pretest and the posttest measurements, the greater the chances of other variables' affecting the dependent variable and thus the posttest measures. This possible source of invalidity was earlier referred to as history.

The other shortcoming of the Pretest-Posttest design is connected with changes resulting from maturation. For example, the mental age of a child increases with time, and this change can affect measures of cognitive performance.

A third possible source of invalidity concerns regression artifacts. These, as discussed in Chapter 4, are pseudoshifts occurring when persons have been selected upon the basis of their extreme scores. It is expected that a regression artifact will occur when cases are selected because they are above or below average with respect to pretest and posttest measures.

The Posttest-Comparison Group Design

The third commonly used pre-experimental design relies on posttest measurement only but does employ a comparison group. (Some refer to this group as a "simulated control group." We use the terms *comparison*

---

3. David Nachmias and Gary T. Henry, "The Utilization of Evaluation Research: Problems and Prospects," in *The Practice of Policy Evaluation*, ed. by David Nachmias (New York: St. Martin's, 1980), pp. 461–476.

group instead of *control group* in those cases in which randomization and experimental manipulation are not performed.) However, the experimental and comparison groups are not formed randomly from a larger representative population; instead, the groups are *intact* before implementation of the independent variable. This design can be symbolized as follows, with a dashed line between the rows representing the two groups indicating intact groups rather than randomly sampled ones:

An example might compare the reading performance of children who participated in Head Start with the performance of a group of children who did not. The latter group is usually chosen to be as similar as possible to the group that was introduced to the independent variable.

One serious problem with this design is that individuals in the two groups might have differed initially with respect to the dependent variable measured (the reading performance); that is, the groups were not equivalent before introduction of the independent variable. Furthermore, possible differences between the groups might have occurred because of a greater willingness of members of one group to participate in the study (the "selection" source of invalidity). Nevertheless, evidence concerning causality cannot be ruled out altogether in cases where additional evidence shows that the two groups do not differ significantly on the average in characteristics relating to the dependent variable.

The internal validity of these pre-experimental designs is weak; too many critical intrinsic and extrinsic variables are not controlled for. Therefore, inferences drawn from pre-experimental designs regarding causal effects are inconclusive. Multivariate statistical analyses, such as the ones discussed in Chapter 14 can improve the inferential power of pre-experimental designs.

QUASI-EXPERIMENTAL DESIGNS

Keeping the classic experimental design as a model of logical proof, scientists have developed a number of quasi-experimental designs. Whereas these designs are weaker on internal validity than are experimental designs, they provide considerably more internal validity than do pre-experimental designs. Unlike experimental designs that rule out the effects of influences other than exposure to an independent variable or a stimulus, quasi-experimental designs do not require randomization and often depend on the possibility that influences other than the treatment can be ruled out by additional empirical evidence and/or data-analysis techniques. The major types of quasi-experimental designs are discussed and exemplified in the following sections.

Contrasted Groups Designs

A common problem in social science research is that in many cases the researcher cannot randomly assign individuals or other units of analysis to experimental and comparison groups. At times, intact comparison groups are used either at the pretest phase only or at the posttest phase. Causal inferences concerning the independent variables are especially vulnerable when groups are compared that are known to differ in some important attributes, such as comparing poor communities with relatively well-to-do ones, groups from different ethnic backgrounds, and males with females. If a posttest-only design is used with such contrasted groups, differences on the posttest measures are likely to be due to initial differences between the groups rather than to the impact of the independent variable. Nevertheless, when differences among such contrasted groups are to be assessed, several elaborations in the research design are possible that can be regarded as safeguards against the intrusion of influences other than the independent variable.

The least elaborated design for *Contrasted Groups* is that in which individuals or other units of analysis are regarded as members of categoric groups. (Categoric group members share some attribute that assigns them to an identifiable category, such as males, Democrats, Catholic, and so on.) Members of each group are measured with respect to the dependent variables. For example, one can compare the reading performances of children residing in different communities. This design can be symbolized in the following way, where $O_1 \ldots O_k$ represent measures on the dependent variable:

$$O_1$$
$$O_2$$
$$O_3$$
$$O_4$$
$$\cdot$$
$$\cdot$$
$$\cdot$$
$$O_k$$

Differences in measurement scores obtained for the above k groups are amenable to straightforward comparative statistical analyses (for example, difference between means). However, because such contrasted groups differ from one another in many ways, difficulties arise when attempts are made to assess the causes for the observed differences.

Relatedly, the groups might differ because of artifacts in the measurement procedures rather than because of any real differences among them. For instance, it has been repeatedly shown that measurements based solely on personal interviews are affected by interviewers' backgrounds: if white interviewers interview both black and white respondents, the presence of the white interviewer might cause the black respondents to give answers that are not representative of their typical views. (See Chapter 8 for a more detailed discussion of this and other problems in interviews.)

One way to reduce the risk of being wrong when making causal inferences based on Contrasted Groups Designs is to obtain supplementary evidence over time regarding the hypothesized differences. Thus, if the same finding is obtained in other settings, and comparisons are made on a number of measures concerning the dependent variables, then such supplementary evidence can increase the inferential powers of a Contrasted Groups Design.

Another procedure that has been employed in comparing the effects of the independent variable on contrasted groups is the matching of individuals from the two groups on one or more variables. Suppose, for example, that an evaluation is conducted of a new method of teaching reading skills in which a comparison is made between the degree of progress shown by children from an extremely poor neighborhood and the progress of children from a wealthy neighborhood in the same city. Pretest measures show significant differences between the two groups before the introduction of the teaching method. The researcher combines pairs of children from the two groups whose scores on reading skills are very similar. With such a procedure, two groups are obtained that have similar average scores on the pretest measures. But such a procedure can be vulnerable. By matching individuals in this manner, the researcher would be selecting children from a lower socioeconomic background with comparatively high scores on reading performance and children with comparatively low scores from higher socioeconomic backgrounds. Regardless of exposure to the independent variable and because of the regression artifact, the findings would indicate that the reading performance of children from the lower socioeconomic background had declined, whereas children from the higher socioeconomic background had improved their reading skills. The major drawback of such a matching procedure is that the problem of whether individuals or other units of analysis have been matched on all relevant and significant factors that can invalidate causal inferences cannot be effectively dealt with.

In some cases in which contrasted groups are compared, measures are available on a number of occasions before and after the introduction of the independent variable. In such cases multiple measures can be obtained before and/or after exposure. Such supplementary data provide a measure of the amount of normal variation in the dependent variable from time to time, irrespective of the independent variable's impact. Suppose, for example, that researchers wish to evaluate the effectiveness of a new approach to teaching reading implemented through the fifth grade in school E. They can compare achievement-test scores in reading for children in the third through seventh grades in that school and in another school (C) in the same community that did not use the new approach. The study is conducted retroactively for students who are currently in the seventh grade and have remained in school from the third grade up to that time. Because schools administer achievement tests each year, the researchers can obtain comparable measures for each of the five years. Evidence for a program effect when there are multiple measures over time consists of a sharp interaction from before to after implementation of the program for the units being compared, as illustrated in Figure 5.1.

Unlike the hypothetical results in Figure 5.1, the findings shown in Figure 5.2 indicate that the independent variable had no effect at all on the individuals in group E beyond what could be expected from the usual course of events, as evidenced in group C. The apparent change in group E is illusory because it is matched by a proportional change in group C. As Jim C. Nunnally suggests, unless striking findings are ob-

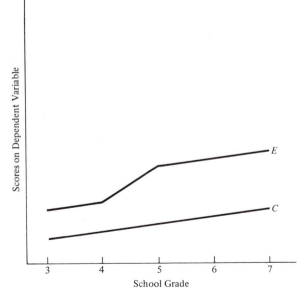

FIGURE 5.1.   Comparison of Two Contrasted Groups Indicating that the Independent Variable Had a Definite Effect

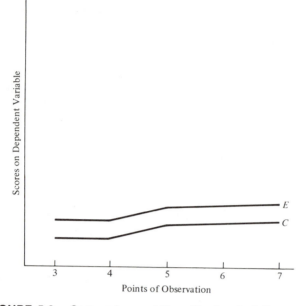

FIGURE 5.2. Comparison of Two Contrasted Groups Indicating that an Independent Variable Had No Effect

tained, like those depicted in the figures, it is usually risky to make any firm inferences concerning cause-and-effect relations from a Contrasted Groups Design.[4]

Planned Variation Designs

Planned Variation Designs involve exposure of individuals to systematically varying kinds of stimuli to assess their causal effects. The Head Start Planned Variation (HSPV) study exemplifies such designs. HSPV was a three-year investigation designed to compare the different effects that different kinds of Head Start centers were having on the development of the academic skills of children from relatively poor families. The study was developed on the assumption that by selecting "sponsors" for different types of programs and by systematically varying the kinds of programs offered to children, one could discover which kinds of programs most benefited which kinds of children.[5]

4. Jim C. Nunnally, "The Study of Change in Evaluation Research: Principles Concerning Measurement, Experimental Designs, and Analysis," in *Handbook of Evaluation Research*, ed. by Elmer L. Struening and Marcia Guttentag (Beverly Hills, Calif.: Sage, 1975), vol. I, p. 131.

5. The following account draws on Herbert I. Weisberg, *Short Term Cognitive Effects of Head Start Programs: A Report on the Third Year of Planned Variation, 1971–1972* (Cambridge, Mass.: Huron Institute, September 1973).

Sponsors selected to participate in the investigation had a substantial amount of variation in their goals and their teaching structures. During the 1971–1972 academic year, eleven sponsors were distributed over a total of twenty-eight sites. For purposes of comparison, eleven of the twenty-eight sites also had "nonsponsored" Head Start classrooms. In addition, three sites had comparison group children who were not enrolled in any program. Children for this comparison group were contacted by direct recruitment and from Head Start waiting lists. Each sponsor had two, three, or four sites. Within each site were variable numbers of classrooms run by the appropriate sponsor. Whereas some sites contained both sponsored classrooms and regular, nonsponsored Head Start classrooms, other sites had only sponsored classrooms.

One major shortcoming of this research design was that a number of important variables were not equally distributed across the sponsors. Herbert I. Weisberg points out that race, age of children, prior preschool experience, and socioeconomic background were all unequally distributed. For example, one sponsor had almost no black children at his site, whereas another sponsor had almost no white children. In spite of this serious source of invalidity, three general inferences were drawn: (1) overall, both the sponsors' programs and the regular Head Start programs tended to accelerate certain kinds of specific academic performance, such as number and letter recognition; (2) pooling the eleven sponsored sets of classrooms and comparing them with the regular, nonsponsored Head Start classrooms showed no large differences; and (3) when the sponsored sets of classrooms were compared among themselves, some differences in performance emerged on the several cognitive tests the children were given. In other words, certain types of curricula seemed to enhance different kinds of cognitive development.

Obviously, these conclusions are suggestive at best because of the unequal distributions of important variables across the sponsors. The confidence in findings obtained with Planned Variation Designs can be increased to a certain extent if the distribution of important variables is equal among the various groups and if measures of the dependent variable are taken on a number of occasions before and after exposure to an independent variable.

Time-Series Designs

In some cases when no comparison group is available for assessing cause-and-effects relations, Time-Series Designs—research designs in which pretest and posttest measures are available on a number of occasions before and after the activation of an independent variable—can be used. Usually the investigator attempts to obtain at least three sets of measures before and after the introduction of the independent variable. A typical time-series design can be represented as follows:

$$O_1 \quad O_2 \quad O_3 \quad X \quad O_4 \quad O_5 \quad O_6$$

Employment of a Time-Series Design makes it possible to separate reactive measurement effects from the effects of an independent variable. A Time-Series Design also enables the researcher to see whether an independent variable has an effect over and above the reactive effects. The reactive effect shows itself at O_3; this can be compared with O_4. An increase at O_4 above the increase at O_3 can be attributed to the independent variable. A similar argument applies for the maturation source of invalidity.

Some authors maintain that history is the most serious problem with this design. They argue that it is plausible that the independent variable did not produce a change in the dependent variable, but rather the change was caused by some other event or combination of events occurring during the study period. Indeed, if there are constantly recurring events other than the independent variable, the making of causal inferences becomes problematic at best. Nevertheless, in concrete research situations, influences other than the independent variable might show up between, say, O_2 and O_3, as well as between O_3 and O_4, making history less of a threat.

A classic study that illustrates the advantages as well as the problems involved with Time-Series Designs is the evaluation of the Connecticut crackdown on speeding following a record number of traffic fatalities in 1955.[6] At the end of 1956 there had been 284 traffic deaths, compared with 324 the year before, a reduction of 12.3 percent. The results are graphed in Figure 5.3, with the intent to magnify differences. Referring to these data, the authorities concluded that "the program is definitely worthwhile." As this inference is based on a sort of pretest-posttest design, a number of plausible rival interpretations could also be advanced. For instance, 1956 might have been a particularly dry year, with fewer accidents due to rain or snow.

A more valid causal inference can be made if the data are presented as part of an extended time series, as illustrated in Figure 5.4. This Time-Series Design controls for maturation. The data permit the rejection of a rival interpretation suggesting that traffic death rates were already going down year after year, which could be a plausible interpretation if the measures were carried out only one year before and after implementation of the program.

Although the extended Time-Series Design takes into account four observations before introduction of the program and three observations after its implementation, it nevertheless fails to control for the effects of

6. Donald T. Campbell, "Reforms as Experiments," *American Psychologist*, 24 (April 1969): 409–429.

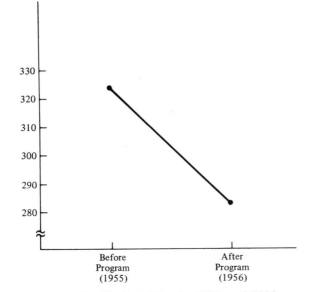

FIGURE 5.3. Traffic Fatalities in 1955 and 1956

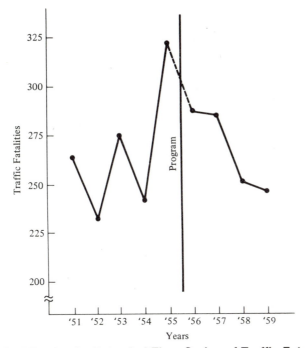

FIGURE 5.4. An Extended Time Series of Traffic Fatalities

SOURCE: Donald T. Campbell, "Reforms as Experiments," *American Psychologist*, 24 (April 1969): 413. Reprinted by permission.

other potential sources of invalidity; for example, history remains a plausible rival explanation. In such a case, one strategy for strengthening the credibility of the inference is to make use of supplementary data if these are available. For example, weather records can be examined to evaluate the rival interpretation that weather conditions were responsible for the decline in traffic deaths.

But time series are unstable even when no independent variables are being introduced. The degree of this normal instability is, according to Campbell, "the crucial issue, and one of the main advantages of the extended time-series is that it samples this instability."[7] In the Connecticut case the authorities had in fact implied that all the change from 1955 to 1956 was due to the crackdown policy. However, as Figure 5.4 indicates, the relatively high preprogram instability makes the policy look ineffective: "The 1955–1956 shift is less than the gains of both 1954–1955 and 1952–1953. It is the largest drop in the series, but it exceeds the drops of 1951–1952, 1953–1954, and 1957–1958 by trivial amounts."[8] Accordingly, one can legitimately advance the argument that the 1955–1956 drop is merely a manifestation of series instabilities. Notwithstanding this plausible interpretation, it can be observed that after the crackdown there are no year-to-year gains, suggesting that the character of the time series has changed.

Regression artifacts also present a serious threat to the validity of Time-Series Designs, especially when these are characterized by instabilities. As a rule it is maintained that with any highly variable time series, if one selects a point that is the "highest so far," the next point, on the average, will be lower or nearer to the general trend. In the previous example the most dramatic shift in the whole series is the upward shift just prior to the crackdown. Thus it is plausible that this caused the implementation of the program rather than, or in addition to, the program's causing the 1956 decline in traffic fatalities. Therefore, at least part of the 1956 drop is an artifact of the 1955 extremity.

Figure 5.5 illustrates a case from which it can be concluded that an independent variable had no effect on the dependent variable. The curve goes up from before the introduction of the independent variable to after its implementation. However, the curve was going up at the same rate before the introduction and continues up at the same rate after implementation.

Interpretation of the hypothetical data in Figure 5.6 is more problematic. The curve goes up from the introduction of the independent variable to after its implementation. However, the great variations before

7. Ibid., p. 413.

8. Ibid.

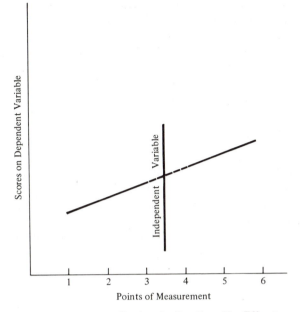

FIGURE 5.5.   A Time Series Indicating No Effect

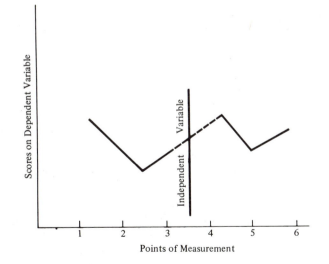

FIGURE 5.6.   A Time Series Illustrating an Illusory Causal Effect

introduction, as well as those observed after its introduction provide no confidence concerning causal effects.

Figures 5.5 and 5.6 illustrate but two different types of findings that could be obtained from a time-series study. They do, however, demonstrate again that Time-Series Designs, as well as other quasi-experimental designs without any comparison group, provide only partial evidence concerning cause-and-effects relations.

Control-Series Designs

We already pointed out that one of the major obstacles in constructing experimental designs is the difficulty of applying random selection procedures in assigning individuals or other units of analysis to experimental and comparison groups. Procedures for matching might also be vulnerable when evidence concerning significant external factors is unavailable. However, nonequivalent comparison groups used in time series provide more reliable evidence on causal effects. Such designs are called Control-Series Designs because they attempt to control those aspects of history, maturation, and test-retest effects shared by the experimental and comparison groups.

Figure 5.7 illustrates these points for the Connecticut speeding crackdown, adding evidence from the fatality rates of neighboring states (the comparison group). To make the two series of comparable magnitude, Campbell presented the data as population-based fatality rates. The Control-Series Design shows that downward trends were present in the neighboring states for 1955–1956 owing to history and maturation (weather, automative safety devices, and so on). However, the data are also indicative of a general trend for Connecticut to rise relatively closer to the other states prior to 1955 and to drop steadily and more rapidly than other states from 1956 onward. With such evidence one can infer that the program had some effect over and above the regression artifact.

COMBINED DESIGNS

The previous sections focused on the weakest and the strongest of the many possible quasi-experimental designs.[9] The stronger designs control in more effective ways for more intrinsic factors (for example, history, maturation, regression artifacts) that might invalidate causal inferences. If the measurement procedures do not vary from one point of measurement to the next, instrument decay can also be ruled out as a source of invalidity. The weakest quasi-experimental designs introduce a greater measure of ambiguity of inference. Nevertheless, they are better suited

9. For other types of quasi-experimental designs, see Thomas D. Cook and Donald T. Campbell, *Quasi-Experimentation: Design and Analysis Issues for Field Settings* (Chicago: Rand McNally, 1979).

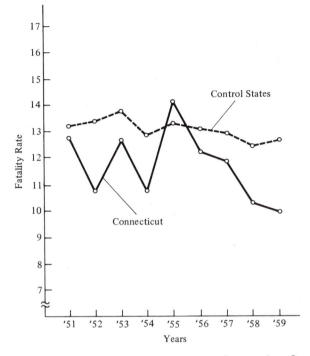

FIGURE 5.7.   A Control-Series Design Comparing Connecticut Traffic Fatalities with Those of Four Other States
SOURCE: Donald T. Campbell, "Reforms as Experiments," *American Psychologist*, 24 (April 1969): 419. Reprinted by permission.

for inferring cause-and-effects relations than are pre-experimental designs. Recently, Robert F. Boruch, among others has systematically elaborated possibilities for combining two or more designs in a single study. Such an approach involves "nesting randomized experiments in a larger framework of quasi-experimental or completely nonquantitative evaluation."[10]

Perhaps one of the most instructive field investigations that combined designs to assess causal effects is that of the Salk vaccine—a preventive medication for paralytic poliomyelitis first experimented with in 1954.[11] In the initial design the idea was to give the vaccine only to

10. Robert F. Boruch, "Coupling Randomized Experiments and Approximations to Experiments in Social Program Evaluation," in *Validity Issues in Evaluative Research*, ed. by Ilene Bernstein (Beverly Hills, Calif.: Sage, 1976), p. 43.

11. The following account leans on Paul Meier, "The Biggest Health Experiment Ever," in *Statistics: A Guide to Unknown*, ed. by Judith M. Tamur et al. (San Francisco: Holden-Day, 1972), pp. 2–13; and K. A. Brownlee, "Statistics of the 1954 Polio Vaccine Trials," *Journal of the American Statistical Association*, 50 (1955): 1005–1013.

those second graders whose parents volunteered them for study and not to give it to first and third graders. Presumably the comparison of results for the experimental group and the comparison groups would be indicative of the vaccine's effectiveness. Such a research design was most vulnerable, however, because polio occurred more frequently in more-sanitary neighborhoods than in unsanitary ones, and the more-sanitary neighborhoods are associated with higher socioeconomic status. People of higher socioeconomic status tend to volunteer more than people of lower socioeconomic status. Consequently, it could have been expected that more volunteers in the second grade would have been prone to have the disease in the first place than second graders in general and the average of the first and third graders. This bias could have invalidated the comparison. Furthermore, if only second graders were vaccinated, physicians might have suspected that some of them had caught paralytic polio because of exposure to the vaccine itself, so that there might have been significant frequency differences in diagnoses in the volunteer and nonvolunteer groups.

Realizing these problems, some state public health officials recommended a controlled field experiment that randomized the vaccine among volunteers from all grade groups. Half the volunteers received the vaccine and half a salt-water injection (placebo), so that the "blindness" of the diagnoses could be protected and physicians could be shielded from their expectations for the outcome in making a diagnosis. In other words, the self-selection source of invalidity would be balanced between the vaccinated and unvaccinated groups of volunteers.

Some states applied the original design, and others, the randomized controlled design. The results of the latter conclusively showed a reduction in the paralytic polio rate from about 57 per 100,000 among the comparison groups to about 16 per 100,000 in the experimental group. In the states where only the second-grade volunteers were vaccinated, the experimental group had about the same rate (17 per 100,000) as those vaccinated in the placebo comparison neighborhoods. The expected bias of an increased rate for volunteers compared with nonvolunteers appeared among the whole group. Among the placebo comparisons, the volunteers who were not vaccinated had the highest rate (57 per 100,000), and those who declined to volunteer had about 36 per 100,000. In the states using the initial pre-experimental design, the first and third graders, who were not asked to volunteer and were not vaccinated, had a rate between the two extremes, 46 per 100,000.

In the Salk vaccine investigation, the two research designs were used simultaneously, and they supported each other. However, in many other situations the use of a quasi-experimental design alone does not provide sufficient confidence in the results. Moreover, when complex problems are studied, one or more of their major components can fre-

After

O_1

O_2

FIGURE 5.8. The Correlational Design

quently be studied experimentally, and the remaining components with quasi-experimental designs.

CORRELATIONAL DESIGNS

The Correlational Design, often referred to as the *cross-sectional study*, is perhaps the most predominant design employed in survey research (see Chapter 8). It is an attempt to approximate the Posttest-Only Control Group Design by utilizing various data-analysis techniques. This design is diagrammed in Figure 5.8. The dotted cell indicates information obtained during the data-analysis stage. The basic comparison between the comparison group and the experimental group is statistical and is based on various cross tabulations and correlational techniques presented in later chapters.

The typical correlational study starts with a sample of individuals who are questioned about their properties and dispositions. For example, Jerold Heiss has attempted to examine the hypothesis that marital instability among blacks is related to a family history of instability.[12] Data from a sample of northern urban blacks were collected on variables such as stability of parental home, marital history, sex, parental socioeconomic status, and age at the point at which the parental home broke up. As a means of measuring the effect of the hypothesized cause (stability of parental home) on the marital history of the respondents, the sample was subdivided into "experimental" and "comparison" groups of respondents with histories of broken and unbroken homes. The percentages of separated and divorced couples in each group were calculated. (For a discussion of methods of percentage analysis, see Chapter 13.) The findings are presented in Table 5.1.

Heiss concluded that those individuals from unstable parental backgrounds are somewhat more likely to experience divorce or separation in their own marriages. This, however, is questionable evidence for accepting the suggested hypothesis. With no before-after comparison or a random assignment of respondents to broken and unbroken homes,

12. Jerold Heiss, "On the Transmission of Marital Instability in Black Families," *American Sociological Review*, 37 (February 1972): 82–92.

TABLE 5.1. Respondents' Marital History by Stability of Parental Home

	Percentage Ever Divorced or Currently Separated
Broken home	39.2%
Unbroken home	31.2

SOURCE: Jerold Heiss, "On the Transmission of Marital Instability in Black Families," *American Sociological Review*, 37 (February 1972): 82–92.

there is no assurance that respondents from broken homes are comparable in all relevant respects to those from unbroken homes. Numerous extrinsic factors could possibly account for the findings. For example, respondents from lower socioeconomic backgrounds might be concentrated in the broken-home group and account for the slightly higher rate of marital instability.

The most common alternative to experimental methods of control is multivariate analysis (see Chapter 14). By examining the original relationship in subcategories of the controlled variables, the researcher performs an operation similar to matching. However, as with matching, the drawback of such a method is that only known and predetermined factors can be controlled. The Correlational Design offers no alternative to randomization, the only technique that disrupts any systematic relationship between the characteristics of the units of analysis and their exposure to the independent variable.

In most correlational designs, the limitations in the manipulation of the independent variable prevent the determination of the time sequence. In some studies, this problem can be resolved on the basis of theoretical and logical considerations—as in our example, where the stability of the parental home is prior to the offspring's divorce or separation. In other studies, however, the direction of influence remains ambiguous.

THE PANEL

A more rigorous solution to the time dilemma in survey research is the Panel Design, in which the same sample is examined at two or more time intervals. Panel studies offer a closer approximation to the before-after condition of experimental designs by studying a group at two or more points in time before and after exposure to the independent variable.

An illustration of the Panel Design is the classic study by Lazarsfeld,

Berelson, and Gaudet on the formation of voting patterns during a presidential campaign.[13] A sample of voters was interviewed once each month in a period from May to November, up to Election Day. The investigators attempted to determine the factors that produce changes in voting intentions during an election campaign. The main advantage of such a study plan was that it enabled the determination of the direction of causation. It was assumed that from time to time various stimuli in the election campaign would change, producing a related change in the voting preferences of the participants. With a comparison of the various measurements of the same respondents taken prior to and after exposure to the agent of change, the time order could be determined.

The main problem of panels is obtaining an initial representative sample of respondents who are willing to be interviewed at set intervals over an extended period. Moreover, even if a researcher succeeds in obtaining the commitment of respondents, there are subsequent dropouts, owing to refusals to continue cooperating and difficulties in tracing respondents who move or change jobs. A serious consequence is that those who dropped out may change in a different way from the rest of the panel, thus affecting the findings. Another problem with repeated interviews with the same group is *panel conditioning*, that is, the risk that repeated measurements may sensitize the respondents. For example, members of a panel may try to appear consistent in the views they express on consecutive occasions. In such cases, the panel becomes atypical of the population it was selected to represent. One possible safeguard to panel conditioning is to give members of a panel only a limited panel life and then to replace them with persons taken randomly from a reserve list.[14]

A COMPARISON OF DESIGNS

The discussion on research designs in this and Chapter 17 has focused on two basic problems of scientific research: inferring causation and generalizing the findings. These problems pose a basic dilemma: to secure unambiguous evidence about causation, one frequently sacrifices generalizability. This is the problematic relation between internal and external validity. Designs that are strong on internal validity tend to be weak on external validity, and vice versa.

13. Paul Lazarsfeld, Bernard Berelson, and Hazel Gaudet, *The People's Choice* (New York: Duell, Sloan & Pearce, 1944).

14. For this and other methods for checking panel conditioning and overcoming problems of sample mortality, see Marion G. Sobol, "Panel Mortality and Panel Bias," *Journal of the American Statistical Association*, 54 (1959): 52–68; and Leslie Kish, *Survey Sampling* (New York: Wiley, 1965).

Perhaps the most serious threat to the internal validity of research designs is adequate control of extrinsic and intrinsic factors. In generalizability, the main issues are the representation of the researched population and of a real social situation. External validity is increased by increasing the heterogeneity of the sample and of the experimental situation. These issues are juxtaposed; as one increases realism and heterogeneity, one may frequently sacrifice control.

This is the point where the weaknesses and advantages of the various designs can be compared. Whereas experiments are strong on control and weak on representation, quasi experiments (especially surveys) are strong on representation but weak on control. Experiments have several advantages. First and foremost, they enable valid causal inferences to be made by exerting a great deal of control, particularly through randomization, over extrinsic and intrinsic variables. The second advantage is their control over the introduction of the independent variable, thus permitting the direction of causation to be determined. These advantages are the shortcomings of quasi experiments and more so of pre-experiments. Lack of adequate control over rival explanations and difficulties in manipulating the independent variable prevent the researcher from drawing unambiguous inferences.

However, although the experiment is accepted as the scientific method par excellence, it has several shortcomings. The most frequent criticism lodged at experiments, especially laboratory experiments, is that they are artificial and removed from real-life situations. It is maintained, as we shall see in Chapter 7, that reality cannot be replicated in experimental settings and, thus, that important issues cannot be analyzed there. A second problem concerns the sample design. In experimental designs, it is difficult to represent a specified population, for many experiments include volunteers or have an incidental sample at best. Nonrepresentative samples prevent the investigator from generalizing to populations of interest and limit the scope of the findings. On the other hand, most correlational designs are carried out in natural settings and permit the employment of probability samples. This allows statistical inferences to be made to broader populations and permits generalizations to real-life situations.

Given that no design can solve simultaneously the problems of control and representation, the investigator is faced with a difficult choice. Although in practice the nature of the study dictates this choice, it is generally accepted that the attainment of internal validity is more crucial than the attainment of external validity. Still, both experimental and quasi-experimental designs can be improved. Experiments can increase external validity by clearly defining the population to be studied and by drawing sampling units from this population following a probability sample design. Correlational studies can greatly improve their internal validity by including auxiliary information as a control against rival hypotheses. Moreover, with recent statistical techniques such as path or causal analysis (see Chapter 14), for example, time sequences can be more clearly specified, and the quality of causal inferences can be greatly improved.

SUMMARY

Randomization together with careful experimental control give scientific research strength and persuasiveness that cannot ordinarily be obtained by other means. However, property-dispositions relations are not readily amenable to experimentation; and social, political and ethical considerations may impede experimenting, or make it impossible to experiment, with stimulus-response relations.

Traditionally, pre-experimental research designs, such as the One-Shot Case Study, the Pretest-Posttest, and the Posttest-Comparison Group, were used when experimentation was impossible. These designs are very weak on internal validity but relatively strong on external validity. More recently, significant developments were made with quasi-experimental designs. These are designs in which some but not all sources of internal validity are controlled for, and therefore their causal inferential powers are greater than those of the pre-experimental designs. We covered some of the strongest quasi-experimental designs, including the Time-Series and the Control-Series. Sometimes designs can be combined so that the inferential powers of the study will increase.

In survey research, Correlational Designs are predominant. These are attempts to approximate the Posttest-Only Control Group Design by using multivariate data-analysis techniques. One solution to the order of events or the time problem inherent in survey research is the panel design in which the same sample of individuals is examined at two or more time intervals. Panel studies offer a closer approximation to the before-after condition of experimental designs by studying the same individuals at two or more points in time before and after exposure to the independent variable. In this sense, they are similar to the Time-Series designs.

KEY TERMS FOR REVIEW

Stimulus-response
  relationship
One-shot case study
Pretest-posttest
  design
Posttest-comparison
  group
Contrasted groups

Planned variation
Time-series design
Extended time-
  series
Control-series
Combined designs
Panel

ADDITIONAL READINGS

Caporaso, James A., and Leslie L. Roos, eds. *Quasi-Experimental Approaches: Testing Theory and Evaluating Policy.* Evanston, Ill.: Northwestern University Press, 1973.

Cook, Thomas D., and Donald T. Campbell. *Quasi-Experimentation: Design and Analysis Issues for Field Settings.* Chicago: Rand McNally, 1979.

Kish, Leslie. "Some Statistical Problems in Research Design." *American Sociological Review,* 24 (1959): 328–338.

Lazarsfeld, Paul F. "Some Episodes in the History of Panel Analysis." In *Longitudinal Research on Drug Abuse,* ed. by D. B. Kandel. New York: Hemisphere, 1978.

McCleary, Richard, and Richard A. Hay. *Applied Time Series Analysis for the Social Sciences.* Beverly Hills, Calif.: Sage, 1980.

Nachmias, David. *Public Policy Evaluation.* New York: St. Martin's, 1979. Chapter 3.

Nesselroade, J. R., and P. B. Baltes, eds. *Longitudinal Research in Human Development: Design and Analysis.* New York: Academic Press, 1978.

Stouffer, Samuel A. "Some Observations on Study Design." *American Journal of Sociology,* 55 (1950): 355–361.

CHAPTER PREVIEW

INTRODUCTION

THE NATURE OF
  MEASUREMENT

  Defining Measurement
  Structure of Measurement

LEVELS OF MEASUREMENT

  Nominal Level
  Ordinal Level
  Interval Level
  Ratio Level

DATA TRANSFORMATION

VALIDITY

  Content Validity
  Empirical Validity
  Construct Validity

RELIABILITY

  Test-Retest Method
  Parallel-Forms Technique
  Split-Half Method

SUMMARY

KEY TERMS FOR REVIEW

ADDITIONAL READINGS

CHAPTER 6
Measurement

INTRODUCTION

When investigators decide upon a research problem and begin to specify the hypotheses that must be examined, they are immediately confronted with the problem of how to design the study and how to measure the variables included in the hypotheses. In the last two chapters we discussed issues of research design. This chapter focuses on measurement, its nature and structure, levels of measurement, and the validity and reliability of measuring instruments. Perhaps the major point to recognize about measurement is that, in the words of Norbert Wiener,

> things do not . . . run around with their measures stamped on them like the capacity of a freight car: it requires a certain amount of investigation to discover what their measures are.[1]

In some cases, this investigation will take the form of a search for a measure within the existing literature; in other cases, the investigator will have to develop a set of measures that will render empirical observations in the form required by the research problem and the research design. Always the researcher has to provide evidence that the measures are valid and reliable.

THE NATURE OF MEASUREMENT

Measurement may be viewed as a procedure in which one assigns numerals, numbers or other symbols, to empirical properties (variables)

---

1. Norbert Wiener, "A New Theory of Measurement: A Study in the Logic of Mathematics," *Proceedings of the London Mathematical Society*, 19 (1920): 181–205. Quoted in *Research Methods: Issues and Insights*, ed. by Billy J. Franklin and Harold W. Osborne (Belmont, Calif.: Wadsworth, 1971), p. 118.

TABLE 6.1.

	Design	Economy	Service
Car A	10	11	10
Car B	13	14	12
Car C	14	14	14
Car D	14	12	13
Car E	10	12	14

according to rules.[2] Let us suppose that someone intends to purchase a new car. Having found that the difference in price among the various compact cars is minute, this individual has decided to make the purchase on the basis of which model best meets the following requirements: design, economical operation, and service. These three features vary. For example, one model may be well designed and economical to operate, but the service supplied by the manufacturer may be unsatisfactory. Accordingly, the buyer has decided to rank each of the three features by five numbers: 10, 11, 12, 13, and 14. Number 10 indicates total dissatisfaction, and number 14 stands for the highest degree of satisfaction. Numbers 11, 12, and 13 indicate increasing degrees of satisfaction with the feature being examined. The buyer examines five models. Table 6.1 summarizes the evaluation of each model according to the three criteria that were set. After examining the scores, the buyer decides to purchase car C because it received the highest score on all three counts, indicating the highest degree of satisfaction.

This is an extremely simplified instance of measurement, but it conveys the idea expressed in the definition. The buyer assigned numerals to objects according to rules. The objects, the numerals, and the rules for assignment were contained in the instructions imposed by the buyer. The numerals, which are the end product of measurement, might be used for comparison, evaluation, and the assessment of relations between the various properties, or variables. For example, the buyer might compute measures of relation between design and economy or between design and service.

Defining Measurement

Further clarification of the three basic concepts used to define measurement—numerals, assignments, and rules—is called for. A numeral is a symbol of the form I, II, III, . . ., or 1, 2, 3, . . . A numeral has no quantitative meaning unless one imputes to it such a meaning. Numerals

---

2. S. S. Stevens, "Mathematics, Measurement and Psychophysics," in *Handbook of Experimental Psychology*, ed. by S. S. Stevens (New York: Wiley, 1951), p. 8.

can be used to label objects such as football players, driving licenses, individuals drawn in a sample from a population, or events. Numerals that are given quantitative meaning become numbers; these enable the use of mathematical and statistical techniques for purposes of description, explanation, and prediction. In other words, numbers are amenable to statistical analyses and mathematical manipulations, which in turn reveal new information about the objects or events being measured.

In the definition of measurement, the term *assignment* means mapping. Numerals or numbers are mapped onto objects or events. To illustrate the mapping idea in measurement, consider Figure 6.1, which shows a number of circles and squares on the left and two numbers on the right; 1 is mapped onto the circles, and 2 onto the squares.

The third concept used to define measurement is that of *rules*. A rule explicates the way in which numerals or numbers are to be assigned to objects or events. A rule might say: "Assign the numerals 10 through 15 to political systems according to how democratic the systems are. If a political system is very democratic, let the number 15 be assigned to it. If a political system is not at all democratic, let the number 10 be assigned to it. To political systems between these limits, assign numbers between the limits." Or suppose that a group is composed of three Democrats and two Republicans and that one uses the following mapping rule: "If an individual is a Democrat, assign him or her 1; if an individual is a Republican, assign her or him 2." The measurement of the variable (party affiliation) is illustrated in Figure 6.2.

Structure of Measurement

Measurement, then, is the assignment of numerals or numbers to objects, events, or variables according to rules. Rules are the most significant component of the measurement procedure because they determine the quality of measurement. Poor rules make measurement meaningless. Measurement is meaningless when it is not tied to reality, and the function of rules is to tie the measurement procedure to reality. Meaningful

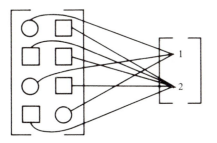

FIGURE 6.1.

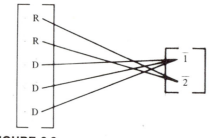

FIGURE 6.2.

measurement is attained only when the measurement procedure has an empirical correspondence with reality. For example, suppose someone is measuring the softness of three objects. If object *A* can scratch *B* and not vice versa, then *B* is softer than *A*. Similarly, if *A* can scratch *B*, and *B* can scratch *C*, then *A* can probably scratch *C*, and one can deduce that object *C* is softer than object *A*. These are observable propositions, and numbers indicating degrees of softness can be assigned to each of those objects after executing a few scratch tests. In this case, the measurement procedure and the number system are isomorphic to reality.

Isomorphism means similarity or identity of structure. In measurement, the crucial question to be asked is whether the numerical system is similar in structure to the structure of objects or events being measured. Are the two similar in some structural aspect? To the physical scientist, the problem of isomorphism is often of secondary concern because the relation between the objects being observed and the numbers assigned to the observations is quite direct. The social scientist, on the other hand, must almost always be alert to the fact that "In order for him to be able to make certain operations with numbers that have been assigned to observations, the structure of his method of mapping numbers to observations must be isomorphic to some numerical structure which includes these operations."[3] If two systems are isomorphic, their structures are the same in the relations and operations they allow for. Thus, if a researcher assigns numbers to objects and then manipulates these numbers by, say, adding them, he or she is implying that the structure of this measurement is isomorphic to the numerical structure known as arithmetic.

Most frequently, social scientists measure *indicators* of properties— not the properties themselves. Variables such as democracy, motivation, hostility, and integration cannot be directly observed; one must infer them from the observation of presumed indicators of the properties. If

3. Sidney Siegel, *Nonparametric Statistics for the Behavioral Sciences* (New York: McGraw-Hill, 1956), p. 22.

elections are held regularly in a political system, one may infer that this is an indicator of the system's democracy. If someone achieves a certain score in a motivation test, one may infer something about this person's level of motivation. In these examples, some identifiable behavior is an indicator of an underlying property. Although the process of measuring directly observable properties is identical to the one for measuring indicators of properties, the rules in the latter are much more difficult to formulate, and the researcher must rely on large inferential leaps. Thus, indicators are specified by operational definitions; after observation of the indicators, numerals or numbers are substituted for the values of the indicators, and statistical and mathematical operations are executed. Obviously, the numerical structure that substitutes indicators must be similar, in its relations and operations, to the structure of indicators; that is, the two must be isomorphic.

LEVELS OF MEASUREMENT

The requirement of isomorphism between numerical systems and empirical properties (or indicators of properties) leads to a distinction among different ways of measuring, that is, to distinct levels of measurement. (The term *scales of measurement* is sometimes used instead of *levels of measurement*. A scale may be thought of as a tool for measuring; a speedometer is a scale, as is a ruler or a thermometer.) The mathematical and statistical operations permissible on a given set of numbers are dependent on the level of measurement attained. Here we will discuss four levels of measurement—nominal, ordinal, interval, and ratio—and the rationale of the operations that are permitted with each level.

Nominal Level

The weakest level of measurement is the nominal level. At this level, numbers or other symbols are used to classify objects or observations. These numbers or symbols constitute a nominal, or classificatory, scale. By means of the symbols 1 and 2, for instance, it is possible to classify a given population into males and females, with 1 representing males and 2 standing for females. The same population can be classified by religion; Christians might be represented by the numeral 6, Jews by 7, and Muslims by 8. In the first case, the population was classified into two categories; in the second, into three. As a rule, when a set of objects can be classified into categories that are exhaustive (that is, they include all objects) and mutually exclusive (that is, with no case in more than one category) and when each category is represented by a different symbol, a nominal level of measurement is attained.

Mathematically, the basic property of the nominal level of measurement is that the properties of objects in one category are equal to each other, but not to anything else in their identical aspect. The logical properties of equivalence are reflexivity, symmetry, and transitivity. Reflexivity means that every object in one of the categories is equal to itself. For example, $a = a$ in the "Christians" category. Symmetry is defined as the relationship when if $a = b$, then $b = a$. Transitivity is the relationship when if $a = b$, and $b = c$, then $a = c$. These three logical properties are operative among objects within the same category, but not necessarily between categories. For instance, these relations will apply to all persons classified as "Christian," but not between "Christians" and "Jews."

At the nominal level, the classification of objects may be equally well represented by any set of symbols. The symbols may also be interchanged without altering any information, if this is done consistently and completely. Accordingly, only statistics that would remain unchanged by such transformation are permissible at the nominal level. These include the mode, measures of qualitative variation, Lambda, and Goodman and Kruskal's tau; these statistics are presented in Chapters 12 and 13.

Ordinal Level

Many properties studied by social scientists are not only classifiable but also exhibit some kind of relation. Typical relations are "higher," "greater," "more desired," "more difficult," and so on. Such relations may be designated by the symbol ($>$), which means "greater than." In reference to particular properties, $>$ may be used to designate "is higher than," "is greater than," "is more desired than," and so on. For instance, it can be hypothesized that France is more democratic than the Soviet Union but less so than England or that Socialist political parties are less dogmatic than Communist parties but more so than religious parties. In general, if (in addition to equivalence) the relation $>$ holds for all pairs of observations engendering a complete rank ordering of objects, an ordinal level of measurement is attained. Consider a property such as "social acceptability." In social acceptability, all members of the upper class are higher than all members of the middle class. All members of the middle class, in turn, are higher than all members of the lower class. The equivalence relation holds among members of the same class, whereas the $>$ relation holds between any pair of classes.

The $>$ relation is irreflexive, asymmetrical, and transitive. Irreflexivity is a logical property wherein it is not true that for any a, $a > a$. Asymmetry means that if $a > b$, then $b \not> a$. Transitivity means that if $a > b$, and $b > c$, then $a > c$. In other words, if a variable such as "conservatism" is measured on the ordinal level, one can infer that if person

a is more conservative than person b, and if b is more conservative than c, then a is more conservative than c; and that the $>$ relation is maintained with regard to all the individuals in the group.

To exemplify measurement at the ordinal level, consider the following common practice of measuring attitudes. Attitudes are measured by means of a series of questions (a test), with the alternative answers being ranked in ascending or descending order. For instance, one of the questions used to measure political alienation is "People like me have a lot of influence on government decisions." The respondent is asked to mark the number representing his or her degree of agreement or disagreement with this statement. The correspondence between the numbers and the answers might be made as in Table 6.2. Other questions on the same attitude are presented to the respondent, who can then be ranked according to his or her responses to all the questions. Suppose a researcher employs ten statements in all, each including four alternative answers, with (1) standing for "definitely agree," (2) for "agree," (3) for "disagree," and (4) for "definitely disagree." The highest score that can be achieved in this test is 40 (that is, a score of 4 on each of the ten questions), and the lowest is 10. To simplify matters, it is assumed that the respondents answered all questions. A respondent whose score is 40 will be regarded as the most alienated and will be ranked first. Another, whose score is nearest to 40—say, 36—will be ranked second, and so on for each individual in the group. The ranking process ends when all the respondents are ranked by their scores on the political alienation questionnaire. Table 6.3 displays hypothetical scores and rankings of seven respondents. An examination of the table reveals that respondent S_6 is the most alienated, whereas respondent S_1 is the least alienated.

The ordinal level of measurement is unique up to a monotonic transformation; that is, any order-preserving transformation does not change the information obtained. It does not matter what numbers one assigns to a pair of objects or to a category of objects so long as one is consistent. It is a matter of convenience whether to use lower numbers for the "more preferred" states, although we do usually refer to excellent performance as "first class" and to progressively inferior performances as "second class" and "third class."

The numbers assigned to ranked objects are called *rank values*. Rank

TABLE 6.2.

Definitely Agree	Agree	Disagree	Definitely Disagree
(1)	(2)	(3)	(4)

TABLE 6.3. Ranking Individuals by Their Scores on a Test of Political Alienation

Respondent	Score	Rank
S_1	10	seventh
S_2	27	third
S_3	36	second
S_4	25	fourth
S_5	20	fifth
S_6	40	first
S_7	12	sixth

values are assigned to objects according to the following rule; the greatest (or the smallest) object is assigned 1; the next in size, 2; the third in size, 3; and so on to the smallest (or greatest) object, which is assigned the last number in a given series. In the last example, S_6 is assigned 1, S_3 is assigned 2, S_2 is assigned 3, S_4 is assigned 4, S_5 is assigned 5, S_7 is assigned 6, and S_1 is assigned 7. It is important to stress that ordinal numbers indicate rank order and nothing more. The numbers do not indicate that the intervals between them are equal, nor do they indicate absolute quantities. It cannot be assumed that because the numbers are equally spaced, the properties they represent are also equally spaced. If two respondents have the ranks 7 and 5, and two others are ranked 4 and 2, one cannot infer that the differences between the two pairs are equal.

Transformations that do not change the order of properties are permissible at the ordinal level. Accordingly, mathematical operations and statistics that do not alter the order of properties are also permissible. For example, a statistic that describes the central tendency of ordinal numbers is the median. The median is not affected by changes in any numbers that are above or below it so long as the number of ranked observations above and below remains the same. Other statistics appropriate for the ordinal level discussed in Chapters 12 and 13 are the range, Gamma, and tau-b and tau-c.

Interval Level

If, in addition to being able to rank order a set of observations in terms of the > relation, one also knows the exact distance between each of the observations, and this distance is constant, then an interval level of measurement has been achieved. In addition to saying that one object is greater than another, one can also specify by how many units the former is greater than the latter. For example, with interval measurement it is possible to say not only that Mike is taller than Bob but also that Mike is, say, four inches taller. To make these quantitative comparisons, one must have a unit of measurement; if a unit of measurement has been established, an interval level of measurement has been achieved. Variables measured at the interval level include height, temperature, time, income, and intelligence quotient. An interval level of measurement, then, is characterized by a common and constant unit of measurement that assigns a real number to all pairs of objects in the ordered set. In this kind of measurement, the ratio of any two intervals (distances) is independent of the unit of measurement.

The structure of the interval level of measurement is such that the differences between observations are isomorphic to the structure of arithmetic. Numbers may be assigned to the positions of the objects so that the operations of arithmetic may be meaningfully executed on the differences between these numbers. The following formal properties are operative at the interval level of measurements:

1. Uniqueness: if a and b stand for real numbers, then $a + b$ and $a \times b$ represent one and only one real number.
2. Symmetry: if $a = b$, then $b = a$.
3. Commutation: if a and b denote real numbers, then $a + b = b + a$, and $ab = ba$.
4. Substitution: if $a = b$ and $a + c = d$, then $b + c = d$; and if $a = b$ and $ac = d$, then $bc = d$.
5. Association: if a, b, and c stand for real numbers, then $(a + b) + c = a + (b + c)$, and $(abc)c = a(bc)$.

Any change in the numbers assigned to the observations must preserve not only their ordering but also their relative differences. In more formal language, the interval level of measurement is unique up to a linear transformation. Thus, the information obtained at this level is not affected if each number is multiplied by a positive constant and then a constant is added to this product. All the common statistics are applicable to interval data.

Ratio Level

Properties that have natural zero points can be measured on the ratio level of measurement. Properties such as weight, time, length, and area have natural zero points and are measured at the ratio level. At this level, the ratio of any two numbers is independent of the unit of measurement. The interval and the ratio levels are similar, and the rules by which numbers are assigned are the same, with one exception. For a ratio level of measurement, we apply the operations and the numbers to the total amount measured from an absolute zero point; for an interval level, we apply the operation to differences from one arbitrary point. A ratio level of measurement, most commonly encountered in the physical sciences, is achieved only when all four of these relations are operationally possible to attain: (1) equivalence, (2) greater than, (3) known distance of any two intervals, and (4) a true zero point.

DATA TRANSFORMATION

Variables that can be measured at a ratio level can also be measured at the interval, ordinal, and nominal levels. As a rule, properties that can be measured at a higher level can also be measured at lower levels, but not vice versa. A variable such as party affiliation can be measured only at a nominal level. The formal properties characterizing each level of measurement are summarized in Table 6.4. For example, whereas the equivalence property exists at each of the four levels, only the ratio level is characterized by a natural zero.

Earlier, we pointed out the kinds of numerical operations and statistics that are, in a strict sense, legitimate and permissible with each level. Some authors tend to deemphasize this question.[4] The problem, however, is significant enough to warrant a few additional comments.

Mathematics and statistics are contentless languages. They deal with numbers and are not concerned with whether the numbers represent the essence of the matter being investigated. Their foremost advantage is in being precise and in enabling researchers to reveal information about phenomena that cannot otherwise be revealed. A question such as "To what extent are a series of variables related?" can be meaningfully and precisely answered by computing measures of relations. Given the numbers, any kind of statistical operation can be performed. Social scientists are concerned with empirical properties, and numbers are used chiefly to gain a better understanding of the relations between these properties. Employing numerical systems and statistics that are not isomorphic to the structure of empirical properties is of little use in advancing our knowledge.

VALIDITY

The problem of validity arises because measurement in the social sciences is, with very few exceptions, indirect. Under such circumstances, researchers are never completely certain that they are measuring the precise property they intend to measure. *Validity* is concerned with the question "Is one measuring what one thinks one is measuring?" For example, does electoral turnout measure political development? Is

4. Paul A. Games, *Elementary Statistics* (New York: McGraw-Hill, 1967).

**TABLE 6.4. Levels of Measurement and Their Characteristic
Properties**

Level	Equivalence	Greater Than	Fixed Interval	Natural Zero
Nominal	Y	N	N	N
Ordinal	Y	Y	N	N
Interval	Y	Y	Y	N
Ratio	Y	Y	Y	Y

agreement with the statement "This world is run by a few people in power, and there is not much the little guy can do about it" an indicator of the variable "alienation"? Clearly, it is always necessary to gather some sort of evidence that provides confidence that a measuring device does, in fact, measure what it appears to measure.

Three basic kinds of validity can be distinguished, each of which is concerned with a different aspect of the measurement situation: content validity, empirical validity, and construct validity. Each of these three types includes several kinds of evidence and has special value under certain conditions.

Content Validity

There are two common varieties of content validity: face validity and sampling validity. *Face validity* rests on the investigators' subjective evaluation as to the validity of a measuring instrument. In practice, face validity does not relate to the question of whether an instrument measures that which the researcher wishes to measure; rather, it concerns the extent to which it measures that which it appears to measure according to the researcher's subjective assessment. For example, an investigator intends to measure the variable "liberalism" by a questionnaire consisting of ten statements. After making up the questionnaire, the researcher reviews each statement to assess its content as to the extent to which it is related to "liberalism." To ascertain this assessment, the researcher might consult a number of specialists (judges). If there is agreement among the judges, the researcher will presumably contend that the questionnaire does not lack face validity and that, consequently, it measures "liberalism." Disagreement among the judges would impair the face validity of a measuring instrument.

The main problem with face validity is that there are no replicable rules for evaluating the measuring instrument, and one has to rely entirely on subjective judgments. Nevertheless, face validity serves a significant function in the process of constructing and formulating measuring instruments. A researcher who constructs an instrument must rely, first and foremost, on his or her own skill and judgment; at later stages, he or she can validate the instrument by performing other validity tests.

The primary concern of *sampling validity* is whether a given population of situations or behavior is adequately sampled by the measuring instrument in question; that is, does the content of the instrument adequately represent the content population of the property being measured? The underlying assumption of sampling validity is that every variable has a content population consisting of an infinite number of items (statements, questions, or indicators) and that a highly valid instrument constitutes a representative sample of these items. In practice, problems arise with the definition of a content population, for this is a theoretical and not an empirical population. (These problems are discussed in Chapter 16, in which sampling techniques are presented.) These problems impair the effectiveness of sampling validity as a test of an instrument's validity. However, sampling validity has an important advantage: it requires the researcher to become acquainted with all the items that are known to belong to the content population. Sampling validity is especially common in innovative research, where investigators attempt to construct instruments and employ them for the first time. After the instrument has been used, its validity can be evaluated by other tests.

Empirical Validity

The concern of empirical validity is with the relations between the measuring instrument and the measurement results. It is assumed that if a certain instrument is valid, then there should exist certain empirical relations between the results produced by the instrument and other properties or variables. Evidence to support the existence of a relation is obtained by measures of correlation appropriate to the level of measurement. (A correlation coefficient is an index of the degree of relation between two measures; see Chapter 13.) Of the various tests designed to evaluate empirical validity, predictive validity is the most widely used. For this reason, it is discussed at some length as follows.

Predictive validity is characterized by prediction to an external measure referred to as a criterion and by checking a measuring instrument against some outcome. In other words, predictive validity is the correlation between the results of a given measurement and an external criterion. For example, one can validate an intelligence test by first obtaining a set of test scores on a group such as college students and by then obtaining the grade-point averages that these students made during their first year of college. A correlation coefficient is then computed between the two sets of measurements. The obtained correlation is usually called the *validity coefficient*. Other criteria that might be used

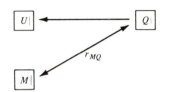

FIGURE 6.3.

to validate intelligence tests are ratings of adjustment, ratings of performance, and units produced in a certain period of time.

The process by which the predictive validity of an instrument is evaluated is illustrated in Figure 6.3. A property (U) is measured by a certain measuring instrument (M), and the researcher desires to evaluate the predictive validity of the instrument. To assess its predictive validity, a criterion (Q) whose validity is undisputed is used. The measurements obtained by M are correlated with the measurements obtained by Q. The size of the validity coefficient (r_{MQ}) measures the predictive validity of the instrument.

Two general points are to be noted when using the predictive-validity test. One relates to the validity of the criterion, and the other concerns the considerations that induce an investigator to use a measuring instrument and not the criterion itself; for example, why not measure grade-point averages directly? In regard to the second point, in some cases the criterion is technically difficult or too expensive to use, and in other cases investigators have to measure a property before they can make use of the criterion. For example, the scholastic ability of a student has to be evaluated prior to his or her admission to a university.

With regard to the validity of the criterion, two common methods are used. One method rests on agreement among researchers that a certain criterion is valid to evaluate a measuring instrument. The agreement is subject to tests of face validity and sampling validity. A somewhat different method is to express the relationship between the instrument and the criterion in terms of the percentage of individuals (or other units of analysis) who would be correctly classified by the instrument according to their known group membership.[5]

Suppose one desires to evaluate the validity of a measuring instrument designed to measure political conservatism. If one has theoretically sound reasons for arguing that people in the lower class are more conservative than people in the middle class, the two groups can be compared as a check of predictive validity. In this case, social class serves as an indirect criterion to the predictive validity of the instrument. If it

5. C. G. Helmstadter, *Research Concepts in Human Behavior* (New York: Appleton-Century-Crofts, 1970).

is empirically observed that persons in the lower-class group are as conservative as persons in the middle-class group, the instrument lacks predictive validity. On the other hand, a relatively high correlation between social class and conservatism will validate the instrument. However, one should be aware that a high correlation is a necessary but not a sufficient condition to the predictive validity of an instrument, because the indirect criterion (social class) may also be related to properties other than political conservatism. Thus, the instrument might measure other properties instead of political conservatism. An indirect criterion, then, is more useful for disvalidating rather than validating a measuring instrument.

Construct Validity

Construct validity involves relating a measuring instrument to an overall theoretical framework in order to determine whether the instrument is tied to the concepts and theoretical assumptions that are employed. Cronbach, an early proponent of construct validity, has observed that "whenever a tester asks what a score means psychologically or what causes a person to get a certain test score, he is asking what concepts may properly be used to interpret the test performance."[6] The theoretical notions one has about the property being measured lead the investigator to postulate various kinds and degrees of relationships between the property and other specified variables. In order to demonstrate construct validity of a measuring instrument, an investigator has to show that these relationships do in fact hold. We shall illustrate the utility of construct validity through Milton Rokeach's research on dogmatism.[7]

On the basis of theoretical reasoning, Rokeach constructed a dogmatism questionnaire. This instrument consists of statements believed to tap close-mindedness, a way of thinking associated with any belief system or ideology regardless of content. Rokeach argued that the ideological orientations of individuals are related to their personalities, thought processes, and behavior. One example among many that can be given is his prediction that dogmatism is related to opinionation. Rokeach undertook an extensive series of investigations aimed at testing his theory and the construct validity of his measuring instruments. In one instance he used what has been called the *known-groups technique*. In this method, groups of people with known characteristics are administered an instrument, and the direction of differences is predicted. Rokeach had college professors and graduate students select friends who, in their opinion, they considered to be open-minded and close-minded.

6. Lee J. Cronbach, *Essentials of Psychological Testing* (New York: Harper & Row, 1960), p. 104.

7. Milton Rokeach, *The Open and the Closed Mind* (New York: Basic Books, 1960).

The dogmatism instrument clearly differentiated the two groups. Although the findings are not clear-cut, they furnish evidence of the construct validity of the dogmatism measure.

Cronbach and Meehl describe the logical process of construct validation in the following way: first, a proposition that an instrument measures a certain property—say, property A—is set forth; second, the proposition is inserted into the present theory of property A; third, working through the theory, one predicts other properties that should be related to the instrument and properties that should exhibit no relation to the instrument; finally, one collects data that empirically confirm or reject the predicted relations. If the anticipated relationships are found, the instrument is considered valid. On the other hand, if the predictions do not hold up, there are three possibilities: (1) the instrument does not measure property A; (2) the theoretical framework that generated the predictions is flawed; or (3) the research design failed to test the predictions properly. The researcher must then make a decision as to which of these three conditions has occurred. Such a decision is based on a careful reconstruction of each of the four steps constituting the validation process.[8]

Campbell and Fiske suggested another method of construct validation involving correlation matrices.[9] This is the *convergent-discriminant* conception of validity, or the *multitrait-multimethod matrix* technique. This method stems from the notion that different methods of measuring the same property should yield similar results, whereas different properties should yield different measurement results regardless of the measuring instrument. Operationally, this means that correlation coefficients among scores for a given property measured by different instruments should be higher than correlations among different properties measured by similar instruments. Evidence of the construct validity of an instrument must, therefore, make use of both a convergent principle—that is, two measures of the same property should correlate highly with one another even though they represent different methods— and a discriminant principle, which implies that two measures should not correlate highly with one another if they measure different properties even though a similar instrument is used. Thus, the validation process requires the computation of intercorrelations among measuring instruments that represent at least two properties, each measured by at least two different instruments.

In view of the distinction between the three types of validity, the

8. Lee J. Cronbach and Paul Meehl, "Construct Validity in Psychological Tests," *Psychological Bulletin*, 52 (1955): 281–302.

9. Donald T. Campbell and Donald W. Fiske, "Convergent and Discriminant Validation by the Multitrait-Multimethod Matrix," *Psychological Bulletin*, 56 (1959): 81–105.

reader is probably concerned as to which validity test to use when evaluating the validity of a given measuring instrument. Although there is no simple solution to this problem, its significance has led a team of experts from different disciplines to recommend that thorough examination of a measuring instrument must include information about the three types of validity.[10] Thus, in the first phase of the construction of a measuring tool, one might evaluate theories that would serve as a foundation for the instrument; next, a content population of items from which a representative sample is to be drawn might be defined; and, finally, the validity of the instrument might be assessed by correlating it with an external criterion.

RELIABILITY

The subject of reliability would not occupy a central place in the methodological literature if the measuring instruments used by social scientists were fully valid. But in many instances, validity evidence is almost entirely lacking; one has to evaluate the measuring instrument with respect to other characteristics and assume its validity. A frequently used method for evaluating an instrument is its degree of reliability.

Reliability is an indication of the extent to which a measure contains *variable errors*, that is, errors that differed from observation to observation during any one measuring instance and that varied from time to time for a given unit of analysis measured twice or more by the same instrument. For example, if one measures the length of a given object in two points of time with the same instrument—say, a ruler—and gets slightly different results, the instrument contains variable errors. Because of the indirect nature of measurements in the social sciences, the errors that occur when social variables are measured are likely to be much greater than those which occur when physical variables are measured. Factors such as momentary absent-mindedness, ambiguous instructions, and technical difficulties (a pencil breaks while the respondent is filling in a questionnaire) may cause the introduction of variable errors. These errors are called variable errors because the amount of error varies from one observation to the next and also because the amount of error is different for a given observation each time it is measured.[11]

Each measurement, then, consists of two components: a *true component* and an *error component*. Reliability is defined as the ratio of the true-score variance in the scores as measured. (The variance is a measure

10. See American Psychological Association Committee on Psychological Tests, "Technical Recommendations for Psychological Tests and Diagnostic Techniques," *Psychological Bulletin Supplement*, 51 (1954), part 2, 1–38.

11. C. G. Helmstadter, *Research Concepts in Human Behavior*, p. 169.

of the spread of observations [scores]; it is a description of the extent to which the observations differ from each other; that is

$$\sigma^2 = \frac{\sum\limits_{i=1}^{N} (x_i - \bar{x})^2}{N}$$

See Chapter 12 for a detailed presentation.) Algebraically, each person's observed score can be represented as

$$x_i = t_i + e_i \tag{6.1}$$

where x_i = score actually obtained by person i

t_i = true score for person i

e_i = amount of error that occurred for person i at the time the measurement was made.

Expressed in variance terms, we get

$$\sigma_x^2 = \sigma_t^2 + \sigma_e^2$$

where σ_x^2 = variance of observed scores

σ_t^2 = variance of true scores

σ_e^2 = variance of errors

Reliability, defined as the ratio of true-score variance to observed-score variance, can be expressed as

$$\text{Reliability} = \frac{\sigma_t^2}{\sigma_x^2} = \frac{\sigma_x^2 - \sigma_e^2}{\sigma_x^2} \tag{6.2}$$

From Equation (6.2) it can be seen that if the measurement involves nothing but error, then $\sigma_x^2 = \sigma_e^2$ and the reliability is zero. On the other hand, when there is no variable error at all, $\sigma_e^2 = 0$, and the ratio defined as reliability becomes

$$\frac{\sigma_x^2}{\sigma_x^2} = 1$$

The reliability measure varies on a scale from zero to one, having the former value when the measurement involves nothing but error and reaching one when there is no variable error at all in the measurement.

In practice, it is impossible to compute directly the true score independently of the amount of error that occurs in any particular measurement. Consequently, the ratio σ_t^2/σ_x^2 has to be estimated. There are three major ways of estimating reliability: the test-retest method, the parallel-forms technique, and the split-half method.

Test-Retest Method

The test-retest method corresponds most closely to the conceptual definition of reliability. A measuring instrument is administered to the same group of persons at two different times, and the correlation between the two sets of observations (scores) is computed. The obtained coefficient is the *reliability estimate*. With this method, error is defined as anything that leads a person to get a different score on one measurement from what he or she obtained on another measurement. Symbolically,

$$r_{xx'} = \frac{S_t^2}{S_x^2} \tag{6.3}$$

where x = performance on the first measurement

x' = performance on the second measurement

$r_{xx'}$ = correlation coefficient between x and x'

S_t^2 = estimated variance of the true scores

S_x^2 = calculated variance of the observed scores

The correlation $r_{xx'}$ provides an estimate of reliability defined as a ratio of the true variance to the observed variance. (For methods of computing the correlation coefficient, see Chapter 13.)

The test-retest method has two main limitations. First, the fact that an individual has been tested on one occasion may influence the measurement on subsequent tests. If the instrument is a questionnaire, the individual may remember specific questions and simply respond the same way as on the first administration, thus yielding a high but overestimated reliability estimate. Second, human properties are continually in a state of flux. It is possible that changes may have occurred in the measured property during the measurement interval, thus lowering the estimate of reliability. The test-retest method, then, may either overestimate or underestimate the true reliability of the instrument, and in many cases it is difficult to determine which has occurred.

Parallel-Forms Technique

One way of overcoming the two limitations inherent in the test-retest method is through the use of the parallel-forms technique. This technique requires two forms of a measuring instrument that may be considered parallel. The two forms are then administered to a group of persons, and the two sets of measures (scores) are correlated to obtain an estimate of reliability. With this technique, there is the problem of determining whether the two forms of an instrument are in fact parallel. Although statistical tests have been developed to determine whether the forms are parallel in terms of statistical measures, the checking with respect to the content of the forms must be made on a judgmental basis.[12]

Split-Half Method

The split-half method estimates reliability by treating each of two or more parts of a measuring instrument as a separate scale. Suppose the measuring instrument is a questionnaire. The questionnaire is separated into two sets, using the odd-numbered questions for one set and the even-numbered questions for the other. Each of the two sets of questions is treated separately and scored accordingly. The two sets are then correlated, and this is taken as an estimate of reliability. To correct the correlation coefficient obtained between the two halves, the following formula, known as the Spearman-Brown prophecy formula, may be applied:

$$r_{xx'} = \frac{2r_{oe}}{1 + r_{oe}} \qquad (6.4)$$

where $r_{xx'}$ = the reliability of the original test

r_{oe} = the reliability coefficient obtained by correlating the scores of the odd statements with the scores of the even statements

This correction assumes that an instrument that is $2n$ questions long will be more reliable than an instrument that is n questions long and that because the length of the instrument has been halved by dividing it into odds and evens, the full instrument will have a higher reliability than would either half.

Cronbach, Rajaratnam, and Glesser introduced a revision to the traditional concept of reliability.[13] These authors maintain that the chief concern of reliability theory is to answer the question "To what universe of potential measurements do we wish to generalize?" Thus, instead of reliability, the notion of generalizability is invoked. Generalizability implies that what one really wants to know about a set of measurements is this: To what extent and with respect to what properties are they like other sets of measurements one might have taken from a given universe of potential measurements? And to what extent and with respect to what properties do they differ from other measurements one might have drawn from that universe of potential measurements? If one asks the likeness and difference questions with respect to a universe of potential meas-

12. Harold Gulliksen, *Theory of Mental Tests* (New York: Wiley, 1950).

13. Lee J. Cronbach, Nageswars Rajaratnam, and Goldine C. Glesser, "A Theory of Generalizability: A Liberalization of Reliability Theory," *British Journal of Statistical Psychology*, 16 (1963): 137–163.

urements, one is asking about the limits of generalizability of the results of one's set of measurements. Whether we consider a particular relation among measurements to be evidence of reliability or generalizability depends on how we choose to define likeness and difference of conditions and measures. The construction of what is same and what is different in sets of measurements depends, in turn, upon the research problem.[14]

SUMMARY

Measurement is the assignment of numerals or numbers to variables, objects, or events according to rules. The most significant concept in this definition is "rules." The function of a rule is to tie the measurement procedure to reality; to establish isomorphism between a certain numerical structure and the structure of the variables being measured. Upon the establishment of isomorphism, mathematical and statistical operations with the numbers that stand for the properties can be executed. The requirement of isomorphism between numerical systems and empirical properties leads to a distinction among four levels of measurement: nominal, ordinal, interval, and ratio. In general, the mathematical operations permissible on a given set of numbers are dependent on the level of measurement obtained.

The notions of validity and reliability are inseparable from measurement theory. Validity is concerned with the question of whether one is measuring what one thinks one is measuring. Traditionally, three basic types of validity have been distinguished, each of which relates to a different aspect of the measurement situation: content validity, empirical validity, and construct validity. To validate a certain measuring instrument, one must look for information about these three types. Reliability is an indication of the extent to which a measure contains variable errors. Operationally, it is assumed that any measure consists of a true component and an error component and that the proportion of the amount of variation in the true component to the total variation measures reliability. This measure can be estimated by one or more of the following methods: test-retest, parallel-forms, and split-half. More recently, the notion of generalizability has been introduced. Generalizability implies that the main concern of reliability is with the extent to which a set of

14. For the statistical expression of the generalizability index, see Lee J. Cronbach, Nageswars Rajaratnam, and Goldine C. Glesser, "A Theory of Generalizability:" A Liberalization of Reliability Theory"; and Goldine C. Glesser, Lee J. Cronbach, and Nageswars Rajaratnam "Generalizability of Scores Influenced by Multiple Scores of Variance," *Psychometrika*, 30 (1965): 395–418.

measurements is like other sets of measurements that might have been drawn from a given universe of potential measurements.

KEY TERMS FOR REVIEW

Measurement	Construct validity
Isomorphism	Known-groups
Indicator	Reliability
Nominal level	The reliability
Ordinal level	measure
Interval level	Test-retest
Face validity	Split-half method
Sampling validity	Generalizability in
Predictive validity	reliability

ADDITIONAL READINGS

Blalock, Hubert M. "The Measurement Problem: A Gap Between the Languages of Theory and Research." In *Methodology in Social Research*, ed. by Hubert M. Blalock and Ann B. Blalock. New York: McGraw-Hill, 1968. Chapter 1.

Jones, Bryan, and Richard Shorter. "The Ratio Measurement of Social Status: Some Cross-Cultural Comparisons." *Social Forces*, 50 (June 1972): 499–511.

Coombs, Clyde H. *A Theory of Data*. New York: Wiley, 1964.

Land, Kenneth C., and Seymour Spillerman, eds. *Social Indicator Models*. New York: Russell Sage, 1975.

Lazarsfeld, Paul F. "Concept Formation and Measurement in the Behavioral Science; Some Historical Observations." In *Concepts, Theory and Explanation in the Behavioral Sciences*, ed. by Gordon J. DiRenzo. New York: Random House, 1966.

Przeworski, Adam, and Henry Teune. *The Logic of Comparative Social Inquiry*. New York: Wiley-Interscience, 1970. Chapter 5.

Whitla, Dean K., ed. *Handbook of Measurement and Assessment in Behavioral Sciences*. Reading, Mass.: Addison-Wesley, 1968.

Wilson, Thomas. "A Critique of Ordinal Variables." In *Causal Models in the Social Sciences*, ed. by Hubert M. Blalock. Chicago: Aldine, 1971. Chapter 24.

PART 2
Data Collection

CHAPTER PREVIEW

CHAPTER 7
Observational Methods

INTRODUCTION

Having decided on the *what* and the *how* of an investigation, we proceed to the data-collection stage. Social science data are obtained when investigators record observations about the phenomena being studied or have the observations recorded for them. In either case, three general forms of data collection may be distinguished: observational methods, survey research, and nonreactive techniques. Each of these three general forms consists of a number of particular methods, the most common of which are discussed in the following chapters. In the present chapter we focus on methods of data collection that rely primarily on observation.

In the first section we discuss the roles of observation in social science research. Next, strategies of observations are presented, and controlled observation in the laboratory and the field are covered and exemplified. The last section describes the participant observation method and the roles the researcher may take during the observation period.

ROLES OF OBSERVATION

Modern social science is rooted in observation. Political scientists observe, among other things, the behavior of occupants of political roles; anthropologists observe simple societies and small communities; social psychologists observe interactions in small groups. In a sense, as the Webbs pointed out, all social research begins and ends with observation:

> An indispensable part of the study of any social institution, wherever this can be obtained, is deliberate and sustained personal observation ... from which the investigator may learn a lot. He clarifies

155

his ideas, which gain in precision and discrimination. He revises his provisional classifications, and tests his tentative hypotheses. What is even more important, the student silently watching a town council or a trade union committee at work, or looking at the conference of politicians and educationists, picks up hints that help him to new hypotheses, to be, in their turn, tried on other manifestations of his subject matter.[1]

The main virtue of observation is its *directness*; it makes it possible to study behavior as it occurs. The researcher does not have to ask people about their own behavior and the actions of others; he or she can simply watch them do and say things. This, in turn, enables the generation of firsthand data that are uncontaminated by factors standing between the investigator and the object of research. For example, when people are asked to report their past behavior, distortions in recall may significantly contaminate the data, but the extent to which an individual is capable of memorizing things has little effect on data collected through observational methods.

Moreover, data collected by observation may describe the observed phenomena as they occur in their *natural settings*. All too many research techniques introduce elements of artificiality into the researched environment. An interview, for instance, is a form of face-to-face interaction, subject to peculiar problems because of the lack of consensus surrounding the roles of researcher and respondent. In such an interaction, the respondents might behave in a way that is not characteristic of their typical behavior (see Chapter 8). Artificiality can be minimized in observational studies, especially when the observed are not aware of their being observed or when they become accustomed to the observer and do not perceive of him or her as an intruder.

Some studies focus on individuals who are unable to give verbal reports or to articulate themselves meaningfully. Elizabeth Gellert has suggested that it is necessary to use observation in studies of children because it is difficult for children to introspect and to remain attentive to lengthy adult tasks.[2] David Riesman and Jeanne Watson used observational methods because the people studied "had no language for discussing sociable encounters, no vocabulary for describing parties except to say that they were 'good' or 'bad,' no way of answering the question 'What do you do for fun?'"[3]

1. Sidney Webb and Beatrice Webb, *Methods of Social Study* (London: Longmans, 1932), p. 158.

2. Elizabeth Gellert, "Systematic Observation: A Method in Child Study," *Harvard Educational Review*, 25 (1955): 179–195.

3. David Riesman and Jeanne Watson, "The Sociability Project: A Chronicle of Frustration and Achievement, in *Sociologists at Work*, ed. by Phillip E. Hammond (New York: Basic Books, 1964), p. 313.

Observational methods might also be used when persons are unwilling to express themselves verbally. Observation demands less active cooperation on the part of the individuals being studied than do verbal reports. Furthermore, verbal reports can be validated and compared with actual behavior through observation. Matilda Riley suggests that even though dispositions to act politically and socially may be best assessed by questionnaire, observational methods are required to assess the "acting out" of these dispositions.[4] Finally, the relationship between a person and his or her environment is often best maintained in observational studies. Opportunities for analyzing the *contextual background* of behavior are improved by the researcher's ability to observe the environment in operation with the observed.

Observation takes many forms. It includes the most casual experiences as well as the most sophisticated laboratory devices, for example, one-way-vision screens, video cameras, and audio-introspectometers. The many forms of observation make it a suitable method for a variety of research purposes. It might be used in exploratory research to gain insights that will subsequently be tested as hypotheses. Observational methods might also be used to collect supplementary data that may interpret or qualify findings obtained by other methods, or they might be used as the primary methods of data collection in descriptive studies.

Observation may take place in natural settings or in the laboratory. A problem such as coalition formation may be studied as it occurs in a real-life situation or in the laboratory room. Observational procedures may range from complete flexibility, guided only by a general problem, to the use of specialized instruments prepared in advance. The researchers may themselves participate in the activities of the group they are observing; they may be viewed as members of the group but minimize their participation; they may be defined as observers who are not part of the group; or their presence might be concealed from the people being observed. Whatever the purpose of the study and the observational procedure used, three major considerations are to be dealt with if the obtained data are to be scientifically meaningful: What to observe; when to observe and how to record; how much inference is required.

TYPES OF BEHAVIOR

The first and most significant consideration concerns a decision with respect to what should be observed. Suppose someone interested in studying the relation between frustration and aggression hypothesizes that frustration causes aggression. To test this hypothesis, frustration and aggression are to be observed. This requires clear and precise opera-

---

4. Matilda W. Riley, *Sociological Research I: A Case Approach* (New York: Harcourt, Brace, 1963).

tional definitions of the two variables. Observable indicators of the variables "frustration" and "aggression," and of other variables in general, might be nonverbal, spatial, extralinguistic, or linguistic.[5]

Nonverbal Behavior

Nonverbal behavior is "the body movements of the organism . . . [and] consists of motor expressions . . . [which] may originate in various parts of the body."[6] Nonverbal behavior has been extensively studied, and it has been repeatedly shown to be a valid indicator of social and psychological processes.[7] Paul Ekman suggests that observations of nonverbal behavior generate data that can serve "to repeat, contradict, or substitute for a verbal message, as well as accent certain words, maintain the communicative flow, reflect changes in the relationship in association with particular verbal messages and indicate a person's feeling about his verbal statement." [8]

Spatial Behavior

Spatial behavior refers to the attempts of individuals to structure the space around them. For example, people move toward, move away from, maintain closeness, and maintain distance. The range, frequency, and outcomes of such movements provide significant data as is illustrated by Chadwick Alger's study on the spatial behavior of the 110 delegates on the Administrative and Budgetary Committee of the United Nations General Assembly.[9] Alger observed 69 of the 70 meetings of this committee during the fall of 1962 and recorded 3,475 private interactions (participants in private conversations, length of private conversations, the name of the initiator of the private conversation, and so on). The author observed that records of private interaction give a different view

5. Karl F. Weick, "Systematic Observational Methods," in *The Handbook of Social Psychology*, ed. by Gardner Lindzey and Elliot Aronson (Reading, Mass.: Addison-Wesley, 1968).

6. Paul Ekman, "A Methodological Discussion of Nonverbal Behavior," *Journal of Psychology*, 43 (1957): 141–149.

7. See, for example, Albert E. Scheflen, "Natural History Method in Psychotherapy: Communicational Research," in *Methods of Research in Psychotherapy*, ed. by Louis A. Gottschalk and Arthur H. Auerbach (New York: Appleton-Century-Crofts, 1966), p. 263–289.

8. Paul Ekman, "Communication through Nonverbal Behavior: A Source of Information about Interpersonal Relationship," in *Affect, Cognition, and Personality*, ed. by Silvan S. Tomkins and Carroll E. Izard (New York: Springer, 1965), p. 441.

9. Chadwick F. Alger, "Interaction in a Committee of the United Nations General Assembly," *Midwest Journal of Political Science*, 10 (1966): 411–447.

of the committee activities than do records of participation in public debate (for example, attendance in meetings and resolution sponsorship). Furthermore, it was found that there was a higher correlation between number of interactions and number of persons in delegation, amount of United Nations support, and the wealth of a nation than there was between number of public speeches and these same measures.

Extralinguistic Behavior

Words, or linguistic content, constitute only a small portion of verbal behavior. Noncontent behaviors such as rate of speaking, loudness, tendency to interrupt, and pronunciation pecularities constitute a fruitful source of data and are generally referred to as extralinguistic behavior. The significance of extralinguistic behavior to the study of human behavior has already been documented in numerous studies. For example, a vocal characteristic such as pitch accurately measures emotional states.[10] The average unit length of spontaneous speech increases as the size of the group increases.[11] These are but two applications of extralinguistic indicators to the study of behavior; they demonstrate the potential significance of noncontent behavior to observational studies.

Linguistic Behavior

The fourth class of variables is termed linguistic behavior, that is, the manifest content of talking and the structural characteristics of talk. Indexes of linguistic behavior have been widely used in studies on social interaction. Robert Bales, for example, devised a system for organizing and coding the process of interaction in groups involved in problem-solving activities. Bales's system, known as "Interaction Process Analysis," or IPA, contains twelve kinds of distinctive behaviors within which the interaction of group members can be coded and analyzed.[12] The IPA code of categories is shown in Table 7.1.

TIMING AND RECORDING

The second major consideration in observational studies concerns the timing and the recording of observations. Obviously, it is impossible to

10. William F. Soskin and Paul E. Kauffman, "Judgment of Emotion in Word-Free Voice-Samples," *Journal of Communication*, 11 (1961): 73–80.

11. William F. Soskin and John P. Vera, "The Study of Spontaneous Talk," in *The Stream of Human Behavior*, ed. by Roger C. Baker (New York: Appleton-Century-Crofts, 1963).

12. Robert F. Bales, "A Set of Categories for the Analysis of Small Group Interaction," *American Sociological Review*, 15 (April 1950): 257–263.

TABLE 7.1. IPA Code of Categories

Social-emotional Area: *Positive*		A	1. Shows solidarity (raises others' status, gives help, reward) 2. Shows tension release (jokes, laughs, shows satisfaction) 3. Agrees (shows passive acceptance, understands, complies)
Task Area: *Neutral*	Answers	B	4. Gives suggestions (direction, implying autonomy for others) 5. Gives opinions (evaluation, analysis, expresses feeling, wish) 6. Gives orientation (information, repeats, clarifies, confirms)
	Questions	C	7. Asks for orientation (information, repetitions, confirmation) 8. Asks for opinions (evaluation, analysis, expression of feeling) 9. Asks for suggestions (direction, possible ways of action)
Social-emotional Area: *Negative*		D	10. Disagrees (shows passive rejection, formality) 11. Shows tension (asks for help, withdraws out of field) 12. Shows antagonism (deflates others' status, defends or asserts self)

SOURCE: Robert F. Bales, "A Set of Categories for the Analysis of Small Group Interaction." *American Sociological Review*, 15 (April 1950): 258. Reprinted with permission.

make continuous observations from the begining to the end of time, so a decision must be made about when to observe. An acceptable approach to this problem is to follow a *time-sampling schedule.* Time sampling refers to the selection of observation units at different points in time. Observation units can be selected in systematic ways so as to ensure representation of a defined population of behavior. For example, one might make one's observations for a fifteen-minute period of each hour randomly selected after stratification by day of the week and hour of the day (see Chapter 16). Time samples have the advantage of assuring the researcher of representative samples of ongoing occurrences. However, they are inadequate when the purpose is to observe events or behavior that occur infrequently.

In addition to developing a time-sampling design, a system for obtaining accurate records of the occurrences has to be devised. Such a system can be constructed by either a deductive approach or an empirical approach. A deductive approach implies that the researcher begins with a conceptual definition, then specifies indicators of the property, and then standardizes and validates the resulting instrument. The deductive approach is implemented when observations are assigned to categories at the time the record is made. On the other hand, the empirical approach requires first the selection of indicators and postpones definitions until some pattern is identified. Each approach involves some risk. With the deductive approach, it is difficult to foresee whether the conceptual definition is precise. The empirical approach, on the other hand, poses difficulties in interpreting the observations. The ideal way to reduce these risks is to combine the two approaches. Karl Weick suggests that "in the ideal sequence, the observer would start with the empirical approach, obtain extensive records of natural events, induce some concepts from the records, and then collect a second set of records which are more specific and pointed more directly at the induced concept."[13]

Regardless of whether the investigator opts for the deductive or empirical approach or combines the two, the categories to which observations are assigned must exhibit certain characteristics. Donald Medley and Harold Mitzel suggest that a *category-system* is to

> limit the observation to one segment or aspect of . . . behavior, and construct a finite set of categories into one and only one of which every unit observed can be classified. The record obtained purports to show, for each period of observation, the total number of units of behavior which occurred and the number classifiable in each category.[14]

In other words, the categories must be explicit, exhaustive, and mutually exclusive. An explicit category is specified in terms of the occurrence to be observed, the situation in which the occurrence takes place, and the event that precedes or follows the observed occurrence. For instance, Edgar Borgatta explicated the "shows tension increase" category in his Interaction Process Scores observational system in the following way:

> In this category are scored the periods of tenseness that grow largely out of impasses or bankruptcy of conversation. Most of the scores that fall into this category are the awkward pauses, which are usually

---

13. Karl E. Weick, "Systematic Observational Methods," p. 102.

14. Donald M. Medley and Harold E. Mitzel, "Measuring Classroom Behavior by Systematic Observation," in *Handbook of Research on Teaching*, ed. by Nathaniel L. Gage (Chicago: Rand McNally, 1963), p. 298.

punctuated by clearing of throats, looking around by one person or another, etc. For the whole group, however, it is sometimes noted that the level of participation grows more tense because of the general personal involvement of the group.[15]

INFERENCE

The third major consideration in observational studies relates to the degree of inference required of the observer. Most records in observation involve inferences. An investigator observes a certain act or behavior; he or she must process this observation and make an inference that the behavior measures a certain variable. Some observational systems require a low degree of observer inference, for example, such straightforward acts as "asks a question," "suggests a course of action," "interrupts another group member," and the like. Many acts, however, require a higher degree of inference. Suppose one observes an adult striking a child. An inference has to be made whether this act represents "aggression," "aggressive behavior," "hostility," "violence," or some other variable. The correctness of such an inference depends to a large extent on the competence of the observer. Well-trained observers are likely to make more reliable inferences, other things being equal.

As a means of increasing the reliability of inferences, training programs applicable to various observational situations were designed. Typically, a program begins with an exposition of the theory, the research hypotheses involved in a given study, and an explanation of the category-system constructed to record the observations. After the trainees have had an opportunity to raise questions, they try to use the category-system on a group that demonstrates the phenomena of the type the observers will be expected to record when the actual data collection begins.[16]

TYPES OF OBSERVATION

The extent to which decisions regarding the types of behavior, timing, and recording and degree of inference are systematically and rigorously implemented is a criterion by which we can distinguish between controlled and noncontrolled observational systems. A controlled observational system is typified by clear and explicit decisions on what, how,

15. Edgar F. Borgatta, "A Systematic Study of Interaction Process Scores, Peer and Self-Assessments, Personality and Other Variables," *Genetic Psychological Monographs*, 65 (1962): 219–291.

16. Roger W. Heynes and Alvin F. Zander, "Observation of Group Behavior," in *Research Methods in the Behavioral Sciences*, ed. by Leon Festinger and Daniel Katz (New York: Holt, Rinehart and Winston, 1945).

and when to observe; a noncontrolled system posits fewer commitments on the part of the researcher and allows greater flexibility. For example, in controlled observation, a time sample is usually drawn prior to observation; in noncontrolled observation, time samples are rarely taken. The choice between controlled and noncontrolled observation depends to a large extent on the research design; that is, controlled observation is most frequently used with experimental research designs and seldom with pre-experimental designs or exploratory studies. In the following sections, controlled and noncontrolled observational systems are discussed.

CONTROLLED OBSERVATIONS

Controlled observations are carried out either in the laboratory or in the field. These two settings share a common concern with respect to the researcher's purpose. In both, the investigator wishes to infer causality by maximizing control over extrinsic and intrinsic variables while employing one of the various experimental research designs and systematically recording observations.

LABORATORY EXPERIMENTATION

The most controlled method of data collection in the social sciences is laboratory experimentation; it involves the introduction of conditions in a controlled environment (laboratory) that simulates certain features of a natural environment. Laboratory experimentation allows the construction of a situation with closely supervised manipulation of one or more variables at a time in order to observe the effects produced.

Classic examples of laboratory experimentation are the Solomon Asch experiments on interpersonal influence. Asch's objective was to examine the social and personal conditions that induce individuals to yield to or resist group pressures when such pressures are perceived to be contrary to fact. Asch developed a procedure for placing an individual in intense disagreement with his or her peers and for measuring the effect of this relationship upon him or her. Eight individuals were instructed to match the length of a given line with one of three unequal lines. Each member of the group was asked to announce her or his judgment publicly. In the midst of the test, one individual found himself or herself suddenly contradicted by the entire group. This contradiction was repeated a number of times during the experiment, because Asch had instructed the seven other members of the group to respond at certain points with wrong judgments. The errors of the majority were large, ranging between 0.50 inch and 1.75 inches. The eighth individual confronted a situation in which a group unanimously contradicted the evidence of her or his senses. This individual, commonly referred to as the critical subject, was the object of investigation. Asch also used a control group in which the errors introduced by the majority were not of the same order encountered under experimental conditions. One of the interesting findings was the marked movement toward the majority: "One third of all the estimates in the critical group were errors identical with or in the direction of the distorted estimates of the majority. The significance of this finding becomes clear in the light of the virtual absense of errors in the control group. . . ."[17]

The Asch experiment exemplifies the two major advantages of laboratory experimentation: it allows rigorous control over extrinsic and intrinsic variables, and it provides unambiguous evidence about causation. Asch eliminated the effects of many variables that might have caused critical subjects to yield to or to resist group pressure; this increased the possibility of observing existing differences due to their experimental treatment. Moreover, Asch could unambiguously specify what caused the movement of his critical subjects toward the majority because he himself controlled and manipulated the independent variable—the seven members of the group who were told when to respond with wrong judgments. Furthermore, Asch varied the experimental treatment in a systematic way, thus allowing for the precise specification of important differences. Finally, the experiment was constructed in a way that enabled a clear detection of the effects of the experimental treatment: the critical subjects had to state their judgments publicly. They had to declare themselves and to take a definite position vis-á-vis their peers. They could not avoid the dilemma by pointing to conditions external to the experimental situation.

Laboratory experiments vary in complexity and design, depending on the research problem and the ingenuity of the experimenter. For example, Morton Deutsch and Robert Krauss developed the "Acme-Bolt trucking game" to study the effects of conflict and threat on bargaining and cooperation.[18] In this experiment, each subject "operates" a trucking firm (Acme or Bolt) through a control box and a visual display panel, with lights showing the movement of trucks. A constant sum of money, minus the cost for the trip's elapsed time, is paid to each player for carrying a load from a starting point to a destination. As shown in Figure 7.1, each subject has two routes to his or her destination: a short main route and a long alternate route. The characteristics of this experiment are such that if a subject takes the alternate route, he or she loses at least

17. Solomon E. Asch, "Effects of Group Pressure upon the Modification Distortion of Judgments," in *Readings in Social Psychology*, ed. by Eleanor Maccoby, Theodore Newcomb, and Eugen Hartley (New York: Holt, Rinehart and Winston, 1958), p. 177.

18. Morton Deutsch and Robert M. Krauss, "The Effect of Threat upon Interpersonal Bargaining," *Journal of Abnormal and Social Psychology*, 61 (1960): 181–189; and "Studies of Interpersonal Bargaining," *Journal of Conflict Resolution*, 6 (1962): 52–76.

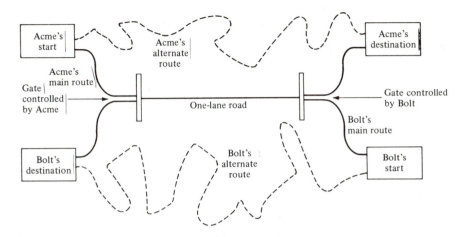

FIGURE 7.1. Subjects' Road Map in the Acme-Bolt Trucking Game
SOURCE: Morton Deutsch and Robert M. Krauss, "The Effect of Threat upon Interpersonal Bargaining." *Journal of Abnormal and Social Psychology*, 61 (1960): 183. Copyright © 1960 by the American Psychological Association. Reprinted by permission.

ten cents on the trip; if both take the main route, they will meet on its one-lane section and be deadlocked unless one of them backs up. The conflict lies in the consideration that it is to each subject's interest to go through the one-lane route before the other, but that some agreement on ensuring access to the main route is mutually beneficial. This problem contains both competitive and cooperative elements, thus providing a basis for the investigation of variables that affect the difficulty with which bargainers can reach an agreement. For instance, the researchers investigated the effect of a threat in the form of "gates" that a subject could close to indicate that the other subject could be prevented from completing her or his trip on the main route. The three basic conditions set in the experiment were such that a gate was possessed by both subjects, only one subject, or neither subject. Deutsch and Krauss hypothesized that the competitive interest provided by gates would introduce elements of self-esteem that would make cooperation most difficult in the two-gate situation and least difficult in the no-gate situation. The results of this experiment supported the hypothesis that the joint outcome— that is, the combined payoff of Acme plus Bolt—was highest in the no-gate case and lowest in the two-gate condition.

To examine the effects of joint or shared rewards in cooperative behavior, Nathan Azrin and Ogden Lindsley used several mechanical instruments to help with their experiment. They first asked pairs of children to play a "game" in which they were reinforced with candy when they made a cooperative response. The children faced one another across a table with a glass partition between them. Each had a metal stylus and a metal plate with three holes. The children were instructed to play the game any way they wanted to by placing the styli in the holes. Next, they were told: "While you are in that room some of these [jelly beans] will drop into this cup. You can eat them here if you want to or you can take them home with you." The children were then left alone. The apparatus used in the experiment was wired so that if the styli were placed in opposite holes within 0.04 second of each other, a red light flashed on the table and a single jelly bean fell into a cup accessible to both children. This was an indication of cooperative response, and the candy served as reinforcement. Azrin and Lindsley report:

> Observation through a one-way vision screen disclosed that leader-follower relationships were developed and maintained in most cases. Almost immediately eight teams divided the candy in some manner. With two teams, one member at first took all the candy until the other member refused to co-operate. When verbal agreement was reached in these two teams, the members then co-operated and divided the candy.[19]

These three experiments illustrate both the significance and the variability in setting the stage for the experiment. Experimenters have to construct a set of procedures that capture the meaning of their conceptualization and that enable the testing of hypotheses. This, in turn, demands the invention of a method of measuring the effect this has on the behavior of the researched individual and the construction of a setting within which the basic manipulations of the independent variables make sense and the measurements are valid and reliable.

Experimental and Mundane Realism

At this point, the reader might question the meaningfulness of laboratory experimentation, as none of the experiments described represents a "real-world" situation. Thus, in the Asch experiment, critical subjects were judging a very clear physical event (the length of lines) and were contradicted by their peers. However, in everyday life, it is almost inconceivable to find oneself in a situation where the unambiguous evidence of one's senses is contradicted by the unanimous judgments of one's peers.

This seeming dilemma is somewhat resolved if a distinction is drawn between two senses in which any given experiment can be said to be realistic.[20] In one sense, an experiment is realistic if the situation is

19. Nathan H. Azrin and Ogden R. Lindsley, "The Reinforcement of Cooperation Between Children," *Journal of Abnormal and Social Psychology*, 52 (1956): 101.

20. Elliot Aronson and James Carlsmith, "Experimentation in Social Psychology," in *The Handbook of Social Psychology*, ed. by Gardner Lindzey and Elliot Aronson.

realistic to the subject, if it involves that individual and has impact on him or her. This kind of realism is commonly termed *experimental realism*. Thus, in the Asch experiment, the critical subjects underwent an experience that caused them to exhibit signs of tension and anxiety. The critical subjects were reacting to a situation that was as "real" for them as any of their ordinary experiences.

The second sense of realism refers to the extent to which events occurring in a laboratory setting are likely to occur in the "real world." This type of realism is called *mundane realism*. An experiment that is high on mundane realism and low on experimental realism does not necessarily yield more meaningful results than one that is high on experimental realism and low on mundane realism. Were Asch to observe interpersonal influences in the "real world," he probably would not have found a situation so clearly structured for observing the effects of group pressure on individual members. Moreoever, if we assume that such a situation could have been found, the effects of intrinsic and extrinsic variables could not have been controlled for, and the obtained findings would have been ambiguous and inconclusive. Experimental realism enables the experimenter to increase the internal validity of the experiment by producing a significant effect within the experimental situation.

Sources of Bias in Laboratory Experiments

Although laboratory experiments operationalize the idea of controlled experimentation and observation in the sense that they are studies in which (1) an investigator interferes with a process, so that (2) random subsets of the units processed are differently treated, and (3) measurements are collected in such a way that variability among units which were treated the same way can be estimated, they have certain limitations. These can be classified into three types: bias due to the demand characteristics of the experimental situation itself; bias due to the unintentional influence of the experimenters; and measurement artifacts.

Demand characteristics. Bias due to demand characteristics comes about when individuals know that they are in an experimental situation and are aware that they are being observed and that certain responses are expected from them. Consequently, individuals may not respond to the experimental manipulation as such, but to their interpretation of what responses these manipulations are supposed to elicit from them. Even if the individual is "told that there are no right or wrong responses, he knows that there are answers that will enhance or diminish his value as a person in the experimenter's eyes."[21] The individual may discover the research hypothesis and respond in a manner consistent with it in an attempt to cooperate with the experimenter. One common way to reduce this source of bias is through deception. Individuals are not told the true

21. Ibid., p. 61.

objective of the experiment but some other credible hypothesis. Thus, if a person modifies behavior so as to support or refute an incorrect hypothesis, the results relating to the true hypothesis might not be affected in a systematic way.[22]

Experimenter bias. Behavior of the experimenter that is not intended to be part of the experimental manipulation but that nevertheless influences individuals who participate in an experiment is termed experimenter bias. When experimenters know what effects they desire from individuals, they may inadvertently communicate their expectations in various ways, for example by showing tension or relief on occasion or by nodding the head. Robert Rosenthal and his colleagues found that when eight of twelve experimenters testing subjects on the same assignment received biased data from their first two subjects (who were accomplices of Rosenthal and his coinvestigators), these early returns influenced the data they collected from subsequent true subjects. The four experimenters who received hypothesis-confirming data from their first two subjects obtained the strongest confirming data from naïve subjects who followed the planted subjects. The four experimenters who received disconfirming data from their first two subjects obtained the most disconfirming data from the naïve subjects who served after the plants. The comparison group of experimenters, who ran only naïve subjects, obtained values between those obtained by the other two groups of experimenters. Accordingly, it was concluded that early returns bias subsequently obtained data.[23]

Attempts to minimize the occurrence of unintentional experimenter bias are directed toward eliminating communication of expectations by using automated procedures such as tape recorders or television cameras that tend to minimize interactions between experimenter and subject. The underlying rationale of such procedures is that bias effects may be reduced if individuals do not interact with the experimenters. Bias effects have also been handled through the use of experimenters with differing expectations regarding the outcome of the investigation. For example, in one study experimenters with different expectations about the effects of the manipulated variables were included as one of the variables in the experimental design. In this case, the researchers assessed whether their own differing expectations produced different outcomes.[24]

22. Ibid., pp. 61–70, for a comprehensive discussion of this and other bias-reducing methods.

23. Robert Rosenthal et al., "The Effects of Early Data Returns on Data Subsequently Obtained by Outcome-Biased Experimenters," *Sociometry*, 26 (December 1963): 487–493.

24. J. Merrill Carlsmith, Barry E. Collins, and Robert L. Helmreich, "Studies in Forced Compliance: I. The Effect of Pressure for Compliance on Attitude Change Produced by Face-to-Face Role Playing and Anonymous Essay Writing," *Journal of Personality and Social Psychology*, 4 (January 1966): 1–13.

Measurement Artifacts. Measurement is a crucial part of the research process. In laboratory experiments, where the effects of an independent variable may be subtle and sensitive, precise measurement is needed to detect such effects. Moreover, measurement procedures are not independent of research design problems, as measurement procedures may create additional interpretations of the obtained data by giving persons who participate in an experiment additional ideas about what is going on, by giving an individual a chance to present himself or herself in a favorable light, and so on.

Measuring instruments may be reactive in the sense that they may change the phenomenon being measured. For instance, the use of cameras in the presence of experimenters may cause the individuals being studied to behave atypically. Relatedly, exposure to the measuring instrument in a pretest may sensitize individuals and affect their posttest scores. Finally, the time of measurement may produce misleading results; that is, a researcher may measure for the effects of independent variables before they have time to affect the dependent variable or after their effects have already waned, thus concealing their actual effect. Carl I. Hovland and his co-authors, for example, found that discredited speakers have no immediate persuasive effect on their listeners, but may have a significant effect a month later, unless the listeners are reminded of the source.[25]

Recording Observations

Observations in the laboratory are recorded on the spot during the experimental session. Often, mechanical devices such as motion pictures, tape recordings, and television are used to obtain an overall view of the occurrences. Next, the units of observation are assigned to a well-structured category-system, such as the one reproduced in Table 7.1. Categorization may also take place during the experimental session if the system of recording is prepared and pretested well in advance. With a well-prepared system of recording and trained observers, the degree of inference required of the observers is minimal.

FIELD EXPERIMENTATION

The major difference between laboratory experimentation and experiments in the field is, as the terms imply, the setting. A laboratory experiment involves the introduction in a controlled environment of conditions that simulate certain features of a natural environment. A field experiment, on the other hand, is a research study in a *natural* situation in which one or more independent variables are manipulated by the

25. Carl I. Hovland, Irving L. Janis, and Harold H. Kelley, *Communication and Persuasion* (New Haven: Yale University Press, 1953).

experimenter under as carefully controlled conditions as the situation permits. In terms of research designs, the contrast between the laboratory experiment and the field study is not sharp. The differences are mostly matters of degree. However, the difficulties involved in controlling intrinsic and especially extrinsic variables are often greater in field experiments.

A classic example of field experimentation is the Lester Coch and John French study on resistance to change.[26] The research objective was to find out why production workers strongly resist changes in methods and jobs and what can be done to overcome this resistance. To this end, participation in planning was regarded as an independent variable that affects production, resignations, and aggression. It was hypothesized that resistance to change could be significantly reduced by increased participation in decisions or processes that lead to change. This hypothesis was tested in the main plant of the Harwood Manufacturing Corporation. Factory workers were divided into three groups. The members of the control group did not participate in any of the discussions and decisions about changes in the plant. Two experimental groups did participate in discussion and decision in different degrees: participation by representation and direct participation. It was found that the no-participation group developed strong resistance after changes in the plant occurred; the group that participated through representation developed very little resistance; and the direct-participation group did not develop any resistance. Moreover, in the direct-participation group, the level of production increased after the changes in the plant occurred. The investigators could infer that the experimental treatment (that is, the degree of participation in discussions and decisions about changes before executing them) was inversely related to resistance to change; the higher the degree of participation, the lower the resistance to change.

The Coch and French study was a field experiment in which the investigators relied mainly on systematic observation within a naturally occurring behavior system. The experimenters intruded in this system by introducing and manipulating one independent variable, the effects of which were clearly observed. This experiment illustrates the main virtue of field experiments: they are appropriate for investigating complex interactions, processes, and changes in natural settings.

As indicated earlier, the main weakness of field experiments is that of control; the control of intrinsic and especially of extrinsic variables is rarely as tight as in laboratory experiments. To meet this problem, French has suggested the following procedures. First, whenever possible, the experiment is to be replicated in the same setting. For example,

26. Lester Coch and John R. P. French, "Overcoming Resistance to Change," *Human Relations*, 1 (1948): 512–532.

French replicated the Harwood Manufacturing Corporation experiment and obtained results similar to those obtained in the original experiment.[27] If replication is not intended, preliminary experiments are conducted in order to ensure that the experimental manipulations produce observable differences. If the experimental manipulations are not sufficiently strong to produce differences, the field conditions are simplified. It has also been recommended that experimental treatments be applied to units of small size (individuals or small groups) rather than large institutions. Smaller units permit easier manipulation and provide opportunities for preliminary experimentation and replication. Finally, the size of the experimental manipulation is reduced by confining it to a relatively short period of time; longer periods increase the chances of unforeseen events taking place.

Procedures for recording observations in field experiments are similar to those in laboratory experimentation. Records are taken on the spot during the experiment. Mechanical instruments such as tape recordings, motion pictures, and television are standard aids in field experimentation. The systematization of data is achieved through the use of observation schedules and category-systems discussed earlier in this chapter.

PARTICIPANT OBSERVATION

The least controlled method of observation is participant observation. This method refers to those "forms of research in which the investigator devotes himself to attaining some kind of membership in or close attachment to an alien or exotic group that he wishes to study."[28] In doing so, the participant observer attempts to share the world view and to adopt the perspective of the people in the situation being observed. His or her role is that of "conscious and systematic sharing, insofar as circumstances permit, in the life activities, and on occasion, in the interests and affects of a group of persons."[29] Direct participation on the part of the observer in the activities of those being studied often entails learning their language, their habits, their work patterns, and the like.

The norms of objectivity, validity, and reliability and the designs for causal inferences are embodied in participant observation, most often implicitly. These are deliberately made unstructured and flexible so as to maximize the understanding of empirical phenomena. Blanche Geer

27. John R. P. French, "Field Experiments: Changing Group Productivity," in *Experiments in Social Process*, ed. by James G. Miller (New York: McGraw-Hill, 1954).

28. Rosalie H. Wax, "Participant Observation," *International Encyclopedia of Social Sciences* (New York: Macmillan 1968), p. 238.

29. Florence Kluckhohn, "The Participant-Observer Technique in Small Communities," *American Journal of Sociology*, 45 (1940): 339–342.

exemplifies the employment of the scientific methodology in the following excerpt:

> My use of hypotheses falls roughly into three sequential types. The first operation consisted of testing the crude yes-or-no proposition. By asking informants or thinking back over volunteered information in the data . . . I stated a working hypothesis in the comments and began the second operation in the sequence: Looking for negative cases or setting out deliberately to accumulate positive ones . . . Working with negatively expressed hypotheses gave me a specific goal. One instance that contradicts what I say is enough to force modification of the hypothesis. . . . The third stage of operating with hypotheses in the field involves two-step formulations and eventually rough models.[30]

In its final stage of development the hypothesis is not of the "X causes Y" type; rather, an all-inclusive set of propositions (a model) is developed to explain the totality of the phenomenon.

Models are constructed with the *analytic induction* method that represents an approximation of the before-after research design. Alfred Lindesmith describes the method of analytic induction as follows:

> The principle which governs the selection of cases to test a theory is that the chances of discovering a decisive negative case should be maximized. The investigator who has a working hypothesis concerning his data becomes aware of certain areas of critical importance. If his theory is false or inadequate, he knows that its weaknesses will be more clearly and quickly exposed if he proceeds to the investigation of those critical areas. This involves going out of one's way to look for negative evidence.[31]

THE ROLES OF THE OBSERVER

Data to be used for analytic induction are collected while the investigator assumes either a complete participant role or a participant-as-observer role.

Complete Participant

A complete participant role means that the observer is wholly concealed, his or her research objectives are not made known, and he or she attempts

---

30. Blanche Geer, "The First Days in the Field," in *Sociologists at Work*, ed. by Phillip Hammond, p. 337.

31. Alfred R. Lindesmith, "Two Comments on W. S. Robinson's 'The Logical Structure of Analytic Induction,'" *American Sociological Review*, 17 (1952): 492.

to become a member of the group under observation. The complete participant interacts with the observed "as naturally as possible in whatever areas of their living interest him and are accessible to him."[32] For example, Leon Festinger, Henry Riecken, and Stanley Schachter studied a group of persons who predicted the destruction of the world. The nature of the group led the authors to believe that if they presented themselves as researchers, then entry to the group would be denied. Consequently, they posed as individuals interested in the activities of the group and became full-fledged members trying to be "nondirective, sympathetic listeners, passive participants who were inquisitive and eager to learn whatever others might want to tell us."[33] Mortimer Sullivan and coauthors investigated the motivations and attitudes of the personnel in a military training program. One of the researchers "enlisted" as a basic trainee and became a full-fledged member of the group. His identity, research objective, and role as a researcher remained unknown to members of the group, including his own commanding officer.[34]

Complete participation has been justified on the grounds that it makes possible the study of ordinarily inaccessible groups or accessible groups that do not reveal to outsiders certain aspects of their culture. In spite of these advantages, and perhaps because of them, the complete participation role has been severely criticized on methodological and ethical points. Kai Erikson rejects all field observations that do not make the role of the researcher and the intent of the study known beforehand because they constitute an invasion of privacy and may harm the observed:

> The sheer act of entering a human transaction on the basis of deliberate fraud may be painful to the people who are thereby misled; and even if that were not the case, there are countless ways in which a stranger who pretends to be something else can disturb others by failing to understand the conditions of intimacy that prevail in the group he has tried to invade.[35]

The complete participation role poses several methodological prob-

32. Raymond L. Gold, "Roles in Sociological Field Observations," *Social Forces*, 36 (1958): 217–223.

33. Leon Festinger, Henry Riecken, and Stanley Schachter, *When Prophecy Fails* (Minneapolis: University of Minnesota Press, 1956), p. 237.

34. Mortimer A. Sullivan, Stuart A. Queen, and Ralph C. Patrick, "Participant Observation as Employed in the Study of a Military Training Program," *American Sociological Review*, 23 (1958): 660–667.

35. Kai T. Erikson, "A Comment on Disguised Observation in Sociology," *Social Problems*, 14 (1967): 368.

lems. First, observers may either become so self-conscious about revealing their true selves that they are handicapped when attempting to
perform convincingly in the pretended role; or they may "go native,"
incorporating the pretended role into their self-conception and losing
the research perspective.[36] Second, the problem of deciding what to
observe is most delicate because the researcher cannot evoke behavior.
For example, the observer must be careful not to ask questions that might
raise the suspicions of the persons observed. Third, recording is not
feasible on the spot; it has to postponed until the observer is alone.
But time lags in reporting introduce selective bias and distortions
through memory. Sullivan and coauthors point out that the disguised
observer had serious problems of reporting and was "never certain
whether his reports were adequate or whether he was 'getting across'
what he was observing."[37]

Participant-as-Observer

In view of these methodological limitations coupled with ethical considerations, participant observers most often assume the participant-as-
observer role. This type of role makes the researcher's presence as a
scientist known to the group being studied, thus minimizing problems
of role-pretending. The participant-as-observer attempts to establish
close relationships with members of the group who subsequently serve
as both informants and respondents. Robert Janes's research illustrates
the participant-as-observer role:

> Field work was begun by visiting town, country and school officials,
> and the newspaper editor to explain the purpose of the study and
> to ask their co-operation. . . . In time social interaction was initiated
> by attending church, joining a veterans' organization, returning visits
> to neighbors, and later spending social evenings with the families
> of several young business men of the community.[38]

A participant-as-observer confronts three major problems: establishing relationships with members of the group, finding resourceful and reliable informants, and maintaining the observer-observed relationship.

Establishing relations with members. The ease with which relationships with members of a group are established depends, to a large
extent, upon the nature of the group and the skills of the researcher.

36. Raymond Gold, "Roles in Sociological Field Observation."

37. Sullivan, Queen, and Patrick, "Participant Observation as Employed in the Study
of a Military Training Program," p. 662.

38. Robert W. Janes, "A Note on the Phases of the Community Role of the Participant
Observer," *American Sociological Review*, 26 (1961): 446–450.

Evans-Pritchard exemplified this point: "Azande would not allow me to live as one of themselves; Nuer would not allow me to live otherwise. Among Azande I was compelled to live outside of the community; among Nuer I was compelled to be a member of it. Azande treated me as a superior; Nuer as an equal."[39]

Finding resourceful and reliable informants. Once relationships with members of the group are established, the participant-as-observer is regarded as a provisional member of the group. He or she learns how to behave in the group and teaches the observed how to act toward him or her. Next, the observer is accepted as a *categorical member* of the group. By this time rapport will have been established, areas of observation will be agreed upon, and informants will be providing information. William Whyte's experiences illustrate several phases in this process:

> I began with a vague idea that I wanted to study a slum district . . . I made my choice on very unscientific grounds: Cornerville best fitted my picture of what a slum district should look like . . . I learned early in my Cornerville period the crucial importance of having the support of key individuals in any groups or organizations I was studying. Instead of trying to explain myself to everyone, I found I was providing far more information about myself and my study to leaders such as Doc than I volunteered to the average corner boy. I always tried to give the impression that I was willing and eager to tell just as much about my study as anyone wished to know, but it was only to group leaders that I made a particular effort to provide really full information . . . Since these leaders had a sort of position in the community that enabled them to observe much better than the followers what was going on and since they were in general more skillful observers than the followers, I found that I had much to learn from a more active collaboration with them.[40]

Intimate relationships with informants may, however, bias the informants' reports, as Whyte himself has observed:

> Doc found this experience of working with me interesting, and yet the relationship had its drawbacks. He once commented: "You've slowed me up plenty since you've been down here. Now, when I do something, I have to think what Bill Whyte would want to know about it and how I can explain it. Before, I used to do things by instinct."[41]

39. Edward E. Evans-Prichard. *The Nuer* (Oxford: Clarendon, 1965), p. 15.

40. William F. Whyte, *Street Corner Society*, 2nd ed. (Chicago: University of Chicago Press, 1955), p. 283–302.

41. Ibid., p. 301.

Maintaining relations. Eventually, the researcher departs from the group being studied, and relationships with members of the group and informants are terminated. The problems arising owing to termination depend on the kinds of relationships established during the study period. If the observed have come to view themselves as friends of the observer, then their demands on him or her will be great. If the investigator has come to regard the observed as friends, his or her ability to maintain objectivity might be impaired. The researcher may overidentify with the observed and start to lose the research perspective.

RECORDING OBSERVATIONS

The participant-as-observer can record his or her observations on the spot during the event. The documentation may take the form of a diary, or it may be a daily record of each event. These original notes are later re-analyzed and placed under the appropriate categories of a category-system. If the study is focused and the objects to be observed are well defined, recording and categorizing can be pursued during the observation period. When constant recording interferes with the quality of observation, devices for remembering things can be designed. For example, Lindgren associated the first outstanding incident that occurred during the observation with a word beginning with a, the next incident with a word beginning with b, and so forth. These key words guided him later when writing up a fuller account of the occurrences.[42]

When notes are not taken on the spot but immediately after the observation, opportunities for distortion and misrepresentation increase. Anselm Strauss and coauthors made use of certain notational conventions to minimize distortions:

> Verbal material recorded within quotations signified exact recall; verbal material within apostrophes indicated a lesser degree of certainty or paraphrasing; and verbal material with no markings meant reasonable recall but not quotation . . . impressions or inferences could be separated from actual observations by the use of single or double parentheses.[43]

Such a recording system is vulnerable to a great amount of observer inference, unlike the recording systems employed in controlled observations.

42. E. J. Lindgren, "Field Work in Social Psychology," *British Journal of Psychology*, 26 (1935): 174–182.

43. Anselm Strauss et al., *Psychiatric Ideologies and Institutions* (New York: Free Press, 1964).

SUMMARY

Observation is considered to be the archetypical method of scientific research. If one wishes to understand, explain, and predict what exists, one can simly go and observe it. But if one's findings are to be systematic, the observations must be carried out with reference to three crucial issues: (1) what to observe, (2) where and when to observe, and (3) how much to infer when recording observations.

Decisions concerning these issues depend on the research problem and the research design. When the researcher's objective is to test a hypothesis experimentally, the units of observations are explicitly defined; a setting is chosen—laboratory or field; a time sample is drawn; and the observations are systematically recorded with as little observer inference as possible. These operations typify controlled observations.

The least controlled method of observation is participant observation. This method refers to those forms of research in which researchers attempt to attain some kind of membership in or close attachment to a group that they wish to study. The research objective is broadly defined; the units of observation are explicated ad hoc and in the field; neither samples of events nor time samples are drawn; and observations are recorded with a great amount of inference.

KEY TERMS FOR REVIEW

Natural setting
Nonverbal behavior
Time-sampling
  schedule
Controlled
  observation
Noncontrolled
  observation
Mundane realism
Demand
  characteristics

Experimenter bias
Field
  experimentation
Participant
  observation
Analytic induction
Complete
  participant
Participant-as-
  observer

ADDITIONAL READINGS

Bales, Robert F. and Stephen P. Cohen. *SYMLOG: A System for the Multiple Level Observation of Groups*. New York: Free Press, 1979.

Brandt, R. *Studying Behavior in Natural Settings*. New York: Holt, Rinehart and Winston, 1972.

Cassell, J. "Risk and Benefit to Subjects of Field Work." *American Sociologist*, 13 (1978): 134–143.

Glaser, Myron. *The Research Adventure: Promise and Problems in Field Work.* New York: Random House, 1972.

Heynes, Roger W., and R. Lippitt. "Systematic Observational Techniques." In *Handbook of Social Psychology,* ed. by Gardner Lindzey. Cambridge, Mass.: Addison-Wesley, 1954. Vol. I, p. 399.

Madron, Thomas W. *Small Group Methods and the Study of Politics.* Evanston, Ill.: Northwestern University Press, 1969.

Rosenthal, Robert. *Experimenter Effects in Behavioral Research.* New York: Appleton-Century-Crofts, 1966.

Wax, Rosalie H. *Doing Fieldwork.* Chicago: University of Chicago Press, 1971.

Zelditch, Morris, Jr. "Some Methodological Problems of Field Studies." *American Journal of Sociology,* 67 (March 1962): 566–576.

CHAPTER PREVIEW

CHAPTER 8
Survey Research

INTRODUCTION

Observational methods of data collection are suitable for investigating phenomena that can be observed directly by the researcher. However, not all phenomena are accessible to the investigator's direct observation; very often, therefore, the researcher must collect data by asking people who have experienced certain phenomena to reconstruct these phenomena for others. The researcher approaches a sample of individuals presumed to have undergone certain experiences and interviews them concerning these experiences. The obtained responses constitute the data upon which the research hypotheses are examined. Three major methods are used to elicit information from respondents: the personal interview, the mail questionnaire, and the telephone survey. These methods can be subsumed under the concept *survey research*. In the following sections, we discuss and evaluate these methods.

THE MAIL QUESTIONNAIRE

The mail questionnaire is regarded as an impersonal survey method. Under certain conditions and for a number of research purposes, an impersonal method of data collection might be found useful. In the following section, we will discuss the advantages and disadvantages of this method.

Advantages

Lower cost. When Claire Selltiz and coauthors wrote that "questionnaires can be sent through the mail, interviewers cannot,"[1] they pointed out one of the chief advantages of the mail questionnaire: it is cheaper than personal interviewing. The mail questionnaire does not require a trained staff of interviewers; all it needs is the cost of planning, sampling, duplicating, mailing, and providing stamped, self-addressed envelopes for the returns. The processing and analysis are usually also simpler and cheaper than those of the personal interview. The lower cost in the administration of a mail questionnaire is particularly evident when the population under study is widely spread geographically. Under such circumstances the cost of interviewing could become prohibitive, and the mail questionnaire may be the only feasible instrument.

Reduction in biasing error. The second major advantage of the mail questionnaire is that it reduces *biasing errors* that might result from the personal characteristics of interviewers and from variabilities in their skills. There are many possibilities for bias in a personal interview situation that may arise because of the nature of the personal interaction between the interviewer and the respondent. This can be completely avoided with a mail questionnaire.

Greater anonymity. The third advantage of the mail questionnaire, greater anonymity, is also associated with the absence of an interviewer. The assurance of anonymity with mail questionnaires is especially helpful when the survey deals with sensitive issues, such as questions about sexual behavior or child abuse. With such questions, a mail questionnaire may elicit a higher response rate than a personal interview.

Considered answers and consultations. Mail questionnaires are also preferable when questions demand a considered (rather than an immediate) answer or if the answer requires consultations of personal documents or of other people.

Accessibility. Finally, the mail questionnaire permits wider geographic contact with minimal cost. For example, when a survey requires a wide coverage and addresses a population that is widely dispersed geographically, interviewing would involve expensive travel cost and time for interviewers.

Disadvantages

Requires simple questions. The mail questionnaire can be used as an instrument for data collection only when the questions are straightforward enough to be comprehended solely with the help of printed instructions and definitions.

1. Claire Selltiz, Lawrence S. Wrightsman, and Stuart W. Cook, *Research Methods in Social Relations*, 3rd ed. (New York: Holt, Rinehart and Winston, 1976), p. 239.

No opportunity for probe. The answers have to be accepted as final; there is no opportunity to probe beyond the given answer, to clarify ambiguous answers, or to appraise the nonverbal behavior of respondents.

No control over who fills out the questionnaire. With a mail questionnaire, researchers have no control over the respondent's environment; thus they cannot be sure that the right person completes the questionnaire. An individual other than the intended respondent may complete it.

Low response rate. The final disadvantage of mail questionnaires—and perhaps their most serious problem—is that they often fail to obtain an adequate response rate. For many mail surveys, the reported response rates are much lower than for personal interviews. The typical response rate for a personal interview is about 95 percent, whereas that for a mail survey is between 20 and 40 percent. Researchers who use mail questionnaires are almost always faced with the problem of how to estimate the effect the nonrespondents may have on their findings. (The response rate is of great significance when making generalizations; see Chapter 17.) The nonrespondents are usually quite different from those who answer the questionnaire. Often they are the poorly educated who may have problems understanding the questions, the elderly who are unable to respond, or those that are more mobile and thus cannot be located. Therefore, the group of nonrespondents is not likely to constitute a representative group of the one originally defined by the investigators and will undoubtedly introduce a serious bias into the study.

Factors Affecting the Response Rate of Mail Questionnaires

The difficulty of securing an acceptable response rate to mail questionnaires requires the use of various strategies that can be taken to increase the response rate. In this section we will discuss these strategies.

Sponsorship. The type of sponsorship of a questionnaire has a significant effect on motivating a respondent to fill out and return the mailing. Therefore, information on sponsorship needs to be included and is usually designated in the cover letter accompanying the questionnaire. Sponsorship affects the response rate by convincing the respondent of the study's legitimacy and value as well as the perceived sanctions with failure to reply.

In general, government-sponsored questionnaires receive the highest response, whereas relatively little-known commerical organizations receive the lowest. Prestigious organizations, such as universities, research institutions, and nonprofit agencies fall somewhat in between.[2]

Inducement to respond. Researchers need to appeal to the respondents and persuade them that they should participate by filling out

2. Kenneth D. Bailey, *Methods of Social Research* (New York: Free Press, 1978), p. 139.

the questionnaires and mailing them back. Several methods can be used, and they vary in their degree of effectiveness. One is to appeal to the respondents' good will, telling them that the researchers need their help. For example, a student conducting a survey for a class project may mention that his or her grade may be affected by the response to the questionnaire.[3]

Another method that has been used quite widely is offering the respondent some reward like a prize or a nominal sum of money (usually no more than $1.00). But, as Kenneth Bailey indicates, the problem with offering money is that some respondents will be indignant that the researchers consider the respondent's time worth so little and thus may not respond at all.[4] However, most often the monetary reward is seen as a symbolic gesture, and the respondents cooperate because they consider the study worthwhile.

Perhaps the most effective strategy is to appeal to the respondents' altrustic sentiments and to convince them of the study's significance. In the following example, the importance of the study and the respondents' potential contribution to its success are expressed in the cover letter accompanying the questionnaire:

> As you know, public service employment is a major part of the federal, state and local strategy to overcome the employment and income problems of economically disadvantaged unemployed people. There is no question that the program is needed throughout the country ... You are probably also aware ... that public service employment programs are quite controversial and their future may be in jeopardy. Part of the reason that these programs are so controversial is that no systematic evaluation of the benefits of these programs for the individuals employed and the communities served has been conducted.
>
> Because this specific evaluation has significant national implication, I strongly urge you to give this enclosed questionnaire your prompt attention and thank you for your cooperation in this evaluation.[5]

Questionnaire format and methods of mailing. Several considerations are involved in designing a mail questionnaire: typography, color, and length and type of cover letter. According to William Goode and Paul Hatt, a slightly larger investment in format and typography (for example, high-quality paper and adequate spacing) will create a great

3. Ibid., p. 141.

4. Ibid., p. 142.

5. Mickey L. Burnim, *An Evaluation of the Public Service Employment Projects in Florida Created Under Title VI of the Comprehensive Employment and Training Act of 1973* (Florida: Department of Community Affairs, 1978), p. 164.

dividend in the number of questionnaires completed and returned.[6] On the other hand, the color of the questionnaire apparently makes little difference in the response rate.[7]

The few studies that have examined the effect of questionnaire length on response rates have found little evidence to indicate that length makes a significant difference. For example, Scott examined this point by sending to one-third of his sample one short (one- to two-page) questionnaire; to another third, a second short questionnaire; and to the remaining third, a long questionnaire, which consisted of the two short ones put together. The response rate for the longer questionnaire was 89.6 percent, whereas for the short ones, it was 90.5 percent.[8] However, there are indications that the effect of length on the response rate differs for short and long questionnaires. If the questionnaire is short, then making it even shorter will increase the response rate. On the other hand, if the questionnaire is over ten pages, length no longer makes a great deal of difference.[9]

Cover letter.   Another factor to be considered in designing the questionnaire is the cover letter. The cover letter must succeed in convincing the respondents to fill out the questionnaire and mail it back. It should therefore identify the sponsor of the study, explain its purpose, tell the respondents why it is important that they fill out the questionnaire, and assure them that the answers will be held in strict confidence. In choosing the style of the letter, the investigator must choose between a formal or a semipersonal letter. It has been shown that the semipersonal letter generates a slightly higher response rate than a formal form letter.

Type of mailing.   An important consideration is the type of mailing to be used. Researchers who neglect to include a stamped, self-addressed envelope receive very few responses. It is unreasonable to expect the respondent not only to fill out the questionnaire, but also to find an envelope and then go to the post office to have it weighed and stamped. Thus, it is a common practice to enclose a stamped, self-addressed envelope. This method is preferable to the business-reply envelope, which generally results in a lower response rate.

Selection of respondents.   The selection of the respondents is largely determined by the nature of the study and the characteristics of

6. William J. Goode and Paul K. Hatt, *Methods in Social Research* (New York: McGraw-Hill, 1957), p. 179.

7. Christopher Scott, "Research on Mail Survey," *Journal of the Royal Statistical Society*, 127, Series A: 143–195.

8. Ibid.

9. Delbert C. Miller, *Handbook of Research Design and Social Measurement* (New York: David McKay, 1977), pp. 79–80.

the population. Thus, beyond the definition of the sampling population, there is very little one can do in the selection process to increase the response rate. However, recognizing that certain characteristics of the respondents are associated with a high or low response rate will help determine whether to use a mail questionnaire to begin with or whether other strategies should be used in order to increase the response rate. The most significant dimension in selecting the respondents is whether they consist of a heterogeneous or a homogeneous group. Heterogeneous groups could consist of many ethnic and racial groups, or of individuals with different levels of income, or of those who live in urban as well as rural locations. Homogeneous groups, on the other hand, consist of individuals with similar background characteristics. Heterogeneous groups are typically used in opinion polls, whereas with more specialized studies, questionnaires are sent to more select groups; for example, to physicians, legislators, city managers, university professors, or members of the Urban League. The response rate for select groups is usually higher than it is for the general population because members of these groups are more likely to identify with the goals of the study and thus will be more motivated to respond. Beyond this distinction, there are certain background characteristics that are associated with differentials in response rate. Respondents who are more educated are more likely to fill out and return questionnaires. Interest or familiarity with the topic under investigation is another important factor in determining the rate of return. Finally, in general, professionals tend to have the highest response rate among all other occupations.

Follow-up. The use of follow-ups with mail questionnaires is by far the most effective method of increasing the response rate. The most common strategy of follow-up is to send a reminder postcard one week after the first mailing to respondents who have not yet replied. The second follow-up consists of another reminder letter and a replacement questionnaire with a return envelope sent at the end of the third week. After seven weeks, another letter with a replacement questionnaire is sent, preferably by certified mail, to those who have not yet responded by that time.

The effectiveness of these follow-up methods was tested on large statewide samples of the general population in four states. Table 8.1 shows the average response rates of the four mailings used in the study.[10] The results obtained by this study reveal the importance of a *multiwave follow-up*. Observe that the final wave increased the response rate by more than 13 percent. Indeed, as Don Dillman points out, "with a

---

10. Adapted from Don A. Dillman, James A. Christensen, Edward H. Carpenter, and Ralph M. Brooks, "Increasing Mail Questionnaire Response: A Four State Comparison," *American Sociological Review*, 39 (October 1974): 755.

TABLE 8.1.   Average Cumulative Response Rates to Four Mailings

Mailing	Time	Average Response Rate
1. First mailing	Week 1	23.8%
2. Post card follow-up	Week 2	42.0
3. First replacement questionnaire	Week 4	59.0
4. Second replacement sent by certified mail	Week 7	72.4

Adapted from Don A. Dillman, James A. Christensen, Edward H. Carpenter, and Ralph M. Brooks, "Increasing Mail Questionnaire Response: A Four-State Comparison," *American Sociological Review*, 39 (October 1974): 755.

mail methodology available which will consistently provide a high response, poor return rate can no more be excused than can inadequate theory or inappropriate statistics.[11]

Although follow-up is clearly an important mechanism in raising the response rate, it raises several problems. First, because follow-up letters and questionnaires are sent only to respondents who have not replied, it is necessary to identify all respondents; thus anonymity cannot be maintained.[12] A way to get around this difficulty is to assure respondents that the replies will be held in strict confidence. Another limitation of the follow-up is that the quality of the response rate declines with successive mailings. Respondents who do not respond the first time might be less likely to take the study seriously and thus may send in an incomplete questionnaire, or their answers may be unreliable. In summary, Table 8.2 rank orders the various procedures discussed so far according to their relative effectiveness in increasing the rate of return. The ranks were determined on the basis of various studies estimating the possible increase of total return of each procedure. Rank could not be determined for the last three procedures.

Evaluating the Response Rate

What is an acceptable response rate for a mail questionnaire? Most investigators attempt to maximize the response rate by using some or all of the strategies that have been discussed in the previous sections. Yet, despite these efforts, many mail surveys achieve a response rate that is not larger than 50 percent. Nonresponse is a serious problem because nonrespondents differ considerably from respondents. For example, it has been shown that mail questionnaires addressed to the general pop-

11. Ibid.

12. C. A. Moser and G. Kalton, *Survey Methods in Social Investigation* (London: Heinemann Educational Books, 1971), p. 266.

TABLE 8.2.   Techniques for Increasing Response Rate

Method	Rank Order*	Optimal Conditions
Follow-up	1	More than one follow-up. Telephone could be used for follow-up.
Inducement	2	Questionnaires containing a token monetary reward produce better results than ones without. However, the population and the type of the questionnaire have to be considered.
Length of questionnaire	3	If a questionnaire is short, then the shorter the better. However, if it is over ten pages, length may cease to be a factor
Sponsorship	4	People the respondent knows produce the best result.
Introductory letter	5	An altruistic appeal seems to produce the best results.
Method of return	Not known	A regular stamped envelope produces better results than business reply envelopes.
Format	Not known	Aesthetically pleasing cover; a title that will arouse interest; an attractive page format.
Selection of respondents	Not known	1. Nonreaders and nonwriters are excluded from participation. 2. Interest in, or familiarity with, the topic under investigation is a major factor in determining the rate of return. 3. The better educated are more likely to return the questionnaires. 4. Professionals are more likely to return questionnaires.

* The numeral 1 indicates the procedure yielding the highest return rate.
Adapted from Delbert C. Miller, *Handbook of Research Design and Social Measurement* (New York: David McKay, 1977), pp. 77–78.

ulation result in an upward bias in social class and education: Individuals who are better educated and of middle-class background are more likely to respond to mail questionnaires.[13] The bias resulting from the non-response may limit the ability to make generalization to the entire population.

The question of what constitutes an acceptable response rate cannot easily be answered. Whereas some investigators consider a response rate of at least 50 percent adequate,[14] most are somewhat more conservative. Bailey maintains that with the proper use of follow-ups, preferably two reminder letters and a telephone call as a third reminder, one should achieve a response rate of approximately 75 percent or more.[15]

Finally, there is some evidence that response rates on mail questionnaires have been declining despite the improvement in follow-up techniques. Some maintain that this is a result of the increased *saturation* in the field. Indeed, in recent years survey research has become a widely used tool, not only of research and marketing organizations, but also of national and local government. Some citizens, though dedicated and loyal to the goals of research, may find themselves faced with a unique decision as to which and how many of the questionnaires they receive each year they should respond to. An attempt to sensitize the questioners to this problem is presented in the following satirical questionnaire for questioners:[16]

BOX 8.1.

Dear Questioner:

You are no doubt aware that the number of questionnaires circulated is rapidly increasing, whereas the length of the working day has, at best, remained constant. In order to resolve the problem presented by this trend, I find it necessary to restrict my replies to questionnaires to those questioners who first establish their *bona fide* by completing the following questionnaire.
1. How many questionnaires, per annum, do you distribute?   ____
2. How many questionnaires, per annum, do you receive?   ____
3. What fraction of the questionnaires you receive do you answer? ____
4. What fraction of the questionnaires you distribute
    are answered?   ____

13. Ibid., p. 263.

14. Earl R. Babbie, *The Practice of Social Research* (Belmont, Calif.: Wadsworth, 1979), p. 335.

15. Bailey, *Methods of Social Research*, p. 153.

16. Samuel Devons, "A Questionnaire for Questioners," *Public Opinion Quarterly*, 39 (1975): 255–256.

Box 8.1 *(Continued)*

 5. Do you think the ratio of the fractions 3:4, should be greater
    than 1; less than 1; any other value? (Please explain.)   ____
 6. What fraction of your time (or effort) do you devote to:
    a. Compiling questionnaires?
    b. Answering questionnaires?   ____
    c. Examining the replies to your own questionnaires?   ____
    d. Examining the replies to other peoples' questionnaires?   ____
    e. Drawing conclusions from questionnaires?   ____
    f. Other activities?   ____
    (a + b + c + d + e + f should add up to 100 percent. If not,   ____
    please explain.)
 7. Do you regard the ratio of (a + b + c + d + e)/f as:
    a. too small? ____
    b. too large? ____
    c. any other ____   (check one only)
 8. Do you ever distribute questionnaires exclusively to people
    who you know distribute questionnaires?   ____
 9. Do you expect answers to questionnaires from people who
    themselves distribute questionnaires about questionnaires?   ____
10. Do you consider it would be of value to distribute a questionnaire
    regarding answers to questionnaires to those individuals
    who receive questionnaires about the distribution of
    questionnaires?
    Yes ____
    No ____   (check one only)
    Any other answer? please explain.
    Replies to this questionnaire *must* be signed. As you may surmise,
they are not suitable, nor will they be used, for statistical purposes.

Source: Samuel Devons, "A Questionnaire For Questioners," *Public Opinion Quarterly,*
39 (1975): 255–256.

THE PERSONAL INTERVIEW

The personal interview can be regarded as a face-to-face interpersonal
role situation in which an interviewer asks respondents questions designed to obtain answers pertinent to the research hypotheses. The questions, their wording, and their sequence define the extent to which the
interview is structured.

The Schedule-Structured Interview

The most structured form is the *schedule-structured interview*, in which
the questions, their wording, and their sequence are fixed and are identical for every respondent. This is done to make sure that when variations
appear between responses, they can be attributed to the actual differences between the respondents and not to variations in the interview.

The researcher attempts to reduce the risk that changes in the wording of questions, for example, might elicit differences in responses. The schedule-structured interview is based on three crucial assumptions:

1. That for any research objective "the respondents have a sufficiently common vocabulary so that it is possible to formulate questions which have the same meaning for each of them."[17]
2. That it is possible to phrase all questions in a form that is equally meaningful to each respondent.
3. That if the "meaning of each question is to be identical for each respondent, its context must be identical and, since all preceding questions constitute part of the contexts, the sequence of questions must be identical."[18]

The Nonschedule-Structured Interview

The second basic form is the focused, or nonschedule-structured, interview. This form has four characteristics:[19]

1. It takes place with respondents known to have been involved in a particular experience.
2. It refers to situations that have been analyzed prior to the interview.
3. It proceeds on the basis of an interview guide specifying topics related to the research hypotheses.
4. It is focused on the subjective experiences regarding the situations under study.

Although the encounter between the interviewer and respondents is structured and the major aspects of the study are explicated, respondents are given considerable liberty in expressing their definition of a situation that is presented to them. The nonschedule-structured interview permits the researcher to obtain details of personal reactions, specific emotions, and the like. The interviewer, having previously studied the situation, is alert and sensitive to inconsistencies and omissions of data that may be needed to clarify the problem.

The Nonscheduled Interview

The least structured form of interviewing is the *nonstructured*, or *nondirective*, interview. Here no prespecified set of questions is employed,

---

17. Stephen Richardson, Barbara S. Dohrenwend, and David Klein, *Interviewing: Its Forms and Functions* (New York: Basic Books, 1965), p. 40.

18. Ibid., p. 43.

19. Robert K. Merton and Patricia L. Kendal, "The Focused Interview," *American Journal of Sociology*, 51 (1946): 541–557.

nor are the questions asked in a specified order. Furthermore, no schedule is used. With little or no direction from the interviewer, respondents are encouraged to relate their experiences, to describe whatever events seem significant to them, to provide their own definitions of their situations, and to reveal their opinions and attitudes as they see fit. The interviewer has a great deal of freedom to probe various areas and to

BOX 8.2. The Schedule-Structured Interview

Interviewer's explanation to the respondent: We are interested in the kinds of problems teenagers have with their parents. We need to know how many teenagers have what kinds of conflicts with their parents. We have a checklist here of some of the kinds of things that happen. Would you think about your own situation and put a check mark to show which conflicts you have had and about how often they have happened. Be sure to put a check in every row. If you have never had such a conflict, then put the check in the first column where it says, "Never."

(Hand respondent the first card dealing with conflicts over the use of the automobile, saying, "If you don't understand any of these things listed or have some other things you would like to mention about how you disagree with your parents over the automobile, let me know and we'll talk about it").

AUTOMOBILE	Never	Only once	More than once	Many times
1. Wanting to learn to drive				
2. Getting a driver's license				
3. Wanting to use the family car				
4. Using it too much				
5. Keeping the car clean				
6. Repairing the car				
7. Driving someone else's car				
8. Want to own a car				
9. The way you drive your own car				
10. Other				

(When the respondent finishes all rows, hand him or her card number 2, saying, "Here is a list of types of conflicts teenagers have with their parents over their friends of the same sex. Do the same with this as you did with the last list.")

Adapted from Raymond L. Gorden, *Interviewing: Strategy, Techniques, and Tactics* (Homewood, Ill.: Dorsey, 1969), pp. 39–40.

BOX 8.3. The Nonschedule-Structured Interview

Instructions to the interviewer: Your task is to discover as many specific kinds of conflicts and tensions between child and parent as possible. The more *concrete* and detailed the account of each type of conflict the better. Although there are four areas of possible conflict that we want to explore (listed in question 3 below), you should not mention any area until after you have asked the first two questions in the order indicated. The first question takes an indirect approach, giving you time to build up rapport with the respondent.

1. What sorts of problems do teenagers have in getting along with their parents?
   (Possible probes: Do they always agree with their parents? Do any of your friends have "problem parents"?
2. What sort of disagreements do you have with your parents? (Possible probes: Do they cause you any problems? In what way do they try to restrict you? Do they like the same things you do?)
3. Have you ever had any disagreement with either of your parents over:
   a. using the family car
   b. friends of the same sex
   c. dating
   d. smoking

Adapted from Gorden, *Interviewing: Strategy, Techniques, and Tactics*, pp. 38–39.

BOX 8.4. The Nonscheduled Interview

Instructions to the interviewer: Discover the kinds of conflicts that the teenager has had with the parents. Conflicts should include disagreements; tensions due to past, present, or potential disagreements; outright arguments and physical conflicts. Be alert for as many categories and examples of conflicts and tensions as possible.

Adapted from Gorden, *Interviewing: Strategy, Techniques, and Tactics*, p. 38.

raise specific queries during the course of the interview. For example, Howard Becker's study of marijuana users is based on such nonscheduled interviews:

> The interviews focused on the history of the person's experience with the drug, seeking major changes in his attitude toward it and in his actual use of it and the reasons for these changes. Generalizations stating necessary conditions for the maintenance of use at each level were developed in initial interviews, and tested again and revised in the light of each succeeding one.[20]

20. Howard S. Becker, "Becoming a Marijuana User," *American Journal of Sociology,* 59 (1953): 235–242.

The differences in interviewing styles in the three types of interviews are illustrated in Boxes 8.2, 8.3, and 8.4 on pp. 192–193: of a schedule-structured interview, a nonschedule-structured interview, and a nonscheduled interview, all concerned with the same research problem. The purpose of the study is to discover the types of conflict between parents and teenagers and their relationship to juvenile crime. The interviews are conducted with two groups of children. One consists of teenagers who have committed no crimes, and the second consists of teenagers who have been known to commit several juvenile crimes.

An interview may be completely structured or nonstructured as illustrated in this example. Alternatively, an interview may consist of structured and nonstructured elements. This will depend upon the purpose of the study. For example, a researcher may use the schedule-structured interview for most questions, but rely on the nonscheduled format for questions that are particularly sensitive.

PERSONAL INTERVIEW VS. MAIL QUESTIONNAIRE

Advantages

Greater flexibility. The interview allows greater flexibility in the questioning process. To the degree that the flexibility increases, the less structured is the interview. The interview allows the interviewer to determine the wording of the questions, to clarify terms that are unclear, to control the order in which the questions are presented, and to probe for additional and more detailed information.

Control of the interview situation. One major advantage of the interview is that it allows greater control over the interviewing situation. An interviewer can ensure that the respondents answer the questions in the appropriate sequence or that they answer certain questions before they are asked subsequent questions. Moreover, in an interview situation, it is possible to standardize the environment in order to ensure that the interview is conducted in private; thus respondents would not have the opportunity to consult one another before giving their answers. It is also possible to record the exact time and place of the interview; this allows the researcher to interpret the answers more accurately, especially in cases in which an important event occurring at the time of the interview may have influenced the respondent's answers.[21]

High response rate. The personal interview results in a higher response rate than the mail questionnaire. Respondents who normally would not respond to a mail questionnaire can easily be reached and interviewed. This includes persons who have difficulties in reading or

21. Bailey, *Methods of Social Research*, p. 158.

writing, or those who do not fully understand the language, or simply those not willing to take the time to write out their answers and mail the questionnaire.

Collection of supplementary information.   An interviewer can collect supplementary information about the respondent. This may include background information about the respondents' personal characteristics and their environment that can aid the researcher in the interpretation of the results. Moreover, an interview situation often yields spontaneous reactions that the interviewer can record and that might be useful in the data analysis stage.

Disadvantages

Higher cost.   The cost of interview studies is significantly higher than that of mail surveys. There are costs involved in the organization required for selecting, training, and supervising interviewers, in paying them, and in the travel time required to conduct interviews. In addition, when interviews follow a nonstructured schedule, the cost of recording and processing the information is very high.

Interviewer bias.   The interview allows for greater flexibility, which is its chief advantage. However, sometimes this leaves room for personal influence and bias of the interviewer. The lack of standardization in the data-collection process makes interviewing highly vulnerable to the bias of the interviewer. Although interviewers are instructed to remain objective and avoid communicating their own personal views, some cues are often given and may influence the answers given by the respondents.[22] Even when verbal cues can be avoided, there are forms of nonverbal communication over which the interviewer may not have full control. Sometimes even the interviewer's race or sex may influence respondents who try to please the interviewer by giving socially desirable answers.

Lack of anonymity.   The interview lacks anonymity, which the mail questionnaire typically provides. Often the interviewer knows all or many of the potential respondents (or at least their name, address, and telephone number). Thus, the respondent may feel threatened or intimidated by the interviewer, especially when the topic or some of the questions are of a sensitive nature.

THE PRINCIPLES OF INTERVIEWING

We now turn to a more detailed discussion of principles and procedures of interviewing. The first step in the interviewing process is getting the

22. John B. Williamson, David A. Konk, and John R. Dalphin, *The Research Craft* (Boston: Little, Brown, 1977), p. 189.

respondent to cooperate and provide the desired information. There are three factors that help in motivating the respondent to cooperate.[23]

1. *The respondents need to feel that their interaction with the interviewer will be pleasant and satisfying.* It is up to interviewers to present themselves to respondents as being understanding and easy to talk to.
2. *The respondents need to see the study as being worthwhile.* The respondents should feel that the study may be beneficial, not only to themselves, but also that it deals with a significant issue and that the respondents' cooperation is very important. Interviewers should interest the respondents in the study by pointing out its significance and the contribution that the respondents can make by cooperating.
3. *Barriers to the interview in the respondents' mind need to be overcome.* Misperceptions that respondents may have must be overcome by interviewers. Some respondents may be suspicious of the interviewers, seeing them as salespeople or as representatives of the government. The interviewers should explain, in a friendly manner, the purpose of the study, the method of selecting respondents, and the confidential nature of the interview.

The Survey Research Center of the University of Michigan provides some useful pointers on how the interviewer should introduce himself or herself to the respondent:

1. *Tell the respondent who you are and whom you represent.*
2. *Tell the respondent what you are doing in a way that will stimulate his or her interest.*
3. *Tell the respondent how he or she was chosen.*
4. *Doorstep instructions should be brief.*
5. *Adapt your approach to the situation.*
6. *Try to create a relationship of confidence and understanding (rapport) between you and the respondent.*

After the initial introduction, the interviewer is ready to begin the interview. There are specific techniques that the interviewer can use in this process:[24]

1. *The questionnaire should be followed, but it can be used informally.*
2. *The interview should be conducted in an informal and relaxed atmosphere and the interviewer should avoid creating the impression that what is occurring is a cross-examination or a quiz.*

23. Institute for Social Research, Survey Research Center, *Interviewer's Manual* (Ann Arbor, Mich.: University of Michigan, 1969), p. 3–1.

24. Ibid., p. 4–1.

3. *The questions should be asked exactly as worded in the question-naire.* This is of particular importance, for even slight changes in the way the questions are presented may change the response obtained. Various studies have shown that even small omissions or changes in the phrasing of questions can distort the results.
4. *Questions should be presented in the same order they are in the questionnaire.* The question sequence has been planned by the researcher to provide continuity and make sure that the respondents' answers will not be influenced by their response to previous questions. Moreover, to standardize the interview, every interviewer should adhere to the same sequence as directed by the investigator.
5. *Questions that are misinterpreted or misunderstood should be repeated and clarified.* In most cases, respondents will not have any problem interpreting or understanding a question. At most, some people would need more time before they respond to a particular question. But occasionally, respondents who have language or hearing problems will have difficulties in understanding a question. The interviewer should then repeat the question. Only on rare occasions should the interviewer reword the question and then only if convinced that otherwise the respondent would misinterpret the question.

Probing

In the *Interviewer's Manual* of the Survey Research Center, University of Michigan, *probing* is defined as "the technique used by the interviewer to stimulate discussion and obtain more information. A question has been asked and an answer given. For any number of reasons, the answer may be inadequate and requires the interviewer to seek more information to meet the survey objectives. Probing is the act of getting this additional information."[25]

Probes have two major functions: (1) They motivate the respondent to elaborate or clarify an answer or to explain the reasons behind the answer; (2) they help focus the conversation on the specific topic of the interview.

In general, the less structured the interview, the more important probing becomes as an instrument for eliciting and encouraging further information.

The following is an illustration of probing used by the interviewer to elicit additional information by "repeating the respondent's statements without including a direct question."[26]

25. Ibid., p. 5–1.

26. Raymond L. Gorden, *Interviewing: Strategy, Techniques and Tactics* (Homewood, Ill.: Dorsey, 1969), p. 286.

RESPONDENT: The main reason I came to Antioch College was because of the combination of high academic standards and the work program. It appealed to me a lot.

INTERVIEWER: It appealed to you a lot?

RESPONDENT: That's right.

INTERVIEWER: Could you tell me a little more exactly why it had this appeal for you?

RESPONDENT: I don't know—it was just that the place sounded less stuffy and straightlaced than a lot of places with just as good an academic program.

INTERVIEWER: You don't like places that are stuffy and straightlaced?

RESPONDENT: You can say that again. A lot of places spend most of their time trying to work out a way of controlling the students, assuming that they are completely incapable of self-control . . .

INTERVIEWER: Why do you suppose Antioch has less supervision by the administration?

RESPONDENT: Well, it is part of the educational philosophy . . .

INTERVIEWER: Let me see if I have grasped the whole picture—you like a school with high academic standards, but one that is not too straightlaced and operates on the assumption that college students can exercise self-control . . .

RESPONDENT: That hits it on the head.

Probing, however, will not work with respondents who refuse to cooperate with the interviewer. This indeed is source of frustration to interviewers and respondents alike. James Reston vividly captures the ridiculous side of probing in the "interview" reprinted in Box 8.5.

Box 8.5 "The Very Last Poll," by James Reston

Q. This is the very last election poll. How are you going to vote?
A. None of your business.

Q. Do you mind telling me how you voted in the last Presidential election?
A. Yes, I mind.

Q. What do think of the candidates running for President?
A. Not much.

Q. Are you leaning one side or the other?
A. I'm not leaning, I'm crying.

Q. What do you think of John Anderson?
A. Best loser since Adlai Stevenson.

Q. What about the Presidential debate in Cleveland?
A. Good show but ridiculous. Presidents don't debate, they decide.

Q. If I may say so, you're an odd character. What are your affiliations?
A. I don't think I have any.

Box 8.5 (Continued)

Q. Look, you must belong to *some* bloc. We're big on blocs this year. Are you an ethnic?
A. *I don't think so, but aren't we all?*

Q. Let me go down my list. You have to be *something*. Are you an Italian?
A. *No.*

Q. A union member?
A. *No.*

Q. A Hispanic?
A. *No, I think I'm one of the other guys—the forgotten majority.*

Q. They may let you vote anyway. What did your mother and father do about politics?
A. *They fought all the time.*

Q. Are you now or have you ever been a card-carrying member of any political party or of the Trilateral Commission or the Council on Foreign Relations?
A. *No.*

Q. Are you a Jew?
A. *My father was an Irish Catholic and my mother was a Presbyterian.*

Q. Wasn't that a little awkward?
A. *It was terrible but wonderful. They had the most glorious battles at home and usually canceled out each other's vote, and . . .*

Q. Please don't go on, I have to find out where you fit in my poll. Are you an evangelical?
A. *I don't know what that means.*

Q. Are you part of the moral majority?
A. *I hope so. I wouldn't want to be a member of the immoral minority.*

Q. Then you must be for Reagan.
A. *I didn't say that.*

Q. Are you against him because he's an actor?
A. *No, all politicians are actors.*

Q. What do you think of his age?
A. *Just right. If he were any younger he might want a second term.*

Q. How do you feel about the candidates?
A. *I feel sorry for them.*

Q. Why?
A. *I think they may be running to please their wives.*

Q. Hmmm—what does that mean?
A. *Well, as I see it, all three candidates in this race are married to very determined and ambitious women. Otherwise, Ronald Reagan and John Anderson might easily have settled happily for retirement. And if Betty Ford, like Ladybird Johnson, hadn't had the good judgment to take her guy back home, the history of the Presidency in the last few years might have been quite different.*

Q. You're raving about the past. Does President Carter scare you?
A. *Only when he smiles.*

Q. Didn't he ask us four years ago "Why not the best?"
A. *That's why I don't fear the worst.*

Q. Didn't he promise us in 1976 a government as good as the people?
A. *Yes.*

Q. Then why are you complaining now?
A. *Because he kept his promise.*

Q. Are you accusing him of being consistent?
A. *My consolation is that they're all inconsistent. Carter, who is really a dove, longing for peace*

Box 8.5 *(Continued)*

and arms control, is pretending to be a hawk. And Reagan, who would like to be a hawk if it didn't interfere with his sleep or create too much mischief, is pretending to be a dove.

Q. Are you saying, then, that the election makes no difference?
A. No.

Q. Are you worried about the lack of leaders in the United States?
A. No, but we're a little short on followers.

Q. Do you believe what Carter and Reagan say about each other? You know, Reagan strolling through the White House playing with the button and Carter dismantling the Pentagon and wrecking the economy?
A. Absolute twaddle. They're driveling and so are you, but I have to go and vote.

Q. Then how are you going to vote?
A. As I said before, its none of your business.

THE TELEPHONE INTERVIEW

The third method to be discussed is the telephone interview, also called the *telephone survey*, which may be characterized as a semipersonal method of collecting information. Not too long ago, telephone surveys were viewed with skepticism or outright distrust. Some texts explicitly warned their readers to avoid this method.[27] The primary reason for the reluctance to use telephone interviewing was the high likelihood of a serious sampling bias. When a substantial proportion of the population had no access to telephones, the sample tended to overrepresent those who were relatively well-off—who could afford a telephone. More recently, however, telephone surveys have gained general acceptance as a legitimate method of data collection in the social sciences.

The main rationale for employing telephone surveys more extensively is that today coverage of more than nine-tenths of the population is likely. In 1958, only 72.5 percent of U.S. households had access to telephones. By 1965, this figure was 80.6 percent, and in 1976, it reached 92.8 percent.[28] In addition, financial pressures have made the telephone survey more attractive. Increasing salaries and fuel costs made the personal interview extremely costly. In comparison, the telephone is convenient, and it produces a very significant cost saving. Moreover, the telephone interview results in a higher response rate than the personal interview. In some metropolitan areas, people are quite nervous about

27. William R. Klecka and Alfred J. Tuchfarber, "Random Digit Dialing: A Comparison to Personal Survey," *Public Opinion Quarterly*, 42 (1978): 105–114.

28. Ibid., p. 106.

opening the doors to strangers. Finding the respondent at home has also become increasingly difficult because of the increased participation in the labor force of married women.[29]

Technological changes and improvement in telephone equipment have also made telephone interviewing easier. It has become possible to draw a random sample of telephone numbers by a process called *random digit dialing*.[30] This method requires the identification of all working telephone exchanges in the targeted geographic area. A potential telephone number is created by randomly selecting an exchange and then appending a random number between 0001 and 999. Additional numbers are created by repeating these two steps. Nonresidential telephones and nonworking numbers are excluded during the interviewing process.[31]

But beyond the obvious advantages of cost and speed that the telephone survey provides, there remains the question of whether telephone surveys are an alternative to face-to-face interviewing. In the first major experiment designed to answer this question, William Klecka and Alfred Tuchfarber replicated a large, personal interviewing survey by means of a random digit dialing telephone survey.[32] The personal interview survey on crime victimization was conducted by the U.S. Bureau of the Census in 1974. The two samples were compared on demographic characteristic measures of crime victimization and attitudes toward crime and the police. The results were very similar, indicating that random digit dialing is an accurate and cost-effective alternative to the personal interview.

Aside from its relative accuracy, telephone interviewing tends to increase the quality of the data. In most cases, telephone interviewers are working from a central office, and their work can be monitored constantly by the supervisory staff. This helps assure that the questions are being asked correctly and that problems can be identified immediately and corrected.

However, the weaknesses of the method cannot be ignored. Telephone interviewing has created a new kind of nonresponse—the "broken off" interview. In about 4 percent of the calls, respondents terminate the interview before it is completed. This is a rare occurrence in personal interviews.[33] Telephone interviews also produce less information; in-

29. Ibid.

30. Ibid.

31. Ibid.

32. Ibid., pp. 105–114.

33. Institute for Social Research, University of Michigan, *Newsletter*, 4:4 (Autumn 1976).

terviewers cannot describe the respondents' characteristics or their environment in detail. Moreover, proportionately more telephone respondents indicate that they feel uneasy about discussing some topics, especially financial status and political attitudes, over the telephone.

In summary, telephone interviewing should be used as an alternative to personal interviewing under certain circumstances—especially when the interview schedule is relatively simple. However, the question of whether personal and telephone interviews are interchangeable remains to be answered. Surveys in the future may be conducted totally by telephone; others may combine telephone and personal interviews so that the two can complement each other and provide greater precision and increased response rate.

COMPARISON OF THREE SURVEY METHODS

In deciding which survey method is best suited for one's research, one has to evaluate which criteria are most significant to the research objective. For example, if a researcher plans a long interview with a representative sample of the general population and wishes to control for nonverbal behavior, and if sufficient funds are available, a form of a personal interview is preferable.[34] On the other hand, if the interview can be simplified, and when funds and speed are an issue, the telephone survey can be used to collect the information. When a rather lengthy questionnaire is to be used, or when it includes threatening or sensitive questions, and especially when the population to be investigated is rel-

TABLE 8.3.   Evaluation of Three Survey Methods

Criteria	Personal interview	Mail	Telephone
Cost	High	Low	Moderate
Response rate	High	Low	High
Control of interview situation	High	Low	Moderate
Applicability to geographically dispersed populations	Moderate	High	Moderate
Applicability to heterogeneous populations	High	Low	High
Obtaining detailed information	High	Moderate	Moderate
Speed	Low	Low	High

34. A sample is representative if the measurements made on its units produce results equivalent to those that would be obtained had the entire population been measured. See Chapter 16.

atively dispersed geographically (and/or when it is a selective population), the mail questionnaire can be considered as an alternative.

Table 8.3 presents some of the comparative advantages and limitations of the three methods of survey research.

CONCLUSION

The survey method is one of the most important data collection methods in the social sciences, and as such it is used extensively to collect information on numerous subjects of research. In recent years, with the public demands for government accountability, there has been an increased emphasis on survey instruments. There are indications that survey research is becoming a widely used tool of various government organizations. Studies of local governments indicate that 50 percent of cities with populations of over 100,000 and counties over 250,000 have used some form of survey. With the growth in the number of surveys conducted, there is also increased criticism of the method. The following comments are quite typical: "Getting things right in social science research is not easy." "The sample of potential respondents was a hodgepodge of various procedures." "I wouldn't trust any survey with a response rate like that." Although sometimes these remarks are justified, often they are not based on facts and are simply a "lip service" to the spirit of criticism. Yet there is no denying that we need a set of criteria that will help us evaluate the usefulness of surveys, detect and control errors in them, and perhaps compensate for these errors wherever possible.[35]

Four decades ago, Edward Deming wrote an article, now a classic, called "On Errors in Survey." In this article, Deming lists thirteen potential errors that should be considered when planning a survey as well as when evaluating its results. The most important factors that might become potential errors in surveys were discussed throughout this chapter: interviewer bias, low response rate, and the difficulty in asking sensitive questions. Reuben Cohen made the following remarks regarding these potential errors in his presidential address to the American Association for Public Opinion Research.

> Some 30 years ago, I was handed a reprint of W. Edward Deming's list of errors in surveys. The message was pretty obvious: Now that you know about them don't make them. With my relative inexperience, and my eternal optimism, I accepted the challenge. My first aproach was to try to do the perfect survey. I am still trying, but I should know better. I quickly discovered Murphy's Law—if any-

35. Gregory Daneke and Patricia Klobus Edwards, "Survey Research for Public Administrators," *Public Administration Review*, 39 (1979): 421–426.

thing can go wrong, it probably will. But I also discovered something else. Even without the time and budget constraints that most of us complain about, there are no perfect surveys. Every survey has its imperfections. The world is not ideally suited to our work. The best we can do is think through the ideal approach to a survey design, or implementation, or analysis problem—what we would do if we had our druthers—then get as close to the ideal as we can within the constraints of time and budget which govern much of our work.

And to those who might be discouraged for these less than perfect goals, we offer the following advice: "Practical work consists in good part of guessing what irregularities, where, and how much one can afford to tolerate. . . The same is true for survey research. It should be done well. It can and should conform well, even if not perfectly, to an ideal approach . . ."[36]

SUMMARY

In this chapter, we discussed the survey as a method of data collection. Three methods were described: the mail questionnaire, the face-to-face interview, and the telephone interview.

The mail questionnaire is regarded as an impersonal survey method. Its major advantages are: lower cost, reduction in biasing error, greater anonymity, and accessibility. Its disadvantages are a low response rate, no opportunity for probing, and the lack of control over who fills out the questionnaire.

The difficulty of securing an acceptable response rate to mail questionnaires calls for the use of various strategies that are known to affect the response rate. Among those, the most effective are the use of follow-up mailings, the sponsorship of the survey, and the appeal of the questionnaire. The questionnaire's format and the methods of mailing used will also affect the response rate.

The personal interview is a face-to-face interpersonal role situation in which an interviewer asks respondents questions designed to obtain answers pertinent to the research hypotheses. The most structured form of interview is the schedule-structured interview in which the questions, their wording, and their sequence are fixed and are identical for every respondent. The nonschedule-structured interview follows an interview guide specifying topics related to the research hypothesis and gives considerable liberty to the respondents to express their views. Finally, the nonscheduled interviews are the least structured form of interview-

---

36. Reuben Cohen, "Close Enough for All Practical Purposes," *Public Opinion Quarterly*, 43 (1979): 420–425.

ing in which no prespecified set of questions is employed. The interviewer has a great deal of freedom to probe various areas and to raise specific queries during the course of the interview.

The third survey method discussed in this chapter is telephone interviewing. This method has gained general acceptance during the last few years as a substitute for personal interviewing. The telephone survey is convenient and produces a significant cost saving. In addition, it sometimes results in a higher response rate than the personal interview. Furthermore, technological change and improvement in telephone equipment have also made telephone interviewing easier, especially using random digit dialing.

KEY TERMS FOR REVIEW

Mail questionnaire
Response rate
Follow-up
Schedule-structured
 interview

Nonscheduled
 interview
Probing
Random digit
 dialing

ADDITIONAL READINGS

Backstrom, Charles, and Gerald Hursh. *Survey Research*. Evanston, Ill.: Northwestern Univ. Press, 1963.

Banaka, William H. *Training in Depth Interviewing*. New York: Harper & Row, 1971.

Dexter, Lewis A. *Elites and Specialized Interviewing: Handbook of Research in Political Behavior*. Evanston, Ill.: Northwestern University Press, 1970.

Glock, Charles, ed. *Survey Research in the Social Sciences*. New York: Russell Sage Foundation, 1967.

Gorden, Raymond L. *Interviewing: Strategy, Techniques, and Tactics*. Homewood, Ill.: Dorsey, 1969.

Hyman, Herbert. *Survey Design and Analysis*. New York: Free Press, 1955.

Maccoby, Eleanor E., and Nathan Maccoby. "The Interview: A Tool of Social Science." In *Handbook of Social Psychology*, ed. by Gardner Lindzey. Reading, Mass.: Addison-Wesley, 1954.

McClosky, Herbert. *Political Inquiry: The Nature and Uses of Survey Research*. New York: Macmillan, 1969.

Oppenheim, N. A. *Questionnaire Design and Attitude Measurement*. New York: Basic Books, 1966.

Phillips, Derek L. *Knowledge from What? Theories and Methods in Social Research*. Chicago: Rand McNally, 1971.

Richardson, Stephen; Barbara S. Dohrenwend; and David Klein. *Interviewing: Its Forms and Functions*. New York: Basic Books, 1965.

Sonquist, John A., and William C. Dunkelberg. *Survey and Opinion Research: Procedures for Processing and Analysis*. Englewood Cliffs, N. J.: Prentice-Hall, 1977.

Weisberg, Herbert F., and Bruce D. Bowen. *An Introduction to Survey Research and Data Analysis*. San Francisco: Freeman, 1977.

CHAPTER PREVIEW

CHAPTER 9
Questionnaire Construction

INTRODUCTION

The last chapter focused on survey research as a method of data collection. In this chapter we discuss the questionnaire as the main instrument in survey research. We start by discussing the foundation of all questionnaires—the question. We then look at the content of questions and differentiate between open-ended, closed-ended, and contingency type questions. We follow by analyzing the format and sequence of questions. The next section introduces possible biases in the wording of questions. In this context we discuss leading, double-barreled, and threatening questions. Finally, in the last two sections, the cover letter accompanying the questionnaire and the instructions included in it are described.

THE QUESTION

The foundation of all questionnaires is the question. The questionnaire must translate the research objectives into specific questions; answers to such questions will provide the data for hypothesis testing. The question must also motivate the respondent so that the necessary information is obtained. It is to these two ends that the question becomes the focus around which the questionnaire is constructed. The major considerations involved in formulating the question are its content, structure, format, and sequence. These issues are examined in the following sections.

CONTENT OF QUESTIONS

Survey questions may be concerned with facts, opinions, attitudes, respondents' motivation, and their level of familiarity with a certain subject. Most questions, however, can be classified into the two general categories of (1) factual questions or (2) opinion and attitude questions.

Factual Questions

Factual questions are designed to elicit objective information from the respondents regarding their background, their environment, their habits, and the like. The most common type of a factual question is the background question, which is asked mainly to provide information by which respondents can be classified, such as sex, age, marital status, education, or income. Such classifications, in turn, may aid in explaining differences in behaviors and attitudes. The following is an example of such a question:

"What was the last grade you completed in school?" (please check one)

_____ 0 to 8 years
_____ 1 to 2 years high school
_____ 3 to 4 years high school: high school graduate __ Yes __ No
_____ 1 to 2 years college
_____ 3 to 4 years college: college graduate __ Yes __ No
_____ 5 or more years college

Other kinds of factual questions are intended to provide information on the respondents' social environment ("Will you please tell me who are the people living in your household?"), their means of transportation ("How do you generally get to work?"), or their leisure activities ("How often do you go to the movies?").[1]

Factual questions are thought to be easier to design than other types of questions. However, even factual questions can present the researcher with problems. Oppenheim refers to several examples of the kind of difficulties that are likely to occur with factual questions.[2] In a housing survey many respondents reported fewer bedrooms than their houses actually contained, simply because they did not think of a den, a playroom, or a guest room as "bedrooms" in the sense intended by the question. Similarly, in a market survey concerning drinking habits, many failed to mention "instant" coffee because they did not consider it as "coffee." These two examples point to a possibly different frame of reference between the investigator and the respondents. A clear definition of what is meant by the concept is always required to avoid this.

1. For examples of other types of factual questions, see C. A. Moser and G. Kalton, *Survey Methods in Social Investigation* (London: Heinemann Educational Books, 1971), pp. 312–314.

2. N. A. Oppenheim, *Questionnaire Design and Attitude Measurement* (New York: Basic Books, 1966), p. 55.

Opinion Questions

The concept "attitude" refers to the sum total of a person's inclinations, prejudices, ideas, fears, and convictions about any specific topic.[3] Opinions, on the other hand, are the verbal expression of attitudes.[4] Thus, a statement such as "The United States should fight communism in the Middle East" would reflect an opinion that is against communism, but an *attitude* about communism would mean a more general orientation of what a person feels and thinks about communism.

An attitude can lead to a tendency to act or react in a certain manner when confronted with certain stimuli. The individual's attitudes are expressed, in speech or behavior, only when the object of the attitude is perceived. A person may have strong attitudes for or against communism, but these are aroused and conveyed only when that person encounters some issue connected with Communists or when he or she is confronted with a stimulus such as a question in an interview.

Attitudes can be described by their content (what the attitude is about), by their direction (positive, neutral, or negative feelings about the object or issue in question), and by their intensity (an attitude may be held with greater or lesser vehemence). To one person, communism may be but of passing interest; to another, it may be of great significance and lead that person to join anti-Communist organizations. One would expect the latter to agree or disagree more strongly than would the former to questions dealing with, say, trade with the Soviet Union.

In general, we are interested in measuring attitudes because they account for the respondent's general inclination. The study of opinion is of interest only in so far as it is a symbol of an attitude. The main difference between asking for opinions and measuring attitudes is that an opinion is generally measured by estimating what proportion of the surveyed population say they agree with a single opinion statement. Attitudes are measured by attitude scales consisting of five to two dozen or more attitude statements, with which the respondent is asked to agree or disagree. An essential requirement of attitude measurement is that such attitude statements be scaled; that is, that the statements be selected and put together from a much larger number of attitude statements according to certain techniques. These techniques, called attitude scaling, will be discussed in Chapter 15.

Survey questions about opinions and attitudes present more problems in construction than questions about facts. It is relatively simple to obtain accurate information on, for example, whether or not a person

3. L. L. Thurstone, "Attitudes Can Be Measured," *American Journal of Sociology*, 33 (January 1928): 529–554.

4. Ibid.

is married or single. One may reasonably assume that the respondent knows whether he or she is married or not. With opinions or attitudes, the assumption that the respondents know cannot always be made. For example, respondents may not have an attitude towards communism, or if they do, it might be largely latent.[5] Moreover, given that many attitudes have various aspects or dimensions, the respondent may *agree* with one aspect and disagree with another. This is why attitudes cannot be measured by a single question. For example, if a respondent strongly disagrees with the statement "Trade with the Soviet Union should be encouraged," this does not imply a broad anti-Communist attitude. This person's disagreement may be due to personal circumstances; for instance, the person may think that trade with the Soviet Union would harm his or her business. By using several attitude statements, one can reduce the effects of one-sided responses.

Finally, answers to opinion and attitude questions are more sensitive to changes in wording, emphasis, and sequence than are those to factual questions. This reflects, in part, the multidimensionality of many attitudes. Questions presented in different ways sometimes reflect different aspects of the attitude and thus result in different answers.

TYPES OF QUESTIONS

The content of the question is only one important aspect in the construction of survey questionnaires. The researcher must also consider the structure of the question and the format of the response categories accompanying the questions. Three types of question structures can be distinguished and will be discussed in the following sections: (1) open-ended questions, (2) closed-ended questions, and (3) contingency questions.

Open-Ended and Closed-Ended Questions

Questions in a questionnaire can be either open-ended or closed-ended. In a closed-ended question, respondents are offered a set of answers from which they are asked to choose the one that most closely represents their views. For example, to measure political conservatism in the United States, Angus Campbell and coauthors used, among other questions, the following closed-ended question:[6]

5. See Moser and Kalton, *Survey Methods in Social Investigation*, p. 317.

6. Angus Campbell, Philip E. Converse, Warren E. Miller, and Donald E. Stokes, *The American Voter* (New York: Wiley, 1960).

"All groups can live in harmony in this country without changing the system in any way."

_____ Strongly agree   __ Disagree

_____ Agree   __ Strongly disagree

Agreement with the question indicated conservatism.

Answers to closed-ended questions can be more elaborate. To measure group cohesiveness, Stanley Seashore[7] asked,

"Do you feel that you are really part of your work group?"

_____ Really a part of my work group

_____ Included in most ways

_____ Included in some ways, but not in others

_____ Don't feel I really belong

_____ Don't work with any one group of people

_____ Not ascertained

Closed-ended questions are easy to ask and quick to be answered; they require no writing by either respondent or interviewer, and their analysis is straightforward. Their major drawback is that they may introduce bias, either by forcing the respondent to choose from given alternatives or by making the respondent select alternatives that might not have otherwise occurred.

Open-ended questions are not followed by any kind of specified choice, and the respondents' answers are recorded in full. For instance, the question "What do you personally feel are the most important problems the government in Washington should try to take care of?" is an open-ended question used frequently in questionnaires designed to study public opinion. The virtue of the open-ended question is that it does not force the respondent to adapt to preconceived answers: having understood the intent of the question, one can express one's thoughts freely, spontaneously, and in one's own language. If the answers to open-ended questions are unclear, the interviewer may probe, that is, ask the respondent to explain further or to give a rationale for something stated earlier. Open-ended questions, then, are flexible: they have possibilities of depth, they enable the interviewer to clear up misunderstandings, and they encourage rapport. However, open-ended questions are difficult to answer and still more difficult to analyze. The researcher has to design a coding frame in order to classify the various answers; in this process, the details of the information provided by the respondent might get lost (see Chapter 11).

7. Stanley E. Seashore, *Group Cohesiveness in the Industrial Work Group* (Ann Arbor: Survey Research Center, Institute of Social Research, University of Michigan), 1954.

The appropriateness of either open-ended or closed-ended questions depends upon a number of factors. Some years ago, Paul Lazarsfeld suggested the use of the following considerations to determine appropriateness:[8]

1. *The objectives of the questionnaire.* Closed-ended questions are suitable when the researcher's objective is to lead the respondent to express agreement or disagreement with an explicit point of view. When the researcher wishes to learn about the process by which the respondent arrived at a particular point of view, an open-ended question is likely to be more appropriate.

2. *The respondent's level of information about the topic in question.* Open-ended questions provide opportunities for the interviewer to ascertain lack of information on the part of the respondent, whereas closed-ended questions do not. Obviously, it is futile to raise questions that are beyond the experiences of respondents.

3. *The extent to which the topic has been thought through by the respondent.* The open-ended question is preferable in situations where the respondents have not yet crystallized their opinions. The use of a closed-ended question in such situations involves a risk that in accepting one of the alternatives offered, the respondent may make a choice that is quite different from an opinion that would have otherwise been expressed had he or she gone through the process of recall and evaluation of past experience.

4. *The ease with which the content of the answer can be communicated by the respondent or the extent to which the respondent is motivated to communicate on the topic.* The closed-ended question requires less motivation to communicate on the part of the respondent, and the response itself is usually less revealing to the respondent (and hence less threatening) than in the case of the open-ended question. The researcher who uses closed-ended questions tends to encounter less frequent refusals to respond.

Sometimes there may be good reasons for asking the same question in both open-ended and closed-ended form. For example, an open-ended answer to the question "Who rules America?" will provide a clear idea of the respondent's perception of the political system and the significance that the person attaches to different power groups. Although this datum is most valuable, it might not allow comparison of one group of respondents with another. Furthermore, one cannot be sure that all information of importance to the respondent has been mentioned; factors such as the inability to articulate thoughts or a momentary lapse of mem-

---

8. Paul F. Lazarsfeld, "The Controversy over Detailed Interviews—An Offer for Negotiation," *Public Opinion Quarterly*, 8 (1944): 38–60.

ory may cause omission of significant points. Therefore, the researcher can ask the same question again, later in the interview, but this time in closed-ended form.

Contingency Questions

Frequently questions that are relevant to some respondents may be irrelevant to others. For example, the question "Check the most important reasons why you are not going to college" obviously applies only to those high school students who are planning to go to college at all. It is often necessary to include questions that might apply only to some respondents and not to others. Some questions may be relevant only to females and not to males; others will only apply to respondents who are self-employed, and so on.

A *contingency question*—a special case of a closed-ended question—is one that applies only to a subgroup of respondents. The relevance of the question to this subgroup is determined by the answer of all respondents to a preceding *filter* question. For example, in a news media survey the filter question might read, "Do you regularly follow the news in the papers?" The contingency question could be, "What recent event do you remember reading about? (Give a brief description.)" The relevance of the second question to the respondent is contingent upon his or her response to the filter question. Only respondents who responded "Yes" to the filter question will find the contingency question relevant. Therefore, the response categories of the filter questions will be 1. Yes (answer the following question); 2. No (skip to question 3).

The formats for filter and contingency questions vary. One alternative, as in the preceding example, is to write directions next to each response category of the filter question. Another common format is to use arrows to direct the respondent either to skip to another question or to answer the contingency question, as in the following example:

"Is this the first full-time job you have held since you graduated from college?"
1. Yes
2. No ⌐

What happened to the job you had before— were you promoted, laid-off, or what? (Check one.)
1. Company folded.
2. Laid off or fired.
3. Job stopped; work was seasonal.
4. Voluntarily quit.
5. Promoted; relocated.
6. Other.

Another format is to box the contingency question and to set it apart from the ordinary questions to be answered by everybody. An example of such a format, taken out of a questionnaire used in a study of high school social climate is shown in Box 9.1.[9]

BOX 9.1.

ANSWER QUESTIONS BELOW IF YOU ARE A SENIOR PLANNING TO GO TO COLLEGE NEXT FALL. NONSENIORS SKIP TO QUESTION 144.

137. Did you take the College Entrance Board Exams?
    ____ yes
    ____ no

138. Do you definitely know yet which college you will attend?
    ____ yes
    ____ no

139. If "yes," how does this school compare to the others you were considering, in each of the following ways?

  1. ☐ 2. ☐ 3. ☐ 4. ☐ Offering the course of study you want.
  1. ☐ 2. ☐ 3. ☐ 4. ☐ General reputation of the school.

SKIP TO QUESTION 151 ON THE NEXT PAGE.

When there are several subgroups to which the questionnaire is addressed and when several contingency questions apply to each subgroup, it is useful to indicate by number which questions the respondent should answer. The instructions are written next to the appropriate response categories in the filter question. This is demonstrated in the following example.

Are you looking for another job at this time?

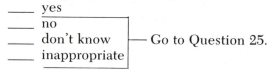

    ____ yes
    ____ no
    ____ don't know — Go to Question 25.
    ____ inappropriate

---

9. James S. Coleman, *The Adolescent Society*, Appendix X, "Spring Students' Questionnaire" (New York: Free Press, 1961), p. 6.

QUESTION FORMAT

In this section we will discuss some of the common techniques of structuring the response categories of closed-ended questions. The general format is to present all possible answers and have the respondent check the appropriate categories. The respondent can either circle his or her answer or check a box or a blank as in the following examples:

"What is your marital status?"

Married	☐ Married	1. Married
Single	☐ Single	2. Single
Divorced	☐ Divorced	3. Divorced
Widowed	☐ Widowed	4. Widowed

Of course, specific directions should be provided as to whether the respondent is to circle a number or check a blank or a box. Among these three methods the least recommended is the blank method because often the respondent will check between the blanks and it will be difficult to tell which category was intended. The method of circling a code number is preferable to the box method because the circled code number can later be punched on cards, and this facilitates the data processing (see, Chapter 11).

Rating

One of the most common formats for questions asked in social science surveys is the rating scale. The rating scale is used whenever respondents are asked to make a judgment in terms of sets of ordered categories, such as "strongly agree," "favorable," or "very often." For example:

"Police should be allowed to conduct a full search of any motorist arrested for an offense such as speeding."
1. Agree strongly
2. Agree
3. Disagree
4. Disagree strongly
5. No opinion

The response categories of such questions are termed "quantifiers"; they reflect the *intensity* of the particular judgment involved. The following sets of response categories are quite common:

1. Strongly agree	1. Too little	1. More
2. Agree	2. About right	2. Same
3. Depends	3. Too much	3. Less
4. Disagree		
5. Strongly disagree		

The numerical codes that accompany these categories are usually interpreted to represent the intensity of the response categories, so that the higher the number, the more intense the response. Yet it should be emphasized that though we assume that the quantifiers involved are ordered by their intensity, it does not imply that the distance between them is equal. Indeed rating scales such as these are most often measured on ordinal levels of measurement, as discussed in Chapter 6.

Despite the difficulty in estimating intensities, we cannot typically ask respondents for exact estimates because most would have a great deal of difficulty with the task. Although it would seem relatively easy to report how many hours in the past week a person watched television, most people have greater difficulty in estimating precisely events of relatively low salience, such as attitudes about foreign policy.[10]

Matrix Questions

The matrix question is a method for organizing a large set of rating questions that have the same response categories. The following is an example of such a device.

Which of the following statements do you (1) strongly agree to, (2) agree with, (3) find that it depends, (4) disagree with, or (5) strongly disagree with:

	Strongly Agree	Agree	Depends	Disagree	Strongly Disagree
My vote gives me all the power I want in governmental affairs	( )	( )	( )	( )	( )
If I complained to a city agency, they would fix up whatever was wrong	( )	( )	( )	( )	( )
I've sometimes wished that government officials paid more attention to what I thought	( )	( )	( )	( )	( )

10. Norman Bradburn and Seymour Sudman, *Improving Interview Method and Questionnaire Design* (San Francisco: Jossey-Bass, 1974), pp. 152–162.

The Card Sort

Another way to measure intensities of judgments is the *card sort*, where the respondent is handed a set of cards with a statement on each card and is asked to sort them into one of seven boxes, depending on his or her degree of agreement with the statement. The following is an example of such a device:

How strongly do you agree or disagree with the following statement: People who are capable of working but don't are a drain on society.

Strongly
Agree

Strongly
Disagree

$+ + +$ $+ +$ $+$ $+ -$ $-$ $- -$ $- - -$

The Semantic Differential

The semantic differential is another type of a rating scale. It measures the respondent's reaction to some object or concept in terms of rating on bipolar scales defined with contrasting adjectives at each end:[11]

$$\text{Good} \; \underline{} \; \underline{} \; \underline{} \; \underline{} \; \underline{} \; \underline{} \; \underline{} \; \text{Bad}$$
$$\quad\quad\quad 3 \quad 2 \quad 1 \quad 0 \quad 1 \quad 2 \quad 3$$

The "0" marks the *neutral position* on the scale, and the positions 1–3 measure the intensities in either direction, with 1 being the slightest reaction and 3 the most intense.

An example of an application of the semantic differential is presented as follows:[12]

Here is a list of pairs of words you might use to describe civil servants. Between each pair is a measuring stick of seven lines. Taking the first pair of words—i.e., "good/bad"—as an example, the line on the extreme left would mean that the civil servant is very good, the next line would mean he or she is fairly good, and so on. The words at the top of your card will help you choose the line you think is appropriate.

---

11. David R. Heise, "The Semantic Differential and Attitude Research," in *Attitude Measurement*, ed. by Gene F. Summers (Chicago: Rand McNally, 1970), pp. 235–253.

12. David Nachmias and David H. Rosenbloom, *Bureaucratic Culture: Citizens and Administrators in Israel* (New York: St. Martin's, 1978), pp. 110–115.

Now will you tell me which line you would use to describe civil servants?

	Very	Fairly	Slightly	Neither	Slightly	Fairly	Very	
Good	_:	_:	_:	_:	_:	_:	_:	Bad
Honest	_:	_:	_:	_:	_:	_:	_:	Dishonest
Efficient	_:	_:	_:	_:	_:	_:	_:	Inefficient
Deep	_:	_:	_:	_:	_:	_:	_:	Shallow
Active	_:	_:	_:	_:	_:	_:	_:	Passive

Ranking

Ranking is used in questionnaires whenever we want to obtain information regarding the degree of importance or the set priorities that people give to a set of attitudes or objects. For instance, in a survey on the quality of life respondents were asked to rank order various dimensions they consider important in life.

"I would like you to tell me what you have found important in life. Would you please look at this card and tell me which of these is most important to *you* as a goal in *your* life, which comes next in importance, which is third, and so forth?"

A prosperous life (having a good income and being able to afford the "good" things in life)
    1st rank
    2nd rank
    3rd rank
    4th rank
A family life (a life completely centered on my family)
    1st rank
    2nd rank
    3rd rank
    4th rank
An important life (a life of achievement that brings me respect and recognition)
    1st rank
    2nd rank
    3rd rank
    4th rank
A secure life (making certain that all basic needs and expenses are provided)
    1st rank
    2nd rank
    3rd rank
    4th rank

Ranking is a useful device in providing some sense of relative order among objects or judgments. This is particularly important given that many properties measured in the social science (for example, "quality of life," "status") cannot be given any precise numerical value. However, with the use of ranking we can at least obtain information regarding their relative order. It should be emphasized, however, that ranking does not provide any information about the distance between the ranks. The difference between, say, rank 1 and rank 2 may not be the same as the difference between rank 2 and rank 3.

SEQUENCE OF QUESTIONS

After the format of questions is determined, consideration should be given to the order in which they are placed in the questionnaire. Two general patterns of question sequence have been found to be most appropriate for motivating respondents to cooperate: the *funnel sequence* and the *inverted funnel sequence.*

The Funnel Sequence

In the funnel sequence, each successive question is related to the previous question and has a progressively narrower scope. For example, if one were interested in finding out how respondents' views of political, economic, and social problems are related to the newspapers they read, one might want to know what sorts of things the respondents think of as problems, what the perceived relative significance of each problem is, how much information they have on the topic, what their sources of information are, and whether certain newspapers have influenced their thinking on the problem. The following questions form a funnel sequence: (1) "What do you think are some of the most important problems facing the nation?" (2) "Of all the problems you have just mentioned, which do you think is the most important one?" (3) "Where have you obtained most of the information about this problem?" (4) "Do you read the *Washington Post?*"

When the objective of the survey is to obtain detailed information and when the respondent is motivated to supply the information, the funnel approach helps the respondent recall details more efficiently. Furthermore, by asking the broadest questions first, the interviewer can avoid imposing a frame of reference before obtaining the respondent's perspective. When the objective of the survey is to discover unanticipated responses, broader questions should be pursued first.[13]

---

13. Raymond L. Gorden, *Interviewing: Strategy, Techniques and Tactics* (Homewood, Ill.: Dorsey, 1969).

The Inverted Funnel Sequence

In the inverted funnel sequence, narrower questions are followed by broader ones. When the topic of the survey does not strongly motivate the respondents to communicate—either because the topic is not important to them or because their experiences are not recent enough to be vivid in their memory—it may be helpful to begin with the narrow questions, which are easier to answer, and reserve the broader (and more difficult) ones until later. If the purpose is to obtain a generalization in the form of a judgment regarding a concrete situation and if the interviewer is unfamiliar with the facts but the respondent knows them, then narrower questions aimed at establishing specific facts should precede questions requiring an overall judgment.[14]

In the following example, an attempt was made to obtain the respondents' judgment regarding the effectiveness of rescue operations during a disaster. To help people make an unbiased judgment, the researcher felt that it was better to deal with the specifics first, later asking for the generalization.[15]

1. How many people were killed in the tornado?
2. How many do you suppose were injured so seriously that they had to go to the hospital?
3. How long was it before most of the injured got to the hospital?
4. Did you see anyone administer first aid by giving artificial respiration or stopping bleeding? Who was it?
5. In general, how well do you think the first aid and rescue operations were carried out?

The *order* in which the questions are presented has been shown to affect the degree to which the respondent is willing to cooperate with the researcher.[16] In addition, question order influences the reliability of the response. For example, there is evidence showing that the position of an item in a list has a significant impact on its being chosen, with items appearing first being endorsed more often.[17] It has been also shown that when respondents are asked to assign numerical values to a set of items (for example, according to their degree of importance), the items appearing first tend to receive a higher rank.

In the following question, respondents are more likely to assign the

14. Ibid., pp. 268–271.

15. Ibid., p. 270.

16. Moser and Kalton, *Survey Methods in Social Investigation*, p. 364.

17. William A. Belson, "The Effects of Reversing the Presentation Order on Verbal Rating Scales," *Journal of Advertising Research*, 6: 4 (1966): 30–37.

first rank to the first category than to the last one simply because it is listed first.

"Among the items below, what does it take to get to be important and looked up to by the other fellows here at school?" (Rank from 1 to 6.)
__ coming from the right family
__ leader in activities
__ having a nice car
__ high grades, honor roll
__ being an athletic star
__ being in the leading crowd

This problem may arise especially in situations where the questions are subjective statements like attitudes, which are not central or salient to the respondent. In such situations the item appearing first tends to form a point of reference for all items that follow. This problem can be overcome by acquainting respondents with the list of items before evaluations are to be made. Alternatively, the order of presentation could be randomized so that the order effects will be randomized, too, and will not result in any systematic bias.[18]

Finally, it should be pointed out that questions that are presented first in the questionnaire should put the respondent at ease; and if an interviewer is present, they should help in creating rapport between the interviewer and the respondent. Thus, the opening question should be easy to answer, preferably interesting, and not deal with sensitive issues. For example, questions about the respondent's drinking habit or sex life, if placed at the beginning, in all likelihood will increase the refusal rate. It is also recommended that open-ended questions be placed later, for they usually require more time and thought and thus may reduce the respondent's initial motivation to cooperate.

AVOIDING BIAS: PITFALLS IN QUESTIONNAIRE CONSTRUCTION

Wording of the Question

The question must be worded so that it is comprehended by the respondent. For example, the researcher's vocabulary might include a word such as *charismatic*, which would not be understood by the proverbial man in the street. If the respondents are individuals from all walks of life, then the interviewer's vocabulary should be understandable by

18. Edwin H. Carpenter and Larry G. Blackwood, "The Effects of Question Position on Responses to Attitudinal Questions," *Rural Sociology*, 44: 1 (1979): 56–72.

the average eighth-grader. Furthermore, words that are subject to a wide variety of interpretation should either be avoided or qualified by specifying their frame of reference. Asking whether one is a liberal might, according to one's interpretation of the term, refer to one's education, one's politics, one's profession, or one's sex life. On the other hand, a question such as "Do you consider yourself liberal? Politically, I mean," instructs the respondent to use the political frame of reference in answering the question. Questions should be worded so that the respondent understands the question and so that the question has one and the same meaning for each respondent unless the researcher desires to assess differentials in meaning.

Response Set

A response set is the tendency to answer all questions in a specific direction regardless of the questions' content.[19] This may be a problem when a set of questions is presented together with the same response format, as in the case of the matrix question and especially when the questions all refer to the same topic. For example, when a set of questions reflects a proabortion attitude, respondents who are against abortion may check all the right-hand response categories simply because they assume that these categories all express objection to abortion. A response set can be avoided by changing the question format, either by varying the response categories for each question or by avoiding the lumping together of questions refering to the same topic.

Leading Questions

The term *leading question* refers to a question phrased in such a manner that it appears to the respondent that the researcher expects a certain answer. A question designed to elicit general attitudes toward social protest might read, "How do you feel about student protest?" The same question phrased in a leading form might read, "You wouldn't say that you were in favor of student protest, would you?" A more subtle form of a leading question might be, "Would you say that you are not in favor of student protest?" This last question makes it easier for respondents to answer *yes* than *no*. In answering *yes*, they are agreeing with the language of the question and are not contradicting the interviewer.

The term *social desirability* refers to the tendency of respondents to agree with questions that support accepted norms or that are perceived as socially desirable. Questions that reflect a socially undesirable behavior or attitude are endorsed less frequently than those high on the

---

19. Kenneth D. Bailey, *Methods of Social Research* (New York: Free Press, 1978), p. 119.

scale of social desirability. For example, Derek Phillips reported that people's scores on a mental health test are directly related to their assessment of the desirability reflected in the items.[20]

Another kind of leading question makes use of words that have become emotionally loaded, either favorably or unfavorably. Terms such as *socialist* or *starvation* make respondents react not so much to the issue posed by the question as to the loaded phrase itself. Consider the following two questions: "The President has made several public statements advocating school integration. Do you think we should integrate our schools?" and "Socialists have always advocated school integration. Do you think we should integrate our schools?" These two questions are loaded, but in different directions; more respondents will tend to agree with the first.

Leading questions are to be avoided if one is looking for undistorted responses. Under certain circumstances, however, leading questions may serve the research objective. The question "Would you favor sending food overseas to feed the starving people of India?" was used to determine the number of people who were so strongly opposed to shipping food to other countries that they rejected the idea even within the strong emotional context of "starving people."[21]

Threatening Questions

Often it is necessary to include questions on topics that the respondent may find embarrassing and thus difficult to answer. These types of questions, denoted as *threatening questions*, are, according to Norman Bradburn and coauthors, "anxiety-arousing questions about, for example, behaviors that are illegal or contra-normative or about behaviors that, though not socially deviant, are not usually discussed in public without some tension."[22] Threatening questions may inquire, for example, about the respondents' gambling habits, about their drinking, whether or not they smoke marijuana or abuse their children, or about their sexual behavior.

There is considerable empirical evidence that threatening questions lead to response bias; that is, to denial of the behavior in question or to underreporting. In general, the reporting of certain behaviors decreases as questions increase in their degree of threat.[23] When presented with

20. Derek L. Phillips, *Knowledge From What?* (Chicago: Rand McNally, 1971), p. 87.

21. Robert I. Kahn and Charles F. Cannell, *The Dynamics of Interviewing* (New York: Wiley, 1957), p. 129.

22. Norman M. Bradburn, Seymour Sudman, Ed Blair, and Carol Stocking, "Question Threat and Response Bias," *Public Opinion Quarterly*, 42 (Summer 1978): 221–234.

23. Ibid.

a threatening question, respondents are caught in a conflict between the role demands of the "good respondent," who responds truthfully to all the questions, and the tendency to present oneself positively. The conflict is usually resolved, not by refusing to answer, but by reporting that one did not engage in that particular activity when one, in fact, did.[24]

As threatening questions may produce biased responses, it is important that researchers first identify whether or not certain questions are threatening. Norman Bradburn and Seymour Sudman suggest that the best method to determine the relative threat of questions is to ask respondents to rate question topics as to how uneasy they thought most people would feel in talking about them.[25] One could also ask about the respondent's own reactions to the questions or rate the degree of difficulty the topics caused in the interview.

Once it is determined which are threatening questions, what should we do about them? In a comprehensive study dealing with response effects to threatening questions in survey research, Bradburn and Sudman propose that the construction of questions makes a great deal of difference.[26] Perhaps the most significant finding in their study was the discovery that the amount of reporting behavior is considerably increased by using a long introduction to the question rather than asking short questions; by an open-ended rather than a closed-ended format; and, to a lesser extent, by letting the respondents pick their own words to talk about the sensitive topics. Their questionnaire contained an item about the number of times in the past year the respondent had become intoxicated. In the short closed form the item read: "In the past year, how often did you become intoxicated while drinking any kind of beverage?" Respondents were asked to classify their response into one of the following categories:

Never
Once a year or less
Every few months
Once a month
Every few weeks
Once a week
Several times a week
Daily

In the open-ended, long form, the respondents were first asked to provide their own word for intoxication: "Sometimes people drink a little

24. Ibid.

25. Bradburn and Sudman, *Improving Interview Methods and Questionnaire Design*, p. 165.

26. Ibid., pp. 14–25.

too much beer, wine, or whiskey so that they act different from usual. What word do you think we should use to describe people when they get that way, so that you will know what we mean and feel comfortable talking about it?" The intoxication item then read: "Occasionally people drink on an empty stomach or drink a little too much and become (respondent's word). In the past year, how often have you become (respondent's word) while drinking any kind of alcoholic beverage?" No response categories were provided for these questions.[27]

Double-Barreled Questions

Double-barreled questions include two or more questions in one. The following item, included in an opinion poll, during the 1979 Iranian crisis is an example:

> "The United States should reduce its dependence on foreign oil and stop selling grain to Iran."
> ____ Agree
> ____ Depends
> ____ Disagree
> ____ Strongly Disagree

The problem with such a question is that it might confuse respondents who agree with one aspect of the question—reducing dependence on foreign oil—but disagree with the other—selling grain to Iran. Many questions that include *and* are very likely doubled-barreled, as in the following statement:

> "The United States should take a harder line at the SALT negotiating table *and* bolster NATO forces in Europe."

> or

> "Would you say that most people are like you *and* can be trusted?"

Both statements include two separate questions that are identified by the use of *and*. Questions with *and* can be used, however, if the dimensions separated by *and* are mutually exclusive and the respondent is asked to select one or to rank them according to some criterion. For instance:

> "At the present time, the country is faced with two major problems—inflation and an energy shortage. Which of these two problems would you say is the most important?"
> 1. Inflation
> 2. Energy shortage

27. Ibid., p. 18.

COVER LETTER

After the questionnaire has been constructed, the next step is to write an introductory statement (for a personal telephone interview) or a cover letter (for a mail questionnaire) in order to explain the purpose of the survey to the respondents and to assure a high response rate. This is of particular importance in mail questionnaires, where the difficulty of securing a high response rate, especially when one needs to ask more than a few simple questions, is well documented (see Chapter 8).

A cover letter must succeed in overcoming any resistance or prejudice the respondent may have against the survey. As such it should (1) identify the sponsoring organization or the persons conducting the study, (2) explain the purpose of the study, (3) tell why it is important

BOX 9.2.

To Program Operators:

The Office of Manpower Planning, Department of Community Affairs, in conjunction with the State Manpower Services Council, has funded a special evaluation of public service employment projects authorized under Title VI of the Comprehensive Employment and Training Act. This evaluation is being conducted by Dr. M. L. Burnim in the Institute for Social Research at Florida State University. The purpose of the evaluation is to determine the impact of public service employment projects on unemployed persons in Florida and to measure the benefit of these projects to the communities in which they are conducted.

As you know, public service employment is a major part of the federal, state, and local strategy to overcome the employment and income problems of economically disadvantaged, unemployed people. There is no question that the program is needed throughout the country to create jobs and training opportunities for the large numbers of people who remain unemployed. You are probably also aware, however, that public service employment programs are quite controversial and their future may be in jeopardy. Part of the reason that these programs are so controversial is that no systemmatic evaluation of the benefits of these programs for the individuals employed and the communities served has been conducted.

Because this specific evaluation has significant national policy implication, I strongly urge you to assist the research team in compiling the necessary data. It is very important that you complete the survey questionnaire transmitted to you as soon as possible.

Thank you for your cooperation.

Sincerely,

Edward A. Feaver, Director
Office of Manpower Planning

BOX 9.3.

Dear Friend:

We are conducting a survey sponsored by the University of Wisconsin-Milwaukee and assisted by the American Civil Liberties Union (ACLU). Our purpose is to learn more about how people like yourself feel about certain aspects of civil liberties and how beliefs are related to behavior. You have been selected at random to participate in this survey—thus your opinions will represent the opinions of thousands of people much like yourself.

Enclosed find a copy of our questionnaire. While it is a bit lengthy and will require about 20 minutes to complete, we hope that you will take the time to complete it and return the questionnaire to us in the enclosed self-addressed envelope. The information you provide will contribute to an important study and may also be used to influence ACLU policy.

A bit about confidentiality. We promise you confidentiality under the academic ethics standards of the American Political Science Association. Your name will not be revealed or associated with your response nor will anyone outside of the project staff here at the University of Wisconsin-Milwaukee be allowed to see your response. Thus, while the ACLU may be interested in the policy implications of our study they will not be furnished with any information which in any way identifies you as an individual. Please note the number in the upper right-hand corner of the questionnaire. This number allows us to temporarily identify you. By referring to this number we will know that you responded to the questionnaire and will not send you the follow-up mailing we will have to send to nonrespondents.

We appreciate your willingness to help us in our research effort. If you would like a copy of our completed study please indicate this on the last page of the questionnaire. We will make certain that you receive a copy of our results. We believe that you will find the questionnaire both interesting and provocative and look forward to receiving your reply.

Sincerely yours,

Richard D. Bingham   James L. Gibson
Associate Professor   Assistant Professor

Enclosures   NOTE: If by some chance you recently received
                         and responded to this questionnaire please
                         return the blank questionnaire to us indicating
                         "duplicate" on the first page.

that the respondent answer the questionnaire, and (4) assure the respondent that the information provided by him or her will be held in strict confidence.

In general, the cover letter for a mail questionnaire needs to be more detailed than the introductory statement in a personal interview. In an interview, the interviewer is always there to explain or persuade the respondent should that become necessary. With a mail questionnaire, the cover letter is all there is, and thus its function is very significant.

Two examples of cover letters used in various mail surveys are shown here. The first, reported in Box 9.2 on p. 228, was used in a mail questionnaire designed and conducted by the Institute of Social Research in Florida State University under the auspices of the State Department of Manpower Planning of Florida to evaluate the Public Service Employment and Training Act, Title VI (CETA).[28]

The second example, reported in Box 9.3, on p. 229, is taken from a study on commitment to civil liberties, conducted by investigators at the University of Wisconsin-Milwaukee.[29] The letter emphasizes the confidentiality of the study and explains in detail how the individual responses will be used (see Box 9.3).

Finally, an important issue is the style used in the cover letter, that is, whether it is a formal or a semipersonal letter. In the two examples given, a form letter was sent out to all respondents included in the sample. Alternatively, rather than addressing the letter to "Dear Friend" or "Dear Respondent," the addressee's address is individually typed at the top of the letter, which also contains an individually typed personalized salutation and is individually signed by the investigator. It has been shown that the semipersonal letter generated a slightly higher response rate than the form letter.[30]

INSTRUCTIONS

Another element to be considered when constructing a questionnaire is the instructions that go with each question or with a set of questions. Instructions should be included with questions that are not self-explanatory; they may range from very simple ones such as "circle the appro-

28. Mickey L. Burnim, *An Evaluation of the Public Service Employment Projects in Florida Created Under Title VI of the Comprehensive Employment and Training Act of 1973* (Tallahassee, Fla.: Florida State University, 1978), p. 164.

29. Richard D. Bingham and James L. Gibson, "Conditions of Commitment to Civil Liberties," Dept. of Political Science, Univ. of Wisconsin, Milwaukee (1979), unpublished.

30. Michael T. Matteson, "Type of Transmittal Letter and Questionnaire Color as Two Variables Influencing Response Rates in a Mail Survey," *Journal of Applied Psychology*, 59 (August 1974): 532–536.

priate category" to more complex instructions that explain how to rank order a set of priorities. When the questionnaire is administered by an interviewer, the instructions are usually written for the interviewer and thus are often short and concise, instructing the interviewer what to do when the respondent provides a certain answer, when to probe for a more detailed answer, or how to clarify a certain question. The following is an example of instructions written for the interviewer:

> Who was your employer on your last job?
> (PROBE FOR CORRECT CATEGORY)
> > Private
> > City
> > County
> > State
> > Federal
> > Self-employed
> > Public, Nonprofit
> > Other _____ (specify)
> > DK

While in an interview study the interviewer is available to answer any questions that may be raised by the respondent, this is not the case with mail questionnaires. There, any questions that remain vague or unclear are likely to result in no response or incorrect answers. Therefore, providing clear instructions is extremely important. The type of instructions vary from general ones introducing the questionnaire or its subsections to specific ones preceding individual questions.

The following is an example of general instructions given at the beginning of a questionnaire on attitudes towards civil liberties:[31]

INSTRUCTIONS: For each of the following questions please mark the answer that comes closest to the way you feel about the issue. There are no "right" or "wrong" answers—please answer the questions as honestly as possible. Answer each of the questions in the order in which it appears. If you wish to make additional comments on any of the specific questions or on the issues in general, use the space at the end of the questionnaire. Your opinions are extremely important for understanding these complex civil liberty issues—we greatly appreciate your cooperation!

The next example, from the same questionnaire, introduces a subsection, presented in a matrix format:

As you know, there are many groups in America that try to get the government or the American people to see things more their way. We

---

31. Bingham and Gibson, "Conditions of Commitment to Civil Liberties."

would like to get your opinions toward what you perceive to be the aims, objectives, or ideas advocated by these groups. In particular, we would like your opinion on how significant the change in the American system of government would be if the ideas of the group were put into practice. Please rate each of the following groups in terms of the nature of the change in our system of government that would follow the implementation of their ideas.

Check only one answer in each column

	Communists	Nazis	Ku Klux Klan
The ideas, if implemented, would create a totally different and much worse system of government	☐	☐	☐
The ideas, if implemented, would significantly change our system of government for the worse	☐	☐	☐
I oppose the ideas, but they would not change our system of government if they were implemented	☐	☐	☐
I support the ideas, but they would not change our system of government if they were implemented	☐	☐	☐
The ideas, if implemented, would significantly change our system of government for the better	☐	☐	☐
The ideas, if implemented, would create a totally different and much better system of government	☐	☐	☐
No Opinion	☐	☐	☐

Finally, the last example is of a specific instruction in replying to a single question.

About how many states have you lived in during your life? (Count only those states that you lived in for at least one year.)

CONSTRUCTING A QUESTIONNAIRE: A CASE STUDY

There are many stages involved in the construction of a questionnaire, beginning with the research problem and going through the process of formulating the questions and considering the format and the type of questions to be used. To illustrate these, we have included in this section a complete questionnaire used in an actual study conducted in 1968 by the Institute for Social Research at the University of Michigan.[32]

The study's objective was to explore the attitudes and perceptions related to urban problems and race relations in fifteen northern cities in the United States. It sought to define the social and psychological characteristics as well as the aspirations of the black and white urban populations. A black sample and a white sample were selected in each of the fifteen cities in the study. Approximately 175 black and 175 white respondents were interviewed in each city. In addition, 366 whites were interviewed in two suburban areas. Altogether, 2,809 black respondents and 2,950 white respondents were interviewed. Individuals interviewed were between the ages of sixteen and sixty-nine and lived in private households.

The study used two questionnaire forms—one for whites and one for blacks. Questions about background characteristics were almost identical in the two forms. The attitudinal questions were also identical in both interview forms, but there was a greater number of questions addressed exclusively to one racial group or to the other. The questionnaires contained attitudinal questions probing the respondent's satisfaction with neighborhood services, their feelings about the effectiveness of the government in dealing with urban problems, the respondents' interracial relationships, their attitude toward integration, and their perception of the hostility between the races. Following in Box 9.4 is a shortened version of the original questionnaire addressed to blacks.

You will notice that the questionnaire starts off with identification numbers for the person being interviewed as well as his or her location. There is also room to provide information on when the interviewer began. Question 1 is an example of an attitude question on degree of satisfaction with services provided by the city. The question was put in a matrix format. Note also that instructions are provided both for the interviewer (Code A below and ask B through E) and the respondent.

Question 2 has a closed-ended and open-ended component (A). Item A is also a contingency question. Questions 3, 5, 6, and 7 are also examples of contingency type questions. The first part is the filter question, and the second is the contingency question, which applies only to those who have checked specific categories in the first part. All questions use a numerical code, which is checked off by the interviewer.

Finally, the last section of the questionnaire is an example of the relative advantage of an interview over other modes of filling out questionnaires (mail, telephone). The interviewer can provide detailed information on the general appearance and attitude of the respondents, which can help in interpreting their response pattern.

32. Angus Campbell and Howard Schuman, *Racial Attitudes in Fifteen American Cities* (Ann Arbor, Mich.: Social Science Archive, 1973).

Box 9.4 Urban Problems Study, January, 1968

```
TIME INTERVIEW
BEGAN:_____AM
              PM
```

City Number ☐☐ v. 3

Segment Number ☐☐☐ v. 9

DULS Line Number ☐☐☐☐ v. 10

Person Number ☐ v. 19

FOR OFFICE USE ONLY

☐☐☐☐☐ v. 2

1. First, I'd like to ask how satisfied you are with some of the main services the city is supposed to provide for your neighborhood. What about the quality of public schools in this neighborhood—are you generally satisfied, somewhat dissatisfied, or very dissatisfied?

(CODE A BELOW, AND ASK B THROUGH E)

	Generally satisfied	Somewhat dissatisfied	Very dissatisfied	Don't know
A. Quality of public schools	1	2	3	8
B. Parks and playgrounds for children in this neighborhood	1	2	3	8
C. Sports and recreation centers for teenagers in this neighborhood	1	2	3	8
D. Police protection in this neighborhood	1	2	3	8
E. Garbage collection in this neighborhood	1	2	3	8

2. Thinking about city services like schools, parks, and garbage collection, do you think your neighborhood gets better, about the same, or worse services than most other parts of the city?

Better ....(ASK A)... 1
About same 2
Worse .... (ASK A)... 3
Don't know 8

A. IF BETTER OR WORSE: What is the reason this neighborhood gets (better/worse) services?

3. If you have a serious complaint about poor service by the city, do you think you can get city officials to do something about it if you call them?

RECODED VALUES

Yes.............(ASK A).... 1
No.............(ASK A).... 5
Don't know .. (ASK A) ... 8

A. Have you ever called a city official with a complaint about poor service?

Yes...........1
No 5

4. In general, do you think (CITY) city officials pay more, less, or the same attention to a request or complaint from a Negro as from a white person?

More 1   1
Less 2   3
Same 3   2
Don't know 8   8

Now let's talk about the problems of (CITY) as a whole.

5. Do you think the Mayor of (CITY) is trying as hard as he can to solve the main problems of the city, or that he is not doing all he could to solve these problems?

Trying as hard as he can 1
Not doing all he coud (ASK A)......X
Don't know 8

A. IF NOT DOING ALL HE COULD: Do you think he is trying fairly hard to solve these problems, or not hard at all?

Fairly hard 2
Not hard at all 3

6. How about the state government? Do you think they are trying as hard as they can to solve the main problems of cities like (CITY), or that they are not doing all they could to solve these problems?

Trying as hard as they can 1
Not doing all they could (ASK A) .. X
Don't know 8

A. IF NOT DOING ALL THEY COULD: Do you think they are trying fairly hard to solve these problems, or not hard at all?

Fairly hard 2
Not hard at all 3

7. How about the federal government in Washington? Do you think they are trying as hard as they can to solve the main problems of cities like (CITY), or that they are not doing all they could to solve such problems?

Trying as hard as they can 1
Not doing all they could (ASK A) .. X
Don't know 8

A. IF NOT DOING ALL THEY COULD: Do you think they are trying fairly hard to solve these problems, or not hard at all?

Fairly hard 2
Not hard at all 3

8. A Negro has been elected Mayor of Cleveland and also of Gary, Indiana. What effect to you think this will have on solving city problems in Cleveland and Gary? Do you think it will make things better, worse, or won't there be much change?

Better 1
Worse 2
Not much change 3
Don't know .... (ASK A) 8

A. IF DON'T KNOW: What would you guess the effect would be—to make things better, worse, or won't there be much change?

Better 1
Worse 2
Not much change 3

9. Have you heard about federal antipoverty programs such as Head Start, the Job Corps, Community Action Centers, and others?

Yes, heard of one or more (ASK A & B)....1
No..5

IF YES, HEARD OF ONE OR MORE:

A. In general, do you think the antipoverty program is doing a good job, a fair job, or a poor job? Why would you say the antipoverty program is doing a (good/fair/poor) job?

Good job..............1
Fair....................2
Poor...................3
Don't know...........8

B. Has anyone in your family taken part in any of these programs in any way?

Yes (ASK C)...........1
No.....................5

C. IF YES TO B: What program(s) and in what way?

Name of Program(s)	Kind of Participation
_____	_____
_____	_____
_____	_____

Now I want to talk about some complaints people have made about the (CITY) police.

10. First, some people say the police don't come quickly when you call them for help. Do you think this happens to people in this neighborhood?

Yes.......(ASK A)...............1
No........(GO TO Q. 11)........5
Don't know .... (ASK A)........8

A. IF YES OR DON'T KNOW: Has it ever happened to you?

Yes.......(ASK B & C)...........1
No........(ASK C).................5

B. IF YES TO A: How long ago was that (the last time)?

_____ years ago

C. IF YES OR NO TO A: Has it happened to anyone you know?

Yes...........1
No...........5

11. Some people say the police don't show respect for people or they use insulting language. Do you think this happens to people in this neighborhood?

Yes.......(ASK A)...............1
No........(GO TO Q. 12)·······5
Don't know.....(ASK A)........8

A. IF YES OR DON'T KNOW: Has it ever happened to you?

Yes.......(ASK B & C)...........1
No........(ASK C)...............5

B. IF YES TO A: How long ago was that (the last time)?

_____ years ago

C. IF YES OR NO TO A: Has it happened to anyone you know?

Yes 1
No 5

<u>RECODED</u>
<u>VALUES</u>

12. Some people say the police frisk or search people without good reason. Do you think this happens often to people in this neighborhood?

Yes.......(ASK A)................1
No........(GO TO Q. 13)........5
Don't know.....(ASK A)........8

A. IF YES OR DON'T KNOW: Has it ever happened to you?

Yes.......(ASK B & C)...........1
No........(ASK C)................5

B. IF YES TO A: How long ago was that (the last time)?

_____ years ago

C. IF YES OR NO TO A: Has it happened to anyone you know?

Yes...........1
No............5

13. Some people say the police rough up people unnecessarily when they are arresting them or afterwards. Do you think this happens to people in this neighborhood?

Yes.......(ASK A)................1
No........(GO TO Q. 14)........5
Don't know.....(ASK A)........8

A. IF YES OR DON'T KNOW: Has it ever happened to you?

Yes.......(ASK B & C)...........1
No........(ASK C)................5

B. IF YES TO A: How long ago was that (the last time)?

_____ years ago

C. IF YES OR NO TO A: Has it happened to anyone you know?

Yes...........1
No 5

14. Do you think Negro citizens are generally given better treatment by Negro policemen, by white policemen, or that it doesn't make much

Negro policemen (ASK A).......1	1
White policemen (ASK A).......2	3
Not much difference 3	2
Don't know......................8	8

A. IF NEGRO OR WHITE POLICEMEN: Why do you think this is?

15. In general, do you think judges in (CITY) are usually harder on   RECODED
Negroes, harder on whites, or that there is not much difference?   VALUES

Harder on Negroes 1	1
Harder on whites 2	3
Not much difference 3	2
Don't know 8	8

16. Do you personally feel safer from crime now than you did two
not asked   or three years ago, or is there no change, or do you feel less safe?
of R

                        Safer today..... 1
                        No change 2
                        Less safe 3

17. Do you think a man can safely walk alone in this neighborhood
not asked   after dark, or would he be wiser not to?
of R

                        Can safely walk along 1
                        Wiser not to 2
                        Don't know 8

18. Here are some complaints you hear sometimes about stores and
merchants. Would you tell me if these things ever happen to you
when you shop in stores in or near this neighborhood?

	Often	Sometimes	Rarely	Never	Don't shop in neighborhood
A. Do you think you are unfairly over-charged for goods often, sometimes, rarely, or never?	1	2	3	4	5 (GO TO B)
B. Do you think you are sold spoiled or inferior goods often, sometimes, rarely, or never?	1	2	3	4	
C. In such stores, are you treated disrespectfully often, sometimes, rarely, or never?	1	2	3	4	

D. IF NEVER SHOP IN NEIGHBORHOOD: Why don't you
                                       shop around
                                       here?

FILL IN ITEMS BELOW IMMEDIATELY AFTER LEAVING RESPONDENT	

A. Total length of interview:
 	
_____ Minutes
	F. What persons over 14 years of age were present during interview? CIRCLE **ALL** THAT APPLY.
	
	v. 63 None 0
	             Spouse 1
	             Parent 2
	             Child over 14 3
	             Other relative or friend ... 4
	             Other (SPECIFY).......... 5

B. Cooperativeness of respondent:
 	
     Very cooperative 1
     Somewhat cooperative ... 2
     Not cooperative 3	

C. Interest of respondent in racial issues:
 	
     Great interest 1
     Ordinary interest 2
     Little interest 3
	G. Neatness of home interior:
	v. 64 Very neat and clean 1
	             Fairly neat and clean 2
	             Fairly messy 3
	             Very messy 4

D. Respondent's skin shade:
 	
     Dark 1
     Medium dark 2
     Medium light 3
     Light 4
	H. Does respondent dress to show "black identity" in any way? CIRCLE **ALL** THAT APPLY.
	             R has "natural (Afro) hair
	v. 65 style 1
	v. 66 R wears "black power button .. 2
	             Other signs of "black
	v. 67 identity" (SPECIFY).......... 3

E. Respondent's understanding of questions:
 	
     Good understanding 1
     Fair understanding 2
     Poor understanding 3
	I. Date of Interview:_____
	v. 69
	
	J. Interviewer's Signature:

K. Please give here a brief description of the respondent, and of any special conditions that affected the interview.	

SUMMARY

The foundation of all questionnaires is the question. The questionnaire must translate the research objectives into specific questions. Answers to these questions will provide the necessary data for hypothesis testing.

Most questions can be classified as either factual or opinion and attitude questions. Factual questions are designed to elicit objective information from the respondent. Opinion and attitude questions, on the other hand, are concerned with inclinations, preference, prejudices, ideas, fears, and convictions. In general, survey questions about opinions and attitudes are much more complex to construct than questions about personal facts. Answers to opinion and attitude questions are more sensitive to changes in wording, emphasis, and sequence than are those to factual questions.

Four types of question structure can be distinguished: (1) open-ended questions, (2) closed-ended questions, (3) contingency questions, and (4) matrix questions. In closed-ended questions, respondents are offered a set of response categories from which they must choose the one that most closely represents their view. Open-ended questions are not followed by any kind of choice and the respondents' answers are recorded in full. A contingency question is one that applies only to a subgroup of respondents. The relevance of the question to this subgroup is determined by the answer of all respondents to a preceding filter question. The matrix question is a method for organizing a large set of items that have the same response categories.

One of the most common formats for questions asked in surveys is the rating scale. It is a judgment made by the respondent in terms of sets of ordered categories. There are several types of rating scales, including the card sort and the semantic differential. Ranking is used in questionnaires whenever the objective is to obtain information regarding the degree of importance or the priorities that people give to a set of attitudes or objects.

Questions must be worded so that they are comprehended by all respondents. A leading question is a question phrased in such a manner that it appears to the respondent that the researcher expects a certain answer. Threatening questions are those that raise the anxiety level of the respondents. Both types of questions may lead to response bias. Leading questions should be avoided, and threatening questions need to be constructed with great sensitivity, using special techniques, such as a long introduction to the question and open-ended rather than closed-ended questions.

KEY TERMS FOR REVIEW

Question	Contingency	Ranking
Factual question	question	Leading questions
Opinion	Filter question	Threatening
Attitude	Rating	questions
Open-ended	Matrix question	Double-barreled
question	Quantifier	questions
Closed-ended	Semantic	
question	differential	

ADDITIONAL READINGS

Babbie, Earl R. *Survey Research Methods.* Belmont, Calif.: Wadsworth, 1973.

Glock, Charles, ed. *Survey Research in the Social Sciences.* New York: Russell Sage Foundation, 1967.

Gorden, Raymond L. *Interviewing: Strategy, Techniques and Tactics.* Homewood, Ill.: Dorsey, 1969.

Hyman, Herbert. *Survey Design and Analysis.* New York: Free Press, 1955.

Kahn, Robert I., and Charles F. Cannell. *The Dynamics of Interviewing.* New York: Wiley, 1957.

Maccoby, Eleanor E., and Nathan Maccoby. "The Interview: A Tool of Social Science." In *Handbook of Social Psychology*, ed. by Gardner Lindzey. Reading, Mass.: Addison-Wesley, 1954.

Oppenheim, N. A. *Questionnaire Design and Attitude Measurement.* New York: Basic Books, 1966.

Richardson, Stephen; Barbara S. Dohrenwend; and David Klein. *Interviewing: Its Forms and Functions.* New York: Basic Books, 1965.

Young, Pauline V. *Scientific Social Surveys and Research.* Englewood Cliffs, N. J.: Prentice-Hall, 1966.

CHAPTER PREVIEW

CHAPTER 10
Unobtrusive Measures

INTRODUCTION

With the exception of the complete participation method, all methods of data collection considered so far take place in either a contrived or a natural setting in which the researched individuals are *aware* of being research subjects. This, we maintained earlier, may introduce errors. The present chapter directs attention to unobtrusive data; that is, data obtained using methods that directly remove the researcher from those being researched. The latter are *not* aware they are the subjects of research, and consequently certain types of errors are avoided. Obviously, unobtrusive methods are not without inherent limitations. *No* method of data collection is without limitations, and as a result more than one method of data collection is needed. Thus, interviews can be supplemented by methods that have different methodological limitations, for example, systematic observation or unobtrusive measures.

In the first section of this chapter we discuss the major types of errors that may be introduced by obtrusive methods such as interviews and questionnaires; we also define and discuss the intent of unobtrusive measures. Next we present several kinds of unobtrusive measures: physical traces, simple observation, and private and public archival records. In the last section we examine content analysis as a method for systematically analyzing data obtained from archival records and documents.

SOURCES OF ERRORS

No data collection method is perfect. Each method has certain advantages but also inherent limitations. With the obtrusive methods discussed in earlier chapters four basic kinds of errors may be introduced by the researched individual: (1) the guinea pig effect, (2) role selection, (3) measurement as change agent, and (4) response sets.

Guinea pig effect.   The guinea pig effect refers to the following fact:

> The measurement process used in the experiment may itself affect the outcome. If people feel that they are "guinea pigs" being experimented with, or if they feel that they are being "tested" and must make a good impression, or if the method of data collection suggests responses or stimulates an interest the subject did not previously feel, the measurement process may distort the experimental results.[1]

Role selection.   Role selection designates those activities that result from the demand characteristics of experimental situations. As discussed in Chapter 7, individuals tend to choose specialized roles while being observed. These, in turn, may not be the roles the researched individuals typically assume.

Measurement as change agent.   Measurement as change agent refers to the possibility that the measurement process itself may induce change in the phenomenon being studied. For example, research in intelligence testing has repeatedly shown that gains in test-passing ability could be traced to experience with previous tests even when no knowledge of the results had been provided.

Response sets.   As discussed in Chapter 8, there are several ways in which bias may be introduced into the data. First, there is the tendency among respondents to endorse a statement more frequently than to disagree with its opposite, generating a source of error known as *acquiescence response set.* Second, the wording of questions may introduce a bias; and third, the sequence of questions may introduce a response bias. Although we discussed methods to minimize these potential sources of errors, they are always present and may confound the findings.

In addition to errors that may be introduced by the researched individuals, there are errors that may be introduced by the investigator. Three major kinds of such errors are (1) interviewer effect, (2) change in the research instrument, and (3) population restrictions.

Interviewer effect.   Interviewer effect refers to the idea that the characteristics of the interviewer may influence the answers of the respondents. Some interviewers' characteristics such as race, sex, or age are easily controllable; others such as nonverbal behavior or the role situation itself are less easily handled and may introduce bias.

---

1. Claire Selltiz, Lawrence S. Wrightsman, and Stuart W. Cook, *Research Methods in Social Relations*, 3rd ed. (New York: Holt, Rinehart and Winston, 1976), p. 101.

Change in the research instrument.   The interviewer or the experimenter may introduce error in the data owing to changes in his or her skills, attitudes, or perceptions: "Just as a spring scale becomes fatigued with use, reading 'heavier' a second time, an interviewer may also measure differently at different times. His skill may increase. He may be better able to establish rapport. He may have learned necessary vocabulary. He may loaf or become bored. . . ."[2]

Population restrictions.   Population restriction derives from the fact that any given data-collection method defines the boundaries of the population that can be studied; for example, illiterate people are excluded from populations studied by mail questionnaires.

UNOBTRUSIVE MEASURES: PURPOSE AND DEFINITION

To a certain extent, errors *known* to be deriving either from the researched individuals or from the investigator can be minimized by a proper research design, valid and reliable measuring procedures, and replication. These, however, provide no absolute guarantee that all error has been eliminated. To cross-validate one's findings, one can use unobtrusive measures. Unobtrusive measures are also used, as is exemplified in the following sections, as a primary data-collection method for some specific research purposes.

An unobtrusive measure is any method of data collection that directly removes the researcher from the set of interactions, events, or behavior being investigated. For example, public archival documents represent an unobtrusive measure because the conditions leading to their production are not influenced by an intruding researcher. Unobtrusive measures avoid the contamination that might arise when investigators and research participants confront one another in data-collection situations. With unobtrusive measures, the individual "is not aware of being tested, and there is little danger that the act of measurement will itself serve as a force for change in behavior or elicit role-playing that confounds the data."[3] These measures range from private and public archives to simple behavior observations of people at work or play; from physical-trace analysis to contrived observations based on mechanical equipment.

PHYSICAL TRACES

Physical traces and evidence left behind by a population are generated without the producer's knowledge of their future use by researchers.

2. Eugene J. Webb et al., *Unobtrusive Measures: Nonreactive Research in the Social Sciences* (Chicago: Rand McNally, 1966), p. 22.

3. Ibid., p. 175.

Eugene Webb and coauthors make a distinction between two broad classes of physical evidence: erosion measures and accretion measures.[4] *Erosion measures* are the natural remnants of some population's activity that has selectively worn certain objects. For example, the wear on library books is an index of their popularity, and the number of miles accumulated by police officers in their patrol cars measures their daily activity. Thus, one can cross-validate the verbal reports of police officers on their daily activities by checking the number of miles accumulated in their patrol cars.

Accretion measures constitute a population's deposit of materials. In this case, the researcher examines those remnants that are left by people and are suggestive of some behavior. For example, Norman Denzin has suggested that deposits of love letters in waste containers be used as a measure of troubled interaction patterns.[5] Samuel Wallace found that hotel clerks assess a person's relationship with legal authorities by the number of possessions that one leaves behind.[6] Settings on the dials of car radios can be used to estimate the popularity of different radio stations by recording the position of the dials when cars are brought in for service.

Physical-trace analysis poses certain difficulties in the collection and interpretation of data: The time needed for collection and the quality of the data pose restrictions. More significant, however, is the fact that in many instances the researcher lacks sufficient data on the population from which the physical traces are drawn to make valid generalizations.

SIMPLE OBSERVATION

Simple observations are the second basic variety of unobtrusive measures. They occur in those situations "in which the observer has no control over the behavior or sign in question, and plays an unobserved, passive and unobtrusive role in the research situation."[7] Although in all other respects simple observations take on the methodology of other observational methods, including participant observation, their peculiarity derives from the fact that the researcher does not intervene in the production of the material. There are four basic types of simple observation: observation of exterior body and physical signs, analysis of expressive movement, physical-location analysis, and observation of language behavior. To some extent these types correspond to the indicators of be-

4. Ibid., pp. 35–52.

5. Norman K. Denzin, *The Research Act* (Chicago: Aldine, 1970), p. 263.

6. Samuel E. Wallace, *Skid Row as a Way of Life* (Totowa, N.J.: Bedminster Press, 1965).

7. Eugene Webb et al., *Unobtrusive Measures*, p. 112.

havior discussed in Chapter 7. The basic difference, however, lies in the methods of observation and in the place of the investigator in the data-collection process.

Observation of Exterior Body and Physical Signs

The first type of simple observation is the observation of exterior body and physical signs that are indicators of behavior or attitudes. Examples of such signs include tattoos, clothing styles, ornamental objects such as jewelry, and other types of possessions. Gregory Stone reports that when one of his respondents was asked if he chose to wear a greater variety or smaller variety of clothes when at work, he replied, "A smaller variety so you look the same every day. So people will identify you. They look for the same old landmark."[8] Phillips has provided multiple indicators of the changes in Miami resulting from the influx of a hundred thousand Cubans. Two years following the Castro revolution, the author observed bilingual street signs, Latin-American foods on restaurant menus, radio broadcasts in Spanish, and services held in Spanish by forty Miami churches.[9] In this study, exterior signs in public places served as indexes of social change.

Analysis of Expressive Movement

A second type of simple observation is the analysis of expressive movement. The focus of observation is on the various features of the body that express the self and on interpretations of social interactions. For example, Glendon Schubert, studying the Supreme Court, has suggested that the speech, grimaces, and gestures of the justices when hearing oral arguments are rich sources of data for students of the Court.[10]

A major problem in the investigation of facial and body gestures is the determination of what a particular gesture conveys. For instance, a smile may mean relief or happiness, and a frown may indicate involvement in thought or disapproval. The meaning of a gesture has to be determined for both the person expressing it and the recipient. The situation in which the gesture is expressed must also be considered. A smile at a funeral probably means something quite different from a smile at a wedding.[11]

8. Gregory P. Stone, "Appearance and the Self," in *Human Behavior and Social Processes*, ed. by Arnold M. Rose (Boston: Houghton Mifflin, 1962), p. 95.

9. R. H. Phillips, "Miami Goes Latin under Cuban Tide," *The New York Times*, March 18, 1962, p. 35.

10. Glendon Schubert, *Quantitative Analysis of Judicial Behavior* (New York: Free Press, 1959).

11. Norman K. Denzin, *The Research Act*, p. 272.

Physical-Location Analysis

Physical-location analysis is the third type of simple observation. The main purpose of this mode of observation is to investigate the ways in which individuals use their bodies in a social space. In Chapter 7, we discussed some indicators of spatial behavior; these, however, are investigated in laboratory settings. Physical-location analysis focuses on behavior that occurs without the researcher's intervention in the conditions that elicit the behavior. To observers of Russian internal politics, for instance, information on who stands next to whom in Red Square reviewing the May Day parade is a clue of stability or change in the power elite. The proximity of a politician to the leader is a direct indication of status; physical position is interpreted as symptomatic of other behavior that gave the politician the status position.

Seating aggregation may be used as an index of interracial relations. In their study of seating aggregation, Campbell, Kruskal, and Wallace used the clustering of blacks and whites as an index of attitude:

> Where seating in a classroom is voluntary the degree to which the Negroes and whites present sit by themselves versus mixing randomly may be taken as a presumptive index of the degree to which acquaintance, friendship and preference are strongly colored by race, as opposed to being distributed without regard to racial considerations.[12]

Observation of Language Behavior

Observations of language behavior represent the fourth form of simple observation. Unobtrusive language analysis focuses on samples of conversations and the interrelationship of speech patterns to locale, to categories of persons present, and to time of day. The analysis combines the study of physical locations with that of expressive movements.

George Psathas and James Henslin examined the rules and definitions employed by cab drivers as they located points of delivery and pickup on the basis of dispatcher messages. These messages were analyzed with regard to the information they conveyed and the action taken by the driver. Each item of information was assigned a special category that represented unique directions for the cab driver. For example, if a driver were told to "drive-up-and-get-out," he must do more than merely drive up. His instructions involve getting out of the cab and actively looking for the passenger in a place where the passenger is presumed to be.[13]

12. Quoted in Eugene Webb et al., *Unobtrusive Measures*, p. 123.

13. George Psathas and James N. Henslin, "Dispatched Orders and the Cab Driver: A Study of Locating Activities," *Social Problems*, 14 (1967): 424–443.

Problems with Simple Observation

Earlier, it was pointed out that the main advantage of simple observation is that the researcher has no part in structuring the observation situation and remains unobserved while observing. This eliminates errors that otherwise could have been introduced by the observed. Simple observation, however, is beset with some particular problems. First, the recorded observations might not represent a wider population, thus limiting the scope of findings. Second, error might be introduced from fallibilities of the observer. The observer may become more attentive as he or she learns the task and becomes involved with it. Third, only certain phenomena can be observed. If the observer is to remain unnoticed, then the settings most amenable to simple observation will be public; private settings are inaccessible to simple observation. Fourth, much of the data collected by simple observation do not generate explanations: "The data . . . don't offer the 'why', but simply establish a relationship."[14] This, in turn, is one of the reasons for using simple observation mainly to supplement data collected by obtrusive methods.

ARCHIVAL RECORDS

The third major form of unobtrusive measures is the analysis of public and private archival records. These data are collected from diverse sources such as actuarial records, political and judicial records, government documents, the mass media, and private records such as autobiographies, diaries, and letters. A large amount of data in the form of public and private archival records is readily available to social scientists. Some of these records have been compiled specifically for purposes of research, whereas others have been prepared for more general use.

Public Records

Four basic varieties of public records may be distinguished. First are actuarial records concerning the demographic characteristics of the population served by the record-keeping agency. These records range from birth and death statistics to records of marriages and divorces. Second are political and judicial records concerning court decisions, legislators' activities, public votes, budget decisions, and the like. Third are governmental and quasi-governmental documents such as crime statistics, records of social welfare programs, and weather reports. Fourth are the various reports, news items, editorials, and other communications produced by the mass media. Each of these four types contains information that has been used for numerous and varied research purposes. In the

---

14. Eugene Webb et al., *Unobtrusive Measures*, p. 127.

following discussions, exemplars of social science research are used to illustrate the many uses of public archival records.

Actuarial records.   Most societies maintain continuing records on births, deaths, marriages, and divorces. Such data have been used by social scientists for both descriptive and explanatory purposes. For example, Webb et al. report that Winston investigated the preference for male offspring in upper-class families by examining birth records. He noted the sex of each child in the birth order of each family. A preference for males was indicated if the male-female ratio of the last child born in families estimated to be complete was greater than that ratio for all children in the same families. The information contained in birth records enabled him to segregate an upper-class sample of parents and to test his hypothesis.[15]

Russell Middleton examined fertility levels with two sets of data: fertility values expressed in magazine fiction and actuarial fertility levels at three different time periods. For 1916, 1936, and 1956, the author estimated fertility values by observing the size of fictional families in eight American magazines. A comparison with population data for the same years showed that shifts in the size of fictional families closely paralleled shifts in the true United States fertility level.[16]

Death records were used in Lloyd Warner's study on death and its accouterments in an American city. Warner investigated official cemetery documents to establish a history of the dead. He found the social structure of the city mirrored in the cemetery. For example, the father was most often buried in the center of the family plot, and headstones of males were larger than those of females. Moreover, a family that had raised its social status moves the graves of its relatives from less prestigious cemeteries to more prestigious ones.[17]

Political and judicial records.   Voting statistics have been used widely to study electoral behavior as well as voting patterns of legislators. Collections such as *A Review of Elections of the World* and *America at the Polls: A Handbook of American Presidential Election Statistics, 1920–1964* provide useful electoral data. (See Institute of Electoral Research, *A Review of Elections of the World* [London: Dillon's University Bookshop, issued biennially]; Richard M. Scammon, ed., *America at the Polls: A Handbook of American Presidential Election Statistics, 1920–1964* [Pittsburgh: University of Pittsburgh Press, 1965].) *The Congressional*

15. Reported in ibid., pp. 57–58.

16. Russell Middleton, "Fertility Values in American Magazine Fiction: 1916–1956," *Public Opinion Quarterly*, 24 (1960): 139–143.

17. Lloyd W. Warner, *The Living and the Dead* (New Haven: Yale University Press, 1959).

Quarterly Almanac has provided periodic information on the U.S. Congress since 1947, including data on the background characteristics of members of Congress, information on major items of legislation, tabulations of roll-call votes, and a survey of political developments. Taylor et al., *World Handbook of Political and Social Indicators* (1972), report cross-national data on 148 political and social measures, such as electoral participation, counts of riots by country per year, numbers of irregular government changes, and inequalities in income distribution.

Research on the social backgrounds of legislators and on their political behavior is also voluminous. The political slant of legislators has been perhaps the most popular research topic. As early as 1949, Nathaniel Gage and Ben Shimberg measured "progressivism" in the U.S. Senate. The authors sampled the senators' votes on eighteen bills evaluated to measure progressivism and found that (1) younger senators are not more progressive than older senators; (2) senators from the same state do not tend to vote the same way; and (3) regional differences are significant in explaining voting differentials.[18]

Duncan MacRae selected a sample of critical votes by consulting the roll calls published in the *New Republic* and the *CIO News*. His assumption was that these sources would publish only reports of votes on issues germane to their presumably liberal readers. From these, MacRae obtained a "liberal index" depending upon the direction of the vote.[19]

Roll-call votes were employed by William Riker and Donald Niemi to examine the question of congressional coalitions. The authors took votes on eighty-seven roll calls, noting whether a member of Congress (1) voted on the winning side, (2) voted on the losing side, (3) did not vote when eligible, and (4) did not vote when ineligible. The rolls were classified into subjects, and an index of coalitions was constructed.[20]

The *Congressional Record* contains information that can be used to study the behavior not only of members of Congress but also of those outside the Congress. For example, it is a common practice for a member of Congress to insert in the *Record* newspaper columns that reflect his or her point of view. In a study of political columnists, Webb employed these data for an estimate of conservatism-liberalism among Washington's columnists. Individual members of Congress were assigned a lib-

18. Nathaniel L. Gage and Ben Shimberg, "Measuring Senatorial Progressivism," *Journal of Abnormal and Social Psychology*, 44 (1949): 112–117.

19. Duncan MacRae, "Some Underlying Variables in Legislative Roll Call Votes," *Public Opinion Quarterly*, 18 (1954): 191–196.

20. William H. Riker and Donald Niemi, "The Stability of Coalitions on Roll Calls in the House of Representatives," *American Political Science Review*, 56 (1952): 58–65.

eral-conservative score by evaluations of their voting record published by two opposing groups—the Conservative Americans for Constitutional Action and the Liberal Committee on Political Action of the AFL-CIO. Columnists were then ordered on the mean score of the members of Congress who placed their articles in the *Record*.[21]

The votes of judicial bodies provide data for a number of research purposes. Glendon Schubert employed statistical analyses of past voting behavior by U.S. Supreme Court justices to predict future votes.[22] Eloise Snyder used past voting behavior in a study of the degree of uncertainty in the whole United States judicial system. In one measure, uncertainty was operationally defined by the number of reversals of lower-court decisions by the Supreme Court.[23] With the precedent principle of *stare decisis*, there should be few reversals if certainty is high.

Dean Jaros and Robert Mendelsohn examined the proposition that the sentencing behavior of judges in lower-level trial courts is the consequence of the playing of a legal-professional role. The authors studied the sentences imposed by three judges of Detroit traffic court during two one-week periods in the summer of 1966. Data were gathered on all complete cases tried during these periods. It was found that social attitudes, professional role considerations, and community values motivate judicial behavior.[24]

Governmental documents. We have already seen the fruitfulness of analyzing governmental documents such as birth and death records. Other governmental and quasi-governmental documents may also serve as a source of data. Lombroso used governmental documents to study the effect of weather and time of year on scientific creativity. He drew a sample of fifty-two physical, chemical, and mathematical discoveries and noted the time of their occurrence. His evidence showed that twenty-two of the major discoveries occurred in the spring, fifteen in the autumn, ten in the summer, and five in winter.[25]

City budgets were the data of Robert Angell's research on the moral integration of American cities. He constructed a "welfare effort index" by computing local per capita expenditures for welfare; he combined this with a "crime index" based on FBI data to get an "integration

21. Eugene J. Webb, "How to Tell a Columnist," *Columbia Journalism Review*, 2 (1963): 20.

22. Glendon Schubert, *Judicial Decision-Making* (New York: Free Press, 1963).

23. Eloise C. Snyder, "Uncertainty and the Supreme Court Decisions," *American Journal of Sociology*, 65 (1959): 241–245.

24. Dean Jaros and Robert I. Mendelsohn, "The Judicial Role and Sentencing Behavior," *Midwest Journal of Political Science*, 11 (1967): 471–488.

25. Reported in Eugene Webb et al., *Unobtrusive Measures*, p. 72.

index."[26] More recently, budgets have been used as indicators of policy committments. The expenditure side of the budget shows "who gets what" in public funds, and the revenue side tells "who pays the cost." The budgetary process provides a mechanism for reviewing governmental programs, assessing their cost, relating them to financial sources, making choices among alternative expenditures, and determining the financial effort that a government will expend on these programs. Davis, Dempster, and Wildavsky examined the federal budget in consecutive periods and identified two variables that explain the greatest portion of budgetary allocations in any year:

1. The agency request for a certain year is a fixed mean percentage of the Congressional appropriation for that agency in the previous year plus a random variable for that year. 2. The Congressional appropriation for an agency in a certain year is a fixed mean percentage of the agency's request in that year plus a variable representing a deviation from the usual relationship between the Congress and the agency for the previous year.[27]

The mass media. The fourth type of public record is the mass media. This is the most easily available source of social science data. Accordingly, research using data obtained from the mass media is voluminous, and only one example will be discussed in the present section. (For other studies using the mass media as a major source of unobtrusive data, see Eugene J. Webb et al., *Unobtrusive Measures: Nonreactive Research in the Social Sciences* [Chicago: Rand McNally, 1966], Chapter 3.)

Oscar Grusky studied the relationship between administrative succession and subsequent change in group performance. From the sports pages, Grusky obtained data on the performance of various professional football teams, as well as the timing of changes in coaches and managers. He found that changing a manager makes a difference in the performance of a team.[28]

The mass media record people's verbal communications; these, in turn, have been analyzed to test a variety of propositions. With the introduction of content analysis, to be discussed shortly, research using the mass media as a primary source of data has rapidly accelerated. Ole Holsti has observed that "during the first two decades of the century,

26. Robert C. Angell, "The Moral Integration of American Cities," *American Journal of Sociology*, 57 (1951): 1–140.

27. Otto A. Davis, M. A. H. Dempster, and Aaron Wildavsky, "A Theory of the Budgetary Process," *American Political Science Review*, 60 (1966): 529–547.

28. Oscar Grusky, "Managerial Succession and Organizational Effectiveness," *American Journal of Sociology*, 69 (1963): 21–31.

an average of approximately 2.5 content-analysis studies appeared each year. During the next three decades, the annual average frequencies rose to 13.8, 22.8, and 43.3 respectively, and by 1950–1958, this figure had more than doubled again to 96.3."[29]

Private Records

Unlike public records, private records are difficult to obtain. Nevertheless, they can be of great value to researchers who wish to gain insights by inspecting the individual's own definition of a situation or an event. Private records include autobiographies, diaries, letters, essays, and the like. *Biographies* are the most frequently used type of private record; they reflect the author's interpretation of his or her personal experiences. The *diary* is a more spontaneous account, as its author is not constrained by task-attitudes that control the production of biographies. Both biographies and diaries are initially directed to one person—the author. *Letters*, on the other hand, have a dual audience—the writer and the recipient—and they often reflect the interaction between them[30]. These three main types of private records are written documents focusing on the author's personal experiences. They are usually produced on the author's own initiative and express his or her personal reflections.

The autobiography. The uniqueness of the autobiography is that it provides a view of a person's life and experiences before they are fragmented by the process of analysis. The investigator may gain an understanding of a person's life in its natural setting, thereby avoiding contamination in the process of problem conceptualization. The autobiography provides "an 'inside picture' of the subject's life, and a side that is neither fully apparent nor fully public."[31]

Gordon Allport distinguished three major types of autobiographies, each of which may serve different research objectives.[32] The first is the *comprehensive autobiography*, which covers a full cycle of the person's life from his or her earliest memory and integrates a large number of experiences. Helen Keller's accounts of her life as a blind deaf-mute exemplify the comprehensive autobiography. The second type is the *topical autobiography*, which focuses on a limited aspect of the person's life. For example, Edwin Sutherland studied only one phase of the life

29. Ole R. Holsti, "Content Analysis," in *The Handbook of Social Psychology*, ed. by Gardner Lindzey and Elliot Aronson (Reading, Mass.: Addison-Wesley, 1968), p. 607.

30. Norman K. Denzin, *The Research Act*, p. 231.

31. Ibid., p. 227.

32. Gordon W. Allport, *The Use of Personal Documents in Psychological Research* (New York: Social Science Research Council, 1942).

of a professional thief:

> The principal part of this book is a description of the profession of theft by a person who had been engaged almost continuously for more than twenty years in this profession. This description was secured in two ways: first, the thief wrote approximately two-thirds of it on topics and questions prepared by me; second, he and I discussed for about seven hours a week for twelve weeks what he had written, and immediately after each conference I wrote in verbatim form . . . all that he had said in the discussion.[33]

The third type is the *edited autobiography*, which is a monitored version of the person's account. The investigator selects only those experiences that are relevant to the research purpose. The purpose of the editing process is to clarify and organize the material so as to illuminate the points relevant to the research hypotheses.

The diary. Diaries provide a firsthand account of the individual's life experiences. Written close to the occurrence of events, they convey immediate experiences unimpaired by distortion of memory. Diaries are not constricted by the fear of public showing; therefore, they reveal events and experiences that were considered significant at the time of their occurrence.

Diaries have been classified into three types. The *intimate journal* is a continuous record of one's subjective perception of his or her experiences over a long period of time. The second type, the *memoir*, is rather impersonal and is written in a relatively short time; it resembles an objective record of the individual's affairs. The third type, the *log*, is also impersonal and contains a record of events, meetings, visits, and other activities of the individuals during a limited period of time.

Some social scientists find the intimate journal rather useful because it contains authentic expressions of one's perceptions over a prolonged period of time. Selltiz et al. exemplify the utility of the personal journal through Bühler's study of adolescents. Bühler compared the diaries of girls in three successive generations and demonstrated that in a period of considerable cultural changes between 1837 and 1910, in which the diaries were written, some basic characteristics of youth, such as the need for intimate relationships, remained unchanged.[34] The intimate journal not only provides a person's subjective perceptions over an extended period, but also allows the investigator to compare two or more time periods in a person's life and to observe continuities and changes.

33. Edwin H. Sutherland, *The Professional Thief* (Chicago: University of Chicago Press, 1937), p. v.

34. Reported in Selltiz et al., *Research Methods in Social Relations*, p. 385.

Letters. Letters are used widely by historians but infrequently by social scientists. One of the earliest attempts to employ letters as a source of social data was the William Thomas and Florian Znaniecki study on the Polish peasant. The authors collected letters sent between Poland and the United States to research the problems that arose when the immigrants moved from the old country to the new society. The letters enabled the investigators to examine, among other things, the persons' personalities and the kinds of interactions they had with the recipients of the letters.[35]

In a more recent study, Lewis Dexter analyzed letters that were sent to members of Congress, thereby examining the nature of public opinion reflected in these letters. One of the interesting findings in this study is that of the hundred letters advocating support for a higher minimum wage, only seventy-five were written by persons eligible to register, and of these only thirty-five were actually registered. In some cases, the letters had been stimulated by interest groups; such letters can be identified by clues such as similarity of phrasing and time of mailing.[36]

AUTHENTICITY

One of the main problems in using private documents is the possibility that they might not be authentic. There are two possible kinds of unauthentic records: records that have been produced by deliberate deceit and records that have been unconsciously misrepresented by the author. Records may be falsified or forged for the sole purpose of gaining prestige or material rewards. For example, writers who claim to have an intimate knowledge of the subject's life can more easily sell an alleged biography to a publishing company; such was the case with the fake biography of Howard Hughes, which was sold in 1972 to a reputable publisher under false pretenses. Several procedures can be used to check whether private records are genuine. First, the authorship should be critically examined. Second, the date of the document has to be established, and dates that are mentioned must be verified. For instance, if the author refers to a particular event, say, a riot, it can be learned whether the event had occurred at the time the document had purportedly been written.

The second kind of authenticity is much more difficult to detect. Documents may not necessarily be false, yet they can easily distort the truth for the following reasons: the authors of letters, diaries, or auto-

35. William I. Thomas and Florian Znaniecki, *The Polish Peasant in Europe and America* (New York: Dover, 1958).

36. Lewis A. Dexter, "Communications-Pressure, Influence or Education?" in *People, Society and Mass Communication*, ed. by Lewis E. Dexter and David M. White (New York: Free Press, 1964).

biographies may not remember the facts; or they may try to please the recipient of the document by exaggerating; or perhaps they are restricted by norms and conventions and thus forced to present a somewhat distorted picture. Stuart Chapin has suggested that the following critical questions be answered before a document is accepted as an authentic record:[37]

1. What did the author mean by a particular statement? What is its real meaning as distinguished from its mere literal meaning?
2. Was the statement made in good faith?
   a. Was the author influenced by sympathy or antipathy to tell an untruth?
   b. Did vanity influence him?
   c. Was he influenced by public opinion?
3. Was the statement accurate?
   a. Was the author a poor observer because of mental defect or abnormality?
   b. Was the author badly situated in time and place to observe?
   c. Was he negligent or indifferent?

With answers to these questions, the investigator will usually be able to eliminate records that are in doubt and accept the rest as credible evidence.

CONTENT ANALYSIS

Data obtained from archival records and documents can be more systematically analyzed with the method of content analysis. One can analyze the content of letters, diaries, newspaper articles, minutes of meetings, and the like. Content analysis is a method of data analysis as well as a method of observation. Instead of observing people's behavior directly, or asking them about it, the researcher takes the communications that people have produced and asks questions of the communications. The content of communication serves as the basis of inference.

Broadly defined, *content analysis* is "any technique for making inferences by systematically and objectively identifying specified characteristics of messages."[38] Objectivity refers here to an analysis that is pursued on the basis of explicit rules that enable different researchers to obtain the same results from the same messages or documents. In a systematic content analysis, the "inclusion or exclusion of content is done according to consistently applied criteria of selection; this require-

37. Stuart F. Chapin, *Field Work and Social Research* (New York: Century, 1920), p. 37.

38. Ole R. Holsti, "Content Analysis," p. 601.

ment eliminates analyses in which only materials supporting the investigator's hypotheses are examined."[39]

Applications of Content Analysis

Although content analysis is always performed on a message, it may also be used to answer questions about other elements of communication. Lasswell formulated the basic question that can be raised by researchers: "Who says what, to whom, how, and with what effect?"[40] More explicitly, a researcher may analyze messages to test hypotheses about (1) characteristics of the text, (2) antecedents of the message, or (3) effects of the communication. These three aspects differ with respect to the questions asked of the data, the dimension of communication analyzed, and the research design.

The most frequent application of content analysis has been to describe the attributes of the message. For example, the concern of one aspect of research on Revolution and Development of International Relations (RADIR) was with the survey of political symbols. Research designs were constructed to enable the testing of hypotheses on "world revolution" by identifying trends in the usage of symbols that express major goal values of modern politics. Editorials from ten prestigious newspapers in the United States, England, France, Germany, and the Soviet Union were analyzed for the period 1890 to 1949. Editorials appearing on the first and the fifteenth day of each month were coded for the presence of 416 key symbols. These symbols included 206 geographical terms, such as names of countries and international organizations, and 210 ideological symbols, such as "equality," "democracy," and "communism." When a symbol appeared it was scored as present, and the expressed attitudes toward it were recorded with reference to one of the following three categories: approval, disapproval, or neutrality. Data from 19,553 editorials were used to trace changing foci of attention and attitude. One of the many reported findings is that symbols of representative governments are used where the practice is under dispute, not where it is an accepted part of the traditions.[41]

In a more recent study of a substantially different subject matter, Maher, McKean, and McLaughlin examined the characteristics of schizophrenic language. The explicit research purpose was to identify the

39. Ibid., p. 598.

40. Harold D. Lasswell, "Detection: Propaganda Detection and the Courts," in Harold D. Lasswell et al., *The Language of Politics: Studies in Quantitative Semantics* (Cambridge, Mass.: MIT Press, 1965), p. 12.

41. Ithiel de Sola Pool, *Symbols of Democracy* (Stanford, Calif.: Stanford University Press, 1952).

systematic differences between language judged to be thought-disordered and language judged to be free from thought disorder. To this end, the authors used documents produced by patients under conditions of spontaneity. The documents ranged from long-term sets of diaries to obscenities scrawled on matchbook covers. A sample of text constituting fifty words was drawn from each document. The samples were coded in accordance with a division of the text into simple thought sequences, or simple units of thought. Each unit included a subject, verb, objects, and modifiers plus the source of the thought, the attributive subject, and the verb. The text was divided into these units, and each word was assigned to categories by its function in the text. Among other findings, the authors report that (1) documents judged to be free from thought disorder used fewer objects per subject than did those judged pathological and (2) documents judged normal contained more qualifiers per verb than those judged pathological.[42]

The second application of content analysis is that in which a text is analyzed in order to make inferences about the sender of the message and about the causes or antecedents of the message. A well-known attenpt to determine the sender's identification is the Mosteller and Wallace study on who wrote *The Federalist Papers*, Nos. 49 to 58, 62, and 63. The authors started with four sets of papers: those known to have been written by Madison, those thought to have been written by Madison or by Hamilton, and those thought to have been written by both. Upon examining the texts of the known set of papers, the investigators were able to select words that differentiated between the two authors. For example, the word *enough* tended to be used by Hamilton but not by Madison. These key differentiating words were then used in combination to attribute authorship of the disputed papers. The data strongly supported the claim of Madison's authorship.[43]

Shneidman inferred personality traits of speakers from logical and cognitive characteristics of their verbal communications. Texts were coded into two category sets: idiosyncrasies of reasoning (which included thirty-two categories consisting of idiosyncrasies of relevance, idiosyncrasies of meaning, and the like) and cognitive manipulations (which consisted of sixty-five styles of thought development, such as switching from normative to descriptive mode). To illustrate the method, Shneidman examined the logical styles of Kennedy and Nixon in their first two television debates and that of Khrushchev in speeches delivered

42. Brendan A. Maher, Kathryn O. McKean, and Barry McLaughlin, "Studies in Psychotic Language," in Phillip J. Stone et al., *The General Inquirer: A Computer Approach to Content Analysis* (Cambridge, Mass.: MIT Press, 1966).

43. Frederick Mosteller and David L. Wallace, *Inference and Disputed Authorship: The Federalist* (Reading, Mass.: Addison-Wesley, 1964).

at the United Nations. He constructed for each idiosyncrasy of reasoning the logical conditions under which idiosyncrasy is controverted or canceled. Inferences regarding psychological characteristics of the message's sender were then drawn. For example, Khrushchev was characterized in the following way:

> He feels that others are prone to misunderstand his position and yet he desires acceptance and will even sacrifice other needs or ends to achieve it. He is moody and needful of approval. . . . He trusts his own instincts, his "natural feel" for things. He is painstaking in certain areas, but in general is impatient and suspicious of detail or subtlety.[44]

Content analysis has also been used to infer aspects of culture and cultural change. David McClelland tested his "need for achievement" theory by analyzing the content of literature in different cultures. An individual with high n-Achievement is someone who wants to succeed, who is nonconforming, and who enjoys tasks that involve elements of risk; n-Achievement is "a sum of the number of instances of achievement 'ideas' or images."[45] The hypothesis that "a society with a relatively high percentage of individuals with high n-Achievement should contain a strong entrepreneurial class which will tend to be active and successful particularly in business enterprises so that the society will grow in power and influence" was tested by scoring samples of literature from different periods of Greek civilization.

The next major application of content analysis is that in which inferences are made about the effects of messages on the recipient. The researcher determines the effects of A's messages to B by content-analyzing B's messages. Alternatively, one can study the effects of communication by examining other aspects of the recipient's behavior. Content analysis serves to delineate the relevant independent variables that are correlated with the recipient's behavior. Bernard Berelson's study is perhaps the earliest attempt to examine the effects of messages on the recipient. During the 1940 presidential campaign, themes of political appeals were identified by content-analyzing public and private media. The public was then surveyed on its reactions to the content of the arguments. The relationship between content and recipients is summarized in the following way:

> Why do people come across arguments and why do they accept them? . . . Mainly, people come across the arguments which the

44. Edwin S. Shneidman, "A Psychological Analysis of Political Thinking," mimeo (Cambridge, Mass.: Harvard University, 1961).

45. David C. McClelland, "The Use of Measures of Human Motivation in the Study of Society," in *Motives in Fantasy, Action and Society,* ed. by John W. Atkinson (Princeton, N.J.: Van Nostrand, 1958).

mediums of communication emphasize; they also tend to see the arguments they want to see and other arguments whose statement is appealing ... people accept the arguments which support their own general position; they also tend to accept the arguments which they see in the public communications and those whose statement is persuasive.[46]

Units and Categories

The content-analysis procedure involves the interaction of two processes: *specification* of the content characteristics to be measured, and *application of the rules* for identifying and recording the characteristics when they appear in the texts to be analyzed. The categories into which content is coded vary with the nature of data and the research purpose. Before discussing general procedures for category construction, we must specify the various recording units used in research and to make a distinction between recording units and context units. The *recording unit* is the smallest body of content in which the appearance of a reference is counted (a reference is a single occurrence of the content element). The *context unit* is the largest body of content that may be examined in characterizing a recording unit. For example, the recording unit may be a single term; but in order to note whether the term is treated favorably, one has to consider the entire sentence in which the term appears (the context unit). Thus, the sentence is taken into account when recording (and subsequently when coding) the term.

Five major *recording units* have been used frequently in content-analysis research: *words* or *terms, themes, characters, paragraphs*, and *items*. The word is the smallest unit generally applied in research. Its application results in a list of frequencies of selected words or terms. For example, Harold Lasswell, in a study on propaganda detection, reports that the *Moscow News* frequently used twenty-seven key political terms during 1938–1939. Eight of these terms and their frequencies are presented in Table 10.1.[47]

For many research purposes, the theme is a useful recording unit. In its simplest form a theme is a simple sentence; that is, subject and predicate. Because in most texts themes can be found in clauses, paragraphs, and illustrations, it becomes necessary to specify which of these places will be searched when using the theme as a recording unit. For example, one may consider only the primary theme in each paragraph

---

46. Bernard Berelson, "The Effects of Print upon Public Opinion," in *Print, Radio, and Film in Democracy*, ed. by Douglas Waples (Chicago: University of Chicago Press, 1942), p. 63.

47. Harold Lasswell, "Detection: Propaganda Detection and the Courts."

TABLE 10.1 Frequency of Use of Key Political Terms

Term	Frequency
Bourgeois	61
Class	92
Class struggle	97
The party	172
Red Army	162
The people	1,136
Revolution	217
Exploitation	54

or count every theme in the text. Themes are most frequently employed in the study of propaganda, attitudes, images, and values.

In some studies, the character is employed as the recording unit. In this case, the researcher counts the number of persons rather than the number of words or themes. This, in turn, enables the examination of traits of characters appearing in various texts.

The paragraph is the fourth recording unit. However, it is rarely used because of difficulties in classifying and coding the various and numerous things implied in a single paragraph.

The item is the whole unit employed by the producer of a message. The item may be an entire article, a book, a speech, or the like. Analysis by the entire item is appropriate whenever the variations within the item are small and insignificant. For example, news stories can often be classified by subject matter such as crime, labor, or sports.

Eventually, recording units are classified and coded into categories. The problem of category construction, as Berelson points out, is the most crucial aspect of content analysis:

> Content analysis stands or falls by its categories. Particular studies have been productive to the extent that the categories were clearly formulated and well adapted to the problem and to the content. Content analysis studies done on a hit or miss basis, without clearly formulated problems for investigation and with vaguely drawn or poorly articulated categories, are almost certain to be of indifferent or low quality as research productions. . . . Since the categories contain the substance of the investigation, a content analysis can be no better than its system of categories.[48]

48. Bernard Berelson, *Content Analysis in Communication Research* (Glencoe, Ill.: Free Press, 1952), p. 147.

Among the types of categories employed frequently in content-analysis research are the following:[49]

"What is said" categories:

SUBJECT MATTER. What is the communication about?
DIRECTION. How is the subject matter treated (for example, favorable-unfavorable; strong-weak)?
STANDARD. What is the basis on which the classification by direction is made?
VALUES. What values, goals, or desires are revealed?
METHODS. What methods are used to achieve goals?
TRAITS. What are the characteristics used in description of people?
ACTOR. Who is represented as undertaking certain acts?
AUTHORITY. In whose name are statements made?
ORIGIN. Where does the communication originate?
LOCATION. Where does the action take place?
CONFLICT. What are the sources and levels of conflict?
ENDINGS. Are conflicts resolved happily, ambiguously, or tragically?
TIME. When does the action take place?

"How it is said" categories:

FORM OR TYPE OF COMMUNICATION. What is the medium of communication (radio, newspaper, speech, television, and so on)?
FORM OF STATEMENT. What is the grammatical or syntactical form of the communication?
DEVICE. What is the rhetorical or propagandistic method used?

Categories must relate to the research purpose, and they must be exhaustive and mutually exclusive. Exhaustiveness ensures that every recording unit relevant to the study can be classified. Mutual exclusivity means that no recording unit can be included more than once within any given category-system. The researcher also has to specify explicitly the indicators that determine which recording units fall into each category. This enables replication, which is an essential requirement of objective and systematic content analysis.

Most content-analysis research is quantitative in one form or another. Quantification may be performed by employing one of the following four systems of enumeration: (1) A *time/space system* that is based on various measures of space (for example, column inches) or units of time (for example, minutes devoted to a news item on the radio) to describe the relative emphases of different categories in the analyzed material. (2) An *appearance system* that calls for searching the material for ap-

49. Ole Holsti, "Content Analysis."

pearance of a certain attribute. The size of the context unit determines the frequency with which repeated recording units occurring in close proximity to each other are counted separately. (3) A *frequency system* in which every occurrence of a given attribute is recorded. The use of the frequency system was exemplified in Table 10.1. (4) An intensity system. This is generally employed in studies dealing with attitudes and values. Methods of quantifying for intensity are based on the construction of attitude scales (see Chapter 15). For example, using the "paired comparison" technique developed by Thurstone, judges decide which possible pair of intensity indicators is rated higher on a scale of attitudes. The judgments are then used to construct categories into which recording units are placed. (The most recent development in content analysis is the programming of computers to process the variety of operations involved in textual analysis. It is beyond the scope of this book to survey these developments, but a good start would be Philip J. Stone et al., *The General Inquirer: A Computer Approach to Content Analysis* [Cambridge, Mass.: MIT Press, 1966].)

SUMMARY

Unobtrusive measures are intended to produce data that are free from errors that either the researched individual or the investigator may introduce when confronting one another in data-collection situations. An unobtrusive measure is any method of data collection that directly removes the researcher from the set of interactions, events, or behavior being studied. With unobtrusive measures the individual is not aware of being researched, and there is little danger that the act of measurement will itself introduce a change in behavior or elicit role playing that biases the data. Unobtrusive measures, like all the methods of data collection, are not perfect, and one should be aware of their limitations relative to other methods.

In this chapter we discussed and exemplified three general types of unobtrusive measures: physical traces, simple observation, and archival records. Physical traces left behind by individuals are generated without their knowledge of how they will be used. Two broad classes of physical traces are erosion measures and accretion measures. Erosion measures are the natural remnants of some population's activity that has selectively worn certain objects. Accretion measures constitute a population's deposit of materials.

Simple observation occurs in those situations in which the observer has no control over the behavior in question and plays an unobserved role in the research situation. There are four basic types of simple observation: observation of exterior body and physical signs, analysis of expressive movement, physical-location analysis, and observation of language behavior.

The third major form of unobtrusive measures is the analysis of public and private archival records. These data are collected from diverse sources, such as actuarial records, political and judicial records, governmental documents, the mass media, and private records, including autobiographies, diaries, and letters. A major problem with private records is the possibility that they are not authentic; they could have been produced by deliberate deceit, or they could have been unconsciously misrepresented by the author. We discussed several procedures that one could take to reduce the risk of using unauthentic private documents.

In the last section we presented content analysis as a method that permits systematic analysis of data obtained from archival records and documents. Instead of observing people's behavior or asking them about it, the investigator takes the communications that people have produced and asks questions of these communications. The content-analysis procedure involves the interaction of two processes: specification of the content characteristics to be analyzed and application of the rules for identifying and recording the characteristics when they appear in the materials to be analyzed. Obviously, the categories into which content is coded vary with the nature of the research problem and the data.

KEY TERMS FOR REVIEW

Acquiescence
  response set
Unobtrusive
  measures
Accretion measures
Simple observation
Physical-location
  analysis

Actuarial records
Topical
  autobiography
Log
Authenticity
Content analysis
Recording units

ADDITIONAL READINGS

Bloch, Marc. *The Historian's Craft*. New York: Vintage, 1953.

Bouchard, J. T. "Unobtrusive Measures: An Inventory of Uses." *Sociological Methods and Research*, 4 (1976): 267–300.

Denzin, Norman K. *The Research Act*. Chicago: Aldine, 1970. Chapter 11.

Gottschalk, Louis; Clyde Kluckhohn; and R. Angell. *The Use of Personal Documents in History, Anthropology, and Sociology*. New York: Social Science Research Council, 1945.

North, Robert C., et al. *Content Analysis.* Evanston, Ill.: Northwestern University Press, 1963.

Spradley, James P. *You Owe Yourself a Drink: The Ethnography of Urban Nomads.* Boston: Little, Brown, 1970.

Turner, Roy, ed. *Ethnomethodology.* London: Harmondsworth, 1974.

Williamson, John B.; David A. Karp; and John R. Dalphin. *The Research Craft.* Boston: Little, Brown, 1977. Chapter 10.

Winks, Robin, ed. *The Historian as Detective: Essays on Evidence.* New York: Harper & Row, 1969.

PART 3
Data Processing and Analysis

CHAPTER PREVIEW

CHAPTER 11
Data Processing

INTRODUCTION

Data processing is the link between data collection and data analysis. It involves the transformation of the observations gathered in the field into a system of categories and the translation of these categories into codes amenable to quantitative analysis. The codes are then recorded on punchcards and processed through computers. This chapter will focus on the major aspects of coding and automatic data processing.

CONSTRUCTING CODING SCHEMES

Coding is the process of classifying responses into meaningful categories. It involves combining detailed information into a limited number of categories that enable simple description of the data and allow for statistical analyses. The main purpose of coding is to simplify the handling of many individual responses by classifying them into a smaller number of groups, each including responses that are similar in content.[1] (In the following discussion, *responses, answers, observations, acts,* and *behavior* are used interchangeably.)

Suppose an investigator has gathered information on the occupations of several hundred individuals. The following are examples of the occupations listed:

Lawyer   Practical nurse
Barber   Migrant farm laborer

1. Paul F. Lazarsfeld and Alan Barton, "Qualitative Measurement in the Social Sciences: Classification, Typologies, and Indices," in *The Policy Sciences*, ed. by Daniel Lerner and Harold D. Lasswell (Stanford, Calif.: Stanford University Press, 1951), pp. 155–192.

Carpenter	Executive
Broker	High school teacher
Elevator operator	Electrician
Veterinarian	Advertising agent

These data are not amenable to analysis without a prior reduction into some system of categories. One acceptable way to classify them is according to the following categories:

1. *Professional and managerial*: lawyer, veterinarian, executive, high school teacher.
2. *Technical and sales*: advertising agent, broker.
3. *Service and skilled labor*: barber, elevator operator, practical nurse, electrician, carpenter.
4. *Unskilled labor*: migrant farm worker.

This system of categories allows for the classification of occupations according to the level of income, prestige, and education that they hold in common, permitting the researcher to handle four well-defined categories rather than several hundred specific occupations. Systems of categories such as this one, used to classify responses or acts that relate to a single item or variable, are referred to as *coding schemes*. The principles involved in the construction of such schemes are discussed in the following sections.

Inductive and Deductive Coding

The previously discussed methods of data collection can be classified according to whether they utilize an inductive or a deductive system of coding. Inductive coding means recording the data as closely as possible to their original detail and postponing categorization: "The observer asks questions about what he is measuring only after he is comfortable that something stable is being measured precisely."[2]

On the other hand, the deductive approach requires that data be recorded according to some preconceived scheme that is applied as the record is being made. With this method, broad categories are employed to classify observations, and original detail is largely disregarded. Most data-collection methods that use a precoded classification system implement a deductive approach.

Examples of deductive coding. In many surveys, categories are constructed in advance, and the respondents are asked to classify themselves. For instance, the following closed-ended question has been pre-

2. Karl E. Weick, "Systematic Observational Methods," in *The Handbook of Social Psychology*, ed. by Gardner Lindzey and Elliot Aronson (Reading, Mass.: Addison-Wesley, 1968), p. 402.

coded, and the respondents place themselves in the appropriate category:

With respect to your own personal role in seeking to bring about changes in your high school and/or in other institutions of our society, which one of the following statements best describes your own position?

1. ☐ I consider myself an activist.
2. ☐ I am in sympathy with most of the activists' objectives, but not with all of their tactics.
3. ☐ I am not emotionally involved, one way or the other.
4. ☐ I am not sure that I approve of what the activists are trying to do, but I have no strong objection to letting them try.
5. ☐ I am in total disagreement with the activists.

Similarly, in controlled observations, the coding scheme employed is prepared in advance, and the observed behavior is systematically recorded. For example, Bales's Interaction Process Analysis is based on the notion that there is a sequence of interactional events that develops within all groups regardless of their function or composition. Observed "acts" are coded into one of twelve categories, which are based on this sequence (see Table 7.1).

Examples of inductive coding. In exploratory research or in pilot studies, data are collected without a predesigned system of categories. Therefore, the coding scheme is constructed on the basis of raw material. With the inductive method of coding, the first step is to select a representative sample of responses and note all the answers to the particular item to be coded. When the selection is sufficiently large and varied for a pattern to emerge, the coding scheme can be constructed. This preliminary scheme is then systematically applied to the data.

The inductive method is most frequently applied to coding responses to open-ended questions or to data obtained from documents or through the method of participant observation. Consider, for example, the responses to the following question, designed to determine the effect of adolscent subculture on academic achievement: "What does it take to get to be a member of the leading crowd?"[3]

Some of the responses were:

Wear just the right things, nice hair, good grooming, and have a wholesome personality.

A good athlete, pretty good looking, common sense, sense of humor.

Money, cars, and the right connections and good personality.

3. James S. Coleman, "Academic Achievement and the Structure of Competition," *Harvard Educational Review*, 29 (1959): 330–351.

Money, clothes, flashy appearance, date older boys, fairly good grades.

Be a sex fiend, dress real sharp, have own car and money, smoke and drink, go steady with a popular boy.

Be a good athlete, have a good personality, be in everything you can, don't drink or smoke.

Athletic ability sure helps.

Have pleasant personality, good manners, dress nicely, be clean, don't swear, be loads of fun.

A nice personality, dress nice without overdoing it.

Good in athletics, wheel type, not too intelligent.

These responses indicate some of the attributes that characterized the adolescent subculture in the late fifties. Responses that were mentioned 10 percent or more of the time were included in a coding scheme employed to analyze the data. The results of this analysis are presented in Table 11.1, in which the major categories of response and their frequencies are listed.

Categories are not always easily identified. Often, the process of constructing a comprehensive coding scheme is a long one and involves switching back and forth between the raw data and the evolving scheme until the latter is applicable and ties in with the general purpose of the study. Paul Lazarsfeld and Alan Barton, examining some general principles of coding, illustrate this process by using some of the coding schemes constructed in the study *The American Soldier*.[4] In an attempt to determine which factors offset combat stress, the investigators of the American soldier drew up a preliminary list of categories on the basis of many responses:

1. Coercive formal authority.
2. Leadership practices—for example, encouragement.
3. Informal group:
   a. Affectional support.
   b. Code of behavior.
   c. Provision of realistic security and power.
4. Convictions about the war and the enemy.
5. Desire to complete the job by winning war, to go home.
6. Prayer and personal philosophies.

These preliminary coding schemes enabled the investigators in this study to classify the raw data and substantially reduce the number of

4. Lazarsfeld and Barton, "Qualitative Measurement," p. 160; Samuel A. Stouffer, *The American Soldier* (New York: Wiley), 1965.

TABLE 11.1. Percentage Distribution of the Criteria for Membership in the Leading Crowd Perceived by Boys and Girls

Criterion for Membership in the Leading Crowd	Boys	Girls
Good personality, being friendly	26.6%	48.7%
Good looks, beauty	14.3	28.9
Having nice clothes	9.0	27.4
Good reputation	17.9	25.9
Having money	7.7	14.2
Good grades, being smart	11.9	11.6
Being an athlete (boys only)	16.3	—
Having a car (boys only)	10.7	—

SOURCE: James S. Coleman, "Academic Achievement and the Structure of Competition," *Harvard Educational Review*, 29 (1959): 333. Reprinted with permission of the publisher.

responses to be analyzed. Yet, a further modification was introduced after it was noted that formal sanctions are often more effective when channeled through informal group sanctions and internal sanctions. Conversely, the norms of the informal groups are influenced by formal sanctions as well as by individual conscience. On this basis, the responses were reanalyzed, and additional information was obtained to produce a modified coding scheme (Table 11.2).

The following responses conform to the modified categories in Table 11.2:

(a) I fight because I'll be punished if I quit.
(b) I fight because it's my duty to my country, the Army, the government; it would be wrong for me to quit.
(c) I fight because I'll lose the respect of my buddies if I quit.
(d) I fight because it would be wrong to let my buddies down.
(e) You have to look out for your buddies even if it means violating orders, or they won't look out for you.
(f) You have to look out for your buddies even if it means violating orders because it would be wrong to leave them behind.
(g) I am fighting because I believe in democracy and hate fascism.

Advantages and disadvantages. Both the deductive and the inductive approaches have their respective shortcomings and advantages. The deductive method has been criticized for violating the continuity and complexity of behavior.[5] A preconstructed coding scheme is often

5. Elizabeth Gellert, "Systematic Observation: A Method in Child Study," *Harvard Educational Review*, 25 (1955): 179–195.

TABLE 11.2. How Norms Bear on Individual Behavior in Combat

Underlying Source of Norms	Channels
Norms of formal authorities	*Direct*: (a) Formal sanctions (b) Internal sanctions *Via group norms*: (c) Informal group sanctions (d) Internal sanctions
Norms of informal groups	(e) Formal group sanctions (f) Internal sanctions
Individual norms	(g) Internal sanctions

SOURCE: Paul F. Lazarsfeld and Alan Barton, "Qualitative Measurement in the Social Sciences: Classification, Typologies, and Indices," in *The Policy Sciences*, ed. by Daniel Lerrer and Harold D. Lasswell (Stanford, Calif.: Stanford University Press, 1951), p. 161. Reprinted with permission.

rigid and does not allow for new insights on the part of the investigator. In addition, omission of descriptive detail may limit reanalysis at a later stage. Conceptual definitions are sometimes imprecise; and when the data are precoded according to these definitions, it is difficult to reclassify them later according to a revised set of categories. Instead, a new set of records must be obtained.[6] However, the deductive approach alerts observers to the dynamics of the situation by directing their attention to predefined and established concepts. Moreover, the observational process may benefit from the omission of superfluous detail.

The chief advantage of the inductive approach is its flexibility and richness, which enable the researcher to generate explanations from the findings. Moreover, it allows for a variety of coding schemes to be applied to the same observation, and it often suggests new categories as well.[7] The shortcoming of this method is that researchers may be bogged down by the mass of details when they try to explain the data. Sometimes too little context is preserved for the coder to determine which details are trivial and can therefore be eliminated.

The preference for either coding strategy depends on the purpose of the investigation. In exploratory studies, where concepts are not well defined, the researcher will be faced by a mass of raw data for which ready-made categories do not exist. The inductive method is then well suited, for it permits concrete categories to be adapted to the data. Con-

6. Weick, "Systematic Observational Methods," pp. 401–402.

7. Ibid.

versely, in studies testing formulated hypotheses, preconstructed categories are derived from the theory, and the deductive approach is applied. Alternatively, it is possible to combine both strategies, starting with the inductive approach and obtaining extensive information from which some concepts are induced and then collecting a second set of data that is better formulated and more specific.

Criteria of Coding Schemes

Whichever method of coding is employed, inductive or deductive, whether the coding scheme is taken from an existing theory or developed from the data, the criteria of a good coding scheme are the same: (a) link to theory, (b) exhaustiveness, (c) mutual exclusiveness, and (d) detail.

Link to theory. The first criterion is that the coding scheme be linked to the theory and the problem under study. Questions and other stimuli may elicit responses that can be classified in terms of different dimensions. Answers to a question such as "In what way are you affected by the energy crisis?" may cover a general concern about the economy, about the consequent changes in life-style, or even about changes in the international system. The researchers have to decide in terms of which dimensions the coding is to be constructed.[8] They may concentrate solely on the political aspects, or they might decide to code in terms of economic considerations. The decision is guided by the aim of the particular study, which will determine the dimensions chosen for coding.

Exhaustiveness. The second criterion of a coding system is that it be exhaustive; that is, the categories must be so constructed that each and every response or behavior can be classified. An example of lack of exhaustiveness would be the classification of marital status into three categories only: "married," "single," and "divorced." If the group had included a widower, then the requirement of exhaustiveness would be violated because this person could not be fitted into the coding scheme. Any classification can become exhaustive by including a category labeled "other" or "miscellaneous." Although this is an accepted solution, it should, if at all possible, be avoided, as it defeats the purpose of the coding process, which is designed to distinguish between cases in terms of the properties under study.[9]

Mutual exclusiveness. The categories must also be mutually exclusive, so that each case is classified only once. This requirement is violated either when some of the categories overlap or when more than one dimension provides a basis for classification. An example of the first

8. C. A. Moser and G. Kalton, *Survey Methods in Social Investigation* (London: Heinemann Educational Books, 1971).

9. Lazarsfeld and Barton, "Qualitative Measurement."

error would be the classification of religious affiliations as Christian, Muslim, Jew, and Catholic. Catholics are also Christians, and each case classified as Catholic could also be assigned to the Christian group. The solution would be to eliminate the Catholic category; or, if a more specific classification of the Christian group is desired, this broad category would have to be further subdivided into all its different denominations.

The second violation may be due to mixing different dimensions in the classification of observations. For example, a coding scheme that codes occupations according to the categories "white collar," "blue collar," "government employee," "union worker," and "self-employed" includes two dimensions, namely, type of work and form of employment. These dimensions cannot be lumped together. The categories could be divided into two separate coding schemes: (a) 1. blue collar, 2. white collar; (b) 1. government employee, 2. union worker, 3. self-employed. Alternatively, these schemes can be combined into a two-dimensional system whose categories would be: (1) blue collar and union worker; (2) blue collar and government employee; (3) blue collar and self-employed; (4) white collar and union worker; (5) white collar and government employee; and (6) white collar and self-employed.

Detail. A further consideration in the construction of a coding scheme is how detailed it should be. In other words, how many categories will the scheme include? On the whole, it is preferable to include too many categories rather than too few, for reducing the number later is easier than splitting an already coded group of responses. However, the number of categories is limited by the number of cases as well as by the anticipated statistical analyses. Categories that include very few cases cannot be retained in the coding scheme unless they represent particularly rare responses of special interest to the researcher.

Purely technical considerations are also likely to dictate the number of categories retained for a final analysis. A very detailed coding scheme will present difficulties when the data are transferred to punchcards. These cards, as we shall see later, consist of eighty columns, each containing twelve categories. Although more than one column could be used if necessary (that is, if there are more than twelve categories), this complicates the analysis and slows it down.

Coding Reliability

In the coding of open-ended questions or other nonstructured material, coders are required to exercise their own judgment in classifying responses according to the coding scheme. However, when given rules cannot be applied automatically, different coders may arrive at different coding. In such instances, the coding process becomes unreliable, a problem that is just as serious as the unreliability of interviewers or observers.

Marvin Sussman and Marie Haug noted that "the largest component of processing error occurs in the coding phase of data analysis."[10] In an independent double coding of 2,775 cases, they found an especially high coding variability in responses to open-ended questions. Similar findings were reported by James Durbin and Alan Stuart.[11] They employed several coders who were given ten different coding operations ranging from purely mechanical tasks to the coding of answers to open-ended questions. Although the items that required automatic coding produced low variability, in the more complex items requiring judgment and interpretation, complete agreement was obtained only on an average of about half the items. To increase coding reliability, one should keep coding schemes as simple as possible, as well as give the coders thorough training. The simplest solution is to compare the codings of two or more coders and resolve all differences by letting them reach a decision concerning problematic items.

Another problem concerning discrepancies in interpretation of responses is much less frequently discussed in the literature. It has to do with differences between the coder and the respondent in interpreting the meaning of the response. This question was formulated in a study attempting to assess whether the respondent and the coder would reach agreement as to the meaning of the response.[12]

In other words, how would the research participants themselves code their answers within the set of categories provided by the researcher? If the research participants, who provide the answers, could also serve as coders, would their coding differ from that of other coders, or would the research participants code their own responses as they are coded by others? Sixty-four college students were asked to complete a questionnaire that included fixed-alternative as well as several open-ended questions. Later on, every research participant independently coded the questionnaires of several other participants as well as his or her own. A research participant's coding of her or his own response was compared with the way that response was coded by others. The comparison revealed significant differences, with a consistent pattern indicating that the coding of a response deviates from the research participant's actual attitudes, the direction of this deviation being determined by the content of the item. The less structured the item, the larger the discrepancy between the respondent's interpretation and that of a coder.

10. Marvin B. Sussman and Marie R. Haug, "Human and Mechanical Error—An Unknown Quantity in Research," *The American Behavioral Scientist*, 11 (1967): 56.

11. James Durbin and Alan Stuart, "An Experimental Comparison Between Coders," *Journal of Marketing*, 19 (1954): 54–66.

12. Kenneth C. W. Kammeyer and Julius A. Roth, "Coding Responses to Open-Ended Questions," in *Sociological Methodology*, ed. by Herbert L. Costner (London: Jossey-Bass, 1971).

These findings raise some serious problems regarding the process of coding nonstructured material. It is clear that such bias might affect relationships between the variables investigated.

CODE BOOK CONSTRUCTION

Once the first step in data processing—the construction of a coding scheme—is completed, the data may be coded according to the specified rules and transferred to one of among the several options available for storing data, such as computer cards or magnetic tapes. First, however, the categories are to be translated into symbols that are amenable to automatic processing and further analysis. These symbols are usually numerical codes utilized either for coding background information (for example, age, income) or information on perceptions, attitudes, and behavior. Information can be coded either in actual numbers or in arbitrary numerical codes representing any agreed-upon meaning. The digit 9 standing for the quantity 9 is an example of an actual number. The same digit can also be assigned to designate properties such as "yes," "no," "U.S.A.," or $100. Researchers are free to assign a digit any meaning they wish, provided that meaning is consistent within the particular coding scheme. However, for items that frequently reappear in various studies, standard coding systems are employed. An example is the coding scheme developed by the Survey Research Center of the University of Michigan, parts of which are reproduced in Table 11.3. The system conforms to U.S. Census Bureau practice and is employed by many investigators in the social sciences.

The coding schemes with their assigned symbols, together with specific coding instructions, may now be assembled in a code book. A code book will identify a specific item of observation and the code number assigned to describe each category included in that item.

In most cases, the code book will identify where the coded information is to be located. For example, if the information is to be transferred to a computer card, the code book will indicate a column·number for each information unit. Table 11.4 is a sample of a code book providing coding instruction on four items. The data in Table 11.5 can be coded by using this code book.

AUTOMATIC DATA PROCESSING

After the coding process, data will be transferred to various devices that are amenable to automatic data processing. In the next sections, we will review some of the most common devices.

TABLE 11.3 Examples of Coding Conventions

Code	Content
A	*The basic scheme*
1	Yes ("good" or most positive)
5	No ("bad" or least positive)
7	Other
8	I don't know
9	Not ascertained
0	Inapplicable (or none)
B	*Agreement*
1	Agree strongly
2	Agree, but not very strongly
3	Not sure; it depends
4	Disagree, but not very strongly
5	Disagree strongly
C	*Age*
	Code actual age
D	*Income*
	Give actual dollar amount
E	*Number of children (or adults)*
	Code actual number
F	*Sex*
1	Male
2	Female
G	*Race*
1	White
2	Black
3	Other

Computer Cards (Punchcards)

The computer card, often referred to as the punchcard, is one of the most common storage devices and is used as a primary means of input. An example of an ordinary punchcard is reproduced in Figure 11.1. The card has eighty columns, each containing digits from 0 to 9, together with two more unmarked positions above the 0, designated as 10 and 11 for the lower and upper positions, respectively. Ordinarily, each item is allocated one column, but one may use more columns if necessary. To

TABLE 11.4. A Code Book Format

Column	Item	Code	
06	City school district	1	Binghamton
		2	Johnston City
		3	Vestal
07	Public or parochial	1	Public
		2	Parochial
08	Name of school	1	C. Fred Johnson
		2	Dickinson
		3	MacArthur
		4	Vestal High
09	Sex of respondent	1	Male
		2	Female

record a digit in a particular column, a hole is punched in that column, in the position required. The first few columns are usually reserved for an identification code. Each case is identified by a number, and that number is punched on every card containing information about that case. If there are 1,000 cases, the first four columns would be used for identification numbers running from 0001 to 1000. If the information on a certain case exceeds one card, more cards can be used, each of which will then contain the case's identification number, as well as an additional column identifying the card number.

The principle involved in using punchcards is easily illustrated by the card reproduced in Figure 11.2, where information on the first case of Table 11.5 is recorded. The codes have been determined by the code book, presented in Table 11.4.

The first five columns identify the case number with a "0" punched in the first four columns and a "1" punched in column 5. A "1" punched

TABLE 11.5. Background Characteristics of Five Respondents

Case number	City school district	Type of school	Name of school	Sex
00001	Binghamton	Public	Dickinson	Male
00002	Johnston City	Parochial	MacArthur	Female
00003	Vestal	Public	Vestal High	Male
00004	Vestal	Public	Vestal High	Female
00005	Johnston City	Parochial	MacArthur	Male

FIGURE 11.1.   A Punchcard

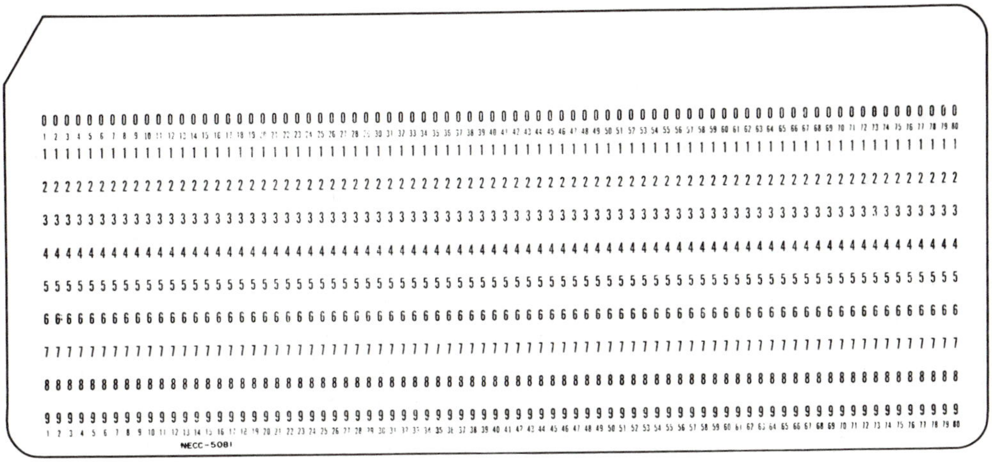

in column 6 indicates that this respondent is from the Binghamton school district; a "1" in column 7 identifies the school as a public school; and the "2" punched in column 8 identifies it as the Dickinson School. Finally, as the first respondent is male, the digit "1" is punched in column 9.

Guidelines for Recording Information on Computer Cards

To conclude the discussion on coding and recording information on punchcards, several suggestions concerning these procedures are listed as follows. These suggestions appear in most data-processing manuals.[13]

1. *Use a "natural" coding scheme.* Digits should run in some familiar ordering, with "high" responses represented by the larger numbers. Thus, responses like "never," "only once," and "more than one time" should be coded 1, 2, and 3 rather than 3, 2, and 1. With items that have no logical ordering, it is advisable to use the larger digit for the most frequent response.
2. *Avoid the use of blank space as coding category.* Many computer programs do not distinguish between blank space and zero punches. Thus a blank space would be interpreted as a zero. The zero, however, is a valid digit to use and is employed to designate "no answer," "no information," and similar categories.

---

13. We have based our discussion on Oliver Benson, *Political Science Laboratory* (Columbus, Ohio: Merril, 1969) and Kenneth Janda, *Data Processing: Applications to Political Research* (Evanston, Ill.: Northwestern University Press, 1965).

FIGURE 11.2. Recording Responses on Punchcards

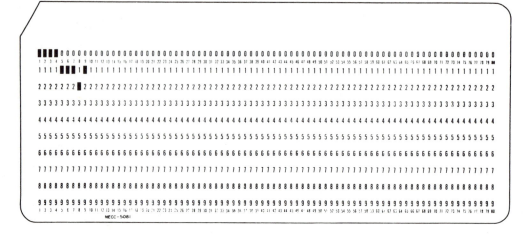

3. *Do not use the "−" and "+" punches.* In computer processing, these punches are not easily interpreted as coding categories.
4. *Use one punch per column.* Sometimes, respondents are allowed to give more than one answer to a question, in which case it seems reasonable to punch all answers in one column. However, this practice complicates computer processing.

Coding Sheets

Not all data lend themselves to direct punching from original material, and information must sometimes be recorded on coding sheets before being punched. The common coding sheet has the same format as the punchcard, with eighty columns, corresponding to the eighty columns on the card. Usually it has twenty-five lines, each line corresponding to one punchcard. The form of recording will depend on the format of the unit records that are employed in processing the data. If it is to be key-punched, horizontal listing is preferable. In this format, the items are listed across the top, with the case numbers down the side. Each item is assigned its own column or columns, the first columns being allocated to the case number. The characteristics of the respondents given in Table 11.5 can be listed on the coding sheet presented in Figure 11.3. The codes have been determined by the code book presented in Table 11.4.

The Keypunch

Information is usually recorded on a punchcard by a keypunch machine. The most common machines are the IBM 24 Card Punch and the IBM

FIGURE 11.3.   A Coding Sheet

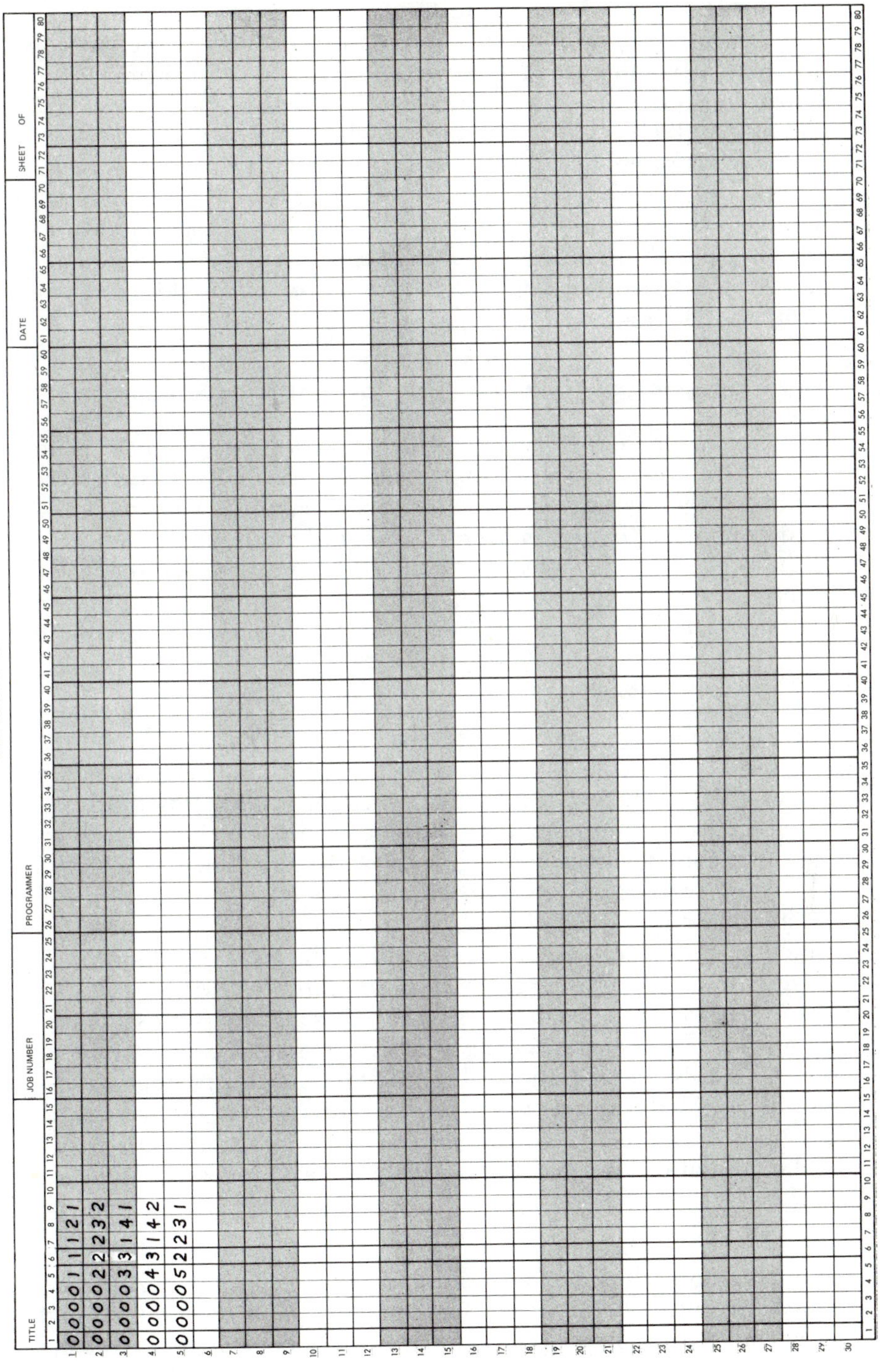

26. The IBM 26 is identical to the 24 but has the additional ability to print the information above the column in which it is punched. The card is punched by operating a typewriterlike keyboard that punches letters, digits, and other special characters. The cards are fed into position by pressing a "feed" button and are punched one column at a time. After each card is punched, the card is automatically positioned for the next column. The card is automatically stacked when completed. Control cards can be prepared and rolled around a drum contained in the machine for punching a large number of cards with the same format. Other functions that can be automatically controlled are skipping columns, printing, ejecting, and feeding cards.

DATA PROCESSING WITH UNIT RECORD EQUIPMENT

Data can be processed either with unit record equipment or with computers. Unit record machines perform specific functions such as sorting, printing, or tabulating. In the last decade, computers have been widely used to perform the functions of unit record equipment. Yet a great deal of the preliminary processing required before data are ready for computer analysis can be accomplished with these machines, and for that reason we shall briefly describe some of the more important units.

The Counter Sorter

The counter sorter is used to sort data into groups, to order it according to sequences, and to tally the cases in each group. This machine can process 650 cards per minute and is useful for large quantities of card input. The machine operates on one column at a time and distributes the cards into stacks according to the hole punched in the column for which the sorter is set. Suppose one wishes to sort out all the female voters from a file of Republican voters. Female is represented by a "2" punched, say, in column 60. To sort out all the females, the sorting mechanism would be positioned to read column 60, and the complete file would be placed in the hopper. When the start key is pressed, the cards are advanced under the sorting mechanism and all cards that have a "2" punch in column 60 will be directed to a special passage. The others will be rejected into the reject pocket. The counter sorter does no computations, but, with its sorting and tallying mechanism, it can do most of the tabulations required at the preliminary processing stage.

The Tabulator

The tabulator, which can add, subtract, and accumulate totals, is mainly used for printing contents of cards. The tabulator operates through control panel wiring. By using a standard listing control panel, the contents of cards can be printed simply by placing them in the hopper and pressing the "start" button. Complex tabulations, as well as some statistical calculations, can also be carried out by the tabulator, but these require fairly complex wiring.

COMPUTER DATA PROCESSING: SYSTEMS AND PROCEDURES

Electronic Computers

The development of electronic computers and their widespread use by social scientists have led to a significant development in the processing and analysis of data. It is far outside our scope to discuss the revolutionary aspects of computers or to provide a general introduction to computer science. Instead, we shall limit ourselves to their function in the social sciences.

Computers can perform all the specialized functions of unit record machines, but at a much higher speed. Indeed, there is little doubt that the most important property of computers is operating speed. In less than twenty years, computing speed has vastly increased, enabling operations previously impossible owing to their size and complexity. It has been noted that "the electronic computer will prove to be the most versatile and influential scientific instrument so far invented. It will play a larger role in the scientific histories of the future than even such obvious challengers as the microscope and the telescope."[14]

Yet, at present, most social scientists use the computer mainly for manipulating or compiling large masses of data. Although the computer has proved to be of tremendous help for these operations, it is not in this capacity that it provides the greatest contribution. Those who predict a glorious future for computers maintain that the main advantage "is its ability to do mathematics in a hurry."[15] Thus, it is in the development of high-powered statistical procedures that computers can be utilized by social scientists.

Input and Output Devices

The computer, however powerful, cannot function alone. Auxiliary media are needed to store and transfer the data from storage devices to the computer or to receive the processed data from the computer and

14. Charles Wrigley, "The University Computer Center," in *Computer Applications in the Behavioral Sciences*, ed. by Harold Borko (Englewood Cliffs, N. J.: Prentice-Hall, 1962), pp. 140–163.

15. Gerald P. Weeg, "The Electronic Computer," in *Automatic Data Processing*, ed. by Richard D. Duke (East Lansing: Michigan State University, 1961), pp. 23–29.

FIGURE 11.4.   High Speed Card Reader

SOURCE: Courtesy of International Business Machines Corporation.

store it. In this section, we shall briefly describe some input and output devices that perform the function of transferring data to the central processing unit or, as in the case of output units, to take the processed results from the computer and make them available to the user.[16]

The punched-card reader.   The card reader is designed to recognize holes punched in a card and to transmit the information to the central processing unit. The reader recognizes only valid characters and usually discontinues reading when an invalid character is read. An example of a high speed card reader is presented in Figure 11.4.

Printer.   One of the most typical output devices is the printer, which communicates results from the computer to the researcher on

16. Elias M. Awad and Data Processing Management Association, *Automatic Data Processing* (Englewood Cliffs, N.J.: Prentice-Hall, 1973), p. 157.

continuous paper forms. A printer translates the computer's character representations into alphabetic or numeric information.[17]

Magnetic tapes.   A different storage and input device is the magnetic tape, which is the most widely used source of secondary storage and of high-speed read-in and write-out capabilities. The main advantage of the magnetic tape over the punchcard is its high speed in reading-in and writing-out information and its relatively reduced data storage space requirement. Most magnetic tapes are made of plastic, coated on one side with a metallic oxide. Bits of information in the form of magnetic fields, referred to as magnetic spots, are recorded on the oxide side of the tape.[18] Magnetic tapes can hold many sets of information denoted as "files." A file is a distinct set of information separated from another by a tape mark.[19] Each file contains several *magnetic records* that are a series of contiguous, magnetically stored items of information.[20]

Tape units.   Reading from and writing on tape are performed by a tape unit (Figure 11.5) at a constant speed. The transfer of information to and from the tape depends on the movement of the tape across the read-write heads and on the number of characters that can be stored on an inch of tape, referred to as *packing density.*[21] Recent computer models have used magnetic tape units capable of storing 1,600 characters per inch.

Magnetic disks.   Magnetic disks are very popular storage and input output devices. They are used primarily for applications requiring large volume data. The magnetic disk unit is similar to the old 45 rpm jukebox record. It consists of five to 100 disks measuring 1½ to 4 feet in diameter, arranged vertically on a common shaft. The most popular disk models have detachable sets of disks called *disk packs.* A disk pack is composed of several platters, each resembling a phonograph record. Information is stored on a disk pack as records and files similar to those used with magnetic tapes.

THE DATA-PROCESSING CYCLE

In the previous sections, we have surveyed some of the most common devices—(the hardware) associated with automatic data processing. In

17. Ibid., pp. 165–168.

18. Ibid., p. 170.

19. William R. Klecka, Norman H. Nie, and C. Hadlai Hull, *SPSS PRIMER, Statistical Package for the Social Sciences Primer* (New York: McGraw-Hill, 1975), p. 9.

20. Ibid.

21. Awad, *Automatic Data Processing*, p. 174.

FIGURE 11.5. Tape Unit

SOURCE: Courtesy of International Business Machines Corporation.

this section, we will discuss the data-processing cycle incorporating some of the devices described previously.

The data processing cycle consists of the following functional components: input device; central processing unit (CPU); central memory and output device. These components are depicted in Figure 11.6.

Input devices. The input devices (possibly a punched card reader) transmits the data to the central processor of the computer to which the device is attached. A computer manipulates data only after they have

FIGURE 11.6. The Data-Processing Cycle

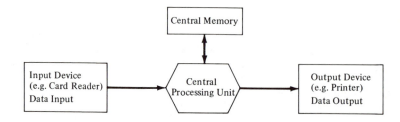

been converted into electrical impulses. The conversion is made after the data have been transferred from documents, such as questionnaires or coding sheets, to acceptable media such as punched cards, magnetic tape or magnetic disks.

Central processing unit. The central processing unit (CPU) is the heart of the computer system, controlling and coordinating all activities. The CPU decides which program to run next, executes the program instructions, and monitors the operation of the input and output devices.

Central memory. The central memory is used to store information during the time the data are being manipulated. The information may include program instructions and data. Unlike other storage media such as cards, tapes, or disks, the central memory stores information only temporarily.

Output devices. The computer produces results in the form of electrical impulses. These are then translated by output devices, such as a printer, to human language, so that the data can be interpreted easily and used effectively. Output data can also be punched on cards or recorded on magnetic tape or magnetic disks for further processing.

TYPES OF DATA PROCESSING

The researcher generally has one or more of these types of data processing available: (1) batch, (2) rapid or remote batch, and (3) interactive. In the following section, we will briefly describe each type and point to the advantages and disadvantages.

Batch processing. In batch computing, the computer handles a job that usually includes a set of data and instructions for processing and analyzing these data. In batch processing, the job is read in with a batch of other jobs and waits its turn before its execution. The turnaround time—the time between reading in and receiving the printed output—ranges between several minutes to 24 hours. The turnaround time depends on how busy the computer is relative to its capacity and length of time needed to run the job.

Rapid batch processing. The "rapid" batch or "remote job entry" batch system has a limit on the amount of computer storage that can be used by the job being processed or by the length of time it can execute. The usual procedure, under such a mode, is to have a card reader, punch, and printer set up in a convenient location, together with keypunch and consultation facilities. With this setup, turnaround time runs between a few seconds to five minutes.

Interactive processing. Interactive processing is a fairly recent method, which allows the researcher to interact directly and continuously with the computer via a teletype or other computer terminals and telephone. Lines with the interactive mode results are printed directly at the axil's terminal. The most important feature of this mode is that turnaround time is almost instantaneous.

Special programs. Despite the complexity of computers, most researchers do not need to know a great deal about computer operations in order to use them. Large libraries of computer programs are provided by most computer installations, and the user only has to learn how to use the appropriate programs. For that, it is not necessary to know computer language or how to write programs. All the necessary information is described in manuals, and the users need only to be familiar with those that contain programs of interest to them.

Most library programs are general-purpose programs, but one now in wide use meets almost all particular needs arising in the processing and analysis of social science data. It is the Statistical Package for the Social Sciences—SPSS. An introduction to this package appears in Appendix H.

SUMMARY

Data processing is a link between data collection and data analysis whereby observations are transformed into codes that are amenable to quantitative analysis. At the first stage of data processing, numerous individual observations are classified into a smaller number of categories so as to simplify the description and analysis of the data. Such systems of categories are referred to as coding schemes.

Coding schemes must be linked to the theory and the problem under study, which dictates the categories to be included in the scheme. The other requirement of a coding scheme is that it be exhaustive and mutually exclusive so that all observations can be classified and that each one can be classified only once. Coding schemes enable the translation of the data into symbols, usually numerals, that allow automatic processing. The translation is usually guided by a code book, which includes the coding schemes with their assigned symbols together with specific coding instructions.

Coded data are processed either with unit record equipment or with computers. Unit record machines, such as the keypunch or the sorter, perform specific functions such as punching or sorting, whereas computers not only perform all these functions with much greater speed but also enable the researcher to use high-powered statistical procedures for analysis.

The data-processing cycle consists of four functional components: input devices, central processing unit, central memory, and output devices. The input devices transmit data from media such as cards, tapes, or disks, to the central processor of the computer. The central processing unit controls and coordinates all activities. It decides which programs to run, executes the program instructions, and monitors the operation of the input and output devices. The central memory is used to store information during the time the data is being manipulated. Output devices translate electrical impulses generated by the computer into human language.

Finally, researchers have one or more of three types of data processing available: batch processing, rapid batch processing, and interactive processing.

KEY TERMS FOR REVIEW

Coding scheme
Deductive coding
Coding reliability
Code book
Coding sheet
Keypunch
Input device

Output device
Central processing
   unit
Central memory
Batch processing
Interactive
   processing

ADDITIONAL READINGS

Armor, David J., and Arthur S. Couch. *Data-Text Primer: An Introduction to Computerized Social Data Analysis*. New York: Free Press, 1972.

Borko, Harold, ed. *Computer Applications in Behavioral Sciences*. Englewood Cliffs, N.J.: Prentice-Hall, 1962.

Davis, Gordon B. *Computer Data Processing*. New York: McGraw-Hill, 1969.

———. *An Introduction to Electronic Computers*, 2nd ed. New York: Macmillan, 1971.

Emerich, Paul L., and J. W. Wilkinson. *Computer Programming for Business and Social Science*. Homewood, Ill.: Richard D. Irwin, 1970.

Gibson, Dana E. *An Introduction to Automated Data Processing*. Elmhurst, Ill.: Business Press, 1972.

Halacy, D. S., Jr. *Computers: The Machines We Think With*, rev. ed. New York: Harper & Row, 1969.

Price, Wilson T. *Introduction to Data Processing*. New York: Holt, Rinehart and Winston, 1972.

CHAPTER PREVIEW

CHAPTER 12

The Univariate Distribution

INTRODUCTION

Within the past three decades, all social science disciplines have experienced a rapid increase in the use of statistics. The role of statistics in the social sciences is an essential one. Without statistics we could not see the patterns and regularities in the phenomena we study. We need statistical methods to organize data, to display information in a meaningful manner, and to describe and interpret the observations in terms that will help us evaluate our hypotheses.

The word *statistics* has a dual meaning. Although it is used to refer to numbers—such as per capita income or batting averages—it is also a field of study. It is the latter usage that will be employed in the following discussion, which will show some of the more basic applications of the statistics field in the social sciences.

The Role of Statistics

The field of statistics involves methods (1) for describing and analyzing data and (2) for making decisions or inferences about phenomena represented by the data. Methods in the first category are referred to as *descriptive statistics*; methods in the second are called *inferential statistics*.

Descriptive statistics enables the researcher to summarize large quantities of data using measures that can be easily interpreted; instead of presenting measures on all observations, one of several statistical measures can be used to summarize the central tendency or dispersion of the data in an attempt to establish a meaningful pattern.

Inferential statistics allows the researcher to make decisions or inferences by interpreting data patterns. The process involves noting whether an expected pattern designated by the theory and hypotheses is actually found in the observations. We might hypothesize, for example, that blue-collar workers are politically more conservative than professionals. In order to decide whether this hypothesis is true, we might survey blue-collar workers and professionals, asking them about their political views. We then make comparisons between these groups, using descriptive statistics, and employ inferential statistics to determine whether the differences between the groups support our expectations.

Both descriptive and inferential statistics help in developing explanations for complex societal phenomena that deal with relationships between variables. Statistics provides the tools to analyze and represent and interpret these relationships.

In this chapter we will explicate the main characteristics of single-variable distributions. In the first section the frequency distribution is defined and described. The second section focuses on measures of central tendency; and the third, on measures of dispersion. The last section deals with the general form of distributions, with a focus on one general theoretical distribution—the normal curve.

THE FREQUENCY DISTRIBUTION

The data that have been coded and prepared for automatic processing are now ready for analysis. The first task is to construct frequency distributions to examine the pattern of response to each of the independent and dependent variables under investigation. (In the following discussion, *responses, answers, observations, cases, acts,* and *behavior* are used interchangeably.) A frequency distribution of a single variable, sometimes referred to as a univariate frequency distribution, is the frequency of observations in each category of a variable. For example, an examination of the pattern of response to the variable "religious affiliation" would involve a description of the number of respondents who claimed they were Protestants, Catholics, or Jews.

To construct a frequency distribution, the researcher simply lists the categories of the variable and counts the number of observations in each. Table 12.1 is an example of the standard form of a univariate frequency distribution. The table has five rows, the first four being the categories of the variable, which appear in the left-hand column, and the right-hand column shows the number of observations in each category. This number is called a *frequency,* and is usually denoted by the letter f. The last row (marked F) is the total of all frequencies appearing in the table. When the categories are mutually exclusive so that each observation is classified only once, the total number of frequencies is equal to the total

TABLE 12.1.   The General Form of a Univariate Frequency Distribution

Category	Frequency (f)
I	f_I
II	f_{II}
III	f_{III}
IV	f_{IV}
Total	F

number of observations (marked N) in the sample. In the following discussion, we shall assume that $F = N$.

With nominal variables, the categories may be listed in any arbitrary order. Thus, the variable "sex" may be described with the category "male" or the category "female" listed first. However, the categories of ordinal variables represent different rankings and are therefore arranged in order. As an illustration, consider the frequency distribution (Table 12.2) from a study that examined the effect of parent-child authority patterns on educational aspirations. The variable "authority patterns" is listed according to the degree of authoritativeness in family relationship.

Frequency Distributions with Interval Variables

When interval variables are to be summarized in frequency distributions, an initial decision must be made as to the number of categories to be used and the cutting points between them. As interval variables are ordinarily continuous, the classification into distinct categories may be quite arbitrary. For example, age may be classified into one-year, two-year, or five-year groups. Similarly, income can be classified in a number of ways.

TABLE 12.2   Authority Patterns in the Family

Authority Patterns	f
Democratic	1,858
Mixed	759
Autocratic	105
Total	2,722

SOURCE: Judie Sinclair and Richard A. Rehberg, "Selected Social Influences on Adolescent Educational Goals" (unpublished).

The intervals are usually of equal width, but the width depends both on the number of observations to be classified and the research purpose. The larger the number of observations, the wider the intervals become. However, wider categories also result in greater loss of detailed information. A general guideline to follow is that the intervals should not be so wide that two measurements included in it have a difference between them that is considered important. For example, if an age difference of one year is not of special significance for cognitive development, but a difference of two is especially important, the interval chosen may be 1–2, 3–4, 5–6. The intervals and their frequency for hypothetical population are presented in the first two columns of Table 12.3.

The *real limits* express the interval boundaries that extend one-half of one year on either side of the interval. The interval width, expressed as w_i, where the subscript i refers to the i-th interval, is the difference between the real limits of the interval:

$$w_i = U_i - L_i \qquad \text{where } U_i \text{ is the upper real limit} \\ \text{and } L_i \text{ the lower real limit.}$$

For the last interval of Table 12.3 the width is:

$$2 = 8.5 - 6.5$$

The midpoint of each interval, symbolized by x_i, is a single value, representing the class interval. It is obtained by adding half the interval width to the lower real limit of a class.[1]

$$x_i = L_i + \frac{w_i}{2}$$

Thus for the second class interval of Table 12.3 the midpoint is:

$$x_i = 2.5 + \frac{2}{2} = 3.5$$

Percentage Distributions

Summarizing the data by constructing frequency distributions of single variables is only the first step in data analysis. Next, the frequencies must be converted into figures that can be interpreted meaningfully. An absolute frequency is meaningless in itself; it needs to be compared with other frequencies. For instance, the significance of 2,000 registered Democrats in one community can be assessed only in relation to the number of all registered voters, to the number of registered Republicans, or to the number of registered Democrats in other communities.

---

1. Herman J. Loether and Donald G. McTavish, *Descriptive Statistics for Sociologists* (Boston: Allyn and Bacon, 1974).

TABLE 12.3. A Frequency Distribution of Family Size

Age in Years	f	Real Limits	Interval Midpoint x_i
1–2	6	0.5–2.5	1.5
3–4	4	2.5–4.5	3.5
5–6	10	4.5–6.5	5.5
7–8	3	6.5–8.5	7.5

Frequencies expressed in comparable numbers are called proportions or percentages. A proportion is obtained by dividing the frequency of a category by the total number of responses in the distribution. When multiplied by 100, a proportion becomes a percentage. Proportions are usually expressed as f_i/N and percentages as $f_i/N \times 100$, with f_i denoting the frequency of category i and N denoting the total number of responses. Both proportions and percentages reflect the relative weight of a specific category in the distribution. For example, the relative weight of the category "autocratic" in Table 12.2 is expressed by the proportion $105/2,722 = 0.038$ or by the percentage $105/2,722 \times 100 = 3.8$ percent. These figures indicate that only about four out of every hundred families in the group have autocratic interaction patterns with their children.

Proportions and percentages permit the comparison of two or more frequency distributions. Note, for instance, the social-class distribution of rural and urban populations displayed in Tables 12.4 and 12.5. Although in absolute numbers the middle class was more predominant in rural areas, the two populations—rural and urban—were unequal numerically; thus, a straightforward comparison of the absolute frequencies is misleading. Instead, to assess the relative weight of the classes within each distribution, the frequencies should be expressed in percentages, which reveal that the impression gained from the absolute frequencies was indeed misleading. Whereas the middle class constituted 75 percent

TABLE 12.4. Social-Class Distribution: Rural Population (in Absolute Frequencies and Percentages)

Social Class	f	Percentage
Upper middle	60	15%
Middle	300	75
Lower	40	10
Total	400	100

TABLE 12.5. Social-Class Distribution: Urban Population (in Absolute Frequencies and Percentages)

Social Class	f	Percentage
Upper middle	20	8%
Middle	200	80
Lower	30	12
Total	250	100

of the rural population, it was 80 percent of the urban group. The new figures make it easier to visualize the frequency of the rural middle class relative to the frequency of the urban middle class.

MEASURES OF CENTRAL TENDENCY

When only a short summary of the data is required, the entire distribution need not be presented. To describe the educational level of Americans by listing the schooling of all citizens of the United States would be rather impractical. Instead, it could be pointed out that most Americans are high school graduates or that the average level of education in the United States is twelve years.

In most distributions, the observations tend to cluster around a central value. For instance, any income distribution can be characterized by the most frequent income or an average income. Similarly, attitude distributions cluster around a certain range. This property can be utilized when attempting to represent a distribution by a single value. The use of such a value not only allows for economy in describing the distribution, but also facilitates comparison of different distributions. One is able to compare the average income in the United States with the average income in England or to contrast the average intelligence of Russian students with that of American students.

Statistical measures that reflect a "typical" or an "average" characteristic of a frequency distribution are referred to as measures of central tendency. The three most commonly used are the mode, the median, and the arithmetic mean.

The Mode

The mode is the category or the observation that appears most frequently in the distribution. It is used as a measure of central tendency mostly with distributions of nominal variables. To identify the mode, one singles out the category containing the largest number of responses. As an illustration, consider the distribution of religious groups presented in Table 12.6. The distribution includes five categories; the first, the Protestant group, is the most predominant. This category is thus the mode of the distribution.

Most distributions are unimodal; that is, they include only one category in which most of the cases are concentrated. At times, however, the distribution is bimodal: it includes two such maximum points. Such a pattern usually exists in distributions that combine two populations. For instance, the distribution of the heights of adults is bimodal; it comprises both men and women, and each sex is characterized by a different typical height.

The advantage of the mode is that it can be easily identified by inspection, and therefore it can be used as a first and quick indicator of the central tendency in a distribution. However, though easy to calculate, the mode is a sensitive indicator. Its position might shift whenever the manner of the distribution's division into categories is altered. Therefore, it is not a very stable measure of central tendency.

The Median

The median is a positional measure that divides the distribution into two equal parts. It is defined as the observation that is located halfway between the smallest and the largest observations in the distribution. For example, in the series 1, 3, 4, 6, 7, the median is 4. The median can be calculated with observations that are ranked according to size, and as such it can be employed with variables that are at least ordinal.

The median is obtained for ungrouped data by locating the middle observation. For an odd number of cases, it is the observation $(N + 1)/2$, where N is the total number of cases. Consider, for example, the fol-

TABLE 12.6. Frequency
Distribution of Religious Groups

Religious Group	f
Protestant	62
Catholic	52
Jewish	10
Muslim	12
Buddhist	2
Total	138

lowing set of nine observations:

$$6, 9, 11, 12, 16, 18, 21, 24, 30$$

$$\uparrow$$

Median

The fifth observation [(9 + 1)/2] divides the distribution in half; the median is therefore the value of the fifth observation, 16. With an even number of observations, the median is located halfway between the two middle observations and is calculated as an average of the observations $N/2$ and $N/2 + 1$. For example, in the following set of observations

$$1, 3, 4, 5, 6, 7, 8, 9$$

$$\uparrow$$

Median

the median is the average of the fourth (8/2) and the fifth (8/2 + 1) observations: (5 + 6)/2 = 5.5

For grouped data, the median is located by interpolating within the interval containing the middle observation. The formula for finding the median is:

$$Md = L_i + \left(\frac{N/2 - \text{Cum } F}{f_i} \right) W_i \qquad (12.1)$$

where Md = median
  L_i = the lower real limit of the interval containing the median
  Cum F = the accumulated sum of the frequencies of all intervals preceding the interval containing the median
  f_i = the frequency of the interval containing the median
  W_i = the width of the interval containing the medium

To illustrate the computation of the median, consider the distribution in Table 12.7. The table shows the age distribution of 134 persons, divided into eight ten-year age groups. Because there are 134 observations ($N = 134$), the median has the value of the sixty-seventh observation (134/2 = 67). The cumulated frequency column shows that there are sixty observations preceding the interval 41–50. The interval 41–50 contains twenty-five more observations. Hence, the sixty-seventh observation is located within the interval 41–50. It is necessary to find the exact age corresponding to the seventh case in this interval. These seven cases constitute 7/25 or 28 percent of the cases in the interval. As the width of the interval is 10 (50.5 − 40.5) we must add 28 percent of 10, namely, 2.8 years, to the lower real limit of the interval containing the median. The median is therefore 40.5 + 2.8 = 43.3. These steps can be

TABLE 12.7. Age Distribution of 134 Cases (Hypothetical)

Age	Real class limits	Frequency	Cumulated Frequency
1–10	0.5–10.5	10	10
11–20	10.5–20.5	12	22
21–30	20.5–30.5	17	39
31–40	30.5–40.5	21	60
41–50	40.5–50.5	25	85
51–60	50.5–60.5	20	105
61–70	60.5–70.5	18	123
71–80	70.5–80.5	11	134
Total		134	134

summarized by employing Equation (12.1):

$$Md = 40.5 + \left(\frac{\frac{134}{2} - 60}{25} \times 10 \right) = 40.5 + \left(\frac{7}{25} \times 10 \right)$$

$$= 40.5 + 2.8 = 43.3$$

An example. An example of the application of the median is given in Table 12.8, which describes the education of twelve groups. The investigators compared the median education of each group. The medians reflect the educational characteristics of twelve different populations, each represented by one single value. For instance, 50 percent of the white rural males completed at least 12.3 years of education; such extended schooling was enjoyed by a smaller ratio of the equivalent black population, whose median was only 8.9 years.

Other Measures of Location

The median is a special case of a more general set of measures of location called *percentiles*. The nth percentile is a number such that n percent of the scores fall below it and $(100 - n)\%$ fall above it. The median is the $n = 50$th percentile; that is, it is a number that is larger than 50 percent of the measurements and smaller than the other 50 percent.[2]

At times, it is useful to identify values that divide the distribution into three, four, or ten groups. For example, the admissions office of a

2. John H. Mueller, Karl F. Schuessler, and Herbert H. Costner, *Statistical Reasoning in Sociology* (Boston: Houghton Mifflin, 1970), pp. 175–177.

TABLE 12.8. Median of Years of Schooling

	White	Black
Males		
Residents of city center	12.1	8.7
Residents of suburbs	12.1	9.7
Residents of rural areas	12.3	8.9
Females		
Residents of city center	12.1	10.5
Residents of suburbs	12.3	10.7
Residents of rural areas	11.8	8.0

university that has decided to accept one-fourth of its applicants will be interested in finding the 25 percent with the highest scores in the entrance examinations. That is, it will locate the seventy-fifth percentile, also called the upper quartile (Q_3), which is the point above which lie 25 percent of the scores.

Equation (12.1) can be adjusted to locate positional values such as the seventy-fifth percentile, the twenty-fifth percentile (also called the lower quartile, or Q_1) or the tenth percentile (D_1). The only adjustment required is multiplying the total number of cases by the required proportion.

For the twenty-fifth percentile, the proportion is $25/100 = \frac{1}{4}$. Thus:

$$Q_1 = L_i + \left(\frac{N/4 - \text{Cum } F}{f_i} \right) W_i \tag{12.2}$$

for the upper quartile, the proportion is $75/100 = \frac{3}{4}$. Therefore

$$Q_3 = L_i + \left(\frac{3N/4 - \text{Cum } F}{f_i} \right) W_i \tag{12.3}$$

and for the tenth percentile

$$D_1 = L_i + \left(\frac{N/10 - \text{Cum } F}{f_i} \right) W_i \tag{12.4}$$

To illustrate the calculation of other measures of location we employ the data contained in Table 12.7 to find the tenth percentile.

$$D_1 = 10.5 + \left(\frac{\frac{134}{10} - 10}{12} \right) 10 = 10.5 + \left(\frac{3.4}{12} \right) 10 = 10.5 + 2.8 = 13.3$$

The Arithmetic Mean

The arithmetic mean is the measure of central tendency most frequently used. It is suitable for representing distributions measured on an interval level and is amenable to mathematical calculations; it also serves as a basis for other statistical measures. The arithmetic mean is defined as the sum total of all observations divided by their number.

In symbolic notations, the mean is defined as:

$$\bar{X} = \frac{\sum\limits_{i=1}^{N} X_i}{N} \tag{12.5}$$

where $\bar{X}$ = the arithmetic mean

$\sum\limits_{i=1}^{N} X_i$ = the sum of total observations

N = the number of observations

According to this equation, the mean ($\bar{X}$) of the series 6, 7, 12, 11, 10, 3, 4, 1, is 54/8 = 6.75.

When the mean is to be computed from a frequency distribution, it is not necessary to add up all the individual observations. Instead, each category can be given its proper weight by multiplying it by its frequency. The following equation can be used:

$$\bar{X} = \frac{\sum\limits_{i=1}^{N} f_i X_i}{N} \tag{12.6}$$

where $\sum\limits_{i=1}^{N} f_i X_i$ = the sum total of all categories multiplied by their respective frequencies.

Table 12.9 presents data on the amount of schooling received by thirty-four individuals. The mean education of this group can be calculated by using Equation (12.6). To calculate the value of $\sum f_i X_i$ (column 3), each category (column 1) is multiplied by its frequency (column 2), and the products are added up. The mean number of years of schooling is therefore:

$$\bar{X} = \frac{278}{34} = 8.18$$

Equation (12.6) can be easily applied to grouped frequency distributions, where the midpoint of the class interval is taken to represent x_i. For example, in the calculation of the mean family size for a group of

TABLE 12.9.   Distribution of Years of Study

(1) Years of Study	(2) f	(3) f_iX_i
2	3	6
3	2	6
6	5	30
8	10	80
10	8	80
12	4	48
14	2	28
Total	$N = 34$	$\Sigma f_iX_i = 278$

respondents presented in Table 12.10, only the midpoint is entered in the calculations.

$$\bar{X} = \frac{51}{18} = 2.83$$

Unlike the mode and the median, the arithmetic mean takes into account all the values in the distribution, making it especially sensitive to extreme values. For example, if one person in a group of ten earns $60,000 annually and each of the others earns $5,000, the mean income of the group would be $10,500, a figure that is not a good representation of the distribution. The mean will thus be a misleading measure of central tendency whenever there are some observations with extremely high or low values.

Comparison of the Mode, Median, and Mean.

The three measures of central tendency just analyzed can be used to represent univariate distributions. However, each has its own characteristics, which both prescribe and limit its use. The mode indicates the point in the distribution with the highest density, the median is the

TABLE 12.10.   Family Size for a Group of Respondents

Family Size	Midpoint	f	f_iX_i
0–2	1	10	10
3–5	4	5	20
6–8	7	3	21
Total		$N = 18$	$\Sigma f_iX_i = 51$

distribution's midpoint, and the arithmetic mean is an average of all the values in the distribution. Accordingly, these measures cannot be mechanically applied. How then does one know when it is preferable to use the mode, the median, or the mean? There is no simple answer to the question; it depends on the objective of the study. For example, if the researcher is investigating the average level of income of a group so as to establish how much each person would receive if all incomes were equally divided, the mean would be most pertinent, as it reflects the highest as well as the lowest income. If, on the other hand, the information is needed to estimate the eligibility of the group to receive financial aid, the mode would be appropriate, for it shows the most typical income and is unaffected by extreme values.

The application of any measure of central tendency also depends on the level of measurement of the variable being analyzed. The mode can represent the distribution of party affiliation, which is a nominal variable. On the other hand, the median can be applied to ordinal variables such as political attitudes. The arithmetic mean is used with interval variables such as income and age. Generally, it is possible to use the measures appropriate for lower levels of measurement, but not for those of higher levels; for instance, income can be represented by the mode, but the arithmetic mean cannot represent the distribution of party affiliation.

MEASURES OF DISPERSION

Measures of central tendency identify the most representative value of the distribution. However, a complete description of the distribution requires that we measure the extent of dispersion about this central value. (In the following discussion, the terms *dispersion, scatter,* and *variation* are used interchangeably.) The actual observations are distributed among many values, and the extent of their spread varies from one distribution to another. For example, two classes may have the same average grade; however, one class may include some excellent students as well as some very poor ones, whereas all the students in the other may be of average ability. Similarly, income distributions with an identical mean may present different patterns of dispersion. In some distributions, most incomes are clustered around the mean; in others, the incomes are widely dispersed. The description of the extent of dispersions about the central value is obtained by several measures designated as measures of dispersion. In this section, we shall discuss the measure of qualitative variation, the range, the mean deviation, the variance, the standard deviation, and the coefficient of variation.

The Measure of Qualitative Variation

The extent of dispersion in nominal distributions can be assessed by means of an index of heterogeneity designated as the measure of qualitative variation. This index reflects the number of differences among the categories of the distribution and is based on the number of categories and their respective frequencies. In general, the larger the number of categories and the greater the overall differences among them, the greater will be the degree of variation. Likewise, the smaller the number of categories and their differences, the smaller will be the variation within the distribution. As an illustration, consider the racial composition of several communities. In an all-white community, there are no racial differences, but in racially mixed communities there will be smaller or larger degrees of variation. The amount of variation will depend on the composition of the community. When most belong to a single racial group, the number of racial differences among the members of the community will be relatively small. Conversely, when most members are divided among several racial groups, the number of differences will be large.

Calculating the total number of differences. The measure of qualitative variation is based on the ratio of the total number of differences in the distribution to the maximum number of possible differences within the same distribution. In order to find the total number of differences in the distribution, the differences between each category and every other category are counted and summed. For instance, in a group of fifty whites and fifty blacks, each of the whites will differ in race from each of the blacks, thereby making a total of 2,500 racial differences. In a group of seventy whites and thirty blacks, there are 2,100 differences. In a group of one hundred whites and no blacks, there are no racial differences.

The procedure for calculating the total number of differences can be expressed in the following equation:

$$\text{Total Observed Differences} = \sum f_i f_j, \quad i \neq j \qquad (12.7)$$

where f_i = frequency of category i
f_j = frequency of category j

For example, in a group of twenty Catholics, thirty Jews, and ten Muslims, there would be $(20 \times 30) + (20 \times 10) + (30 \times 10) = 1,100$ religious differences.

Calculating the maximum possible differences. The total of observed differences is meaningful only in relation to the maximum possible number of differences, for each distribution has a different number of categories and of frequencies. Relating the observed differences to the maximum possible differences has the effect of controlling for these factors. The maximum number of differences occurs when each category in the distribution has an identical frequency. Thus, the maximum number of frequencies is computed by finding the number of differences that would be observed if all frequencies were equal. Symbolically:

$$\text{Maximum Possible Differences} = \frac{n(n - 1)}{2} \left(\frac{F}{n}\right)^2 \qquad (12.8)$$

where n = the number of categories in the distribution
F = total frequency

In the previous example of twenty Catholics, thirty Jews, and ten Muslims, the maximum possible differences are

$$\left(\frac{3 \times 2}{2}\right) \left(\frac{60}{3}\right)^2 = 1,200$$

The measure of qualitative variation is the ratio between the total observed differences and the maximum possible differences. In other words,

$$\text{Measure of Qualitative Variation} = \frac{\text{Total Observed Differences}}{\text{Maximum Possible Differences}}$$

Symbolically, the measure is expressed in the following equation:

$$\text{Measure of Qualitative Variation} = \frac{\sum f_i f_j}{\frac{n(n - 1)}{2} \left(\frac{F}{n}\right)^2} \qquad (12.9)$$

The measure of variation for the last example is:

$$\text{Measure of Qualitative Variation} = \frac{1,100}{1,200} = .92$$

The measure of qualitative variation varies between zero and one. Zero indicates the absence of any variation, whereas one reflects maximum variation. The measure will be zero whenever the total observed differences are zero. It will take the value of one when the number of observed differences is equal to the maximum possible differences.

An application of the measure of qualitative variation is the Nachmias and Rosenbloom work on representative bureaucracy. The investigators used the measure to compare the degree of social integration in selected Federal agencies in 1970.[3] Their results are presented in Table 12.11, where selected federal agencies are ranked according to the degree of integration in their general schedule work force. The table con-

---

3. David Nachmias and David H. Rosenbloom, "Measuring Bureaucratic Representation and Integration," *Public Administration Review*, 33 (1973): 590–597.

TABLE 12.11. The Social Integration of the General Schedule Work Forces of Selected Federal Agencies, 1970

Agency	Percentage					Total	Measure of Variation
	Black	Spanish Surnamed	American Indian	Oriental	Other		
EEOC	49.9	9.5	.8	.9	38.9	748	.71
Government Printing Office	53.6	.4	.2	.3	45.6	1,548	.63
State	31.5	2.2	.3	.9	65.1	5,810	.60
Labor	25.7	1.7	.4	.5	71.7	10,535	.52
GSA	24.1	1.6	.2	1.0	73.2	18,931	.51
HEW	21.3	1.5	2.4	.7	74.1	94,502	.51
CSC	23.0	2.3	.2	.7	73.8	5,216	.50
VA	22.0	1.8	.2	1.0	75.1	115,997	.48
HUD	18.6	1.5	.3	.7	78.9	14,721	.43
Interior	4.0	1.7	12.7	.8	80.9	50,725	.41
Post Office	17.9	.6	.1	.6	80.7	2,775	.40
Small Business Administration	11.6	5.4	.4	.5	82.0	4,272	.39
Commerce	14.5	.6	.1	.8	84.0	29,115	.34
Treasury	12.3	1.5	.1	.7	85.4	82,318	.32
GAO	13.6	.6	.1	.4	85.3	4,598	.32
Justice	9.6	2.4	.1	.4	87.5	36,947	.28
Army	8.7	2.2	.2	1.0	87.9	237,914	.27
Defense (entire)	7.8	2.4	.2	1.0	88.7	600,044	.26
Navy	8.0	1.3	.2	1.3	89.3	158,986	.25
Air Force	4.6	4.3	.3	.7	90.1	151,217	.23
Agriculture	5.5	1.3	.3	.5	92.3	81,437	.18
Transportation	5.4	1.1	.3	.5	92.8	58,690	.17
NASA	2.7	.6	.1	.6	96.0	27,278	.10

SOURCE: U.S. Civil Service Commission, *Minority Group Employment in the Federal Government*, November 30, 1970.

tains information that clearly indicates the utility of the measure. If an agency were proportionally representative of the social composition of the society as a whole, its measure of variation would be about .30. Thus more than half of the agencies in Table 12.11 are more integrated in terms of their social composition than is the society at large.

The Range and the Interquartile Range

The range measures the distance between the highest and lowest values of the distribution. For example, in the following set of observations

$$4, 6, 8, 9, 17$$

the range is the difference between 17 and 4; that is, 13 (17 − 4 = 13). This measure requires that observations be ranked according to size; thus, it can be applied in cases where the distribution is at least on an ordinal level of measurement. The range has a special significance when a dearth of information produces a distorted picture of reality. For instance, two factories with annual average wages of $15,000 have different pay ranges; one has a range of $2,000, and the other has a range of $9,000. Without the additional information supplied by the range, one would get the impression that the wage scales in both factories were identical. The range is a useful device for gaining a quick impression of the data. However, it is a crude measure of dispersion because it takes into account only the distribution's two extreme values. Thus, it is sensitive to changes in one single score.

An alternative to the range is the interquartile range, which is the difference between the lower and upper quartiles (Q_1 and Q_3). It measures the spread in the middle half of the distribution, and is less affected by extreme observations. The lower and upper quartiles will vary less from distribution to distribution than will the most extreme observations; thus, the interquartile range is a more stable measure of dispersion than is the range.[4] To illustrate the interquartile range, consider the data in Table 12.7. The lower quartile (Q_1) for these data is 27.76, and the upper quartile (Q_3) is 58.75. These values were calculated with Equations 12.2 and 12.3. The interquartile range is thus 58.75 − 27.76 = 30.99. This figure indicates that the range of the middle half of this age distribution is 30.99. The principle of the interquartile range can be applied to any part of the distribution. For example, one can calculate the range between the tenth and ninetieth percentiles to measure the dispersion of the middle 80 percent of the observations.

Limitations of the range and interquartile range as measures of dispersion. The various measures of dispersion discussed above have a major drawback in that, being based on two values alone, they reflect

4. Hubert M. Blalock, *Social Statistics*, 2nd ed. (New York: McGraw-Hill, 1972), pp. 77–79.

only the dispersion in some defined section of the distribution. Some measure must be devised that will reflect the aggregate dispersion in the distribution. However, to measure aggregate dispersion it is necessary to establish the deviation of all the values in the distribution from some criterion. In other words, some norm is to be decided upon that will permit one to determine which value is higher, or lower, than expected. For example, the evaluation of income as "high" or "low" is meaningful only in relation to some fixed criterion. Income evaluated as "high" in India would be considered "low" in the United States.

Any of the measures of central tendency analyzed so far can be chosen as a norm. It is possible to measure deviations from the mode, the median, or the arithmetic mean; however, the latter is used as a basis for calculation of measures of dispersion that are employed more extensively.

Measures of Dispersion Based on the Mean

The simplest way to obtain a measure of deviation is to calculate the average deviation from the arithmetic mean:

$$\text{Average deviation} = \frac{\sum_{i=1}^{N} (X_i - \bar{X})}{N}$$

where X_i = each individual observation
$\bar{X}$ = arithmetic mean
N = total number of observations

However, the sum of the deviations from the mean is always equal to zero; thus, the average deviation will be zero, for its numerator will always be zero. This property of the mean can be bypassed in two ways: by ignoring the signs and taking the deviations' absolute values or by squaring the deviations. The mean deviation is obtained with the first method; the standard deviation, with the second.

The Mean Deviation

The mean deviation makes use of every observation in the distribution. It is computed by taking the difference between each observation and the mean, summing the absolute value of these deviations, and dividing the sum by the total number of observations. Symbolically, the measure is expressed in Equation (12.10):

$$\text{Mean deviation} = \frac{\sum_{i=1}^{N} |X_i - \bar{X}|}{N} \qquad (12.10)$$

where X_i = each individual observation

$\bar{X}$ = arithmetic mean

N = total number of observations

$||$ = the absolute difference

For example, to compute the mean deviation of the scores

$$2, 4, 6, 8, 10$$

we first calculate the mean

$$\bar{X} = \frac{2 + 4 + 6 + 8 + 10}{5} = \frac{30}{5} = 6$$

We then subtract the mean from each score and obtain the following deviations:

$$-4, -2, 0, +2, +4$$

These deviations are summed by ignoring the signs and dividing by the number of scores:

$$\text{Mean deviation} = \frac{4 + 2 + 0 + 2 + 4}{5} = \frac{12}{5} = 2.4$$

This figure indicates that the mean difference between each score and the arithmetic mean is 2.4.

The advantage of the mean deviation is that it takes into account all the observations in the distribution. However, absolute values are not amenable to arithmetic manipulations; thus, the mean deviation, which is based on such values, cannot be applied when further mathematical calculations are required.

The Variance and the Standard Deviation

The computation of the variance and standard deviation is similar to the mean deviation, except that, instead of taking the deviation's absolute values, they are squared and then summed and divided by the total number of observations. The definitional formula for the variance is:

$$s^2 = \frac{\sum\limits_{i=1}^{N} (X_i - \bar{X})^2}{N} \tag{12.11}$$

where s^2 = variance.

In other words, the arithmetic mean is subtracted from each score; the differences are then squared, summed, and divided by the total number of observations. The numerical example of Table 12.12 illustrates the various steps involved in the computation of the variance. Applying

Equation (12.11) to the data, we get

$$s^2 = \frac{200}{5} = 40$$

In a simpler computational formula of the variance, the squared mean is subtracted from the squared sum of all scores divided by the number of observations; that is,

$$s^2 = \frac{\sum\limits_{i=1}^{N} X_i^2}{N} - \bar{X}^2 \qquad (12.12)$$

Equation (12.12) is applied to the same data of Table 12.12

$$s^2 = \frac{605}{5} - 81 = 121 - 81 = 40$$

In reflecting squared deviations, the variance expresses the average dispersion in the distribution not in the original units of measurement but in squared units. This problem is bypassed by taking the square root of the variance, thereby transforming the variance into the standard deviation. The standard deviation is a measure expressing dispersion in the original units of measurement. Symbolically, the standard deviation is expressed in Equations (12.13) and (12.14), corresponding to Equations (12.11) and (12.12) respectively:

$$s = \sqrt{\frac{\sum\limits_{i=1}^{N} (X_i - \bar{X})^2}{N}} \qquad (12.13)$$

$$s = \sqrt{\frac{\sum\limits_{i=1}^{N} X_i^2}{N} - \bar{X}^2} \qquad (12.14)$$

where s = standard deviation

For the previous example, the value of the standard deviation is—using Equation (12.13)—

$$s = \sqrt{\frac{200}{5}} = \sqrt{40} = 6.3$$

The Variance and the Standard Deviation for Grouped Data

Very often the data are grouped, and then a different procedure for computing the variance and the standard deviation has to be employed.

TABLE 12.12.   Computation of the Variance

X_i	$X_i - \bar{X}$	$(\bar{X}_i - \bar{X})^2$	X_i^2
3	−6	36	9
4	−5	25	16
6	−3	9	36
12	3	9	144
20	11	121	400
Total		200	605

$\bar{X} = 9$

Equation (12.15) can be applied to grouped data where the interval's midpoint is represented by X_i and f_i stands for the corresponding frequencies.[5]

$$s^2 = \frac{\sum f_i X_i^2 - (f_i X_i)^2/N}{N} \tag{12.15}$$

This formula is applied to the data of Table 12.13.

$$s^2 = \frac{1094 - (136)^2/20}{20} = \frac{1094 - 18496/20}{20} = \frac{1094 - 924.8}{20}$$

$$= \frac{169.20}{20} = 8.46$$

We can now obtain the standard deviation by simply taking the square root of 8.46. Thus

$$s = \sqrt{8.46} = 2.91$$

TABLE 12.13.   Age Distribution of 20 Respondents

Age	Midpoint X_i	f	X_i^2	$f_i X_i^2$	$f_i X_i$
1–3	2	4	4	16	8
4–6	5	3	25	75	15
7–9	8	10	64	640	80
10–12	11	3	121	363	33
Total		20		$\Sigma f_i X_i^2 = 1094$	$\Sigma f_i X_i = 136$

5. Loether and McTavish, *Descriptive Statistics for Sociologists*, p. 154.

The Standard Deviation: Advantages and Applications

The standard deviation has various advantages over other measures of dispersion. First, it is more stable from sample to sample. (On sampling, see Chapter 16.) Second, it has some important mathematical properties that enable the researcher to obtain the standard deviation for two or more groups combined. Furthermore, its mathematical properties make it a useful measure in more advanced statistical work, especially in the area of statistical inferences (see Chapters 16 and 17).

The application of the standard deviation as a research device is illustrated in the following example. Table 12.14 compares differences in feelings of life satisfaction among persons of several countries, using the mean and standard deviation of the variable "life satisfaction" in each country.

The mean scores are almost identical, implying that satisfaction with life is similar in the countries studied. However, there are differences in the standard deviations of each country. The relatively low standard deviations in England, Germany, and the United States indicate that these countries are homogeneous as far as satisfaction is concerned; that is, people have a satisfaction score which is close to their group's mean score. In Italy, however, the dispersion is greater, suggesting that the degree of satisfaction reflected by the mean is not common to all the Italians in the group studied.

The Coefficient of Variation (V)

Standard deviations cannot be compared in absolute magnitudes in instances where the distributions compared have very different means. A standard deviation of 2, for instance, would convey a different meaning in relation to a mean of 6 than to a mean of 60. Therefore, the degree of dispersion must be calculated relative to the mean of the distribution. This principle is implemented in the *coefficient of variation*, which reflects relative variation. Symbolically, the coefficient of variation is defined as follows:

$$V = \frac{s}{\bar{X}} \qquad (12.16)$$

TABLE 12.14.   Mean and Standard Deviation on an Index of Life Satisfaction in Four Western Nations (Hypothetical Data)

England (903)		*Germany* (950)		*Italy* (998)		*USA* (980)	
Mean	SD	Mean	SD	Mean	SD	Mean	SD
6.7	1.0	6.7	1.2	6.6	3.2	6.5	1.3

NOTE: The figures in parentheses denote the number of persons interviewed in each group.

TABLE 12.15. Political Participation in Four Countries: Mean and Standard Deviation.

England (963)		Germany (955)		Italy (995)		USA (970)	
Mean	SD	Mean	SD	Mean	SD	Mean	SD
4.75	2.7	5.4	2.9	2.8	2.8	5.64	2.7

SOURCE: Giuseppe di Palma, *Apathy and Participation* (New York: Free Press, 1970), p. 220. Copyright © 1970 by The Free Press, a division of Macmillan Publishing Co., Inc. Reprinted with permission of the publisher.
NOTE: The figures in parentheses denote the number of cases; scores ranged from 0 to 12.

where V = coefficient of variation
$\quad$ s = standard deviation
$\quad$ $\bar{X}$ = arithmetic mean.

To illustrate the application of the coefficient of variation, consider the data in Table 12.15 from di Palma's comparative investigation on political behavior. Presented are the means and standard deviations of the variable "political participation." In absolute magnitudes, there are no significant differences among the standard deviations in the four countries. However, there are substantial differences between the means, indicating varying degrees of participation in each country. In Italy, for example, the mean participation is much lower than in the other countries, but the degree of dispersion is almost identical. Intuitively, however, it seems that a deviation of 2.8 has a greater significance in relation to a mean of 2.8 than to a mean of 4.75 or 5.4. To correct for these discrepancies, the standard deviations were converted into coefficients of variation. The results are displayed in Table 12.16. It is noticed that, indeed, the relative deviation from the mean is higher in Italy than in other countries, reflecting the lower degree of homogeneity in political participation.

TYPES OF FREQUENCY DISTRIBUTIONS

The discussion of univariate distributions has thus far been limited to descriptive measures reflecting central tendencies and dispersion. The

TABLE 12.16. Mean Political Participation and Coefficient of Variation in Four Countries.

England (963)		Germany (955)		Italy (995)		USA (970)	
Mean	V	Mean	V	Mean	V	Mean	V
4.75	0.57	5.4	0.54	2.8	1.00	5.65	0.48

SOURCE: The figures in parentheses denote the number of cases.

next step in describing a distribution is to identify its general form. Distributions may have distinctive forms with few low scores and many high scores, with many scores concentrated in the middle of the distribution, or with many low scores and few high scores.

The simplest way to describe a distribution is by a visual representation. Examples of different forms are presented in Figure 12.1.

The values of the variable are represented along the baseline, and the area under the curve represents the frequencies. For example, in distribution *a*, the frequency of the interval 25–35 is represented by the area under the curve in that interval. The distribution (Figure 12.1a) is a symmetrical distribution; that is, the frequencies at the right and left tails of the distribution are identical, so that if the distribution is divided into two halves, each will be the mirror image of the other. This usually means that most of the observations are concentrated at the middle of the distribution, and that there are few observations with very high or very low scores. An example of a symmetrical distribution is the height of men. Few men are very short or very tall; most are of medium height. Many other variables tend to be distributed symmetrically, and this form of distribution plays an important role in the field of statistical inference.

In nonsymmetrical distributions, there are more extreme cases in one direction of the distribution than in the other. A nonsymmetrical distribution in which there are more extremely low scores is referred to as a negatively skewed distribution (Figure 12.1b). When there are more extremely high scores, the distribution is positively skewed (Figure 12.1c). Most income distributions are positively skewed, with few families having extremely high incomes.

Skewness can also be identified according to the positions of the measures of central tendency. With symmetrical distributions, the mean will coincide with the median and the mode; with skewed distributions, there will be discrepancies between these measures. In a negatively skewed distribution, the mean will be pulled in the direction of the lower scores; in a positively skewed distribution, it will be located closer to

FIGURE 12.1. Types of Frequency Distributions

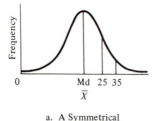 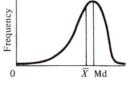 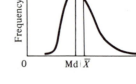

a. A Symmetrical
   Distribution

b. A Negatively Skewed
   Distribution

c. A Positively Skewed
   Distribution

the high scores. This property of skewed distributions makes the choice of an average value a critical issue. Since the mean is pulled in the direction of the extreme scores, it loses its typicality, and hence its usefulness as a representative measure. In such instances, it might be useful to employ the median or the mode instead.

The Normal Curve

One type of symmetrical distribution is called the *normal curve*; it has great significance in the field of statistics. A normal curve is shown in Figure 12.2. Its principal properties are as follows:

1. it is symmetrical and bell-shaped;
2. the mode, the median, and the mean coincide at the center of the distribution;
3. the curve is based on an infinite number of observations; and
4. a single mathematical formula describes how frequencies are related to the values of the variable.

The fifth property of the normal curve is its most distinct characteristic. *In any normal distribution, a fixed proportion of the observations lies between the mean and fixed units of standard deviations.* The proportions can be seen in Figure 12.2. The mean of the distribution divides it exactly in half: 34.13 percent is included between the mean and one standard deviation to the right of the mean; the same proportion is included between the mean and one standard deviation to the left of the mean. The plus signs indicate standard deviations above the mean; and the minus signs, standard deviations below the mean. Thus, between $\bar{X} \pm 1s$ are included 68.26 percent of all observations in the distribution; between $\bar{X} \pm 2s$ are 95.46 percent of the observations; and between $\bar{X} \pm 3s$ are 99.73 percent of the observations.

FIGURE 12.2.   Proportions Under the Normal Curve

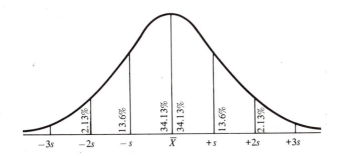

In any univariate distribution that is normally distributed, the proportion of observations included within fixed distances of the mean can be determined. For example, in a distribution of intelligence with a mean of 110 and a standard deviation of 10, 68.26 percent of all cases have an intelligence quotient between $110 \pm 1s$—that is, between 100 and 120—and 95.46 percent have a score that is not below 90 and does not exceed 130.

Standard Scores

To evaluate the proportion of observations included within an interval desired, one must express observations in standard deviation units. For instance, to find the proportion of cases that have an IQ between 110 and 130, one has to determine how many standard deviations away from the mean the score of 130 is located. Observations are converted into standard deviation units by means of Equation (12.17):

$$Z = \frac{X_i - \bar{X}}{s} \qquad (12.17)$$

where Z = number of standard deviation units
X_i = any observation
$\bar{X}$ = arithmetic mean
s = standard deviation

Z, sometimes referred to as a *standard score*, expresses the distance between a specific observation (X_i) and the mean in terms of standard deviation units. A Z of 2 means that the distance between the mean of the distribution and X_i is two standard deviations. For example, in a distribution with a mean of 40 and a standard deviation of 5, the score of 50 is expressed as follows:

$$Z = \frac{50 - 40}{5} = \frac{10}{5} = 2$$

The score of 50 lies two standard deviations above the mean. Similarly, 30 is two standard deviations below the mean:

$$\frac{30 - 40}{5} = \frac{-10}{5} = -2$$

To determine the proportion of observations that lie between the mean and any observation in the distribution, special tables have been constructed for the standard form of the normal curve. The tables show proportions for various Z values. In the left-hand column are listed the first two digits of Z; the third digit is shown across the top. Thus, for example, the proportion included between the mean and a Z of 1 is .3413, or 34.13 percent; the value for a Z of 1.65 is .4505. Only one-half of the

FIGURE 12.3.

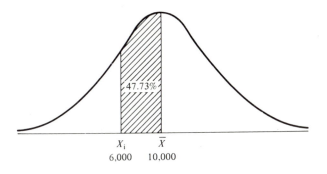

X_i : 6,000   X̄ : 10,000

curve's proportions is given, because the curve is symmetrical. Thus, the distance between the mean and a Z of −1.0 is identical to the area between the mean and a Z of 1.0. To use the table, one first finds the appropriate Z score for any particular observation by Equation (12.17), and then consults Appendix C.

To illustrate the use of the standard normal table, suppose the distribution of income in a particular community is normal, its mean income is $10,000, and the standard deviation is $2,000. We want to determine what proportion of the people in this community have an income between $6,000 and $10,000. First, $6,000 is converted into standard deviation units:

$$Z = \frac{6{,}000 - 10{,}000}{2{,}000} = -2$$

Next, it is seen in Appendix C that .4773 of all observations are included between the mean and a Z of 2. In other words, 47.73 percent of all people in the community earn between $6,000 and $10,000 a year. This is shown in Figure 12.3.

What proportion of the community earns between $11,000 and $15,000? Both figures are converted into standard scores:

$$Z_1 = \frac{11{,}000 - 10{,}000}{2{,}000} = 0.5$$

$$Z_2 = \frac{15{,}000 - 10{,}000}{2{,}000} = 2.5$$

Appendix C indicates that .4938 is included between the mean and 2.5 standard deviation units, and .1915 between the mean and 0.5 units. Therefore, the area included between $11,000 and $15,000 is .4938 − .1915 = .3023 (30.23 percent). This is shown in Figure 12.4.

FIGURE 12.4.

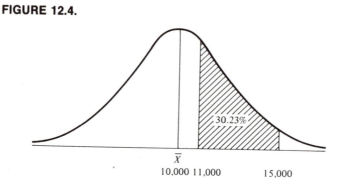

$\overline{X}$
10,000 11,000   15,000

SUMMARY

The preliminary stage of analysis consists of quite ordinary methods designed to provide a straightforward description of the data. Once coded, each item is summarized in some tabular form, and measures such as averages and percentages are calculated to describe its main characteristics. It is common to begin the analysis by showing how the respondents are distributed on all the items of the investigation. A distribution might show, for instance, that twenty of the eighty respondents included in a sample are males, and the rest are females; that forty-six are Democrats, twenty are Republicans, and fourteen do not identify with any party. Such listings of the number of observations that fall into each of several categories are termed frequency distributions. Frequencies are often converted into proportions or percentages; these are helpful in assessing the weight of a single category in relation to other categories of the distribution or in relation to other distributions.

Often, it is useful to obtain some average value that is representative of the distribution. For example, one may need to answer such questions as "What is the most typical political orientation of this group of respondents?" or "What is their average income?" These questions can be answered by using measures of central tendency. The three commonly used statistical measures of central tendency are the mode, the median, and the arithmetic mean.

Measures of central tendency can be misleading if they are not accompanied by measures of dispersion that describe the amount of dispersion in the distribution. Whereas the measures of central tendency reflect the most typical or average characteristics of the group, the measures of dispersion indicate how many members of the group deviate from it and the extent of the deviation. Whereas a small deviation denotes that most responses are clustered around the measure of central tendency, a large deviation indicates that the measure is a poor representation of the distribution.

Finally, one of the important steps in examining a distribution is the identification of its general form. Certain kinds of forms are characteristic of different empirical phenomena. For instance, many income distributions have few extremely high incomes; most incomes are concentrated in the middle or lower ranges. Such distributions are skewed toward the higher values. On the other hand, intelligence distributions are typically symmetrical; most scores are concentrated in the middle range, with very few extremely high or extremely low scores.

KEY TERMS FOR REVIEW

Descriptive
  statistics
Inferential statistics
Midpoint
Mode
Median
Measure of
  qualitative
  variation

Interquartile range
Mean deviation
Variance
Coefficient of
  variation
Skewed distribution
Normal curve
Standard score

ADDITIONAL READINGS

Anderson, R. Theodore, and Morris Zelditch, Jr. *A Basic Course in Statistics*, 2nd ed. New York: Holt, Rinehart and Winston, 1968, pp. 17–89.

Handel, Judith D. *Introductory Statistics for Sociology*. Englewood Cliffs, N.J.: Prentice-Hall, 1978.

Huff, Darrell. *How to Lie with Statistics*. London: Victor Gollancz, 1964.

Iversen, Gudmund R. *Statistics for Sociology*. Dubuque, Iowa: William C. Brown Co., 1979.

Langley, Russell. *Practical Statistics*, rev. ed. New York: Dover, 1970, Chapter 4.

Freeman, Linton C. *Elementary Applied Statistics*. New York: Wiley, 1965, pp. 29–67.

Palumbo, Dennis J. *Statistics in Political and Behavioral Science*. New York: Appleton-Century-Crofts, 1969, Chapters 2 and 3.

Zeller, Richard A., and Edward G. Carmines. *Statistical Analysis of Social Data*. Chicago: Rand McNally, 1978.

CHAPTER PREVIEW

INTRODUCTION

THE CONCEPT OF
   RELATIONSHIP

   How to Construct a Bivariate
     Table
   The Principle of Covariation—An
     Example
   Precentaging Bivariate Tables
   Median and Mean as Covariation
     Measures

THE MEASUREMENT OF
   RELATIONSHIP

   Proportional Reduction of Error
     Principle

NOMINAL MEASURES OF
   RELATIONSHIP

   Guttman Coefficient of
     Predictability (lambda—λ)
   Goodman and Kruskal's Tau (τ_b)

ORDINAL MEASURES OF
   RELATIONSHIP

   The Pair Concept
   Types of Pairs
   Gamma (γ or G)
   Kendall's Tau-b and Tau-c

INTERVAL MEASURES OF
   RELATIONSHIP

   Prediction Rules
   Linear Regression
   The Criterion of Least Squares
   Errors of Prediction
   Pearson's Product Moment
     Correlation Coefficient (r)

SUMMARY

KEY TERMS FOR REVIEW

ADDITIONAL READINGS

CHAPTER 13
Bivariate Analysis

INTRODUCTION

Once single variables have been summarized and their pattern of distribution described, the researcher confronts the next task in the analysis of data: examining the pattern of relationship between the variables under investigation. This chapter examines different methods for measuring bivariate relationships between variables. The first section discusses the concept of relationship; the second section describes nominal measures of relationship; the third section deals with ordinal measures of relationship; and the last section presents interval measures of relationship.

THE CONCEPT OF RELATIONSHIP

Each of us, whether scientist or layperson, is aware of what relationships are. We know that, in the world around us, things go together. It is observed that as children grow, their weight increases; that cities tend to be more polluted than rural areas; and that the crime rate is higher in central cities than in suburbs. Each of these observations is a statement of a relationship: between age and weight, between degree of urbanization and pollution, and between living conditions and crime.

To say that people who live in slums are usually unskilled is to describe a relationship between living conditions and occupation. This statement can be made only if it is known that people who have better living conditions are also trained for skilled work. In other words, to state a relationship between X and Y is to say that certain categories of the variable X go with certain categories of the variable Y. This—the

323

principle of covariation—is basic to the notion of association and relation, and it refers to the idea that observations can be placed in several categories simultaneously. For example, lower-class people are also often Democrats, and highly educated individuals have higher incomes.

The first step in examining a relationship between two variables is the construction of a bivariate table. The steps involved in the construction of bivariate tables are discussed in the following section.

How to Construct a Bivariate Table

A bivariate table is one in which two variables have been cross-classified. It consists of rows and columns, where the categories of one variable are labels for the rows and the categories of the second variable are labels for the columns. Usually, the independent variable is the column variable, and the dependent variable is the row variable.[1] As an illustration of how a bivariate table is constructed, observe the data presented in Box 13.1. Sixteen individuals have been listed by their sex and their job satisfaction scores. These observations have been tallied and classified by their joint position on sex and job satisfaction into the appropriate cells in Table 13.1. The table is a 3-by-2 table because it has three rows and two columns, each representing a category of either the variable sex or the variable job satisfaction. The fourth row represents the column totals; and the third column, the row totals. Usually, bivariate tables are set up with the independent variable listed across the top (column variable) and the dependent variable listed at the left side of the table (row variable). However, this convention is not always adhered to.

The Principle of Covariation—An Example

The principle of covariation is demonstrated in Tables 13.2, 13.3, and 13.4. These tables summarize information on two variables: religious denomination and social class.[2] Table 13.2 illustrates a pattern of perfect covariation of the variables. It is observed that all the Catholics are classified into the low social-class category, that all Jews belong to the middle class, and that the Protestants occupy the high social-class category. The two variables covary because specific categories of the variable "religious denomination" go with specific categories of the variable "social class."

The same pattern recurs in Table 13.3, but to a lesser extent because not all members of a given religious denomination belong to the same

1. Herman J. Loether and Donald G. McTavish, *Descriptive Statistics for Sociologists* (Boston: Allyn and Bacon, 1974), pp. 174–176.

2. John H. Mueller, Karl F. Schuessler, and Herbert L. Costner, *Statistical Reasoning in Sociology* (Boston: Houghton Mifflin, 1970), pp. 242–248.

BOX 13.1.

Sex	Job Satisfaction
Male = M	High = H
Female = F	Medium = M
	Low = L

Id Number	Sex	Job Satisfaction
1	M	H
2	M	H
3	F	H
4	M	M
5	F	L
6	F	L
7	F	L
8	M	M
9	M	H
10	F	M
11	M	H
12	M	H
13	M	L
14	F	M
15	F	L
16	F	H

TABLE 13.1.   Satisfaction by Sex

	Sex		
Job Satisfaction	Male	Female	Row Totals
High	5	2	7
Medium	2	2	4
Low	1	4	5
Column Totals	8	8	16

TABLE 13.2.   Social Class by Religious Denomination (Perfect Covariation)

	Religious Denomination			
Social Class	Catholic	Jewish	Protestant	Total
Upper	0	0	8	8
Middle	0	8	0	8
Lower	8	0	0	8
Total	8	8	8	24

**TABLE 13.3. Social Class by Religious Denomination
(Moderate Covariation)**

| Social Class | Religious Denomination | | | |
	Catholic	Jewish	Protestant	Total
Upper	0	2	6	8
Middle	1	6	1	8
Lower	7	0	1	8
Total	8	8	8	24

class. Yet it can still be said that most members of a particular religion belong to a particular social stratum.

When variables are not related, it is said that they are independent of each other, that is, that they do not "go together." Table 13.4 illustrates this point. There is no clear pattern for any of the religious groups in the table. Catholics can be upper, middle, or lower class, because they are more or less equally distributed among the three classes; the same goes for the Jews and the Protestants. One cannot say anything about a person's socioeconomic status on the basis of his or her religion.

Tables 13.2, 13.3, and 13.4 are examples of bivariate distributions arranged in tabular form. The bivariate distribution consists of the categories of two variables and their joint frequencies. Its components are displayed in the bivariate tables of our example. Each table has two dimensions, one per variable. The variables are divided into a number of categories; for example, the variable "social class" has been divided into the categories "upper," "middle," and "lower," and the variable "religious denomination" into "Catholic," "Jewish," and "Protestant." The cells of the table constitute an intersection between two categories, each of one variable. The frequencies in each cell are of those observations that have two traits in common. For example, Table 13.4 shows two Catholics from the upper class, three from the middle class, and three from the lower class. The Jews have three members of the upper class, two members in the middle class, and three in the lower class; finally, there are three Protestants in the upper class, three in the middle class, and two in the lower class.

The bivariate table can also be visualized as a series of univariate distributions.[3] By splitting each table down its columns and taking each column separately, we will have divided each bivariate distribution into three univariate distributions, representing the class standing of Protestants, Catholics, and Jews. In a comparison of the three univariate

3. Theodore R. Anderson and Morris Zelditch, Jr., *A Basic Course in Statistics* (New York: Holt, Rinehart and Winston, 1968), chapter 6.

TABLE 13.4.   Social Class by Religious Denomination (Near Zero Covariation)

	Religious Denomination			
Social Class	Catholic	Jewish	Protestant	Total
Upper	2	3	3	8
Middle	3	2	3	8
Lower	3	3	2	8
Total	8	8	8	24

distributions derived from, say, Table 13.3, it is seen that each distribution differs from the others in its pattern of dispersion. In the Protestant distribution, most of the respondents tend to cluster at the upper extremity of the distribution; the Jews are clustered in the center; and the Catholics tend toward the lower section. This is even more pronounced in Table 13.2, where the tendency becomes absolute (that is, all Protestants are upper class, and so on). In Table 13.4, on the other hand, there is practically no difference among the three distributions, the dispersion being identical in each. Thus, the amount of covariation in a bivariate table can be determined by a comparison of the univariate distributions that constitute the table. The larger the difference, the higher the degree of covariation of the two variables.

Percentaging Bivariate Tables

A generally useful way of summarizing a bivariate table and comparing its univariate distributions to assess relationship is by expressing its frequencies as percentages. Percentaging tables is appropriate whenever the variables are nominal, but the use of percentages is predominant even when the variables being analyzed are ordinal or interval. In Table 13.5, the observations of students' social class and track assignment have

TABLE 13.5.   Distribution Between Tracks by Father's Occupation

	Father's Occupation	
	Blue Collar	White Collar
College prep	249	484
Noncollege prep	269	99
Total	518	583

SOURCE: Walter E. Schafer and Carol Olexa, *Tracking and Opportunity* (New York: Chandler, 1971).

TABLE 13.6.   Distribution Between Tracks by Father's Occupation

	Father's Occupation	
	Blue Collar	White Collar
College prep	48%	83%
Noncollege prep	52	17
Total	100 (518)	100 (583)

been cross-tabulated to examine the hypothesis that social class, measured by father's occupation, determines the assignment of secondary school students to different tracks. The table has been set up in the conventional way: father's occupation (the independent variable) is at the top of the table, and track assignment (the dependent variable) is on the left-hand side.

Each occupational group can be visualized as a univariate distribution, and its frequencies transformed into percentages by using the total number of cases in each distribution as a base for percentaging (that is, 518 blue-collar students and 583 white-collar students each represent 100 percent). The percentages are presented in Table 13.6. The next step is a comparison of the univariate distributions to determine the extent of covariation between father's occupation and track assignment. Whereas the computation of percentages goes down the columns, the comparison cuts across the rows. The proportion of blue-collar students assigned to the college-prep tracks is compared with the proportion of white-collar students so assigned (48 percent and 83 percent). The percentages of blue-collar and white-collar students assigned to the noncollege-prep track can also be compared.

Table 13.6 displays a clear pattern of covariation: a blue-collar occupation is associated with a noncollege-prep track, and a white-collar occupation with a college-prep track. The two univariate distributions differ in their pattern of distribution between tracks; most students from white-collar backgrounds are in the college-prep tracks, whereas the blue-collar students are more or less equally divided, with a slight tendency toward the noncollege-prep tracks.

Whenever one variable is considered the independent variable and the other the dependent one, the percentages should be computed in the direction of the independent variable. If track assignments were considered an independent variable and father's occupation the dependent variable (which seems unlikely in this example), then percentages would be computed across the rows instead of along the columns.

Median and Mean as Covariation Measures

When the variables of a bivariate distribution are ordinal, the medians of the various univariate distributions can be used as measures of covariation. The hypothetical data of Table 13.10 will illustrate this point. One hundred and twenty-two individuals were classified according to their race and attitude toward education. The dependent variable "at-

BOX 13.2. The Principles of Table Reading

Social Scientists make considerable use of statistical tables as a way of presenting research results. The following discussion may be useful for the student as a quick guide to table reading.[4]

1. *Look for the title.* The title describes the information that is contained in the table. In Table 13.7, the title tells about differences in preferred sports between socioeconomic strata.

2. *Examine the source.* The source of the data is usually written at the bottom of the table, as is shown in Table 13.7. Identifying the source will help in assessing the reliability of the information as well as in finding the original data in case further information is needed.

TABLE 13.7. Socioeconomic Differences in the Designation of Spectator or Participant Sports as Favorites by Metropolitan Residents

| | Socioeconomic Strata | | | |
Favorite Sport	Upper (percent)	Middle (percent)	Lower (percent)	Totals (percent)
Spectator	35.6	57.1	54.7	48.8
Participant	64.4	42.9	45.3	51.2
	100.0	100.0	100.0	100.0
	(N = 188)	(N = 175)	(N = 172)	(N = 535)

SOURCE: Adapted from Gregory P. Stone, "Some Meanings of American Sport: An Extended View," in *Sociology of Sport: Proceedings of the C.I.C. Symposium on the Sociology of Sport*, ed. Gerald S. Kenyon (Chicago: Athletic Institute, 1969, p. 10).

3. *Determine in which direction the percentages have been computed.* This step is a crucial one and should be carefully observed. It is important to examine whether the percentages have been computed down the columns, across the rows, or on the basis of the whole table. Or, is the table an abbreviated one, in which the percentages, as presented, do not add up to 100 percent? The direction is determined by examining where the 100 percent or total cases have been inserted. In Table 13.7, the percentages have been computed down the column. On the other hand, in Table 13.8, the percentages have been computed in the opposite direction, across the rows.

4. This discussion is based on Roberta G. Simmons, "Basic Principles of Table Reading," in Morris Rosenberg, *The Logic of Survey Analysis* (New York: Basic Books, 1968), pp. 251–258.

BOX 13.2. (Continued)

TABLE 13.8. Level of Education in Relation to Social Class

Social Class	Did not finish high school	Graduated from high school but did not enter college	Entered college but did not finish	Completed a four-year college program
Upper and Upper Middle	0	10	10	80
Lower Middle	2	10	26	62
Working	10	24	37	29

Adapted from: Robert J. Havighurst and Bernice Neugarten, *Society and Education,* 3rd ed. (Boston: Allyn & Bacon, 1967), Table IV–1 and III–5.

4. *Make Comparisons.* Comparing the percentage differences in the table is a quick method for assessing the extent of a relationship between the variables. Comparisons are always made in a direction opposite to the one in which the percentages have been computed. If the percentages have been computed down the column, as in Table 13.7, then we compare percentages across the rows. The proportion of members in the upper strata who favor spectator sport is compared to the proportion of the middle and lower strata who favor spectator sport (35.6 to 57.1 to 54.7). The proportion of each of the socioeconomic strata who favor participant sport can also be examined (64.4 to 42.9 to 45.3). There are social class differences in the designation of spectator or participant sports as favorites. Individuals from the upper class are more likely to favor participant sports than those from the middle and lower strata.

Often, for the sake of simplicity, only part of the table is presented. Table 13.9 is an example. It is important to observe that the two percentages in this table do not add up to 100 percent, and that they are to be compared directly to one another. They represent the different proportion of individuals in the two categories of the independent variable (race) who belong to one response category of the dependent variable (family status).

TABLE 13.9. Family Status of Black and White College Goers

Race	Percentage of Each Group with High Family Status	
Black	10.0	(N = 872)
White	32.2	(N = 6,403)

SOURCE: Based on Gail E. Thomas, "The Influence of Ascription, Achievement and Educational Expectations on Black-White Postsecondary Enrollment," *The Sociological Quarterly,* 20 (Spring 1979): 209–222.

TABLE 13.10. Attitude Toward Education by Race

| Attitude Toward Education | Race | | | |
	Mexican-American	Black	White	Total
1	5	15	20	40
2	10	10	10	30
3	15	4	5	24
4	20	6	2	28
Total	50	35	37	122

titude toward education" is on the left-hand side, and each racial group is assumed to be a univariate distribution. The variable "attitude toward education" is ranked from 1, expressing a positive attitude, to 4, a negative attitude. The appropriate summary measure for ordinal data is the median, which can be utilized to summarize each of the three distributions: the Mexican-Americans, the blacks, and the whites. Among whites, the median is 1, among blacks it is 2, and among the Mexican-Americans it is 3. Thus, the whites show the most positive attitude toward education, blacks' attitudes are intermediate, and Mexican-Americans display the most negative attitude. The fact that the pattern in each distribution is different indicates a relationship or covariation between race and attitudes toward education.

With interval variables, the arithmetic mean can be used as a comparative measure. Table 13.11 is a bivariate distribution of intelligence test scores by age. Each age group can be visualized as a distribution and summarized by the arithmetic mean. Table 13.12 presents the arithmetic means of the distribution. Each pair of means can be compared. It is noted that average scores rise with age, a fact that permits one to deduce that the variables "age" and "intelligence" covary.

TABLE 13.11. Intelligence Test Scores by Age (Hypothetical Data)

| IQ Test Scores | Age | | | | |
	6–10	11–15	16–20	21–25	Total
0–4	10	6	4	1	21
5–9	8	10	3	2	23
10–14	6	7	8	8	29
15–19	4	3	3	10	20
Total	28	26	18	21	93

**TABLE 13.12.   Mean of IQ Test
Scores in Four Age Groups**

Age Group	Mean
6–10	7.7
11–15	8.3
16–20	9.8
21–25	13.4

THE MEASUREMENT OF RELATIONSHIP

So far, the extent of covariation of two variables has been assessed by comparing the univariate distributions that constitute the bivariate table. However, there are various statistical techniques that allow the researcher to assess the extent to which two variables are associated by a single summarizing measure. Such measures of relationship, often referred to as correlation coefficients, reflect the strength and the direction of association between the variables and the degree to which one variable can be predicted from the other.

The notion of prediction is inherent in the concept of covariation. When two variables covary, it is possible to use one to predict the other; when they do not, information about one will not enable the prediction of the other. As an illustration, consider Tables 13.2, 13.3, and 13.4 again; assume that no information is available about the religious denomination of the 24 persons and that the social status of each one is to be guessed. Generally, the best guess will be the most frequent category. However, since in all three tables the frequencies of all the categories are identical, any category can be arbitrarily selected. Suppose the middle class is chosen as the best guess. Since only eight cases in each table do in fact belong to the middle class, there will be sixteen errors out of twenty-four guesses in each of the three tables.

Religious denomination can be used to predict social class only if it is likely to reduce the number of errors in prediction. Suppose it is predicted that all Protestants are upper class, all Jews are middle class, and all Catholics are lower class. In Table 13.2, this prediction is accurate in each of the twenty-four cases; in Table 13.3, there are five errors; in Table 13.4, there are sixteen errors.

The advantage of employing religious denomination to predict social class can be calculated by subtracting the new number of errors from the previous total. In Table 13.2, the advantage is absolute because the reduction in the number of errors is the greatest ($16 - 0 = 16$). In Table 13.3, a considerable advantage is gained, the number of errors being reduced by 11 ($16 - 5 = 11$). In Table 13.4, there is no change in the

number of errors, despite the employment of religious denomination
(16 − 16 = 0).

Proportional Reduction of Error Principle

The strength of the association between social class and religious denomination can be assessed by calculating the proportional reduction
in prediction error when using one variable to predict another. The
proportional reduction of error is defined as follows.[5]

$$\frac{b - a}{b} \tag{13.1}$$

where b = original number of errors (before employing the independent variable as a predictor)

     a = new number of errors (after employing the independent var-
iable as a predictor)

Using Equation (13.1), you can calculate the proportional reduction in
errors of prediction from Tables 13.2, 13.3, and 13.4.

For Table 13.2: $\dfrac{16 - 0}{16} = \dfrac{16}{16} = 1$

For Table 13.3: $\dfrac{16 - 5}{16} = \dfrac{11}{16} = .69$

For Table 13.4: $\dfrac{16 - 16}{16} = \dfrac{0}{16} = 0$

The proportional reduction of error is absolute in Table 13.2, as
reflected in the magnitude of the coefficient 1, expressing a perfect
relationship between the variables "religious denomination" and "social
status." The number of errors in Table 13.3 has been reduced by almost
70 percent, following the employment of religious denomination as a
predictor. This is expressed by the coefficient .69. In Table 13.4, there
is no advantage in using religious denomination. The coefficient (0)
expresses the absence of any association between the two variables.

Any measure of association can be developed along similar lines,
provided it is based on two kinds of rules:[6] (a) *rules that allow the
prediction of the dependent variable on the basis of an independent
variable and (b) rules that allow the prediction of the dependent variable independently of an independent variable.* On this basis, any meas-

5. John H. Mueller et al., *Statistical Reasoning in Sociology*, p. 248.

6. Herbert L. Costner, "Criteria for Measures of Association," *American Sociological
Review*, 30 (1965): 341–353.

ure of association can be defined as in Equation (13.2):

$$\text{Measure of Association} = \frac{\text{Error by Rule (b)} - \text{Error by Rule (a)}}{\text{Error by Rule (b)}} \quad (13.2)$$

Most of the measures of relationship introduced in this chapter will be analyzed according to this definition. In the following sections we discuss lambda and Goodman and Kruskal's tau, which measure the relation between nominal variables. Next, we introduce gamma and Kendall's tau-b and tau-c as ordinal coefficients. In the last section, Pearson's r as an interval measure of relation is discussed.

NOMINAL MEASURES OF RELATIONSHIP

Guttman Coefficient of Predictability (lambda—λ)

The correlation lambda (λ), also known as the Guttman coefficient of predictability, is suitable for calculating relationships between nominal variables.[7] To illustrate its calculation, suppose one is interested in predicting the party identification of non-Southern whites during the 1960s. One possibility is to use the distribution of party identification during 1960, thereby making use of prediction rule (b). The univariate distribution of party identification is presented in Table 13.13.

The most effective way of guessing the party identification of each of these 900 voters, on the basis of the distribution given earlier, is to use a measure of central tendency that will yield the smallest number of errors in prediction. As party identification is a nominal variable, the mode is the most appropriate. As Democrats are the most frequent category ($f = 378$), the best guess is that each voter identified with the Democratic party, for the number of errors will not exceed 522 (234 Independents and 288 Republicans). Any other guess would magnify the number of errors. When guessing voters' party identification on the basis of the dependent variable alone, the most frequent category is chosen. According to this rule (b), the number of errors is 522 out of 900 guesses, that is, 58 percent.

The percentage of error might be reduced if another variable, "1956 party identification," is used as a predictor. Information is available on each of the 900 voters regarding their party identification in 1956. On this basis, it is possible to construct a bivariate table (Table 13.14) where all voters are classified according to two variables: their party identifi-

7. Louis Guttman, "An Outline of the Statistical Theory of Prediction," in *The Prediction of Personal Adjustment*, ed. by Paul Horst (New York: Social Science Research Council, 1941: Bulletin 48.

**TABLE 13.13.   1960 Party
Identification among Non-
Southern Whites*

Non-Southern Whites	f
Democrat	378
Independent	234
Republican	288
Total	900

SOURCE: Adapted from Angus C. Campbell et al., *Elections and the Political
Order* (New York: Wiley, 1966), p. 232.
* The original data appear in percentages. Owing to differences in rounding
in the original table, the total frequencies are not identical.

cation in 1956 and in 1960. With this additional information, one can
predict the party identification of non-Southern whites prior to the elections of 1960 on the basis of their 1956 party identification. First, take
those who declared themselves Democratic in 1956; there were 324
respondents, 279 of whom gave the same identification in 1960. As this
is the most frequent category, it is assumed that anyone who identified
with the Democratic party in 1956 did so again in 1960. With this assumption, forty-five errors of predictions are made because forty-five of
the 324 identified themselves otherwise in 1960.

Two hundred and seventy voters identified themselves as Independents in 1956; 144 of them did so again in 1960. It can, therefore, be
assumed again that whoever identified themselves as Independents in
1956 did so in 1960 as well. With this assumption, the number of errors

**TABLE 13.14.   1956 and 1960 Party Identification among Non-Southern
Whites**

Party Identification, 1960	Party Identification, 1956			1960 Overall
	Democrat	Independent	Republican	
Democrat	279	81	18	378
Independent	45	144	45	234
Republican	*	45	243	288
1956 overall	324	270	306	900

SOURCE: Angus C. Campbell et al., *Elections and the Political Order* (New York: Wiley,
1966), p. 225.
* Less than half of 1 percent.

is 81 + 45 = 126, the number who did not identify themselves as Independents. Finally, for those 306 who identified with the Republicans in 1956, it is assumed that the preference patterns did not change; as a result, 45 + 18 = 63 errors are made.

The total number of errors made by using the new rule (a) is

$$45 + 126 + 63 = 234$$

Two hundred and thirty-four errors out of 900 predictions is 26 percent of 900. Using an independent variable as a predictor leads to a decrease in the error of prediction, as expressed in the magnitude of the correlation, which can now be calculated:

$$\text{error stemming from rule (b)} = 522$$

$$\text{error stemming from rule (a)} = 234$$

$$\text{lambda } (\lambda) = \frac{522 - 234}{522} = .55$$

Thus, 55 percent of the errors of prediction concerning party identification in 1960 were eliminated by utilizing the identification pattern during the 1956 elections.

Lambda is an asymmetrical coefficient, as it reflects relationships between variables in one direction only. In practice, it is often represented as λ_a, "a" indicating that it is asymmetrical. The coefficient .55 expresses the relationship between party identification in 1956 and 1960, with that of 1956 serving as an independent variable. The correlation coefficient can also be calculated in the opposite direction, with 1960 serving as the independent variable. The method of calculation is identical: we compute the number of errors made when estimating 1956 identification patterns without reference to 1960 data and then calculate the advantage obtained by gauging the 1956 data from those of 1960.

An alternative procedure for computing lambda. Lambda can also be computed by a slightly simpler procedure using Formula (13.3)[8]

$$\lambda_a = \frac{\sum f_i - F_d}{N - F_d} \tag{13.3}$$

where f_i = the modal frequency within each category of the independent variable

F_d = the modal frequency in the marginal totals of the dependent variable

N = the total number of cases

8. Linton C. Freeman, *Elementary Applied Statistics* (New York: Wiley, 1965), p. 74.

We can now repeat our calculation of the correlation between the data from 1956 and those from 1960, with the 1956 party identification serving as the independent variable.

$$\sum f_i = 279 + 144 + 243 = 666$$

$$F_d = 378$$

$$N = 900$$

$$\lambda_a = \frac{666 - 378}{900 - 378} = \frac{288}{522} = .55$$

To summarize, the magnitude of lambda expresses the proportional reduction in error of estimate when switching from rule (b) to rule (a). The strength of the association between the two variables reflects the improvement in prediction attainable with the aid of a second variable. Lambda may range from 0 to 1.0; zero indicates that there is nothing to be gained by shifting from one prediction rule to another, whereas 1.0 reflects the fact that the use of an independent variable permits the dependent variable to be predicted without any error at all.

Limitations of lambda. Lambda has a limitation in situations where the modal frequencies of the independent variable are all concentrated in one category of the dependent variable. In such a case, lambda will always be zero even in instances where the two variables are in fact related. For example, in the bivariate distribution presented in Table 13.15, it can be seen that place of residence is associated with self-esteem. More residents of rural areas (75 percent) have high self-esteem than do residents of cities (66 percent). However, because the sum of all modal frequencies of the variable place of residence ($\sum f_i = 300 + 200$) is equal to the modal frequency of the marginal totals of the variable self-esteem ($F_d = 500$), lambda will take on the value of zero. Such a pattern of distribution is likely to occur when the marginal totals of the dependent variable are extremely uneven. Lambda would

TABLE 13.15. Place of Residence and Self-Esteem

Self-Esteem	Place of Residence		
	Rural Areas	Cities	Total
High	300	200	500
Low	100	100	200
Total	400	300	700

then be inappropriate and a different measure of association such as Goodman and Kruskal's tau is preferable.

Goodman and Kruskal's Tau (τ_b)

Goodman and Kruskal's tau (τ_b) measures association between nominal variables and can be applied in situations when lambda is inappropriate. Like lambda, tau is an asymmetrical coefficient and is based on the same principle of minimizing error of prediction by introducing a predictor— the independent variable. Tau ranges from 0 to 1.0 with 0 implying no reduction in error and 1.0 indicating prediction with no error. The main difference between lambda and tau is in the method of computing error, which is more restrictive in the case of tau.

In order to illustrate the computation of tau, let us go back to Table 13.14. Party identification in 1960 is to be predicted from its marginal distribution, while maintaining the observed distribution. Following this rule, 378 cases would be assigned to the category "Democrat," 234 to "Independent," and 288 to "Republican." Although the predicted marginal distribution is identical to the observed one, the cases assigned by this rule to the respective categories would not necessarily be the same cases that actually belong to these categories. Thus, it is expected that in the long run, some cases will be misclassified. The error in misclassification is computed as follows: for the category "Democrat" there are 378 cases who may belong to this category but 522 who would be wrongly assigned. The error in prediction is then:

$$\frac{522}{900} \times 378 = 219.24$$

Similarly, for the category "Independent," there are

$$\frac{666}{900} \times 234 = 173.16 \text{ errors}$$

and for the "Republican" category,

$$\frac{612}{900} \times 288 = 195.84 \text{ errors}$$

The total number of errors obtained when predicting party identification in 1960 with no prior knowledge is then:

$$219.24 + 173.16 + 195.84 = 588.24$$

Next, we calculate the number of errors when prediction is made with knowledge of the independent variable—1956 party identification. Cases are assigned to cells on the basis of the observed frequencies. Thus, of the 324 cases who voted Democratic in 1956, 279 will be assigned to the category "Democrat" and 45 to the category "Independent." For this column the number of errors would be:

$$\left(\frac{45}{324} \times 279\right) + \left(\frac{279}{324} \times 45\right) = 77.5$$

For the category "Independent," the total number of errors is:

$$\left(\frac{189}{270} \times 81\right) + \left(\frac{126}{270} \times 144\right) + \left(\frac{225}{270} \times 45\right)$$
$$= 56.7 + 67.2 + 37.5 = 161.4$$

Similarly, for the category "Republican," there are:

$$\left(\frac{288}{306} \times 18\right) + \left(\frac{261}{306} \times 45\right) + \left(\frac{63}{306} \times 243\right)$$
$$= 16.94 + 38.38 + 50.03 = 105.35 \text{ errors.}$$

The total sum of errors obtained when the 1956 party identification is used to predict the 1960 party identification is:

$$77.5 + 161.4 + 105.35 = 344.25$$

Tau is defined as follows:

$$\tau_b = \frac{S_1 - S_2}{S_1} \tag{13.4}$$

where S_1 = total sum of errors obtained when no predictor is used

S_2 = total sum of errors obtained when a predictor is used

Accordingly,

$$\tau_b = \frac{588.24 - 344.25}{588.24} = .41$$

Note that tau has a smaller numerical value than lambda; this is a function of its more restrictive method for computing error.

ORDINAL MEASURES OF RELATIONSHIP

When both variables of a bivariate distribution are ordinal, the construction of a measure of relationship is based on the principal property of the ordinal scale, by which observations can be ranked in relation to the variables being measured. With a single variable, one is generally interested in evaluating the relative position of the observations on the variable. For example, professions can be ranked according to the amount of prestige they command; and students, according to their relative degree of political tolerance. The same principle can be applied with two variables. Here, the interest is in examining whether the ranking of observations on each of the variables is identical, similar, or different. Every two observations are compared, and it is noted whether one that is ranked high on one variable is as high with regard to the other. For instance, one can examine whether the ranking of professions by their prestige in the 1950s resembles their ranking in the 1970s or whether persons with a conservative orientation on foreign affairs show a similar tendency on internal issues.

When observations display the same order on both variables, the relationship is said to be positive; when the order is inverse, so that the observation ranking highest on one variable is the lowest on the second variable, the relationship is negative. When there is no clear pattern in the relative position of the observations on both variables, then the variables are said to be independent of each other. Consider the following example: if all military personnel with high rank are also more liberal on political issues than the lower-ranking officers, then one may say that military rank and political liberalism are positively related. If, however, the high-ranking officers are less liberal, the association is negative. When some high officers are liberal and others are not, then rank and liberalism are independent of each other.

The Pair Concept

Most ordinal measures of relationship are based on the *pair* as a unit of analysis and its relative ranking on both variables. For example, we can compare every pair of officers in terms of their rank and liberalism. The number of pairs that can be formed out of N cases is obtained by Formula (13.5):

$$\binom{N}{2} = \frac{N(N-1)}{2} \tag{13.5}$$

Suppose six officers are classified according to their rank and degree of liberalism. The observations are presented in Table 13.16. According to

TABLE 13.16. Liberalism by Rank (Hypothetical Data)*

	Rank (X)		
Liberalism (Y)	Low	High	Total
Low	$2(_{11})$	$1(_{12})$	3
High	$1(_{21})$	$2(_{22})$	3
Total	3	3	6

* The numbers in parentheses designate the cell numbers.

Formula (13.5), fifteen pairs can be formed out of six observations:

$$\binom{6}{2} = \frac{6(5)}{2} = 15$$

Table 13.17 lists the fifteen pairs according to cell number and rank on each of the variables. The first column designates the pair's number;

TABLE 13.17. Relative Position of Officers in Rank and Liberalism

Pair	From Cell	Rank of Officer (X)	Degree of Liberalism (Y)	Order
1	a 11	L	L	Tie on X and Y
	b 11	L	L	
2	a 11	L	L	Tie on Y
	b 12	H	L	
3	a 11	L	L	Tie on Y
	b 12	H	L	
4	a 11	L	L	Tie on X
	b 21	L	H	
5	a 11	L	L	Tie on X
	b 21	L	H	
6	a 11	L	L	Same
	b 22	H	H	
7	a 11	L	L	Same
	b 22	H	H	
8	a 11	L	L	Same
	b 22	H	H	
9	a 11	L	L	Same
	b 22	H	H	
10	a 12	H	L	Inverse
	b 21	L	H	
11	a 12	H	L	Tie on X
	b 22	H	H	
12	a 12	H	L	Tie on X
	b 22	H	H	
13	a 21	L	H	Tie on Y
	b 22	H	H	
14	a 21	L	H	Tie on Y
	b 22	H	H	
15	a 22	H	H	Tie on X and Y
	b 22	H	H	

the second column, the cell number (with "a" designating the first member of the pair, and "b" the second member); and the third and fourth columns, their rank and liberalism. The last column describes the relative position of the pair on the two variables.

For instance, the first pair, designated as tied on X and Y, consists of two officers, both classified in cell 11. These officers have the same rank and share the same political views. Pairs tied on Y are officers of different ranks and sharing the same political views; pairs tied on X are officers of the same rank but of different political views; pairs designated as "same" are officers who have the same relative position on both variables, so that if one has the highest rank, that officer would be the most liberal as well. Pairs designated as "inverse" have a different relative position on both variables, so that if one has the highest rank, that officer would be the least liberal of the pair.

Types of Pairs

From the total number of pairs that can be constructed from N observations, the following groups can be distinguished:

1. Pairs that display the same order on both X and Y; they will be denoted as Ns.
2. Pairs that display an inverse order on X and Y; they will be denoted as Nd.
3. Pairs tied on X, denoted as Tx.
4. Pairs tied on Y, denoted as Ty.
5. Pairs tied on X and on Y, denoted Txy.

1. To find Ns in the general bivariate table, the frequency in every cell is multiplied by the total of all the frequencies in the cells below it and to its right, and the products are added up. In Table 13.16, the number of pairs displaying the same ranking on both variables is $2 \times 2 = 4$.

2. To calculate Nd in the general bivariate table, the frequency in each cell is multiplied by the total of all the frequencies in the cells below it and to its left, and the products are added up. In Table 13.16, the number of pairs displaying different rankings on the two variables is $1 \times 1 = 1$.

3. To find the number of pairs tied on $X(Tx)$, the frequency in every cell is multiplied by the total of all the frequencies in the cells in that column, and the products are added up. The number of pairs tied on X is $(2 \times 1) + (1 \times 2) = 4$.

4. To find the number of pairs tied on $Y(Ty)$, the frequency in each cell is multiplied by the sum of the frequencies in the cells in that row, and the products are added up. The number of pairs tied on Y in Table 13.16 is $(2 \times 1) + (1 \times 2) = 4$.

5. To work out the number of pairs that are tied on X and Y (Txy), all the pairs that can be created from every cell, by means of the formula $\binom{N}{2}$, are added up. In Table 13.16, the ties on X and Y are:

$$\text{Cell 11: } \frac{2(1)}{2} = 1$$

$$\text{Cell 12: } \frac{1(0)}{1} = 0$$

$$\text{Cell 21: } \frac{1(0)}{1} = 0$$

$$\text{Cell 22: } \frac{2(1)}{2} = 1$$

The total number of pairs of all kinds that can be constructed out of N observations is:

$$\binom{N}{2} = Ns + Nd + Tx + Ty + Txy$$

In our example:

$$\binom{6}{2} = 4 + 1 + 4 + 4 + 2 = 15$$

Gamma (γ or G)

Gamma, a coefficient used for measuring the association between ordinal variables, was developed by Leo Goodman and William Kruskal.[9] It is a symmetrical statistic, based on the number of same-order pairs (Ns) and the number of different-order pairs (Nd). Tied pairs play no part in the definition of gamma.

The coefficient is defined by Formula (13.6)[10]

$$\gamma = \frac{0.5(Ns + Nd) - Min\,(Ns, Nd)}{0.5(Ns + Nd)} \tag{13.6}$$

To illustrate the calculation of gamma, consider the data presented in Table 13.18 on class standing and political tolerance of students. If these two variables are associated, it will be possible to predict students' political tolerance on the basis of their class standing with a minimum of error.

First, the number of pairs that can be constructed from 1,032 observations is counted. With tied pairs excluded, the overall number of

9. Leo A. Goodman and William H. Kruskal, "Measure of Association for Cross Classification," *Journal of the American Statistical Association,* 49 (1954): 732–764.

10. John H. Mueller et al., *Statistical Reasoning in Sociology,* p. 282.

TABLE 13.18.   Political Tolerance of College Students by Class Standing

	Class Standing						
	Fresh-man	Sopho-more	Junior	Senior	Graduate Student (Full time)	Graduate Student (Part time)	Total
Less tolerant	30	30	34	33	40	15	182
Somewhat tolerant	66	75	79	79	120	45	464
More tolerant	28	51	59	63	151	34	386
Total	124	156	172	175	311	94	1,032

pairs that can be constructed from a bivariate table is $Ns + Nd$. Ns and Nd are calculated according to the definitions presented previously.

$$Ns = 30(75 + 51 + 79 + 59 + 79 + 63 + 120 + 151 + 45 + 34)$$
$$+ 66(51 + 59 + 63 + 151 + 34)$$
$$+ 30(79 + 59 + 79 + 63 + 120 + 151 + 45 + 34)$$
$$+ 75(59 + 63 + 151 + 34)$$
$$+ 34(79 + 63 + 120 + 151 + 45 + 34)$$
$$+ 79(63 + 151 + 34) + 33(120 + 151 + 45 + 34)$$
$$+ 79(151 + 34) + 40(45 + 34) + 120(34)$$
$$= 157,958$$

$$Nd = 15(120 + 151 + 79 + 63 + 79 + 59 + 75 + 51 + 66 + 28)$$
$$+ 45(151 + 63 + 59 + 51 + 28)$$
$$+ 40(79 + 63 + 79 + 59 + 75 + 51 + 66 + 28)$$
$$+ 120(63 + 59 + 51 + 28)$$
$$+ 33(79 + 59 + 75 + 51 + 66 + 28)$$
$$+ 79(59 + 51 + 28) + 34(75 + 51 + 66 + 28) + 79(51 + 28)$$
$$+ 30(66 + 28) + 75(28)$$
$$= 112,882$$

The total number of pairs (tied pairs excluded) is $Ns + Nd = 157,958 + 112,882 = 270,840$.

Next, the relative political tolerance of the students is determined on the basis of the dependent variable alone—rule (b). To find the relative position of each of the 270,840 pairs, some random system can be used. (As the univariate distribution of the variable "political tolerance" does not provide information about the relative political tolerance of the students, it cannot be used as a basis of prediction.) For example, members of each pair can be labeled as heads or tails, and by flipping a coin it is decided which member is more tolerant. When this process is repeated for each pair, it can be expected that in the long run 50 percent of the guesses about the relative position of the students will be accurate, whereas the other 50 percent will be erroneous. Hence, prediction rule (b) will produce $Ns + Nd/2 = 135,420$ errors.

Prediction rule (a) states that if there are more pairs displaying the same order (Ns), an identical ranking for all the pairs will be predicted. In that case, the number of errors will be Nd, that is, the number of pairs whose ranking is different on the two variables. In the same way, should the number of inverted pairs (Nd) be greater, pairs will be given a different ranking, whereupon the number of errors will equal Ns, that is, the number of pairs with identical ranking.

The calculations based on the information in Table 13.18 indicate that the number of pairs with the same ranking is greater than the number of those whose ranking is inverted $(Ns > Nd)$. Hence, the relative position of political tolerance for each pair will be predicted on the basis of its member's class standing, so that the student with the greater seniority exhibits greater tolerance. If Mary is a sophomore and John is a freshman, Mary will be more tolerant than John. As not all pairs display the same order, the number of errors made by such a prediction rule is $Nd = 112,882$.

The relationship between class standing and political tolerance can now be asserted, using the general formula for measures of association:

$$\frac{b - a}{b}$$

where $b = 0.5(Ns + Nd)$

$a = Min\ (Ns, Nd)$

Accordingly,

$$\gamma = \frac{0.5(Ns + Nd) - Nd}{0.5(Ns + Nd)} = \frac{135,420 - 112,882}{135,420} = \frac{22,538}{135,420} = .17$$

A value of .17 for γ reflects the advantage gained by using the variable "class standing" in predicting political tolerance. By the use of this variable, 17 percent of the total number of errors were eliminated.

Another formula for gamma. Gamma can also be calculated by using Formula (13.7)

$$\gamma = \frac{Ns - Nd}{Ns + Nd} \qquad (13.7)$$

This formula reflects the relative predominance of same-order or different-order pairs. When same-order pairs predominate, the coefficient is positive; when different-order pairs predominate, it is negative. When the ranking on both variables is identical, the number of same-order pairs (Ns) will equal the total number of pairs because Nd will be zero. Gamma will then equal 1.0.

$$\gamma = \frac{Ns - 0}{Ns + 0} = \frac{Ns}{Ns} = 1.0$$

A coefficient of 1.0 indicates that the dependent variable can be predicted on the basis of the independent variable without any error. When $Ns = 0$, the coefficient will be negative, but prediction is still accurate:

$$\gamma = \frac{0 - Nd}{0 + Nd} = \frac{-Nd}{Nd} = -1.0$$

When the number of different-order pairs is equal to the number of same-order pairs, gamma is zero:

$$\gamma = \frac{Ns - Nd}{Ns + Nd} = \frac{0}{Ns + Nd} = 0$$

A gamma of zero reflects that there is nothing to be gained by using the independent variable to predict the dependent variable.

Limitations of gamma. The main weakness of gamma as a measure of ordinal association is the exclusion of ties from its computation. Hence, it will reach a value of ± 1 even under conditions of less than perfect association. For example, a perfect relationship was described early in the chapter as in the following table:

50	0
0	50

$\gamma = 1$

However, because gamma is based on untied pairs only, it becomes 1 under the following conditions as well:

50	50
0	50

$\gamma = 1$

In general, in marginal distributions that are uneven, with a concentration of many observations in few categories, there will be many tied pairs, and gamma will be based on a smaller proportion of pairs. This is especially acute in 2 × 2 tables, where the proportion of untied pairs will be small, even when all marginal frequencies are equal. Although there is no simple solution to the problem of ties, it is advisable to have as many categories as possible of the two variables, thereby to minimize the number of tied pairs and maximize the number of pairs on which gamma is based.

Kendall's Tau-b and Tau-c

With many ties, a different measure that handles the problem of ties can be used. It is Kendall's tau-b, defined as follows:

$$\tau_b = \frac{Ns - Nd}{\sqrt{(Ns + Nd + Ty)(Ns + Nd + Tx)}} \qquad (13.8)$$

Tau-b varies from -1 to $+1$ and is a symmetrical coefficient. It has the same numerator as gamma, but has a correction factor for ties in its denominator (Ty and Tx). For example, for the following bivariate distribution

$$x$$

	30	70	100
y	30	20	50
	60	90	150

we get:

$$Ns = 600 \qquad Ty = 2{,}700$$
$$Nd = 2{,}100 \qquad Tx = 2{,}300$$

Therefore,

$$\tau_b = \frac{600 - 2{,}100}{\sqrt{(600 + 2{,}100 + 2{,}700)(600 + 2{,}100 + 2{,}300)}} = \frac{-1{,}500}{5{,}196} = -.29$$

Note that under the same conditions, gamma gives a considerably higher figure than tau-b:

$$\gamma = \frac{600 - 2{,}100}{600 + 2{,}100} = \frac{-1{,}500}{2{,}700} = -.56$$

Gamma will always exceed tau-b when there are tied pairs. With no ties, its value will be identical with tau-b.

Tau-b reaches a maximum of ±1 when the number of rows (r) and columns (c) are equal. For rectangular tables, tau-c, a variant of tau-b, can be substituted. Tau-c is defined thus:

$$\tau_c = \frac{Ns - Nd}{\frac{1}{2}N^2(M - 1)/m}$$ (13.9)

$$m = Min\ (r, c)$$

Both tau-b and tau-c are difficult to interpret as measures that designate a proportional reduction of error in prediction. In this respect, they are less satisfactory than gamma.

INTERVAL MEASURES OF RELATIONSHIP

At lower levels of measurement, the ability to make predictions is restricted, even when the variables considered are associated. At most, one can point out an interdependence of certain categories or properties, such as the fact that Catholics tend to vote Democratic; or, one can expect the same relative position of observations on two variables, for instance, that military rank is associated with liberalism. However, predictions of this type are imprecise, and there is frequently a need for more accurate predictive statements, as for example, when one wishes to predict individuals' future income on the basis of their level of education or a city's crime rate from its racial composition.

Prediction Rules

When the variables being analyzed are at least interval, one can be more precise in describing the nature and the form of the relationship. Precise prediction rules are quite frequently made in the natural sciences in the form of prediction functions. For instance, there are functions that express the relationship between acceleration distance and time in the form $K = PV/T$; or between voltage resistance and current in the form $C = V/R$.

In the social sciences, however, prediction functions are expressed in much simpler terms. Most relationships can in fact be formulated in terms of a linear function rule. A function is said to be linear when pairs of X,Y values fall exactly into a function that can be plotted as a straight line. All such functions have rules of the form $Y = a + bX$, where a and b are constant numbers.

For example, there is a perfect linear relationship between the distance and the time that a car travels at a fixed speed (Table 13.19). If its speed is sixty miles per hour, it will go sixty miles in one hour, or X miles in Y time. The linear function expresses the relationship between the time and the distance that the car travels. Such a function takes the form of $Y = 1X$, reflecting the fact that a change of one unit of distance (miles) will bring about a change of one unit of time (minutes). The constant 1 preceding X in the formula is called b, or the slope, expressing the number of units of change in Y accompanying one unit of change in X.

Linear Regression

This method of specifying the nature of a relationship between two variables is referred to as regression analysis. The task of regression is to find some algebraic expression by which to represent the functional relationship between the variables. The equation $Y = a + bX$ is a linear regression equation, meaning that the function describing the relation between X and Y is that of a straight line. Ordinarily, the observations of X and Y—and the regression line connecting them—are displayed in the form of a graph. The variables X and Y are represented by two intersecting axes. Each observation is entered as a dot at the point where the X and Y scores intersect. In Figure 13.1, we have entered the observations from Table 13.19 to illustrate the graphical presentation of bivariate observations and the functional form describing their interrelationship. The independent variable, X, is placed on the horizontal axis; Y, the dependent variable, on the vertical axis; and each observation is plotted at the intersection of the two axes. For example, the last observation of Table 13.19 is plotted at the intersection of the two axes on the score 15, to represent its score of 15 on the two variables.

The regression line does not always pass through the intersection of the X and Y axes. When a straight line intersects the Y axis, there is a need for another constant to be introduced into the linear regression equation. This constant is symbolized by the letter a and is called the Y intercept. The intercept reflects the value of Y when X is zero. Each of the three regression lines in Figure 13.2 has different values for a and b. The three different values of a (6, 1, 2) are reflected in the three different intersections of the lines. The different values of b (-3, 0.5, 3) reflect the steepness of the slopes. The higher the value of b, the steeper the slope. Finally, the sign of b expresses the direction of the relationship between X and Y: when b is positive, an increase in X is

TABLE 13.19. Distance by Time

X (Miles)	Y (Time in Minutes)
1	1
3	3
5	5
10	10
15	15

FIGURE 13.1. Regression of Y on X

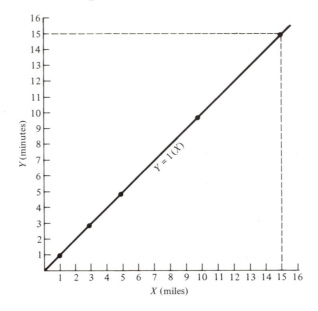

accompanied by an increase in Y; when b is negative, Y decreases as X increases (Figure 13.2, I).

Most relationships in the social sciences can be fairly well expressed by the linear function. Thus, for example, the equation $Y = 2,000 + 1,000X$ expresses the relation between income and education; a is the initial yearly salary ($2,000) for individuals who had no education at all, and b (1,000) stands for an increment of $1,000 for each additional year of education. Using this prediction rule, we could expect individuals having ten years of schooling to make $12,000 a year.

FIGURE 13.2.

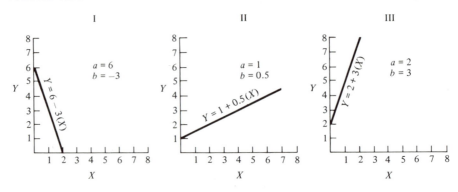

The Criterion of Least Squares

The regression equation, however, is only a prediction rule; thus, there are discrepancies between actual observations and the ones predicted. The goal is to construct such an equation that the deviations, or error of prediction, will be at a minimum. If a specific criterion is adopted in determining a and b of the linear equation, it is possible to create a function that will minimize the variance around the regression line. This is the criterion of least squares, which minimizes the sum of the squared differences between the observed Y's and the Y's predicted with the regression equation. According to this criterion, a and b can be calculated by the following formulas:

$$b = \frac{\sum_{i=1}^{N} (X_i - \bar{X})(Y_i - \bar{Y})}{\sum_{i=1}^{N} (X_i - \bar{X})^2} \qquad (13.10)$$

$$a = \frac{\sum_{i=1}^{N} Y_i - b \sum_{i=1}^{N} X_i}{N} = \bar{Y} - b\bar{X} \qquad (13.11)$$

A more convenient formula for computing b is as follows:

$$b = \frac{N \sum XY - (\sum X)(\sum Y)}{N \sum X^2 - (\sum X)^2} \qquad (13.12)$$

An illustration. As an illustration of the construction of a precise prediction rule for interval variables, consider the series of observations in Table 13.20 on per capita GNP and the percentage of the urban population living in cities with a population of over 20,000. These observations were assembled from sixteen countries, with the aim of exploring the relationship between the degree of urbanization (as an indicator of modernization) and per capita GNP. The variable to be predicted (the dependent variable) is "per capita GNP," and the independent variable is the "percentage of urban population."

To predict the per capita GNP of any country, without any additional information, a value that will produce the smallest possible number of errors is chosen as an estimate for each country in the distribution. The arithmetic mean is the best guess for every interval distribution because the mean of its squared deviations is lower than for any other value. The average per capita GNP, according to the data, is

$$\bar{Y} = \frac{\sum_{i=1}^{N} Y_i}{N} = 146$$

TABLE 13.20.   GNP Per Capita and Percentage of the Urban Population in Cities of Over 20,000

Country	Percentage of Urban (x)	Per Capita GNP (y)	xy	x^2	y^2
Nepal	4.4	45	198.0	19.36	2,025
Afghanistan	7.5	50	375.0	56.25	2,500
Laos	4.0	50	200.0	16.00	2,500
Burma	10.0	57	570.0	100.00	3,249
Libya	18.4	60	1,104.0	338.56	3,600
Pakistan	11.8	70	826.0	139.24	4,900
Bolivia	19.4	99	1,920.6	376.36	9,801
Iran	21.0	108	2,268.0	441.00	11,664
Jordan	25.5	129	3,289.5	650.25	16,641
Egypt	29.1	142	4,132.2	846.81	20,164
Iraq	23.6	156	3,681.6	556.96	24,336
Syria	38.8	173	6,712.4	1,505.44	29,929
Turkey	18.2	220	4,004.0	331.24	48,400
Spain	39.8	293	11,661.4	1,584.04	85,849
Japan	43.1	306	13,188.6	1,857.61	93,636
Chile	46.3	379	17,547.7	2,143.69	143,641
Total	360.9	2,337	71,679.0	10,962.81	502,835

SOURCE: Adapted from Bruce M. Russet et al. *World Handbook of Political and Social Indicators* (New Haven: Yale University Press, 1964), pp. 294–298.

To assess the prediction error, subtract each observation from the mean (to calculate the deviations), and square the deviations. The sum of the squared deviations, referred to as total variation about $\bar{Y}$, is selected as an estimate of error of prediction—rule (b)—because it produces the minimum of errors. The total variation about $\bar{Y}$ is defined as in Equation (13.13):

$$\text{Total variation} = \sum_{i=1}^{N} (Y_i - \bar{Y})^2 \tag{13.13}$$

The next step is to reduce the errors of prediction of per capita GNP by employing a second variable, "percentage of urban," as a predictor. This can be accomplished by constructing a prediction rule in the form of a regression equation that will best describe the relationship between these two variables and that will allow us to predict per capita GNP on the basis of percentage of urban population with a minimum of error.

The observations of Table 13.20 can be displayed in a scatter diagram, which is a graphic device providing a first approximation of the relationship between the two variables (Figure 13.3). Each dot represents an observation that has a fixed X and Y characteristic. For example, the dot designated as A represents Chile, with a per capita GNP of $379 and 46.3 percent of its urban population in cities of over 20,000. Next, a line that best approximates the trend the dots display is drawn. Obviously, several such lines can be drawn between the dots, but only one, the line of least squares, comes as close as possible to all the individual observations. Before drawing this line, calculate the constants a and b:

$$b = \frac{16(71,679) - (360.9)(2,337)}{16(10,962.81) - 130,248.81} = 6.7$$

$$a = 146 - 6.7(22.6) = -5.42$$

The resulting linear equation is therefore:

$$Y = -5.42 + 6.7X$$

The estimated regression line can now be drawn and applied to predict per capita GNP for every level of urban population. For example, if a country had only 10 percent of its urban population in cities of over 20,000 inhabitants, its per capita GNP is expected to be $Y = -5.42 + 6.7(10) = 61.58$.

FIGURE 13.3. GNP Per Capita and Percentage of Urban Population

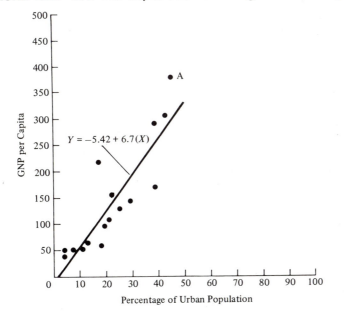

Errors of Prediction

One can see from Figure 13.3 that most of the out observations are spread around the regression line. The deviations of the actual observations from the predicted ones represent the errors produced when using the prediction rule specified above in predicting per capita GNP on the basis of the percentage of urban population.

The error involved in predicting per capita GNP from percentage of urban population can be estimated by measuring the deviations of the actual observations from the regression line. The predicted per capita GNP for each country is subtracted from the actual observations recorded in Table 13.20. For example, for Nepal, the predicted per capita GNP according to the prediction rule $Y = -5.42 + 6.7X$ is $-5.42 + 6.7(4.4)$ $= -5.42 + 29.48 = 24.06$. The actual per capita GNP of Nepal is 45; the error of prediction is thus $45 - 24.06 = 20.94$.

The sum of the squared errors of prediction is the variation unexplained by the independent variable. It is defined in Formula (13.14):

$$\text{Unexplained variation} = \sum_{i=1}^{N} (Y_i - Y_p)^2 \qquad (13.14)$$

where Y_i = actual observations

Y_p = predicted observations

Another measure of error that is widely used is the *standard error of estimate (Sy.x)*. It is based on the *unexplained variation* around the regression line and is defined as:

$$Sy.x = \sqrt{\frac{\sum_{i=1}^{N} (Y_i - Y_p)^2}{N}} \qquad (13.15)$$

The standard error of estimate closely parallels the standard deviation, discussed in Chapter 12.

Pearson's Product Moment Correlation Coefficient (r)

It is noted that there are two measures of variability for Y. The first, the total variation about $\bar{Y}$, is the error obtained when one predicts Y with no prior knowledge of X—rule (b). (Rule (b) is the total variation about $\bar{Y}$.) The second, the unexplained variation (as defined by equation (13.14), is the error obtained when using linear regression as the prediction rule—rule (a). For the data in Table 13.20, the figures are these:

$$\text{Total variation} = 161,487$$

$$\text{Unexplained variation} = 34,088$$

These two estimates of error enable the construction of an interval measure of association that reflects a proportional reduction in error when one shifts from the first prediction rule—(b), the mean—to the second—(a), the linear regression equation—to evaluate Y. This measure, r^2, is defined in Equation (13.16):

$$r^2 = \frac{\text{Total Variation} - \text{Unexplained Variation}}{\text{Total Variation}} \tag{13.16}$$

In our example,

$$r^2 = \frac{161,487 - 34,088}{161,487} = .789$$

The unexplained variation is subtracted from the original error of prediction to evaluate the proportional reduction in error. The proportional reduction in error is reflected by r^2 when X is used to predict Y. When the percentage of urban population is used to predict per capita income, the proportional reduction in error is 78.9 percent. Unexplained variation of zero means that the regression equation eliminated all errors in predicting Y, and r^2 then equals 1, meaning that any variation in Y can be explained by X. On the other hand, when the unexplained variation is identical to the total variation, r^2 is zero, indicating complete independence between X and Y.

Conventionally, it is the square root of r^2, r, designated as Pearson's product moment correlation coefficient or Pearson's r, rather than r^2, that is used as a coefficient of correlation. Pearson's r ranges from -1.0 to $+1.0$, where a negative coefficient indicates inverse relations between the variables. A simple formula for computing r is:

$$r = \frac{N \sum XY - (\sum X)(\sum Y)}{\sqrt{[N \sum X^2 - (\sum X)^2][N \sum Y^2 - (\sum Y)^2]}} \tag{13.17}$$

The size of r^2 or r is determined by the spread of the actual observations around the regression line. Thus, if all the observations are on the line, r will be 1.0; if they are randomly scattered, r will approximate zero. Figure 13.4 illustrates the possibilities of a strong positive relationship, a weak positive relationship, and no relationship. However, when r or r^2 approximates or equals zero, one should not rush to the conclusion that the variables are not related. The relationship may be curvilinear—that is, it cannot be described by a straight line—so that a coefficient based on the linear model would not give a correct picture of the statistical relationship. In general, a careful scrutiny of the scatter diagram will give an indication as to what extent the observations display a linear or a curvilinear trend or whether they are just scattered at ran-

FIGURE 13.4.

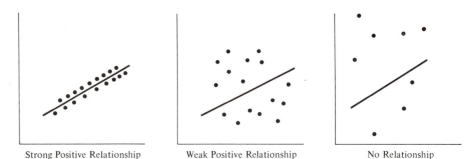

| Strong Positive Relationship | Weak Positive Relationship | No Relationship |

dom. When the data are clearly nonlinear, the *eta coefficient* can be employed instead of Pearson's r.[11]

SUMMARY

This chapter focused on the nature of relationships between two variables and on the construction of measures of relationship. It was demonstrated that when variables are related, they vary together so that specific categories of one variable "go together" with specific categories of the second or that there is some correspondence in the relative position of the two variables. Sometimes, when interval variables are related, it is possible to describe the relationship by employing specific functions enabling exact predictions.

A relationship between two variables can be assessed by comparing the univariate distributions constituting the bivariate table, using summary measures such as the median or the mean. Alternatively, associations can be described by special measures of relationships that reflect the relative utility of using one variable to predict another.

Measures of relationship usually correspond to the variables' level of measurement. Nominal relations are assessed by lambda, or by Goodman and Kruskal's tau. Either gamma or Kendall's tau is used to calculate relations between ordinal variables. Finally, Pearson's r is an interval measure of relationship that reflects the proportional reduction of error when one shifts from the mean as a prediction rule to the linear regression equation.

11. It is beyond the scope of this text to discuss curvilinear relations. See Mordecai Ezekiel and Karl A. Fox, *Methods of Correlation and Regression Analysis*, 3rd ed. (New York: Wiley, 1959), chap. 6.

KEY TERMS FOR REVIEW

Proportional
  reduction of error
Guttman coefficient
  of predictability
Goodman and
  Kruskal's tau
Gamma

Kendall's tau-b
Error of prediction
Regression line
Criterion of least
  squares
Pearson's *r*

ADDITIONAL READINGS

Acton, Forman S. *Analysis of Straight-Line Data*. New York: Wiley, 1959.

Blalock, Hubert M. *Social Statistics*, 2nd ed. New York: McGraw-Hill, 1972, Chapters 17–18.

Handel, Judith D. *Introductory Statistics for Sociology*. Englewood Cliffs, N.J.: Prentice-Hall, 1978.

Iversen, Gudmund R. *Statistics for Sociology*. Dubuque, Iowa: William C. Brown, 1979.

Tufte, Edward R. *Data Analysis for Politics and Policy*. Englewood Cliffs, N.J.: Prentice-Hall, 1974, chapters 1–3.

Walker, Helen M., and Joseph Lev. *Elementary Statistical Methods*, 3rd ed. New York: Holt, Rinehart and Winston, 1969, Chapters 12–14.

Wallis, W. Allen. "How to Read a Table." In Billy J. Franklin and Harold W. Osborne, eds. *Research Methods: Issues and Insights*. Belmont, Calif.: Wadsworth, 1971, pp. 418–432.

Weisberg, Herbert F. "Models of Statistical Relationships." *American Political Science Review*, 67 (December 1974): 1638–1655.

Zeisel, Hans. *Say It with Figures*, 5th ed. New York: Harper and Row, 1968.

Zeller, Richard A., and Edward G. Carmines. *Statistical Analysis of Social Data*. Chicago: Rand McNally, 1978.

CHAPTER PREVIEW

CHAPTER 14

Control, Elaboration and Multivariate Analysis

INTRODUCTION

The examination of a bivariate relationship is but the first step in data analysis. Next, the substantive implications of the findings are evaluated, and causal inferences may be drawn. The bivariate measure of a relation is limited to the establishment of covariation and its direction. To interpret the findings and to assess the causal priorities of the investigated variables, one introduces other variables into the analysis. Suppose one finds a relationship between parents' age and child-rearing practices; that is, older parents tend to be more restrictive with their children than younger parents. What interpretation can be given to this finding? One may claim that the variables are causally related and that increasing age of parents is associated with a shift from permissive toward restrictive attitudes. However, alternatively, it is a possibility that a difference in child-rearing practices is due, not to a difference in age, but rather to a difference in orientation: Older parents were exposed to an orientation stressing restriction, whereas younger parents behave according to a more liberal orientation advocating more permissive practices. In other words, the relationship between parents' age and child-rearing practices is due to the fact that the variables "age" and "child-rearing practices" are both associated with a third variable, "orientation."

An observed correlation between two or more variables does not, of itself, permit the investigator to make causal interpretations. A bivariate relationship may be the product of chance, or it may exist because the variables are related to a third, unrevealed variable. Furthermore, the phenomenon under investigation can often be explained by more than a single independent variable. In either case, the introduction of additional variables serves the purpose of clarifying and elaborating the original relationship.

This chapter focuses on the analysis of more than two variables. The analysis of more than two variables serves three major functions in empirical research: control, elaboration, and prediction. The first function substitutes for the mechanism of experimental control when such is lacking. The second clarifies bivariate relationships by introducing intervening or conditional variables. The third is served by analyzing two or more independent variables to account for the variation in the dependent variable. This chapter discusses ways in which a third variable may enter into empirical research. In the first three sections, we consider the strategy of controlling for a third variable and elaboration. The fourth section deals with multivariate counterparts to the bivariate measures of relations. In the last section, some techniques of causal modeling are examined.

CONTROL AND ELABORATION

The Concept of Control

An association between two variables is not a sufficient basis for an inference that the two are causally related. Other variables need to be ruled out as alternative explanations of the relation. For example, a relationship between height and income can probably be accounted for by the variable "age." Age is related to both income and height, and this joint relationship produces a statistical relationship that has no causal significance. The original relation between height and income is said to be spurious. Spuriousness is a concept that applies to situations where an extraneous variable produces a "fake" relation between the independent and dependent variables. It is essential that an investigation uncover the extraneous factors contaminating the data in this way. Thus, in validating bivariate associations, an important step is to rule out the largest possible number of variables that might conceivably explain the original association. This is achieved by a process denoted as *control*, a basic principle in all research designs. With experimental designs, control is accomplished by dividing research participants into experimental and control groups, the allocation being made by a process of randomization. The logic of controlled experimentation assures the researcher that all extraneous variables have been controlled and that the two groups differ only with regard to their exposure to the independent variable. However, social scientists find it difficult to manipulate social groups and to apply experimental treatment prior to observations. Consequently, they lack control over numerous factors that throw doubt on any association between independent and dependent variables employed in the investigation.

In quasi-experimental designs, statistical techniques substitute for the experimental method of control. These techniques are employed during data analysis rather than at the data-collection stage. There are two major methods of statistical control. The first entails subgroup comparisons and is accompanied by the technique of cross tabulation. The second technique, partial correlation, employs mathematical procedures to readjust the value of a bivariate correlation coefficient.

METHODS OF CONTROL

Cross Tabulation as a Control Operation

The cross-tabulation method of control can be compared to the mechanism of matching, which is employed in experiments. In both techniques, the investigator attempts to equate the groups examined with respect to variables that may bias the results. With matching, research participants are equated *prior* to their exposure to the independent variable. This is done by a physical allocation to the experimental and control groups, resulting in pairs that are identical with respect to the controlled factors. With cross tabulation, research participants are allocated to the respective groups only *during the analysis stage.* Thus, whereas matching is a physical control mechanism, cross tabulation is a statistical operation.

Cross tabulation involves the division of the sample into subgroups according to the categories of the controlled variable. The original bivariate relation is then reassessed within each subgroup. The division into subgroups removes the biasing inequality by computing a measure of relationship for groups that are internally homogeneous with respect to the biasing factor.

Generally, only variables that are associated with both the independent variable and the dependent variable will bias the results. Thus, only variables that show an association with the independent and dependent variables under investigation are selected as control variables.

An illustration. The following example illustrates the steps involved in controlling for a third variable through cross tabulation. Suppose a sample of 900 respondents is selected to test the hypothesis that people from urban areas are politically more liberal than rural dwellers. The data obtained are presented in Table 14.1. It is observed that 50 percent of urban residents are liberal, compared with only 28 percent of the respondents from rural areas. Thus, it may be concluded that political liberalism is associated with place of residence. Next, the problem is whether such a result suffices for acceptance of the suggested hypothesis. The question is whether the association obtained is real (in which case the hypothesis may be supported) or is based on an accidental relation with a third variable (in which case the relationship is spurious).

TABLE 14.1. Political Liberalism by Urban-Rural Location

Political Liberalism	Urban Area	Rural Area
High	50% (200)	28% (140)
Low	50% (200)	72% (360)
Total	100% (400)	100% (500)

One such additional variable might be education, which is associated with both place of residence and political liberalism, as reflected in the hypothetical bivariate distributions of Tables 14.2 and 14.3.

Partial Tables

To control for education, one divides the 900 persons into two groups according to their level of education (high, low). Within each group, urban-rural location is cross-tabulated with political liberalism. The original bivariate association is then estimated in each of the subgroups. The controlled data are summarized in Table 14.4.

The resulting two bivariate tables of Table 14.4 are referred to as partial tables because each one reflects only part of the total association. Each pair of parallel cells in the two partial tables adds up to the corresponding cell in the original table (Table 14.1). For example, the 180 highly educated respondents who come from urban areas and are liberals, plus the 20 respondents who are urban liberals with a low level of education, together constitute the 200 respondents in the original bivariate table who are liberal and from urban areas.

TABLE 14.2. Education by Urban-Rural Location

Education	Urban Area	Rural Area
High	75% (300)	20% (100)
Low	25% (100)	80% (400)
Total	100% (400)	100% (500)

TABLE 14.3.   Political Liberalism by Education

Political Liberalism	Education	
	High	Low
High	60%	20%
	(240)	(100)
Low	40%	80%
	(160)	(400)
Total	100%	100%
	(400)	(500)

To assess the partial association, compute a measure of relationship for each of the control groups and compare it with the original result. Appropriate measures are selected in the same way as for regular bi-variate distributions. Difference of percentages, gamma, or Pearson's r can be used, depending on the level of measurement.

The value of the partial association can be either identical or almost identical to the original one, it can vanish, or it can change. For the examination of spurious relationships, only the first two possibilities are relevant. When the partial association is identical or almost identical to the original one, one may conclude that the control variable does not account for the original relation. If it vanishes, the original association is said to be spurious. (A third variable may intervene between the dependent and independent variables, in which case the partial association will also vanish [or approximate zero]. An example will be considered in the next section.) When the partial association does not vanish

TABLE 14.4.   Political Liberalism by Urban-Rural Location, Controlling for Education (Spurious Relationship)

Political Liberalism	High Education		Low Education	
	Urban Area	Rural Area	Urban Area	Rural Area
High	60%	60%	20%	20%
	(180)	(60)	(20)	(80)
Low	40%	40%	80%	80%
	(120)	(40)	(80)	(320)
Total	100%	100%	100%	100%
	(300)	(100)	(100)	(400)

but is different from the original one, then it is said that the relationship is elaborated. Elaboration is considered in a later section.

The original association is spurious.   In the example of Table 14.4, education completely accounts for the relation between residence and liberalism, for there is no difference between rural and urban residents in their degree of liberalism within either of the two educational groups. Sixty percent of the highly educated rural residents, like 60 percent of the highly educated urban residents, are politically liberal. Within the low-education group, 20 percent are liberal wherever they reside. The overall association between the independent and dependent variables is completely accounted for by the association of each with education. This pattern can be presented graphically, as in Figure 14.1.

Education determines both political liberalism and place of residence. That is, people who are educated tend to live in cities and are generally politically liberal. There is no inherent link between political liberalism and place of residence, and the association between them is spurious.

The original association is nonspurious.   The control of a third variable may lead to entirely different results. In the hypothetical example of Table 14.5, the original bivariate association remains unchanged by the educational level. In the total sample, as well as in each educational group, 50 percent of urban residents are liberal, compared with 28 percent of rural residents. This result indicates that the overall relationship between the two original variables is not accounted for by the control variable. The investigator can be confident that education is an irrelevant factor with respect to this particular association.

In practice, the results are not as clear-cut as presented here. It is very rare for associations either to vanish or to remain identical with the original results. Often, the partial tables show a clear decrease in the size of the original relationship; at times, the reduction is slight. This is because of the numerous factors that can account for a bivariate association. In the above example, other variables such as income, party identification, or religious affiliation might conceivably explain the relationship between urban-rural location and political liberalism. This characteristic of variables has been referred to as "block-booking."[1] It refers to the multidimensionality of human beings and of their social interaction. When a comparison is made between people in terms of social class, only one dimension is tackled. People may differ thoroughly from each other in a great many things, and all these other factors may enter into the phenomenon to be explained. The block-booked factors become our control variables; but when we control for only one or some

1. Morris Rosenberg, *The Logic of Survey Analysis* (New York: Basic Books, 1968), pp. 26–28.

FIGURE 14.1.

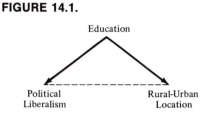

of them, the rest may still explain the remaining residual in the dependent variable.

The procedure, then, is to hold constant all other variables that may be relevant to the subject of investigation. The selection of these variables is a logical and theoretical operation, the only statistical guideline being the requirement that the potential control factor be related to both the independent and dependent variables. Of course, one can never be completely sure that all relevant variables have been introduced into the analysis. However, the more relevant factors controlled for, the greater the confidence that the relationship is not spurious.

Partial Correlation as a Control Operation

The cross-tabulation control operation is quite popular in empirical research, and it is applied to all levels of measurement. However, it has a drawback that limits its use when the number of cases is relatively small. The cross-tabulation method of control entails a subdivision of the sample into progressively smaller subgroups, according to the number of categories of the controlled factor. This reduces the number of cases serving as a basis for computing the coefficient, thus rendering its

TABLE 14.5. Political Liberalism by Urban-Rural Location, Controlling for Education (Nonspurious Relationship)

| *Political Liberalism* | *High Education* | | *Low Education* | |
	Urban Area	Rural Area	Urban Area	Rural Area
High	50%	28%	50%	28%
	(50)	(35)	(150)	(105)
Low	50%	72%	50%	72%
	(50)	(90)	(150)	(270)
Total	100%	100%	100%	100%
	(100)	(125)	(300)	(375)

validity and reliability questionable. This is particularly acute when there are several variables controlled simultaneously.

A second method of control, not limited by the number of cases, is the partial correlation. This is a mathematical adjustment of the bivariate correlation, designed to cancel out the effect of the control variable on the independent and dependent variables. The logic underlying the calculation of this measure of association is similar to that of cross tabulation. The original association between the independent and dependent variables is reassessed so that it reflects a direct association, independent of the variables' association to a third extraneous factor.

Suppose a correlation is found of $r = .60$ between self-esteem and educational expectation. To test the nature of this association, it is reasonable to introduce an additional variable, "social class," which is related to both self-esteem ($r = .30$) and educational expectation ($r = .40$). Partial correlation can be used to obtain a measure of association with the effect of social class removed. The formula for calculation of the partial correlation coefficient is given in Equation (14.1):

$$r_{12.3} = \frac{r_{12} - (r_{13})(r_{32})}{\sqrt{1 - r_{13}^2} \sqrt{1 - r_{13}^2}} \qquad (14.1)$$

where X_1 = independent variable

X_2 = dependent variable

X_3 = control variable

The symbol on the right-hand side of the dot indicates the variable to be controlled. Thus, $r_{12.3}$ is the correlation between variables 1 and 2 controlling for variable 3. Similarly, a partial coefficient between variables 1 and 3 controlling for 2 would be denoted as $r_{13.2}$. A partial with one control is referred to as a *first-order partial* to distinguish it from a bivariate correlation, often denoted as a zero-order correlation. A partial with two controls is referred to as *second-order partial*, and so on. When more than one variable is controlled for simultaneously, their numbers are added to the right of the dot. Thus, controlling for variables 3 and 4 would be expressed as $r_{12.34}$.

The partial correlation for self-esteem and educational expectation can now be calculated:

$$r_{12.3} = \frac{.60 - (.30)(.40)}{\sqrt{1 - (.30)^2} \sqrt{1 - (.40)^2}} = \frac{.48}{\sqrt{.7644}} = \frac{.48}{.87} = .55$$

where X_1 = self-esteem

X_2 = educational expectation

X_3 = social class

Notice that the total correlation between the original variables appears first in the numerator of the formula. The effect of the correlation between the control variable and each of the original ones is then subtracted from it. The result is standardized by two correction factors in the denominator, which reflect the variation explained in the independent and dependent variables by the control variable.[2]

The squared partial correlation reflects the proportion of variation left unexplained by the control variable and explained by the independent variable. Thus, about 30 percent $[(.55)^2 \times 100]$ of the variation in educational expectation was explained by self-esteem after removing the effect of social class.

In contrast to the cross-tabulation method of control, the partial correlation yields a single summarizing measure that reflects the degree of correlation between two variables controlling for a third. Thus, variation in the partial associations by different categories of the controlled variable is not reflected in the partial correlation because it averages out the different partials. This property of the measure is its main disadvantage, as it might obscure otherwise essential information. In cases where the investigator suspects that there are significant differences between the partials of the various subgroups, it is advisable to use the cross-tabulation technique instead.

A partial correlation may be employed to control for more than one variable. The formulas for higher-order coefficients have a similar logic, where the lower-order partial replaces the zero-order correlation in the original first-order formula. Following are the formulas for second-order and third-order partial correlation coefficients:

Second-order partial correlation:
$$r_{12.34} = \frac{r_{12.3} - (r_{14.3})(r_{24.3})}{\sqrt{1 - r_{14.3}^2}\,\sqrt{1 - r_{24.3}^2}} \qquad (14.2)$$

Third-order partial correlation:
$$r_{12.345} = \frac{r_{12.34} - (r_{15.34})(r_{25.34})}{\sqrt{1 - r_{15.34}^2}\,\sqrt{1 - r_{25.34}^2}} \qquad (14.3)$$

The Concept of Elaboration

The mechanism of control discussed in the preceding section is designed to uncover factors that might invalidate the original bivariate association. When such a mechanism is applied, there are two alternative outcomes: the partial association is zero, or close to it, in which case it can be concluded that the original relationship is spurious; or the partial association is almost identical to the original one, in which case the in-

---

2. Hubert M. Blalock, *Social Statistics*, 2d ed. (New York: McGraw-Hill, 1972), pp. 433–440.

vestigators may be satisfied that the bivariate association has a substantive significance. In the first instance, the investigators are likely to turn to other factors that can be employed as independent variables and repeat the process of validating the relationship, if a relationship is observed. On the other hand, if they are convinced that the relationship observed is nonspurious, they can proceed to a more advanced stage of analysis and elaborate the bivariate association. Elaboration usually involves the introduction of other variables to determine the links between the independent and dependent variables or the specification of the conditions under which the association takes place.

An illustration. Let us illustrate the meaning of elaboration with some concrete examples. For a long time it has been argued that social class determines the mobility orientations of adolescents. Various investigators have attempted to provide an explanation for this association. Some have maintained that the difference between social classes is reflected in different cultural backgrounds, and that it is this difference that largely accounts for the variation in mobility orientations.[3] Others indicated that lower and middle classes adopt different child-rearing practices that influence the motivation to achieve.[4]

What is the meaning of the different interpretations suggested? The association between class and mobility orientations is explained by cultural background or by child-rearing practices. In the first interpretation, cultural background is determined by social class, whereas mobility orientations are dependent upon cultural background. In the second interpretation, child-rearing practices determine mobility orientations and are themselves determined by social class. These relationships may be represented schematically as follows:

Social Class → Cultural Background → Mobility Orientations

Social Class → Child-rearing Practices → Mobility Orientations

In the two alternative interpretations, the third variable (cultural background or child-rearing practices) provides a link between social class and mobility orientations. The third variable is said to intervene between the two original variables.

In another set of studies, it was demonstrated that women are less likely to vote than men.[5] It was suspected that the amount of interest in

3. Herbert H. Hyman, "The Value System of Different Classes: A Social Psychological Contribution to the Analysis of Stratification," in *Class, Status and Power* ed. by Richard Bendix and Seymour M. Lipset (Glencoe, Ill.: Free Press, 1953), pp. 488–499.

4. Elizabeth Douvan and Joseph Adelson, *The Adolescent Experience* (New York: Wiley, 1966), pp. 341–354.

5. Paul F. Lazarsfeld, Bernard Berelson, and Hazel Gaudet, *The People's Choice* (New York: Columbia University Press, 1968), p. 48.

politics might account for the difference in involvement. Women, it was believed, are less interested in politics and thus less likely to vote in elections. However, when interest was controlled for, it was found that this interpretation was only partially true. Indeed, among women, noninterest is accompanied by nonvoting. But this does not hold among men. Men tend to vote even if their interest is rather limited. In this example, the original bivariate association is pronounced only under certain conditions, that is, among noninterested citizens. The control variable is thus said to be a *conditional variable*.

These two types of interpretations, which are among the most common ones, elaborate the original bivariate relationship. In the first case, the elaboration answers the question "*Why* are the independent and dependent variables related?" In the second case, the elaboration specifies under *what* conditions the relationship will hold.

Elaboration, like control, involves holding a third variable constant and reexamining the original association. This can be accomplished by using either cross tabulation or partial correlation coefficients.

Intervening Variables

Let us start with the first case, in which the controlled variable is said to intervene between the independent and dependent variables. The data summarized in Table 14.6 examine the relationship between social class and intention to vote. The findings in Table 14.6 demonstrate that these two variables are associated: persons from the upper class are more likely to vote in an election than are those in lower classes. The investigators hypothesized that this association could be explained with the variable "political interest." That is, it was claimed that social class affects voting indirectly through political interest. Upper-class people tend to be more interested in politics and consequently are more likely to vote.

As a means of testing this hypothesis, political interest was held constant, and the original relationship was reexamined. If, as suggested,

TABLE 14.6   Social Class and Intention to Vote

Intention to Vote	Social Class	
	Upper	Lower
Will not vote	6%	15%
Will vote	94%	85%
Total	100%	100%
	(1,600)	(2,000)

TABLE 14.7.   Social Class and Intention to Vote by Political Interest

| | Political Interest | | | | | |
| | Great | | Medium | | Low | |
Intention to Vote	Upper Class	Lower Class	Upper Class	Lower Class	Upper Class	Lower Class
Will not vote	2%	2%	6%	6%	35%	35%
Will vote	98%	98%	94%	94%	65%	65%
Total	100%	100%	100%	100%	100%	100%
	(480)	(500)	(960)	(1,120)	(160)	(380)

social class has only an indirect influence on voting, then when the intermediate link is controlled for, the association between social class and voting should disappear. The results in Table 14.7 confirm the hypothesis: among groups with identical political interest, social class does not influence the propensity to vote. The original relationship vanishes when political interest is controlled for. The order of the variables, which can be inferred from the data, is displayed diagramatically as follows:

Social Class → Political Interest → Voting

The conditions for the interpretation given above require that the control variable be associated with both the independent and dependent variables; and that when controlled for, the original relationship should vanish (or diminish considerably) in all categories of the control variable. To the reader who exclaims that these were the identical conditions required for declaring the relationship spurious, we can only confirm that this is indeed the case. The statistical tests in both cases are identical, but the interpretation is significantly different. With a spurious interpretation, the statistical results invalidate an hypothesis about the relationship between the independent and dependent variable; an intervening interpretation, on the other hand, clarifies and explains such a relationship. How, then, can a distinction be made between the two?

Morris Rosenberg maintains that the difference is a theoretical issue rather than a statistical one and that it lies in the assumed causal relationship among the variables.[6] With a spurious interpretation, it is assumed that there is no causal relation between the independent and dependent variables; in the intervening case, the two are indirectly related through an intermediate link, the control variable. The difference between the two interpretations is presented graphically in Figure 14.2.

In the first case (a), the control variable precedes both independent

6. Morris Rosenberg, *The Logic of Survey Analysis*, pp. 54–66.

FIGURE 14.2. Spurious and Intervening Interpretations

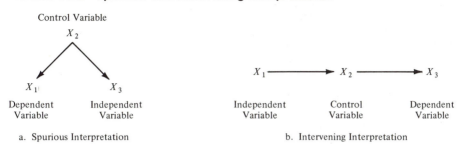

a. Spurious Interpretation   b. Intervening Interpretation

and dependent variables; in the second (b), the independent variable is first in the time sequence. Only factors that precede the independent variable in time can be invalidating factors; that is, only when a factor precedes the independent variable can one say that it determines both the independent variable and the dependent variable. In the last example, political interest is not likely to precede social class; thus, we are satisfied with the intervening interpretation. However, the time sequence cannot always be determined accurately. For instance, one's self-esteem can determine one's popularity, which in turn influences one's occupational achievement. But self-esteem may also intervene between popularity and achievement. In both cases, the statistical test will yield the same result. In such a situation, both interpretations are feasible, and the investigator might have to introduce other factors that will help to reject one of these two possibilities.

Conditional Variables

The second type of interpretation involves a specification of conditions or contingencies necessary for the occurrence of the relationship. We will illustrate the meaning of conditional interpretation using the example on voting behavior. Paul Lazarsfeld, Bernard Berelson, and Hazel Gaudet found that nonvoting is associated with sex; their findings are reported in Table 14.8.

The data reflect a clear pattern of association. The greatest proportion of nonvoters is found among women: 18 percent of all women abstained from voting, compared with 2 percent of all men. To gain further insight, the investigators controlled for the variable "interest in politics." The results are presented in Table 14.9.

It is observed that among the categories of the control variable, "level of interest," the association differs considerably. Whereas it has virtually disappeared in the high-interest category, it is pronounced in the low-interest group. In other words, "the less a group is interested in the election, the greater will be the amount of deliberate non-voting

TABLE 14.8. Voting and Sex

Voting	Men	Women
Voted	98%	82%
Did not vote	2%	18%
Total	100%	100%
	(1,294)	(1,418)

SOURCE: Paul F. Lazarsfeld, Bernard Berelson, and Hazel Gaudet, *The People's Choice* (New York: Columbia University Press, 1968), p. 48.

among women as compared with men."[7] The difference, it is maintained, is due to difference in socialization patterns that put more social pressure on men to go to the polls, even if they are not interested in the events of the campaign and the election results. In this example, the control variable, "level of interest," is a conditional factor that specifies a condition facilitating a relationship between sex and voting behavior.

Conditional relationships such as this one are quite common in social science research and can be inferred whenever the relative size or direction of the original bivariate relationship is more pronounced in one category of the control variable than in another. The presence of such differences between subgroups reflects the nature of social reality, where each variable can be broken down into various components. Indeed, many conditional factors are associated with almost any two-variable relationships. This makes the analysis of conditional relationships one of the most important aspects of statistical analysis.

TABLE 14.9. Voting and Sex by Level of Interest

	Level of Interest					
	Great		Medium		None	
Voting	Men	Women	Men	Women	Men	Women
Voted	99%	98%	98%	87%	83%	44%
Did not vote	1%	2%	2%	13%	17%	56%
Total	100%	100%	100%	100%	100%	100%
	(449)	(328)	(789)	(852)	(56)	(238)

SOURCE: Paul F. Lazarsfeld, Bernard Berelson, and Hazel Gaudet, *The People's Choice* (New York: Columbia University Press, 1968), p. 48.

---

7. Paul F. Lazarsfeld, Bernard Berelson, and Hazel Gaudet, "Political Interest and Voting Behavior," in *The Language of Social Research*, ed. by Paul F. Lazarsfeld and Morris Rosenberg (New York: Free Press, 1955), p. 158.

Interest and concern as a condition. Herbert Hyman analyzed the various factors that are generally considered conditions for most bivariate associations and classified them into three major groups.[8] The first class involves variables that specify relationship in terms of interest and concern. In many situations, interest and concern specify the conditions under which the effectiveness of an independent variable is more or less pronounced. For instance, consider the finding that self-esteem is associated with intensity of political discussion.[9] Adolescents with low self-esteem, who are more self-conscious, tend to avoid expressing their political views. Taking into account the level of political interest, it is observed that the relationship holds only among those who are interested in politics. Those who are not interested in politics also do not discuss politics, even though they might have a high degree of self-esteem. Thus, the utilization of the conditional factor helps to clarify the original findings. People tend to differ in their interests, which, in turn, affect their attitudes and behavior patterns. Thus, social stimuli are likely to have differential effects on them, and the identification of these differing patterns may prove to be essential to the social scientist.

Time and place as a condition. The second class of factors specifies associations in terms of time and place. A relationship between two variables can vary according to the time and place at which it is studied. Gabriel Almond and Sidney Verba, for example, in their five-nation study, found a positive relationship between education and the belief that one would receive equal treatment at the hands of government.[10] Less educated people were less likely to expect equal treatment than were highly educated people. However, when this association was examined in several countries, it was found that this was not equally true in all of them. In the English-speaking countries (the United States and Britain), there is hardly any difference among educational levels. In Germany, the difference is greater; in Italy and Mexico, the differences are substantial. These findings specify that the nature of the social system and its effect on attitudes and beliefs are different in the various countries.

Specification by time is meaningful, especially when the dynamic aspect of a relationship is considered. Often, a relationship that holds at one time will be diminished or changed at another. An example is the general process of development and socialization. The family is known

8. Herbert H. Hyman, *Survey Design and Analysis* (New York: Free Press, 1955), p. 295–311.

9. Morris Rosenberg, "Self-Esteem and Concern with Public Affairs," *Public Opinion Quarterly*, 26 (1962): 201–211.

10. Gabriel A. Almond and Sidney Verba, *The Civic Culture* (Princeton, N.J.: Princeton University Press, 1963), pp. 69–75.

to affect various behavioral patterns in children. This effect is pronounced, especially at the early stages, when the child is more exposed and more vulnerable to his or her family. At later stages, however, other aspects of socialization play an important role, and the family's influence diminishes. Thus, a relationship between family characteristics and behavioral orientations would not stay constant if examined at different times.

Background characteristics as a condition. The last class of factors is background characteristics of the units of analysis. Often, associations are likely to differ for persons or groups that do not share the same characteristics. Thus, the relation between class position and voting behavior is different for men and for women, and the effect of teachers' encouragement on self-esteem is not identical for black and white children. These distinctions are perhaps the most common among the types of specifications employed in the social sciences. In fact, some researchers employ such control variables as "social class," "level of education," "sex," and "age" almost automatically, reexamining all relationships obtained.

MULTIVARIATE ANALYSIS

Multiple Relationships

Up to this point, consideration has been given only to situations in which one independent variable is said to determine the dependent variable being studied. However, in real situations, it is seldom that only one variable is relevant to what is to be explained. Often, various variables are directly associated with the dependent variable. Population change, for example, is explained by four variables: "birth rate," "death rate," "immigration rate," and "emigration rate." Similarly, a well-known theory of delinquency employs the variables "barrier to legitimate opportunities" and "degree of exposure to illegitimate opportunities" to account for rates of delinquency.[11] Thus, there are often several independent variables, each of which may contribute to the prediction of the dependent variable.

The simultaneous effect of several independent variables on the dependent variable can be assessed by constructing a multiple regression equation, which describes the amount of linear relationship between the dependent and independent variables. The equation is pre-

---

11. Richard Cloward and Lloyd E. Ohlin, *Delinquency and Opportunity* (New York: Free Press, 1960), chapters 4, 6.

sented in Formula (14.4)

$$Y_1 = a_{1.23} + b_{12.3}X_2 + b_{13.2}X_3 \qquad (14.4)$$

where Y_1 represents the dependent variable and X_2 and X_3 the independent variables. Designated as partial regression coefficients, $b_{12.3}$ and $b_{13.2}$ are the slopes of the regression line for each independent variable, controlling for the other. Thus, $b_{12.3}$ reflects the amount of change in Y_1 associated with a given change in X_2, holding X_3 constant, and $a_{1.23}$ designates the intercept point on the Y_1 axis for both X_2 and X_3.

Just as in the two-variable situation, the constants of the multiple linear regression equation are estimated so as to minimize the average square error in prediction. This is accomplished by using the least-square criterion to obtain the best fit to the data. The computing formulas for $b_{12.3}$, $b_{13.2}$, and $a_{1.23}$ are presented in Equations (14.5), (14.6), and (14.7):

$$b_{12.3} = \frac{b_{12} - (b_{13})(b_{32})}{1 - b_{23}b_{32}} \qquad (14.5)$$

$$b_{13.2} = \frac{b_{13} - (b_{12})(b_{23})}{1 - b_{32}b_{23}} \qquad (14.6)$$

$$a_{1.23} = \bar{Y}_1 - b_{12.3}\bar{X}_2 - b_{13.2}\bar{X}_3 \qquad (14.7)$$

Note that b_{32} is not the same as b_{23}. The regression coefficient is asymmetrical, so the subscripts are not interchangeable.

To illustrate the computation of the multiple-regression constants using Equations (14.5), (14.6), and (14.7), we shall attempt to estimate the simultaneous effect of education and self-esteem on the extent of political liberalism.

Designating liberalism as Y_1, education as X_2, and self-esteem as X_3, the following are the hypothetical b coefficients for the simple bivariate effect of these variables upon each other:

$b_{12} = 0.7 \rightarrow$ effect of education on liberalism

$b_{13} = 1.3 \rightarrow$ effect of self-esteem on liberalism

$b_{32} = 0.5 \rightarrow$ effect of education on self-esteem

$b_{23} = 1.8 \rightarrow$ effect of self-esteem on education

These coefficients are substituted into Equations (14.5) and (14.6):

$$b_{12.3} = \frac{0.7 - (1.3)(0.5)}{1 - (1.8)(0.5)} = .50$$

$$b_{13.2} = \frac{1.3 - (0.7)(1.8)}{1 - (0.5)(1.8)} = .40$$

To compute the constant a, the mean values of the three variables are obtained:

$$\text{Mean score of self-esteem } (\bar{X}_3) = 5.8$$
$$\text{Mean score of liberalism } (\bar{Y}_1) = 6.5$$
$$\text{Mean score of education } (\bar{X}_2) = 8.9$$

According to Equation (14.7):

$$a_{1.23} = 6.5 - (0.5)(8.9) - (0.4)(5.8) = -.27$$

With the obtained values of $b_{12.3}$, $b_{13.2}$ and $a_{1.23}$, the complete multiple regression equation for predicting liberalism on the basis of education and self-esteem would therefore be:

$$Y_1 = -0.27 + 0.5X_2 + 0.4X_3$$

It indicates the extent of political liberalism that would be expected, on the average, with a given level of education and a given level of self-esteem. For example, for a person with ten years of schooling and a self-esteem score of eight, the expected level of liberalism would be:

$$Y_1 = -0.27 + (0.5)(10) + (0.4)(8) = 7.93$$

As the b coefficients reflect the net effect of each variable, they can be compared so as to denote the relative importance of the independent variables. However, since each variable is measured on a different scale in different units, *b must be standardized to be comparable*. The standardized equivalent of the b coefficient is called the *beta weight*, or the *beta coefficient*; it is symbolized as β. The beta weights are obtained by multiplying b by the ratio of the standard deviation of the independent variable to the standard deviation of the dependent variable. Thus, $\beta_{12.3}$ would be expressed as:

$$\beta_{13.2} = b_{13.2} \frac{s_3}{s_1} \tag{14.8}$$

For the previous example, the standard deviations are:

$$s_1 \text{ (liberalism)} = 3$$
$$s_2 \text{ (education)} = 4.1$$
$$s_3 \text{ (self-esteem)} = 2.2$$

Accordingly:

$$Y_1 = -0.27 + 0.5 \left(\frac{4.1}{3} \right) X_2 + 0.4 \left(\frac{2.2}{3} \right) X_3$$

Therefore, the multiple regression equation, expressed in beta coefficients is:

$$X_1 = -0.27 + 0.68X_2 + 0.29X_3$$

This would indicate that for every increase of one standard deviation in education, liberalism increases by 0.68 standard deviation; and with an increase of one standard deviation in self-esteem, liberalism increases by 0.29 standard deviation. When the relative importance of the two factors is compared, it is evident that education contributes more (0.68) to liberalism than does self-esteem (0.29).

Just as with simple regression, one needs to estimate how well the multiple-regression rule fits the actual data. In simple regression, the fit (or the relative reduction of error) was measured using r^2, which is defined as the ratio of the variation explained to the total variation in the dependent variable. Similarly, when the prediction is based on several variables, an estimate of the relative reduction of error is based on the ratio of the variation explained with various variables simultaneously to the total variation. This measure, R^2, is termed the *coefficient of multiple determination* and designates the percentage of the variation explained by all the independent variables in the multiple-regression equation. The square root of R^2 indicates the correlation between all independent variables taken together with the dependent variable; it is thus denoted as the *coefficient of multiple correlation*.

For the three-variable case, the formula for R^2 is presented in Equation (14.9):

$$R_{1.23}^2 = \frac{r_{12}^2 + r_{13}^2 - 2r_{12}r_{13}r_{23}}{1 - r_{23}^2} \tag{14.9}$$

In the multiple correlation coefficient, note that the symbol for the dependent variable is to the left of the dot, whereas all the independent variables are placed to the right. For instance, the multiple correlation coefficient between the dependent variable Y_1 and X_2, X_3, X_4 would be designated as $R_{1.234}$.

As an example, let us calculate the percentage of variation explained in modernization (Y_1), using education (X_2) and urbanization (X_3) as predictors. The hypothetical zero-order correlations are: $r_{12} = .60$; $r_{13} = .50$; $r_{23} = .20$. $R_{1.23}^2$ is then

$$R_{1.23}^2 = \frac{.60^2 + .50^2 - 2(.60)(.50)(.20)}{1 - .20^2} = \frac{.49}{.96} = .51$$

This means that 50 percent of the variation in modernization is accounted for by the combined effect of education and urbanization. Note the $R_{1.23}$ ($\sqrt{R_{1.23}^2}$), which is .714, is larger than either r_{12} or r_{23}. R always reaches maximum value relative to the zero-order coefficients when the independent variables employed are not correlated. When the correlation between the independent variables is zero, R^2 is simply the sum of the squared zero-order correlations. For example, when r_{23} is zero, we get:

$$R_{1.23}{}^2 = r_{12}{}^2 + r_{13}{}^2$$

When the intercorrelation between the independent variables is high, the obtained multiple coefficient would not ordinarily be much larger than the largest zero-order correlation. In such a case, using the other independent variables would not improve the prediction, and the investigator would be better off omitting the variable from the prediction equation. In other words, to improve the prediction, one should introduce the greatest possible number of relevant independent variables that are *independent of each other*.

CAUSAL MODELS

The discussion has focused on methods of control that provide an interpretation of the relation between two variables. It was indicated that a "real" relationship is one that does not prove to be spurious. This is determined by the time sequence of the variables and the relative size of the partial associations.

These two elements—the size of the partials relative to the original bivariate associations and the assumed time order between the variables—have been suggested by Paul Lazarsfeld as the kind of evidence required for inferring causation: "We can suggest a clear-cut definition of the causal relation between two attributes. If we have a relationship between X and Y, and if for any antecedent test factor c the partial relationship between X and Y does not disappear, then the original relationship should be called a causal one."[12] Although one can never directly demonstrate causality from correlational data, it is possible to make causal inferences concerning the adequacy of specific causal models. Herbert Simon and Hubert Blalock suggested a method that enables such inferences. This method involves a finite set of explicitly defined variables, assumptions about how these variables are interrelated causally and assumptions about the effect of outside variables on the variables included in the model.[13]

The Simon-Blalock method can be applied to situations involving three or more variables. To simplify matters, however, our discussion

12. Paul F. Lazarsfeld, "The Algebra of Dichotomous Systems," in *Studies in Items Analysis and Prediction*, ed. by Herbert Solomon (Stanford, Calif.: Stanford University Press, 1959), p. 146.

13. Herbert A. Simon, *Models of Man: Social and Rational* (New York: Wiley, 1957); Hubert M. Blalock, *Causal Inference in Nonexperimental Research* (Chapel Hill: University of North Carolina Press, 1964).

will be limited to the three-variable case. Later on, we shall illustrate the analysis of models involving four variables.

A Three-Variable Model

Theoretically, there could be six causal connections between three variables X_1, X_2, and X_3. These possibilities are diagrammed in Figure 14.3. (The direction of causality is indicated by an arrowhead.) A simplifying assumption rules out two-way causation, either directly in the form $X_1 \rightleftarrows X_2$ or indirectly in the form shown in the second part of the figure. This assumption limits the number of causal connections between three variables to three. Furthermore, under this assumption a dependent variable cannot determine any of the variables preceding it in the causal sequence. Thus, in a causal system having three variables X_1, X_2, and X_3—where X_1 is the independent variable, X_2 the intervening variable, and X_3 the dependent variable—X_2 cannot determine X_1, and X_3 cannot determine X_2 or X_1.

The problem of adequately representing a system that rules out two-way causation can be handled by a recursive system of equations. This system allows variables to be arranged hierarchically in terms of their causal priorities. Thus, the previously described causal system having three variables X_1, X_2, and X_3 could be described as follows:

$$X_1 = e_1$$
$$X_2 = b_{21}X_1 + e_2$$
$$X_3 = b_{31.2}X_1 + b_{32.1}X_2 + e_3$$

FIGURE 14.3.   Causal Connections Among Three Variables

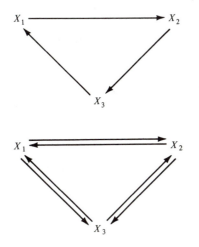

FIGURE 14.4.

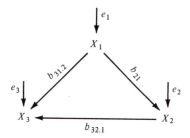

This set of equations indicates that X_1 depends only on outside variables represented by e_1; that X_2 depends on X_1 and other outside factors; and that X_3 depends on X_1 and X_2, as well as on outside factors. The e_1's designate the outside factors and are commonly referred to as *error terms*. The particular causal ordering represented by these equations is diagrammatically presented in Figure 14.4.

It is noted that the equations are simple linear regression equations indicating the relation of each variable to another. (We assume linearity and additive effects of the independent variables.) We have used the conventional notation for regression coefficients, where b_{21}, for instance, measures the effect of X_1 on X_2; and $b_{31.2}$ measures the effect of X_1 on X_3 when X_2 is held constant. (The constant "a" has been omitted from each of the equations. This can be done whenever each variable is measured in standardized form.) Any slope involves controls only for variables that have explicitly appeared in the equation; thus, b_{21} does not involve any controls for the remaining variables, whereas $b_{31.2}$ and $b_{32.1}$ each control for the other variable.

In addition to the a priori assumption of no reciprocal causation, another assumption involves the error terms (e_1) included in each of the equations. It is assumed that the errors are uncorrelated; that is, that "all other" factors influencing the dependent variable are unrelated to the other independent variables in the system.[14]

Having satisfied these two assumptions and if one can also assume that the model diagrammed in Figure 14.4 is theoretically sound, it is possible to study each equation separately and to use ordinary least-square procedures to estimate the three coefficients b_{21}, $b_{31.2}$, and $b_{32.1}$. However, one can rarely assume that a given model is correct. Rather, one proceeds by making causal inferences concerning the adequacy of models by eliminating those that make predictions inconsistent with the

14. Herbert A. Simon, "Spurious Correlation: A Causal Interpretation," *Journal of the American Statistical Association*, 49 (1954): 467–479.

data. In our recursive system, however, the number of unknowns is the same as the number of equations, so that each of the coefficients can be estimated uniquely, regardless of the data. To test the adequacy of a model, reduce the number of unknowns by setting one or more of the b's equal to zero. This imposes conditions that the data must satisfy for the equations to be mutually consistent. A coefficient equal to zero is equivalent to saying that there is no direct link between the two variables concerned. Thus, going back to the original diagram (Figure 14.4), if we set $b_{21} = 0$, we are saying that there is no direct causal link between X_1 and X_2; $b_{31.2} = 0$ implies that X_1 and X_3 are not directly related; similarly, $b_{32.1} = 0$ means that X_3 and X_2 have no direct link. These three alternatives are presented in Figure 14.5. Each of these three alternative models imposes a specific condition that the equations must satisfy. In Model I, $b_{21} = 0$; in Model II, $b_{31.2} = 0$; and in Model III, $b_{32.1} = 0$. The corresponding arrows (b_{21}, $b_{31.2}$, $b_{32.1}$) have been eliminated in each of the three diagrams.

The conditions imposed on each of the specific models are the predictions that should hold true if a model is correct. These predictions can be expressed in terms of correlation coefficients; that is, the vanishing of a b is equivalent to the vanishing of the comparable correlation coefficient. Thus, $b_{21} = 0$ implies that $r_{21} = 0$; $b_{32.1} = 0$, that $r_{32.1} = 0$; and $b_{31.2} = 0$, that $r_{31.2}$ should be zero as well.

The predictions derived from the models to be tested are always in terms of vanishing partials or zero-order coefficients that are set to zero. Predictions are always in terms of coefficients that reflect the uniqueness of the model under study. In other words, models are tested not in terms of their causal links, but rather by a test of the relationship between all pairs of unconnected variables. This means that the number of predictions for each causal model is a function of the number of variables in the system and the number of coefficients that were set to zero. The

FIGURE 14.5. Three Causal Models

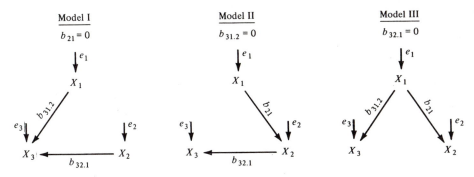

number of predictions that can be derived can be determined by Formula (14.10):

$$P = \frac{n(n-1)}{2} - K \qquad (14.10)$$

where P = number of predictions

n = number of variables

K = number of nonzero coefficients (or the number of causal arrows)

In our example, $n = 3$ and $K = 2$ in each of the models; thus,

$$P = \frac{3(2)}{2} - 2 = 1$$

This method for drawing causal inferences is demonstrated in the following example on political behavior and its determinants.[15] It is hypothesized that the social characteristics of an individual's father (X_1) and the father's party identification (X_2) are the causal determinants of the individual's partisan attitudes (X_3). The alternative causal priorities of the variables are expressed in three alternative models.

The first causal model suggests that the social characteristics of the father directly influence both his own party identification as well as his child's partisan attitudes. This causal ordering is displayed in Figure 14.6. This model implies that there is no causal link between one's partisan attitudes and one's father's party identification and that the statistical association between them is due to a third factor—the father's

FIGURE 14.6.

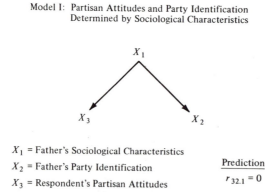

Model I: Partisan Attitudes and Party Identification Determined by Sociological Characteristics

X_1 = Father's Sociological Characteristics

X_2 = Father's Party Identification

X_3 = Respondent's Partisan Attitudes

Prediction

$r_{32.1} = 0$

---

15. This example is based on Arthur S. Goldberg, "Discerning a Causal Pattern among Data on Voting Behavior," *American Political Science Review*, 60 (1966): 913–922. Because we are limited to a three-variable case, several modifications were made.

social characteristics, which determine them both. Thus, the correlation between them is expected to vanish when the third factor is held constant.

In Model II (Figure 14.7), the party identification of the father intervenes between his own social characteristics and his child's partisan attitudes. In this model, there is a direct link between the party identification of the parent and the partisan attitudes of the respondent, but no direct link between the father's social characteristics and the partisan attitudes. The prediction of this model is therefore $r_{31.2} = 0$.

Finally, a hypothetical alternative is one in which the parent's social characteristics and his party identification are assumed to be independent causes of a person's partisan attitudes. In such a case, we would expect the zero-order relation between the two independent variables to approach zero. The last model is presented in Figure 14.8.

If we make use of the intercorrelations between the variables, the three alternative models can be tested. The matrix of correlations is given in Table 14.10. The predictions and the empirical results are summarized in Table 14.11.

The correlation between the father's social characteristics and his party identification is numerically larger than would be expected if the variables were not causally related. Model III is thus eliminated as implausible. Model I provides a better fit to the data, but the discrepancy between the prediction and the empirical results is still substantial. The prediction for Model II, however, fits the actual results fairly well and thus receives our support. It is noted that one can proceed only by the elimination of implausible models rather than by establishing directly

FIGURE 14.7.

Model II: Father's Party Identification Intervening Between
Sociological Characteristics and Respondent's
Partisan Attitudes

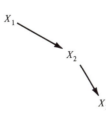

X_1 = Father's Sociological Characteristics

X_2 = Father's Party Identification

X_3 = Respondent's Partisan Attitudes

Prediction

$r_{31.2} = 0$

FIGURE 14.8.

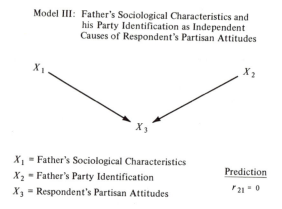

Model III: Father's Sociological Characteristics and
his Party Identification as Independent
Causes of Respondent's Partisan Attitudes

X_1 = Father's Sociological Characteristics

X_2 = Father's Party Identification

X_3 = Respondent's Partisan Attitudes

Prediction

$r_{21} = 0$

the validity of any particular model. The criterion of rejection and acceptance is empirical, and the models that provide the best predictions are supported.

The extension of the technique discussed earlier to a four-variable model is quite straightforward. Using the underlying logic, one can work out the prediction equations for any particular four-variable model. With four variables, there are six pairs of relationships and 2^6 (64) alternative

TABLE 14.10. Intercorrelations Between Father's Sociological Characteristics, Father's Party Identification, and Respondent's Partisan Attitudes

	X_2	X_3
X_1	.454	.318
X_2		.453

X_1 = · Father's sociological characteristics

X_2 = Father's party identification

X_3 = Respondent's partisan attitudes

TABLE 14.11. Predictions and Empirical Results for Models I, II, and III

	Prediction	Empirical Results
Model I	$r_{32.1} = 0$	.366
Model II	$r_{31.2} = 0$	.141
Model III	$r_{21} = 0$	.454

models. Some of these models are trivial; still, the number of significant ones is quite large. Thus, it is virtually impossible to compare a set of data against all possible models; the researcher can proceed only by selecting models that are theoretically plausible and then testing them against the data.

A Four-Variable Model

Before concluding, we shall discuss briefly a four-variable model to illustrate how the method can be applied in more complex cases. In a study on adolescent achievement variables, data from 1,455 male high-school freshmen were used to evaluate the tenability of the causal ordering of adolescent achievement variables: "socioeconomic status," "mobility attitudes," "measured intelligence," and "educational expectations."[16] In Model I, which is consistent with a traditional perspective of sociology, adolescents' educational expectations are linked with socioeconomic status via mobility attitudes and measured intelligence. In Model II, mobility attitudes and measured intelligence are linked with socioeconomic status via educational expectation. These two perspectives are depicted in Figure 14.9.

As is evident from the diagrams depicting the two models, some of the arrows connecting the variables have been eliminated, which is equivalent to setting the parallel coefficients to zero. In Model I, mobility attitudes and measured intelligence are not directly connected; thus, the coefficient indicating the path from X_2 to $X_3 \rightarrow r_{32.1}$ is set to zero. Similarly, X_4 is not directly influenced by X_1, which is equivalent to saying that $r_{41.23} = 0$. In Model II, the arrow connecting socioeconomic status and mobility attitudes is missing. Therefore, $r_{21.34} = 0$. Similarly, socioeconomic status and measured intelligence are not directly related; thus, $r_{31.4} = 0$.

FIGURE 14.9. Two Temporal Sequences of Adolescent Achievement Variables

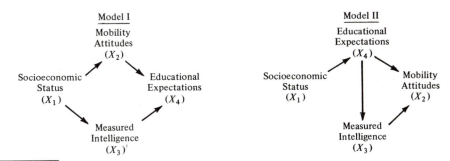

Model I

Mobility Attitudes (X_2)

Socioeconomic Status (X_1)

Educational Expectations (X_4)

Measured Intelligence (X_3)

Model II

Educational Expectations (X_4)

Socioeconomic Status (X_1)

Mobility Attitudes (X_2)

Measured Intelligence (X_3)

16. Richard A. Rehberg, Walter E. Schafer, and Judie Sinclair, "Toward a Temporal Sequence of Adolescent Achievement Variables," *American Sociological Review*, 35 (1970): 34–48.

We can now write the predictions and the empirical values obtained in Rehberg, Shafer, and Sinclair's data. In Table 14.12, the original zero-order associations are summarized; in Table 14.13, the predictions and the empirical tests are presented.

As is evident from the empirical results, there is little support for Model I. The correlations between mobility attitudes and intelligence and between socioeconomic status and educational expectations remain substantial after removing the effect of the control variables. On the other hand, the data support the two predictions of Model II. Partialing out the influence of intelligence and educational expectations virtually eliminates the relationship between the variables (X_1 to X_2, and X_1 to X_3). The empirical test thus renders Model II more tenable than Model I.

Concluding the discussion on causal inference, we note that the technique has both advantages and limitations. Its value lies in providing a framework that enables the researcher to evaluate causal relations between several variables simultaneously and to eliminate models that are not supported by the data. The great limitation of the technique is that it depends on several a priori assumptions that may well be untenable. Because the validity of the model being tested hinges on the validity of the required assumptions, the technique cannot be applied to situations where the reasonableness of the assumptions cannot be ascertained.

TABLE 14.12. Zero-Order Correlations

	X_2	X_3	X_4
X_1	.120	.210	.390
X_2		.210	.390
X_3			.420

X_1 = Socioeconomic status
X_2 = Mobility attitudes
X_3 = Measured intelligence
X_4 = Educational expectations

TABLE 14.13. Predictions and Empirical Results

	Prediction	*Empirical Values*
Model I	$r_{32.1} = 0$	.191
	$r_{41.23} = 0$	.341
Model II	$r_{21.34} = 0$	.029
	$r_{31.4} = 0$	.050

SUMMARY

In this chapter we have discussed analysis with three or more variables. Multivariate analysis has three basic functions: control, interpretation, and prediction. Statistical control is a substitute for experimental control and is accomplished through cross tabulation or partial correlation. With cross tabulation, an attempt is made to equate groups exposed to the independent variable with those not exposed, in all relevant matters. The selection of relevant control variables is based on theoretical as well as statistical considerations. It is required that the control variable be associated with both independent and dependent variables. The partial correlation is a method of statistically adjusting the zero-order correlation to cancel out the effect of the control variable on the independent and dependent variables.

When the mechanism of control is applied to a bivariate association, it can either cancel out the original relationship or have no effect on it. In the first case, the association is either spurious or mediated by the control variable; in the second case, the association is considered real and is subject to further analysis. Whereas a spurious interpretation invalidates a bivariate association, an intervening interpretation clarifies it and explains how the independent and dependent variables are related. A second class of interpretation specifies the conditions under which the association holds. Specification can be made according to interest and concern, time and place, and specific qualifications or characteristics.

Multiple regression and correlation comprise a technique for assessing the simultaneous effect of several independent variables on the dependent variable under study. In multiple regression, a prediction rule is estimated that evaluates the extent of change produced in the dependent variables by an independent variable, holding other relevant independent variables constant. The multiple correlation estimates the degree of fit of the prediction equation with the empirical data. R^2, the multiple correlation coefficient, measures the amount of variance in the dependent variable explained by the independent variables employed.

To make causal inferences, one can employ a method that uses correlational techniques. This, the Simon-Blalock method, assumes that the causal system is recursive and that the variables outside of the system are uncorrelated with the determinants of the dependent variable. Predictions are based on links between variables that are assumed to be zero. Assuming that some of the links in the system are unrelated imposes conditions that the data must satisfy for the prediction equations to be mutually consistent. Causal models are not tested directly; rather, inadequate models are eliminated.

KEY TERMS FOR REVIEW

Spurious relation
Partial tables
Partial correlation
Cross tabulation
Elaboration
Intervening
variable
Control variable

Conditional
variable
Multiple
Regression
coefficient
Coefficient of
multiple
determination

ADDITIONAL READINGS

Baggaley, Andrew R. *Intermediate Correlational Methods.* New York: Wiley, 1964, Chapters 4–5.

Blalock, Hubert M., ed. *Causal Models in the Social Sciences.* Chicago: Aldine-Atherton, 1971.

Blalock, Hubert M. *Theory Construction.* Englewood Cliffs, N.J.: Prentice-Hall, 1969.

Cohen, Jacob. "Multiple Regression as a General Data-Analytic System." *Psychological Bulletin,* 70 (December 1968): 426–443.

Heise, David R. *Causal Analysis.* New York: Wiley, 1975.

Hilton, Gordon. *Intermediate Politometrics.* New York: Columbia University Press, 1976.

Hirschi, Travis, and Hanan Selvin, "False Criteria of Causality in Delinquency Research." *Social Problems,* 13 (1966): 254–268.

Mosteller, Frederick, and John W. Tukey. *Data Analysis and Regression.* Reading, Mass.: Addison-Wesley, 1977.

Palumbo, Dennis, Jr. *Statistics in Political and Behavioral Science.* New York: Appleton-Century-Crofts, 1969, Chapter 10.

Sonquist, John A. *Multivariate Model Building.* Ann Arbor, Mich.: Institute for Social Research, 1970.

CHAPTER PREVIEW

CHAPTER 15

Index Construction and Scaling Methods

INTRODUCTION

In Chapter 6, we defined measurement as a procedure in which the researcher assigns symbols or numbers to empirical properties according to rules. We also discussed the structure of measurement, the idea of isomorphism, the four levels of measurement, and techniques for assessing validity and reliability. We are now in a position to discuss more advanced topics, namely, index construction and scaling.

Indexes and scales are measuring instruments. They are constructed to represent more validly the complexities inherent in human behavior. Indeed, concepts such as power, equity, freedom, intelligence, or bureaucracy are extremely difficult to measure because, among other things, they are composites of several empirical properties. Indexes and scales are means of measuring such complex phenomena.

Indexes and scales refer in most cases to composite measures constructed through the combination of two or more items or indicators. For example, socioeconomic status is a common index constructed by the combination of three indicators: income, education, and occupation.

Scales and indexes are employed in the social sciences for several reasons. First, they enable several variables to be represented by a single score that reduces the complexity of the data. Second, scales and indexes provide quantitative measures that are amenable to greater precision and statistical manipulation. Finally, indexes and scales increase the reliability of measurement. A score on a scale or index is considered to be a more reliable indicator of the property being measured than is a measure based on a response to one question or item alone. An example is something most students encounter daily. Students would not like to have an exam grade determined by their answer to a single multiple-choice or true-false question. First, the full universe of content of the material or topic being measured is not likely to be covered, and, second, a misinterpretation or mistake on any one question is less likely to lead to a wrong conclusion about the student's views on the topic if there are a larger number of questions. Multiple-item scales and indexes are, therefore, used to increase the reliability of the measurement and to obtain greater precision.

Scales differ from indexes by the greater rigor in their construction. Whereas indexes are constructed by the simple accumulation of scores, greater attention is paid in scales to the test of validity and reliability. Moreover, most scales involve the underlying *principle of unidimensionality*. This principle implies that the items comprising the scale should reflect a single dimension and belong on a continuum presumed to reflect one and only one concept.

Item analyses used in some scaling techniques identify questions or items that do not belong with the others in the set. Other scaling techniques permit us to rank order items by level of difficulty or intensity. Also, some scaling methods produce interval level scales, thereby avoiding the limitations imposed by nominal or ordinal type data.

Before one constructs a new scale, it is important that a survey of the literature be made to ascertain if an appropriate scale is already available. The sources listed in the additional readings at the end of the chapter provide a comprehensive source of information on scales available in the social sciences.

In the following section we discuss the logic of index construction and present several techniques for constructing indexes. The Thurstone and Likert scaling techniques are discussed next. These two types of scales are concerned with the measurement of attitudes on an ordinal and interval level of measurement. Then Guttman scaling, or the scalogram analysis as a method for scaling, is presented and exemplified. The Guttman technique can be applied to nominal and ordinal levels of analysis.

INDEX CONSTRUCTION

The combination of two or more items or indicators yields a composite measure, usually referred to as an *index*. For example, the Consumer Price Index (CPI) is a composite measure indicating changes in retail prices. The retail prices that make up the index are divided into eight major groups: food, housing, apparel, transportation, medical care, personal care, reading and recreation, and other goods and services. The approximately 400 commodities and services that are included were selected as being representative of the price trends of subgroups of related items and include the cost of diverse commodities and services, such as rice, men's work gloves, women's wool suits, rent, mortgage interest, gasoline, and haircuts. The 400 commodities and services are collected from fifty urban areas selected to be representative of those city characteristics that affect the way in which families spend their money; factors such as city size, climate, population density, and income level are taken into consideration. Within each city, price quotations are obtained from those sources from which families of wage and salary workers purchase goods and services. For each item, the prices reported by the various sources are combined, with appropriate weights, to ascertain average price changes for the city. Index numbers are prepared monthly for the country and for each of five large cities, and quarterly for the other cities.[1]

Four major problems are involved in constructing indexes: definition of the purpose for which the index is being compiled, selection of sources of data, selection of base, and selection of methods of aggregation and weighting.

Definition of Purpose

Essential to the process of index construction are these questions: What does one attempt to measure, and how is the measure going to be used? Logically speaking, if A is an index of X, then A may be only one of several indexes of X. Thus, some kind of supporting evidence is needed to make the case that the values of A correspond to the values of X. Most often, X is a broad concept like public welfare or political participation. Such concepts consist of a complex combination of phenomena and are subject to differing interpretations. Accordingly, no single indicator will cover all the dimensions of a concept, and a number of indicators have to be developed. Each indicator, in turn, serves a specific purpose that must be explicated prior to construction of the index.

Selection of Data

Obtrusive and/or unobtrusive methods of data collection may be used to construct indexes. Decisions as to which source of data to use depend on the purpose of the index and on the research design employed. As suggested in Chapter 5, for some types of quasi-experimental designs both obtrusive and unobtrusive data are required. Under either circumstance, the investigator must ascertain that the data pertain strictly to the

1. The following description is based on U.S. Bureau of Labor Statistics, *The Consumer Price Index: A Short Description of the Index as Revised* (Washington, D.C.: U.S. Government Printing Office, 1964) and William H. Wallace, *Measuring Price Changes: A Study of Price Indexes* (Richmond, Va.: Federal Reserve Bank of Richmond, 1970).

phenomenon being measured. This involves issues of validity and reliability, which were discussed in Chapter 6.

Selection of Base

For comparative purposes, indexes are expressed in the form of a proportion, a percent, or a ratio. A proportion is defined as the frequency of observations in any given category (f_i) divided by the total number of observations (N), or f_i/N. A proportion may range from zero to 1. A proportion becomes a percent when multiplied by 100 $(f_i/N \times 100)$, and a percent, by definition, may range from zero to 100. A ratio is a fraction that expresses the relative magnitude of any two sets of frequencies. To find the ratio between two frequencies, take the first frequency and divide by the second. For example, if a group consisted of 500 females and 250 males, the ratio of females to males is found by dividing 500 by 250, or 2/1.

To illustrate the use of these measures, consider Table 15.1, which reports the frequencies, proportions, and percents of selected criminal offenses in a New Jersey city by sources of official data.[2] The one, crime in New Jersey (CNJ), is compiled annually by the office of the state's attorney general. The other source was compiled from the municipal court dockets (MCD) in the city.

An examination of the table reveals a serious ambiguity in the meaning of crime data. There are differences in the amounts of officially recognized crime: CNJ reports more offenses than do court dockets. This is consistent with the fact that court dockets report information from a

TABLE 15.1. Selected Offenses and Source of Information

Selected Offenses	CNJ			MCD		
	f	Proportion	%	f	Proportion	%
Armed robbery	23	.04	4	0	.00	0
Robbery	17	.03	3	5	.01	1
Atrocious assault	13	.02	2	2	.007	.07
Simple assault	223	.40	40	250	.89	89
Break and entry	206	.37	37	1	.003	.3
Larceny	78	.14	14	24	.09	9
Total	560	1.00	100	282	1.00	100

2. The frequencies are reported in W. Boyd Littrell, "The Problem of Jurisdiction and Official Statistics of Crime," in *Current Issues of Social Policy*, ed. by W. Boyd Littrell and Gideon Sjoberg (Beverly Hills, Calif.: Sage, 1976), p. 236.

higher jurisdiction than does CNJ. CNJ reports offenses that are known to police, whereas court dockets report cases in which offenders have been identified, arrested, and booked on official complaints. Given that many offenses occur for which offenders are not apprehended, one would expect attrition of cases as these move upward through the levels of jurisdiction. However, the data for the "Simple assault" category are most problematic because it appears that municipal courts heard more cases of specific offenses than were known to the police in a city where the courts and the police shared jurisdiction. This indeed is improbable, and an index based on such data would be misleading.

Shifting the base. Often it is necessary to shift the base of an index number series from one time period to another. For instance, shifting the base is necessary if indexes of one series are to be compared with those of another series meaningfully. One method for shifting the base is to divide all the indexes in the original series by the original value of the index for the new base period and multiply by 100. This is illustrated with hypothetical data in Table 15.2. To obtain the new index (with base 1969) for 1969, we divide the original index (with base 1973) for 1969 by 70 and then multiply by 100. This results in (70/70) × 100 = 100. The new index for 1970 equals (80/70) × 100 = 114.3, and so on, until the complete new series is obtained.

Methods of Aggregation and Weighting

A common method for constructing indexes is by computing aggregate values. The aggregates can be either simple or weighted, depending on the purpose of the index.

TABLE 15.2. Changing the Base of an Index Number

Year	Values of Old Index (1973 = 100)	Values of New Index (1969 = 100)
1969	70	100.0
1970	80	114.3
1971	60	85.7
1972	95	135.7
1973	100	142.9
1974	115	164.3
1975	120	171.4
1976	118	168.6
1977	105	150.0

Simple aggregates. Table 15.3 illustrates the construction of a simple aggregative price index. The prices of each commodity (C_i) in any given year are added to give the index for that year. As noted earlier, it is convenient to designate some year as a base, which is set equal to 100. In this example all the indexes are expressed in the last row as a percentage of the 1973 number, obtained by dividing each of the numbers by the value in the base period ($20.13) and multiplying by 100. Symbolically,

$$PI = (\sum p_n / \sum p_o) \times 100 \qquad (15.1)$$

where *PI* stands for price index; p refers to the price of an individual commodity; o, to the base period at which price changes are measured; and n refers to the given period that is being compared with the base. The formula for a particular year (for instance 1977, with 1973 being the base) is:

$$PI_{73,77} = \sum p_{77} / \sum p_{73} \times 100 \qquad (15.2)$$

Thus,

$$PI_{73,77} = [(6.10 + 7.18 + 7.90 + 6.80)/$$
$$(3.21 + 5.40 + 6.62 + 4.90)]$$
$$\times 100 = (27.98/20.13) \times 100 = 139.00$$

Weighted aggregates. Simple aggregates may conceal the relative influence of each indicator of an index. To prevent such misrepresentation, one employs weighted aggregates often. To construct a weighted aggregative price index for the data in Table 15.3, take a list of the quantities of the specified commodities, and calculate to determine what this aggregate of goods is worth each year at current prices. This means that each unit price is multiplied by the number of units, and the re-

TABLE 15.3. Construction of Simple Aggregative Index Numbers (Hypothetical Data)*

Commodities	1973	1974	1975	1976	1977
C_1	$ 3.21	$ 4.14	$ 4.90	$5.80	$ 6.10
C_2	5.40	5.60	5.10	6.40	7.18
C_3	6.62	8.10	9.00	8.35	7.90
C_4	4.90	5.40	5.10	7.25	6.80
Aggregate value	$20.13	$23.24	$24.10	$27.80	$27.98
Index number†	100.00	115.45	119.72	138.10	139.00

*Prices are per unit.
†Percent of 1973.

TABLE 15.4.   Construction of Aggregative Index Weighted by Consumption in 1973

Commodities	1973 Con-sump-tion*	Value of 1973 Quantity at Price of Specified Year				
		1973	1974	1975	1976	1977
C_1	800	$2,568	$3,312	$3,920	$4,640	$4,880
C_2	300	1,620	1,680	1,530	1,920	2,154
C_3	450	2,979	3,645	4,050	3,758	3,555
C_4	600	2,940	3,240	3,060	4,350	4,080
Aggregate value		$10,107	$11,877	$12,560	$14,668	$14,669
Index†		100.0	117.5	124.3	145.1	145.1

*Hypothetical quantity units of consumption.
†Percent of 1973.

sulting values are summed for each period. Symbolically,

$$PI = \sum p_n q / \sum p_o q \times 100 \qquad (15.3)$$

where q represents the quantity of the commodity marketed, produced, or consumed, that is, the quantity weight, or multiplier. The procedure, using the quantities in 1973 as multipliers, is illustrated in Table 15.4. Because the total value changes while the components of the aggregate do not, these changes must be due to price changes. Thus the aggregative price index measures the changing value of a fixed aggregate of goods.

A Delinquency Index: An Example

An example of index construction in the field of criminology is the Sellin and Wolfgang Index of Delinquency. Evaluating crime-control policies requires at least three major types of information: data on the incidence of crimes, data on the response of the justice system, and data on social and demographic characteristics. With respect to incidence of crimes, a major problem is that offenses are varied in nature and magnitude. Some result in death, others inflict losses of property, and still others cause merely inconvenience. Yet the traditional way of comparing, say, one year's crime with another has been simply to count offenses, disregarding differences in content, shape, and size. Such unweighted indexes are misleading. A police report that indicates merely an overall decline or increase in the total number of offenses committed may be misleading if there are significant changes in the type of offenses committed. For example, a small decline in auto theft but a large increase in armed robbery should lead to a decline in an unweighted crime index because reported auto thefts are usually much greater in absolute numbers than are reported armed robberies.

In a genuine attempt to tackle this problem in the area of delinquency, Thorsten Sellin and Marvin E. Wolfgang developed a system of weighting by describing 141 carefully prepared accounts of different crimes to three samples of police officers, juvenile court judges, and college students.[3] The accounts of the different crimes included various combinations, such as death or hospitalization of the victim, type of weapon, and value of property stolen, damaged, or destroyed. For example, "The offender robs a person at gunpoint"; "The victim struggles and is shot to death"; "The offender forces open a cash register in a department store and steals five dollars"; "The offender smokes marijuana." Members of the samples were asked to rate each of these on a "category scale" and a "magnitude estimating scale," and their ratings were used to construct the weighting system. For example, a crime with the following "attributes" would be given the following number of points:

A house is forcibly entered	1
A person is murdered	26
The spouse receives minor injury	1
Between $251 and $2,000 are taken	2
Total score	30

With such an index, comparisons over time and between different communities can be carried out more meaningfully, taking into account the seriousness of the crimes committed.

Attitude Indexes (Arbitrary Scales)

Attitude indexes, also referred to as arbitrary scales, involve a battery of questions that are selected on an a priori basis. Numerical values are assigned arbitrarily to the item or question responses, and these values are summed to obtain total scores. These scores are then interpreted as indicating the attitude of the respondent. Consider the following five statements designed to measure alienation:

1. Sometimes I have the feeling that other people are using me.
   □ Strongly agree   □ Disagree
   □ Agree   □ Strongly disagree
   □ Uncertain
2. We are just so many cogs in the machinery of life.
   □ Strongly agree   □ Disagree
   □ Agree   □ Strongly disagree
   □ Uncertain

3. Thorsten Sellin and Marvin E. Wolfgang, *The Measurement of Delinquency* (New York: Wiley, 1964).

3. The future looks very dismal.
   ☐ Strongly agree   ☐ Disagree
   ☐ Agree   ☐ Strongly disagree
   ☐ Uncertain
4. More and more, I feel helpless in the face of what's happening in the world today.
   ☐ Strongly agree   ☐ Disagree
   ☐ Agree   ☐ Strongly disagree
   ☐ Uncertain
5. People like me have no influence in society.
   ☐ Strongly agree   ☐ Disagree
   ☐ Agree   ☐ Strongly disagree
   ☐ Uncertain

Suppose we arbitrarily score responses in the following way: Strongly agree = 4; Agree = 3; Uncertain = 2; Disagree = 1; and Strongly disagree = 0. Thus, a respondent who answers, "Strongly agree," to all five statements will have a total score of 20, indicating a high degree of alienation; a respondent who answers, "Strongly disagree," to all five statements will have a total score of zero, indicating that that person is not alienated. In reality, most respondents will obtain scores between these two extremes, and the researcher has to work out a scoring system classifying respondents according to their degree of alienation. For example, respondents who score zero to 6 are not alienated; respondents who score from 7 to 13 are somewhat alienated; and those who score between 14 and 20 are most alienated.

This index is also termed an *arbitrary scale* because there was nothing about the procedure to guarantee that any one statement or item tapped the same attitude as the other items. Is item 3 tapping the same aspect of alienation as does item 5? Does item 4 correspond to the remaining items? Will another researcher who uses the index get the same findings? That is, is the index reliable? These central questions are addressed in the following sections discussing scaling methods.

SCALING METHODS

Thurstone Scales

Among the scales in which attitude statements (hereafter "items") are determined by judges, Thurstone's technique of *equal-appearing intervals* is the most significant contribution. Earlier, we suggested that scaling involves ranking individuals according to a classificatory system. The Thurstone technique was developed to accomplish this in such a way that the intervals between the rankings assigned by the scale would approximate equal intervals.

The general procedure of the Thurstone technique is to ask judges to rank items into categories. The researcher then selects from these categories a number of items (usually fifteen to twenty) to form the scale. Items are selected from each of the ordered categories, giving preference to items on whose ranking the judges agreed. The procedure involves five steps: (1) compiling scale items, (2) having judges order the possible items, (3) computing the average value for each item, (4) selecting the specific scale items and computing the ogive values (cumulative percentage values), and (5) testing the relevancy of the items.

Compiling scale items. First, the researcher composes a large number of items concerning the attitude to be measured. The items should cover the entire range of attitudes, from extremely favorable to extremely unfavorable, including neutral items. Each item should refer to the present; express only one idea; be brief, unambiguous, and relevant; and be in a form that permits it to be endorsed or rejected in terms of a definitely expressed attitude. Each item is written on a separate slip of paper.

Ordering items. The second step is to have judges rank the items into a number of categories according to how favorable or unfavorable the items are to the attitude being investigated. Judges should be selected by a probability sampling design so that their views represent the population to be scaled (see Chapter 16). Each judge ranks each item on a scale according to favorableness of the item to the attitude, usually in seven or eleven categories. Thus, a given item might be ranked in the third category by one judge and in the eleventh by another. Each judge compiles seven or eleven sets; these are combined into one master set of seven or eleven categories (all items in set 1 for each judge are placed in master set 1, and so on).

Computing the median. In the third step, the slips are regrouped by item. Suppose a given item had slips in sets 5, 9, 10, 11. All the slips for this item are collected and put aside. Each item thus has a set of slips whose number corresponds to the number of judges. For each item the median value is calculated. All items with a median 1 are placed in the 1 category; all those with median 2 are placed in the 2 category; and so on, up to seven or eleven.

Selecting scale items. The fourth step is to select the specific items to be used in the final scale. Two criteria are applied. First, the full range of the scale has to be represented, which is done by ensuring that at least one item is selected from each of the final seven or eleven categories. Second, items in each category are selected according to how much agreement there was among judges that the item belongs in that category; the items that are selected in this way have the least dispersion. To identify the items with the least dispersion, Thurstone used the "Q value" method. These Q values are measures of dispersion based on computing graphic medians and *ogive values.* Hypothetical data on one item are presented in Table 15.5 and illustrated in Figure 15.1, in which

TABLE 15.5. Hypothetical Data on the Distribution of Judges' Selections for One Item

Category Number	Number of Judges	Cumulative Percentage
1	0	0
2	10	3.3
3	20	10.0
4	35	21.7
5	60	41.7
6	80	68.4
7	49	84.7
8	30	94.7
9	15	99.7
10	1	100.0
11	0	100.0
	N = 300	

the vertical axis stands for the cumulative percentage of judges and the horizontal axis for category numbers (eleven categories are used). It should be noted that a graph of Q values is to be constructed for each item.

From Figure 15.1, one can see that 21.7 percent of the judges ranked

FIGURE 15.1. Graph of Q Values for Data in Table 15.5

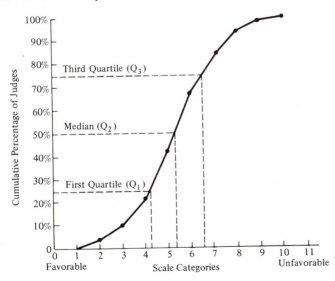

the item in category 4 or lower, 84.7 percent ranked it in category 7 or lower, and 99.7 percent ranked it in category 9 or lower. The 0.217, 0.847, 0.997, and so on levels are the ogive levels. The graphic median can be calculated by reading the category number that corresponds to the 0.50 level; in this example, the graphic median is 5.3. The median value represents the scale value of the item.

A (quartile) dispersion is the difference between the category numbers corresponding to the 0.75 level and the 0.25 level, or $Q_3 - Q_1$. This difference is known as the Q value, or *coefficient of ambiguity*. In our example, the coefficient of ambiguity equals $6.5 - 4.2$, or 2.3. If that is the lowest Q value for any item in that particular category, that item will be selected for the final scale because it reflects the highest degree of agreement among the judges. A low value of the coefficient of ambiguity indicates a low degree of ambiguity in regard to an item.

Testing relevancy. The fifth step concerns relevancy. Each item should be relevant. Relevancy is determined by plotting the responses of each item against all other items. Generally, judges tend to be consistent in their evaluations of the various items in a scale. For example, if a number of judges endorse items with scale values around 2.0, they will not usually endorse items that deviate markedly from this value, for example, items with scale values of 6.0 or 7.0. If responses to a given item are markedly inconsistent, the item is irrelevant and should be eliminated from the scale.

The final scale is made up of a battery of fifteen to twenty unambiguous, relevant items arranged randomly, representing a graded series of values from "extremely favorable" to "extremely unfavorable." The reliability and the validity of the scale can be evaluated by any of the methods discussed in Chapter 6.

Likert Scales

Another method of scale construction is generally referred to as the technique of *summated rating*, or Likert scaling. Likert scales are much simpler than Thurstone scales. Although in Likert scales there is no attempt to attain a near-interval level of measurement, it has not been empirically shown that Thurstone scales are much different in this regard. Likert scales do not rely on judges' opinions and are widely used in the professional literature.

Six steps can be distinguished in the construction of a Likert scale: (1) compiling possible scale items, (2) administering items to a random sample of respondents, (3) computing a total score for each respondent, (4) determining the *discriminative power* (DP) of items, (5) selecting the scale items, and (6) testing reliability.

Compiling possible scale items. In the first step, the researcher compiles a series of items that express a wide range of attitudes from extremely positive to extremely negative. Each item calls for checking one of five fixed-alternative expressions such as "strongly agree," "agree," "undecided," "disagree," and "strongly disagree." (Occasionally, three, four, six, or seven fixed-alternative expressions are used. Other expressions such as "almost always," "frequently," "occasionally," "rarely," and "almost never" are also used.) In this five-point continuum, weights of 1, 2, 3, 4, 5 or 5, 4, 3, 2, 1 are assigned, the direction of weighting being determined by the favorableness or unfavorableness of the item.

To measure attitudes toward employment of older people, Wayner Kirchner developed a twenty-four-item scale using the Likert method. The following four items illustrate the scoring technique.[4]

1. Most companies are unfair to older employees.
   - ☐ Strongly agree   ☐ Disagree
   - ☐ Agree   ☐ Strongly disagree
   - ☐ Undecided
2. I think that older employees make better employees.
   - ☐ Strongly agree   ☐ Disagree
   - ☐ Agree   ☐ Strongly disagree
   - ☐ Undecided
3. In a case where two people can do a job about equally well, I'd pick the older person for the job.
   - ☐ Strongly agree   ☐ Disagree
   - ☐ Agree   ☐ Strongly disagree
   - ☐ Undecided
4. I think older employees have as much ability to learn new methods as do other employees.
   - ☐ Strongly agree   ☐ Disagree
   - ☐ Agree   ☐ Strongly disagree
   - ☐ Undecided

This scale was scored by assigning weights for response alternatives to positive items (acceptance of hiring older persons). The weights were assigned as follows: Strongly agree—5; Agree—4; Undecided—3; Disagree—2; Strongly disagree—1. If negative items (that is, items indicating rejection of employment of older persons) had been included in the scale, their weights would have been reversed.

Administering all possible items. In the second step, a large number of respondents, selected randomly from the population to be measured, are asked to check their attitudes on the list of items.

Computing a total score. In this step, a total score for each respondent is calculated by summing the value of each item that is

4. Wayne K. Kirchner, "The Attitudes of Special Groups Toward the Employment of Older Persons," *Journal of Gerontology*, 12 (1957): 216–220.

checked. Suppose a respondent checked "Strongly agree" in item 1 (score 5); "Undecided" in item 2 (score 3); "Agree" in item 3 (score 4); and "disagree" in item 4 (score 2). His or her total score is $5 + 3 + 4 + 2 = 14$.

Determining the discriminative power. In the fourth step, the researcher has to determine a basis for the selection of items for the final scale. This can be done either with the *internal consistency method*—that is, correlating each item with the total score and retaining those with the highest correlations—or with *item analysis.* Both methods yield an internally consistent scale. With either method, the problem is to find items that consistently separate those who are "high" on the attitude continuum from those who are "low." With item analysis, each item is subjected to a measurement of its ability to separate the "highs" from the "lows." This is called the discriminative power (*DP*) of the item. In calculating the *DP*, we sum the scored items for each respondent and place the scores in an array, usually from the lowest to the highest scores. Next, we compare the range above the upper quartile (Q_1) with that below the lower quartile (Q_3), and the *DP* is calculated as the difference between the weighted means of the scores above Q_1 and of those who fall below Q_3, as illustrated in Table 15.6.

Selecting the scale items. The *DP* value is computed for each of the possible scale items, and those items with the largest *DP* values are selected. These are the items that best discriminate among individuals expressing differing attitudes toward the measured attitude.

Testing reliability. Reliability of the scale can be tested in much the same manner as in other measuring procedures. For example, we can select enough items for two scales (at least one hundred) and divide them into two sets, constituting two scales. The split-half reliability test can be then used (see Chapter 6).

Guttman Scaling

The Guttman scaling technique, first developed by Louis Guttman in the early 1940s, was designed to incorporate an empirical test of the

TABLE 15.6. DP Computing Table for One Item

Group	Number in Group	1	2	3	4	5	Weighted Total*	Weighted Mean†	DP ($Q_1 - Q_3$)
High (top 25%)	9	0	1	2	3	3	35	3.89	
									2.00
Low (bottom 25%)	9	1	8	0	0	0	17	1.89	

*Weighted total = score × number checking that score.

†Weighted mean = $\dfrac{\text{weighted total}}{\text{number in group}}$

TABLE 15.7. A Hypothetical Perfect Guttman Scale*

	Items in the Scale			Total Score
Respondent	Item 1 Admit to close kinship by marriage	Item 2 Admit to the same social club	Item 3 Admit as a neighbor	
A	+	+	+	3
B	+	+	−	2
C	+	−	−	1
D	−	−	−	0

* + indicates agreement with the statement; − indicates disagreement.

unidimensionality of a set of items as an integral part of the scale-construction process. Guttman suggested that if the items comprising the scale tap the same attitudinal dimension, they can be arranged so that there will be a continuum that indicates varying degrees of the underlying dimension. More explicitly, Guttman scales are unidimensional and cumulative. Cumulativeness implies that "the component items can be ordered by degree of difficulty and that the respondents who reply positively to a difficult item (question) will always respond positively to less difficult items or vice versa."[5] If we take an example from the physical world, we know that if an object is four feet long, it is longer than one foot and longer than two and three feet. In the social world we know that if a Mexican-American father would not mind if his daughter married a black American, he also would not mind having this person belong to the social club he belongs to. Similarly, if he would not object to accepting this person as a member of his club, he would not mind having him live in his neighborhood. The scale that would result from administering these three items to a group of respondents is illustrated in Table 15.7. This scale is unidimensional as well as cumulative: the items are unidimensionally ranked on a single underlying dimension, and the scale is cumulative in that none of the respondents has a − (disagreement) response before a + (agreement) response or a + response after a − response. Thus, information on the position of any respondent's last positive response allows the prediction of all his or her other responses to the item.

In practice, a perfect Guttman scale is rarely obtainable. In most cases, inconsistencies are present. Consequently, it is necessary to establish a criterion for evaluating the unidimensional and cumulative assumptions. Guttman developed the *coefficient of reproducibility (CR)*

5. Norman Nie, Dale H. Bent, and Hull C. Hadlai, *Statistical Package for the Social Sciences* (New York: McGraw-Hill, 1970), p. 529.

which measures the degree of conformity to a perfect scalable pattern:

$$CR = 1 - \frac{\Sigma_e}{Nr} \tag{15.4}$$

where CR = coefficient of reproducibility

Σ_e = total number of inconsistencies

Nr = total number of responses (number of responses × number of items)

A CR of .90 is the minimum standard for accepting a scale as unidimensional.

How to construct a Guttman scale. In this section we will discuss the major steps involved in constructing a Guttman scale: (1) selecting scale items, (2) recording responses on a scalogram sheet, (3) calculating the coefficient of reproducibility, and (4) refining the scale.

Selecting scale items. In discussing the considerations involved in discovering and selecting items for a Guttman scale, Gorden lists three conditions that must be met, in the following order:[6]

1. There must actually be an attitude toward the object (class of objects, event or idea) in the minds of the people in the population to be sampled and tested.
2. A set of statements about the object must be found which have meaning to the members of the sample and which elicit from them a response that is a valid indicator of that attitude.
3. The items in this set of statements or questions must represent different degrees along a single dimension.

Attitude scale items are selected by a variety of methods from all available sources: newspapers, books, scholarly articles, and the researcher's own knowledge of the problem. Interviewing experts as well as a subgroup of respondents will also help in securing good items. After a large set of potential items is compiled, a preliminary selection of items must be made. Items should be selected that clearly relate to the attitude being measured and that cover the full continuum from strongly favorable to strongly unfavorable statements. Two to seven response categories may be constructed for each statement. The most common formats are Likert-type items with five-point scale, as in the following example:

"Please indicate how much you agree or disagree with the following statement: Nowadays a person has to live pretty much for today and let tomorrow take care of itself."

---

6. Raymond L. Gorden, *Unidimensional Scaling of Social Variables* (New York: Macmillan, 1977), p. 46.

1. Strongly agree
2. Agree
3. Undecided
4. Disagree
5. Strongly disagree

Recording responses on a scalogram sheet. The items selected for Guttman scaling are usually included in a questionnaire and administrated to a sample of the target population. Before the answers to the questionnaire are scored, items should be arranged so that higher numbers will consistently stand for either the most positive or most negative feelings. Items that do not correspond to this pattern should be reversed.

Next, the responses to all items are added to obtain a total score, which can be put on the front page of the questionnaire. The questionnaires are then arranged in rank order, with the highest total score on the top. The scores are recorded on a scalogram sheet, as in Figure 15.2 on p. 408, where the responses of a sample of fifteen respondents to ten items have been recorded.[7] The respondents have been arranged according to the rank order of their total scores, ranging from 47 to 32. The items have been arranged according to the scale order expected by the researcher.

Calculating the coefficient of reproducibility. The coefficient of reproducibility is defined as the extent to which the total response pattern on a set of items can be reproduced if only the total score is known. This depends on the extent to which the pattern of responses conform to a perfectly scalable pattern as was demonstrated in Table 15.7. As you have noticed, the pattern of responses presented in the scalogram sheet of Figure 15.2 deviates considerably from a perfectly scalable pattern. The extent of the deviation will be assessed by calculating the coefficient of reproducibility.

Choosing cutting points. In the calculation of inconsistencies, each item in the scale is considered independently of all other items. In a perfectly scalable pattern, we would expect in each item to see a downward progression from one column to another, that is, from 5 to 1 without ever reversing direction. You will notice that there are deviations from such a pattern in each of the items. To count these deviations, we establish *cutting points*, which are the points in the column where the pattern would shift from one response category (column) to another if the items were perfectly scalable.[8] The cutting points are presented in Figure 15.2. You will notice that for item 1, for example, there is only

---

7. This discussion is based on Gorden, *Unidimensional Scaling of Social Variables*, pp. 100–108.

8. Ibid., pp. 117–118.

FIGURE 15.2. Responses of Fifteen Respondents to Ten Items

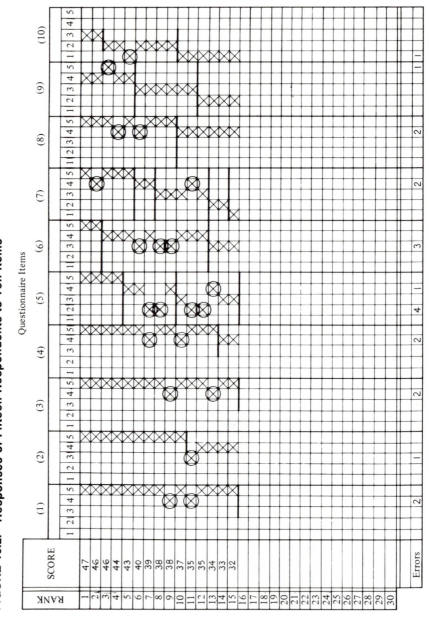

one pattern of response, 5, and thus the cutting point is below the last case. For item 2, the pattern shifts from 5 to 4 between the tenth and eleventh case, and that is where the cutting point has been placed. Responses that deviate from the pattern as indicated by the cutting point are circled and counted as errors. The number of errors for each column is recorded in the last row of the scalogram sheet. We can now calculate the error of reproducibility, which is the ratio of total number of inconsistencies to total response.

$$\text{Error of Reproducibility: } \frac{\Sigma_e}{Nr}$$

where Σ_e = total number of inconsistencies

Nr = total number of responses (number of responses × number of items)

The error of reproducibility for the data in Figure 15.2 is

$$\frac{\Sigma_e}{Nr} = \frac{21}{15 \times 10} = \frac{21}{150} = 0.14$$

We can now calculate the coefficient of reproducibility following Equation (15.4).

$$CR = 1 - 0.14 = 0.86$$

The obtained coefficient of reproducibility is below the required .90 criterion, and thus we will attempt to refine the scale and increase the coefficient of reproducibility.

Refining the scale.   The scale can be refined by rejecting items that have a relatively high number of errors as well as by collapsing adjacent response categories into one, in items where the response pattern vacillates among those categories.[9] The new pattern is presented in the revised scalogram sheet in Figure 15.3. In the revised sheet, item 5 has been rejected and crossed out. In addition, category 4 of items 1 and 3 has been collapsed into category 5. In item 6, category 3 is combined with category 4. Following these changes, all responses have been re-scored and the revised scores entered in their new rank order.

With these changes, the number of errors has been reduced to $\Sigma_e = 9$. We can now recalculate the coefficient of reproducibility:

$$CR = 1 - \frac{9}{135}$$

$$= 1 - 0.067 = 0.93$$

9. Ibid., chapter 5.

FIGURE 15.3.   Refining a Guttman Scale

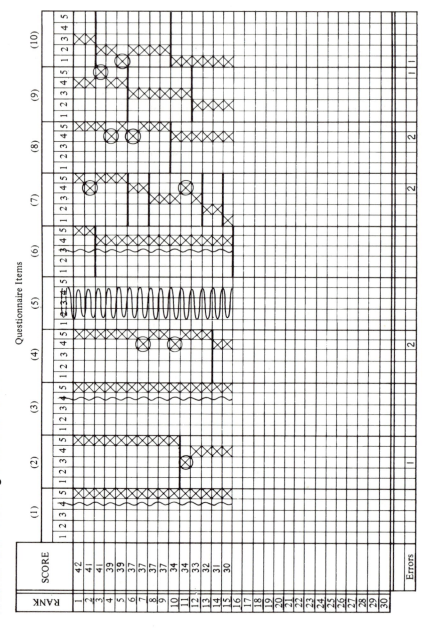

As observed, the revised coefficient meets the .90 criterion of scalability and unidimensionality.

Guttman Scale Application: An Example

After the development of the Guttman scale and its refinement, the results can be presented to describe the distribution of the variable measured. The scale can also be related to other variables in the study. An example of the development and application of a Guttman scale is Wanderer's study on riot severity in American cities.[10] This is a particularly interesting application of the Guttman scaling technique because it is based on behavioral indicators rather than on attitudes. The investigator analyzed seventy-five riots and civil criminal disorders reported to have taken place during the summer of 1967. Information used in the construction of the scale was provided by the mayors' offices at the request of a U.S. Senate subcommittee. The scale includes the following items of riot severity: killing, calling of the National Guard, calling of the state police, sniping, looting, interference with firefighters, and vandalism. These items are ordered from most to least severe or from least to most frequently reported. The coefficient of reproducibility of this Guttman scale of riot severity is .92. The scale and the distribution of the cities along the scale are presented in Table 15.8. Cities are organized

TABLE 15.8. A Guttman Scale of Riot Severity

Scale Type	% Cities (n = 75)	Items Reported
8	4	No scale items
7	19	"Vandalism"
6	13	All of the above and "interference with firefighters"
5	16	All of the above and "looting"
4	13	All of the above and "sniping"
3	7	All of the above and "called state police"
2	17	All of the above and "called National Guard"
1	11	All of the above and "law officer or civilian killed"
Total	100%	

Based on Jules J. Wanderer, "An Index of Riot Severity and Some Correlates," *American Journal of Sociology*, 74 (March 1969): 503, Table 1.

10. Jules J. Wanderer, "An Index of Riot Severity and Some Correlates," *American Journal of Sociology*, 74 (March 1969), p. 503.

into eight scale types according to the degree of severity, with 8 indicating the least severe and 1 the most severe riot activity.

At the second stage of the analysis the researcher treated riot severity, as measured by the Guttman scale, as a dependent variable and examined a set of independent variables in terms of their relationship to riot severity. For example, a relationship was found between the percentage increase of nonwhites, and riot severity as measured by the scale; that is, once a riot takes place, the greater the percentage increase of nonwhites, the greater the severity of the riot.

The Guttman scale of riot severity developed in this study suggests that the events that constitute riots and civil-criminal disorders are not erratic or randomly generated. On the contrary, if one employs the property of Guttman scales, the sequence of events for levels of riot severity may be predicted.

SUMMARY

In this chapter we discussed the logic and techniques of index construction and several scaling techniques. We started out by discussing index construction. An index is a composite measure of two or more indicators or items. An example is the Consumer Price Index (CPI), which is a composite measure indicating changes in retail prices. Four major problems are involved in constructing indexes: definition of the purpose for which the index is being compiled, selection of sources of data, selection of the base, and selection of methods of aggregation and weighting.

Scaling is a method of measuring the amount of a property possessed by a class of objects or events. It is most often associated with the measurement of attitudes. Attitude scales consist of a number of attitude statements with which the respondent is asked to agree or disagree. Scaling techniques are applied to the problem of ordering the selected statements along some sort of continuum. They are methods of forming a series of qualitative facts into quantitative series. All the scales discussed in this chapter are either assumed to be unidimensional or tested for unidimensionality. This means that the items comprising the scale should belong on a continuum, which is presumed to reflect one and only one concept.

The Thurstone technique of scaling was developed as a method of ranking individuals in such a way that the intervals between the rankings would approximate equal intervals. The general procedure of the Thurstone technique is to ask judges to rank items into categories. The researcher then selects from these categories a number of items to form the scale. The procedure of selection involves five steps: compiling scale items, having judges order the possible items, computing the average value for each item, selecting the specific scale items and computing the cumulative percentage values, and finally testing the relevancy of the scale.

Another method of scale construction discussed in this chapter is the technique of summated rating or Likert scaling. The technique involves the compiling of possible scale items, administering them to a random sample of respondents, computing a total score for each respondent, determining the discriminative power of each item, and selecting the final scale items.

The final method of scaling discussed is the Guttman scaling technique. This method was designed to incorporate an empirical test of the unidimensionality of a set of items as an integral part of the scale-construction process. A Guttman scale is unidimensional as well as cumulative. The items are unidimensionally ranked on a single underlying dimension, and the scale is cumulative in that information on the position of any respondent's last positive response allows the prediction of all his or her other responses to the items. To measure the degree of conformity to a perfect scalable pattern, Guttman developed the coefficient of reproducibility. A coefficient of reproducibility of .90 is the conventional minimum standard for accepting a scale as unidimensional.

KEY TERMS FOR REVIEW

Index
Weighted aggregate
Unidimensionality
Attitude index
Thurstone scale
Equal-appearing
  interval
Likert scale

Discriminative
  power
Coefficient of
  reproducibility
Error of
  reproducibility
Guttman scale

ADDITIONAL READINGS

Bonjean, Charles M.; Richard J. Hill; and S. Dale M. Lenmore. *Sociological Measurement: An Inventory of Scales and Indices.* San Francisco: Chandler, 1967.

Hannan, Michael T. *Aggregation and Disaggregation in Sociology.* Lexington, Mass.: Lexington Books, 1971.

Maranel, Gary M. *Scaling: A Sourcebook for Behavioral Scientists.* Chicago: Aldine, 1974.

Miller, Delbert C. *Handbook of Research Design and Social Measurement.* New York: David McKay, 1970.

Reeder, Leo G.; Linda Ramacher; and Sally Gorelnik. *Handbook of Scales and Indices of Health Behavior.* Pacific Palisades, Calif.: Goodyear, 1976.

Riley, Matilda W.; J. W. Riley Jr.; and Jackson Toby. *Sociological Studies in Scale Analysis: Applications, Theory, Procedures.* New Brunswick, N.J.: Rutgers University Press, 1954.

Robinson, John P.; Jerrold G. Rusk; and Kendra B. Head. *Measures of Political Attitudes.* Ann Arbor: Institute for Social Research, University of Michigan, 1968.

Robinson, John P., and Phillip R. Shaver. *Measures of Social Psychological Attitudes.* Ann Arbor: Institute for Social Research, University of Michigan, 1969.

Shaw, Marvin E., and Jack M. Wright. *Scales for the Measurement of Attitudes.* New York: McGraw-Hill, 1968.

Straus, Murray A. *Family Measurement Techniques.* Minneapolis: University of Minnesota Press, 1969.

Wallace, William H., *Measuring Price Changes: A Study of Price Indexes.* Richmond, Va.: Federal Reserve Bank of Richmond, 1970.

PART 4

Inferential Methods

CHAPTER PREVIEW

CHAPTER 16

Sampling and Sample Designs

INTRODUCTION

Usually, data are collected in order to make generalizations. For example, what is the pattern of racial attitudes in American cities? What is the level of political trust among Americans? Are Americans today more conservative than they were in the sixties? Questions of this kind call for generalizations. But only rarely does a study include observations of *all* respondents or *all* events that are defined by the research problem. A familiar example are the polls used to predict the outcome of elections. Pollsters attempt to achieve two things: (1) to predict from a relatively small group of respondents how the population of voters would vote if the election were held at the time the poll was taken and (2) to predict how the electorate will vote when the actual election is held. Both of these predictions involve employing a subset of the total electorate (a sample) and predicting the behavior of the entire set (the electorate or population).

The purpose of this chapter is to explain in general terms the principles underlying sampling theory. We do not attempt to present the theory itself in rigorous terms; rather, we attempt to acquaint the student with some basic principles and the commonly used sampling designs.

In the first section we discuss the aims of sampling. We then follow with definitions and discussions of central concepts: population, the sampling unit, sampling frame, and the sample. In a special section we discuss the considerations involved in determining the sample size. The section on sampling designs describes procedures of probability and nonprobability sampling designs. Finally, in the last section, nonsampling errors are discussed.

AIMS OF SAMPLING

The drawing of conclusions from data generally requires researchers to rest their case on partial information. In a survey, it is impractical to interview all possible respondents; in a controlled experiment, it is impossible to test the hypothesis on all potential subjects. However, inferences based on a subset of the whole aggregate may nonetheless be fairly accurate. Well-selected subsets may reflect precisely the characteristics of the aggregate. With a few thousand survey votes, one can predict the voting intentions of millions of voters. When the data are partial and used to characterize the whole, the subset is called a *sample*, and the whole is called a *population*. A specified value of the population, such as the average income, is called a *parameter*; its counterpart in the sample is termed a *statistic*. The chief aim of sampling is to make an inference about a parameter that is unknown from a sample statistic that can be measured.

In order to arrive at accurate estimates of parameters, the researcher should deal effectively with the following: (1) the definition of the population, (2) the size of the sample, and (3) the sample design.

THE POPULATION

A population is the aggregate of all cases that conform to some designated set of specifications.[1] For example, by the specifications "people" and "residing in Britain," we define a population consisting of all people who reside in Britain. Similarly, by the specifications "students" and "enrolled in state universities in the United States," we define a population consisting of all students enrolled in state universities in the United States. One may similarly define populations consisting of all households in a given community, all the registered voters in a particular precinct, all the case records in a file. A population may be a group of people, houses, records, legislators, and so on. The specific nature of the population depends on the purpose of investigation. If one is studying voting behavior in a presidential election, the population is all those who registered to vote. On the other hand, if one is investigating consumer behavior in a particular city, the population might be all the households in that city.

One of the first problems facing a researcher who wishes to estimate a population value from a sample value is the determination of the population involved. If one is interested in voting behavior in Britain and wishes to draw a sample so as to predict how the election will turn out,

1. Isidor Chein, "An Introduction to Sampling," in Claire Selltiz et al., *Research Methods in Social Relations* (New York: Holt, Rinehart and Winston, 1959).

one must not include anyone under eighteen in the sample. The population of voters in Britain is not the same as the population of Britain. Even "all British citizens eighteen years of age or older" is not an adequate definition of the population of voters because the individual is required to meet certain standards set by the law before the election is held. Individuals who do not meet these standards are not eligible to vote; hence, they are not part of the population of voters. The population, then, has to be defined in terms of (1) content, (2) extent, and (3) time. One may wish to specify (1) all persons over eighteen years of age living in private dwelling units (2) in England (3) on May 28, 1981.

The Sampling Unit

A single member of a population (for example, a voter or a household) is referred to as a *sampling unit*. Usually, sampling units have numerous traits, one or more of which may interest the researcher in particular. For example, if the population is defined as all third-graders in a town attending public school on a particular day, the sampling units are all third-graders. Third-graders, however, have many traits, including grades, habits, opinions, and expectations. A researcher may be interested only in a single trait such as arithmetic grades or two or more traits, for example, arithmetic grades, IQ scores, and motivation.

A sampling unit is not necessarily an individual. It may be an event, a city, or a nation. For example, in a cross-cultural study of role-differentiation in the nuclear family, Morris Zelditch used ethnographic reports as his source of data.[2] In his study the sampling units were societies. Zelditch compiled a list of all societies for which ethnographers had reported relevant data. He then utilized these findings to examine the different societies at different periods of time. Other investigations may focus on rural counties or on city blocks, and so on.

Finite and Infinite Populations

A population may be finite or infinite, depending upon whether the sampling units are finite or infinite. By definition, a *finite population* contains a countable number of sampling units, for example, all registered voters in a particular city in a given year. On the other hand, an *infinite population* consists of an endless number of sampling units, such as an unlimited number of coin tosses. Sampling designed to produce information about some trait of a finite population is usually termed *survey sampling*.

2. Morris Zelditch, Jr., "Role Differentiation in the Nuclear Family: A Comparative Study" in *Family Socialization and Interaction Process*, ed. by Talcot Parsons and Robert F. Bales (New York: Free Press, 1955).

Sampling Frame

Once the population has been defined, steps should be taken to draw a sample that will represent the population. The actual procedures involve a selection of a sample from a complete list of sampling units. The list of the sampling units that is used in the selection of the sample is called a *sampling frame*. Ideally, the sampling frame includes all sampling units in the population; however, very rarely does such a physical list actually exist, and thus a list that is assumed to be equivalent is substituted for it. For example, in a large national study, it would be virtually impossible to obtain a complete and accurate listing of all individuals residing in the United States. These difficulties are encountered even by a huge organization such as the Census Bureau, which counts the entire nation every decade. For example, the 1980 census cost at least $1 billion and required 180 million forms printed on 5,000 tons of paper. The 3.3 billion individual answers were collected and processed by nearly 300,000 Census Bureau workers and transferred to 5,000 miles of microfilm for electronic scanning. Yet for all its efforts, the census missed large numbers of the nation's residents. An increasingly transient life-style in the United States has made the compilation of mailing lists more difficult in 1980 than ever before. Frequently, it is easier to obtain a list of residence addresses than a list of names. These can then be used as a sampling frame.[3]

In smaller-scale studies, the sampling frame may be based on telephone directories, city directories, or membership lists that are held by many private and public organizations.

The correspondence between a sampling frame and the sampling population is extremely important. A sample can be only as accurate as the sampling frame from which it was drawn. Indeed, every aspect of the sample design—the population coverage, the stages of sampling, and the actual selection process—is influenced by the sampling frame. Before the sample selection is undertaken, the investigator must evaluate the sampling frame for possible faults. Leslie Kish provides a useful classification of typical problems in sampling frames: (1) incomplete frames, (2) clusters of elements, and (3) blank foreign elements.[4]

Incomplete frames. The problem of incomplete frames occurs when sampling units included in the population are missing from the list. For example, if the population includes all new residents in a community, a sampling frame based on the multiple listing service in the area would be incomplete because it consists only of new homeowners and does not include renters.

---

3. Kenneth D. Bailey, *Methods of Social Research* (New York: Free Press, 1978), pp. 73–75.

4. Leslie Kish, *Survey Sampling* (New York: Wiley, 1965), Section 2.7.

Faced with a problem of an incomplete sampling frame, the sampler should try to find a supplemental list. For example, it may be possible to compile a list of all new renters in the community by using the city directory, which sometimes identifies new residents in the community as homeowners or renters.

Clusters of elements.   The second potential problem of a sampling frame is the clusters of elements. This problem occurs when sampling units are listed in clusters rather than individually. For example, the sampling frame may consist of city blocks, whereas the study focuses on individuals, heads of households. A possible solution of this problem would be to take a sample of blocks and then to list all the individual households in each of the selected blocks. The selection of individuals from each household (most households include more than one individual) would be according to prespecified criteria, such as any individual over eighteen or only heads of households.

Blank foreign elements.   The problem of blank foreign elements is quite common and occurs when the sampling units of the frame are not included in the original population, for example, when the population is defined as consisting only of eligible voters whereas the frame contains some individuals who are too young to vote. This is often a problem when the listing used as a frame is outdated. Another example, often encountered with the use of city directories, is the failure to list residents when an address in the directory is given. This does not necessarily mean that nobody lives at that address, but possibly the residents have recently moved to a new address and could not be located. These cases should be treated as blanks and simply omitted from the sample. It is advisable to select a slightly larger sample initially in order to compensate for such omissions.

Errors in Sampling Frames: A Historical Example

Our discussion of errors in sampling frames could not be complete without citing perhaps the most notorious example of sampling failure in the history of sampling: the 1936 *Literary Digest* poll. In 1936, Franklin Delano Roosevelt, completing his first term of office as President of the United States, was running against the Republican candidate Alfred Landon of Kansas. The *Literary Digest* magazine, in the largest poll in history, consisting of about 2.4 million individuals, predicted a victory for Landon by 57 percent to 43 percent. Despite this decisive prediction, Roosevelt won the election by a huge landslide—62 percent to 38 percent for Landon.[5]

The error was enormous, the largest ever made by any polling organization, despite the very large sample size. The major reason for the

5. David Freedman, Robert Pisani, and Roger Purves, *Statistics* (New York: Norton, 1978), pp. 302–307.

error was found in the sampling frame. The *Digest* had mailed questionnaires to ten million people, names and addresses coming from various sources such as telephone directories and club membership lists. In 1936, however, few *poor* people had telephones, nor were they likely to belong to clubs. Thus, the sampling frame was incomplete and systematically excluded the poor. This omission was of particular significance in 1936 because in that year the poor voted overwhelmingly for Roosevelt, while the well-to-do voted mainly for Landon.[6] Thus the sampling frame did not accurately reflect the voting that actually occurred on election day.

SAMPLE SIZE

A *sample* is any subset of sampling units from a population. A subset is any combination of sampling units that does not include the entire set of sampling units that has been defined as the population. A sample may be one sampling unit, all but one sampling unit, or any number in between.

There are various common misconceptions about the necessary size of a sample. One is that the sample should be a regular proportion (often put at 5 percent) of the population; another is that the sample should total about 2,000; still another is that any increase in the sample size will increase the precision of the sample results. No such rule-of-thumb method is adequate. The size of the sample is properly estimated by deciding what level of accuracy is required and, hence, how large an error is acceptable.

Standard Error

The notion of the error margin, or standard error, is central to sampling theory and to the understanding of how to determine a sample size. (Some statisticians use the term *sampling error* for *standard error*.) The basic idea of standard error can be clarified by considering a small hypothetical population and confining the discussion to what is termed *simple random sampling*. This is a method for selecting sampling units whereby each possible sample of n units from a population of N units has an equal chance of being selected.

Suppose that the population consists of five individuals earning $500, $650, $400, $700, and $600 per month, so that the population's mean monthly income (denoted by μ) is $570. A sample of two is drawn ($n = 2$) with the purpose of estimating μ. Suppose also that the draw results in the selection of the two individuals earning $500 and $400. The sample

6. Ibid.

mean (denoted by $\bar{x}$) is therefore \$450; this is taken as an estimate of μ, the population mean. Because in this example it is already known that μ is \$570, one can see that the estimate of \$450 is inaccurate. Had the selection fallen upon the two members earning \$650 and \$700, the estimate of μ would have been \$675, which is also inaccurate. The accuracy of a sample estimate refers to its closeness to the correct population value; but because the latter is usually unknown, the actual accuracy of the sample estimate cannot be assessed. Nevertheless, its probable accuracy can be estimated.[7]

Consider all the samples of size $n = 2$ that could have been selected from this population. It is assumed that sampling is without replacement; that is, having selected the first individual, one selects the second individual from the remaining four; after selecting the second individual, one selects a third individual from the remaining three, and so on. Table 16.1 presents the ten possible samples and the estimate of μ derived from each. If this process continued indefinitely, each of the samples given in Table 16.1 would be drawn over and over again. The distribution resulting from the value of $\bar{x}$ derived from this infinite number of samples is called the *sampling distribution of the mean*. Because each of the ten samples has an equal chance of being selected and therefore

TABLE 16.1.   Estimates of the Population's Mean

Possible Samples of $n = 2$ (Incomes of Individuals Selected)	$\bar{x}$ (Estimate of μ)
500 and 650	575
500 and 400	450
500 and 700	600
500 and 600	550
650 and 400	525
650 and 700	675
650 and 600	625
400 and 700	550
400 and 600	500
700 and 600	650
Total	5,700

---

7. C. A. Moser and G. Kalton, *Survey Methods in Social Investigation* (London: Heinemann Educational Books, 1971), pp. 63–64.

in the long run occurs an equal number of times, the average of the estimates derived from all the possible samples is 5,700/10 = 570, which is equal to the population mean, μ.

The average of the estimates of a population parameter obtained from an infinite number of samples is called the expected value of the estimator (in our example it is 570). The estimator is the method of estimating the population parameter from the sample statistic (which, in our example, is the sample mean). An estimate, on the other hand, is the value obtained by using the method of estimation for a specific sample. If the expected value of the estimator is equal to the population parameter, the estimator is unbiased; if not, it is biased. The difference between the expected value and the true population value $(E\bar{x} - \mu)$ is termed the bias. Although in the above example the sampling was random and the sample mean was unbiased, the estimates all differ somewhat from each other and from μ. This is so because each estimate rests on one sample, and each sample consists of different observations. In practice, the estimate of a population parameter is based on only one sample, and one can estimate from any random sample how big the differences (sampling fluctuations) are likely to be on the average. This estimate is based on a measure indicating the spread of the sampling distribution. The most common measure of the spread of any distribution is the standard deviation or its square, the variance (see Chapter 12). The standard deviation of the sampling distribution in our example is

$$[(575 - 570)^2 + (450 - 570)^2 + (600 - 570)^2 + (550 - 570)^2$$

$$+ (525 - 570)^2 + (675 - 570)^2 + (625 - 570)^2 + (550 - 570)^2$$

$$+ (500 - 570)^2 + (650 - 570)^2]/10 = \sqrt{4,350} = 65.95$$

The standard deviation of the sampling distribution of means is called the standard error of the mean [denoted $S.E.(\bar{x})$], and serves as a criterion for evaluating the probable accuracy of one's estimate. The $S.E.(\bar{x})$ can be estimated from a single sample and can be represented by the following formula:

$$S.E.(\bar{x}) = \sqrt{\frac{\sigma^2}{n} \cdot \frac{N - n}{N - 1}}$$

where σ = the standard deviation in the population

N = the number of units in the population

n = the number of units in the sample

One can use a modified definition of the population standard deviation, S, rather than σ.[8] The modified standard deviation is defined as

$$S = \sqrt{\frac{\sum_{i=1}^{N} (x_i - \mu)^2}{N - 1}}$$

With this definition,

$$S.E.(\bar{x}) = \sqrt{\frac{S^2}{n} \cdot \frac{N - n}{N}} = \sqrt{\frac{S^2}{n} \left(1 - \frac{n}{N}\right)} \tag{16.1}$$

If the population is very large relative to the sample, the factor $1 - n/N$, which is called the finite population correction, approximates unity and can be omitted. (In this case, the formula becomes $S.E.(\bar{x}) = S/\sqrt{n}$). In the present example, it obviously cannot be omitted, and we calculate the standard error from Equation (16.1), with $N = 5$, $n = 2$ and

$$S^2 = \frac{(500-570)^2 + (650-570)^2 + (400-570)^2 + (700-570)^2 + (600-570)^2}{4}$$

$$= \frac{58,000}{4} = 14,500$$

Therefore,

$$S.E.(\bar{x}) = \sqrt{\frac{14,500}{2} \cdot \frac{5-2}{5}} = \sqrt{4,350} = 65.95$$

which agrees with the previous result.

The formula for the standard error of the mean is based on two factors: the value of n (that is, sample size) and the value of S or σ (that is, the variability in the population). In practice, however, the value of S is almost never known, and one has to substitute for S the standard deviation of incomes calculated from the sample (to be denoted s) and then estimate the standard error from Formula (16.1). Thus,

$$s = \sqrt{\frac{1}{n-1} \sum_{i=1}^{n} (x_i - \bar{x})^2}$$

is an unbiased estimate for S, and its value can be calculated from the sample. The term *unbiased estimate* refers to the fact that as one draws more and more samples from the same population and finds the mean of all these unbiased estimates, the mean of these unbiased estimates

8. Ibid., pp. 66–67.

approaches the population value. Sample means, then, are unbiased estimates of the population mean.

Confidence Intervals

One more concept needs to be introduced before discussing the method by which a sample size is determined. This concept is *confidence interval,* and it was first proposed by Neyman.[9] In the preceding discussion, the point was made that the population mean is equal to the mean of all the sample means that can be drawn from a population and that one can estimate the standard deviation of these sample means. If the distribution of sample means is normal or approximates normality, we can use the properties of the normal curve to estimate the location of the population mean. If one knew the mean of all sample means (the population mean) and the standard deviation of these sample means (standard error of the mean), one could compute Z scores and determine the range within which any percentage of the sample means can be found. Between $-1Z$ and $+1Z$, one would expect to find 68 percent of all sample means; between $-1.96Z$ and $+1.96Z$, one would expect to find 95 percent of all sample means; and between $-2.58Z$ and $+2.58Z$, one would expect to find 99 percent of all sample means (see Chapter 12). However, it is this mean of the population that is unknown and that one wishes to estimate on the basis of a single sample.

The normal curve can be used for this purpose. A sample mean that was $+1.96Z$ scores (or standard errors of the mean) above the population mean has a .025 probability of occurrence; 97.5 percent of all sample means will be smaller than $+1.96$ standard errors of the mean. If it is a rare event for a sample mean to be 1.96 or more standard errors of the mean above the population mean, it is just as rare for the population mean to be 1.96 standard errors of the mean below a given sample mean. But one does not know whether the sample mean is larger or smaller than the true mean of the population. Nevertheless, if we were to construct an interval of -1.96 to $+1.96$ about the sample mean, we could have great confidence that the population mean is located somewhere in that interval. We do not expect that the sample mean will in fact be as far as ± 1.96 standard errors of the mean away from the population mean, and we are confident that the population mean is no further than this from the sample mean. If we construct an interval of ± 1.96 standard errors of the mean about the sample mean, we expect the population mean to be within this interval with 95 percent confidence. There is a 5 percent chance that we are wrong; that is, that the population mean

9. Jerzy Neyman, *Outline of a Theory of Statistical Estimation Based on the Classical Theory of Probability,* Philosophical Transaction of the Royal Society, series A, Vol. 236, 1937.

FIGURE 16.1. Normal Curve: Percent Areas From the Mean to Specified Standard Error Distances

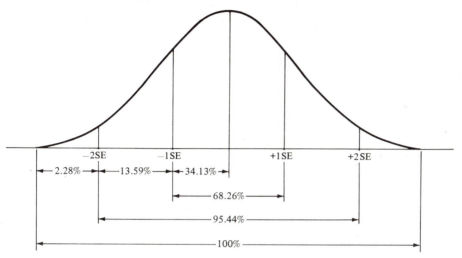

is not within the interval (see Figure 16.1). If one does not wish to run a 5 percent risk of being incorrect, one can use a different confidence interval. The chance that the population mean will be within +2.58 and −2.58 standard errors of the sample mean is 99 out of 100, and this is the 99 percent confidence interval. The width of the confidence interval around the sample mean is decided by the researcher. The confidence interval can be made extremely narrow if the researcher is willing to run a large risk of being wrong. The researcher could use an interval of ±.68 standard errors of the mean and have only a 50 percent chance of being correct in assuming that the population mean is within the interval.

To sum up: if a given sampling distribution is known to be approximately normal, one is able to infer that about 68 percent of the sample estimates of which it is comprised will lie between its mean and one standard error, about 95 percent between its mean and twice the standard error, and so on. This knowledge is put to use by phrasing statements about population estimates in forms such as the following: given that the sample mean, $\bar{x}$, is an unbiased estimator of the population mean, μ, one can be 68 percent confident that the range $\bar{x} \pm S/\sqrt{n}$ includes the population mean, and one's confidence would be approximately 95 percent that the range $\bar{x} \pm 2(S/\sqrt{n})$ includes μ, and so on.

Determining the Sample Size

We are now in a position to deal with the size of samples. If cost and other practical limitations do not enter into the decision about the sample size, there is no difficulty in determining the desired size. Recall Formula (16.1) for the standard error of the mean:

$$S.E.(\bar{x}) = \sqrt{\frac{S^2}{n}\left(1 - \frac{n}{N}\right)}$$

Ignoring the finite population correction, we get

$$S.E.(\bar{x}) = \frac{S}{\sqrt{n}} \tag{16.2}$$

where S is the standard deviation of the variable under study in the population. Inverting, we then have

$$n = \frac{S^2}{[S.E.(\bar{x})]^2} \tag{16.3}$$

In order to calculate the sample size, n, the researcher has to have some idea of the standard deviation in the population and must also decide how big a standard error can be tolerated. If, for example, a random sample is to be drawn from a population consisting of 10,000 sampling units, and $S^2 = .20$, and the desired $S.E.(\bar{x}) = .016$, the estimated sample size is

$$n = \frac{.20}{.000256} = 781.25$$

If the sample size represents a sizable proportion of the population, the finite population correction has to be included. In such cases, the final sample size is calculated by

$$n' = \frac{n}{1 + \left(\dfrac{n}{N}\right)} \tag{16.4}$$

where N is the population size. In our example, if $N = 10,000$, then

$$n' = \frac{781.25}{1 + \dfrac{781.25}{10,000}} \cong 725$$

Formulas (16.3) and (16.4) illustrate the principle involved in estimating the size of a sample. In practice, decisions concerning the sample size are more complicated. The first difficulty relates to the precision required. Researchers must decide how precise they want their sample results to be, that is, how large a standard error they can tolerate. Second, the decision on a sample size is also governed by the way the results are to be analyzed. Third, if more than one variable is to be studied, a sample that is adequate for one variable may be unsatisfactory for another.

Fourth, in order to use Formula (16.3) one needs an estimate of S, which, by definition, leads only to a rough estimate of the required sample size.[10]

SAMPLE DESIGNS

In the last two sections, we discussed sampling problems in relation to the definition of the population and the size of the sample. The third sampling problem arises in connection with the method of securing a representative sample. The essential requirement of any sample is that it be as representative as possible of the population from which it is drawn. A sample is said to be representative if the analyses made on its sampling units produce results equivalent to those that would be obtained had the entire population been analyzed.

Probability and Nonprobability Sampling

In modern sampling theory, a basic distinction is made between probability and nonprobability sampling. The distinguishing characteristic of probability sampling is that one can specify for each sampling unit of the population the probability that it will be included in the sample. In the simplest case, each of the units has the same probability of being included in the sample. In nonprobability sampling, there is no way of specifying the probability that each unit has of being included in the sample, and there is no assurance that every unit has some chance of being included. If a set of units has no chance of being included in the sample, a restriction on the definition of the population is implied; that is, if the traits of this set of units are unknown, then the precise nature of the population also remains unknown.[11] Accordingly, only probability sampling makes possible representative sampling designs.

A properly executed sample design can guarantee that, if a researcher were to repeat the study on a number of different samples drawn from a given population, his or her findings would not differ from the true population figures by more than a specified amount. A probability sample design makes it possible for the researcher to estimate the extent to which the findings based on one sample are likely to differ from what he or she would have found by studying the entire population. With a probability sample design, it is possible to attach estimates of standard errors to the sample results.

10. It is beyond the scope of this chapter to discuss these and more advanced issues. See Kish, *Survey Sampling;* Taro Yamane, *Elementary Sampling Theory* (Englewood Cliffs, N.J.: Prentice-Hall, 1967); Moser and Kalton, *Survey Methods in Social Investigation.*

11. Chein, "An Introduction to Sampling."

In spite of the great advantage of probability samples, social scientists do sometimes employ nonprobability samples. The major advantages of nonprobability samples are convenience and economy, which, under certain circumstances, may outweigh the risks involved in not using probability sampling. Also, when a population cannot be defined because of factors such as a nonavailable list of the population, the researcher may be forced to use a nonprobability sample.[12]

Nonprobability Sample Designs

Three major designs of nonprobability samples have been used by social scientists: convenience samples, purposive samples, and quota samples.

Convenience samples.   A convenience sample is obtained when the researcher selects whatever sampling units are conveniently available. Thus, a college professor may select students in his class; a researcher may take the first 200 people she or he meets on the street who are willing to be interviewed. There is no way of estimating the representativeness of convenience samples, and one cannot attach estimates of standard errors to the sample results.

Purposive samples.   With purposive samples, occasionally referred to as judgment samples, the sampling units are selected subjectively by the researcher, who attempts to obtain a sample that appears to him or her to be representative of the population. The chance that a particular sampling unit will be selected for the sample depends upon the subjective judgment of the researcher. Because it is impossible to determine precisely why each different researcher judges each sampling unit he or she selects to contribute to the representativeness of the sample, it is impossible to determine the probability of any specific sampling unit being included in the sample. Purposive samples have been used with some success in attempts to forecast election turnouts. In the United States, for example, a number of small election districts in each state are selected, their election returns in previous years having approximated the overall state returns. All the eligible voters in the selected districts are interviewed on their voting intentions, and the forecast is based on these reports. The underlying (and indeed risky) assumption is that the selected districts are still representative of their respective states.

Quota samples.   The chief aim of quota samples is the selection of a sample that is as closely as possible a replica of the population. For example, if it is known that the population has equal numbers of Catholics and Protestants, the researcher selects an equal number of Protestants and Catholics in the sample. If it is known that 15 percent of the

12. Moser and Kalton, *Survey Methods in Social Investigation*, p. 127.

population is black, 15 percent of the total sample is black. In quota sampling, interviewers are given an assignment of quota groups specified by traits such as sex, age, social class, and ethnicity. For example, an interviewer may be instructed to interview fifteen individuals, of whom six live in the suburbs and seven in the central city. Seven have to be men and six women; of the seven men (and the same quota for women) exactly three should be married and four single. It is obvious that disproportions between the sample and the population are likely to occur in traits that have not been included as part of the specifications for the interviewers' quotas. In addition to the major shortcomings of quota samples (the impossibility of estimating sampling errors), two other limitations are significant: (1) within the quota groups, interviewers may fail to secure a representative sample of interviewees, and (2) the method makes strict control of field work difficult.[13]

Quota sampling was a rather popular method used by polling organizations up until the presidential elections of 1948, the year the polls incorrectly predicted that Thomas E. Dewey would be elected president.[14] Three major polls predicted the outcome of the election and all three had declared Dewey the winner. Yet on election day President Harry S. Truman won with almost 50 percent of the popular vote, whereas Dewey got just over 45 percent.

All three polls used quota sampling, taking into consideration traits that they assumed influenced voting such as place of residence, sex, age, race and income. Although this is a sensible assumption, there are many factors that influence voting besides the ones sampled in the 1948 election. Moreover, no quota was set on Republican or Democratic votes because the distribution of political opinion was exactly what these polling organizations did not know and were trying to find out.[15]

Finally—and perhaps the most serious problem—within the assigned quotas, the interviewers were free to choose anybody they liked. This left a lot of room for discretion, which in turn created a significant bias.

Probability Sample Designs

Earlier, it was pointed out that in contrast to nonprobability sampling, probability sample designs permit one to specify for each sampling unit the probability that it will be included in the sample, in a single draw from the population, and accordingly to attach estimates of standard

13. Ibid., pp. 133–134.

14. Freedman et al., *Statistics*, pp. 302–307.

15. Ibid., pp. 305–307.

errors to the sample results. In the following pages, we consider four major designs of probability samples: simple random sampling, systematic sampling, stratified sampling, and cluster sampling.

Simple random samples. Simple random sampling is the basic probability sampling design, and it is incorporated into all the more elaborate probability sampling designs. Simple random sampling is a sampling procedure that gives each of the N sampling units of the population an equal and known nonzero probability of being selected. To ensure this requirement, one uses one of the following two basic procedures: (1) The *lottery method.* Each member of the population is represented by a disk; the disks are placed in an urn and mixed well; and a sample of the desired size is drawn. (2) The use of a *table of random digits*, such as that reproduced in Appendix B. The operational procedure is quite simple. Each sampling unit of the population is listed and given a number, from 0 to N. The table of random digits is entered at some random starting point. Each digit that appears in the table is read in order (up, down, or sideways; the direction does not matter, so long as it is consistent). Whenever a digit that appears in the table of random digits corresponds to the number of a sampling unit in the list, that sampling unit is selected for the sample. This process is continued until the desired sample size is reached. The selection of any given sampling unit places no limits on which other sampling units can be selected.

Either of these two procedures ensures that every sampling unit of the population has an equal and known probability of being included in the sample; this probability is n/N, where n stands for the size of the sample and N for the size of the population.[16] For example, if the population consists of 50,389 eligible voters in a town and a simple random sample of 1,800 is to be drawn, the probability of each sampling unit of the population being included in the sample is 1,800/50,389, or .036.

Systematic samples. Systematic sampling consists of selecting every Kth sampling unit of the population after the first sampling unit is selected at random from the first K sampling units. Thus, if one desires to select a sample of 100 persons from a population of 10,000, one takes every hundredth individual ($K = N/n = 10,000/100 = 100$). The first selection must be determined by some random process, such as the use of a table of random digits. Suppose the fourteenth person were selected; the sample would then consist of individuals numbered 14, 114, 214, 314, 414, and so on.

Systematic sampling is much simpler than simple random sampling. When interviewers who are untrained in sampling are to execute the sampling in the field, it is much simpler to instruct them to select every

16. For the mathematical proof, see Kish, *Survey Sampling,* pp. 39–40.

BOX 16.1.

How to Draw a Random Sample

The Problem

Let us assume that in a cost-containment study of an area hospital, patients' records are to be examined. There are $N = 100$ patients' records from which a simple random sample of $n = 10$ is to be drawn.

1. We can number the accounts, beginning with 001 for the first account and ending with 100 representing the hundredth account. Notice that we have three-digit numbers in our population. If the total number of records were 1,250, we would need four-digit numbers. In our case we need to select three-digit random numbers in order to give every record the same known chance of selection.

2. Now refer to Appendix B and use the first column. You will notice that each column has five-digit numbers. If we drop the last two digits of each number and we proceed down the column, we obtain the following three-digit numbers

104	854	521	007*
223	289	070*	053*
241	635	486	919
421	094*	541	005*
375	103	326	007
779	071*	293	690
995	510	024*	259
963	023*	815	097*
895	010*	296	

The last number listed is 097 from line 35 (column 1). We do not need to list more numbers since we already have ten different numbers that qualify for our sample (007 appears twice but is selected only once). The starred numbers are the records chosen for our sample. These are the only numbers that fall between the range we specified, 001–100.

We now have ten records in our simple random sample. Let us list them:

094	070	005
071	024	097
023	007	
010	053	

3. We need not start with the first row of column 1. We can select any starting point such as, for example, the seventh row of column 2. We can also choose to progress in any way we want down the columns, across them, or diagonally as long as we decide ahead of time on what our plan will be.

BOX 16.2.

How to Draw a Systematic Sample

The Problem

A social scientist is interested in investigating the relationship between marital status and grade point average of students in a larger urban campus ($N = 35,000$). As the information needed can be obtained from the students' records, a sample of say $n = 700$ records needs to be selected. Although a simple random sample may be selected, using the method described in the previous section, this would require a great deal of work. Alternatively we could use the following procedure:
1. The first step is to determine the sampling interval, K. As $N = 35,000$ and the sample size $n = 700$, K is 35,000/700; that is, $K = 50$.
2. We now select the first record at random from the first $K = 50$ records listed and then select every fiftieth record thereafter until a sample size of 700 is selected. This method is called a 1–in–50 systematic sample.

Kth person from a list than to have them use a table of random digits. Also, whenever a population is too large or a large sample is to be drawn, the use of systematic sampling is more convenient.

With systematic sampling, each sampling unit in the population has a $1/K$ probability of being included in the sample; hence, the sample mean is an unbiased estimate of the population mean. However, the variance of the sample may not be a good estimate of the population variance, for one is, in effect, dividing the sample units into strata, each of K size. There may be a systematic pattern in the data occurring at every Kth unit, and this will bias the sample. For example, if dwelling units or blocks are selected and the first chosen is a corner house, every Kth element may also be a corner house. This may introduce a bias since corner house are usually larger. In cases where the population exhibits a systematic pattern, if the list can be thoroughly shuffled first, problems may be alleviated; the subsequent selection can then be treated as a simple random sample.[17]

Stratified samples. Stratified sampling is used primarily to ensure that different groups of a population are adequately represented in the sample, so that the level of accuracy in estimating parameters is increased. Furthermore, all other things being equal, stratified sampling reduces the cost of execution considerably. The underlying idea in stratified sampling is that already existing knowledge of the population is used "to divide it into groups such that the elements within each group

---

17. For some other procedures for avoiding problems caused by systematic patterns in populations, see William Cochran, *Sampling Techniques*, 2nd ed. (New York: Wiley, 1963).

are more alike than are the elements in the population as a whole."[18] If a series of homogeneous groups can be sampled in such a way that, when the samples are combined, they constitute a sample of a more heterogeneous population, then increased accuracy will result. For example, suppose that it is known that there are 700 whites, 200 blacks, and 100 Mexican-Americans in a given population. If a random sample of 100 persons were drawn, one would probably not get exactly 70 whites, 20 blacks, and 10 Mexican-Americans; the proportion of Mexican-Americans, especially, might be relatively either too large or too small. On the other hand, a stratified sample of 70 whites, 20 blacks, and 10 Mexican-Americans would assure better representation of these groups. It should be emphasized that stratification does not imply any departure from the principle of randomness because a probability sample is subsequently drawn within each stratum.

The necessary condition for division into homogeneous strata is that the criteria for division be correlated with the variable being studied. A second condition is that the criteria used do not require so many subsamples as to increase the size of the sample over that required by a simple random sample.[19] Suppose a researcher who wants to estimate the average family income in a small town knows the traits of all the families in the population. As it has already been established that income correlates with occupation, education, ethnicity, age, and sex, these would become logical bases for stratification. However, if all these bases were used, the value of stratified sampling would diminish, for the number of subsamples would become enormous. Consider what would happen if there were four categories of occupation, three of education, three of race, three of age, and two of sex. The number of subsamples would then equal $4 \times 3 \times 3 \times 3 \times 2$, or 216. Because a statistically satisfactory frequency in the smallest cell could not possibly be less than around ten cases, this would require a minimum of 2,160, assuming that the frequencies in all cells were equal. No one could consider such a number as a sample of a small town. To solve this problem, one assumes that many such stratification bases occur as associated factors. Thus, if social status is chosen to stand for occupation, education, and ethnicity, the number of subsamples can be reduced to 4 (social-status groups) $\times$ 3 (age groups) $\times$ 2 (sex groups) = 24 subsamples. This is a more usable sample design, and the researcher would obtain a more representative sample than the one obtainable with a simple random sample.

Sampling from the different strata can be either proportional or dis-

18. Morris H. Hansen, William N. Hurwitz, and William G. Madow, *Sampling Survey Methods and Theory* (New York: Wiley, 1953), p. 40.

19. William J. Goode and Paul K. Hatt, *Methods in Social Research* (New York: McGraw-Hill, 1952), pp. 221–222.

BOX 16.3.

How to Draw a Stratified Sample

The Problem

   In a study of revitalization in an urban neighborhood, the attitudes of new residents toward their community is to be examined. It is anticipated that the attitudes of homeowners may differ from those of renters. Therefore, as a means of assuring proper representation of both groups, it is decided to use a proportional stratified random sample with two strata: homeowners and renters.
1. The population consists of $N = N_1 + N_2$ with N_1 denoting new homeowners and N_2 new renters. $N_1 = 200$ and $N_2 = 300$. Therefore $N = 500$. It is decided to select a proportional sampling fraction of 1/10 from each stratum. Thus $N_1 = 20$ homeowners and $N_2 = 30$ renters will be included in the sample.
2. The procedure of simple random sampling described in a preceding section is applied separately to the homeowner and renter lists.

---

proportional. If one draws into the sample the same number of sampling units from each stratum, or a uniform sampling fraction (n/N), the sample is known as a *proportionate stratified sample*. The sample size from each stratum is proportional to the population size of the stratum. On the other hand, if there are variable sampling fractions (that is, the total number in each stratum is different), the sample is a *disproportionate stratified sample*. Most often, researchers will use a disproportionate stratified sample when they wish either to assess the differences between two or more particular strata or to analyze one stratum intensively. When a disproportionate stratified sample is used, a mean computed for the population based on the means of all the strata would have to be weighted in accordance with the number in each stratum. In this case, the population mean can be defined as

$$\bar{X} = W_1\bar{X}_1 + W_2\bar{X}_2 + \cdots + W_n\bar{X}_n = \sum_{i=1}^{n} W_i\bar{X}_i$$

where $\bar{X}$ is the estimated mean based on strata; W_n is the weight of each stratum (computed as $W_i = N_i/N$, where N_i is the number of elements in the ith stratum and N is the total number in the population); and $\bar{X}_n$ is the mean for each stratum.

   Cluster samples.   Large-scale survey studies rarely make use of simple, systematic, or stratified random samples because of the enormous expense associated with them; instead, they make use of cluster sampling. A researcher arrives at the set of sampling units to be included in the sample by first sampling larger groupings, called *clusters*. The clusters are selected by a simple or stratified sample. If not all the sampling units in these clusters are to be included in the sample, the final selection from within the clusters is also carried out by a simple or stratified sampling procedure.

Suppose that the research objective is to study the political attitudes of adults in the various election districts of a city, that there is no single list available containing all the names, and that it is too expensive to compile a list. However, a list or a map of the election districts is readily available. A researcher can randomly select election districts from the list (first-stage cluster sampling). Within each of the districts, the researcher may then select blocks at random (second-stage cluster sampling) and interview all the persons in these blocks. The researcher may also use a simple random sample within each block selected, in which case a three-stage cluster sample will be obtained. (This sampling method is also called *area probability sampling* or just *area sampling*.) Similarly, a survey of urban households may take a sample of cities; within each city that is selected, a sample of districts; and within each selected district, a sample of households.

Moser and Kalton suggest three general points about clustering.[20]

BOX 16.4.

How to Draw a Cluster Sample[21]

The Problem

The purpose of the study is to interview residents of an urban community. No list of resident adults is available, and thus cluster sampling is used as the sampling design.

Stage 1
1. The area to be covered is defined using an up-to-date map. Boundaries are defined, and areas that do not include dwelling units are excluded.
2. The entire area is divided into blocks. Boundary lines should not bisect dwellings and should be easily identifiable by fieldworkers.
3. Blocks are numbered, preferably serially and in serpentine fashion.
4. A simple random or a systematic sample of blocks is selected, using the appropriate procedure.

Stage 2
1. All dwelling units in each of the selected blocks are listed and numbered. The delineation sometimes requires fieldworkers to ensure that all new constructions are listed.
2. A single random or a systematic sample of dwelling units is selected.
3. Selected individuals within each selected dwelling unit are interviewed. The selection usually follows the investigator's "guidelines".

---

20. Moser and Kalton, *Survey Methods in Social Investigation*, pp. 101–102.

21. Based in part on Matilda White Riley, *Sociological Research: Exercises and Manual* (New York: Harcourt, Brace & World, 1963), Vol. 2, p. 172.

First, the decision to call a particular aggregate of units a cluster depends on the unit of analysis. Thus, an area can be called a cluster because it contains a number of households, the household being the unit of enquiry. On the other hand, if the area is the unit of enquiry, it cannot be called a cluster. Second, clusters need not necessarily be natural aggregates such as districts, schools, or classes. Clustering does take advantage of existing groupings of the population, but artificial clusters can also be made, as when researchers impose grids onto maps. Third, in any one sample design, several levels of clusters may be used. In the last example, cities, districts, and households were used.

Probability Sampling: A Summary

These four designs of probability sampling do not exhaust the range of probability sampling procedures, and the reader is advised to consult Russell Ackoff and Leslie Kish for other designs.[22] However, these are the basic designs most commonly used by social investigators. By way of a summary, a brief description of the four designs is given in Table 16.2.

Probability Sampling: An Example

To illustrate the entire process of sampling, this section describes the procedures employed by the Institute for Social Research (ISR) at the University of Michigan, in its national surveys.[23] The sampling procedure involves three sampling designs: cluster sampling, stratified sampling, and simple random sampling.

ISR is among the largest university-based social science research organization in the United States. Research projects run by the institute are sponsored by governmental organizations, private business, and public service organizations. Surveys of economic behavior, mental health, and political behavior are often conducted by the organization. Many of the studies conducted by ISR involve large nationwide samples. The following are the steps roughly followed by the center in drawing a national sample.[24] (See Figure 16.2.)

Step 1.   The entire geographical area of the United States is divided into small areas called *primary sampling units* (PSU). The PSUs are generally counties or metropolitan areas. Out of the entire list of PSUs, seventy-four are selected by stratified random sampling to assure ade-

22. Russell Ackoff, *The Design of Social Research* (Chicago: University of Chicago Press, 1953); Kish, *Survey Sampling.*

23. Survey Research Center, *Interviewer's Manual* (Ann Arbor: Institute for Social Research, The University of Michigan, 1969), Chapter 8.

24. Based on Survey Research Center, *Interviewer's Manual*, Chapter 8.

TABLE 16.2. Description of Four Probability Samples

Type of Sampling	Description
Simple random	Assign to each sampling unit a unique number; select sampling units by use of a table of random digits.
Systematic	Determine the sampling interval (N/n); select the first sample unit randomly; select remaining units according to interval.
Stratified Proportionate	Determine strata; select from each stratum a random sample proportionate to the size of the strata in the population.
Disproportionate	Determine strata; select from each stratum a random sample of the size dictated by analytical considerations.
Cluster	Determine the number of levels of clusters; from each level of clusters select randomly; ultimate units are groups.

quate representation of different types of areas such as rural areas, large and middle-sized cities, as well as areas from the north, south, east, and west.

Step 2. Each of the seventy-four selected PSUs is further subdivided into a smaller area. For example, take a hypothetical PSU consisting of two large cities, six medium-sized towns, and the rural remainder of the county. It would be divided into three strata: (1) large cities, (2) smaller cities and towns, and (3) rural areas. Units within these strata are called *sample places*. One or more sample places are selected within each strata.

Step 3. Each sample place is further divided into *chunks*. A chunk is defined as an area having identifiable boundaries; for example, in urban areas, a chunk is equivalent to a block, whereas in rural areas it is an area bounded by roads or county lines. Within each sample place, chunks are randomly selected.

Step 4. At this stage the interviewers play a major role in the sampling process. They visit each sample chunk, listing all the dwelling units, and suggest how the chunk can be divided into areas each containing four to twelve dwelling units. These areas are called *segments*. Segments are then randomly selected from each chunk.

Step 5. At the last stage, dwelling units are selected from each segment to be included in the final sample. The selection of dwelling units varies. When a segment includes only a few dwelling units, all are to be included in the study. If the segment contains more dwelling units,

FIGURE 16.2.   Drawing a National Sample

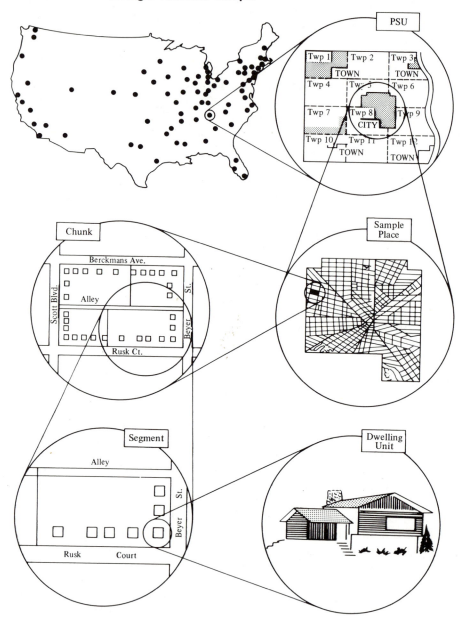

SOURCE: *Interviewer's Manual* (rev. ed., 1976), Survey Research Center, Institute for Social Research, the University of Michigan, p. 8–2.

only a specified fraction of the dwellings located within that segment will be included in the study.

NONSAMPLING ERRORS

Sampling theory is essentially concerned with the error introduced by the sampling procedure. In a perfect design, this error is minimized for an individual sample. The error in estimates refers to what is expected in the long run if a particular set of procedures is followed. However, even if the sampling error is minimized, there are other sources of error, for example, measurement error (see Chapter 6). In survey research, the most pervasive error is the *nonresponse error*. Nonresponse is defined as those observations that are not carried out because of refusal to answer, not-at-homes, lost forms, and so on. Nonresponse can introduce a substantial bias into the findings.

You recall the *Literary Digest* poll of 1936. We discussed the errors made by the *Digest* in the sampling frame selection process. Yet the *Digest* failed not only at this stage but also later on when it based its estimates on a very low response rate. The results of the poll were based on the response of 2.4 million people, out of ten million originally selected to be included in the sample.[25] This biased the results considerably because there was evidence showing that the nonrespondents tended to vote for Roosevelt whereas, among the respondents, over half favored Landon.

Generally, the amount and kind of bias is related to the following conditions:

1. The greater the nonresponse proportion, the greater will be the biasing effects. The response proportion can be computed with Formula (16.5):

$$R = 1 - \frac{(n - r)}{n} \qquad (16.5)$$

For example, if the original sample size is 1,200, and 1,000 responses are actually obtained, the response rate is $1 - (1,200 - 1,000)/1,200 = 0.83$, and the nonresponse rate is 0.17, or 17 percent.

2. The seriousness of the nonresponse bias depends on the extent to which the population mean of the nonresponse stratum differs from that of the response stratum.[26] In symbols,

$$\mu_1 - \mu = \mu_1 - (R_1\mu_1 + R_2\mu_2)$$
$$= \mu_1(1 - R_1) - R_2\mu_2$$
$$= R_2(\mu_1 - \mu_2)$$

25. Freedman et al., *Statistics*, pp. 302–307.

26. Moser and Kalton, *Survey Methods in Social Investigation*, pp. 166–167.

where N_1 is a "response stratum," N_2 a "nonresponse stratum," $N_1/N = R_1$, and $N_2/N = R_2$.

3. Each of the following nonresponse types affects the sample results in a different way. (These types apply to entire schedules as well as to parts of an interview or questionnaire or to single questions.)

a. *Uninterviewables:* every selected sample is likely to include some people who are ill, illiterate, or have language barriers.
b. *Not found:* this includes people who have moved and those who are inaccessible, for instance, who cannot make an appointment.
c. *Not-at-homes:* some people are out when the interviewer calls, but could be reached by re-calling.
d. *Refusals:* some people refuse to cooperate and will not answer survey questions. Refusals may also vary with the type of question being asked.

The proportion of nonrespondents varies in relation to factors such as the nature of the population, the type of data-collection method being used, the kinds of questions being asked, the skill of the interviewers, and the number of call-backs that can be made. A poorly designed and administered interview schedule might yield a very low response rate. To estimate the effect of nonresponse, collect information about the nonrespondents on call-backs. Based on such knowledge, imputations can be made. Suppose, for example, that voters are surveyed to estimate the proportions that identify with one party or another and that the survey has a 10 percent nonresponse rate. This can be corrected with information about the education or income of the nonrespondents.[27] Suppose that 10 percent amounts to 300 voters and that, of these, 70 percent have incomes of about $12,000 a year. If one knew that, in general, 90 percent of the people in this income level are Democrats, one might estimate that $.70 \times 300 \times .90 = 189$ are Democrats. However, there is no way of computing the possible error of this estimate. Imputation can be used to correct for nonresponse only if the response rate is relatively low.

SUMMARY

Inferential statistics is concerned with making predictions from one set of data either to a future state or to a larger population. In this chapter, the focus was on drawing population estimates from sample statistics. In order to arrive at accurate estimates of parameters, the researcher has to deal effectively with three problems: (1) definition of the population,

---

27. Dennis J. Palumbo, *Statistics in Political and Behavioral Science* (New York: Appleton-Century-Crofts, 1969), p. 359.

(2) determination of the sample size, and (3) selection of a representative sample.

A population has to be defined in terms of (1) content, (2) extent, and (3) time. A sample is any subset of sampling units from the population. A sample may be one sampling unit, all but one sampling unit, or any number in between. The determination of a sample size is essentially dependent on the value of the standard error and on the width of the confidence interval that is set by the researcher. The confidence interval can be made extremely narrow if the researcher is willing to run a large risk of being wrong or extremely wide if the researcher opts to run a negligible risk.

Upon the definition of a population and the determination of the size of the sample, a representative sampling design has to be selected. A sample is representative if the analyses made on its units produce results equivalent to those that would be obtained had the entire population been analyzed. Most often, researchers use probability sampling designs because they can specify for each unit of the population the probability of its being included in the sample. Four basic probability samples were considered—simple random sample, systematic sample, stratified sample, and cluster sample—the characteristics of which were summarized in Table 16.2.

In survey research, in addition to sampling error, nonresponse error is most pervasive. Nonresponse is defined as those measurements that are not carried out because of refusal to answer, not-at-homes, lost forms, and so on. Nonresponse can introduce a substantial bias into the findings, and some of the methods for estimating bias were briefly discussed.

KEY TERMS FOR REVIEW

Population
Parameter
Statistic
Sampling unit
Sampling frame
Sample
Standard error
Unbiased estimate

Confidence interval
Probability sample
Quota sample
Simple random
    sample
Stratified sample
Cluster sample
Nonresponse bias

ADDITIONAL READINGS

Cochran, William G.; Frederick Mosteller; and John W. Tukey, "Principles of Sampling." *Journal of the American Statistical Association*, 49 (March 1954): 13–35.

Edwards, W. Demin. *Sample Design in Business Research*. New York: Wiley, 1960.

Granovettes, Mark. "Network Sampling: Some First Steps." *American Journal of Sociology*, 81 (May 1976): 1287–1303.

Hansen, Morrise H.; William N. Hurwitz; and William G. Madow. *Sampling Survey Methods and Theory*. New York: Wiley, 1953.

Kish, Leslie. *Survey Sampling*. New York: Wiley, 1965.

Mace, Arthur F. *Sample Size Determination*. New York: Reinhold, 1964.

Mendenhall, William; Lyman Ott; and Richard L. Scheaffer. *Elementary Survey Sampling*. Belmont, Calif.: Wadsworth, 1971.

Morns, J. Slonim. *Sampling in a Nutshell*. New York: Simon & Schuster, 1966.

Stuart, Alan. *Basic Ideas in Scientific Sampling*, 2nd ed. New York: Hafner, 1976.

Sudman, Seymour. *Applied Sampling*. New York: Academic Press, 1976.

Yamane, Taro. *Elementary Sampling Theory*. Englewood Cliffs, N.J.: Prentice-Hall, 1967.

CHAPTER PREVIEW

CHAPTER 17
Hypothesis Testing

INTRODUCTION

In the previous chapter, we introduced the general idea of inferential statistics, which deal with the problem of evaluating population characteristics when only the sample evidence is given. It was demonstrated that sample statistics may give good estimates of particular population parameters, but that virtually any estimate will deviate from the true value owing to sampling fluctuations. The process of statistical inference enables investigators to evaluate the accuracy of their estimates.

A second use of inferential statistics is the assessment of the probability of specific sample results under assumed population conditions. This type of inferential statistics is called *hypothesis testing* and will occupy us throughout this chapter. With estimation, a sample is selected to evaluate the population parameter; with the testing of hypotheses, on the other hand, assumptions about the population parameter are made in advance, and the sample then provides the test of these assumptions. With estimation, the sample provides information about single population parameters such as the mean income or the variance of education; with hypothesis-testing, an inference is usually being made about relationships among variables—as, for example, the relationship between education and income or between occupation and particular political attitudes.

This chapter describes the strategy of hypothesis-testing by focusing on concepts such as the sampling distribution, type I and type II errors, and the level of significance. We then consider several methods of testing hypotheses about the relationship between two variables: difference

447

between means, Pearson's r, the Mann-Whitney test, and the Chi-square test.

THE STRATEGY OF TESTING HYPOTHESES

The first step in testing a hypothesis is to formulate it in statistical terms. We have already discussed how to draw a hypothesis from a theory or how to formulate a research problem as a hypothesis. However, in order to test the hypothesis, one must formulate it in terms that can be analyzed with statistical tools. For example, if the purpose of the investigation is to establish that educated individuals have higher incomes than do non-educated individuals, the statistical hypothesis might be that there is a positive correlation between education and income or that the mean income of a highly educated group will be larger than the mean income of a group with a lower level of education. In both cases, the statistical hypothesis is formulated in terms of descriptive statistics (such as a correlation or a mean) as well as a set of specifying conditions about these statistics (such as a positive correlation or a difference between the means).

The statistical hypothesis always applies to the population of interest. In the preceding example, no inferences would be necessary if the population could be directly tested; then, any difference between the means (or a positive correlation of any size) would support the hypothesis. However, sample results are subject to sampling fluctuations, which would account for the difference between the means or for the positive coefficient. Thus, a result in line with the hypothesis may imply either that the hypothesis is true or that it is false, with the results being due to chance factors. On the other hand, a deviation between the sample results and the expected population value could mean either that the hypothesis is false or that it is true, with the difference between the expected and obtained values being due to chance. Table 17.1 illustrates these four possibilities.

TABLE 17.1. Alternative Interpretations of Sample Results

Hypothesis Is	Sample Results	
	According to Expectation	Deviation from Expectation
True	*Results validate hypothesis*	*Results due to sampling fluctuation*
False	*Results due to sampling fluctuation*	*Results validate hypothesis*

Whether a sample result is according to expectation or deviates from expectation, either case can imply that the hypothesis is either *true* or *false*. Therefore, sample results cannot be interpreted directly; a decision rule is needed to enable the researcher to reject or retain a hypothesis about the population on the basis of sample results. The procedure of statistical inference enables the researcher to determine whether a particular sample result falls within a range that can occur by chance or that it could not possibly be a result of chance. This procedure involves the following steps listed, which are discussed in some detail:

1. Formulate a null hypothesis and a research hypothesis.
2. Choose a sampling distribution and a statistical test according to the null hypothesis.
3. Specify a significance level (α), and define the region of rejection.
4. Compute the statistical test, and reject or retain the null hypothesis accordingly.

NULL AND RESEARCH HYPOTHESIS

There are two statistical hypotheses involved in the process of testing hypotheses. The first is the *research hypothesis*, which is usually symbolized by H_1. The second, symbolized by H_0, is the *null hypothesis*; the null hypothesis (H_0) is determined by H_1, which is really what one wants to know; H_0 is the antithesis of H_1.

Suppose the research hypothesis states that Catholics have larger families than do Protestants. With the mean score for the size of family in the Catholic population designated as μ_1, and in the Protestant population as μ_2, the research hypothesis would be:

$$H_1 : \mu_1 > \mu_2$$

The null hypothesis would be:

$$H_0 : \mu_1 = \mu_2$$

The null hypothesis can be expressed in several different ways. However, it is usually an expression of no difference or no relationship between the variables. Both the null hypothesis and the research hypothesis are expressed in terms of the population parameters, not in terms of the sample statistics. The null hypothesis is the one that is tested directly; the research hypothesis is supported when the null hypothesis is rejected as being unlikely.

The need for two hypotheses arises out of a logical necessity: the null hypothesis is based on negative inference in order to avoid the *fallacy of affirming the consequent*—that is, one must eliminate false hypotheses rather than accept true ones. For instance, suppose theory

A implies empirical observation *B*. When *B* is false, one knows that *A* must also be false. But when *B* is true, *A* cannot be accepted as true, because *B* can be an empirical implication of several other theories that are not necessarily *A*. Acceptance of *A* as true would be the fallacy of affirming the consequent.

Durkheim's theory of suicide may serve as an illustration. One of its propositions (*A*) is that people in individualistic situations are more likely to commit suicide. The empirical observation (*B*) derived from this proposition is that the suicide rate will be higher among single than among married individuals. If *B* proves to be false (if there is no difference in the suicide rates of married and single persons), then theory *A* is false. But what if *B* is true? *A* cannot be accepted as true; there are many other explanations for *B* that are not necessarily *A*. For instance, the higher suicide rate of single persons might be explained not by individualism, but rather by their excessive drinking, which may lead to depression and to suicide. Thus, observation *B* might imply that A_1, another theory, is true.

Usually, many alternative theories might explain the same observations; the researcher has to select the most credible one. Thus, the credibility of a theory can be established only by the elimination of all alternative theories: "For any given observation which is an implication of A, say B_1, there will be *some of* the possible alternative theories which will imply not-B_1. If we then demonstrate B_1, these alternative theories are falisfied. This leaves us with *fewer alternative possible theories* to our own."[1]

THE SAMPLING DISTRIBUTION

Having formulated a specific null hypothesis, the investigator proceeds to test it against the sample results. For instance, if the hypothesis states that there is no difference between the means of two populations ($\mu_1 = \mu_2$), the procedure would be to draw a random sample from each population, compare the two sample means ($\bar{X}_1$ and $\bar{X}_2$), and make an inference from the samples to the populations. However, the sample result is subject to sampling error; therefore, it does not always reflect the true population value. If samples of the same size are drawn from the population, each sample will usually produce a different result.

In order to determine the accuracy of the sample statistic, one has to compare it to a statistical model that gives the probability of observing such a result. Such a statistical model is called a *sampling distribution*. A sampling distribution of a statistic is obtained by drawing a large

1. Arthur L. Stinchcombe, *Constructing Social Theories* (New York: Harcourt, Brace & World, 1968), p. 20.

number of random samples of the same size from the defined population, computing the statistic for each sample, and plotting the frequency distribution of the statistic. We have seen in Chapter 16 an example of such a distribution: the sampling distribution of the mean. It is possible to construct a sampling distribution of any other statistic, for example, of the variance (s^2), of the standard deviation (s), of the difference between means $(\bar{X}_1 - \bar{X}_2)$, or of proportions (p).

As an illustration, let us go back to Durkheim's theory on suicide. The hypothesis to be tested is that single people have a relatively higher suicide rate than does the general population. One way of evaluating the proportion of suicide among single people is by comparing the number of suicides in this group to the average proportion in the population at large. Suppose the records of health centers indicate that the national suicide rate in the adult population is 2 out of every 100, or .02. The research hypothesis would then imply that the rate of suicide among single people is higher than .02. Thus

H_1: The proportion of suicides among single people > .02.

The null hypothesis would state that the proportion of suicides among single people is the same as the national average. Therefore:

H_2: The proportion of suicides among singles = .02

Suppose that a sample of 100 is drawn from the records on single persons' suicides and that the rate of suicide is .30. Is this result sufficiently larger than .02 to justify the rejection of the null hypothesis? To assess the likelihood of obtaining a rate of .30 under the assumption of the null hypothesis, it is compared to a distribution of suicide rates of the adult population. Let us assume that 1,000 random samples of 100 each are drawn from the records on suicide and that the suicide rate is computed for each sample. The obtained hypothetical sampling distribution[2] is presented in Table 17.2. This sampling distribution may serve as a statistical model for assessing the likelihood of observing a suicide rate of .30 among single people if their rate were equivalent to that of the adult population. The probability of observing any particular result can be determined by dividing its frequency in the distribution by the total number of samples. The obtained probabilities are displayed in the third column of Table 17.2. For example, the suicide rate of .38–.39 occurred five times; therefore, the probability that any sample of size n = 100 will have this suicide rate is 5/1,000 or .005; that is, we would expect to obtain such a result in approximately 0.5 percent of the samples of 100 drawn from the population. Similarly, the probability of obtaining

2. Such a distribution is often denoted as an experimental sampling distribution because it is obtained from observed data.

TABLE 17.2. Hypothetical Sampling Distribution of Suicide Rates for 1,000 Random Samples (Sample: *n* = 100)

Suicide Rate	Number of Samples (*f*)	Proportion of Samples ($p = f/n$)
.40 or more	0	.000
.38–.39	5	.005
.36–.37	10	.010
.34–.35	10	.010
.32–.33	10	.010
.30–.31	15	.015
.28–.29	50	.050
.26–.27	50	.050
.24–.25	50	.050
.22–.23	150	.150
.20–.21	200	.200
.18–.19	150	.150
.16–.17	100	.100
.14–.15	100	.100
.12–.13	50	.050
.10–.11	15	.015
.08–.09	10	.010
.06–.07	10	.010
.04–.05	10	.010
.02–.03	5	.005
.01 or less	0	.000
Total	1,000	1.000

a rate of .30–.31 is .015, or 1.5 percent. The probability of obtaining a rate of .30 or more is equal to the sum of the probabilities of .30–.31, .32–.33, .34–.35, .36–.37, .38–.39, and .40 or more; that is, .015 + .010 + .010 + .010 + .005 + .000 = .050. Thus, we would expect 5 percent of all samples of 100 drawn from this population to have a suicide rate of .30 or more.

LEVEL OF SIGNIFICANCE AND THE REGION OF REJECTION

Following the construction of the sampling distribution, the likelihood of the result of .30 (given the assumption of the null hypothesis) can now be evaluated. The decision as to what result is sufficiently unlikely to justify the rejection of the null hypothesis is quite arbitrary. Any set of extreme results can be selected as a basis for rejection of the null hypothesis. The range of these results is designated as the *region of rejection*. The sum of the probabilities of the results included in the region of rejection is denoted as the *level of significance*, or α. It is customary to set the level of significance at .05 or .01, which means that the null hypothesis is to be rejected if the sample outcome is among the results that would have occurred no more than 5 percent or 1 percent of the time.

Figure 17.1 graphically represents the sampling distribution of Table 17.2 and the region of rejection with α = .05. The region of rejection includes all the suicide rates of .30 and above. The sum of the probabilities of these results is equal to the level of significance, .05.

The obtained sample result of .30 falls within the region of rejection;

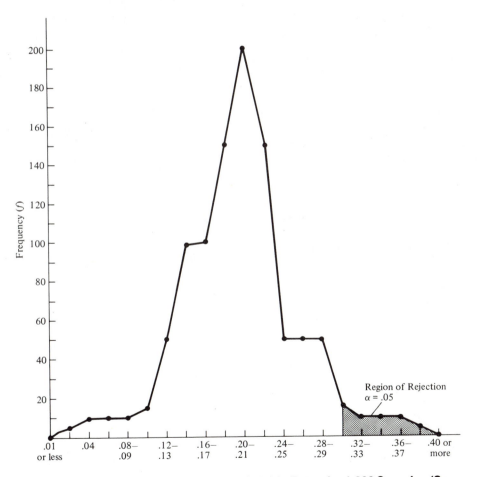

FIGURE 17.1. Sampling Distribution of Suicide Rates for 1,000 Samples (Sample: *n* = 100)

thus, the null hypothesis can be rejected at the .05 level of significance. The rejection of the null hypothesis lends support to the research hypothesis that the suicide rate of single people is higher than the rate in the general adult population.

One-Tailed and Two-Tailed Tests

In the preceding example, the set of extreme results was selected from the right tail of the sampling distribution. However, extreme sample outcomes are also located at the left-hand tail. In Table 17.2 the probability of a suicide rate of .11 and below is equal to the probability of obtaining a rate of .30 and above; in both cases, it is .05.

A statistical test may be *one-tailed or two-tailed*. In a two-tailed test, the region of rejection is located at both left and right tails. In a one-tailed test, extreme results leading to the rejection of the null hypothesis can be located at either tail.

The decision to locate the region of rejection in one or two tails will depend on whether H_1 implies a specific direction to the predicted results and whether it specifies large or small values. When H_1 predicts larger values, the region of rejection will be located at the right tail of the sampling distribution (as in the example on suicide). When H_1 implies lower values, the left tail is selected as a region of rejection. For instance, suppose the research hypothesis had implied that single people have a lower suicide rate than does the general adult population; that is,

H_1: proportion of suicide in single population $< .02$.

The results considered unlikely under this hypothesis are at the left tail of the distribution. At the .05 level of significance, the critical region will consist of the following rates: .10–.11, .08–.09, .06–.07, .04–.05, .02–.03, .01 or less. The sum of the probabilities of these results is .015 + .010 + .010 + .010 + .005 + .000 = .050. Figure 17.2 presents the right-tail and left-tail alternatives.

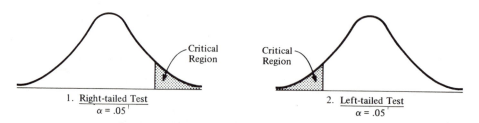

1. Right-tailed Test
α = .05

2. Left-tailed Test
α = .05

FIGURE 17.2.   Right-Tail and Left-Tail Tests

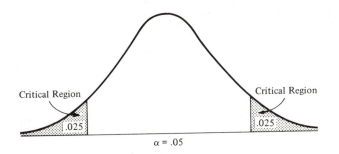

FIGURE 17.3. A Two-Tailed Test

There are occasions when the direction of the research hypothesis cannot be predicted accurately. For example, we may have suspected that single persons have a different suicide rate but were unable to specify the direction of the difference. The research hypothesis would have been expressed as:

H_1: proportion of single persons' suicide $\neq .02$.

When H_1 cannot be accurately specified, H_0 is rejected whenever extreme values in either direction are obtained. In such a case, the statistical test is designated as a *two-tailed test*, and the level of significance is divided in two. Thus, a .05 level of significance would mean that H_0 will be rejected if the sample outcome falls among the lowest 2.5 percent or the highest 2.5 percent of the sampling distribution. This alternative is diagrammed in Figure 17.3.

Let us select the .05 level of significance and make use of a two-tailed test in the suicide example. The critical region will consist of the alternatives .34–.35, .36–.37, .38–.39, .40 or more (.010 + .010 + .005 = .025) and .06–.07, .04–.05, .02–.03, .01 or less (.010 + .010 + .005 = .025). With a two-tailed test, a sample result of .30 is not included in the region of rejection; thus, the null hypothesis would not have been rejected in this case. With a one-tailed test, the null hypothesis is more likely to be rejected because there is a greater probability that the sample result will fall within the critical region.

Type I and Type II Errors

In statistical hypothesis-testing, the entire population is not measured directly, so the statistical test can never prove if the null hypothesis is true or false. The only evidence it provides is whether the sample result is sufficiently likely or unlikely to justify the decision to retain or to reject the null hypothesis.

The null hypothesis can be either true or false, and in both cases it can be rejected or retained. If it is true and is rejected nonetheless,

TABLE 17.3.   Alternative Decisions in Hypotheses-Testing

Decision	Hypothesis Is True	Hypothesis Is False
Reject hypothesis	Type I error	No error
Accept hypothesis	No error	Type II error

the decision is in error. The error is the *rejection of a true hypothesis—a type I error*. If the null hypothesis is false but is retained, the error committed is the *acceptance of a false hypothesis*; this error is designated as a *type II error*. These four alternatives are presented schematically in Table 17.3.

The probability of rejecting a true hypothesis—a type I error—is defined as the *level of significance*. Thus, in the long run, an investigator employing the .05 level of significance will falsely reject 5 percent of the true hypotheses he or she tests. Naturally, one would be interested in minimizing the error of rejecting a true hypothesis by making the level of significance as low as possible. However, type I errors and type II errors are inversely related. Thus, a decrease in the error of rejecting a true hypothesis leads to an increase in the probability of retaining a false one. Under these conditions, the selection of α is determined by (1) the type of problem one is investigating and (2) the consequences of rejecting a true hypothesis or retaining a false one. If, for example, the subject of investigation is the effect of an experimental teaching method on the achievement of disadvantaged children, where the results of the study will determine the implementation of the method throughout the school system, the researcher should carefully consider the consequences of making a mistake. Suppose the null hypothesis states that the new teaching method has negative effects. If it were to be rejected when it is actually true, the consequences could be very severe; hundreds of thousands of disadvantaged children would be harmed. If, on the other hand, it is not rejected when it is actually false, the implementation of the new method will be postponed until further evidence is available. Therefore, in this case it would be preferable to minimize α because the implications of rejecting a true hypothesis are more severe than those of retaining a false one.

When a study does not have practical implications, the selection of α will be arbitrary, but the choice will usually be governed by accepted conventions. The significance levels commonly used in social science research are .001, .01, and .05.

PARAMETRIC AND NONPARAMETRIC TESTS OF SIGNIFICANCE

In the following sections we shall discuss selected tests that are most common in social science research. The tests are divided into two major groups: parametric tests and nonparametric tests. A *parametric test* is a statistical test based on several assumptions about the parameters of the population from which the sample was drawn. Among the most important ones are the assumptions that (1) the observations must be drawn from a normally distributed population and (2) that the variables are measured on at least an interval scale.[3] The results of a parametric test are meaningful only in so far as these assumptions are valid.

A *nonparametric statistical test* is one whose model neither specifies the normality condition nor requires an interval level of measurement. There are certain assumptions associated with most nonparametric tests; however, they are weaker and fewer than those associated with parametric tests.

In practice, one need not go through the laborious procedure of constructing a sampling distribution. In many instances, sampling distributions have been constructed by previous researchers and are known in advance. Moreover, there are distributions that can be used as approximations of certain sampling distributions. For example, the sampling distribution of the mean closely approximates the normal curve distribution, which can therefore be used in testing hypotheses about means.

In the discussion of specific tests that follows, reference will be made to existing sampling distributions that have been constructed in advance or that approximate the desired distribution. The sampling distributions that are employed in this section are provided in Appendixes C through G.

Selected Parametric Tests

Difference between means. Many hypotheses in empirical research involve a comparison between populations. For example, to assess the relationship between social class and voting, one could compare different social classes with respect to their voting patterns. Similarly, in comparing blacks and Mexican-Americans with respect to achievement, one is relating ethnicity to achievement.

When the dependent variable being investigated is measured on an interval scale, a comparison of means can be used to reflect the amount of relationship between two variables (see Chapter 13). To assess the significance of a difference between means, use the *difference-between-means test.*

To illustrate the testing of hypotheses about the difference between means, let us center around a concrete problem for which data are presented in Table 17.4, showing the mental health test scores of two samples. One is of hospitalized mental patients, and the other is of mentally

3. Sidney Siegel, *Nonparametric Statistics for the Behavioral Sciences* (New York: McGraw-Hill, 1956), pp. 2–3.

TABLE 17.4. Mean Scores of Mental Health Scale of Receiving Ward Patients and College Students

	Receiving Ward Patients	*College Students*
n	101	126
$\bar{X}$	6.10	3.60
s	4.52	3.04

SOURCE: Jerome G. Manis et al., "Validating a Mental Health Scale," *American Sociological Review*, 28 (1963): 108–116.

healthy college students. The investigation was designed to evaluate the validity of a mental health scale. The assumption that the scale accurately measures mental health would lead to the research hypothesis that on a mental health scale, mental patients have a higher score (a high score on the test reflects mental illness) than do college students; that is,

$$H_1: \mu_1 > \mu_2,$$

where μ_1 is the mean score of the population of mental patients and μ_2 the mean of college students. The null hypothesis could state that there is no difference in the mean score of the two populations; that is,

$$H_0: \mu_1 = \mu_2$$

Inspection of the data reveals a difference between the two sample means of 2.50 (6.10–3.60). Although this difference is in the expected direction, its probability of occurrence under the assumption of the null hypothesis has to be determined. If such a difference is unlikely to occur, assuming that the population means are identical, we shall reject the null hypothesis.

The selection of the appropriate sampling distribution for testing the difference between means depends on the sample size. When each sample is larger than 30 ($n > 30$), the sampling distribution of the difference between means approaches normality, and, thus, the normal curve (Appendix C) can be used as the statistical model. The procedure is similar to the one employed in estimating population means (see Chapter 16). One can translate the difference between the means to standard Z scores and then determine its probability of occurrence according to the normal curve distribution. For a two-tailed test, using the .05 level of significance, the critical region expressed in Z scores includes all the positive scores of 1.96 and above or all the negative scores of −1.96 and below, whose likelihood of occurrence is .025. For a one-tailed test, the critical region contains all scores of 1.65 and above or

-1.65 and below. Similarly, for the .01 level of significance, Z is ± 2.58 and ± 2.33, respectively.

To test the null hypothesis on the mental health test scores, we can select a right-tail test because H_1 is a directional hypothesis implying large values. The level of significance selected will be .01; any value larger than 2.33 will lead to the rejection of the null hypothesis.

To determine the significance of the difference between the means using the normal curve, one must convert the difference to standard scores. This can be accomplished using a test statistic denoted as t, which is defined in Formula (17.1):

$$t = \frac{(\bar{X}_1 - \bar{X}_2) - (\mu_1 - \mu_2)}{\hat{\sigma}_{\bar{x}_1 - \bar{x}_2}} \tag{17.1}$$

where $\bar{X}_1 - \bar{X}_2$ = difference between the sample means

$\mu_1 - \mu_2$ = the means of the sampling distribution of the difference between means

$\hat{\sigma}_{\bar{x}_1 - \bar{x}_2}$ = an estimate of the standard error[4] of the sampling distribution of the difference between the means

Like Z, t measures deviations from the means in terms of standard deviation units; $\bar{X}_1 - \bar{X}_2$ replaces X, $\mu_1 - \mu_2$ replaces $\bar{X}$, and $\hat{\sigma}$ replaces s. Z, however, cannot be calculated when the variances of the two populations (σ_1^2 and σ_2^2) are unknown. That is, t substitutes for Z whenever sample variances (s_1^2 and s_2^2) are used as estimates of the populations' parameters. Because the populations' variances are almost never available, for all practical purposes, the t statistic is used to transform mean differences to standard scores. The t is normally distributed when $n > 30$; thus, the normal distribution can be employed whenever each sample size is > 30. However, when $n \leq 30$, the normal approximation is not appropriate and the sampling distribution of t has to be used.

The estimate of the standard error ($\hat{\sigma}_{\bar{x}_1 - \bar{x}_2}$) can be obtained by two methods. The first assumes that the two *population variances are equal*—for instance, $\sigma_1^2 = \sigma_2^2$—and, thus, the variances of the two samples are combined into a single estimate of σ_1^2 or σ_2^2. The standard error under these conditions is as follows:

$$\hat{\sigma}_{\bar{x}_1 - \bar{x}_2} = \sqrt{\frac{n_1 s_1^2 + n_2 s_2^2}{n_1 + n_2 - 2}} \sqrt{\frac{n_1 + n_2}{n_1 n_2}} \tag{17.2}$$

where n_1 and n_2 are sample sizes of sample 1 and sample 2, respectively, and s_1^2 and s_2^2 are variances of sample 1 and sample 2.

---

4. The standard error is the standard deviation of the sampling distribution; see Chapter 16 for a discussion of this concept.

When there is no basis for assuming that the population variances are identical, it is not possible to pool the sample variance. In this instance, the estimation for the two variances is separate, and the obtained formula for the standard error is

$$\hat{\sigma}_{\bar{x}_1 - \bar{x}_2} = \sqrt{\frac{s_1^2}{n_1 - 1} + \frac{s_2^2}{n_2 - 1}} \tag{17.3}$$

To calculate t for the data summarized in Table 17.4, we assume that $\sigma_1^2 = \sigma_2^2$ and estimate the pooled estimate of the standard error:

$$\hat{\sigma}_{\bar{x}_1 - \bar{x}_2} = \sqrt{\frac{(101)(4.52)^2 + 126(3.04)^2}{101 + 126 - 2}} \sqrt{\frac{101 + 126}{(101)(126)}} = .50$$

As under the null hypothesis it has been assumed that $\mu_1 = \mu_2$, the definition of t reduces to

$$t = \frac{\bar{X}_1 - \bar{X}_2}{\hat{\sigma}_{\bar{x}_1 - \bar{x}_2}} \tag{17.4}$$

We obtain the following result for our example:

$$t = \frac{6.1 - 3.6}{.50} = \frac{2.5}{.50} = 5$$

Referring to the normal curve table (Appendix C), we observe that the value of t is in fact greater than the value needed for rejection (2.33) at the .01 level of significance. In other words, the difference between the sample mean of mental patients and that of college students is not likely to be due to sampling error. Accordingly, we reject H_0 and conclude that the difference between the samples reflects different degrees of mental health, and that the measuring scale is therefore valid.

The t distribution.   When either or both of the sample sizes are less than 30, the normal curve does not approximate the sampling distribution of the difference between means. As a result, using the normal curve to determine the probability of H_0 will yield inaccurate conclusions, and the sampling distribution of t has to be used instead. The t is actually a family of curves, each determined by the sample size. Thus, for a sample size of 7, t has a different distribution from that for a sample size of 10. The sampling distribution of t is reproduced in the Appendix D. The values in this table are given in terms of the significance level (one tail and two tails) and the degrees of freedom (df).

Degrees of freedom (df).   The concept of degrees of freedom is a basic one and will be used in other statistical tests. It refers to the number of free choices one can make in repeated random samples that constitute sampling distribution. If, for example, one is allowed to pick two numbers freely, there are two degrees of freedom. If, on the other hand, the two numbers must sum to 20, there is only one free choice or one degree of freedom, for after the first number has been freely chosen, the second number is determined by the sum total. The number of degrees of freedom of the t distribution is limited by the fact that for each sample, the population variance has to be estimated, and there are only $n - 1$ quantities that are free to vary. The number of degrees of freedom is then equal to $n - 1$ for each sample. Thus, to test a hypothesis about difference between two samples, df is equivalent to $(n_1 - 1) + (n_2 - 1) = n_1 + n_2 - 2$.

To illustrate the use of the t table, we shall test the hypothesis that achievement is associated with assignment to tracks in a secondary school. The data are summarized in Table 17.5. The investigators hypothesized that achievement and track assignment were related so that a college preparatory track had more students that were high achievers than did a noncollege track. The null hypothesis to be tested is that the means of the two populations are identical whereas the research hypothesis states that the mean achievement of the college preparatory track (μ_1) is higher than that of the noncollege track (μ_2):

$$H_0: \mu_1 = \mu_2$$

$$H_1: \mu_1 > \mu_2$$

We can proceed with the same procedure in calculating the standard error and the t ratio, using Equations (17.2) and (17.4):

$$\hat{\sigma}_{\bar{x}_1 - \bar{x}_2} = \sqrt{\frac{13(23.6)^2 + 6(12.2)^2}{13 + 6 - 2}} \sqrt{\frac{13 + 6}{(13)(6)}} = 10.8$$

$$t = \frac{48.3 - 20.5}{10.8} = \frac{27.8}{10.8} = 2.574$$

The obtained t can now be compared with the appropriate value in the sampling distribution of t. The number of degrees of freedom for sample sizes of 13 and 6 is 17 ($13 + 6 - 2$). At the .01 level of significance with a one-tailed test (right tail), the t for which H_0 will be rejected is 2.567.

TABLE 17.5. Mean Achievement of Students in College Preparatory and Noncollege Tracks

	College Preparatory Track	Noncollege Track
n	13	6
$\bar{x}$	48.3	20.5
s	23.6	12.2

A t larger than 2.567 is unlikely to occur if H_0 is true. As 2.574 is larger than 2.567, the null hypothesis is rejected, and the investigator can conclude that the difference in achievement between the two tracks is statistically significant.

A significance test for Pearson's r.   The correlation coefficient Pearson's r—like $\bar{X}$, Md, or b—is a statistic obtained from sample data; as such, it is just an estimate of a population parameter. Pearson's r corresponds to the population correlation denoted as ρ or rho. As a sample statistic, r is subject to sampling fluctuations; the test of its statistical significance is an assessment of the likelihood that the obtained correlation is due to sampling error. For example, a researcher may test the hypothesis that liberalism is correlated with income and draw a random sample of 24, obtaining an r of .30. It is probable that in the population these two variables are not correlated at all and that the obtained coefficient is a result of chance factors. In other words, is an r of .30 large enough to make the hypothesis of no relation unlikely?

The strategy of testing such a hypothesis is similar to that used in the difference-of-means test; the null hypothesis states that the correlation in the population is zero; and the research hypothesis, that it is different from zero:

$$H_0: \rho = 0$$

$$H_1: \rho \neq 0$$

Testing the significance of r when ρ is zero.   When ρ is assumed to be zero under the null hypothesis, the statistical significance of r can be tested using the normal curve or the t distribution depending on the sample size.

When n is larger than 50, the sampling distribution of r is approximated by the normal curve, with a mean of zero and a standard error defined as:

$$\sigma_r = \frac{1}{\sqrt{n-1}} \tag{17.5}$$

The standard score Z is obtained by subtracting from r the mean of the sampling distribution (0) and dividing by the standard error. The definition of Z is given by Equation (17.6):

$$Z = r \bigg/ \frac{1}{\sqrt{n-1}} = r\sqrt{n-1} \tag{17.6}$$

As an example, suppose that a sample of 101 observations produced a correlation of $r = .50$ between social class and delinquency. For one, to reject the null hypothesis at the .05 level of significance, Z must be smaller than -1.96 or larger than 1.96 ($-1.96 > Z > 1.96$).

$$Z = .50\sqrt{101-1} = 5$$

The null hypothesis of no correlation is rejected, and the relationship between social class and delinquency is said to be significant.

When n is less than 50, the significance of r can be tested using the t distribution with $n - 2$ degrees of freedom,[5] where t is defined as:

$$t = \frac{r\sqrt{n - 2}}{\sqrt{1 - r^2}} \qquad (17.7)$$

To illustrate the use of t in testing the significance of Pearson's r, let us suppose that a correlation of .30 between income and years of schooling is obtained from a sample of $n = 24$ ($df = 2$). The t is equal to:

$$t = \frac{.30\sqrt{22}}{\sqrt{1 - .30^2}} = 1.475$$

From the distribution of t in Appendix D, we see that at the .05 level of significance for a two-tailed test and with 22 df, the value of t required to reject the null hypothesis is 2.074. As the obtained t is smaller than this value, the null hypothesis cannot be rejected, and the relationship between income and political participation is said to be not significant.

Testing the significance of r when ρ is not zero. When ρ is different from zero, the sampling distribution of r is skewed, and the normal curve or t approximations cannot be used. In that case, a different procedure is employed; it is applicable to high and low r's and can be used with large or small samples. With this procedure (developed by R. A. Fisher), r is transformed into another statistic, Fisher's z,[6] having a distribution that is approximately normal for all sample sizes and all values of ρ. z is related to r by the following formula:

$$z = 1.151 \log_{10} \frac{1 + r}{1 - r} \qquad (17.8)$$

The standard error of Fisher's z is equal to:

$$\sigma_z = \frac{1}{\sqrt{n - 3}} \qquad (17.9)$$

The transformation of r to Fisher's z or vice versa can be made by reference to Appendix E. The table is entered with values of r and their corresponding z's. For example, if $r = .85$, $z = 1.256$; for $z = 2.185$,

---

5. The significance of r is also a test of the significance of the regression coefficient, which is zero when r is zero. The regression involves two constants, a and b; therefore, two degrees of freedom are lost in determining the line.

6. Fisher's z has no connection with the standard score Z used with the normal curve.

r = .975. The transformed r's can now be used to construct a standard Z score by the following expression:

$$Z = \frac{z_r - z_\rho}{\sigma_z} \qquad (17.10)$$

where z_r = Fisher's z for r

z_ρ = Fisher's z for ρ

σ_z = standard error of Fisher's z

As an example, let us test the null hypothesis that the correlation between occupational aspiration and occupational attainment is ρ = .70, against the alternative research hypothesis that ρ > .70. A sample of 252 cases drawn at random gives a correlation of r = .81. The hypothesis is tested with the .05 level of significance and is right-tailed. From Appendix E we find that for r = .81, z = 1.127. Similarly, ρ of .70 is equivalent to a z of .867. The standard error of z is:

$$\sigma_z = \frac{1}{\sqrt{249}} = .063$$

The standard Z score is then:

$$Z = \frac{1.127 - .867}{.063} = \frac{.260}{.063} = 4.127$$

To reject the null hypothesis at the .05 level with a one-tailed test, a standard score of at least 1.65 is required. As the obtained standard Z score is larger than this value, the null hypothesis is rejected.

Selected Nonparametric Tests

The Mann-Whitney test. The Mann-Whitney test is applicable whenever we wish to test the null hypothesis that two samples have been drawn from the same population against the alternative research hypothesis that the populations differ from each other.[7] The only assumptions required in making this test are that the two samples are independently and randomly drawn and that the level of measurement of the variables under investigation is at least ordinal.

Suppose we have sampled 13 males (n_1 = 13) and 14 females (n_2 = 14) and have given each one a score reflecting their level of alienation:

Male sample: 5, 7, 10, 13, 19, 24, 25, 28, 30, 32, 33, 36, 37

Female sample: 1, 3, 4, 6, 9, 12, 14, 15, 17, 18, 20, 21, 22, 23

7. Siegel, *Nonparametric Statistics*, pp. 116–126.

If we assume that the population of females is identical to the population of males with respect to level of alienation, it is expected that the values in the two samples will be similar. If the values have similar magnitudes, males will have larger alienation scores in approximately one-half of the male-female pairs; in the rest of the pairs, the females' scores will exceed the males.' We can count the number of pairs in which the scores of males exceed the scores of females and designate it as U; the number of pairs for which the opposite is true is designated U'. If the null hypothesis of identical populations were true, we would expect U and U' to be approximately equal.[8]

To determine U, we can use the following equation:

$$U = n_1 n_2 + \frac{n_2(n_2 + 1)}{2} - R_2 \tag{17.11}$$

where n_1 = sample size of sample 1

n_2 = sample size of sample 2

R_2 = the sum of ranks for sample 2

The ranks are obtained by arranging all the scores in order of magnitude. For instance, the first three females (1, 3, 4) head the scale, with rank 4 being the first male (score 5). Thus, the ranks for males are 4, 6, 8, 10, 15, 20, 21, 22, 23, 24, 25, 26, 27, and the ranks for females are 1, 2, 3, 5, 7, 9, 11, 12, 13, 14, 16, 17, 18, 19. To determine U', we subtract U from the total number of pairs

$$U' = n_1 n_2 - U \tag{17.12}$$

For our data,

$$U = (13)(14) + \frac{14(14 + 1)}{2} - 147 = 140$$

$$U' = (13)(14) - 140 = 182 - 140 = 42$$

To evaluate the significance of H_0, we compare the smaller of the two values U or U' with the significant values of the sampling distribution of U in the Appendix F.[9] At the .05 level, we need a U of 50 or smaller when direction is not predicted or 56 or smaller when direction is predicted. In either case, the obtained value (42) is smaller and enables us to reject the null hypothesis.

The sampling distribution of U approaches normality when the sam-

---

8. John H. Mueller, Karl F. Schuessler, and Herbert L. Costner, *Statistical Reasoning in Sociology* (Boston: Houghton Mifflin, 1970), p. 423.

9. For situations in which one of the samples is smaller than 9, another table of probabilities is used.

ples' size increases. When either of the samples is larger than 20, we can compute standard scores and use the normal distribution. The mean of the sampling distribution would then be:

$$\mu_U = \frac{n_1 n_2}{2}$$

and the standard error would be:

$$\sigma_U = \frac{\sqrt{n_1 n_2 (n_1 + n_2 + 1)}}{12}$$

Z is obtained using the following formula:

$$Z = \frac{U - n_1 n_2/2}{\sqrt{n_1 n_2 (n_1 + n_2 + 1)/12}} \tag{17.13}$$

The Chi-square test (χ^2). This section discusses a general test designed to evaluate whether the difference between observed frequencies and expected frequencies under a set of theoretical assumptions is statistically significant.

The Chi-square test is most often applied to problems in which two nominal variables are cross-classified in a bivariate table. The data summarized in Table 17.6 are an example of a research problem to which the Chi-square test is applicable. Table 17.6 is a bivariate table in which the religious denominations of wife and husband have been interrelated. When the frequencies are converted to percentages (in parentheses), it is observed that whereas 93 percent of the Catholic wives married Catholic husbands, only 24 percent of the Protestant wives, and none of the Jewish wives, had a Catholic husband. We want to examine whether such differences are statistically significant. Under the null hypothesis we assume that there are no differences among the three groups of wives in their pattern of selection; that is, we would expect Catholic, Protestant, or Jewish wives to have the same proportion of Catholic, Protestant, or Jewish husbands. We then compute the frequencies, given this

TABLE 17.6.   Religious Denominations of Husband and Wife

Husband	Wife			
	Catholic	Protestant	Jewish	Total
Catholic	(93%) 271	(24%) 20	0	291
Protestant	(6%) 17	(74%) 61	0	78
Jewish	1	(2%) 1	(100%) 66	68
Total	289	82	66	437

SOURCE: August B. Hollingshead, "Cultural Factors in the Selection of Marriage Mates," *American Sociological Review*, 15 (1950): 619–627.

TABLE 17.7. Religious Denominations of Husband and Wife: Expected Frequencies

Husband	Wife			
	Catholic	Protestant	Jewish	Total
Catholic	192	55	44	291
Protestant	52	14	12	78
Jewish	45	13	10	68
Total	289	82	66	437

assumption, and compare them with the observed frequencies. If the differences between the observed and expected frequencies are so large as to occur only rarely (5 percent or 1 percent of the time), the null hypothesis is rejected.

The statistic used to evaluate these differences is Chi-square (χ^2), which is defined as:

$$\chi^2 = \sum \frac{(f_0 - f_e)^2}{f_e} \tag{17.14}$$

where f_0 = observed frequencies

f_e = expected frequencies

To compute the expected frequencies for any cell, use the following formula:

$$f_e = \frac{(\text{row total})(\text{column total})}{n} \tag{17.15}$$

For Table 17.6, the expected frequency for the Catholic-Catholic pair is equal to

$$\frac{(289)(291)}{437} = 192$$

Table 17.7 is the reconstructed table containing frequencies we would expect if religious denominations of husband and wife were not related.

Calculating Chi-square (χ^2). To compute χ^2, subtract the expected frequencies of each cell from the observed frequencies, square them, and divide by the expected frequency of the cell, and then sum for all cells. These calculations are summarized in Table 17.8. Note that χ^2 would have been zero if the observed frequencies were identical with the expected frequencies. That is, the larger the difference between what is observed and what would be expected were the hypothesis of no relations true, the larger will be the value of χ^2.

TABLE 17.8. Calculation of χ^2 for Data of Tables 17.6 and 17.7

f_o	f_e	$f_o - f_e$	$(f_o - f_e)^2$	$\dfrac{(f_o - f_e)^2}{f_e}$
271	192	79	6241	32.5
17	52	-35	1225	23.5
1	45	-44	1936	43.0
20	55	-35	1225	22.3
61	14	47	2209	157.8
1	13	-12	144	11.1
0	44	-44	1936	44.0
0	12	-12	144	12.0
66	10	56	3136	313.6
				$\chi^2 = 659.8$

To evaluate the χ^2 statistic obtained, we need to compare it to the sampling distribution of χ^2, and to observe whether the value of 659.8 is large enough and thus unlikely if the null hypothesis is true. The sampling distribution of χ^2 is reproduced in Appendix G. There are two factors that determine the distribution: (1) the level of significance (α), and (2) the number of degrees of freedom. Thus, χ^2 is really a family of distributions, each determined by different parameters. We shall select for this problem a level of significance of .01, which means that only if we obtain a χ^2 larger than what we would expect to find in no more than 1 out of 100 of our samples will the null hypothesis be rejected.

The number of degrees of freedom of the χ^2 sampling distribution is set by the number of cells for which expected frequencies can be selected freely. For any bivariate table, the cells that can be determined arbitrarily are limited by the marginal total of both variables. Thus, in a table of 2×2, for instance, there is only one cell that is free to vary, the three others being predetermined by the marginal totals. Generally, we can compute the number of degrees of freedom using the following formula:

$$df = (r - 1)(c - 1) \qquad (17.16)$$

where r = number of rows

  c = number of columns

Thus,

in a 2×2 table, $df = (2 - 1)(2 - 1) = 1$

in a 3×3 table, $df = (3 - 1)(3 - 1) = 4$

in a 4×3 table, $df = (4 - 1)(3 - 1) = 6$

The probabilities under H_0 are given at the top of each column in Appendix G, and the row entries indicate the number of degrees of freedom. The probabilities are the appropriate ones for a right-tailed test; even though the research hypothesis did not imply a specific direction, we are usually interested in the upper tail of the distribution because regardless of the direction, a relationship means that we would obtain a Chi-square value larger than would be expected by chance.

For our example, with 4 df and .01 level of significance, the entry is 13.277, indicating that a value of 13.277 will occur in only 1 percent of the samples. Our obtained sample result of 659.8 is much larger than that and is obviously very unlikely under the null hypothesis. In fact, even higher levels of significance—of .001, for example ($\chi^2 = 18.465$)—calls for the rejection of the null hypothesis.

THE TEST OF SIGNIFICANCE CONTROVERSY

In the last two decades, social scientists have engaged in a debate over the uses and misuses of statistical tests of significance. The controversy has centered around several specific issues. In this section, we briefly outline three major ones: the problem of sampling, the confusion between substantive and statistical significance, and the criteria for selecting a level of significance.[10]

The Problem of Sampling

The first issue raises two fundamental questions: First, can significance tests be applied to nonprobability samples? Second, is there any meaning to these tests when the unit of analysis is a population rather than a sample? It is recalled that statistical tests of significance enable the researcher to infer about population characteristics on the basis of evidence obtained from a sample. The sample statistic is compared with a theoretical model—a sampling distribution—to evaluate its likelihood of occurrence under specified conditions. The controversy regarding sampling has evolved around the legitimacy of applying tests of significance to nonprobability samples. Those who oppose the application of the tests under these conditions maintain that only when probability samples are drawn from a specified population can a sample statistic be compared with a sampling distribution to assess its likelihood of occurrence under the conditions specified by the null hypothesis. As the condition of probability sampling is not often met in social research, it

10. For a comprehensive documentation of these and other aspects of the controversy, see Denton E. Morrison and Ramon E. Henkel, eds., *The Significance Test Controversy* (Chicago: Aldine, 1970).

is argued that in most cases, tests of significance are inappropriately used.[11]

Advocates of statistical tests, on the other hand, argue that even with nonprobability samples, the tests are a useful device given that any set of data is subject to measurement error and this error can be assumed to be random. Furthermore, it can be assumed that nonprobability samples have been drawn from a hypothetical population that includes all possible samples that could have been drawn under equivalent circumstances. Finally, even when tests of significance are not being used as a device enabling generalizations to a population, they are useful in providing a screen for results that are worth further exploration[12]

A related question is the applicability of tests of significance in studies employing the entire population. A typical case is the selection of one unit, for example, a precinct or a school, and including in the study all the cases in that unit. Obviously, the attempt to generalize to the population by using statistical tests is inappropriate because the whole population is already included. However, it is often claimed that the unit can be conceived of as a subuniverse.[13] That is, an attempt is being made to generalize the findings to other units of the same kind, for example, other precincts or other schools. The main criticism lodged at such an approach is that unless other units to which inferences are being made can be assumed to be identical to the researched population, generalizations on the basis of statistical significance are inappropriate.

Statistical and Substantive Significance

The issue of statistical versus substantive significance derives from a confusion between two independent concepts: statistical significance and theoretical significance. Findings may show statistical significance without confirming substantive hypotheses, or they may have a substantive meaning without being statistically significant. Although substantive and statistical significance may coincide, a problem of interpretation arises when they do not. The error of confusing the two is committed when a relatively weak relationship between a number of variables is given a theoretical interpretation because it is statistically

11. Santo F. Camilleri, "Theory, Probability and Induction in Social Research," *American Sociological Review*, 27 (1962): 170–178; Robert McGinnis, "Randomization and Inference in Sociological Research," *American Sociological Review*, 23 (1958): 408–414; Denton E. Morrison and Ramon E. Henkel, "Significance Tests Reconsidered," *American Sociologist*, 4 (1969): 131–140.

12. David Gold, "Statistical Tests and Substantive Significance," *American Sociologist*, 4 (1969): 42–46.

13. Johan Galtung, *Theory and Methods of Social Research* (New York: Columbia University Press, 1967), pp. 358–388.

significant or when relationships of considerable magnitude and of theoretical importance are rejected for lack of statistical significance.[14] As statistical significance can be a function of sample size as well as of random fluctuations, this approach may lead to the rejection of what is theoretically important and to the elaboration of the trivial.[15]

Investigators who use statistical tests to test substantive hypotheses too often have accepted weak associations just because they were found to be statistically significant. Consequently, complex interpretations and theorizing were based on rather small, but statistically significant, differences.

The view that statistical tests of significance can be utilized to assess substantive significance holds that statistical tests provide a method by which investigators can screen substantive findings. David Gold maintains:

> A meaningful and useful interpretation can be given to a test of significance applied to any set of data. . . . A test of significance can be viewed as an attempt to fit observed data to a model. The model is that of a random process which, for a given set of data, can generate a sampling distribution of a statistic whose characteristics are known. A decision about the substantive significance or importance, not statistical significance, of an observed relationship can be made on the basis of the degree to which the model provides a good fit. In the absence of other explicit criteria, the degree of fit can be taken as an explicit minimum criterion which any relationship taken to be important must meet and which is superior to subjective variable judgments of importance.[16]

Gold and others who have taken the same stance claim that tests of significance can be used as a necessary (but not sufficient) condition for substantive significance.[17] In other words, relationships that are too weak to be statistically significant should not be considered worthy of further investigation. This view has been criticized as fostering an atheoretical view of the social sciences. That is, it promotes a false notion of what should be considered a sufficient basis for substantive significance by putting variables in a quantitative competition rather than in a competition based on theory.[18]

14. Hanan C. Selvin, "A Critique of Tests of Significance in Survey Research," *American Sociological Review*, 22 (1957): 519–527.

15. Galtung, *Theory and Methods of Social Research*, p. 374.

16. Gold, "Statistical Tests," p. 43.

17. James Davis, "Review of Robert K. Merton et al., The Student Physician," *American Journal of Sociology*, 63 (1958): 445–446.

18. Morrison and Henkel, "Significance Tests Reconsidered."

Criteria for Selecting a Level of Significance

Adherence to a statistical rather than a theoretical criterion in evaluating empirical results leads to another problem that is the third issue in the significance-test controversy. This is the issue of selecting a level of significance. As was pointed out in previous sections, most researchers select the .05, .01, or .001 levels of significance in assessing their research results. These levels are conventionally selected usually regardless of the type of problem under investigation.[19] Employing a conventional level of significance does have certain advantages of avoiding ambiguity and of providing a consistent criterion for evaluating research findings; that is, findings can be easily compared with regard to their statistical significance. However, the disadvantages of arbitrarily adhering to a given level of significance might outweigh the advantages. By indiscriminately selecting significance levels as cutting points between either rejecting the null hypothesis or failing to reject it, one enforces a dichotomy on a probabilistic continuum, thereby losing important nuances and often rejecting results supported either by the theory or by previous findings just because they fail to attain significance by a small fraction.[20]

Alternative procedures for setting and reporting levels of significance have been suggested by Johan Galtung,[21] James Skipper et al.,[22] and Sanford Labovitz.[23] It is argued that the choice of a level of significance can be decided upon rationally only when the cost of the decision can be evaluated in advance. As in the social sciences the cardinal decision has to do with whether to publish the findings, researchers should report the obtained level of significance rather than choose an arbitrary level.[24] Sanford Labovitz has suggested several criteria to consider when choosing a significance level.[25] First, the selection should be dictated either by the practical consequences of rejection or relative to a body of knowledge and to theory. For example, when the practical consequences of committing a type I error are serious, it is advisable to select

19. James K. Skipper, Jr., Anthony L. Guenther, and Gilbert Nass, "The Sacredness of .05: A Note Concerning the Uses of Statistical Levels of Significance in Social Science," *American Sociologist*, 2 (1967): 16–18.

20. Morrison and Henkel, "Significance Tests Reconsidered."

21. Galtung, *Theory and Methods of Social Research*, pp. 379–383.

22. Skipper et al., "The Sacredness of .05."

23. Sanford Labovitz, "Criteria for Selecting a Significance Level: A Note on the Sacredness of .05," *American Sociologist*, 3 (1968): 200–222.

24. Skipper et al., "The Sacredness of .05."

25. Labovitz, "Criteria for Selecting a Significance Level."

a small level of significance. Similarly, findings that have no theoretical or empirical support would be assessed on the basis of a small level of rejection so as to avoid a hasty rejection of the null hypothesis.

The sample size is another criterion in selecting a level of significance. With large samples, variables that are only slightly correlated will be statistically significant. For example, in a sample of 1,000 cases or more, a correlation of .10 is significant at the .01 level. However, such a relationship is of little substantive meaning. Therefore, it is generally advisable to select a small level of significance with large samples but not with small samples where large differences may not be statistically significant.

The controversy over tests of significance demonstrates more than anything else that the application of the tests in empirical research cannot be a matter of routine. Problems arise both with regard to the method of application and in the interpretation given to the findings. There are many situations in which nonprobability samples are used, or when the total population is studied. Under these circumstances, the application of significance tests can be misleading. Caution should be taken also in the interpretation of relationships that prove to be statistically significant. Tests of significance are relatively insensitive to the strength of association between variables, especially in large samples. Thus, substantive interpretations should be given in terms of the size of association, and interpretations regarding generalizations are to be expressed in terms of levels of significance.

SUMMARY

Statistical inference refers to a procedure that allows the investigator to decide between two hypotheses about a population parameter on the basis of a sample result.

The first step in testing a hypothesis is to formulate it in statistical terms. The statistical hypothesis always applies to the population of interest. There are two statistical hypotheses involved in the process of testing hypotheses. The first is the research hypothesis, which is symbolized by H_1. The second, symbolized by H_0, is the null hypothesis, which is set up for logical purposes. The null hypothesis is the one that is tested directly. The research hypothesis is supported when the null hypothesis is rejected as being unlikely.

The need for two hypotheses arises out of a logical necessity. The null hypothesis is based on negative inference in order to avoid the fallacy of affirming the consequent; that is, one must eliminate false hypotheses rather than accept true ones.

After formulating a specific null hypothesis, the investigator proceeds to test it against the sample result; it is compared to a statistical model that gives the probability of observing such a result. Such a statistical model is called a sampling distribution. A sampling distribution of a statistic is obtained by drawing a large number of random samples of the same size from the defined population, computing the statistic for each sample, and plotting the frequency distribution of the statistic.

The sampling distribution allows us to estimate the probability of obtaining the sample result. This probability is called the level of significance, or α, which is also the probability of rejecting a true hypothesis (type I error). When the likelihood of obtaining the sample result is very small under the assumptions of the null hypothesis, H_0 is rejected, and the rejection adds to our confidence in the research hypothesis.

Statistical tests are divided into two major groups: parametric tests and nonparametric tests. A parametric test is a statistical test based on several assumptions about the parameters of the population from which the sample was drawn. Among the most important ones are the assumption that the observations must be drawn from a normally distributed population and that the variables are measured on at least an interval scale. A nonparametric statistical test is one whose model does not specify the normality condition or require an interval level measurement. The difference-between-means test and a significance test for Pearson's r were discussed as examples of parametric tests. The Mann-Whitney test and the Chi-square are nonparametric tests of significance.

KEY TERMS FOR REVIEW

Null hypothesis
Sampling
  distribution
Region of rejection
Level of
  significance
One-tailed test

Two-tailed test
Type I error
Type II error
Parametric tests
Nonparametric tests
t test
Chi-square

ADDITIONAL READINGS

Blalock, Hubert M. *Social Statistics*, 2nd ed. New York: McGraw-Hill, 1972, chapters 8–15.

Bradley, James V. *Distribution-Free Statistical Tests*. Englewood Cliffs, N.J.: Prentice-Hall, 1968.

Caulcott, Evelyn. *Significance Tests*. London: Routledge & Kegan Paul, 1973.

Cohen, Jacob. *Statistical Power Analysis for Behavioral Sciences*. New York: Academic Press, 1969.

Edgington, E. "Statistical Inference and Non-Random Samples." *Psychological Bulletin*, 66: 6 (1966): 485–487.

Garson, David G. *Political Science Methods*. Boston: Holbrook, 1976, Chapter 10.

Zeller, A. Richard, and Edward C. Carmines. *Statistical Analysis for Social Data*. Chicago: Rand McNally, 1978, Chapters 11–14.

PART 5

The Ethics of Social Science Research

CHAPTER PREVIEW

478

CHAPTER 18
Ethical Concerns in Social Science Research

INTRODUCTION

In Chapter 1, we argued that the social sciences are both scientific and humanistic and that social scientists are observers as well as participants in the subject matter of their disciplines. Social science research is not conducted in isolation. Researchers are constantly interacting with a complex and demanding sociopolitical environment that formally and informally influences their research decisions. A central component of this environment is the relationship between ethical considerations and research.

This chapter deals with the ethics of conducting social science research and with ways to ensure the rights and welfare of persons and communities that are the subjects of the studies of social scientists. In the first section, we discuss the reasons for the recent concerns with research ethics. Next, three case studies—on obedience to authority, on police behavior, and on the characteristics of college students—are presented to exemplify some central ethical concerns. The ethical dilemma of social scientists—the conflict between the right to research and the right of research participants to self-determination, privacy, and dignity—is discussed in the following section. There we also suggest a costs-benefits framework for making ethical decisions in particular situations. Informed consent and the right to privacy are two common and important ethical issues; we discuss them in the next sections. In the last section, we discuss professional codes of ethics and include a composite code for social scientists.

479

WHY RESEARCH ETHICS?

As the scope of the social sciences has expanded and as our methods of research and analyses have become more sophisticated, there has been a heightened concern with the ethics of conducting social science research. Issues related to the research participants' rights and welfare and the researchers' obligations have been discussed within each of the social science professions, and most scientific societies have adopted ethical codes that cover their particular domains.

Obviously, conducting research that may encroach upon the rights and welfare of research participants is not the intent or the major interest of most investigators. The objective of most social scientists is to contribute to the development of systematic, verifiable knowledge. The research process, as discussed throughout this book, is the overall scheme of activities in which scientists engage in order to produce systematic and verifiable knowledge. However, each of the principal stages of the research process (see Figure 1.1) may involve ethical considerations in addition to the purely scientific ones.

Ethical issues arise from the kinds of problems social scientists investigate and the methods used to obtain valid and reliable data. They may be evoked by the research problem itself (for example, genetic engineering, determinants of intelligence, policy evaluation); the setting that the research takes place in (for example, a hospital, prison, or public school); the procedures required by the research design (for example, exposure of the experimental group to conditions that may have negative effects on the participants); the method of data collection (for example, covered participant observation); the kinds of persons serving as research participants (for example, poor, children, politicians, or mental patients); and the type of data collected (for example, sensitive information). To exemplify more concretely these arguments, let us examine three studies.

Obedience to Authority Study

The Milgram study is an important and controversial case worth describing in some detail. To find the conditions under which individuals would fail to obey instructions from a person in a position of authority, a controlled laboratory experiment was conducted.[1]

Two people came to a psychology laboratory to work together in a study of learning processes. One was to be a "teacher" and the other a "learner." The real experimental participant was the teacher, who was told that the objective of the experiment was to study the effect that

---

1. The following discussion is based on Stanley Milgram, *Obedience to Authority* (New York: Harper & Row, 1974).

punishment would have on learning. However, the learner, who was seated in a chair with his arms strapped to prevent movement and an electrode attached to his wrist, had been instructed beforehand on how to react. The individual conducting the experiment told him that he was to learn a list of pairs of words. If he made an error, he would receive a shock. The teacher observed all this and was then taken into the main experimental room and instructed how to use an impressive-looking shock generator that had an array of thirty switches labeled from 15 to 450 volts. The switches were also labeled from "slight shock" to "danger—severe shock"; at level 28 (420 volts), the label indicated "XXX" in red.

The teacher was then told that he would "teach" the person in the other room by reading to him paired words, such as "nice—day" or "blue—box." The teacher read a stimulus word and then four possible responses. The learner indicated which of the possible responses was correct by pressing one of four switches. If the response was correct, the teacher went on to the next set. If the response was incorrect, he was to administer a shock to the learner. The teacher was also instructed to move one level higher on the shock generator whenever a wrong response was given. However, no actual shocks were ever given to the learner.

The major dependent variable in these experiments was obedience—the refusal of the teacher to follow the instructions of the person in authority, the investigator, who encouraged him to continue to administer increasingly severe shocks to the learner, who continued to make errors or failed to respond. The instructions took the form of statements, such as "You must go on. The experiment requires that you go on. I'll take the responsibility." The learner continued to give the same set of reactions to the experimental procedure. He indicated no discomfort until the 75-volt shock, at which time he gave a little grunt. The same was true for the 90-volt and the 105-volt shocks, but at the 120-volt shock, the learner shouted that the shocks were painful. At 135 volts, he groaned painfully, and at 150 volts shouted that he wanted to be released and refused to continue. He gave similar responses but with greater intensity to subsequent shocks, and at 180 volts, he cried out that he couldn't stand the pain. At 270 volts he screamed in agony, and at 300 volts, he refused to continue giving answers. After 330 volts, the learner was no longer heard from.

The results of the experiments defy common morality. In most conditions, a substantial number of research participants were obedient and continued to provide quite painful and dangerous shocks to the learner in compliance with the experimenter's instructions. In one experiment, twenty-six of the forty research participants continued the shocks to the maximum of 450 volts; five gave 300 volts before quitting, and eight gave between 315 and 360 volts.

Another important finding in this study was the extent to which the experimental experience provided a high level of stress for the *teacher* rather than for the learner, who was never actually shocked. According to Milgram, "Subjects were observed to sweat, bite their lips, groan, and dig their fingernail into their flesh. These were characteristic, rather than exceptional, responses to the experiment."[2] There was substantial evidence that the stress for the research participants, usually those who were obedient, was extreme. Such stress was acknowledged by both the teachers and the experimenters. Aware of the possibility that the research procedures might have lasting negative effects on the participants, the investigator took two measures. First, all participants were later provided with a complete, true description of the purposes and the mechanics of the experiment they had just participated in, and a friendly encounter between the teacher and the learner ensued. Second, one year after the experiment, a psychiatric interview was conducted with a sample of the participants; no negative effects were detected.

A number of ethical criticisms have been raised concerning these experiments. First, the teachers were under the illusion that they were inflicting pain upon another individual. Thus, their right to full and truthful information about the experiment had been denied. The participants were *initially deceived* about the true purpose of the research. Second, the participants suffered extreme stress; they became extremely upset and nervous and some even had uncontrollable seizures. Third, some critics charged that as the results were made known, participants might be overwhelmed with guilt when they realized what the results might have been had they really administered electric shocks. Fourth, the experiment was criticized on the grounds that "it could easily affect an alteration in the subject's . . . ability to trust adult authorities in the future," to undermine the participants' trust in authority. Lastly, it was maintained that because the participants derived no benefit from being in the obedience study, the experiments should not have been carried out.[3] Although Milgram has responded to these ethical concerns, the issues raised by the critics are indeed valid and important.[4]

Police Behavior Study

In the 1960s, charges of police brutality were frequent in communities throughout the United States. Such charges and indeed police behavior

2. Stanley Milgram, "Behavioral Study of Obedience," *Journal of Abnormal and Social Psychology*, 67 (1963): 375.

3. For a more detailed discussion of these criticisms, see Diana Baumrind, "Some Thoughts on Ethics of Research: After Reading Milgram's Behavioral Study of Obedience," *American Psychologist*, 19 (1964): 421–423.

4. For Milgram's responses, see his *Obedience to Authority*, pp. 193–202.

toward the public in general had not until then been studied systematically. Albert Reiss decided to observe how police treated citizens.
He knew, however, that had the true purpose of the study been known
to the individual police officers who were being observed, it would have
curtailed police brutality. Reiss, therefore, led the officers to believe that
the study mainly concerned the reactions of citizens to the police. In the
course of the study, Reiss recorded a substantial amount of mistreatment
and brutality on the part of the police.[5]

   This study raised three important ethical issues: first, deception had
been used to gain access to observations that otherwise would have been
closed to the researcher. (The individual police officers had not known
the true purpose of the study, nor had they known that *they* were the
primary units of observation and analysis.) Second, and relatedly, the
police officers had not agreed to take part in the study. They had not
exercised fully informed consent because they had not known that they
were the subjects of investigation. And third, studies of this type could
generate distrust in participants to the extent that future investigators
would find it difficult to obtain information and to gain the cooperation
of participants such as police officers.

Characteristics of College Students Study

A project that had a considerable impact upon the development of ethical
issues in survey research was the American Council of Education project
on the characteristics of college students.[6] Designed during the period
of student unrest on college campuses in the 1960s, its purpose was to
provide information on the attitudes and behavior of college undergraduates during and after their college years. This longitudinal study involved repeated measures of the same individuals and of hundreds of
thousands of respondents. Controversy over the project was heightened
when measures related to political orientations and activism were included in the survey questionnaire. Substantial attention was drawn to
the questions of the possible uses of the data and to the suspicion that
school administrators or government agencies might be able to identify
activist students by having access to the questionnaire. In this case, the
major ethical issue was the participants' anonymity and the confidentiality of the data. These, in turn, are closely related to concerns over
participants' rights and welfare, as will be discussed shortly.

5. Albert J. Reiss, *The Police and the Public* (New Haven: Yale University Press,
1971), and "Police Brutality—Answers to Key Questions," *Transaction*, 5 (1968): 10–19.

6. See Robert F. Boruch, "Education Research and the Confidentiality of Data: A
Case Study," *Sociology of Education*, 44 (1971): 59–85, and J. Walsh, "A.C.E. Study on
Campus Unrest: Questions for Behavioral Scientists," *Science*, 165 (1969): 1243–1245.

BALANCING OF COSTS AND BENEFITS

These three cases illustrate that important ethical issues arise before and after the conducting of research. The issues raised by these studies are common and frequent. Research that employs deception as a part of the experiment has become commonplace because it offers methodological and practical advantages. Unobtrusive measures are collected routinely without the knowledge of the observed individuals, and the confidentiality of survey data cannot always be maintained.

In many cases, social scientists face a conflict between two rights: the right to research and to acquire knowledge, and the right of individual research participants to self-determination, privacy, and dignity. A decision not to conduct a planned research project because it interferes with the participants' welfare is a limit on the first of these rights. A decision to conduct a research despite an ethically questionable practice (for example, deception) is a limit on the second right. This is the ethical dilemma of social science research.

There are no right or wrong answers to this dilemma. The values people attach to the benefits and costs of social science research depend heavily on their background, convictions, and experience. For example, whereas policy analysts give heavy weight to the benefits that can come from accurately predicting the effects of public policies, civil libertarians are always alert to possible dangers to individual freedom, privacy, and self-determination. They tend to doubt that the benefits of any study justify taking even small risks of invading individual rights.

Nonetheless, in planning a research project, researchers have the obligation to weigh carefully the potential benefits or contributions of a proposed project against the costs to individual participants. Such costs include affronts to dignity, anxiety, embarrassment, loss of trust in social relations, loss of autonomy and self-determination, and lowered self-esteem. The potential benefits of a given study are advances that may accrue to theoretical or practical knowledge, gains to the research participant (including monetary compensation), satisfaction in making a contribution to science, and increased understanding of the researched phenomena.

The process of balancing potential benefits against possible costs is necessarily subjective and must remain a matter for the individual researcher to determine. Scientists make individual judgments about research practice in light of their own values. Our choices are related to our values, and we should weigh these values carefully when making ethical decisions. Furthermore, ethical decisions are to be made individually in each case because the process by which decisions are made is as important as the final choice. The ethical researcher "is educated about ethical guidelines, carefully examines moral alternatives, exercises judgment in each situation, and accepts responsibility for his choice."[7] Within the context of costs versus benefits, two central problems that most often concern investigators are those of informed consent and privacy.

INFORMED CONSENT

There is now wide acceptance of the doctrine that research involving human participants should be performed with the *informed consent* of the participants. Informed consent is absolutely essential whenever participants are exposed to substantial risks or are asked to forfeit personal rights. In fact, the United States Department of Health and Human Services guidelines governing research supported under its grants require that a signed consent form should be completed if research participants are placed "at risk."[8] More than eight hundred major research institutions have voluntarily agreed to comply with federal guidelines in review of all research conducted in their institutions, whether funded by the federal government or not. The informed consent policy does not *preclude* the conduct of social science research that involves risk, but it does require the use of informed participants. When research participants are to be exposed to pain, to physical or emotional injury, to an invasion of privacy, or to physical or psychological stress, or when they are asked to surrender temporarily their autonomy (for example, in drug research), then informed consent must be fully guaranteed. Participants should know that their involvement is voluntary at all times, and they should receive a thorough explanation beforehand of the benefits, rights, risks, and dangers involved as a consequence of their taking part in the research project.

Reasons for Informed Consent

The idea of informed consent derives from cultural values and from legal considerations. It rests upon the high preference we give to freedom and to self-determination. Persons should be free to determine their own behavior because freedom is a good in itself. Holders of this view might even argue, as did John Locke, that being free is a natural right, and restrictions on freedom must be carefully justified and agreed to. When persons involved in research risk a limitation of their freedom, they must be asked to consent to this limitation.

7. Eduard Diener and Rick Crandall, *Ethics in Social and Behavioral Research* (Chicago: University of Chicago Press, 1978), pp. 4–5.

8. U. S. Department of Health, Education and Welfare, Public Health Service and National Institutes of Health, *The Institutional Guide to D.H.E.W. Policy on Protection of Human Subjects*, DHEW Publication (NIH): 72–102 (December 2, 1971).

Furthermore, allowing each individual to decide whether to participate in a research project reflects a respect for the right of self-determination and shifts part of the responsibility to the participant for any
negative effects that might occur in the course of the study. Another
reason for consent is based on the argument that mature individuals are
best able to promote their own well-being. Because people will protect
their own interests, allowing them freedom of choice about participation
in research builds into the situation a safeguard against hazardous research procedures.[9] Finally, from the researchers' perspective, informed
consent reduces their legal liability because participants will have voluntarily agreed to take part in the research project.

The Meaning of Informed Consent

Although there is now wide acceptance of the principle of informed
consent, there are wide variations in implementation. This is mainly a
result of disagreements about what informed consent means in individual cases. Questions like these—"What is an informed participant?"
"How do we know that a person understands the information that is
given?" "How much information should be given?" "What if it is extremely important that participants do not know if they are in the experimental or control group?"—are obviously difficult, and there are no
standard answers to them. It is possible and useful, however, to clarify
the intent of the informed consent principle in general terms, to point
out its major elements, and to discuss some issues involved in its
implementation.

Eduard Diener and Rick Crandall define informed consent as "the
procedure in which individuals choose whether to participate in an investigation after being informed of facts that would be likely to influence
their decision."[10] This involves four elements: competence, voluntarism,
full information, and comprehension.

Competence

A basic assumption associated with the principle of informed consent
is that any decision made by a responsible, mature individual *who is
given the relevant information* will be the correct decision. However,
because there are many persons who are not mature and responsible,
the problem becomes one of systematically identifying them.

In general, persons are said not to have the capacity to provide
consent on the basis of two criteria—either they have inadequate mental

9. Diener and Crandall, *Ethics in Social and Behavioral Research*, p. 36.

10. Ibid., p. 34.

capacity, or they are in situations where there is some question about their ability to exercise self-determination. Those considered incompetent include young children, comatose medical patients, and mental patients. When such participants may receive direct benefits from their involvement in a research project (for example, therapeutic treatment), it is considered appropriate for the guardians, parents, and others responsible for such participants to make decisions for them. When direct benefits are not expected and there is some risk of negative effects, many would suggest that the research be prohibited altogether.[11]

Voluntarism

Adherence to the principle of informed consent will enhance the freedom of participants to choose whether or not to take part in a research project and will guarantee that exposure to known risks is undertaken voluntarily. But establishing the conditions under which an individual is considered to be deciding on the basis of free will is a complex undertaking. In research situations that involve institutional settings such as prisons, mental institutions, hospitals, or public schools, substantial influence from persons in positions of authority is involved. For example, a patient in care of a physician-researcher may consent to a treatment because that patient is physically weak or in other ways under the influence of the physician. In fact, the ethics of medical experimentation emphasize voluntary consent, but, until recently, researchers have not realized the subtle nature of some infringements on that voluntarism. The context for the careful explication of the need for truly voluntary consent has been set forth in the Nuremberg Code: "This means that the person involved should have legal capacity to give consent; should be so situated as to be able to exercise free power of choice, without the intervention of any element of force, fraud, deceit, over-reaching, or other ulterior form of constraint or coercion."[12]

In order to establish conditions conducive to voluntary consent, some have suggested that the researcher create an egalitarian relationship with the participants and view the research endeavor as a joint adventure in an exploration of the unknown.[13] Other scientists suggest that the presence of a third, neutral party during the informed-consent procedure will minimize possibilities for coercion. Still others advise that participants be allowed to consult with others after a request for consent is made and before a decision is reached.

11. Paul D. Reynolds, *Ethical Dilemmas and Social Science Research* (San Francisco: Jossey-Bass, 1979), p. 91.

12. Reprinted ibid., p. 436.

13. Ibid., p. 93.

Full Information

To be adequate, consent must be voluntary and informed. Consent may be uninformed yet given voluntarily or fully informed yet involuntary.

In practice, it is impossible to get a fully informed consent. This would require the transmission of endless technical and statistical details. Furthermore, in many situations the researchers themselves do not have full information on the consequences associated with research projects. If, in Paul Reynolds' words, "there were full information, there would be no reason to conduct the research—research is only of value when there is ambiguity about a phenomenon."[14] This, however, should not imply that the entire informed-consent philosophy is inapplicable. Instead, the strategy of *reasonably informed consent* has been adopted.

The federal guidelines are based on the idea of reasonably informed consent. The guidelines call for six basic elements of information to be transmitted for consent to be reasonably informed:[15]

1. A fair explanation of the procedures to be followed and their purposes.
2. A description of the attendant discomforts and risks reasonably to be expected.
3. A description of the benefits reasonably to be expected.
4. A disclosure of appropriate alternative procedures that might be advantageous to the participant.
5. An offer to answer any inquiries concerning the procedures.
6. An instruction that the person is free to withdraw his or her consent and to discontinue participation in the project at any time without prejudice to the participant.

Some of the elements of information included in these guidelines are obviously controversial. For example, disclosure of the research purpose could invalidate the findings; this was the case in the Milgram experiments and the Reiss study. There is also disagreement over how much information must be disclosed. In fact, a study by Resnick and Schwartz illustrates a situation in which giving complete information was found to be undesirable. These authors resolved to tell participants everything about a verbal conditioning experiment before it began, giving them information that usually is not made explicit. The authors telephoned participants before the study and gave a lengthy, detailed explanation about the research procedures. Many participants never showed up for the study. Contrary to the findings in most verbal conditioning studies, those who did come were not positively conditioned.

14. Ibid., p. 95.

15. HEW, *Institutional Guide to DHEW Policy*, p. 7.

The study showed that giving participants too much information has destructive effects on the research outcomes.[16]

Questions concerning the criteria for deciding what information should be given to participants have become of crucial importance. One criterion is the legal framework of what a "reasonable and prudent person" would want to know. There must be full disclosure of all aspects that a person concerned about his or her own welfare would need to know before making a decision. Participants have an unconditional right to know of any potential danger or of any rights to be lost during the study.

A more operationally applicable criterion to determine what information may be relevant to participants is to let a committee representative of potential participants make a selection or else a committee representative of both investigators and participants. Another procedure is to interview surrogate participants systematically and allow them to determine what is relevant information.[17]

Comprehension

The fourth element of informed consent, comprehension, refers to "confidence that the participant has provided knowing consent when the research procedure is associated with complex or subtle risks."[18] Clearly, an elaborate description of the project, even if it is provided in nontechnical language, may be difficult to comprehend fully.

A number of suggestions have been made for ways to ensure that comprehension has occurred. They include the use of highly educated participants who are most likely to understand the information, the availability of a consultant to discuss the study with the participant, and also a time lag between the request for participation and the decision to take part in the study. A common procedure is to provide an independent measure of comprehension by questioning the participants or by asking them to respond to questionnaires that test whether they know the information.[19]

The Responsibility of the Scientist

The practice of informed consent is the most general solution to the problem of how to promote social science research without encroaching

16. H. J. Resnick and T. Schwartz, "Ethical Standards as an Independent Variable in Psychological Research," *American Psychologist*, 28 (1973): 134–139.

17. For this and other procedures, see Reynolds, *Ethical Dilemmas and Social Science Research*, pp. 95–96.

18. Ibid., p. 97.

19. Ibid.

upon individual rights and welfare. In principle, if all the conditions associated with informed consent—competence, voluntarism, full information, and comprehension—are present, researchers will be relatively confident that the rights and welfare of research participants have been given appropriate attention.

The principle of informed consent should not, however, be made an absolute requirement of all social science research. Although usually desirable, it is not absolutely necessary in studies where no danger or risk is involved. The more serious the risk to research participants, the greater becomes the obligation to obtain informed consent. At the same time, investigators are assumed to retain responsibility for possible negative effects for participants, even if the latter consented to take part in the research. Informing participants will never totally shift responsibility from investigators to those taking part in the research project.

PRIVACY

Invasions of privacy are of great concern to all, especially in a time when there are incursions from many quarters and when information is relatively easily obtained. The right to privacy, that is, "the freedom of the individual to pick and choose for himself the time and circumstances under which, and most importantly, the extent to which, his attitudes, beliefs, behavior, and opinions are to be shared with or withheld from others,"[20] may easily be violated during an investigation or after its completion.

In the study of the American Council on Education on the characteristics of college students, we saw that respondents were requested to give private, sensitive information that could have been used by campus administrators and government authorities to identify campus activists. The data were placed in computer storage and made available to anyone willing to pay a small user's fee. To protect their research participants, the researchers separated the identification of the participants from their responses in the data bank. But there still existed the possibility that government might subpoena the information. In this study, the researchers requested private information from students, but they could not guarantee confidentiality in the political climate of the time. Subsequently, the sensitive information was made "subpoena-free" by storing the code that linked the data to individual respondents abroad.

Dimensions of Privacy

Privacy may be considered from three different perspectives: the sensitivity of information being given, the setting being observed, and dis-

20. M. O. Ruebhausen and Oliver G. Brim, "Privacy and Behavioral Research," *American Psychologist*, 21 (1966): 423–444.

semination of the information.[21] Before discussing methods for safe-guarding privacy, we will find it useful to discuss aspects of the question of privacy.

Sensitivity of information. Sensitivity of information refers to how personal or potentially threatening the information being given to the researcher is. Certain kinds of information are more personal than others and may be potentially more threatening. As the American Psychological Association states, "Religious preferences, sexual practices, income, racial prejudices, and other personal attributes such as intelligence, honesty, and courage are more sensitive items than 'name, rank, and serial number.'"[22] The greater the sensitivity of the information, the more safeguards are called for to protect the privacy of the research participants.

The settings being observed. The setting of a research project may vary from very private to completely public. For example, the home is considered one of the most private settings in our culture, and intrusions into people's homes without their consent are forbidden by law. However, the extent to which a particular setting is public or private is not always crystal clear and thus may lead to ethical controversies. For example, to study the nature of the activities of male homosexuals engaging in brief, impersonal sexual encounters in public locations (rest rooms), Humphreys assumed the role of a covert participant. He adopted the voyeuristic role of a "watch queen" (warning participants of approaching police, teenagers, or "straight" males), thus gaining confidence of the participants and access to their behavior. The license plates of 134 vehicles used by the participants were recorded, and fifty were interviewed in their homes as part of a legitimate social-health survey one year later.[23] Critics charged that although the study was conducted in a public rest room, the participants did not initiate sexual activities ("private acts") until they were assured that the setting was temporarily "private."

Dissemination of information. The third aspect of privacy concerns the ability to match personal information with the identity of research participants. Information about income remains relatively private if only a single investigator is informed of it. But when information is publicized with data and names communicated through the media, privacy is seriously invaded. The more people who can learn about the information, the more concern there must be about privacy.

It is not uncommon for a whole town or a small community to be able to identify participants in a research project even when fictitious

21. Diener and Crandall, *Ethics in Social and Behavioral Research*, pp. 55–57.

22. American Psychological Association, *Ethical Principles in the Conduct of Research with Human Subjects* (Washington, D.C.: Ad hoc Committee on Ethical Standards in Psychological Research, American Psychological Association, 1973), p. 87.

23. Laud Humphreys, *Tearoom Trade: Impersonal Sex in Public Places* (Chicago: Aldine, 1970).

names are used. For example, Arthur Vidich and Joseph Bensman describe in *Small Town in Mass Society* the intimate and sometimes embarrassing details of the lives of the residents in a small town in upstate New York.[24] Although the town and the residents were given fictitious names, the individual descriptions in the book were easily recognizable by those involved. Not only was this aspect of the study severely criticized,[25] but the townspeople staged a parade in which each wore a mask on which was written the fictitious name given to him or her by the researcher—a clear indication that the whole town knew the identity of the participants in the book. At the end of the parade came a manure spreader, with an effigy of the researcher looking into the manure.[26]

Sensitivity about information, about the setting of a research project, and about the extent of the dissemination of information obtained are three important aspects that must be considered when deciding how private certain information is and what safeguards must be used to protect research participants.

Like most rights, privacy can be voluntarily relinquished. Research participants may voluntarily surrender their right of privacy by either allowing a researcher access to sensitive topics and settings or by agreeing that the research report may identify them by name. In the latter cases, the informed consent of participants is necessary. Obviously, when observations are made without the participants' knowledge (as is the case of unobtrusive observation), no informed consent is possible.

Two common methods used to protect participants are the use of anonymity and confidentiality. The obligation to protect the anonymity of research participants and to keep research data confidential is an all-inclusive one. It should be fulfilled at all costs unless arrangements to the contrary are made with the participants in advance.

ANONYMITY

Applying the right of anonymity requires that the identity of individuals be separated from the information they give. In other words, a participant is considered anonymous when the researcher or other persons cannot identify particular information with a particular participant. If the information is given anonymously, with the researcher unable to associate a name with the data, then the privacy of the participant is secured even though sensitive information may be revealed. For example, anonymity is maintained in a mail survey in which no identification numbers are

24. Arthur J. Vidich and Joseph Bensman, *Small Town in Mass Society* (Garden City, N.Y.: Doubleday, 1960).

25. Urie Bronfenbrenner, "Freedom and Responsibility in Research: Comments," *Human Organization*, 18 (1959): 49–52.

26. Diener and Crandall, *Ethics in Social and Behavioral Research*, p. 62.

given to the questionnaires before their return. On the other hand, a respondent to a personal interview cannot be considered anonymous because an interviewer collects data from an identifiable respondent.

One procedure for ensuring anonymity is simply not to acquire names and other means of identifying participants in a research project. Alternatively, participants may be asked to use an alias of their own creation or to transform well-remembered data (for example, by subtracting their birthday from their social security number). Anonymity may be enhanced if names and other identifiers are linked to the information by a code number. Once the data have been prepared for analysis, anonymity can be maintained by separating identifying information from the research data. Further safeguards include the prevention of duplication of records, passwords to control access to data, or automatic monitoring of the use of files.[27]

CONFIDENTIALITY

Participants in social science research are commonly told that the information they provide will be treated as confidential; that is, that even though researchers are able to identify a particular participant's information, they would not reveal it publicly. Although investigators have a strict moral and professional obligation to keep the promise of confidentiality, there are circumstances in which it may be difficult or even impossible to do so. One of the most important of such situations is when information is subpoenaed by judicial authorities or legislative committees.

In the data collection stage, participants should be given clear, accurate statements about the meaning and limits of confidentiality. The greater the jeopardy posed by the information itself and the greater chances of subpoena or audit of individual data, the more explicit should be the explanation given to participants. Donald Campbell and coauthors offer these suggestions for possible explanations: Where the material solicited involves no obvious jeopardy to respondents, a vague, general promise of confidentiality is acceptable. For example,

> These interviews will be summarized in group statistics so that no one will learn of your individual answers. All interviews will be kept confidential. There is a remote chance that you will be contacted later to verify the fact that I actually conducted this interview and have conducted it completely and honestly.[28]

27. For an excellent discussion of these and other procedures, see Reynolds, *Ethical Dilemmas and Social Science Research*, pp. 167–174.

28. Donald T. Campbell et al., "Protection of the Rights and Interests of Human Subjects in Program Evaluation, Social Indicators, Social Experimentation, and Statistical Analyses Based Upon Administrative Records: Preliminary Sketch." Northwestern University, mimeographed, 1976.

Where full and honest answers to the question could jeopardize a respondent's interests in the case of subpoena, the respondent should be so informed. For example,

> These interviews are being made to provide average statistical evidence in which individual answers will not be identified or identifiable. We will do everything in our power to keep your answer completely confidential. Only if so ordered by Court and Judge would we turn over individually identified interviews to any other group or government agency.[29]

In order to assure outsiders access to data without compromising the confidentiality requirement, a number of techniques have been developed. These include the following: (1) *Deletion of identifiers*—for example, deleting the names, social security numbers, and street addresses from the data released on individuals. (2) *Crude report categories*—for example, releasing county rather than census-tract data, year of birth rather than date, profession but not speciality within profession, and so on. (3) *Microaggregation*—that is, construction of average persons from data on individuals and the release of these data, rather than data on individuals. (4) *Error inoculation*—deliberately inoculating error into individual records while leaving the aggregate data unchanged. One method of doing this is adding random error whose distribution and parameters are specified beforehand.[30]

PROFESSIONAL CODES OF ETHICS

Regulations guiding social science research now exist at several levels. Legal statutes, ethics review committees, the personal ethics of the individual researcher, and ethical codes of the professional associations are all important regulatory mechanisms. In this section, we introduce the idea of professional codes of ethics and furnish a composite ethical code for social scientists.

Most of the major professional societies of social scientists have developed codes of ethics to assist their members. These codes comprise the consensus of values within the profession. They help the individual researcher because they delineate and explicate what is required and what is forbidden. Ethical codes are written to cover the specific problems and issues that are frequently encountered in the types of research carried out within a particular profession. Codes sensitize the researcher

29. Ibid.

30. See Henry W. Riecken and Robert F. Boruch, *Social Experimentation* (New York: Academic Press, 1979), pp. 258–269.

to obligations and to problem areas where there is agreement about proper ethical practice.

Paul Reynolds has put together a useful composite code of ethics based on statements appearing in twenty-four codes related to the conduct of social science research. Most represent codes adopted by national associations of social scientists. This composite code is reported in the following box. (The figure after each item represents the number of different ethical codes in which the statement occurred.)

BOX 18.1.   A Code of Ethics for Social Scientists

Principles

General Issues Related to the Code of Ethics

1. The social scientist(s) in charge of a research project is (are) responsible for all decisions regarding procedural matters and ethical issues related to the project whether made by themselves or subordinates (7).

2. Teachers are responsible for all decisions made by their students related to ethical issues involved in research (1).

3. All actions conducted as part of the research should be consistent with the ethical standards of both the home and host community (1).

4. Ethical issues should be considered from the perspective of the participant's society (2).

5. If unresolved or difficult ethical dilemmas arise, assistance or consultation should be sought with colleagues or appropriate committees sponsored by professional associations (2).

6. Any deviation from established principles suggests: (a) that a greater degree of responsibility is being accepted by the investigator, (b) a more serious obligation to seek outside counsel and advice, and (c) the need for additional safeguards to protect the rights and welfare of the research participants (2).

Decision to Conduct the Research

7. Research should be conducted in such a way as to maintain the integrity of the research enterprise and not to diminish the potential for conducting research in the future (3).

8. Investigators should use their best scientific judgment for selection of issues for empirical investigation (1).

9. The decision to conduct research with human subjects should involve evaluation of the potential benefits to the participant and society in relation to the risks to be borne by the participant(s)—a risk-benefit analysis (2).

10. Any study which involves human subjects must be related to an important intellectual question (4).

11. Any study which involves human subjects must be related to an important intellectual question with humanitarian implications, and there should be no other way to resolve the intellectual question (2).

12. Any study which involves human participants must be related to a very important intellectual question if there is a risk of permanent, negative effects on the participants (2).

BOX 18.1. *(Continued)*

13. Any study involving risks as well as potential therapeutic effects must be justified in terms of benefits to the client or patient (2).

14. There should be no prior reason to believe that major permanent negative effects will occur for the participants (1).

15. If the conduct of the research may permanently damage the participants, their community, or institutions within their community (such as indigenous social scientists), the research may not be justified and might be abandoned (2).

Conduct of the Research

16. All research should be conducted in a competent fashion, as an objective, scientific project (4).

17. All research personnel should be qualified to use any procedures employed in the project (7).

18. Competent personnel and adequate facilities should be available if any drugs are involved (4).

19. There should be no bias in the design, conduct, or reporting of the research—it should be as objective as possible (4).

Effects on and Relationships with the Participants

Informed Consent

General

20. Informed consent should be used in obtaining participants for all research; investigators should honor all commitments associated with such agreements (10).

21. Participants should be in a position to give informed consent; otherwise it should be given by those responsible for the participant (2).

22. Informed consent should be used if the potential effects on participants are ambiguous or potentially hazardous (7).

23. If possible, informed consent should be obtained in writing (1).

24. Seek official permission to use any government data, no matter how it was obtained (1).

Provision of information

25. Purposes, procedures, and risks of research (including possible hazards to physical and psychological well-being and jeopardization of social position) should be explained to the participants in such a way that they can understand (7).

26. Participants should be aware of the possible consequences, if any, for the group or community from which they are selected, in advance of their decision to participate (1).

27. The procedure used to obtain the participant's name should be described to him or her (1).

28. Sponsorship, financial and otherwise, should be specified to the potential participants (2).

29. The identity of those conducting the research should be fully revealed to the potential participants (2).

30. Names and addresses of research personnel should be left with participants so that the research personnel can be traced subsequently (1).

BOX 18.1. *(Continued)*

31. Participants should be fully aware of all data gathering techniques (tape and video recordings), photographic devices, physiological measures, and so forth), the capacities of such techniques, and the extent to which participants will remain anonymous and data confidential (2).

32. In projects of considerable duration, participants should be periodically informed of the progress of the research (1).

33. When recording videotapes or film, subjects should have the right to approve the material to be made public (by viewing it and giving specific approval to each segment) as well as the nature of the audiences (1).

Voluntary consent

34. Individuals should have the option to refuse to participate and know this (1).

35. Participants should be able to terminate involvement at any time and know that they have this option (3).

36. No coercion, explicit or overt, should be used to encourage individuals to participate in a research project (6).

Protection of Rights and Welfare of Participants
General issues

37. The dignity, privacy, and interests of the participants should be respected and protected (8).

38. The participants should not be harmed; welfare of the participants should take priority over all other concerns (10).

39. Damage and suffering to the participants should be minimized through procedural mechanisms and termination of risky studies as soon as possible; such effects are justified only when the problem cannot be studied in any other fashion (8).

40. Potential problems should be anticipated, no matter how remote the probability of occurrence, to ensure that the unexpected does not lead to major negative effects on the participants (1).

41. Any harmful aftereffects should be eliminated (4).

42. The hopes or anxieties of potential participants should not be raised (1).

43. Research should be terminated if danger to the participants arises (3).

44. The use of clients seeking professional assistance for research purposes is justified only to the extent that they may derive direct benefits as clients (1).
Deception

45. Deceit of the participants should only be used if it is absolutely necessary, there being no other way to study the problem (3).

46. Deception may be utilized (1).

47. If deceit is involved in a research procedure, additional precautions should be taken to protect the rights and welfare of the participants (2).

48. After being involved in a study using deception, all participants should be given a thorough, complete, and honest description of the study and the need for deception (5).

49. If deception is not revealed to the participants, for humane or scientific reasons, the investigator has a special obligation to protect the interests and welfare of the participants (1).

BOX 18.1. *(Continued)*

Confidentiality and anonymity

50. Research data should be confidential and all participants should remain anonymous, unless they (or their legal guardians) have given permission for release of their identity (15).

51. If confidentiality or anonymity cannot be guaranteed, the participants should be aware of this and its possible consequences before involvement in the research (4).

52. Persons in official positions (studied as part of a research project) should provide written descriptions of their official roles, duties, and so forth, (which need not be treated as confidential information) and provided with a copy of the final report on the research (1).

53. Studies designed to provide descriptions of aggregates or collectivities should always guarantee anonymity to individual respondents (1).

54. 'Privacy' should always be considered from the perspective of the participant and the participant's culture (1).

55. Material stored in data banks should not be used without the permission of the investigator who originally gathered the data (1).

56. If promises of confidentiality are honored, investigators need not withhold information on misconduct of participants or organizations (1).

57. Specific procedure for organizing data to ensure anonymity of participants (details omitted) (1).

Benefits to Participants

58. A fair return should be offered for all services of participants (1).

59. Increased self-knowledge, as a benefit to the participants, should be incorporated as a major part of the research design or procedures (1).

60. Copies or explanations of the research should be provided to all participants (2).

61. Studies of aggregates or cultural subgroups should produce knowledge which will benefit them (1).

Effects on Aggregates or Communities

62. Investigators should be familiar with, and respect, the host cultures in which studies are conducted (1).

63. Investigators should cooperate with members of the host society (1).

64. Investigators should consider, in advance, the potential effects of the research on the social structure of the host community and the potential changes in influence of various groups or individuals by virtue of the conduct of the study (1).

65. Investigators should consider, in advance, the potential effects of the research and the report on the population or subgroup from which participants are drawn (1).

66. Participants should be aware, in advance, of potential effects upon aggregates or cultural subgroups which they represent (1).

67. The interests of collectivities and social systems of all kinds should be considered by the investigator (1).

Interpretations and Reporting of the Results of the Research

68. All reports of research should be public documents, freely available to all (4).

BOX 18.1. *(Continued)*

69. Research procedures should be described fully and accurately in reports, including all evidence regardless of the support it provides for the research hypotheses; conclusions should be objective and unbiased (14).

70. Full and complete interpretations should be provided for all data and attempts made to prevent misrepresentations in writing research reports (6).

71. Sponsorship, purpose, sources of financial support, and investigators responsible for the research should be made clear in all publications related thereto (3).

72. If publication may jeopardize or damage the population studied and complete disguise is impossible, publication should be delayed (2).

73. Cross-cultural studies should be published in the language and journals of the host society, in addition to publication in other languages and other societies (2).

74. Appropriate credit should be given to all parties contributing to the research (9).

75. Full, accurate disclosure of all published sources bearing on or contributing to the work is expected (8).

76. Publication of research findings on cultural subgroups should include a description in terms understood by the participants (2).

77. Whenever requested, raw data or other original documentation should be made available to qualified investigators (1).

78. Research with scientific merit should always be submitted for publication and not withheld from public presentation unless the quality of research or analysis is inadequate (1).

Reprinted with permission from Paul Davidson Reynolds, *Ethical Dilemmas and Social Science Research* (San Francisco: Jossey-Bass, 1979), Appendix 4, pp. 443–448.

SUMMARY

The fact that the social sciences are both scientific and humanistic raises a fundamental ethical dilemma: How are we to develop systematic, verifiable knowledge when research procedures may infringe upon the rights and welfare of individuals?

There are no absolute right or wrong answers to this dilemma. The values that we attach to the potential benefits and costs of social science research depend on our backgrounds, convictions, and experience. Nonetheless, a broad consensus has been emerging as is evident from the ethical codes of professional societies. These codes delineate what is required and what is forbidden. Although they sensitize researchers to the obligations and to problem areas where there is agreement about proper ethical practice, there is no substitute for the personal code of ethics of the individual investigator. The ethical researcher is educated about ethical guidelines, thoroughly examines the costs and potential benefits of the research project, exercises judgment in each situation, and accepts responsibility for his or her choice.

Within this ethical decision-making framework, two common issues were discussed: informed consent and privacy. Informed consent is the most general solution to the problem of how to promote social science research without encroaching upon individual rights and welfare. It is the procedure in which individuals choose whether to participate in a research project after being informed of the facts that would be likely to influence their decision. Informed consent involves four basic elements: competence, voluntarism, full information, and comprehension. The more serious the risk to research participants, the greater becomes the obligation to obtain informed consent.

The right to privacy can be easily violated during an investigation or after its completion. In deciding how private given information is, one should consider three criteria: the sensitivity of the information, the setting being observed, and the extent of dissemination of the information. Two common ways to protect the privacy of research participants are to maintain their anonymity and to keep the data confidential.

KEY TERMS FOR REVIEW

Research deception
The ethical
    dilemma
Ethical researcher
Informed consent
Competence
Voluntarism
Reasonably
    informed consent

Comprehension
Right to privacy
Sensitivity of
    information
Anonymity
Confidentiality
Codes of ethics

ADDITIONAL READINGS

Bermant, Gordon; Herbert C. Kelman; and Donald P. Warwick, eds. *The Ethics of Social Intervention.* New York: Wiley, 1978.

Boruch, Robert F. "Strategies for Eliciting and Merging Confidential Social Research Data." *Policy Sciences,* 3 (1972): 275–297.

————. "Assuring Confidentiality of Responses in Social Research: A Note on Strategies." *American Sociologist,* 6 (1971): 308–311.

Cassell, J. "Risk and Benefit to Subjects of Fieldwork." *American Sociologist,* 13 (1978): 134–143.

Carroll, D. J. "Confidentiality of Social Science Research and Data: The Popkin Case." *Policy Sciences,* 6:3 (1973): 268–280.

Katz, J. *Experimentation with Human Beings.* New York: Russell Sage Foundation, 1972.

Kelman, Herbert C. *A Time to Speak: On Human Values and Social Research.* San Francisco: Jossey-Bass, 1968.

Lappe, M. "Accountability in Science." *Science*, 187 (1975): 696–698.

Nejelski, P. *Social Research in Conflict with Law and Ethics.* Cambridge, Mass.: Ballinger, 1976.

Rainwater, Lee, and David J. Pittman, "Ethical Problems in Studying a Politically Sensitive and Deviant Community." *Social Problems*, 19 (Spring 1967): 357–366.

Toulmin, Stephen. *Reason in Ethics.* Cambridge, England: Cambridge University Press, 1970.

Glossary

Accretion Measures: Unobtrusive measures using deposited physical material.

Actuarial Records: Public records concerning the demographic characteristics of the population served by the record-keeping agency.

Ad Hoc Classificatory System: A level of theory with arbitrary categories constructed to organize and summarize empirical observations.

Anonymity: The protection of research participants by separating specific identities from the information given.

Arithmetic Mean: The sum total of all observations divided by their number.

Attitude: A concept that refers to the sum total of a person's inclinations, prejudices, ideas, fears, and convictions about any specific topic.

Attitude Index: A series of questions selected on an a priori basis, the scores of which are interpreted as indicating the attitude of the respondent.

Authenticity: The quality of genuineness regarding private records.

Axiomatic System: One form of a theoretical system that contains a set of concepts and definitions, a set of existence statements, a set of relational statements divided into axioms and theorems, and a logical system used to relate concepts with statements and to deduce theorems from axioms.

Batch Processing: A type of data processing in which the computer handles a set of data and instructions for processing and analyzing these data.

Central Memory: A computer device used to store information during the time the data is being manipulated.

Central Processing Unit: A unit that controls and coordinates activities of the computer system, such as executing the program instructions and monitoring the operation of the input and output devices.

Chi-Square: A test statistic that allows one to decide whether observed frequencies are essentially equal to, or significantly different from, frequencies predicted by a theoretical model. The outcome of the test allows decisions as to whether or not frequencies are distributed equally among categories, whether or not a distribution is normal, or whether or not two variables are independent.

Closed-Ended Question: A question that offers respondents a set of answers from which they are asked to choose the one that most closely represents their views.

Codebook: A book compiled by the researcher identifying a specific item of observation and the code number assigned to describe each category included in that item.

Coding: Assigning codes in the form of numerals (or other symbols) for each category of each variable in a study.

Coding Reliability: The extent of agreement between different coders when classifying their individual responses according to the coding scheme.

Coding Scheme: A system of categories used to classify responses or behaviors that relate to a single item or variable.

Coefficient of Multiple Determination: A measure indicating the proportion of variation explained by all the independent variables in the multiple-regression equation.

Coefficient of Reproducibility: A measure that indicates how precisely a score on a Guttman scale can be used to reproduce the scores on the items that compose the scale; the fewer the number of errors in predicted item scores, the higher the coefficient of reproducibility.

Combined Designs: The merging of two or more research designs into a single study to increase the inferential powers of that study.

Concept: An abstraction representing an object, a property of an object, or a certain phenomenon that scientists use to describe the empirical world.

Conceptual Definition: A definition that describes a concept by using primitive and derived terms.

Conceptual Framework: A level of theory in which descriptive categories are systematically placed within a broad structure of explicit and assumed propositions.

Conditional Variable: A contingency necessary for the occurrence of the relationship between the independent and dependent variable.

Confidence Interval: A measure that specifies the range of values within which any percentage of the sample means is located.

Confidentiality: The protection of the identity of research participants.

Content Analysis: A method of data analysis that permits systematic, quantitative analysis of observations obtained from archival records and documents.

Context of Justification: Those activities of scientists as they attempt to logically and empirically verify claims for knowledge.

Contingency Question: A question that applies only to a subgroup of respondents because it is relevant only to certain people.

Continuous Variables: Variables that do not have a minimal size unit.

Contrasted-Groups: The comparison of groups that are known to differ in some important attributes.

Control Group: The group in an experimental research design that is not exposed to the independent variable.

Control-Series: A quasi-experimental design that attempts to control those aspects of history, maturation, and test-retest effects shared by the experimental and comparison groups.

Control Variable: A variable that is controlled for, or held constant, in order to examine whether it affects the relationship between independent and dependent variables.

Cover Letter: The letter that accompanies a mail questionnaire.

Criterion of Least-Squares: The criterion that minimizes the sum of the squared vertical distances between the regression line and actual observations.

Cross-Tabulation: A table showing the relationship between two or more variables by presenting all combinations of categories of variables.

Deductive Explanation: An explanation that accounts for a phenomenon by demonstrating that it can be deduced from an established universal generalization.

Degree of Freedom: A characteristic of the sample statistic that determines the appropriate sampling distribution.

Dependent Variable: The variable that the researcher wishes to explain.

Discrete Variables: Variables with a minimal size unit.

Discriminative Power: A measure of each item's ability to separate the "highs" from the "lows" on an attitude continuum when selecting items for the Likert scale.

Double-Barreled Questions: Questions that include two or more questions in one, thus confusing respondents who might agree with one aspect of the question but disagree with the other.

Ecological Fallacy: An error that results from analyzing groups but making inferences on the behavior of individuals.

Elaboration: A method of introducing other variables to the analysis in order to determine the links between the independent and dependent variables.

Empirical Observations: Observations that rely on perceptions, experience, and behavior.

Epistemology: The study of the foundations of knowledge, especially with reference to its limits and validity.

Equal-Appearing Interval: A method of ranking individuals in such a way that the intervals between the rankings assigned by the scale would approximate equal intervals.

Erosion Measure: An unobtrusive measure based on the wearing away of physical materials.

Experimental Group: The group exposed to the independent variable in an experimental research design.

Extended Time-Series: A research design that presents the data as part of a broadened time-series, and therefore controls for maturation.

External Validity: The extent to which the research findings can be generalized to larger populations and applied to different settings.

Extrinsic Factors: Biases resulting from the differential recruitment of research participants to the experimental and control groups.

Factorial Design: A research design that allows one to examine simultaneously the effects of two or more independent variables on the dependent variable. This design also allows one to detect interaction between the variables.

Factual Question: A question designed to elicit objective information from respondents regarding their background, their environment, and their habits.

Fallacy of Reification: The error of treating concepts as though they are the actual phenomena.

Field Experimentation: An experimental study conducted in the field as contrasted to a laboratory experiment.

Frequency Distribution: The frequency (number of times) of observations in each value of a variable.

Funnel Technique: A technique of questionnaire construction in which the questionnaire begins with general queries and then "funnels down" to more specific items.

Gamma: A coefficient of association indicating the magnitude and direction between ordinal variables.

Guttman Coefficient of Predictability (also known as lambda): A measure of association indicating the magnitude and direction between nominal variables.

Hypothesis: A tentative answer to a research problem, expressed in the form of a relation between independent and dependent variables.

Independent Variable: The variable hypothesized to explain variations in the dependent variable.

Index: A composite measure of two or more indicators or items.

Informed Consent: The agreement of an individual to participate in a study after being informed of facts that would be likely to influence his or her responses.

Input Device: The component of the data processing cycle that transmits data from media such as cards, tapes, or disks to the central processor of the computer.

Interaction Process Analysis (also known as the Bales category system): A set of twelve categories used to code interaction in groups. The analysis is a highly structured observational technique, using both structured observational categories and a structured laboratory setting.

Interactive Processing: A method of data processing that allows the researcher to interact directly and continuously with the computer via a teletype or other computer terminals and telephone.

Intersubjectivity: A norm of scientific methodology that states that knowledge must be transmittable so that scientists can understand and evaluate the methods of other scientists and perform similar observations in order to verify empirical generalizations.

Interval Level: The level of measurement achieved (1) when each observation falls into exhaustive and mutually exclusive measurement categories; (2) when measurement categories can be ordered; and (3) when the intervals between adjacent categories are equal.

Intervening Variable: An intermediate variable between an independent variable and a dependent variable. The independent variable affects the dependent variable through the intervening variable.

Intrinsic Factors: Changes in units under study that occur during the study period, changes in the measuring instrument, or the reactive effect of the observation itself.

Isomorphism: Similarity or identity in structure.

Leading Questions: Questions phrased in such a manner that the respondent believes that the researcher expects certain answers.

Level of Measurement: Refers to the degree that characteristic numbers describe characteristics of the measured variable. The higher the level of measurement, the more statistical methods are applicable.

Level of Significance: The probability of rejecting a true null hypothesis, that is, the possibility of making a Type I error.

Likert Scale: A type of summated rating scale designed to assist in excluding questionable items from the scale.

Linear Relation: A relation between two variables X and Y of the form $Y = ax + b$, where a and b are constant values. The graph of a linear relation is a straight line.

Log: A record of events, meetings, visits, and other activities of an individual in a given period of time.

Magnitude of a Relation: The extent to which variables covary positively or negatively.

Mail Questionnaire: An impersonal survey method in which questionnaires are mailed to respondents; the responses constitute the data upon which research hypotheses are tested.

Matching: A method of control that involves equating the experimental and control groups on extrinsic variables that are presumed to relate to the research hypothesis.

Matrix Question: A method of organizing a large set of rating questions that have the same response categories.

Measure of Qualitative Variation: An index of heterogeneity based on the ratio of the total number of differences in the distribution to the maximum number of possible differences within the same distribution.

Measurement: A procedure in which the researcher assigns numbers or other symbols to empirical properties according to rules.

Measures of Central Tendency: Statistical measures that reflect a typical or an average characteristic of a frequency distribution.

Measures of Dispersion: A family of statistics whose objective is to convey information of the dispersion or spread of a distribution.

Median: A measure of central tendency defined as the point above and below which 50 percent of the observations fall.

Methodology: A system of explicit rules and procedures upon which research is based and against which claims for knowledge are evaluated.

Mode: A measure of central tendency defined as the most frequently occurring observation category in the data.

Model: An abstraction from reality that serves to order and simplify our view of the reality while still representing its essential characteristics.

Multiple Relations: The simultaneous effect of several independent variables on the dependent variable.

Negative Relation: A direction which indicates that as value of one variable increases, the value of another decreases.

Nominal Level: The level of measurement which requires that the measurement categories be exhaustive and mutually exclusive. This is the lowest level of measurement.

Nonparametric Tests: Statistical tests that require either no, or very few, assumptions about the population distribution.

Nonresponse Bias: Bias that occurs when persons do not respond to a survey and are therefore not represented in the total sample.

Nonscheduled Interview: The least structured form of interviewing; no prespecified set of questions is employed, nor is an interview schedule used. The interviewer has a great deal of freedom to probe various areas, and to raise specific queries during the course of the interview.

Normal Distribution: A type of symmetrical distribution of great significance in the field of statistics. It is a mathematically defined curve. Under certain circumstances, it is permissible to treat frequency distributions of variables as close approximations of the normal distribution.

Normal Science: The routine verification of dominant paradigms in any historical period.

Null Hypothesis: A statement of no relationship between variables; the null hypothesis is rejected when an observed statistic appears unlikely under the null hypothesis.

One-Shot Case Study: An observation of a single group or event at a single point of time, usually subsequent to some phenomena that allegedly produced change.

Open-Ended Question: A question that is not followed by any kind of specified choice; the respondents' answers are recorded in full.

Operational Definition: A set of procedures that describe the activities one should perform in order empirically to observe a phenomena.

Opinion: The verbal expression of an attitude.

Ordinal Level: The level of measurement achieved (1) when each observation falls into exhaustive and mutually exclusive measurement categories, and (2) when the categories can be ordered.

Ostensive Definition: A definition that conveys the meaning of a concept by indicating examples.

Panel: A design in survey research that offers a closer approximation to the before-after condition of experimental designs by interviewing the same group at two or more points in time.

Parameter: A specified value of the population.

Parametric Tests: Hypotheses tests based on assumptions about the parameter values of the population.

Partial Correlation: A method of statistical control that involves a mathematical adjustment of the bivariate correlation, designed to cancel out the effect of other variables on the independent and dependent variables.

Partial Tables: Tables that reflect only part of the total association between the independent and dependent variables.

Participant Observation: Nonstructured observation in which the researcher is a member of the group being studied and participates in the group's activities.

Pearson Product-Moment Correlation Coefficient: A statistic that specifies the magnitude and direction of relation between two interval-level variables. Also called the Pearson r, or simply r, it is the most commonly used statistic in correlational analysis.

Physical Location Analysis: A type of simple observation that focuses on the ways in which individuals use their bodies in a social space.

Planned Variation: A research design involving the exposure of individuals to systematically varying values of the independent variable in order to assess their causal effects.

Population: The aggregate of all cases that conform to some designated set of specifications.

Positive Relation: A direction which indicates that as value of one variable increases, the value of another also increases.

Posttest: The measurement taken after exposure to the independent variable.

Predictive Validity: Validation of a measure by prediction to an external criterion.

Pretest: The measurement taken prior to the introduction of the independent variable.

Pretest-Posttest Design: A pre-experimental design that compares the measures of the dependent variable before and after exposure to the independent variable.

Primitive Term: A concept that contains shared agreement as to its meaning, but that cannot be conceptually defined.

Probabilistic Explanation: Accounting for a phenomena by using generalizations that express an arithmetical ratio between phenomena, or generalizations that express tendencies.

Probability Sample: A sample design that permits one to specify for each sampling unit the probability that it will be included in the sample.

Probing: The technique used by an interviewer to stimulate discussion and obtain more information.

Proportional Reduction of Error Principle: A method used to measure the magnitude of the relations between two variables. One variable is used to predict the values of another.

Quantifiers: The response categories of the rating scale that reflect the intensity of the particular judgment involved.

Quartile: A percentile that is an even multiple of .25.

Quota Sample: The selection of a nonprobability sample that is as closely as possible a replica of the population.

Random Digit Dialing: Drawing a random sample of numbers by selecting an exchange, and then appending random numbers between 0001 and 9999.

Randomization: A method of control which helps to offset the confounding effects of known as well as unforeseen factors by randomly assigning cases to the experimental and control groups.

Rating: A judgment made by the respondent in terms of sets or ordered categories such as "strongly agree," "favorable," or "very often."

Ratio Level: The level of measurement that has a unique zero point.

Rationalism: A school of thought which holds that the totality of knowledge can be acquired only by strict adherence to the forms and rules of logic.

Region of Rejection: The area under the sampling distribution specified by the null hypothesis that covers those values of the observed statistic that lead to the rejection of the null hypothesis. In one-tailed tests, there is one region of rejection; in a two-tailed test, there are two regions of rejection.

Regression Coefficient: A measure indicating the amount of change in the dependent variable associated with a given change in one of the independent variables.

Relation: Joint occurrence or covariation between two or more variables.

Reliability: The consistency of a measuring instrument.

Replication: The repetition of an investigation in an identical way as a safeguard against unintentional error or deception.

Research Design: The program that guides the investigator in the process of collecting, analyzing, and interpreting observations.

Research Problem: An intellectual problem calling for an answer in the form of a scientific inquiry.

Research Process: The overall scheme of scientific activities in which scientists engage in order to produce verifiable knowledge.

Revolutionary Science: The abrupt development of a rival paradigm which is accepted only gradually by a scientific community.

Right to Privacy: The freedom of individuals to choose for themselves the time, the circumstances under which, and the extent to which their beliefs and behavior are to be shared or withheld from others.

Sample: Any subset of sampling units from a population.

Sampling Distribution: A theoretical distribution that can be specified for any statistic that can be computed for samples from a population.

Sampling Frame: The list of the sampling units that is used in the selection of the sample.

Sampling Unit: A single member of a sampling population; or, in cluster sampling, a collection of sampling units.

Schedule-Structured Interview: An interview in which the questions, their wording, and their sequence are fixed and identical for every respondent.

Semantic Differential: A type of rating scale that measures the respondent's reaction to some object or concept in terms of rating on bipolar scales defined with contrasting adjectives at each end.

Simple Observation: A type of unobtrusive measure that occurs in situations in which the observer remains unnoticed by the observed.

Simple Random Sample: A basic probability sampling design that gives each of the sampling units of the population an equal chance of being selected for the sample.

Skewed Distribution: A distribution in which more observations fall on one side of the mean than the other.

Split-Half Method: A method of assessing the reliability of an instrument by dividing items into two equivalent parts and correlating scores in one part with scores in the other.

Spurious Relation: An apparent relation between the independent and dependent variables that is found to be false because both are caused by a third variable. When the third variable is controlled for, the apparent relationship between the dependent and independent variables disappears.

Standard Deviation: A commonly used measure of variability whose size indicates the dispersion of a distribution.

Standard Error: The standard deviation of a sampling distribution.

Standard Score: An individual observation that belongs to a distribution with a mean of zero and a standard deviation of 1.

Stratified Random Sample: A probability sampling design in which the population is first divided into homogeneous strata within each of which sampling is conducted.

Systematic Sample: A sample in which every *k*th case is selected (usually with a random start) where *k* is a constant.

t Test: A hypothesis test that uses the *t*-statistic and the *t*-distribution in order to decide whether to reject or retain the null hypothesis.

Taxonomy: A level of theory that consists of a system of categories constructed to fit the empirical observations so that relationships among categories can be described.

Test-Retest Method: A method of assessing the reliability of an instrument by administering it twice to the same group of people and correlating the scores.

Theoretical System: Systematic combinations of taxonomies, conceptual frameworks, descriptions, explanations, and predictions in a manner that provides structure for a complete explanation of empirical phenomena.

Threatening Questions: Questions that respondents may find embarrassing or sensitive.

Thurstone Scale: An attitude scaling procedure in which proposed scale items are determined by judges in an attempt to construct an interval scale.

Time-Series Design: A quasi-experimental design in which pretest and posttest measures are available on a number of occasions before and after exposure to an independent variable.

Topical Autobiography: A private record that focuses on a limited aspect of a person's life.

Type I Error: The rejection of a true null hypothesis.

Type II Error: The acceptance of a false null hypothesis.

Unidimensionality: A principle which implies that the items comprising a scale reflect a single dimension and belong on a continuum that reflects one and only one theoretical concept.

Units of Analysis: The entities to which our concepts pertain and which influence subsequent research design, data collection, and data analysis decisions.

Validity: When referring to measurement, the degree to which the measuring instrument measures what it is supposed to measure.

Variance: A measure of quantitative variation reflecting the average dispersion in the distribution. It is the squared standard deviation.

Verstehen: Understanding; the notion that social scientists can understand human behavior through empathy.

Weighted Aggregate: A method of constructing an index with the purpose of specifying the relative influence of each indicator or item.

APPENDIX A. The summation sign Σ

In statistics it is frequently necessary to make use of formulas involving sums of numerous quantities. As a shorthand substitute for writing out each of these sums at length, the Greek letter Σ (capital sigma), which means to summate or add, is used. As a rule, whenever Σ appears it means that *all* quantities appearing to the right of it should be summed.

If we want to add ten scores, we can always write

$$X_1 + X_2 + X_3 + X_4 + X_5 + X_6 + X_7 + X_8 + X_9 + X_{10}$$

or the same expression can be shortened to

$$X_1 + X_2 + \ldots + X_{10}$$

which means the same thing. The three dots (. . .) mean "and so on." This same instruction may be put in still another way:

$$\sum_{i=1}^{10} X_i$$

When Σ is used it instructs us to add up everything that follows (X_i) starting with the case specified below the Σ symbol $(i = 1)$ and ending with the case specified above (10). This example may be read as follows: add up (Σ) all the observations (X_i) ranging from the first $(i = 1)$ through the tenth (10). If we want only to sum the observations 4 and 5 $(X_4 + X_5)$, we can write

$$\sum_{i=4}^{5} X_i$$

and if we wish to indicate that all of some unspecified number of cases should be added together, we can use N to symbolize the unspecified number of cases and write

$$\sum_{i=1}^{N} X_i$$

This says: sum all the observations from the first to the Nth; it is a general instruction for the addition of all cases regardless of their number. When this general instruction is intended, and when the range of values to be summed is obvious, it is customary to omit the notation of limits and write

$$\sum X_i$$

or even

$$\sum X$$

This indicates that the summation is to extend over all cases under consideration.

Rules for the use of Σ

There are a number of rules for the use of Σ. For example,

$$\sum_{i=1}^{N} (X_i + Y_i) = \sum_{i=1}^{N} X_i + \sum_{i=1}^{N} Y_i$$

which says that the summation of the sum of the two variables (X and Y) is equal to the sum of their summations. It makes no difference whether one adds each X_i to each Y_i and

517

then sums their total from 1 to N, or sums all the X_i's and all the Y_i's and adds their sums; the result is the same.

Another rule is expressed in the following equation:

$$\sum_{i=1}^{N} kX_i = k \sum_{i=1}^{N} X_i$$

A constant k may be moved across the summation sign. That is to say, if we are instructed to multiply each of a series of numbers by a constant

$$kX_1 + kX_2 + \ldots + kX_N$$

we can simply sum our numbers and multiply that sum by the constant; the result is the same.

A third rule is the following:

$$\sum_{i=1}^{N} k = kN$$

The summation of a constant is equal to the product of that constant and the number of times it is summed.

Another rule states that

$$\left(\sum_{i=1}^{N} X_i\right)^2 = (X_1 + X_2 + \ldots + X_N)^2$$

$$= X_1^2 + X_2^2 + \ldots + X_N^2 + 2X_1X_2$$

$$+ 2X_1X_3 + \ldots + 2X_{N-1}X_N$$

$$\neq X_1^2 + X_2^2 + \ldots + X_N^2$$

That is, we must distinguish between

$$\sum_{i=1}^{N} X_i^2 \text{ and } \left(\sum_{i=1}^{N} X_i\right)^2$$

APPENDIX B.   Random digits

Line/Col.	(1)	(2)	(3)	(4)	(5)	(6)	(7)	(8)	(9)	(10)	(11)	(12)	(13)	(14)
1	10480	15011	01536	02011	81647	91646	69179	14194	62590	36207	20969	99570	91291	90700
2	22368	46573	25595	85393	30995	89198	27982	53402	93965	34095	52666	19174	39615	99505
3	24130	48360	22527	97265	76393	64809	15179	24830	49340	32081	30680	19655	63348	58629
4	42167	93093	06243	61680	07856	16376	39440	53537	71341	57004	00849	74917	97758	16379
5	37570	39975	81837	16656	06121	91782	60468	81305	49684	60672	14110	06927	01263	54613
6	77921	06907	11008	42751	27756	53498	18602	70659	90655	15053	21916	81825	44394	42880
7	99562	72905	56420	69994	98872	31016	71194	18738	44013	48840	63213	21069	10634	12952
8	96301	91977	05463	07972	18876	20922	94595	56869	69014	60045	18425	84903	42508	32307
9	89579	14342	63661	10281	17453	18103	57740	84378	25331	12566	58678	44947	05585	56941
10	85475	36857	53342	53988	53060	59533	38867	62300	08158	17983	16439	11458	18593	64952
11	28918	69578	88231	33276	70997	79936	56865	05859	90106	31595	01547	85590	91610	78188
12	63553	40961	48235	03427	49626	69445	18663	72695	52180	20847	12234	90511	33703	90322
13	09429	93969	52636	92737	88974	33488	36320	17617	30015	08272	84115	27156	30613	74952
14	10365	61129	87529	85689	48237	52267	67689	93394	01511	26358	85104	20285	29975	89868
15	07119	97336	71048	08178	77233	13916	47564	81056	97735	85977	29372	74461	28551	90707
16	51085	12765	51821	51259	77452	16308	60756	92144	49442	53900	70960	63990	75601	40719
17	02368	21382	52404	60268	89368	19885	55322	44819	01188	65255	64835	44919	05944	55157
18	01011	54092	33362	94904	31273	04146	18594	29852	71585	85030	51132	01915	92747	64951
19	52162	53916	46369	58586	23216	14513	83149	98736	23495	64350	94738	17752	35156	35749
20	07056	97628	33787	09998	42698	06691	76988	13602	51851	46104	88916	19509	25625	58104
21	48663	91245	85828	14346	09172	30168	90229	04734	59193	22178	30421	61666	99904	32812
22	54164	58492	22421	74103	47070	25306	76468	26384	58151	06646	21524	15227	96909	44592
23	32639	32363	05597	24200	13363	38005	94342	28728	35806	06912	17012	64161	18296	22851
24	29334	27001	87637	87308	58731	00256	45834	15398	46557	41135	10367	07684	36188	18510
25	02488	33062	28834	07351	19731	92420	60952	61280	50001	67658	32586	86679	50720	94953

APPENDIX B.   Random digits (continued)

Line/Col.	(1)	(2)	(3)	(4)	(5)	(6)	(7)	(8)	(9)	(10)	(11)	(12)	(13)	(14)
26	81525	72295	04839	96423	24878	82651	66566	14778	76797	14780	13300	87074	79666	95725
27	29676	20591	68086	26432	46901	20849	89768	81536	86645	12659	92259	57102	80428	25280
28	00742	57392	39064	66432	84673	40027	32832	61362	98947	96067	64760	64584	96096	98253
29	05366	04213	25669	26422	44407	44048	37937	63904	45766	66134	75470	66520	34693	90449
30	91921	26418	64117	94305	26766	25940	39972	22209	71500	64568	91402	42416	07844	69618
31	00582	04711	87917	77341	42206	35126	74087	99547	81817	42607	43808	76655	62028	76630
32	00725	69884	62797	56170	86324	88072	76222	36086	84637	93161	76038	65855	77919	88006
33	69011	65795	95876	55293	18088	27354	26575	08625	40801	59920	29841	80150	12777	48501
34	25976	57948	29888	88604	67917	48708	18912	82271	65424	69774	33611	54262	85963	03547
35	09763	83473	73577	12908	30883	18317	28290	35797	05998	41688	34952	37888	38917	88050
36	91567	42595	27958	30134	04024	86385	29880	99730	55536	84855	29080	09250	79656	73211
37	17955	56349	90999	49127	20044	59931	06115	20542	18059	02008	73708	83517	36103	42791
38	46503	18584	18845	49618	02304	51038	20655	58727	28168	15475	56942	53389	20562	87338
39	92157	89634	94824	78171	84610	82834	09922	25417	44137	48413	25555	21246	35509	20468
40	14577	62765	35605	81263	39667	47358	56873	56307	61607	49518	89656	20103	77490	18062
41	98427	07523	33362	64270	01638	92477	66969	98420	04880	45585	46565	04102	46880	45709
42	34914	63976	88720	82765	34476	17032	87589	40836	32427	70002	70663	88803	77775	69348
43	70060	28277	39475	46473	23219	53416	94970	25832	69975	94884	19661	72828	00102	66794
44	53976	54914	06990	67245	68350	82948	11398	42878	80287	88267	47363	46634	06541	97809
45	76072	29515	40980	07391	58745	25774	22987	80059	39911	96189	41151	14222	60697	59583
46	90725	52210	83974	29992	65831	38857	50490	83765	55657	14361	31720	57375	56228	41546
47	64364	67412	33339	31926	14883	24413	59744	92351	97473	89286	35931	04110	23726	51900
48	08962	00358	31662	25388	61642	34072	81249	35648	56891	69352	48373	45578	78547	81788
49	95012	68379	93526	70765	10592	04542	76463	54328	02349	17247	28865	14777	62730	92277
50	15664	10493	20492	38391	91132	21999	59516	81652	27195	48223	46751	22923	32261	85653

51	16408	81899	04153	53381	79401	21438	83035	92350	36693	31238	59649	91754	72772	02338
52	18629	81953	05520	91962	04739	13092	97662	24822	94730	06496	35090	04822	86774	98289
53	73115	35101	47498	87637	99016	71060	88824	71013	18735	20286	23153	72924	35165	43040
54	57491	16703	23167	49323	45021	33132	12544	41035	80780	45393	44812	12515	98931	91202
55	30405	83946	23792	14422	15059	45799	22716	19792	09983	74353	68668	30429	70735	25499
56	16631	35006	85900	98275	32388	52390	16815	69298	82732	38480	73817	32523	41961	44437
57	96773	20206	42559	78985	05300	22164	24369	54224	35083	19687	11052	91491	60383	19746
58	38935	64202	14349	82674	66523	44133	00697	35552	35970	19124	63318	29686	03387	59846
59	31624	76384	17403	53363	44167	64486	64758	75366	76554	31601	12614	33072	60332	92325
60	78919	19474	23632	27889	47914	02584	37680	20801	72152	39339	34806	08930	85001	87820
61	03931	33309	57047	74211	63445	17361	62825	39908	05607	91284	68833	25570	38818	46920
62	74426	33278	43972	10119	89917	15665	52872	73823	73144	88662	88970	74492	51805	99378
63	09066	00903	20795	95452	92648	45454	09552	88815	16553	51125	79375	97596	16296	66092
64	42238	12426	87025	14267	20979	04508	64535	31355	86064	29472	47689	05974	52468	16834
65	16153	08002	26504	41744	81959	65642	74240	56302	00033	67107	77510	70625	28725	34191
66	21457	40742	29820	96783	29400	21840	15035	34537	33310	06116	95240	15957	16572	06004
67	21581	57802	02050	89728	17937	37621	47075	42080	97403	48626	68995	43805	33336	21597
68	55612	78095	83197	33732	05810	24813	86902	60397	16489	03264	88525	42786	05269	92532
69	44657	66999	99324	51281	84463	60563	79312	93454	68876	25471	93911	25650	12682	73572
70	91340	84979	46949	81973	37949	61023	43997	15263	80644	43942	89203	71795	99533	50501
71	91227	21199	31935	27022	84067	05462	35216	14436	29891	68607	41867	14951	91696	85065
72	50001	38140	66321	19924	72163	09538	12151	06878	91903	18749	34405	56087	82790	70925
73	65390	05224	72958	28609	81406	39147	25549	48542	42627	45233	57202	94617	23772	07896
74	27504	96131	83944	41575	10573	08619	64482	73923	36152	05184	94142	25299	84387	34925
75	37169	94851	39117	89632	00959	16487	65536	49071	39782	17095	02330	74301	00275	48280

APPENDIX B. Random digits (continued)

Line/Col.	(1)	(2)	(3)	(4)	(5)	(6)	(7)	(8)	(9)	(10)	(11)	(12)	(13)	(14)
76	11508	70225	51111	38351	19444	66499	71945	05422	13442	78675	84081	66938	93654	59894
77	37449	30362	06694	54690	04052	53115	62757	95348	78662	11163	81651	50245	34971	52924
78	46515	70331	85922	38329	57015	15765	97161	17869	45349	61796	66345	81073	49106	79860
79	30986	81223	42416	58353	21532	30502	32305	86482	05174	07901	54339	58861	74818	46942
80	63798	64995	46583	09785	44160	78128	83991	42865	92520	83531	80377	35909	81250	54238
81	82486	84846	99254	67632	43218	50076	21361	64816	51202	88124	41870	52689	51275	83556
82	21885	32906	92431	09060	64297	51674	64126	62570	26123	05155	59194	52799	28225	85762
83	60336	98782	07408	53458	13564	59089	26445	29789	85205	41001	12535	12133	14645	23541
84	43937	46891	24010	25560	86355	33941	25786	54990	71899	15475	95434	98227	21824	19585
85	97656	63175	89303	16275	07100	92063	21942	18611	47348	20203	18534	03862	78095	50136
86	03299	01221	05418	38982	55758	92237	26759	86367	21216	98442	08303	56613	91511	75928
87	79626	06486	03574	17668	07785	76020	79924	25651	83325	88428	85076	72811	22717	50585
88	85636	68335	47539	03129	65651	11977	02510	26113	99447	68645	34327	15152	55230	93448
89	18039	14367	61337	06177	12143	46609	32989	74014	64708	00533	35398	58408	13261	47908
90	08362	15656	60627	36478	65648	16764	53412	09013	07832	41574	17639	82163	60859	75567
91	79556	29068	04142	16268	15387	12856	66227	38358	22478	73373	88732	09443	82558	05250
92	92608	82674	27072	32534	17075	27698	98204	63863	11951	34648	88022	56148	34925	57031
93	23982	25835	40055	67006	12293	02753	14827	23235	35071	99704	37543	11601	35503	85171
94	09915	96306	05908	97901	28395	14186	00821	80703	70426	75647	76310	88717	37890	40129
95	59037	33300	26695	62247	69927	76123	50842	43834	86654	70959	79725	93872	28117	19233
96	42488	78077	69882	61657	34136	79180	97526	43092	04098	73571	80799	76536	71255	64239
97	46764	86273	63003	93017	31204	36692	40202	35275	57306	55543	53203	18098	47625	88684
98	03237	45430	55417	63282	90816	17349	88298	90183	36600	78406	06216	95787	42579	90730
99	86591	81482	52667	61582	14972	90053	89534	76036	49199	43716	97548	04379	46370	28672
100	38534	01715	94964	87288	65680	43772	39560	12918	86537	62738	19636	51132	25739	56947

Abridged from *Handbook of Tables for Probability and Statistics*, Second Edition, edited by William H. Beyer (Cleveland: The Chemical Rubber Company, 1968.) Copyright The Chemical Rubber Co., CRC Press, Inc. Reprinted with permission.

APPENDIX C. Areas under the normal curve

Fractional parts of the total area (10,000) under the normal curve, corresponding to distances between the mean and ordinates which are Z standard-deviation units from the mean.

Z	.00	.01	.02	.03	.04	.05	.06	.07	.08	.09
0.0	0000	0040	0080	0120	0159	0199	0239	0279	0319	0359
0.1	0398	0438	0478	0517	0557	0596	0636	0675	0714	0753
0.2	0793	0832	0871	0910	0948	0987	1026	1064	1103	1141
0.3	1179	1217	1255	1293	1331	1368	1406	1443	1480	1517
0.4	1554	1591	1628	1664	1700	1736	1772	1808	1844	1879
0.5	1915	1950	1985	2019	2054	2088	2123	2157	2190	2224
0.6	2257	2291	2324	2357	2389	2422	2454	2486	2518	2549
0.7	2580	2612	2642	2673	2704	2734	2764	2794	2823	2852
0.8	2881	2910	2939	2967	2995	3023	3051	3078	3106	3133
0.9	3159	3186	3212	3238	3264	3289	3315	3340	3365	3389
1.0	3413	3438	3461	3485	3508	3531	3554	3577	3599	3621
1.1	3643	3665	3686	3718	3729	3749	3770	3790	3810	3830
1.2	3849	3869	3888	3907	3925	3944	3962	3980	3997	4015
1.3	4032	4049	4066	4083	4099	4115	4131	4147	4162	4177
1.4	4192	4207	4222	4236	4251	4265	4279	4292	4306	4319
1.5	4332	4345	4357	4370	4382	4394	4406	4418	4430	4441
1.6	4452	4463	4474	4485	4495	4505	4515	4525	4535	4545
1.7	4554	4564	4573	4582	4591	4599	4608	4616	4625	4633
1.8	4641	4649	4656	4664	4671	4678	4686	4693	4699	4706
1.9	4713	4719	4726	4732	4738	4744	4750	4758	4762	4767
2.0	4773	4778	4783	4788	4793	4798	4803	4808	4812	4817
2.1	4821	4826	4830	4834	4838	4842	4846	4850	4854	4857
2.2	4861	4865	4868	4871	4875	4878	4881	4884	4887	4890
2.3	4893	4896	4898	4901	4904	4906	4909	4911	4913	4916
2.4	4918	4920	4922	4925	4927	4929	4931	4932	4934	4936
2.5	4938	4940	4941	4943	4945	4946	4948	4949	4951	4952
2.6	4953	4955	4956	4957	4959	4960	4961	4962	4963	4964
2.7	4965	4966	4967	4968	4969	4970	4971	4972	4973	4974
2.8	4974	4975	4976	4977	4977	4978	4979	4980	4980	4981
2.9	4981	4982	4983	4984	4984	4984	4985	4985	4986	4986
3.0	4986.5	4987	4987	4988	4988	4988	4989	4989	4989	4990
3.1	4990.0	4991	4991	4991	4992	4992	4992	4992	4993	4994
3.2	4993.129									
3.3	4995.166									
3.4	4996.631									
3.5	4997.674									

SOURCE: Harold O. Rugg, *Statistical Methods Applied to Education* (Boston: Houghton Mifflin, 1917), appendix table III, pp. 389–390. Reprinted with the kind permission of the publisher.

APPENDIX C.   Areas under the normal curve (*continued*)

Z	.00	.01	.02	.03	.04	.05	.06	.07	.08	.09
3.6	4998.409									
3.7	4998.922									
3.8	4999.277									
3.9	4999.519									
4.0	4999.683									
4.5	499.966									
5.0	4999.997133									

APPENDIX D.   Distribution of *t*

df	Level of significance for one-tailed test					
	.10	.05	.025	.01	.005	.0005
	Level of significance for two-tailed test					
	.20	.10	.05	.02	.01	.001
1	3.078	6.314	12.706	31.821	63.657	636.619
2	1.886	2.920	4.303	6.965	9.925	31.598
3	1.638	2.353	3.182	4.541	5.841	12.941
4	1.533	2.132	2.776	3.747	4.604	8.610
5	1.476	2.015	2.571	3.365	4.032	6.859
6	1.440	1.943	2.447	3.143	3.707	5.959
7	1.415	1.895	2.365	2.998	3.499	5.405
8	1.397	1.860	2.306	2.896	3.355	5.041
9	1.383	1.833	2.262	2.821	3.250	4.781
10	1.372	1.812	2.228	2.764	3.169	4.587
11	1.363	1.796	2.201	2.718	3.106	4.437
12	1.356	1.782	2.179	2.681	3.055	4.318
13	1.350	1.771	2.160	2.650	3.012	4.221
14	1.345	1.761	2.145	2.624	2.977	4.140
15	1.341	1.753	2.131	2.602	2.947	4.073
16	1.337	1.746	2.120	2.583	2.921	4.015
17	1.333	1.740	2.110	2.567	2.898	3.965
18	1.330	1.734	2.101	2.552	2.878	3.922
19	1.328	1.729	2.093	2.539	2.861	3.883
20	1.325	1.725	2.086	2.528	2.845	3.850
21	1.323	1.721	2.080	2.518	2.831	3.819
22	1.321	1.717	2.074	2.508	2.819	3.792
23	1.319	1.714	2.069	2.500	2.807	3.767
24	1.318	1.711	2.064	2.492	2.797	3.745
25	1.316	1.708	2.060	2.485	2.787	3.725
26	1.315	1.706	2.056	2.479	2.779	3.707
27	1.314	1.703	2.052	2.473	2.771	3.690
28	1.313	1.701	2.048	2.467	2.763	3.674
29	1.311	1.699	2.045	2.462	2.756	3.659
30	1.310	1.697	2.042	2.457	2.750	3.646
40	1.303	1.684	2.021	2.423	2.704	3.551
60	1.296	1.671	2.000	2.390	2.660	3.460
120	1.289	1.658	1.980	2.358	2.617	3.373
∞	1.282	1.645	1.960	2.326	2.576	3.291

SOURCE: Appendix D is abridged from Table III of R. A. Fisher and F. Yates, *Statistical Tables for Biological, Agricultural and Medical Research* published by Longman Group Ltd. London (1974) 6th edition (previously published by Oliver & Boyd Ltd. Edinburgh) and by permission of authors and publishers.

APPENDIX E. Values of z for given values of r

r	.000	.001	.002	.003	.004	.005	.006	.007	.008	.009
.000	.0000	.0010	.0020	.0030	.0040	.0050	.0060	.0070	.0080	.0090
.010	.0100	.0110	.0120	.0130	.0140	.0150	.0160	.0170	.0180	.0190
.020	.0200	.0210	.0220	.0230	.0240	.0250	.0260	.0270	.0280	.0290
.030	.0300	.0310	.0320	.0330	.0340	.0350	.0360	.0370	.0380	.0390
.040	.0400	.0410	.0420	.0430	.0440	.0450	.0460	.0470	.0480	.0490
.050	.0501	.0511	.0521	.0531	.0541	.0551	.0561	.0571	.0581	.0591
.060	.0601	.0611	.0621	.0631	.0641	.0651	.0661	.0671	.0681	.0691
.070	.0701	.0711	.0721	.0731	.0741	.0751	.0761	.0771	.0782	.0792
.080	.0802	.0812	.0822	.0832	.0842	.0852	.0862	.0872	.0882	.0892
.090	.0902	.0912	.0922	.0933	.0943	.0953	.0963	.0973	.0983	.0993
.100	.1003	.1013	.1024	.1034	.1044	.1054	.1064	.1074	.1084	.1094
.110	.1105	.1115	.1125	.1135	.1145	.1155	.1165	.1175	.1185	.1195
.120	.1206	.1216	.1226	.1236	.1246	.1257	.1267	.1277	.1287	.1297
.130	.1308	.1318	.1328	.1338	.1348	.1358	.1368	.1379	.1389	.1399
.140	.1409	.1419	.1430	.1440	.1450	.1460	.1470	.1481	.1491	.1501
.150	.1511	.1522	.1532	.1542	.1552	.1563	.1573	.1583	.1593	.1604
.160	.1614	.1624	.1634	.1644	.1655	.1665	.1676	.1686	.1696	.1706
.170	.1717	.1727	.1737	.1748	.1758	.1768	.1779	.1789	.1799	.1810
.180	.1820	.1830	.1841	.1851	.1861	.1872	.1882	.1892	.1903	.1913
.190	.1923	.1934	.1944	.1954	.1965	.1975	.1986	.1996	.2007	.2017
.200	.2027	.2038	.2048	.2059	.2069	.2079	.2090	.2100	.2111	.2121
.210	.2132	.2142	.2153	.2163	.2174	.2184	.2194	.2205	.2215	.2226
.220	.2237	.2247	.2258	.2268	.2279	.2289	.2300	.2310	.2321	.2331
.230	.2342	.2353	.2363	.2374	.2384	.2395	.2405	.2416	.2427	.2437
.240	.2448	.2458	.2469	.2480	.2490	.2501	.2511	.2522	.2533	.2543
.250	.2554	2565	.2575	.2586	.2597	.2608	.2618	.2629	.2640	.2650
.260	.2661	.2672	.2682	.2693	.2704	.2715	.2726	.2736	.2747	.2758
.270	.2769	.2779	.2790	.2801	.2812	.2823	.2833	.2844	.2855	.2866
.280	.2877	.2888	.2898	.2909	.2920	.2931	.2942	.2953	.2964	.2975
.290	.2986	.2997	.3008	.3019	.3029	.3040	.3051	.3062	.3073	.3084
.300	.3095	.3106	.3117	.3128	.3139	.3150	.3161	.3172	.3183	.3195
.310	.3206	.3217	.3228	.3239	.3250	.3261	.3272	.3283	.3294	.3305
.320	.3317	.3328	.3339	.3350	.3361	.3372	.3384	.3395	.3406	.3417
.330	.3428	.3439	.3451	.3462	.3473	.3484	.3496	.3507	.3518	.3530
.340	.3541	.3552	.3564	.3575	.3586	.3597	.3609	.3620	.3632	.3643
.350	.3654	.3666	.3677	.3689	.3700	.3712	.3723	.3734	.3746	.3757
.360	.3769	.3780	.3792	.3803	.3815	.3826	.3838	.3850	.3861	.3873
.370	.3884	.3896	.3907	.3919	.3931	.3942	.3954	.3966	.3977	.3989
.380	.4001	.4012	.4024	.4036	.4047	.4059	.4071	.4083	.4094	.4106
.390	.4118	.4130	.4142	.4153	.4165	.4177	.4189	.4201	.4213	.4225

SOURCE: From *Statistical Tables and Problems* by Albert E. Waugh, table A11, pp. 40–41. Copyright 1952 by McGraw-Hill Book Company. Used with permission of McGraw-Hill Book Company.

APPENDIX E. Values of z for given values of r *(continued)*

r	.000	.001	.002	.003	.004	.005	.006	.007	.008	.009
.400	.4236	.4248	.4260	.4272	.4284	.4296	.4308	.4320	.4332	.4344
.410	.4356	.4368	.4380	.4392	.4404	.4416	.4429	.4441	.4453	.4465
.420	.4477	.4489	.4501	.4513	.4526	.4538	.4550	.4562	.4574	.4587
.430	.4599	.4611	.4623	.4636	.4648	.4660	.4673	.4685	.4697	.4710
.440	.4722	.4735	.4747	.4760	.4772	.4784	.4797	.4809	.4822	.4835
.450	.4847	.4860	.4872	.4885	.4897	.4910	.4923	.4935	.4948	.4961
.460	.4973	.4986	.4999	.5011	.5024	.5037	.5049	.5062	.5075	.5088
.470	.5101	.5114	.5126	.5139	.5152	.5165	.5178	.5191	.5204	.5217
.480	.5230	.5243	.5256	.5279	.5282	.5295	.5308	.5321	.5334	.5347
.490	.5361	.5374	.5387	.5400	.5413	.5427	.5440	.5453	.5466	.5480
.500	.5493	.5506	.5520	.5533	.5547	.5560	.5573	.5587	.5600	.5614
.510	.5627	.5641	.5654	.5668	.5681	.5695	.5709	.5722	.5736	.5750
.520	.5763	.5777	.5791	.5805	.5818	.5832	.5846	.5860	.5874	.5888
.530	.5901	.5915	.5929	.5943	.5957	.5971	.5985	.5999	.6013	.6027
.540	.6042	.6056	.6070	.6084	.6098	.6112	.6127	.6141	.6155	.6170
.550	.6184	.6198	.6213	.6227	.6241	.6256	.6270	.6285	.6299	.6314
.560	.6328	.6343	.6358	.6372	.6387	.6401	.6416	.6431	.6446	.6460
.570	.6475	.6490	.6505	.6520	.6535	.6550	.6565	.6579	.6594	.6610
.580	.6625	.6640	.6655	.6670	.6685	.6700	.6715	.6731	.6746	.6761
.590	.6777	.6792	.6807	.6823	.6838	.6854	.6869	.6885	.6900	.6916
.600	.6931	.6947	.6963	.6978	.6994	.7010	.7026	.7042	.7057	.7073
.610	.7089	.7105	.7121	.7137	.7153	.7169	.7185	.7201	.7218	.7234
.620	.7250	.7266	.7283	.7299	.7315	.7332	.7348	.7364	.7381	.7398
.630	.7414	.7431	.7447	.7464	.7481	.7497	.7514	.7531	.7548	.7565
.640	.7582	.7599	.7616	.7633	.7650	.7667	.7684	.7701	.7718	.7736
.650	.7753	.7770	.7788	.7805	.7823	.7840	.7858	.7875	.7893	.7910
.660	.7928	.7946	.7964	.7981	.7999	.8017	.8035	.8053	.8071	.8089
.670	.8107	.8126	.8144	.8162	.8180	.8199	.8217	.8236	.8254	.8273
.680	.8291	.8310	.8328	.8347	.8366	.8385	.8404	.8423	.8442	.8461
.690	.8480	.8499	.8518	.8537	.8556	.8576	.8595	.8614	.8634	.8653
.700	.8673	.8693	.8712	.8732	.8752	.8772	.8792	.8812	.8832	.8852
.710	.8872	.8892	.8912	.8933	.8953	.8973	.8994	.9014	.9035	.9056
.720	.9076	.9097	.9118	.9139	.9160	.9181	.9202	.9223	.9245	.9266
.730	.9287	.9309	.9330	.9352	.9373	.9395	.9417	.9439	.9461	.9483
.740	.9505	.9527	.9549	.9571	.9594	.9616	.9639	.9661	.9684	.9707
.750	.9730	.9752	.9775	.9799	.9822	.9845	.9868	.9892	.9915	.9939
.760	.9962	.9986	1.0010	1.0034	1.0058	1.0082	1.0106	1.0130	1.0154	1.0179
.770	1.0203	1.0228	1.0253	1.0277	1.0302	1.0327	1.0352	1.0378	1.0403	1.0428
.780	1.0454	1.0479	1.0505	1.0531	1.0557	1.0583	1.0609	1.0635	1.0661	1.0688
.790	1.0714	1.0741	1.0768	1.0795	1.0822	1.0849	1.0876	1.0903	1.0931	1.0958

APPENDIX E. Values of z for given values of r (continued)

r	.000	.001	.002	.003	.004	.005	.006	.007	.008	.009
.800	1.986	1.1014	1.1041	1.1070	1.1098	1.1127	1.1155	1.1184	1.1212	1.1241
.810	1.1270	1.1299	1.1329	1.1358	1.1388	1.1417	1.1447	1.1477	1.1507	1.1538
.820	1.1568	1.1599	1.1630	1.1660	1.1692	1.1723	1.1754	1.1786	1.1817	1.1849
.830	1.1870	1.1913	1.1946	1.1979	1.2011	1.2044	1.2077	1.2111	1.2144	1.2178
.840	1.2212	1.2246	1.2280	1.2315	1.2349	1.2384	1.2419	1.2454	1.2490	1.2526
.850	1.2561	1.2598	1.2634	1.2670	1.2708	1.2744	1.2782	1.2819	1.2857	1.2895
.860	1.2934	1.2972	1.3011	1.3050	1.3089	1.3129	1.3168	1.3209	1.3249	1.3290
.870	1.3331	1.3372	1.3414	1.3456	1.3498	1.3540	1.3583	1.3626	1.3670	1.3714
.880	1.3758	1.3802	1.3847	1.3892	1.3938	1.3984	1.4030	1.4077	1.4124	1.4171
.890	1.4219	1.4268	1.4316	1.4366	1.4415	1.4465	1.4516	1.4566	1.4618	1.4670
.900	1.4722	1.4775	1.4828	1.4883	1.4937	1.4992	1.5047	1.5103	1.5160	1.5217
.910	1.5275	1.5334	1.5393	1.5453	1.5513	1.5574	1.5636	1.5698	1.5762	1.5825
.920	1.5890	1.5956	1.6022	1.6089	1.6157	1.6226	1.6296	1.6366	1.6438	1.6510
.930	1.6584	1.6659	1.6734	1.6811	1.6888	1.6967	1.7047	1.7129	1.7211	1.7295
.940	1.7380	1.7467	1.7555	1.7645	1.7736	1.7828	1.7923	1.8019	1.8117	1.8216
.950	1.8318	1.8421	1.8527	1.8635	1.8745	1.8857	1.8972	1.9090	1.9210	1.9333
.960	1.9459	1.9588	1.9721	1.9857	1.9996	2.0140	2.0287	2.0439	2.0595	2.0756
.970	2.0923	2.1095	2.1273	2.1457	2.1649	2.1847	2.2054	2.2269	2.2494	2.2729
.980	2.2976	2.3223	2.3507	2.3796	2.4101	2.4426	2.4774	2.5147	2.5550	2.5988
.990	2.6467	2.6996	2.7587	2.8257	2.9031	2.9945	3.1063	3.2504	3.4534	3.8002

r	z
.9999	4.95172
.99999	6.10303

APPENDIX F. Table of critical values of *U* in the Mann-Whitney test

Critical values of U at $\alpha = .001$ with direction predicted or at $\alpha = .002$ with direction not predicted

N_1 \ N_2	9	10	11	12	13	14	15	16	17	18	19	20
1												
2												
3									0	0	0	0
4		0	0	0	1	1	1	2	2	3	3	3
5	1	1	2	2	3	3	4	5	5	6	7	7
6	2	3	4	4	5	6	7	8	9	10	11	12
7	3	5	6	7	8	9	10	11	13	14	15	16
8	5	6	8	9	11	12	14	15	17	18	20	21
9	7	8	10	12	14	15	17	19	21	23	25	26
10	8	10	12	14	17	19	21	23	25	27	29	32
11	10	12	15	17	20	22	24	27	29	32	34	37
12	12	14	17	20	23	25	28	31	34	37	40	42
13	14	17	20	23	26	29	32	35	38	42	45	48
14	15	19	22	25	29	32	36	39	43	46	50	54
15	17	21	24	28	32	36	40	43	47	51	55	59
16	19	23	27	31	35	39	43	48	52	56	60	65
17	21	25	29	34	38	43	47	52	57	61	66	70
18	23	27	32	37	42	46	51	56	61	66	71	76
19	25	29	34	40	45	50	55	60	66	71	77	82
20	26	32	37	42	48	54	59	65	70	76	82	88

SOURCE: D. Auble, "Extended Tables for the Mann-Whitney Statistic," *Bulletin of the Institute of Educational Research at Indiana University*, vol. 1, no. 2, Tables 1, 3, 5 and 7, 1953, with the kind permission of the publisher; as adapted in S. Siegel, *Non-parametric Statistics*, New York: McGraw-Hill, 1956, table K.

APPENDIX F.   Table of critical values of *U* in the Mann-Whitney test (*continued*)

Critical values of *U* at $\alpha = .01$ with direction predicted or at $\alpha = .02$ with direction not predicted

N_1 \ N_2	9	10	11	12	13	14	15	16	17	18	19	20
1												
2					0	0	0	0	0	0	1	1
3	1	1	1	2	2	2	3	3	4	4	4	5
4	3	3	4	5	5	6	7	7	8	9	9	10
5	5	6	7	8	9	10	11	12	13	14	15	16
6	7	8	9	11	12	13	15	16	18	19	20	22
7	9	11	12	14	16	17	19	21	23	24	26	28
8	11	13	15	17	20	22	24	26	28	30	32	34
9	14	16	18	21	23	26	28	31	33	36	38	40
10	16	19	22	24	27	30	33	36	38	41	44	47
11	18	22	25	28	31	34	37	41	44	47	50	53
12	21	24	28	31	35	38	42	46	49	53	56	60
13	23	27	31	35	39	43	47	51	55	59	63	67
14	26	30	34	38	43	47	51	56	60	65	69	73
15	28	33	37	42	47	51	56	61	66	71	76	82
16	31	36	41	46	51	56	61	66	71	76	82	87
17	33	38	44	49	55	60	66	71	77	82	88	93
18	36	41	47	53	59	65	70	76	82	88	94	100
19	38	44	50	56	63	69	75	82	88	94	101	107
20	40	47	53	60	67	73	80	87	93	100	107	114

Critical values of *U* at $\alpha = .025$ with direction predicted or at $\alpha = .05$ with direction not predicted

N_1 \ N_2	9	10	11	12	13	14	15	16	17	18	19	20
1												
2	0	0	0	1	1	1	1	1	2	2	2	2
3	2	3	3	4	4	5	5	6	6	7	7	8
4	4	5	6	7	8	9	10	11	11	12	13	13
5	7	8	9	11	12	13	14	15	17	18	19	20
6	10	11	13	14	16	17	19	21	22	24	25	27
7	12	14	16	18	20	22	24	26	28	30	32	34
8	15	17	19	22	24	26	29	31	34	36	38	41
9	17	20	23	26	28	31	34	37	39	42	45	48
10	20	23	26	29	33	36	39	42	45	48	52	55
11	23	26	30	33	37	40	44	47	51	55	58	62
12	26	29	33	37	41	45	49	53	57	61	65	69
13	28	33	37	41	45	50	54	59	63	67	72	76
14	31	36	40	45	50	55	59	64	67	74	78	83
15	34	39	44	49	54	59	64	70	75	80	85	90
16	37	42	47	53	59	64	70	75	81	86	92	98
17	39	45	51	57	63	67	75	81	87	93	99	105
18	42	48	55	61	67	74	80	86	93	99	106	112
19	45	52	58	65	72	78	85	92	99	106	113	119
20	48	55	62	69	76	83	90	90	105	112	119	127

APPENDIX F.   Table of critical values of *U* in the Mann-Whitney test (*continued*)

Critical values of U at $\alpha = .05$ with direction predicted or at $\alpha = .10$ with direction not predicted

N_1 \ N_2	9	10	11	12	13	14	15	16	17	18	19	20
1											0	0
2	1	1	1	2	2	2	3	3	3	4	4	4
3	3	4	5	5	6	7	7	8	9	9	10	11
4	6	7	8	9	10	11	12	14	15	16	17	18
5	9	11	12	13	15	16	18	19	20	22	23	25
6	12	14	16	17	19	21	23	25	26	28	30	32
7	15	17	19	21	24	26	28	30	33	35	37	39
8	18	20	23	26	28	31	33	36	39	41	44	47
9	21	24	27	30	33	36	39	42	45	48	51	54
10	24	27	31	34	37	41	44	48	51	55	58	62
11	27	31	34	38	42	46	50	54	57	61	65	69
12	30	34	38	42	47	51	55	60	64	68	72	77
13	33	37	42	47	51	56	61	65	70	75	80	84
14	36	41	46	51	56	61	66	71	77	82	87	92
15	39	44	50	55	61	66	72	77	83	88	94	100
16	42	48	54	60	65	71	77	83	89	95	101	107
17	45	51	57	64	70	77	83	89	96	102	109	115
18	48	55	61	68	75	82	88	95	102	109	116	123
19	51	58	65	72	80	87	94	101	109	116	123	130
20	54	62	69	77	84	92	100	107	115	123	130	138

APPENDIX G.   Distribution of χ^2

Probability

df	.99	.98	.95	.90	.80	.70	.50	.30	.20	.10	.05	.02	.01	.001
1	$.0^3157$	$.0^3628$	.00393	.0158	.0642	.148	.455	1.074	1.642	2.706	3.841	5.412	6.635	10.827
2	.0201	.0404	.103	.211	.446	.713	1.386	2.408	3.219	4.605	5.991	7.824	9.210	13.815
3	.115	.185	.352	.584	1.005	1.424	2.366	3.665	4.642	6.251	7.815	9.837	11.341	16.268
4	.297	.429	.711	1.064	1.649	2.195	3.357	4.878	5.989	7.779	9.488	11.668	13.277	18.465
5	.554	.752	1.145	1.610	2.343	3.000	4.351	6.064	7.289	9.236	11.070	13.388	15.086	20.617
6	.872	1.134	1.635	2.204	3.070	3.828	5.348	7.231	8.558	10.645	12.592	15.033	16.812	22.457
7	1.239	1.564	2.167	2.833	3.822	4.671	6.346	8.383	9.803	12.017	14.067	16.622	18.475	24.322
8	1.646	2.032	2.733	3.490	4.594	5.527	7.344	9.524	11.030	13.362	15.507	18.168	20.090	26.125
9	2.088	2.532	3.325	4.168	5.380	6.393	8.343	10.656	12.242	14.684	16.919	19.679	21.666	27.877
10	2.558	3.059	3.940	4.865	6.179	7.267	9.342	11.781	13.442	15.987	18.307	21.161	23.209	29.588
11	3.053	3.609	4.575	5.578	6.989	8.148	10.341	12.899	14.631	17.275	19.675	22.618	24.725	31.264
12	3.571	4.178	5.226	6.304	7.807	9.034	11.340	14.011	15.812	18.549	21.026	24.054	26.217	32.909
13	4.107	4.765	5.892	7.042	8.634	9.926	12.340	15.119	16.985	19.812	22.362	25.472	27.688	34.528
14	4.660	5.368	6.571	7.790	9.467	10.821	13.339	16.222	18.151	21.064	23.685	26.873	29.141	36.123
15	5.229	5.985	7.261	8.547	10.307	11.721	14.339	17.322	19.311	22.307	24.996	28.259	30.578	37.697

df														
16	5.812	6.614	7.962	9.312	11.152	12.624	15.338	18.418	20.465	23.542	26.296	29.633	32.000	39.252
17	6.408	7.255	8.672	10.085	12.002	13.531	16.338	19.511	21.615	24.769	27.587	30.995	33.409	40.790
18	7.015	7.906	9.390	10.865	12.857	14.440	17.338	20.601	22.760	25.989	28.869	32.346	34.805	42.312
19	7.633	8.567	10.117	11.651	13.716	15.352	18.338	21.689	23.900	27.204	30.144	33.687	36.191	43.820
20	8.260	9.237	10.851	12.443	14.578	16.266	19.337	22.775	25.038	28.412	31.410	35.020	37.566	45.315
21	8.897	9.915	11.591	13.240	15.445	17.182	20.337	23.858	26.171	29.615	32.671	36.343	38.932	46.797
22	9.542	10.600	12.338	14.041	16.314	18.101	21.337	24.939	27.301	30.813	33.924	37.659	40.289	48.268
23	10.196	11.293	13.091	14.848	17.187	19.021	22.337	26.018	28.429	32.007	35.172	38.968	41.638	49.728
24	10.856	11.992	13.848	15.659	18.062	19.943	23.337	27.096	29.553	33.196	36.415	40.270	42.980	51.179
25	11.524	12.697	14.611	16.473	18.940	20.867	24.337	28.172	30.675	34.382	37.652	41.566	44.314	52.620
26	12.198	13.409	15.379	17.292	19.820	21.792	25.336	29.246	31.795	35.563	38.885	42.856	45.642	54.052
27	12.879	14.125	16.151	18.114	20.703	22.719	26.336	30.319	32.912	36.741	40.113	44.140	46.963	55.476
28	13.565	14.847	16.928	18.939	21.588	23.647	27.336	31.391	34.027	37.916	41.337	45.419	48.278	56.893
29	14.256	15.574	17.708	19.768	22.475	24.577	28.336	32.461	35.139	39.087	42.557	46.693	49.588	58.302
30	14.953	16.306	18.493	20.599	23.364	25.508	29.336	33.530	36.250	40.256	43.773	47.962	50.892	59.703

For larger values of df, the expression $\sqrt{2\chi^2} - \sqrt{2df - 1}$ may be used as a normal deviate with unit variance, remembering that the probability for χ^2 corresponds with that of a single tail of the normal curve.

SOURCE: Appendix G is reprinted from Table IV of R. A. Fisher and F. Yates, *Statistical Tables for Biological, Agricultural and Medical Research*, published by Longman Group Ltd. London (1974) 6th edition (previously published by Oliver & Boyd Ltd. Edinburgh) and by permission of the authors and publishers.

APPENDIX H. An Introduction to SPSS

prepared by Claire L. Felbinger

Introduction

This appendix is designed to assist students in preparing and executing computerized data analysis using one of the most widely available and used software packages: the Statistical Package for the Social Sciences (SPSS).[1] SPSS, designed especially for the analysis of social science data, contains most of the common routines employed by social scientists. Indeed, almost all the data analysis procedures described in this text can be executed by SPSS subprograms. Of particular interest to social scientists is the program's capacity to easily handle the reccuring needs of data analysis. For instance, SPSS enables the researcher to recode variables, to deal with missing values, to sample, weight, and select cases, and to compute new variables and effect permanent or temporary transformations.

This treatment is intended to supply the novice analyst with the tools necessary to set up an SPSS file and execute basic types of analysis. It is not by any means an exhaustive display of either the variety of subprograms available or the intricacies of the more highly powered types of analysis possible within SPSS. Rather, the examples used are intended to parallel the work covered in the text. Students are encouraged to refer to the SPSS manual for information on other available subprograms and for a more detailed explanation of the ones covered in this appendix.

The data set used in the examples is a subset of Sidney Verba and Norman Nie's *Political Participation in America*.[2] A sample codebook containing the variables used is found at the end of this appendix. We will use these data to build a permanent SPSS file, clean the data, and execute statistical procedures in much the same way as if we were actually involved in a research project. Hence, we will assume that the data are prepared (as in Chapter 11) in machine readable form, clean

1. Norman H. Nie, C. Hadali Hull, Jean G. Jenkins, Karin Steinbrenner, and Dale Brent, *Statistical Package for the Social Sciences*, 2nd ed. (New York: McGraw-Hill, 1975).

2. Sidney Verba, Norman Nie, Principal Investigators, *Political Participation in America* (ICPSR Study Number 7015) (Ann Arbor, Mi: Inter-University Consortium for Political and Social Research, 1976). An extensive discussion of the use of these data in the analysis of citizen participation can be found in Verba, Sidney, and Nie, *Participation in America: Political Democracy and Social Equality*. (New York: Harper & Row, 1972).

the data by using univariate distributions (Chapter 12), perform bivariate (Chapter 13) and multivariate (Chapter 16) analysis with hypothesis testing (Chapter 17), and construct scales (Chapter 15).

Preparing The Data

We have prepared the data as discussed in Chapter 11. In particular, we have assembled a data set that contains 2,549 cases having 1 card (deck) per case. All the decks associated with each case are together and in order (i.e., Case 1—Deck 1; Case 1—Deck 2, . . . , Case N—Deck 0). To access SPSS at your particular research facility, it is necessary to supply additional cards known as Job Control Language (JCL) cards. These cards are unique to your facility. They grant access to the computer, initiate accounting procedures, assign tape or disk space, access the SPSS software, and perform other functions. Although the SPSS manual supplies some general JCL information,[3] it is advisable that you contact consultants at your facility as to the proper JCL, because site requirements vary from one facility to another.

Setting Up An SPSS File

The language of SPSS is logical and quite simple. You will find a consistency in the language and patterns employed that match your expectations. You will call for a task to be done (control) and alert the system as to how you want it accomplished (specification). The first fifteen columns of a punchcard (the control field) are set aside for commands, while columns sixteen to eighty (the specification field) allow you to determine how the transformation or analysis will be carried out. If your specification takes up more than the sixty-four columns between sixteen and eighty, you may continue on the next card, provided you *do not* break within a word or logical connector, and that you begin the continuation in column sixteen. Remember, a computer cannot read English and interpret your needs; it only reacts to signals (characters) for which it has been programmed. Therefore, be careful to punch commands, variable names, and the like exactly as designated.

The first step is to set up and save a file containing not only our data, but also information concerning the type of information contained, where it is located, and what you plan to call it. Following is a list of control cards in the order of their inclusion in the program. Table 1 summarizes these control cards and their structure.

---

3. See Nie et al., *Statistical Package for the Social Sciences*, pp. 585–630.

TABLE 1. Format Specifications for SPSS File Data-Definition Cards[a]

Control Field (Begin Column 1)	Specification Field (Begin Column 16)
[b]RUN NAME	RUN title of up to 64 characters
[c]FILE NAME [GET FILE]	Alphanumeric label of up to 8 characters [FILE NAME]
VARIABLE LIST	VARIABLE NAME, VARIABLE NAME (each of up to 8 characters)
N OF CASES	Number of Cases or UNKNOWN
INPUT MEDIUM	DISK or CARD or TAPE must be specified
INPUT FORMAT	FIXED (Format list)[d]
[b]VAR LABELS	VARNAME, $label_1$/ $VARNAME_2$, $label_2$ . . . (labels have a 40 character maximum)
[b]VALUE LABELS	VARNAME or $list_1$ ($value_1$) $label_1$ ($value_2$) $label_2$. . . / VARNAME or $list_2$ . . . / . . . .
[b]MISSING VALUES	$VARNAME_1$ (value $list_1$) $VARNAME_2$ (value $list_2$) . .
READ INPUT DATA	No specification
(FIRST PROCEDURE	INSERTED HERE)
SAVE FILE	No specification required
FINISH	

[a] See below for a sample setup runstream using the Verba-Nie data.
[b] Optional control cards.
[c] Substituted for FILE NAME on subsequent runs.
[d] See below for discussion of format list.

A Discussion and Explanation of Table 1.

1. RUN NAME—This control allows you to label your run. The label is printed across the top of each page of SPSS output.
2. FILE NAME—This control names and labels your file. On subsequent runs, you will access your particular SPSS file by substituting a GET FILE card for the FILE NAME card.

3. VARIABLE LIST—This card names the variables in the order defined on the subsequent INPUT FORMAT card. When naming variables by number (e.g., V1, V2, . . . VN), you may assign names "V1 TO VN" on the specification field.

4. N OF CASES—This control specifies the number of different cases included in your data file. If tape or disk is the INPUT MEDIUM, the specification UNKNOWN may be used. However, when input is in the form of cards or when a subfile structure is used,[4] the exact number of cases must be specified.

5. INPUT MEDIUM—This control alerts the system as to the form of the readable input data. You must state the device (CARD, DISK, TAPE) on which your data are stored and provide the appropriate JCL to access any noncard data.

6. INPUT FORMAT—This control states the organization of your cases, the type and location of your variables on the INPUT MEDIUM. (Formatting procedures will be discussed in the next section.)

[The following three control cards are optional.]

7. VAR LABELS—This optional control allows you to further describe your variable. It augments your VARIABLE LIST. This option is quite handy if you choose to assign V-numbers as variable names.

8. VALUE LABELS—This control allows you to associate a label with each value of a variable. For example, if the coded values 1, 2, 3 stand for the terms low, medium, and high respectively, then when that particular variable is used in a procedure, its coded value will have its associated label next to it on the printed output.

9. MISSING VALUES—This control defines which values for variables are designated as missing. There exists a RECODE facility to designate blanks as missing.[5] The ability to declare MISSING VALUES enables the researcher to include or exclude in statistical procedures those variables that contain missing values.

10. READ INPUT DATA—This card switches control from the program to the system. It alerts the system that the data should be read into the file at that time. If the INPUT MEDIUM is CARD, the cards are inserted into the runstream at this point. Note that the specification field is empty.

11. SAVE FILE—This control saves your data and their labels and/or modifications as a permanent system file. We wish to SAVE the FILE at this point since we know we will access this file at a later date for other purposes. Having SAVEd the FILE, we can eliminate

4. Nie et al., *Statistical Package for the Social Sciences*, p. 39.

5. Nie et al., *Statistical Package for the Social Sciences*, p. 92.

many of the steps used to set up the file and start right off with the procedures we choose.

12. FINISH—This control specifies that you have completed all SPSS commands. It transfers control back to the system. (Various updates of SPSS do not require this card. In these cases, the program itself will generate a FINISH command when a non-SPSS character/word is encountered.)

The Input Format Card

The INPUT FORMAT card consists of the words INPUT FORMAT in the control field followed by the specification of FIXED, BINARY, or FREEFIELD followed by the format list.[6] In most social science research, as in our data set example, the format will usually be FIXED, i.e., we placed the variables on the same deck and in the same column field for each case. The format list consists of FORTRAN-like format elements of the form nFw.d where:

n = the number of consecutive variables with the exact format
F = FIXED format field
w = the field width in columns counting the sign $(+, -)$ of the value and decimal point if they are punched on the raw data cards.
d = number of digits interpreted or punched right of the implied decimal point

with the following symbols designating the location of the variables

nX = skip "n" columns
Tn = transfer or tabulate to column "n"
  / = skip to the next record (deck).

Suppose we have a data set that contained four variables: a respondent's identification number, the respondent's monthly salary, the respondent's total years of education, and the respondent's age. In the sample case, we have respondent 146 who earns $1,280.50 per month, has a college degree, and who is 28 years old. Further, the codebook is set up such that the data would be set up in columns (2–5), (8–13), (14–15), (16–17), respectively. The sample case may look like that in Figure 1. If each case is set up in the same manner, then the format is FIXED and the format card would read:

1   16
INPUT FORMAT   FIXED (1X, F4.0, T8, F6.2, 2F2.0)

6. For additional format specifications, see Nie et al., *Statistical Package for the Social Sciences*, pp. 41, 176, 177.

FIGURE 1. Card Image Coding Scheme for Sample Respondent 146

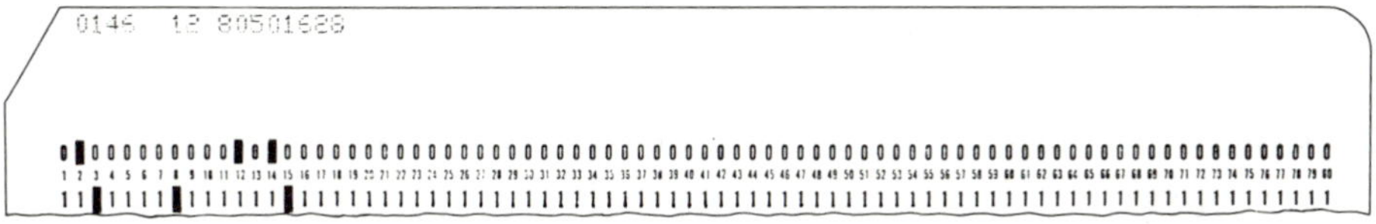

This means, "Skip the first column; read an identification number whose maximum column width is four; tabulate to column eight; read a six digit wide salary figure with two of those places to the right of the implied decimal point; read the next two variables as two column width digits." See the sample deck set up below for a more elaborate INPUT FORMAT.

Data Modification and Procedures

Once we have assembled the necessary JCL and SPSS data-definition cards, we are ready to take the final step in file setup—instructing the computer to "do" something with the information we have supplied. The two generic processes we will be concerned with in this treatment are DATA MODIFICATIONS and PROCEDURES.

In general, when we wish to manipulate or transform our data in any way, we employ DATA MODIFICATIONS. PROCEDURES, on the other hand, instruct the computer to calculate statistics for us. The DATA MODIFICATIONS included for our purposes are RECODE, COMPUTE, SELECT IF, and ASSIGN MISSING. The PROCEDURES are FREQUENCIES, CONDESCRIPTIVE, CROSSTABS, GUTTMAN, PEARSON CORR, SCATTERGRAM, and LIST FILEINFO.

A PROCEDURE card is required in the runstream which sets up the SPSS file. It precedes the READ INPUT DATA card (see Table 1). Subsequent runs will not usually require a READ INPUT DATA. Thus, the general progression in your runstream will be to GET FILE, apply DATA MODIFICATIONS, and execute PROCEDURES.

The Initial Run

Our initial run should be executed with two goals in mind. First, it is necessary to determine whether the input data has been translated into SPSS exactly as we planned. Secondly, we are concerned with determining whether any stray or illegal punches slipped past the verification. SPSS will copy print an INPUT FORMAT that will include the VARIABLE LIST by variable name, the deck number, columns, and format of each variable as you declared its field. This information should be checked carefully with your codebook to assure you have properly

TABLE 2. SPSS File Data Setup For Verba-Nie Data

[Insert initial JCL here]

1	16
RUN NAME	SET UP VERBA-NIE DATA
FILE NAME	POLPART
VARIABLE LIST	V1 TO V31
N OF CASES	UNKNOWN
INPUT MEDIUM	TAPE
INPUT FORMAT	FIXED (F1.0, F4.0, 3F1.0, F7.0, 2F1.0, 2F2.0, 21F1.0
VAR LABELS	V1 DECK NUMBER/V2 RESPONDENT NUMBER/V3 SEX OF RESPONDENT/V4 RACE OF RESPONDENT/V5 EDUCATIONAL LEVEL OF RESPONDENT/ . . . V29 DOES R. READ TIME MAGAZINE/V30 DOES R. READ READERS DIGEST/V31 DOES R. READ SATURDAY EVENING POST
VALUE LABELS	V3 (1) MALE (2) FEMALE (0) NA/V4 (1) WHITE (2) BLACK (3) ORIENTAL (4) AMERICAN INDIAN (5) LATIN AMERICAN (8) OTHER (0)NA/V5 (1)NO SCHOOLING (2) GRAMMAR OR ELEMENTARY (3) SOME HIGH SCHOOL (4) COMPLETED HIGH SCHOOL (5) COLLEGE INCOMPLETE (6) COLLEGE, GRADUATED (7) HIGHER THAN COLLEGE (9) DK (0) NA/ . . . V24 to V31 (1) YES (2) NO (0) INAPPROPRIATE

TABLE 2.   SPSS File Data Setup For Verba-Nie Data (*continued*)

READ INPUT DATA

FREQUENCIES   GENERAL = ALL

SAVE FILE

FINISH

[Insert Concluding JCL Here]

---

transferred the data. Assuming the format is correct, we will insert a PROCEDURE to provide FREQUENCIES or univariate distributions for each variable. This output will enable us to determine the extent of cleaning (Chapter 12) necessary prior to generating statistical information.

The format of the FREQUENCIES card is:

```
1               16
FREQUENCIES     GENERAL = VARNAME₁, VARNAME₂,
                .....,  VARNAMEₙ
```

where adjacent variables may be accessed by stating $VARNAME_1$ TO $VARNAME_n$ and all variables can be included by simply punching ALL after the = sign. Table 2 shows the actual setup of the Verba-Nie data we are using in this appendix.

Cleaning the Data

Once we have verified that our INPUT FORMAT was correct and all the data are in their intended form, we use the printout generated from FREQUENCIES to determine whether there are any illegal responses listed for each of our variables. For example, if a variable was coded "V24: 1 = Yes, 2 = No, 0 = Inappropriate" and we find a "7" listed in the FREQUENCIES for that variable, then we can permanently erase that illegal response using a RECODE in a subsequent run combined with a MISSING VALUES and SAVE FILE in the runstream. We will RECODE the incorrect value to another value that we designate as missing or incorrect. The choice as to the designated value depends on which responses are possibly correct for the particular variable. In the above example, "0" is a valid response to V24; therefore, we chose to designate "9" as the value representing a missing or incorrect response to V24. However, when a missing response was punched from the survey, the keypuncher skipped the column rather than punch a "9" for that case. Because SPSS reads all blanks as zeroes, we also need to differentiate between a "0" (inappropriate) and a "blank" (Missing). The RECODE facility can handle both these transformations. The format would be:

```
1                              16
RECODE                         V24 (BLANK = 9) (7 = 9)

MISSING VALUES                 V24 (9)

.
.
      [Insert remainder of modifications, then procedures]
.

SAVE FILE

FINISH
```

When we have processed each variable in this fashion, we can generate a complete and up-to-date data definition description of our variables (including VARIABLE LIST, LABELS, MISSING VALUES) by a procedure called LIST FILEINFO:

```
1                              16
LIST FILEINFO                  COMPLETE
```

The more complete job you do at defining your data via optional labeling the better the LIST FILEINFO functions as a revised codebook. At this point, we are ready to begin analysis of the data.

Univariate Distributions (Chapter 12)

You recognized the output from the FREQUENCIES as a univariate distribution of groups of responses for each variable. Now that the data are cleaned, you can repeat this procedure and generate summary univariate statistics including the mean, standard error, median, mode, standard deviation, variance, kurtosis, skewness, range, minimum and maximum values. If we wish to generate all of these statistics for a subset of our variables, the runstream would include:

```
1                              16
FREQUENCIES                    GENERAL = V2, V6, V23, V28 to V34

STATISTICS                     ALL
```

If you wish to select only some of the available statistics, thus saving some computer time, you may specify the number code of the statistics you require in the specification field.[7]

You may wish to generate the same summary statistics on an interval variable (e.g., family income or city population) and not be concerned with seeing the actual frequency distribution. The CONDESCRIPTIVE procedure is invoked thus:

```
1                                  16
CONDESCRIPTIVE                     V9
```

Note: No STATISTICS card is necessary with the CONDESCRIPTIVE procedure.

Bivariate Distributions (Chapter 13)

As we learned in Chapter 13, bivariate analysis enables us to see the association or relationship between two variables; we can observe how one variable covaries with another. Using bivariate statistics, we can determine not only if a relationship exists at all (significance test), but also the strength and direction of those relationships (measures of association).

Nominal and Ordinal Measures. The CROSSTABS procedure is specifically designed to generate bivariate tables and statistics for nominal and ordinal level variables and is of the form:

```
1                       16
CROSSTABS               TABLES = VARIABLE₁ BY VARIABLE₂
                        [BY VARIABLE₃]/VARIABLE₄ BY
                        VARIABLE₅ [BY VARIABLE₆]/ . . .
```

$TABLES = VARIABLE_1 \ BY \ VARIABLE_2 \ [BY \ VARIABLE_3]/VARIABLE_4 \ BY \ VARIABLE_5 \ [BY \ VARIABLE_6]/ \ldots$

Variables 1 and 4 are dependent variables (printed down the left hand column as has been the convention in this book) of different sets of tables; Variables 2 and 5 are independent variables of their respective tables; and Variables 3 and 6 function as control variables (see below) generating one table for each value of the control. The use of controls is optional.

Suppose we wish to examine the relationship between educational level and interest in politics. We would make the following command:

```
1                       16
CROSSTABS               TABLES = V13 BY V11

STATISTICS              1, 4, 6, 7, 8
```

7. See Nie et al., *Statistical Package for the Social Sciences*, p. 201. Also, you may construct histograms and vary the form of the output by designating OPTIONS 9 (pp. 201, 217).

which would produce Table 3. Let us look at the boldly out-lined cell. Here is how we would interpret the numbers in the cell which contains persons who have completed high school (V11, value 4) and who are slightly interested in politics (V13, value 2). The number 324 means that there are 324 respondents (count) who have both those characteristics. Thirty-six point two percent of those who are slightly interested are in the "completed high school" category (row percent) while 41.8 percent of those who have completed high school (column percentage) are only slightly interested in politics. The N of 324 out of the total N of 2,549 accounts for 12.7 (total) percent of the respondents in the sample. The uppermost left hand description cell (COUNT, ROW PCT, COL PCT, TOT PCT) lists the order of the figures within internal cells.

Notice that Table 3 has 5 rows and 8 columns. We know that the value of our coefficients, for example, Chi-square (χ^2), are a function of the number of cells in the table. As it stands, the table contains cells representing the answer "Don't Know." We can choose to exclude this response group and treat it as if it were missing data by "collapsing" the categories either by using a RECODE or a SELECT IF command.[8] We would get exactly the same results if we put either of the following cards before the CROSSTABS card:

1	16
RECODE	V13 (8 = 9)/V11 (8 = 9)

or

SELECT IF	(V13 LT 8 OR V11 LT 8)

Although we would normally use the RECODE modification to merge the "Don't Knows" into the MISSING VALUES category, we introduce the SELECT IF card as a way to call only a subset of cases to be included in the procedure. By using the SELECT IF card, we do not transform the data but eliminate cases which reply "Don't Know" (by implication those coded 9 = missing). Often in social science research, we wish to examine relationships among a subset of our sample. In CROSSTABS, this can be accomplished by including a third (control) variable in the TABLES = specification. However, if we are only interested in one category of the control variable (or if we are using another procedure which does not allow a method of control) the SELECT IF is the handiest way to segregate such a subset. The format of the SE-

---

8. If you use a TRANSFORMATION of your data to collapse your categories, do not use a SAVE FILE card or else these transformations will be permanent modifications. Instead, omit the SAFE FILE or perform temporary transformations. See Nie et al., *Statistical Package for the Social Sciences*, pp. 94, 101.

TABLE 3.   Sample CROSSTABS – Table of Interest in Politics by Educational Level of Respondent

SPSS BATCH SYSTEM   10/29/80   PAGE

FILE   POLCON   (CREATION DATE = 10/27/80)

```
* * * * * * * * * * * * * * * * * * * C R O S S T A B U L A T I O N   O F  * * * * * * * * * * * * * * * * * * * * * * * * *
V13       INTEREST IN                      POLITICS       BY V11          EDUCATIONAL LEVEL OF RESPONDENT
* * * * * * * * * * * * * * * * * * * * * * * * * * * * * * * * * * * * * * * * * * * * * * * * * * *  PAGE 1
```

Each cell: COUNT / ROW PCT / COL PCT / TOT PCT

V13	V11 NO SCHOO LING 1.	GRAMMAR OR ELEME 2.	SOME HIG H 3.	COMPLETE D HIGH S 4.	COLLEGE, INCOMPLE 5.	COLLEGE, GRADUATE 6.	HIGHER T HAN COLL 7.	DK 9.	ROW TOTAL
0. NA	10 / 4.4 / 41.7 / .4	117 / 51.5 / 17.5 / 4.6	55 / 24.2 / 10.5 / 2.2	33 / 14.5 / 4.3 / 1.3	10 / 4.4 / 3.1 / .4	2 / .9 / 1.3 / .1	0 / .0 / .0 / .0	0 / .0 / .0 / .0	227 / 8.9
1. NOT INTERESTED	10 / 1.6 / 41.7 / .4	219 / 34.9 / 32.7 / 8.6	145 / 23.1 / 27.8 / 5.7	193 / 30.7 / 24.9 / 7.6	44 / 7.0 / 13.7 / 1.7	17 / 2.7 / 10.8 / .7	0 / .0 / .0 / .0	0 / .0 / .0 / .0	628 / 24.6
2. ONLY SLIGHTLY IN	2 / .2 / 8.3 / .1	172 / 19.2 / 25.7 / 6.7	181 / 20.2 / 34.7 / 7.1	324 / 36.2 / 41.8 / 12.7	127 / 14.2 / 39.7 / 5.0	60 / 6.7 / 38.0 / 2.4	29 / 3.2 / 37.2 / 1.1	1 / .1 / 100.0 / .0	896 / 35.2
3. SOMEWHAT INTERES	2 / .3 / 8.3 / .1	159 / 20.1 / 23.7 / 6.2	139 / 17.5 / 26.6 / 5.5	226 / 28.5 / 29.1 / 8.9	139 / 17.5 / 43.4 / 5.5	79 / 10.0 / 50.0 / 3.1	49 / 6.2 / 62.8 / 1.9	0 / .0 / .0 / .0	793 / 31.1
9.	0 / .0 / .0 / .0	3 / 60.0 / .4 / .1	2 / 40.0 / .4 / .1	0 / .0 / .0 / .0	0 / .0 / .0 / .0	0 / .0 / .0 / .0	0 / .0 / .0 / .0	0 / .0 / .0 / .0	5 / .2
COLUMN TOTAL	24 / .9	670 / 26.3	522 / 20.5	776 / 30.4	320 / 12.6	158 / 6.2	78 / 3.1	1 / .0	2549 / 100.0

CHI SQUARE = 323.92414 WITH 28 DEGREES OF FREEDOM   SIGNIFICANCE = .0000

LAMBDA (ASYMMETRIC) = .06413 WITH V13 DEPENDENT.   = .06373 WITH V11 DEPENDENT.

LAMBDA (SYMMETRIC) = .06392

KENDALL'S TAU B = .24348   SIGNIFICANCE = .0000

KENDALL'S TAU C = .22602   SIGNIFICANCE = .0000

GAMMA = .32631

LECT IF card is below:

```
1                        16
SELECT IF                (VAR NAME [LOGICAL CONNECTOR]
                         value)
```

where the logical connectors are

Connector	Meaning
EQ	is equal to
LT	less than
LE	less than or equal to
GT	greater than
GE	greater than or equal to

and the "value" can be a number or another variable name. The SELECT IF may become more complex by forming logical compound sentences connected by AND (all conditions must apply for case inclusion) or OR (any condition can be met for case inclusion).

Finally, we can use the SELECT IF and RECODE in conjunction with each other to select cases and collapse categories. For example, the cards

```
1                        16
SELECT IF                (V3 EQ 1 AND V4 EQ 2)

RECODE                   V13 (8 = 9) V11 (8 = 9)

CROSSTABS                TABLES = V13 BY V11

STATISTICS               1, 4, 6, 7, 8
```

would produce Table 4 whose respondents were all black males. (Note that the variables on the SELECT IF card need not appear on the PROCEDURE card.)

If your research question centers around black males with the exclusion of other categories by sex and race, and if your data set is so designed that the other categories are included, this is an appropriate way to select your cases and perform a bivariate analysis.

Interval Measures (Chapter 13). The subprogram PEARSON CORR calculates the Pearson Product-Moment Correlation, an associational statistic appropriate for interval variables, and tests for significance using a one-tailed *t*-test. In most cases, coefficients generated by PEARSON CORR are equivalent to the Spearman Rank-Order Coefficients produced by NONPAR CORR when variables are measured at the ordinal level. Therefore, we present PEARSON CORR as appropriate for or-

TABLE 4. CROSSTABS Table of Interest by Educational Level of Black Males

```
SPSS BATCH SYSTEM                                                    10/27/80          PAGE

FILE   POLCON   (CREATION DATE = 10/27/80)

* * * * * * * * * * * * * * * * * * * *   C R O S S T A B U L A T I O N   O F   * * * * * * * * * * * * * * * * * * * *
    V13      INTEREST IN                        POLITICS          BY V11      EDUCATIONAL LEVEL OF RESPONDENT
* * * * * * * * * * * * * * * * * * * *                                              * * * * * * * * *   PAGE 1
```

V13	V11 COUNT ROW PCT COL PCT TOT PCT	NO SCHOO LING 1.	GRAMMAR OR ELEME H 2.	SOME HIG H 3.	COMPLETE D HIGH S 4.	COLLEGE, INCOMPLE 5.	COLLEGE, GRADUATE 6.	HIGHER T HAN COLL 7.	ROW TOTAL
1. NOT INTERESTED		0 .0 .0 .0	16 53.3 34.8 15.2	5 16.7 22.7 4.8	7 23.3 31.8 6.7	1 3.3 20.0 1.0	1 3.3 16.7 1.0	0 .0 .0 .0	30 28.6
2. ONLY SLIGHTLY IN		1 3.4 50.0 1.0	10 34.5 21.7 9.5	7 24.1 31.8 6.7	8 27.6 36.4 7.6	1 3.4 20.0 1.0	2 6.9 33.3 1.9	0 .0 .0 .0	29 27.6
3. SOMEWHAT INTERES		1 2.2 50.0 1.0	20 43.5 43.5 19.0	10 21.7 45.5 9.5	7 15.2 31.8 6.7	3 6.5 60.0 2.9	3 6.5 50.0 2.9	2 4.3 100.0 1.9	46 43.8
COLUMN TOTAL		2 1.9	46 43.8	22 21.0	22 21.0	5 4.8	6 5.7	2 1.9	105 100.0

```
CHI SQUARE =  7.49823 WITH 12 DEGREES OF FREEDOM    SIGNIFICANCE = .8230
LAMBDA (ASYMMETRIC) = .01695 WITH V13 DEPENDENT.           = .00000 WITH V11 DEPENDENT.
LAMBDA (SYMMETRIC) = .00847
KENDALL'S TAU B = .04926   SIGNIFICANCE = .2808
KENDALL'S TAU C = .05034   SIGNIFICANCE = .2808
GAMMA = .07201
NUMBER OF MISSING OBSERVATIONS = 12
```

dinal-ordinal, ordinal-interval and interval-interval variables. The series

1	16
PEARSON CORR	V6, V8, V13, V7
OPTIONS	3
STATISTICS	1

will produce one table showing the means and standard deviation of the variables and one table including the coefficients, the N upon which the calculations were based, and the significance level. This is illustrated in Table 5.

You may wish to plot a Scatter Diagram to visually assess the relationship between two of your variables. The subprogram SCATTERGRAM will plot these relationships for you and also calculate the Pearson's r, r-squared, significance of r, standard error of the estimate, the intercept with the vertical axis, and the slope. The series

1	16
SCATTERGRAM	V6, V13
STATISTICS	ALL

will produce the output graphically displaying the relationship between participation and interest in politics.

Multivariate Analysis (Chapter 14)

The three major functions of multivariate analysis, as we learned in Chapter 14, are control, interpretation, and prediction. Mechanically, the first two functions are covered by using control variables in the equations; the subprograms CROSSTABS and PARTIAL CORR can provide for these controls. Prediction is enhanced by REGRESSION.

Multivariate CROSSTABS. This appendix presented above the basic format of the CROSSTABS card. The portion in brackets indicates the control variable(s). For instance, resultant output from a bivariate table controlling for sex would consist of two tables having the same dependent and independent variables but differing as to the respondents' gender: for the first table, all cases are men and for the second, all are women. A control variable with four values would generate four tables.

PARTIAL CORR. Partial Correlations are conceptually similar to multivariate CROSSTABS in that the effects of other variables are controlled when analyzing the relationship between the original variables.

TABLE 5. Pearson's Correlations between Selected Participation Variables

SPSS BATCH SYSTEM

10/27/80   PAGE 19

FILE   POLCON   (CREATION DATE = 10/27/80)

------------------- P E A R S O N   C O R R E L A T I O N   C O E F F I C I E N T S -------------------

	V6	V8	V13	V7
V6	1.0000 (2549) P=*****	-.0739 (2549) P= .000	.4026 (2544) P= .000	-.0752 (2549) P= .000
V8	-.0739 (2549) P= .000	1.0000 (2549) P=*****	-.0586 (2544) P= .003	.0941 (2549) P= .000
V13	.4026 (2544) P= .000	-.0586 (2544) P= .003	1.0000 (2544) P=*****	-.0521 (2544) P= .009
V7	-.0752 (2549) P= .000	.0941 (2549) P= .000	-.0521 (2544) P= .009	1.0000 (2549) P=*****

(COEFFICIENT / (CASES) / SIGNIFICANCE)

(A VALUE OF 99.0000 IS PRINTED IF A COEFFICIENT CANNOT BE COMPUTED)

Whereas CROSSTABS physically removes the effects by partitioning the cases based on values of the control, PARTIAL CORR statistically removes the effects. This difference can be very important when controlling for more than one variable because physical separation reduces cell frequencies. Thus, when the analysis calls for more than one control or when the N is relatively small, we advise the use of PARTIAL CORR.

The input

1	16
PARTIAL CORR	V6 WITH V8, V13, V17 BY V3, V4 (1, 2)
STATISTICS	ALL

would compute zero-order, first-order, and second-order partials for each unique combination of the dependent variable (V6) and independent variables (V8, V13, V17). The controls will be for V3 and V4 individually and simultaneously. A maximum of five (5) orders may appear within the parentheses. The order may not exceed the number of control variables. An example of PARTIAL CORR output is Table 6.

REGRESSION (Multiple Relationships). Oftentimes, there are a number of independent variables each of which is hypothesized to contribute to the explained variance of a single dependent variable. Multiple REGRESSION is the SPSS subprogram which handles such simultaneous effects.

The commands for REGRESSION consist of the declaration of the variables included in the analysis and how the processing should take place. For our purposes, the general format of the sequence of cards is:

1	16
REGRESSION	VARIABLES = DEPENDENT VAR, INDEPENDENT VAR_1, INDEPENDENT VAR_2, . . . INDEPENDENT VAR_N
	REGRESSION = DEPENDENT VAR WITH INDEPENDENT VAR_1, INDEPENDENT VAR_2, . . . INDEPENDENT VAR_N (even number)
STATISTICS	1, 2, 3

Because REGRESSION is an asymmetric statistic, we must state which of our variables is dependent so that we can regress Y on X. The even number (any one between 2–98) in parentheses states that all independent variables be entered into the equation simultaneously.[9] Given

9. One can calculate Stepwise Hierarchical Regression by placing an odd number in the parentheses. In stepwise regression, variables are entered into the equation based on

the numbers in the STATISTICS specification field, the following statistics will be calculated and printed: a correlation matrix, means and standard deviations for each variable in the VARIABLES = list with the number of valid cases.[10] A Summary Table is also printed.

The REGRESSION sequence below is used to generate the output in Table 7:

```
1               16
REGRESSION   VARIABLES = V6, V8, V13, V17, V3, V4
             REGRESSION = V6 WITH V8, V13, V17, V3, V4(2)

STATISTICS   1, 2, 3
```

Notice that in Table 7 all variables were entered into the equation in one step. Also notice that you receive an Analysis of Variance for the set, a statement of the standard error, and some summary statistics which are also contained in Summary Table 8. Table 8 can tell you at a glance the values of R, R^2, the change in R^2 attributable to each variable's inclusion, the Pearson's r between each independent variable and the dependent variable, each b, Beta and the intercept a.

Measurement: Variable, Scale and Index Construction (Chapter 15)

In Chapter 15, we discussed methods for measuring respondents' attitudes. We tapped these attitudes by constructing scales and indices with indicators of particular attitudes. SPSS has the facility to assist in a variety of ways the construction of uni- and multidimensional scales. Students are encouraged to explore options in FACTOR analysis, IF transformations, and COUNT operations as their expertise in methodology increases. However, for purposes of this treatment, we will only explore basic additive and GUTTMAN scaling techniques.

Basic Composite Measures. Often in social science research it is convenient to create or transform variables, for example by weighting, per capitizing, or otherwise performing mathematical operations on existing variables. The COMPUTE transformation is probably the most useful and universal facility in SPSS to satisfy these needs. The card format is quite simple in that you use logical mathematical expressions

---

their inclusion level (Nie et al., *Statistical Package for the Social Sciences*, pp. 344–345) and percent of unexplained variance, one at a time. For variations on inclusion types and levels, plus calculating residuals, see ibid., pp. 342–367.

10. The default in REGRESSION is listwise deletion of missing cases. This means that if there is missing data on any variable in the VARIABLES = list, the case will be deleted. For other options, see ibid., pp. 353–355.

TABLE 6. PARTIAL CORRelations of Selected Participation Variables Controlling for the Effects of Two Variables Separately and Simultaneously

```
SPSS BATCH SYSTEM                                          10/27/80        PAGE 14

FILE  POLCON (CREATION DATE = 10/27/80)

-------------------PARTIAL   CORRELATION   COEFFICIENTS-------------------

CONTROLLING FOR...       V3        V4

                   V8         V13        V17

V6              -.1069      .3961      .6268
                ( 2540)    ( 2540)    ( 2540)
                P= .000    P= .000    P= .000

(COEFFICIENT/(D.F.)/SIGNIFICANCE)        (A VALUE OF 99.0000 IS PRINTED IF A COEFFICIENT CANNOT BE COMPUTED)

-------------------PARTIAL   CORRELATION   COEFFICIENTS-------------------

CONTROLLING FOR...       V3

                   V8         V13        V17

V6              -.1177      .3987      .6257
                ( 2541)    ( 2541)    ( 2541)
                P= .000    P= .000    P= .000

(COEFFICIENT/(D.F.)/SIGNIFICANCE)        (A VALUE OF 99.0000 IS PRINTED IF A COEFFICIENT CANNOT BE COMPUTED)

-------------------PARTIAL   CORRELATION   COEFFICIENTS-------------------

CONTROLLING FOR...       V4

                   V8         V13        V17

V6              -.0642      .3999      .6271
                ( 2541)    ( 2541)    ( 2541)
                P= .001    P= .000    P= .000

(COEFFICIENT/(D.F.)/SIGNIFICANCE)        (A VALUE OF 99.0000 IS PRINTED IF A COEFFICIENT CANNOT BE COMPUTED)
```

TABLE 7.   Inclusion of Variables in a Multiple REGRESSION of Participation on Respondent Characteristics

```
FILE     POLCON    (CREATION DATE = 10/27/80)

* * * * * * * * * * * * * * * * * * * * * * * * * M U L T I P L E   R E G R E S S I O N   * * * * * * * * * * * * * * * * * * * * * * * * * VARIABLE LIST 1
                                                                                                                                           REGRESSION LIST 1
DEPENDENT VARIABLE. .      V6      SUMMARY PARTICIPATION               SCORE

VARIABLE(S) ENTERED ON STEP NUMBER 1. .      V4     RACE OF RESPONDENT
                                             V8     OCCUPATION OF RESPONDENT
                                             V13    INTEREST IN                       POLITICS
                                             V17    ATTEND POLITICAL MEETINGS
                                             V3     SEX

MULTIPLE R              .67926         ANALYSIS OF VARIANCE    DF      SUM OF SQUARES      MEAN SQUARE          F
R SQUARE               .46139         REGRESSION               5.      9608782.17786     1921756.43557     434.82941
ADJUSTED R SQUARE      .46033         RESIDUAL              2538.     11216853.62689      4419.56408
STANDARD ERROR        66.47980
```

```
------------ VARIABLES IN THE EQUATION ------------                    ------------ VARIABLES NOT IN THE EQUATION ------------

VARIABLE         B          BETA     STD ERROR B      F                 VARIABLE      BETA IN     PARTIAL     TOLERANCE      F

V4          -.8901277+001   -.04787    2.75282     10.456
V8          -.9471820+000   -.03642     .43181      4.811
V13          .2420015+002    .25411    1.44648    279.906
V17          .1281861+003    .55857    3.45893   1373.407
V3          -.7925241+001   -.04377    2.98055      7.070
(CONSTANT)  -.1739688+003
```

```
ALL VARIABLES ARE IN THE EQUATION
STATISTICS WHICH CANNOT BE COMPUTED ARE PRINTED AS ALL NINES.
```

TABLE 8. Multiple REGRESSION Summary Table of Participation on Respondent Characteristics

FILE   POLCON   (CREATION DATE = 10/27/80)

*   M U L T I P L E   R E G R E S S I O N   *

DEPENDENT VARIABLE . . .   V6   SUMMARY PARTICIPATION   SCORE

VARIABLE LIST 1
REGRESSION LIST 1

SUMMARY TABLE

VARIABLE		MULTIPLE R	R SQUARE	RSQ CHANGE	SIMPLE R	B	BETA
V4	RACE OF RESPONDENT	.07507	.00564	.00564	-.07507	-.8901277+001	-.04787
V8	OCCUPATION OF RESPONDENT	.09866	.00973	.00410	-.07422	-.9471820+000	-.03642
V13	INTEREST IN POLITICS	.40815	.16658	.15685	.40262	.2420015+002	.25411
V17	ATTEND POLITICAL MEETINGS	.67815	.45989	.29331	.62605	.1281861+003	.55857
V3	SEX	.67926	.46139	.00150	-.07059	-.7925241+001	-.04377
(CONSTANT)						-.1739688+003	

to create your composite measure (for instance, you can add (+), subtract
(−), multiply (*), divide (/), exponentiate (**N)).[11] It is also quite flexible
in that the operands may be variable names, real numbers, or integers.
The general form of the COMPUTE card is:

```
1                       16
COMPUTE                 COMPUTED VARIABLE
                        = ARITHMETIC EXPRESSION
```

If you COMPUTE new variables or indices and use a SAVE FILE, the
computed variables become permanent variables added to your file.

When new variables are computed, cases with missing data on any
variable-operand will not have a resultant value for the new variable.
SPSS allows you to ASSIGN a MISSING value for these cases. The value
you ASSIGN MISSING should not be a valid value for your computed
variable.[12] The general form of the ASSIGN MISSING card is quite
similar to the MISSING VALUES card:

```
1                       16
ASSIGN MISSING          COMPUTED VARIABLE (value)
```

Let us construct a scale (Likert) of political activity using our Participation Data Set. The variables we will use are V13, V14, V15, V18,
and V19. We assume by choice of a Likert Scale that all of these variables
tap the same unidimensional concept—political activity—and that each
of the variables contributes equally to the concept; they are equally
weighted. We can then place our respondents on a continuum between
politically inactive and politically active. In our case the variables are
all constructed in such a way that a low value on a variable denotes
inactivity and a high value activity. Otherwise, it would be necessary
to RECODE the variables to reflect the presence of an inverted scale.
However, we do have two problems prior to computing the scale. First,
because cases with missing data on any variable will be excluded, we
need a method to alleviate the effects of the missing data. Second, in
three of our scales 1 = inactivity, whereas in the other two 0 = inactivity.
We can RECODE the variables to handle both these problems. The
construction of our Likert Scale, ACTIVE, is captured in the following

---

11. See Nie et al., *Statistical Package for the Social Sciences*, for the complete listing
of operators.

12. If you do assign a valid response to the ASSIGN MISSING, then not only will
missing values be declared, but a real value will be recoded to a missing value.

runstream:

```
1              16
RECODE         V13, V14, V15, V18, V19 (8, 9 = 0)
               (Changes "Don't Knows" and Missing to
               (a zero value to maximize the N of
               (cases on ACTIVE.

RECODE         V15, V18 (0 = 1) (1 = 2) (2 = 3) (3 = 4)
               (Causes all inactivity scores to be 1
               (and activity to be 4

COMPUTE        ACTIVE = V13 + V14 + V15 + V18 + V19
```

Since we coded all missing cases as "0", there will be no missing values on ACTIVE. However, if we wished to reflect the missing data (especially when we have very few missing values) as missing, and drop those cases with missing values on any variable, we would delete the first RECODE and add the following after the COMPUTE:

```
1                    16
ASSIGN MISSING       ACTIVE (0) (Since "0" is an invalid answer.)
```

Variables 14 through 16 measure media exposure. This can be scaled in the same way as we scaled ACTIVE. Additionally, we can use the COMPUTE to index behaviors or instances of behaviors. For example, Variables 24 through 31 ask which magazines, if any, respondents regularly read. If we were interested in determining how many magazines were read by each respondent, we would submit the following:

```
1                    16
COMPUTE              NMAGS = V24 + V25 + V26 + V27 + V28
                     + V29 + V30 + V31

ASSIGN MISSING       NMAGS (9)
```

GUTTMAN SCALE. Up to this point, our unidimensional scales are all additive, i.e., they are assumed to be measuring part of the same underlying concept. Additionally, like the operation of addition, the variable orderings were commutative, that is, V13 + V14 were the same conceptually as V14 + V13. Some unidimensional scales account for interrelationships and/or operating characteristics of component items; these are more complicated. They affix an unequal weight to items along the continuum and assume an ordering by degree of difficulty. GUTTMAN scaling is one example of a cumulative, unidimensional scale.

Let us return to our ACTIVE index. One may argue that some of the political activities are less costly than others. For example, it takes less time and effort to be (passively) interested in politics (V13) than to (actively) vote in a local election (V19). Likewise, it is even more costly to work for a party or candidate (V15) because this calls for a sustained action. Consequently, we can consider using a GUTTMAN SCALE. The general format of the GUTTMAN SCALE card is:

```
1                       16
GUTTMAN SCALE           SCALE NAME = VARIABLE NAME
                        (division point)
                        VARIABLE NAME (division
                        point) . . .
```

where: division point = the value of the variable greater than or equal to which a case must have to be considered as "passing" an item.

(Note: A maximum of twelve variables and three division points may be declared.)

The commands necessary to produce the GUTTMAN SCALE in Table 9 are:

```
1                       16
GUTTMAN SCALE           ACTSCALE = V13(2.5), V14(1.5), V15(1.5),
                        V18(2.5), V19(2.5)

OPTIONS                 1

STATISTICS              2, 3, 4
```

OPTIONS 1 causes missing data to be entered into all scales and computations like we did by recoding missing and "Don't Knows" to 0. The default is deletion of cases with any missing values. The STATISTICS include the coefficient of reproducability, the minimum marginal reproducability and the percent improvement achieved by GUTTMAN SCALE.

We use GUTTMAN SCALE to determine the scalability of the items in ACTSCALE. In this instance, we choose decision points based on a performance/nonperformance dichotomy allowing the algorithm to arrange items from most difficult (V18) to least difficult (V19). Under the table (SUMS) we can see the number of persons who pass the performance criterion (the number under "1" in each variable category) and those who do not (the number under "0"). Cases are arranged along the ACTSCALE (5–0) depending on how many and in what order of difficulty persons are politically active. Within each cell we can see the number of persons in each category who are performers or nonperformers.

Upon examination of the output we see that the items do not form a cumulative scale; the coefficient of reproducability is 0.86. However, if they did we could COMPUTE scale scores for each of our cases by

TABLE 9.   GUTTMAN SCALE to Determine the Scalability of Activity Scale (ACTSCALE) Items

```
                                                          10/31/80    PAGE  2
FILE     POLCON      (CREATION DATE = 10/27/80)

* * * * * * * * * * * * *  G U T T M A N   S C A L E  (ACTSCALE)  U S I N G * * * * * * * * * * * * *
V13      INTEREST IN              POLITICS            DIVISION POINT =   2.50
V14      ATTEMPT TO               MANIPULATE VO       DIVISION POINT =   1.50
V15      WORK FOR           A POLITICAL PARTY         DIVISION POINT =   1.50
V18      ATTEND POLITICAL MEETINGS                    DIVISION POINT =   2.50
V19      VOTING HISTORY                               DIVISION POINT =   2.50
* * * * * * * * * RESP = 1 FOR VALUES EQUAL TO DIVISION POINT AND ABOVE * * * * * * * * * * *

ITEM..  V18          V15          V13          V14          V19

RESP..   0      1  |  0      1  |  0      1  |  0      1  |  0      1  | TOTAL
  ----|··ERR----|·ERR----|·ERR ·---|·ERR ·---|ERR ·----|
A    |     |       |       |       |       |
C  5 |   0    147 |  0    147 |  0    147 |  0    147 |  0    147 |  147
T    |----ERR |       |       |       |       |
S    |     |       |       |       |       |
C  4 | 118    98 | 25    191 | 52    164 | 17    199 |  4    212 |  216
A    |     |----ERR |       |       |       |
L    |     |       |       |       |       |
E  3 | 318    87| 216    189 | 177   228| 85    320 | 14    391 |  405
     |     |       |---- ERR·|       |       |
     |     |       |       |       |       |
   2 | 542    45 | 479    108| 390   197 | 284   303| 66    521 |  587
     |     |       |       |----ERR |       |
     |     |       |       |       |       |
   1 | 800     7 | 796    11 | 745    62 | 746    61 | 141   666 |  807
     |     |       |       |       |----ERR |
     |     |       |       |       |       |
   0 | 387     0 | 387     0· 387     0 | 387     0 | 387     0 |  387
     |--------|--------|--------|--------|--------|
SUMS   2165   384  1903   646  1751   798  1519  1030   612  1937  2549
PCTS     85    15    75    25    69    31    60    40    24    76
ERRORS    0   237    25   308   229   259   386    61   225     0   1730


     2549 CASES WERE PROCESSED
        0 (OR    .0 PCT) WERE MISSING


STATISTICS..

COEFFICIENT OF REPRODUCIBILITY = .8643
MINIMUM MARGINAL REPRODUCIBILITY = .7277
PERCENT IMPROVEMENT = .1365
```

a (1) RECODE of the original variables reflecting the performance = 1/nonperformance = 0 dichotomy, (2) COMPUTE an additive index of the dichotomized variables, and (3) ASSIGN a MISSING value or zero to cases having missing data on any of the items. The use of GUTTMAN SCALE to determine scalability in conjunction with the COMPUTE statement lends reliability to your additive scale.

Conclusion

The SPSS and other statistical package manuals may seem complicated and imposing upon first inspection. It is with this in mind that the

Introduction to SPSS was designed—to assist students in taking that first big step into computerized data analysis. We hope that this treatment will encourage the researcher to pick and choose portions of those packages which lend themselves to his or her data needs and methodological expertise. A package like SPSS has many capabilities and potentials which grow with the abilities of the individual researcher. Thus, we encourage you to explore these potentials with the help of the manual as your skills increase.

CODEBOOK: Political Participation in America

VAR 01	DECK IDENTIFICATION NUMBER IS '1'	NO MISSING DATA CODES DK 1 COL 1 WIDTH 1

VAR 02	INTERVIEW NUMBER	NO MISSING DATA CODES DK 1 COL 2–5 WIDTH 4

INTERVIEW NUMBER

VAR 03	SEX OF R	MD = 0 DK 1 COL 6 WIDTH 4

SEX OF RESPONDENT

   1. MALE
   2. FEMALE

   0. NA

VAR 04	RACE OF R	MD = 0 DK 1 COL 7 WIDTH 1

RACE OF RESPONDENT
   1. WHITE
   2. BLACK
   3. ORIENTAL
   4. AMERICAN INDIAN
   5. LATIN AMERICAN (INCLUDING MEXICAN, CUBAN, PUERTO RICAN, ETC.)
   6. OTHER

   0. NA

VAR 05	R'S FATHER'S LEVEL OF EDUCATION	MD = 0 OR GE 9 DK 1 COL 8 WIDTH 1

WHAT IS THE LAST GRADE OR YEAR IN SCHOOL WHICH YOU COMPLETED?

Codebook (continued)

1. NO SCHOOLING
2. GRAMMAR OR ELEMENTARY (1–8 YEARS)
3. SOME HIGH SCHOOL (9–11) YEARS)
4. COMPLETED HIGH SCHOOL (12 YEARS)
5. COLLEGE, INCOMPLETE
6. COLLEGE, GRADUATED
7. HIGHER THAN COLLEGE

9. DK
0. NA

VAR 06   SUMMARY PRTCN INDEX   MD = LE 999999
                                                               DK 1 COL 9–14
                                                               WIDTH 7

RESPONDENT'S SCORE ON SUMMARY PARTICIPATION INDEX

999999 – MISSING

VAR 07   MARITAL STATUS OF R   NO MISSING DATA CODES
                                                                 DK 1 COL 15
                                                                  WIDTH 1

ARE YOU MARRIED, WIDOWED, DIVORCED, SEPARATED, OR NEVER MARRIED?

1. MARRIED
2. WIDOWED
3. DIVORCED
4. SEPARATED
5. NEVER MARRIED

VAR 08   OCC OF R: STATUS   MD = 0 OR GE 9
                                                                 DK 1 COL 16
                                                                  WIDTH 1

OCCUPATION OF RESPONDENT—OCCUPATIONAL STATUS
– IF RESPONDENT IS EMPLOYED, SELF-EMPLOYED, UNEMPLOYED, OR RETIREE—
Q. 8A. WHAT KIND OF WORK (DO YOU/DID YOU) NORMALLY DO?
Q. 8B. IN WHAT KIND OF BUSINESS OR INDUSTRY (IS/WAS) THAT?

. . . .

THE INTERVIEWER WAS INSTRUCTED TO PROBE FOR AN EXACT DESCRIPTION OF THE OCCUPATION.
1. GOVERNMENT SERVICE: THIS INCLUDES ALL POSITIONS IN THE GOVERNMENT—ELECTED AND APPOINTED OFFICIALS, POLICEMEN, POSTMEN, BUREAUCRATS, OFFICE WORKERS, MAINTENANCE MEN IN GOVERNMENT EMPLOY, ETC. IT INCLUDES ALL ENGAGED IN GOVERNMENTAL SERVICES OR WORKING FOR BUREAUS AND ORGANIZATIONS ENGAGED IN SUCH SERVICES. IT DOES NOT INCLUDE THOSE WORKING FOR GOVERNMENT-OWNED INSTITUTIONS WHICH PROVIDE OTHER SERVICES (SEE CODE 2).

Codebook (continued)

2. EMPLOYMENT IN THE NON-PROFIT SECTOR: THE RESPONDENT WORKS FOR A NON-PROFIT ORGANIZATION SUCH AS A UNION, COOPERATIVE, RELIGIOUS ORGANIZATION, PRIVATE SCHOOL, ETC. THIS ALSO INCLUDES WORKING IN GOVERNMENT-OWNED ENTERPRISES THAT PROVIDE SERVICES WHICH MIGHT ALSO BE PERFORMED IN THE PRIVATE SECTOR—NATIONALIZED INDUSTRIES, GOVERNMENT TRADING COMPANIES, GOVERNMENT FARMS, MINES, SCHOOLS, HOSPITALS, ETC.
3. EMPLOYMENT IN THE PRIVATE SECTOR: ALL INDIVIDUALS EMPLOYED BY ANOTHER INDIVIDUAL, GROUP, OR ORGANIZATION ENGAGED IN PROFIT-MAKING ACTIVITIES.
4. PRIVATE SELF-EMPLOYMENT: ALL INDIVIDUALS WHO WORK FOR THEIR PERSONAL PROFIT AND WHO MAY OR MAY NOT EMPLOY OTHERS WHILE DOING SO. THIS CATEGORY INCLUDES DOCTORS, LAWYERS, SERVICEMEN OR REPAIRMEN WHO OPERATE THEIR OWN BUSINESSES, PEDDLERS, AS WELL AS BUSINESSMEN WHO OWN THEIR OWN BUSINESSES REGARDLESS OF THE SIZE OF THAT BUSINESS.
5. FAMILY EMPLOYMENT: ALL INDIVIDUALS EMPLOYED BY THEIR KIN IN AN ENTERPRISE THAT CONSISTS ENTIRELY OF PREDOMINANTLY FAMILY MEMBERS. WORKERS ON FAMILY OR KIN-GROUP OWNED FARMS OR FAMILY BUSINESSES, ETC., ARE INCLUDED.
6. EMPLOYMENT IN THE PRIVATE SECTOR GENERALLY, AS OPPOSED TO GOVERNMENT SERVICE, BUT NOT ENOUGH INFORMATION AVAILABLE TO DISTINGUISH BETWEEN CATEGORIES 3, 4, AND 5 AND CERTAIN ASPECTS OF CATEGORY 2 (PRIVATE HOSPITALS, SCHOOLS, ETC.).
9. UNASCERTAINED OR AMBIGUOUS STATUS: NA DK
0. INAP., CODED 7–9

VAR 09   R'S FAMILY INCOME 1ST YR   MD = GE 88
                                                  DK 1 COL 17–18
                                                  WIDTH 2

WILL YOU PLEASE LOOK AT THIS CARD AND TELL ME WHICH FIGURE COMES CLOSEST TO YOUR TOTAL FAMILY INCOME FOR THE PAST YEAR—BEFORE TAXES, THAT IS? JUST TELL ME THE LETTER NEXT TO THE FIGURE THAT FITS YOU BEST.

THE INTERVIEWER WAS INSTRUCTED TO HAND THE RESPONDENT A CARD LISTING THE FIGURES CODED BELOW.

IF THE INTERVIEWER GAVE AN ESTIMATE OF THE RESPONDENT'S FAMILY INCOME, THAT AMOUNT WAS CODED, UNLESS CODE 88, "REFUSED" WAS ALSO CIRCLED.

01. LESS THAN $1,000
02. $1,000 TO $1,999
03. $2,000 TO $2,999
04. $3,000 TO $3,999
05. $4,000 TO $4,999
06. $5,000 TO $5,999

Codebook (continued)

```
07.  $6,000 TO $6,999
11.  $7,000 TO $7,999
21.  $8,000 TO $8,999
31.  $9,000 TO $9,999
41. $10,000 TO $14,999
51. $15,000 TO $19,999
61. $20,000 TO $24,999
71. $25,000 OR MORE

88.  REFUSED
98.  NA
99.  DK
```

VAR 010	AGE OF R	MD = 0
		DK 1 COL 19–20
		WIDTH 2

HOW OLD WERE YOU ON YOUR LAST BIRTHDAY?

IF THE RESPONDENT REFUSED TO ANSWER, AND THE INTERVIEWER RECORDED A GUESS, THAT AGE WAS CODED.

IF THE RESPONDENT REFUSED TO ANSWER, AND THE INTERVIEWER RECORDED A GUESS, THAT AGE WAS CODED.

17 YEARS OLD

89 YEARS OLD

00. NA OR REFUSED

VAR 011	R'S LEVEL OF EDUCATION	MD = 0 OR GE 9
		DK 1 COL 21
		WIDTH 1

WHAT IS THE LAST GRADE OR YEAR IN SCHOOL WHICH YOU COMPLETED?

1. NO SCHOOLING
2. GRAMMAR OR ELEMENTARY (1–8 YEARS)
3. SOME HIGH SCHOOL (9–11 YEARS)
4. COMPLETED HIGH SCHOOL (12 YEARS)
5. COLLEGE, INCOMPLETE
6. COLLEGE, GRADUATED
7. HIGHER THAN COLLEGE

9. DK
0. NA

Codebook (continued)

VAR 012   R'S PARTY: REP/DEM/IND   MD = 0 OR GE 9
                                                 DK 1 COL 22
                                                 WIDTH 1

GENERALLY SPEAKING, DO YOU USUALLY THINK OF YOURSELF AS A
REPUBLICAN, A DEMOCRAT, AN INDEPENDENT, OR WHAT?

    1. DEMOCRAT
    2. REPUBLICAN
    3. INDEPENDENT, OR NO PARTY
    8. OTHER, MINOR PARTY

    9. DK
    0. NA

VAR 013   R HOW INTERESTED IN POLT   MD = 0 OR GE 9
                                                   DK 1 COL 23
                                                   WIDTH 1

HOW INTERESTED ARE YOU IN POLITICS AND NATIONAL AFFAIRS—ARE
YOU VERY INTERESTED, SOMEWHAT INTERESTED, ONLY SLIGHTLY
INTERESTED, OR NOT AT ALL INTERESTED?

    1. NOT INTERESTED
    2. ONLY SLIGHTLY INTERESTED
    3. SOMEWHAT INTERESTED
    4. VERY INTERESTED

    9. DK
    0. NA

VAR 014   R TRY INFLUENCE VOTE   MD = 0 OR GE 9
                                               DK 7 COL 24
                                               WIDTH 1

DURING ELECTIONS DO YOU EVER TRY TO SHOW PEOPLE WHY THEY
SHOULD VOTE FOR ONE OF THE PARTIES OR CANDIDATES? DO YOU DO
THAT OFTEN, SOMETIMES, RARELY, OR NEVER?

    1. NEVER
    2. RARELY
    3. SOMETIMES
    4. OFTEN

    9. DK
    0. NA

VAR 015   R WORK FOR PARTY OR CAND   MD = GE 9
                                                   DK 1 COL 25
                                                   WIDTH 1

HAVE YOU DONE OTHER WORK FOR ONE OF THE PARTIES OR
CANDIDATES IN MOST ELECTIONS, SOME ELECTIONS, ONLY A FEW, OR
HAVE YOU NEVER DONE SUCH WORK?

Codebook (continued)

```
        0. NEVER
        1. ONLY A FEW
        2. SOME ELECTIONS
        3. MOST ELECTIONS

        9. NA
```

VAR 016   R BELONG POLITICAL GROUP   MD = GE 8
                                               DK 1 COL 26
                                               WIDTH 1

    DO YOU BELONG TO ANY POLITICAL GROUPS?

        0. NO
        1. YES

        8. NA

VAR 017   R ATTEND POLTL MEETINGS   MD = 0
                                               DK 1 COL 27
                                               WIDTH 1

    IN THE PAST THREE OR FOUR YEARS HAVE YOU ATTENDED ANY
    POLITICAL MEETINGS OR RALLIES?

        1. NO
        2. YES

        0. NA

VAR 018   HOW OFN R ATND POLTL MTG   MD = 0 GE 8
                                               DK 1 COL 28
                                               WIDTH 1

    IF RESPONDENT HAS ATTENDED ANY POLITICAL MEETINGS IN THE PAST
    THREE OR FOUR YEARS—

    ABOUT HOW MANY TIMES HAS R ATTENDED POLITICAL MEETINGS OR
    RALLIES IN THE PAST THREE OR FOUR YEARS?

        0. NEVER
        1. ONCE
        2. TWO OR THREE TIMES
        3. MORE THAN THREE TIMES

VAR 019   R ALWAYS VOTE LCL ELECTN   MD = 0 OR GE 9
                                               DK 1 COL 29
                                               WIDTH 1

    WHAT ABOUT LOCAL ELECTIONS? DO YOU ALWAYS VOTE IN THOSE, DO
    YOU SOMETIMES MISS ONE, OR DO YOU RARELY VOTE, OR DO YOU
    NEVER VOTE?

        1. NEVER VOTE
        2. RARELY VOTE

Codebook (continued)

---

    3. SOMETIMES MISS
    4. VOTE IN ALL

    9. DK
    0. NA

VAR 020   R MAKE PLTL CONTRIBUTION   MD = 0
                                                     DK 7 COL 30
                                                     WIDTH 1

IN THE PAST THREE OR FOUR YEARS, HAVE YOU CONTRIBUTED MONEY TO A POLITICAL PARTY OR CANDIDATE OR TO ANY OTHER POLITICAL CAUSE?

    1. NO
    2. YES

    0. NA

VAR 021   HOW OFTEN WATCH TV NEWS   MD = GE 7
                                                      DK 1 COL 31
                                                     WIDTH 1

IF RESPONDENT EVER WATCHES TELEVISION—

HOW OFTEN DO YOU WATCH THE NEWS BROADCASTS ON TELEVISION— EVERY DAY, A FEW TIMES A WEEK, ABOUT ONCE A WEEK, LESS THAN ONCE A WEEK, OR NEVER?

    0. NEVER
    1. LESS THAN ONCE A WEEK
    2. ONCE A WEEK
    3. A FEW TIMES A WEEK
    4. EVERY DAY

    7. INAP.
    8. NA
    9. DK

VAR 022   HOW OFTEN READ NEWSPAPER   MD = GE 8
                                                      DK 1 COL 32
                                                     WIDTH 1

AND HOW OFTEN DO YOU READ THE NEWSPAPER—EVERY DAY, A FEW TIMES A WEEK, ONCE A WEEK, LESS THAN ONCE A WEEK, OR NEVER?

    0. NEVER
    1. LESS THAN ONCE A WEEK
    2. ONCE A WEEK
    3. A FEW TIMES A WEEK
    4. EVERY DAY

    8. NA
    9. DK

Codebook (continued)

VAR 023   READ MAGAZINES REGULARLY   MD = GE 2
                                                   DK 1 COL 33
                                                 WIDTH 1

ARE THERE ANY MAGAZINES YOU READ REGULARLY?

WHATEVER THE RESPONDENT UNDERSTANDS AS "REGULARLY" WAS THE OPERATIVE DEFINITION HERE. IF THE RESPONDENT SAID HE/SHE MISSED READING AN ISSUE OF A PARTICULAR MAGAZINE NOW AND THEN, THE INTERVIEWER WAS INSTRUCTED TO CODE THE MAGAZINE AS REGULARLY READ, BUT A MAGAZINE WAS NOT CODED AS REGULARLY READ IF THE RESPONDENT SAID SHE/HE READ IT NOW AND THEN.

    0. NO
    1. YES

    2. NA

VAR 024   R READ LIFE REGULARLY   MD = 0
                                                 DK 1 COL 34
                                             WIDTH 1

IF THERE ARE ANY MAGAZINES RESPONDENT READS REGULARLY—

WHICH ONES ARE THEY?

DOES THE RESPONDENT READ LIFE MAGAZINE REGULARLY?

IN THE QUESTIONNAIRE ABOVE QUESTION WAS ACCOMPANIED BY A LIST OF MAGAZINES AND THE INTERVIEWER WAS INSTRUCTED TO CIRCLE EACH MAGAZINE ON THE LIST MENTIONED BY THE RESPONDENT. THE LIST INCLUDED: LIFE, LOOK, NEWSWEEK, NEW YORKER, READER'S DIGEST, SATURDAY EVENING POST, TIME AND U.S. NEWS AND WORLD REPORT. THE INTERVIEWER WAS ALSO INSTRUCTED TO RECORD UP TO THREE OTHER MAGAZINES MENTIONED BY THE RESPONDENT. FOR PURPOSES OF ADDITIONAL CLARITY, EACH MAGAZINE ON THE LIST HAS BEEN CODED AS A SEPARATE VARIABLE IN THIS CODEBOOK. THE THREE ADDITIONAL MAGAZINES HAVE ALSO BEEN CODED SEPARATELY.

    1. YES
    2. NO

    0. INAP.

VAR 025   R READ LOOK REGULARLY   MD = 0
                                                 DK 1 COL 35
                                             WIDTH 1

IF THERE ARE ANY MAGAZINES RESPONDENT READS REGULARLY?

DOES THE RESPONDENT READ LOOK MAGAZINE REGULARLY?

SEE VAR NO. 024 FOR FULL QUESTION TEXT AND EXPLANATORY NOTE.

Codebook (continued)

```
        1. YES
        2. NO

        0. INAP., CODED 0 OR 2 IN VAR NO. 024
------------------------------------------------------------------------------

VAR 026        READ NEWSWEEK REGULARLY        MD = 0
                                              DK 1 COL 36
                                              WIDTH 1

    IF THERE ARE ANY MAGAZINES RESPONDENT READS REGULARLY—

    DOES RESPONDENT READ NEWSWEEK REGULARLY?

    SEE VAR NO. 024 FOR FULL QUESTION TEXT AND EXPLANATORY NOTE.

        1. YES
        2. NO

        0. INAP., CODED 0 OR 2 IN VAR NO. 024
------------------------------------------------------------------------------

VAR 027        READ NEW YORKER REGULARLY      MD = 0
                                              DK 1 COL 37
                                              WIDTH 1

    IF THERE ARE ANY MAGAZINES RESPONDENT READS REGULARLY—

    DOES THE RESPONDENT READ THE NEW YORKER REGULARLY?

    SEE VAR NO. 024 FOR FULL QUESTION TEXT AND EXPLANATORY NOTE

        1. YES
        2. NO

        0. INAP., CODED 0 OR 2 IN VAR NO. 024
------------------------------------------------------------------------------

VAR 028        READER'S DIGEST REGULAR        MD = 0
                                              DK 1 COL 38
                                              WIDTH 1
    IF THERE ARE ANY MAGAZINES RESPONDENT READS REGULARLY—

    DOES THE RESPONDENT READ THE READER'S DIGEST REGULARLY?

    SEE VAR NO. 024 FOR FULL QUESTION TEXT AND EXPLANATORY NOTE.

        1. YES
        2. NO

        0. INAP., CODED 0 OR 2 IN VAR NO. 024
------------------------------------------------------------------------------

VAR 029        SATURDAY EVENING POST          MD = 0
                                              DK 1 COL 39
                                              WIDTH 1

    IF THERE ARE ANY MAGAZINES RESPONDENT READS REGULARLY—

    DOES THE RESPONDENT READ THE SATURDAY EVENING POST
    REGULARLY?
```

Codebook (continued)

SEE VAR. NO. 024 FOR FULL QUESTION TEXT AND EXPLANATORY NOTE.

    1. YES
    2. NO

    0. INAP., CODED 0 OR 2 IN VAR NO. 024

VAR 030   R READ TIME REGULARLY   MD = 0
                                                DK 1 COL 40
                                              WIDTH 1

IF THERE ARE ANY MAGAZINES RESPONDENT READS REGULARLY—

DOES THE RESPONDENT READ TIME MAGAZINE REGULARLY?

SEE VAR. NO. 024 FOR FULL QUESTION TEXT AND EXPLANATORY NOTE.

    1. YES
    2. NO

    0. INAP., CODED 0 OR 2 IN VAR NO. 024

VAR 031   US NEWS & WORLD REPORT   MD = 0
                                                DK 1 COL 41
                                            WIDTH 1

IF THERE ARE ANY MAGAZINES RESPONDENT READS REGULARLY—

DOES THE RESPONDENT READ U.S. NEWS AND WORLD REPORT
REGULARLY?

SEE VAR. NO. 024 FOR FULL QUESTION TEXT AND EXPLANATORY NOTE.

    1. YES
    2. NO

    0. INAP., CODED 0 OR 2 IN VAR NO. 024

Reprinted with permission of the Inter-University Consortium for Political and Social Research, Ann Arbor, Michigan.

Author Index

Subject Index